Central Asia in World War Two

Central Asia in
World War Two

*The Impact and Legacy of Fighting for
the Soviet Union*

Vicky Davis

BLOOMSBURY ACADEMIC

LONDON • NEW YORK • OXFORD • NEW DELHI • SYDNEY

BLOOMSBURY ACADEMIC
Bloomsbury Publishing Plc
50 Bedford Square, London, WC1B 3DP, UK
1385 Broadway, New York, NY 10018, USA
29 Earlsfort Terrace, Dublin 2, Ireland

BLOOMSBURY, BLOOMSBURY ACADEMIC and the Diana logo are trademarks of
Bloomsbury Publishing Plc

First published in Great Britain 2023

Cover design by Annabel Hewitson
Image on cover: War Memorial in Bazar Korgon, Kyrgyzstan. Photography credit to
the author.

A catalogue record for this book is available from the British Library.

A catalog record for this book is available from the Library of Congress.

ISBN: HB: 978-1-3503-7229-0
PB: 978-1-3503-7228-3
ePDF: 978-1-3503-7230-6
eBook: 978-1-3503-7231-3

Typeset by Deanta Global Publishing Services, Chennai, India

To find out more about our authors and books visit www.bloomsbury.com and sign up for
our newsletters.

In memory of
Chinara Seidimatova
Saide Kvirikashvili
Muedin Settarov
and Sanie Zevadinova

CONTENTS

FIGURES

All photographs are by the author, unless otherwise credited.

MAPS

NOTES ON THE TEXT

Transliteration and translations

Very few words are in their original ethnic minority languages. Most of the words which are not in English are transliterated from Russian, the unifying language of the Soviet Union. Transliteration from the Cyrillic alphabet is according to the *Slavonic and East European Review* system, based on a modified Library of Congress convention. The only exception is the use of 'j' instead of 'dzh', in view of the frequency of this combination of letters in Central Asian words and names, although the usual 'dzh' combination is retained for Russian names. All translations from the Russian are mine, unless quoted from other sources in English.

Archival and newspaper references

All archival references refer to documents held in the Issyk-Kul' State Archives, Karakol, Kyrgyzstan (IKSA). They are noted in the format IKSA:a/b/c/d, where 'a' refers to the *fond* (collection), 'b' refers to the *opis'* (description), 'c' refers to the *delo* (file) and 'd' is the *list* (individual sheet) number. Most material consulted was in Russian.

References to the Kyrgyz newspaper *Issyk-Kul'skaia Pravda* are abbreviated to IKP.

ABBREVIATIONS

ALZHIR	a labour camp for women in Akmolinsk
CIS	Commonwealth of Independent States
CSTO	Collective Security Treaty Organization
GKO	State Defence Committee
GULag	the extensive network of forced labour camps
HEP	hydro-electric power
IKP	*Issyk-Kul'skaia Pravda*
IKSA	Issyk-Kul' State Archives
MPVO	anti-aircraft defence units
MTS	co-operative machine tractor station
NATO	North Atlantic Treaty Organization
NCO	non-commissioned officer
NKO	People's Commissariat of Defence
NKVD	Commissariat of Internal Affairs governing the secret police, the precursor to the KGB
POW	prisoner of war
RKKA	the Red Army of Workers and Peasants, referred to as 'the Red Army'
SADUM	Spiritual Administration of the Muslims of Central Asia
SAVO	the Central Asian Military District based in Tashkent
SSR	Soviet Socialist Republic
TASS	the official Soviet state news agency
TsOKS	Central Combined Cinema Studio
USSR	Union of Soviet Socialist Republics, referred to as 'the Soviet Union'

GLOSSARY

Aardakh	the 'exodus' of deported Chechens to Central Asia
agitprop	(political) agitation and propaganda
aksakal	village elder
akyn	bard
atala	thin soup
Basmachi	Central Asian rebels opposing Soviet rule
chuchuk	horsemeat sausage
detsad	nursery school or kindergarten
dombra	traditional type of lute
druzhba narodov	friendship of the peoples
eldashy	comrades
evakopunkt	reception centre for evacuees
fel'dsher	medical orderly, paramedic
glasnost'	transparency of government
Glavlit	Main Directorate for Literary and Publishing Affairs, responsible for censorship
Great Patriotic War	the Second World War in which the Soviet Union officially participated with the Allies from 1941 to 1945
iusupy	derogatory term for Central Asians in Russian
Jadidism	political movement for Islamic reform and education
jailoo	alpine pasture
jigit	lad
jihad	Islamic holy war or campaign
kalpak	traditional felt hat
Kara gün	the 'black day', on which the Crimean Tatars were deported
Karlag	Karaganda Labour Camp
kinoteatr	cinema
kolkhoz	collective farm
Komsomol	Communist Party youth organization
komuz	traditional stringed instrument

korenizatsiia	policy of indigenization, whereby an ethnic minority could retain its own culture and partial self-governance on its home territory
Kresy	the eastern borderlands of Poland
kulak	wealthy peasant
likpunkt	education centre promoting literacy
makhorka	rough tobacco
mankurt	mythical slave without memory of the past
mat' geroina	heroine mother
natsmen	(member of) an ethnic minority
obligatsii	war bonds
obrazovanie	formal education
plov	traditional dish of rice and meat
podvig	(military) exploit
pokhoronka	notification of death
Rodina	Motherland
samovar	traditional hot water urn used for making tea
shtrafbatal'on	penal battalion
Sovinformbiuro	Soviet Information Bureau, the official news agency
sovkhoz	state collective farm
spetspereselentsy	special settlers, a euphemism for deportees
Stakhanovite	prize-winning worker setting production records
Stavka	Stalin and his chiefs of staff
subbotnik	day of voluntary work for the common good
Sürgün	exile of the Crimean Tatars
tyndyk	the ventilation hole at the apex of a yurt
Untermensch	racially inferior sub-human
untragbar	unacceptable
Urkun	the revolt and flight in 1916 of thousands of Kazakhs and Kyrgyz to China and Mongolia in the face of threatened tsarist conscription during the First World War
Virgin Lands Campaign	the post-war Soviet drive to open up new tracts of land in the Soviet Union to increase agricultural production
vospitanie	social and moral upbringing
zek	prisoner, usually in a GULag camp

PLACE NAMES

Central Asia in the book comprises the former Kazakh, Kyrgyz, Uzbek, Tajik and Turkmen Soviet Socialist Republics, formerly known as Russian Turkestan. Often in the Soviet period, though, the term 'Central Asia' excluded Kazakhstan. Similarly, it did not include the Caucasus region.

For the purposes of this book, however, the Kazakh, Kyrgyz, Tajik, Turkmen and Uzbek Soviet Socialist Republics will be called by the modern names of the five successor states of the Soviet Union: Kazakhstan, Kyrgyzstan, Tajikistan, Turkmenistan and Uzbekistan respectively. At the time, the Kyrgyz SSR was often referred to as Soviet Kirgiziia.

The citizens of the respective republics are similarly referred to as Kazakhs, Kyrgyz, Tajiks, Turkmens and Uzbeks, regardless of ethnicity.

Central Asia as a whole is referred to as the 'region'. An *oblast'* is a province within a republic, while a *raion* is one of many districts within a province.

Names of towns and regions in the Soviet era and today

Throughout the book the names of towns and cities appear as they were known in the Russian language at the time, with the exception of the cities of Moscow, Warsaw and Yalta which retain the English versions of their names. If they have a different name today, then the modern name appears in brackets after the wartime name on its first mention. The following places have changed their names since the war; the contemporaneous, wartime name is listed first, followed by the more recent version(s).

Akmolinsk	Founded as Akmola. After the war it was renamed Tselinograd during the Virgin Lands campaign, Astana in 1998, Nur-Sultan in 2019, reverting to Astana in 2022
Aktiubinsk	Aktobe
Alma-Ata	Known as (Fort) Vernyi prior to 1921 and since 1993 known as Almaty

Chimkent	Shymkent
Danzig	Gdansk
Dneprodzerzhinsk	Kamianske
Dnepropetrovsk	Dnipro
Frunze	The wartime capital of Kyrgyzstan, previously called Pispek and now known as Bishkek
Gur'ev	Atyrau
Iman	Dal'nerechensk
Jambul	Taraz
Jarkent	Renamed Panfilov in 1942 and reverted to Jarkent on independence
Khar'kov	Kharkiv
Kiev	Kyiv
Kiubyshev	Samara
Königsberg	Kaliningrad
Krasnovodsk	Turkmenbashi
Krivii Rog	Kryvyi Rih
Leningrad	Known as Petrograd immediately prior to the 1917 revolution and now known as St Petersburg.
Leninogorsk	Ridder
L'vov	L'viv
Moldavia	Moldova, the majority of pre-war Bessarabia
Nikolaev	Mykolaiv
Pahlevi	Bandar-e Anzali
Przheval'sk	Karakol
Rybach'e	Balykchy
Sazanovki	Anan'evo
Stalinabad	Dushanbe
Stalingrad	(formerly Tsartisyn) Volgograd
Stalino	Donetsk
Voroshilovgrad	Luhansk

MAP 1 *The Union of Soviet Socialist Republics in 1941.*

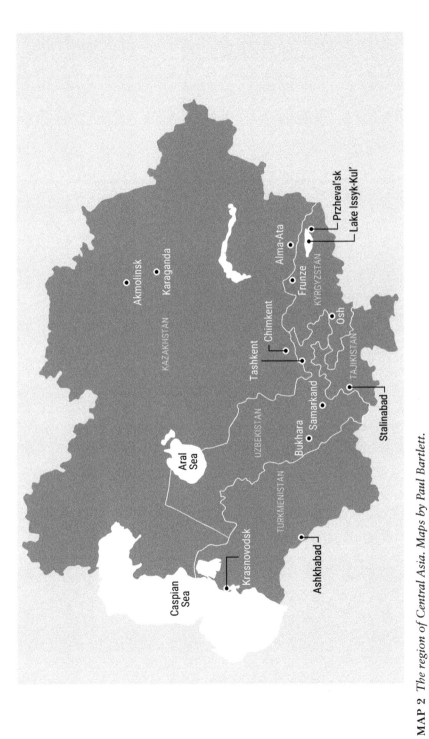

MAP 2 *The region of Central Asia. Maps by Paul Bartlett.*

PART I

Fighting for the Soviet Union

1

War in the wind

The young man stood with his comrades from the collective farm, looking back at the Tien Shan mountains, where he had so far spent his entire life. Jumabek Rakhmanov was born in the remote village of Toktoian in the Issyk-Kul' province of Soviet Kyrgyzstan, not far from the borders with Kazakhstan and China. Like many others, he wasn't quite sure of his exact date of birth, as it was not obligatory to register births at the time.[1] His parents had told him that he was born in 1919, but official records indicated 1922.[2] In any case, shortly after the start of war, most young men who had not previously been called up were conscripted once they reached the age of nineteen or twenty, and his turn had definitely come.[3]

Rakhmanov had already travelled the many kilometres from his collective farm in the Tiup district to reach Pristan' Przheval'sk, the main landing stage at the eastern end of the majestic Lake Issyk-Kul'. It was the first time that he had left his home, and he was already missing his young wife and family. Looking back, he could almost make out the outskirts of the big market town of Przheval'sk which he had reached on horseback. Now his father had returned home with the horse, leaving him standing in the bitter winter wind, the *Ulan*, waiting for the barge to carry him across the water. As the tugboat pulled the barge out onto the open waters, he and his new comrades huddled together for warmth on the deck for the slow 180-kilometre journey into the teeth of the wind. Their immediate destination was Rybach'e (Balykchy), the main port at the western end of the second-largest mountain lake in the world. Once back on land, the group would be loaded onto trucks and trains taking them to the muster station in Tokmak for official registration and medical screening, before their military training began in earnest.

Rakhmanov had no choice but to leave his home in answer to Moscow's call. While a minority of his comrades went to war because they felt that it was their patriotic duty as Soviet citizens, most Central Asians simply could not avoid the bureaucracy of conscription into the Red Army: the Soviet Union was depending on its ethnic minorities to supplement the ranks of its Slavic citizens being decimated by the advancing enemy. From all over

Soviet Central Asia, young men took a last bite of bread from a fresh loaf, leaving it hanging from the ceiling or wall until the day of their return.[4]

And yet there remained a dark shadow in most homes. This was a region of the Soviet Union with a long tradition of oral history. Close-knit families still recalled the terrible events of 1916, when indigenous men from Central Asia were targeted by their imperial Russian overlords for labour battalions during the First World War. At that time it was clear that many Central Asians had still not come to terms with the Russian occupation and colonization of the region in the second half of the nineteenth century. Internal tensions were evident, as it became obvious from increasing Russian demands on the region that it had lost its economic and political independence, with a visible military presence of around 125,000 of the tsar's troops ready to quash any potential rebellion. Furthermore, cultural and religious differences between the ruling Orthodox Christian settlers and their Muslim Central Asian subjects remained almost insurmountable.[5]

It was against this uneasy background that Central Asians recalled with relief Tsar Alexander II's promise never to conscript them for military duties. However, they were all too well aware of the increasing demands for additional taxes, while their crops, cotton, horses and camels were requisitioned for the war. By the summer of 1916 it was obvious that the war was dragging on to the detriment of Russia and that more manpower was needed to replace the Russian troops who had fallen in Europe. Even so, the conscription call issued in the summer of 1916 to a quarter of a million men came as a shock, especially as they were exactly those able-bodied men heavily involved in bringing in the much-needed annual harvest.[6]

Unrest and increased animosity towards the Russians spread across the region, developing into a significant, prolonged uprising against conscription in the eastern parts. Anti-colonial emotions came to a head as locals bearing primitive weapons attacked Russian and Cossack villages, bridges and the new railway lines constructed to assist the colonial powers with the movement of goods and men. They stood no real chance of success against the might of the Russian empire, though. Retaliation was relentless and brutal, particularly in the area around Lake Issyk-Kul', with its high concentration of Russian settlers.[7]

In the face of almost certain death at home, over 170,000 Kyrgyz citizens headed for the border in the mass winter exodus across treacherous mountain passes to China and Mongolia, known locally as the *Urkun*. Almost 60 per cent of the original refugees lost their lives as they fell into gorges, starved or froze to death on the trek.[8] To make matters worse, the Chinese were not over-enthusiastic about the arrival of a motley crowd of destitute foreigners. Once they heard that the conscription was no longer being enforced, many of the refugees decided to undertake the hazardous return journey the following summer, only to face armed Russian reprisals.[9]

Thanks to this popular resistance to their over-demanding colonial overlords, the population of Central Asia was decimated. Seventy per cent of the population of the Przheval'sk area died in the course of one year, while up to half a million Kazakh citizens remained in China. In all, it is estimated that a quarter of a million nomads and farmers died across the region, in contrast to the mere 3,000 Russian soldiers and settlers killed in the rebellion.[10]

Better conditions were supposedly heralded in Central Asia by the Russian Revolution of 1917, which was claimed to release Central Asia from imperial Russian domination. With the subsequent formation of the USSR (Union of Soviet Socialist Republics) in 1922, the region embarked on a period of transition from its old status as an imperial colony to its new position as an integral part of the Soviet Union. By the onset of the Second World War, the five young Soviet Socialist Republics were only just getting used to their new identity as full members of the huge umbrella state.[11]

Following a long history of difficult relationships with imperial Russia and more recently the Soviet Union, how would the population of Central Asia react at the outbreak of a second world war, when, once again, they were called to fight for a power which was not always accepted as being their own? To whom would the people pledge their loyalty? Certainly they could be expected to fight for their families and their clan, but would they be ready to defend their new state, their new 'homeland'? Could Moscow do enough to keep the ethnic minorities of Central Asia onside throughout the war, such that they would be willing to serve on behalf of the Soviet Union, the so-called Fatherland, and to fight alongside the other Soviet republics against a common enemy, even if there was little else they had in common? Since the formation of the Soviet Union, the population of Central Asia had become Sovietized in many ways, but had also undergone a particularly prolonged social and economic upheaval in the two decades before the war. By the onset of war in 1941, to what extent did they feel citizens of the USSR, when so much complex history lay behind them?

As in Rakhmanov's case, the sons of the *Urkun* generation were largely prepared to answer the call to defend the new Soviet Fatherland – resigned if not enthusiastic, as they and their families became embroiled in the four-year common struggle for survival. It is indeed quite amazing that there was any stamina left in the region's population, after the introduction of collectivization in the early 1930s with its subsequent toll, to cope with the heavy demands which the war years would bring. Mutual mistrust between Moscow and its distant citizens in Central Asia remained throughout the Second World War, leading to sometimes different perceptions of the conflict, different vested interests and – in the aftermath – a different attitude to remembrance between Russia and the independent republics of Central Asia today.

Scope of the book

Surprisingly little is known in the West about the role of Central Asia in the Second World War. The region as a whole has been largely overlooked by historians, who have tended, if anything, to concentrate on its centuries-old position at the hub of the ancient Silk Road. Indeed, very few of the Western tourists travelling to Central Asia to admire its architecture or ski in its mountains would be able to identify its republics as having fought alongside the Allies as part of the former Soviet Union. This work plugs the gap in Eurocentric history by shedding light on the region's strategic involvement in the Second World War, claiming for Central Asia its rightful place in this key period of Soviet and world history.

Thanks to Central Asia's position at the southern extremity of the Soviet Union, it was neither occupied nor particularly endangered directly by the enemy during the war. On the periphery of historical interest also, its wartime experience has mainly been incorporated and subsumed into that of the Soviet Union as a whole. Indeed, the history of its ethnic minorities was never of particular interest to Soviet academics, just as it has often been swept up within a 'Russian' narrative by most Eurocentric scholars. Only recently has a handful of specialized studies shed light on various individual facets of Central Asia during the Second World War.[12] However, Central Asia played a major overall role in wartime, once the western regions of the Soviet Union were occupied. Without this precious region and its people in the rear, the Red Army would have struggled to regain its advantage after the sudden Nazi invasion. This book for the first time gives credit to Central Asians for their invaluable contribution to the war effort as a whole.

The experiences of ethnic minorities in wartime are placed at the very heart of this study of the impact of war on some of the most vulnerable citizens of the Soviet Union – not only the indigenous peoples of Central Asia but also those people evacuated or deported to the region from the western Soviet Union. In many ways, though, the experience of Soviet Central Asia was representative of much that happened in the Second World War across all the non-occupied regions of the Soviet Union. With the increased state exploitation of its resources, Central Asia had much in common with Siberia and the Urals. Wartime deprivation such as requisitions and acute hunger were suffered across the Soviet Union. In this respect, the lives of the people of Central Asia serve to highlight the typical issues faced by Soviet citizens, cementing their wartime unity of purpose. However, in Central Asia recent memories of anti-colonial struggles and its different linguistic, cultural and religious backgrounds could well have adversely affected the necessary unity of the Soviet peoples. The tension between the region's distinctive tradition and the new Soviet modernity imposed on all its people – not only those who went to war – was a recipe for potential friction which could well have undermined the war effort.

The war also introduced issues unique to Central Asia, such as its deployment as a dumping ground for evacuees, deportees and prisoners. It is much too simplistic, though, to make sweeping generalizations across a region which was not always affected uniformly by the war. Some western areas of Kazakhstan, for instance, were much closer to the front line and prioritized for transport links, while other parts of the Kazakh republic were so far removed from the action that they were developed for the incarceration and exploitation of unfortunate prisoners and deportees. Uzbekistan was the state's destination of choice for the majority of evacuees, bearing the brunt of the influx of women and children seeking refuge from enemy occupation. New factories were established in cities with good electricity and water supply, while the region's rural areas were all severely depleted of their crops and animals for the war effort.

The demographic changes in Central Asia were largely representative of the whole of the Soviet Union, with decreases in births and a large increase in deaths. In addition, though, the impact of the population displacement across the region was immense – reminiscent of the movement along the trails of the ancient Silk Road, but on a far larger scale. In this respect, Central Asia became the veritable crossroads of the Soviet Union, as vast waves of population movements swept across the region. Where Russian settlers had in the previous century travelled east to colonize the region, followed by internal prisoners dispatched to the camps of the GULag, during the war troops and supplies moved rapidly westwards to the front line, just as millions of prisoners of war, wounded soldiers, evacuees, refugees and finally deportees travelled east away from danger or foreign influence. The dramatic ethno-dynamic changes of war caused huge stresses on this region of the Soviet Union above all others, which could have undermined the existing fault lines and caused the collapse of traditional society. On the other hand, any unification of purpose during the war would inevitably lead to an acceleration of the integration of Central Asia into the Soviet Union. Only time would tell how a society at war would react to such prolonged strain.

The challenges faced by Central Asians were exacerbated by Moscow's perception of the region as a safe space in the rear, providing an area free from enemy bombardment in which to accommodate the evacuated industrial infrastructure which was key to winning the war and the future viability of the Soviet project. The mighty Soviet state desperately needed this vast region on the periphery, while remaining suspicious of its majority Muslim population which could potentially have turned against Joseph Stalin's rule of steel at any stage. Its busy propaganda machine made sure that the region was kept largely in line with a war effort which demanded so much of its citizens, while being singled out for special praise wherever possible. The population was far more exposed to Soviet ideals than ever before, broadcast by the mass media and epitomized by the Russian language and culture imported by evacuees.

In partial recompense for its sacrifices, much of Central Asia received substantial amounts of inward state investment. Not only was its infrastructure modernized but its people continued to benefit hugely from the pre-war Soviet education and equality drive which accelerated through the war years with new schools and fresh opportunities for all parts of society. In addition, conscripted Central Asian servicemen gained first-hand knowledge of the Russian language and traditions with the subsequent post-war opportunity for advancement within the communist system. In this way, the region experienced a rapid step-change in modernization and politicization thanks to the homogenizing effects of the war on all Soviet society.

The following chapters explore in depth the experience of Central Asians both in the armed forces and on the home front. This work does not flinch from examining the previously taboo subjects largely unmentioned in Soviet studies – the treatment of prisoners of war on both sides, issues of desertion, collaboration and anti-Semitism, plus the inhumanity of the waves of deportation to which many Soviet citizens were subjected. More than anything, though, this book examines the interaction of the dominant Soviet state with its Asian citizens on the southern borderlands. While Moscow found itself in crucial need of the Central Asian republics during the war, it remained intent on using the circumstances of war to accelerate its campaign of Sovietizing this Asian society and completing its ideological aim of bringing enlightened socialism to the masses.

This work is the social history of over 300 individuals swept up in the whirlwind of war by a state which was careless of the number of lives exacted in order to secure victory. It is an analysis of a worldwide conflict as it affected these ordinary citizens of Central Asia on a day-to-day, individual scale. Their role in this remote region of the Soviet Union had important implications for their communities and republics for decades to come. The following chapters are peppered with examples of ordinary men and women whose lives were affected by the course of a war dictated from a capital thousands of kilometres away, a war which was not really 'theirs' at all. Now is the time to claim their place in a critical moment of history hitherto dominated by the totalitarian state in which they lived.

Sources and structure

The material for this book was researched between 2017 and 2020 during a series of visits to Central Asia and despite curtailment due to the prevalent health conditions which prevented further planned forays into the field. Sources include archival documents and photographs, contemporaneous press coverage, Soviet-era history books, museum exhibitions, memoirs, literature and films. Most of the sources were produced in the Russian language, the lingua franca of the Soviet Union and the medium of most official publications at the time.

Although the bulk of this material was obtained on the ground, it is nonetheless important to question the reliability of such evidence. Handwritten or typed documents retained in local archives no doubt contain largely correct information, but they are still subject to the emphasis and terminology of their Soviet authors – writers who would sometimes have been trying to boost their importance, extenuate themselves or pull the wool over the eyes of a superior. In most cases, however, there is no reason not to accept the facts and figures contained in the official reports or on the pink and grey slips of coarse paper or card used out of necessity by the region's middle managers in times of universal paper shortages. Furthermore, this documentary evidence is typical of the administrative work ubiquitous in the wartime Soviet Union and representative of work taking place behind the scenes across Central Asia.

Newspapers, on the other hand, were always considered to be propaganda tools and therefore their articles sometimes need to be taken with a pinch of salt. While covering precious pages of newsprint with details of speeches made by Comrade Stalin in Moscow and relayed to the regions by TASS (the official Soviet state news agency), journalists also sought out examples of model Soviet behaviour amongst the local population, while openly criticizing managers, farms or factories for falling below desired standards. Local editors were at the beck and call of the Soviet propaganda machine and therefore subject to demands from above to print mainly positive news about the war effort. Published facts and figures may well have been distorted to emphasize the military success of the Red Army or the economic output of local workers in an effort to boost citizens' morale. If this is understood at the outset, then it is possible to read between the lines in certain cases in order to extract small gems of information which successfully illustrate life in wartime.

Histories of the region in wartime published while Leonid Brezhnev was General Secretary of the Communist Party of the Soviet Union (1964–82) are the only other written sources available. They, however, are prone to the politically required hype of the time. Kerimbaev's superficially authoritative history of the war in Kyrgyzstan, written in 1980 at the height of the Brezhnev-era war cult, is the one main source in that country, a comprehensive account of sometimes biased information, glorifying the many almost unbelievable feats of combatants and civilians alike.[13] This book informs all subsequent histories appearing in Kyrgyzstan, including contemporary school textbooks which concentrate on highly propagandized personal stories of local people. In the same way, modern histories of the other republics tend to reproduce without question Soviet-era data from similar sources, relying on probably overly patriotic tales of heroes and their exploits to attract their readership, while omitting salient information on the many so-called 'blank spots' in the history of the Second World War.

Indeed, it is these lacunae in the war narrative in Soviet Central Asia which are of such interest to the Western researcher. As academics in the region often remain fixated on their local war heroes, very little is mentioned about subjects which still remain taboo and are once again difficult to access from material in the main Soviet war archives based in Moscow. It is here that local archives are so invaluable, offering a unique insight into day-to-day problems in the rear.

Western histories often casually mention millions of Soviet deaths, even though these statistics may also be misleading: numbers vary according to different sources, and it is sometimes impossible to judge exactly how many men were lost in various theatres of war, for example, or how many people died from starvation in the rear. The loss of human lives was immense, but wildly different figures are quoted, which I have attempted to untangle in the text. This uncertainty is just one indication of the chaos of war, the retrospective counting of bodies and the ignorance of authorities about how some isolated families may have quietly succumbed to malnutrition. On the other hand, it is likely that some of the more insignificant figures recorded in the archives with some attention to detail are factually correct – the numbers of children living in a certain orphanage or the numbers of Jewish evacuees benefiting from education in a particular village, for instance.

I was privileged to gain access to some personal letters written by private Soviet individuals during or shortly after the war. There remain also some key witnesses who were alive during the war and can still testify to the conditions pertaining to their childhood. I have occasionally included their testimony, either as related directly to me – often with the help of a trusted interpreter – or through their stories passed down to younger family members. Memory brings its own unreliability, however, with the benefit of the rose-tinted spectacles of hindsight and potential flaws introduced by the repeated recounting of a wartime trajectory which may at the time have been in need of some embellishment. The passage of time renders some accounts unreliable, although they may be based on a skeleton of sometimes remarkable truth. I have included very few of these narratives in this work, often with a word of caution. Other personal information was gleaned from post-war memoirs and documented interviews with war veterans collected by local historians, which are verifiable and useful for illustrative purposes.[14]

Wanderlust and curiosity fuelled my first visit to Central Asia. By the time I left, I was determined to return to the region to take advantage of the opportunities presented to me to research its recent past. Since those early days, I have benefited from the assistance of numerous new friends and colleagues, who have in turn introduced me to others able to help with my research. I should particularly like to acknowledge the support of the team at the NGO 'WPU Erayim', based in Bishkek and working with international partners across the region. Through them I met the wonderful Chinara Seidimatova, director of the Archives in Kyrgyzstan's Issyk-Kul' province, who generously provided me with a desk and support team. Here in Karakol, not far from the Chinese border, I was at liberty to immerse myself in the treasure trove of hundreds of dusty, drab Soviet-era folders and newspapers. If much of this work focuses on Kyrgyzstan, it is thanks to the wealth of historical material hidden in the Issyk-Kul' archives: pure gold, in fact! Drawing on these previously undiscovered archival documents, this work reveals the true impact of war in Central Asia.

Far removed from the centre of the former Soviet Union, I was able to absorb and re-live the quotidian matters of wartime life in this remote part of Central Asia. This work is therefore not a state-centric overview of political decisions and military manoeuvres; rather, it weaves together the threads of many individual lives, to consider the point of view of ordinary citizens – the individual people behind the statistics – who were caught up in Soviet history through no fault of their own. Small bit-players in a worldwide drama, they were flung around by a storm which engulfed their region and their homes, as families struggled to survive the impact of the Second World War far away from the front line.

Part I of the book examines the war from the point of view of the combatants. From the preparations for war and regional conscription process, we probe into the world of draft-dodging and the population's misgivings in Chapter 2. Chapter 3 scrutinizes the experience of the region's ill-equipped soldiers at the fighting front, covering their successes and failures on the front line and in the ideological battlefield. Not only heroes appear in the survey, though. Prisoners of war, deserters, penal and labour battalions also feature in the overall tapestry of the wartime trajectory of Central Asian troops. Women also played a valuable role in the conflict, not only in tending the thousands of war wounded who eventually made their way back home to start a new life in Central Asia. From Leningrad (St Petersburg) to Manchuria, the region's troops saw active service, despite often suffering racial discrimination and prejudice.

Part II delves into domestic life on the home front, showing that the human cost of war was not confined to losses on the battlefield. Chapter 4 considers those left behind to labour in the fields and factories, providing the sometimes forced labour building the infrastructure necessary to increase the scale of production for the wartime economy. Society in wartime is dissected in Chapter 5, with the huge disruption to the family unit. The very real problems faced in towns and villages are analysed, including issues of community health under the severe conditions of rationing and universal malnutrition. Children, whose development the state prioritized, continued in education, despite the ubiquitous problems and shortages faced by the education system and their families. However, some occasional leisure time permitted the relaxation offered by theatres, the cinema, literature and the arts, all influenced by the state's propaganda machine as scrutinized in Chapter 6. As the mass media took over the dissemination of information from the banned mosques and clerics, the people of Central Asia, as elsewhere in the Soviet Union, received mainly the news as propagated to its citizens by the regime.

The huge impact on the region of the population displacement of civilians is the subject of Part III. Chapter 7 explores the evacuation on an unprecedented scale of industry, higher education and intellectuals from the occupied western regions to Central Asia, including Jewish refugees and hundreds of thousands of children, many of them unaccompanied. Even worse, Chapter 8 charts the successive waves of oppressed ethnic minorities who were deported from the fringes of the Soviet Union to be re-housed under punitive conditions in Central Asia. Poles, Koreans, Greeks, Crimean Tatars and Chechens were uprooted and transported to what was usually a hostile reception, while also changing the balance of society and the composition of the region's population for decades to come. The cruel treatment and fate of the deportees conclude the evaluation of Central Asia during the war years.

The final chapter examines the legacy of the Second World War on the region through its memorial film and literature, and the various aspects of remembrance of the war. The legacy of the war is understandably muddied: state by state, province by province, here is a complex mnemonic situation in need of untangling. Lasting remembrance of the war is still tangible in Central Asia through its monuments, rituals of commemoration and, less visibly, through its political relations with Russia. Most importantly today, though, is the attitude of the region's people to their own history through the lessons taught in schools and material studied in universities, as the younger generation considers its Soviet legacy. As the region matures into its post-Soviet identity over eighty years after the war, have its various republics actually been able to reclaim a narrative which depicts them not merely as a minor part of the former Soviet Union?

Who owns history? Is it the all-powerful state or the regions; the centre or the periphery; the dominant race or the ethnic minority; the general or the rank-and-file soldier; the war correspondent or the junior officer? Usually it is the dominant state, the author or film-maker who controls the narrative. In this work I have stitched together a colourful patchwork of personal stories to produce a three-dimensional picture of a region at war. Replete with examples of small people, of Central Asians and others impacted by the war, the book serves as a social history of the war years.

The scope of this book ranges from the Caspian Sea in the west to the Mongolian border in the east; from the Siberian heartlands in the north to the Afghan border in the south. It emphasizes the interconnectedness and interdependence of the Soviet regions, as the nomads of Central Asia – only newly incorporated into the Soviet Union – embarked on long and hazardous journeys to the Soviet Western Front, while those at home accepted hundreds of thousands of evacuees and deportees from distant regions of the Soviet Union. We start our quest for further insight into the life of the ordinary person in wartime on the Soviet–Chinese border – in the frontier town of Przheval'sk, today's Karakol, on the shore of Kyrgyzstan's Lake Issyk-Kul'.

Notes

1   According to the director of the Issyk-Kul' State Archives.

2   Information from the Rakhmanov family archives and extended interview on 22 May 2018.

3   E. S. Kaptagaev, Ch. M. Seidimatova, et al., eds, *Sbornik: Issyk-kul'tsy v gody Velikoi Otechestvennoi voiny (1941–1945gg.)* (Karakol: Issyk-Kul'skii oblastnoi gosudarstvennyi arkhiv, 2015), 209.

4   Timur Dadabaev, *Identity and Memory in Post-Soviet Central Asia: Uzbekistan's Soviet Past* (London and New York: Routledge, 2016), 65.

5   E. D. Sokol, *The Revolt of 1916 in Russian Central Asia* (1954) (Baltimore: Johns Hopkins University Press, 2016), 11 and 38; and Shoshana Keller, *Russia and Central Asia: Coexistence, Conquest, Convergence* (Toronto and London: University of Toronto Press, 2020), 12.

6   Sokol, *The Revolt of 1916 in Russian Central Asia*, 67–8 and 73–4; Keller, *Russia and Central Asia*, 141; and Christopher Robbins, *In Search of Kazakhstan: The Land that Disappeared* (Croydon: Profile, 2008), 35.

7   The full history of these events can be found in Aminat Chokobaeva, 'When the Nomads Went to War: The Uprising of 1916 in Semirech'e'. In *The 1916 Central Asian Revolt: Rethinking the History of a Collapsing Empire in the Age of War and Revolution*, eds A. Chokobaeva, C. Drieu and A. Morrison, 145–69 (Manchester: Manchester University Press, 2019); and Sokol, *The Revolt of 1916 in Russian Central Asia*.

8   Ibid., 111–15, 120–2, 124 and 127–32.

9   Ibid., 126 and 130–4; and Keller, *Russia and Central Asia*, 142.

10 Sokol, *The Revolt of 1916 in Russian Central Asia*, 144 and 156–7; Keller, *Russia and Central Asia*, 12 and 142; and Robbins, *In Search of Kazakhstan*, 36.

11 G. Hosking, *Russia and the Russians: A History from Rus to the Russian Federation* (London: Allen Lane, Penguin, 2001), 428 and 431; Ali İğmen, *Speaking Soviet with an Accent: Culture and Power in Kyrgyzstan* (Pittsburgh: University of Pittsburgh, 2012), 26; and Keller, *Russia and Central Asia*, 162 and 165–9.

12 See notably: Roberto Carmack, *Kazakhstan in World War II: Mobilization and Ethnicity in the Soviet Empire* (Lawrence: University Press of Kansas, 2019); Jeff Eden, *God Save the USSR: Soviet Muslims and the Second World War* (Oxford: Oxford University Press, 2021); and Rebecca Manley, *To the Tashkent Station: Evacuation and Survival in the Soviet Union at War* (Ithaca and London: Cornell University Press, 2009).

13 S. K. Kerimbaev, ed., *Sovetskii Kirgizstan v Velikoi Otechestvennoi voine 1941–1945 gg* (Frunze: ILIM, 1980).

14 B. Z. Esenaliev, ed., *Zhenishke dank / Slava Pobede* (Bishkek: Kutaalam, 2015); and Sam Tranum, ed., *Life at the Edge of the Empire: Oral Histories of Soviet Kyrgyzstan* (Poland: CreateSpace, 2012).

2

Preparing for war

It is all too often assumed that the Soviet Union was totally unprepared for war against Nazi Germany, resulting in the surprise attack of Operation Barbarossa in June 1941 and the enemy's rapid advance towards Moscow, Leningrad and Ukraine. In fact, the situation at the outbreak of war was not quite so clear-cut.

The Soviet Union under Stalin had been preparing for war throughout most of the 1930s. Successive five-year plans had prioritized increasing the industrialization intended to build socialism, which had resulted in the output of civilian industries increasing by 160 per cent. At the same time, munitions production grew seventy-fold, even if the quality suffered with the hasty push for expansion. More and more military equipment and armaments were manufactured, while workforces were placed on a military footing early in 1941.[1]

Workers were moved from civilian enterprises to the munitions industry to effect a rapid re-armament of the country. An emphasis was also placed on the exploitation of raw materials and the production of refined metals and fuels, while expertise in precision engineering and associated technical skills was increased. By June 1941 the production lines were humming as the new, formidable T-34 tanks, aircraft, guns, rifles and ammunition left the factories. Despite this huge push, many soldiers were left with obsolete weapons, or worse – no armaments at all. Furthermore, several key factories were located in the western part of the country, the first to fall after the invasion.[2]

Moreover, during the purges of the late 1930s a high percentage of talented Soviet generals were accused of treason and either executed or sent to Siberia by the Stalin regime, while thousands of more junior commanders were arrested.[3] With a depleted, demoralized, ineffective and largely uncoordinated leadership, the remaining commanding officers exercised understandable caution, as junior – often relatively inexperienced and poorly trained – officers had been untested in war. They were also let down by poor communications, relying on old field telephones rather than more dependable radio equipment, and were all too often left to face an enemy with superior tanks and weapons.[4]

Most of all, though, Adolf Hitler, the Nazi leader, achieved an element of surprise in the launch of Operation Barbarossa, which clearly affected Stalin's grip on the immediate situation, leading to his silence and considerable political uncertainty during the first few days of the invasion. However, things could have been much worse, had the country not already been on a war footing with 5.4 million trained men serving in the armed forces, 6 per cent of the working population.[5]

One of these was Nikolai Liashchenko, a career officer who was born in 1908 and joined the Red Army as a volunteer in 1929 at the height of the Sino-Soviet conflict over the Chinese Eastern Railway. Leaving his village of Sazonovka on the banks of Lake Issyk-Kul', he joined other young men from across the Soviet Union in the far east of the country. Upon his return, Liashchenko went as an officer cadet to the Lenin Military Academy in Tashkent. The 1917 revolution had opened the door to study for Central Asians, and his educational background and membership of the Komsomol, the Communist Party's youth movement, no doubt helped him to obtain a place.[6]

As a junior officer in his first command, Liashchenko was posted to the Kara-Kum desert area of Kazakhstan in 1931 to help quell the insurgent bands of *Basmachi* rebels promoting a style of pan-Turkic Islamic nationalism in conflict with the new communist ideology propagated by Vladimir Lenin, the Bolshevik leader of the 1917 revolution. Following a spell in the far east of Siberia, where the state was worried about a possible conflict with Japan, he was posted as a lieutenant to Spain, where the Soviets were fighting against Franco's fascists in the civil war. Recalled to Moscow two years later when promoted to major, Liashchenko attended staff college at the Frunze Academy, preparing for a higher leadership role as officer training in the Soviet Union was stepped up. There, he built on his previous military experience with courses in the use of newly developed military artillery, although his staff training was rudely interrupted by the outbreak of war. With others in his generation of middle-ranking officers, he had narrowly escaped the purges which had curtailed the careers and even lives of many of his seniors, plus teachers and military theorists from the academy.[7]

Other officers in a similar position had seen action in various spheres in the years before Hitler's invasion. Experience in the air and the logistics of supplying an army across vast distances was gained during the largely successful border skirmishes in Manchuria and Mongolia against Japanese expansionism into Siberia, culminating in the decisive Battle of Khalkhin Gol in the summer of 1939. The Soviet–German non-aggression pact of August 1939, signed by foreign ministers Viacheslav Molotov and Joachim von Ribbentrop, might have suggested a peaceful time ahead, but the Soviet Union's own enthusiasm for colonial expansion to the west was confirmed the following month. Driving into eastern Poland, the Baltic States and

Bessarabia thanks to military and political co-operation with Nazi Germany, Red Army officers gained further valuable experience in modern warfare.

Universal conscription in the Soviet Union became a fact of life from the beginning of September 1939, when Stalin started to plan his foray into Eastern Europe, thanks to Nazi Germany. National military service was compulsory for young men, with well-organized conscription in successive annual tranches according to their year of birth. The conscription season usually started in October in Central Asia so that men were signed up and ready for training by the following January. Soviet men were generally called up at the age of nineteen unless they were at university or in reserved occupations.[8] However, Central Asians were found to be weaker and physically less developed than most, so that in Kyrgyzstan national service was often delayed until men reached the age of twenty or even twenty-one.[9]

The Kyrgyz military archives reveal a successful conscription operation in the Issyk-Kul' province in the autumn of 1939 'at a high political-ideological level'. This was retrospectively and rather optimistically attributed to a series of motivational meetings held with young men and their parents before they joined up, which included talks by veterans of the wars in Spain and Manchuria. Additionally, over 40 per cent of the men were in the Komsomol and so had already received a basic introduction to military training. However, half of them had not completed school: only 35 per cent had finished primary school, with merely two or three years of education under their belt. The claim by the military authorities that the new recruits were 'highly literate' must therefore be taken with a pinch of salt, as 6 per cent were judged to be illiterate and 37 per cent 'barely literate'.[10] All of these trainee soldiers would benefit in theory from further training in Frunze (Bishkek) in literacy and the Russian language, although the efficacy of this educational campaign was often questioned by regional authorities.

Stalin has been credited with using the non-aggression pact to play for time, fearing correctly that Germany would turn eventually from its war with France and the West to face the Soviet Union itself. Any delaying tactics, even siding with Hitler, would give him time to prepare the Red Army for the greater conflict to come. The badly judged war with Finland during the winter of 1939–40 exposed the overall lack of preparedness, efficiency, equipment, tactical skill and training of the Red Army. The deficiencies of the Soviet forces were demonstrated by the rapid and costly loss of over 126,000 men. The winter war in arctic conditions indicated to Stalin the serious shortcomings of the Red Army, but his response came too late, just as the true weakness of the Soviet Union was exposed to Hitler.[11]

By January 1940 older men born from 1903 to 1913 as well as the usual generation of 1918 and 1919 were being conscripted in Kyrgyzstan, at the height of the war with Finland. Secret files demonstrate the urgent need to boost Soviet forces in Murmansk and Leningrad in the north of the country as the Red Army was engaged simultaneously on several fronts. The initially boosted reserves of Soviet forces and equipment were rapidly depleted, and all units held in the rear were quickly mobilized to the front. By May 1940 the conscription age in Kyrgyzstan was officially lowered to nineteen in a drive to strengthen forces as rapidly as possible.[12]

In January 1941 Kyrgyz air club cadets were sent for air force officer training as soon as they had completed their course in a push to supplement the ranks of qualified pilots. By the time war broke out against Germany the Central Asian republics were already on a war footing with long lists of existing, relatively experienced servicemen already compiled – men who would then not return home for the duration of the war.[13]

By the summer of 1941, the deployment of trained troops on the Soviet western borders was in place, even if a proportion of men were on summer leave. However, they were sparsely spread with no depth to their formations – not an ideal position with which to repel a determined German invasion. Stalin was relying on a rapid Soviet counter-attack to take his troops directly into enemy territory and no defensive strategy, reserves or fortifications were in place.[14] While still playing for political time in order to prepare for a war with Germany, Stalin eventually accelerated work in the western Soviet Union to improve the infrastructure necessary for the movement of troops. Even in distant Kyrgyzstan, an inventory of all cars and other vehicles was being ordered as part of a flurry of secret pre-mobilization orders three weeks before the outbreak of war.[15] However, the time for preparations finally ran out on 22 June when Germany suddenly invaded the Soviet Union and the Great Patriotic War began in earnest.

'War has started'

Of course, war did not come as a complete surprise to many citizens of the Central Asian republics, particularly those living in towns where newspapers were available in local libraries. Literacy had increased dramatically under Soviet rule, and by 1941 many children completed at least three years of primary education. Although Paris was a good 6,000 kilometres away from Tashkent, people were aware that a war was being waged in distant Europe, just as they recalled that a non-aggression pact had been signed between the Soviet Union and Nazi Germany two years previously.[16]

However, the editor tended to relegate news of the war in Europe to the back page of the modest provincial broadsheet *Issyk-Kul'skaia Pravda* (Issyk-Kul' Truth), printed several times a week in both Kyrgyz and Russian-language versions. In the summer of 1941, only the determined reader would learn of de Gaulle's men fighting in Syria, the sinking of British ships, English deaths in London and Kent following German bombing, or of the retaliatory air attacks on the Ruhr, northern France, Belgium and Rotterdam.[17] The headlines concentrated on items closer to home and the pervading communist ideology, such as the positive spin on improvements in roads and infrastructure, agricultural technology and industrial productivity.[18] Most people were thus led to believe that the Soviet Union was immune to the distant conflict. If, however, a war did occur, then the official state line was that the powerful Soviet troops, with modern tanks and aircraft at their disposal, would more than deal with any German hostility. While some more patriotic citizens were therefore complacent at the breakdown of the non-aggression pact, others had regarded it optimistically as a safety net and reacted with undisguised anger at the German invasion.[19]

Most of the rural population in Kyrgyzstan still led a semi-nomadic life, following the seasons. When Germany launched Operation Barbarossa and invaded the western Soviet Union with powerful massed forces, many Kyrgyz were living temporarily with their animals up on the *jailoo*, the rich alpine summer grazing meadows. The press, following Stalin's lead, was silent for a few days until 'War has started' was broadcast all over the front page of *Issyk-Kul'skaia Pravda*, as it was throughout the Soviet Union. Drumming up support for the motherland and communism, the state order for mobilization issued hastily on 22 June was reproduced on page two of the 25 June edition, calling up all men not already serving in the armed forces in the main Soviet republics of Russia, Ukraine and the Caucasus, but not in Central Asia or the far east of Siberia. The state was not yet ready to test the loyalty of these peripheral parts of the Soviet Union, recalling no doubt the *Urkun* rebellion of 1916 in Kyrgyzstan and the *Basmachi* rebellion in Uzbekistan in the 1920s. The government similarly granted itself the power to draft unemployed or otherwise employed men and women into the defence industry and to increase the length of the working day to twelve hours, while promptly cancelling all forthcoming holidays.[20]

As the focus of the press turned immediately to the invasion of the western Soviet Union, the existing war in Europe was crowded out, undeserving of paper and print columns. However, the press was again silent for over a month, as the reality of war took hold and the censor deemed it prudent not to divulge the speedy advance of the enemy into the Baltic States, Soviet Belarus and Ukraine. Increasingly desperate rumours filled the information vacuum, including whispers that there had been skirmishes on the eastern Turkish border and that Central Asia may be absorbed into a larger Turkish protectorate. Officials displayed concern that these invented stories may have been propagated by the Nazis, invoking fear of the 'enemy within'.[21] Betraying increasing twitchiness, and perhaps also wishing to keep the men on their toes and alert to the reality of war, Moscow hurriedly put out a call to destroy any secret information securely, keeping it safe from prying eyes, including past copies of the army newspaper in Kyrgyzstan, *Frunzevets*. Men were reminded that it was forbidden to cut out articles and then dispose of them carelessly. They were for the eyes of servicemen only and must never fall into unsafe hands or be given to waste paper processors for disposal. Today, used copies would have simply been shredded.[22]

The awful reality in the western regions of the Soviet Union was still not close enough to home to overly concern the population of Central Asia, who went on for the time being with their normal summer lives far from urban centres and the front line. Some men, though, responded to the emergency by promptly volunteering for military service, as nearly 1,000 joined up in Tashkent alone in the first week of the war. This number largely comprised ethnic Russians working in the capital city of Uzbekistan, but even more responded in Samarkand, perhaps because it was a little closer to the danger. In contrast, very few men volunteered from the more Asian cities of Fergana and Andijan.[23]

Years later, at the height of the Brezhnev-era war cult, only politically correct and often inflated memories were documented, recalling the apparently spontaneous gathering on 22 June in Frunze of over 3,000 workers, all vowing 'to our Party and our government our readiness to defend the Motherland'. Even a 57-year-old man seemed determined to join his son already serving in the Red Army. By the next day, as the town formed its own war commission, 250 miners were allegedly already on their way to the front.[24]

Military and political leaders in Tashkent tried to drum up further support for the war, once the state had decided that Asians were desperately needed at recruiting stations.[25] The state issued internal passports – essentially identity cards – to its citizens, including the defined 'nationality' or ethnicity of the bearer as a virtually immutable status. The Soviet Union was officially a multinational, multiethnic state, where all nationalities were recognized as equal in the 'brotherhood of peoples', thus rendering all men liable for the defence of the country. As recruitment started in earnest, the propaganda machine offered carrots to counter the sticks accompanying the draft papers.

By August 1941 the local press in the large Issyk-Kul' province of Kyrgyzstan was starting to deploy examples of Russian patriotism, comparing for the first time the conflict in the western Soviet Union with Napoleon's invasion of 1812, subsequently termed the Patriotic War.[26] In this way citizens became accustomed to calling the new conflict the 'Great Patriotic War', *Uluu Ata-Mekendik sogush* in Kyrgyz or *Velikaia Otechestvennaia voina* in Russian. The photograph of a smiling and successful young Russian airman was the first example of a regular series of images intended to attract volunteers and conscripts.[27]

The recruiting campaign was deliberately targeted at specific audiences.[28] If Issyk-Kul' residents were to be enticed to the recruiting stations by a positive image, in Tashkent, a thousand kilometres to the west, a healthy fear of the enemy was felt to be the key to increasing numbers. Moscow had learnt that it was necessary to incorporate local examples into their recruitment campaign, so young men who previously had not understood the very real danger to their families far from the front learnt that their role could well save their homeland from invasion by the barbaric enemy. The fourteenth-century Uzbek hero Amir Timur (known in the West as

Tamerlane) was invoked to remind men of their fearless national role model, while well-known figures from literature and architectural examples were deployed by the propagandists to remind the people of just what was at stake if the enemy reached Central Asia. By the beginning of July 3,000 Tashkent citizens had volunteered for military service, despite misgivings on the part of Communist Party officials, who feared that Uzbeks may not be willing to fight for the Soviet Union.[29]

Conscription

Jumabek Rakhmanov was just one of the estimated 35,000 men to leave their homes in the Issyk-Kul' province to travel into the unknown.[30] He was on his way to fight a distant war on what Westerners call the Eastern Front, but which for Soviets was the Western Front.

Of the overall pre-war population of Kyrgyzstan of around 1.6 million people, 365,000 (about 23 per cent) would serve in the RKKA, *Raboche-Krest'ianskaia Krasnaia Armiia*, the Red Army of Workers and Peasants – known as the Red Army for short.[31] Over 34 million men in total fought for the Soviet Union during the war years, including over 1.2 million Kazakh citizens – mainly ethnic Slavs – who were called up for active service, representing a similar 20 per cent of the total population of 6 million.[32] The figures for Uzbekistan are comparable, with 1.4 million leaving home out of a population of 7 million. Statistics for Turkmenistan and Tajikistan indicate a slightly lower percentage of conscripts: around 300,000 left from each of these smaller Central Asian republics, indicative, perhaps, of a lower degree of trust in the south of the region on the part of the Soviet authorities. In general, however, most small villages and families were affected, losing – for the moment at least – the cream of their able-bodied men.[33]

The first men to leave were mainly patriotic volunteers, as conscription was not introduced into Central Asia until later than most areas of the Soviet Union. Central Asians were reprieved for a while, no doubt as the government still suspected some disloyalty from its Muslim citizens or those living close to the Chinese border.[34] In much of the rest of the country, all men born between 1905 and 1918 were called up by emergency decree on the first day of the war, to join the 1919–22 cohort already serving.

Every military commissariat across Kyrgyzstan finally received secret instructions from the *Narodnyi komissariat oborony* (NKO), the People's Commissariat for Defence, to start conscription on 18 September 1941. For the next four weeks, the following categories of men were to be conscripted:

- the standard cohort of those born in 1922 (aged nineteen);
- those born in 1921 and earlier, if they had not already been called up due to poor health or exceptional family circumstances;

- younger men born in 1923 with middle or higher education;
- and any person with medical training.[35]

The GKO (*Gosudarstvennyi komitet oborony*), the State Defence Committee, decided to start mobilization from 1 October of all Soviet males aged from sixteen to fifty. However, these age criteria did not yet apply to ethnic Central Asians. By then, a total of only 1,623 men, including 236 Jews, had been conscripted in the Issyk-Kul' province. Very few older men were called up, just over 3 per cent of the overall number, as most were already in the army or had been exempted from service for valid reasons. By the end of the year all men under thirty-five were liable for conscription. Some disorganization in the recruitment process was demonstrated, as several distinctly older men were called up by mistake, as were some hospital patients who were obviously unfit for service. In a desperate attempt to meet the quota from Central Asia demanded by the State Defence Committee, 500 political prisoners from the prison camp at Tambovsk on the Russo-Kazakh border were conscripted into the army, as were some common criminals serving prison sentences for minor infractions.[36]

During the first months of the war the conscription process remained rather chaotic, as the military and civil authorities tried to identify men liable for service. Those in charge of the operation in Alma-Ata (Almaty), the capital of Kazakhstan, were severely reprimanded by regional military inspectors, who judged their operation to be lacking in efficiency. Some men attending the recruitment centre there were forced to go without food or medical support, thus prejudicing their readiness for training and active service.[37]

As the war progressed, the organization of conscription became more streamlined, often spearheaded by key personnel working in collective farms.[38] Specific data was collected about each man: his name, place and year of birth, attitude to communism, education and degree of literacy, knowledge of Russian, medical history, place of work and field of specialist training. Most of this information was collected from the village elder or workplace before the actual conscription instructions were issued.[39] Political lectures lauding communism and venomizing Nazi Germany were delivered to prospective conscripts through their Komsomol organization or collective farm.[40] In order to spur on recruitment, a sergeant in the famous Panfilov Division was invited to give a motivational pre-conscription talk to young Komsomol members in the Kyrgyz town of Przheval'sk in August 1942.[41]

The pace of conscription accelerated towards the end of 1942 as the Battle of Stalingrad was in full swing, Soviet losses were high, and the outcome of the war was in the balance.[42] The conscription age was officially reduced to eighteen to increase the supply of replacement manpower, and by the autumn of 1943 consistently high numbers of young men were being processed by Major Staroluvtsev, the head of recruitment in the town of Przhevasl'k. A total of 1,145 men joined the army in the Issyk-Kul' province in the month of October alone, a significant number of new troops to supplement those conscripted from other areas across Central Asia.[43]

New conscripts

Most conscripts from Central Asia, and indeed from across the Soviet Union as a whole, had typically worked as farmers, tractor drivers, teachers, bakers or veterinary assistants. Factory workers, less common in Central Asia, were in contrast mainly redeployed to the defence industry. In general, young men were conscripted directly into the army, while older men were deployed in less strategic – but equally physically demanding – construction battalions, building and mending roads and railway lines. Volunteers who had previously served in the army were accepted with alacrity, while others were processed in a more measured response.[44]

Communist Party officials were quickly conscripted into the army in an effort to instil and maintain ideological discipline and morale, although evidence suggests that party leaders often contrived to stay in their own region, where they were able to continue their political work without exposing themselves to danger.[45] Similarly the search for qualified pilots continued, although less trusted Central Asians were rarely eligible for more elite military placements, for example, as paratroopers.[46] At the same time, at the other end of the spectrum, prison camps were constantly scoured for dispensable inmates to serve as cannon fodder on the front line.[47]

Even more valuable were those with technical expertise, especially telegraph and radio communications specialists.[48] Teachers and university students from Kyrgyzstan were amongst the first to be called up for officer training, being rapidly deployed to active service, where their brief military training unfortunately rarely imbued the necessary survival skills.[49] After some unfortunate – if foreseeable – losses, more enlightened orders were issued to spare university students from conscription until they had finished their course. Similarly exempt were shipbuilding workers and students at the shipbuilding institute evacuated to Kyrgyzstan from occupied Ukraine.

Arguably most valuable, however, were medically qualified personnel, who served both at the front and at muster stations. At first, medical students had to finish their studies before deployment in the field, although this instruction was soon relaxed as men with any medical training at all were needed behind the battle lines. Former university students and medical personnel already conscripted into the armed services were urgently instructed to stay there, despite the need for medical services in the civilian population on the home front.[50]

Some men were excused conscription if their expertise was required locally or if they were working in reserved industries such as munitions, aviation or shipbuilding factories. From 1942, men working in reserved occupations were excused from active service for at least one further year.[51] Those in the so-called 'black' metal industry were also deemed to be more valuable in their factories at home, so anybody employed in iron and steel production was definitely exempt from conscription, as they were responsible for the raw materials needed for the continued output of vital military equipment.[52]

Some individuals decided to alter their date of birth, always rather vague in Central Asian records, so that they could remain at home for another year.[53] Others, though, anxious to serve their country, volunteered earlier than necessary, with one man leaving for the front aged fourteen, five years younger than the usual nineteen or twenty.[54] Responsibility for elderly parents in Central Asia traditionally lies with the youngest son, but often the eldest son in the family was spared from military service if a younger son was already in the army, a matter of shame for some men, but relief for their parents.[55] Despite some concessions for family responsibility, many families were left entirely without their menfolk as they were conscripted in successive drafts.

Physical fitness was important for military service, although those volunteering or conscripted from Central Asia failed to meet the state's criteria more often than their counterparts in the European regions of the Soviet Union. Men were supposed to be at least 150 centimetres tall for most regiments, although infantry rifle divisions preferred their soldiers to be a more unrealistic 175 centimetres. Physical development was relatively slow in Central Asia, and some, otherwise fit, young men's call-up was postponed until they met the required minimum height and weight requirements.[56]

Medical examinations at recruitment and muster points screened out men unfit for military service before they embarked on their basic training. While ethnic Slavs living in Central Asia were relatively fit, it was generally acknowledged that ethnic Kazakh and Kyrgyz men did not benefit from as good a diet or health service, often living far away from the medical facilities in urban centres. In most parts of Kyrgyzstan, therefore, a significant percentage of sick men arrived at the muster point. While overall in the Issyk-Kul' province 4.3 per cent of conscripts were rejected on medical grounds, in some areas the figure was much higher, for example, 17.8 per cent in the more remote Tan' Shan' district.[57] In the Jeti-Oguz district, the procedures for medical screening were so poorly organized that up to 40 per cent of relatively elderly men were by default exempted from military service.[58] In addition, some men from rural areas were ill equipped to deal with life in the army, arriving barefoot and wearing ragged clothes. In many cases clothes had to be provided for them before they were officially accepted.[59]

Already in 1940 medical reception centres had been required to clean up their act, as extra measures were put in place to prepare them for the processing of large numbers of men in sanitary conditions and with a functioning canteen. Medical literature and advice were on offer – sadly all too often to men who lacked adequate literacy – on the prevention of common diseases such as tuberculosis, gonorrhoea, bronchitis and malaria.[60] Each reception centre was supposed to be supervised by one military commander and two doctors. Early snags in the system, which allowed too many doctors to be mobilized to the front such that there was no ear specialist left in the Issyk-Kul' province, for example, were gradually overcome. A dearth of experienced doctors continued in Kazakhstan, however, particularly in Alma-Ata. Inspections of medical centres continued to reveal shortcomings, for example, the overly long time taken to treat men until they were fit for service and the alleged waste of time by some doctors, who insisted on treating conscripts as individuals rather than potential fighting machines.[61]

Procedures for medical intervention improved noticeably as the war progressed. The communal baths in Przheval'sk were opened on a daily basis from eight o'clock in the morning to midnight, alongside a dedicated disinfection unit. Beds were reserved in specialist medical institutions for treatment and a prolonged recovery if necessary, such that in Kazakhstan in April 1944, only 2.1 per cent of new conscripts were in need of medical treatment.[62] Thanks to this screening, many potential conscripts benefited from early medical intervention and life-saving treatment previously not accessible to them. Young Nikolai Nefedov from the Tiup district of the Issyk-Kul' province, for instance, was due to take up automobile training in the army before joining a motorized regiment, but complained of overall weakness and pain throughout his body. Upon learning that he had previously contracted brucellosis while working as a veterinary technician in Kazakhstan, doctors immediately dispatched him to a hospital specializing in infectious diseases for six weeks before proceeding with his conscription.[63]

Overall across the region around 14 per cent of potential conscripts were exempt from service on medical grounds. While a few healthy individuals attempted to bribe their way out of conscription by the illegal purchase of an exemption certificate, many men were sent home genuinely suffering from chronic illnesses, for example, epilepsy or dermatitis.[64] The philosophy of the medical centres was, ideally, to ensure that the men were fit for service before sending them off to the front. Many of course returned home wounded, needing further medical treatment. Later in the war, men who previously had been deemed unfit and not liable for conscription underwent a re-evaluation under amended criteria. For example, in March 1942 the army was accepting men blind in one eye for non-manual work in the rear, while those with chronic gastritis were still sent to construction brigades. By 1944 medical rejections in the Issyk-Kul' province included those 17 per cent of men who were shorter than 150 centimetres, two men with one leg shorter than the other, two who were not sufficiently developed physically, one convalescent, one post-operative man, one with dermatitis and one with a particularly bad boil or furuncle.[65]

This medical intervention, while welcome, was compromised once in the army by the poor sanitation inherent in such a large-scale operation, especially when the men reached Tashkent, the largest city in Central Asia and therefore home to the headquarters of SAVO, the Central Asian

Military District.[66] Further west in Samarkand (Uzbekistan) and north in Karaganda (Kazakhstan), conditions were also ripe for the spread of disease and discontent. Once in military barracks, the new recruits suffered harsh conditions in cramped and crowded living conditions. Many men who had at first accepted this rite of passage with some stoical fatalism also became disillusioned with the constant barrage of political indoctrination, dated equipment and a lack of experienced officers.[67]

If some men were deemed unfit for active service for physical reasons, others did not qualify as they held a nationality seen to be suspicious by the political and military authorities. Many ethnic Germans had lived in Kyrgyzstan for generations since the end of the nineteenth century, having emigrated and settled in Central Asia in order to practise their Mennonite faith. More ethnic Germans joined them in the region from 1936, victims of Stalin's purges; they were often sent to the Karaganda corrective labour camp in Kazakhstan (familiarly known as Karlag). Many others, around 1 million in total and notably the Volga Germans, were deported from other areas of the Soviet Union as war broke out, usually deployed to labour camps and treated as prisoners. The Mennonites of the Chui valley in Kyrgyzstan, living in villages around Talas and Kant, automatically became 'enemies of the people' after the outbreak of war with Germany. In particular, shortly after receiving a medal from the Soviet Union for fighting against the Germans in 1941, one man was stripped of his award and transferred to construction work.[68]

In addition to ethnic Germans, suspicion also fell on certain refugees to the region. Finns, Romanians, Hungarians and those born in Bessarabia were not welcome in the armed forces on the grounds of their questionable loyalty, in contrast with other – more ethnically trustworthy – refugees. Nationalities of whom the authorities were suspicious were used to form non-military construction columns, including Koreans who had been deported to Kazakhstan from the Vladivostok area before the war, when they were deemed to have been potential Japanese collaborators or spies.[69] From this point of view, the slight delay in conscription of ethnic Central Asians confirmed their place on a higher rung of the Soviet loyalty ladder than many, if not quite as near the top as their Slavic compatriots from Russia, Ukraine or Belarus.

Police records were checked before conscription: a known criminal carrying weapons could obviously pose a danger to the Soviet Union. The NKVD (secret police) were also suspicious of anybody whose parents had been repressed in 1937 and 1938, in addition to many Kyrgyz and Kazakhs whose family had lived for a period in China after the 1916 exodus. They were considered to be potentially dangerous as their relations had resisted conscription in the First World War. One man of Dungan nationality was deemed to be fit for manual work only, as both his parents had been arrested in the purges; another man's father had been executed as a counter-revolutionary for making contact with relations in China, leaving his son inacceptable for service in the Red Army. On the other hand, one Chinese man who had entered the Soviet Union and taken Soviet citizenship in 1940 found that he was in fact liable for conscription. It is difficult to judge which men fared the worst.[70]

Not only men were conscripted into the army, however. Central Asia was key in providing horses for the front – animals which were transported by train to the battlefield and then used in cavalry and artillery divisions. The Issyk-Kul' province of Kyrgyzstan sent more than their fair share, if largely unwillingly, alongside the other republics of Central Asia and even Mongolia, a close geographical and political neighbour of the Soviet Union, lying very much within the Soviet sphere of influence.

Much reliance was placed on horses, with sometimes more concern for their welfare than for the troops themselves. At the start of the war, the main issue was to send sufficient qualified vets to the front as well as large quantities of saddles and fodder. Military orders ensured in December 1941 that 40 tons of hay were transported by boat across Lake Issyk-Kul' to Rybach'e, and thence by train to the west, destined no doubt to keep the animals alive as they helped in the defence of Moscow. Every village sent four or five animals each year, although of the 59,000 collected in the province in February 1942, only 2,250 were deemed fit for service, a sorry figure embarrassingly classified as top secret in the official returns.[71] Perhaps this was because the local Przhevalsky horses were too small and lightweight for duties at the front, just like many of the local men. Urgent plans for obtaining more horses were underway by January 1943, although no doubt their owners were reluctant to part with the animals which were so necessary for the home front.

Many older men were also loath to leave their often starving families and their duties at home to join the army when called. Large families were common in Central Asia, but some parents were reticent to permit all their sons to leave the household. This was far from the semi-organized resistance demonstrated in 1916: twenty-five years after the *Urkun* most Central Asians had become resigned to Soviet authority. Despite the harshness of collectivization, the clampdown on religious activity and the Stalinist purges, most had benefited from Soviet rule which brought with it increased opportunities.[72] Others, though, had much to lose by fighting a war, with a genuine fear of leaving their families to struggle alone. Some even fled into the mountains or sought protection from friends and family to avoid an uncertain future after conscription.

The authorities began to clamp down on draft-dodging as early as August 1941, but had become increasingly concerned at the loss of potential conscripts by the winter, when counter-measures were stepped up. Military commanders in charge of key transit railway stations were instructed to watch out for draft-dodgers, deserters and spies who may be lurking amongst the crowds of legitimate travellers. As the problem increased during the autumn, top secret orders were issued from the regional headquarters of the NKO in Tashkent on how to arrest soldiers on the run. Not surprisingly, the NKVD were also enlisted to track down individual deserters, conducting regular searches of bazaars, parks, collective farms, workers' hostels and cinemas in an effort to arrest those who had put themselves outside the law. It was admitted, however, that it was more difficult to pursue and punish deserters if they subsequently found a useful job in industry.[73]

The penalty for desertion was severe, even if the men had not yet officially joined up or were desperate to see their families before leaving for the front. Many were subjected by the NKVD to a court trial and sentenced to death. Some were punished for desertion, even if it turned out that they were unfit for service in any case; others were targeted, although they did not appear on the official conscription lists either by design or by omission. Already in July 1941 a certain Sharshe Samarkov was arrested in Przheval'sk for desertion, and five other young conscripts were sent to court and sentenced to six months in prison for draft-dodging combined with the lesser charge of hooliganism.[74]

At this early stage, most absconders were avoiding conscription, although a few were already in the army. Evidence suggests that it was the older men who were most reluctant to join up, as they had family responsibilities and were more able to escape into hiding, whereas younger men had fewer options and were possibly more willing to answer the patriotic call. In the summer of 1942 around 1 per cent of all men served with conscription papers failed to appear at the mustering station without good reason. As the war progressed, disillusionment spread and 1,982 men from the Issyk-Kul' province failed to arrive at the muster station in 1943, a large proportion of whom were over the age of forty. Statistics sent to Tashkent reveal that the most popular months for evasion were June and July, when the mountain weather was clement. The authorities decided that the most effective counter-measure would be to place the onus on the chairmen of the local collective farms to ensure that their men arrived for registration, while increasing the amount of political input received by potential conscripts in order to convince them of their duty to the motherland. However, in the first quarter of the following year forty-two men avoided conscription from the Tiup district alone, again mostly in the older age bracket of 25–40.[75]

Many Kyrgyz in rural areas still did not feel part of the Soviet state, and in the early days of the war there were some small-scale protests against conscription, although nowhere near the scale of the 1916 rebellion. Some men were helped in their escape from prison, and many sought refuge in the high mountains. A few managed to reach the relative safety of the Chinese border, while others stayed in Kyrgyzstan, aided by friends and family, but sometimes resorting to raiding nearby settlements to steal cows and horses. A certain 21-year-old conscript, Takhtakhun Dushimbiev, was executed by firing squad for desertion even before leaving the Issyk-Kul' province. His family, too, suffered badly for his crime, with all their rights to financial support immediately withdrawn.[76]

In contrast, some so-called deserters were vindicated. Iakov Bubnov of Przheval'sk was unjustly taken for a deserter in the spring of 1942, when he had legitimately been given a six-month leave of absence from conscription on medical grounds. Swept up in the NKVD searches, he was finally exonerated by a medical commission. Fifteen genuine draft-dodgers, on the other hand, were captured in the mountains and sentenced to ten years in a strict prison camp in Siberia. At least they were eventually able to return home, unlike many of their serving compatriots who fell in battle.[77]

Many men also fled the army once they reached the muster stations, and the full impact of military life was brought home by the inadequacies of the reception areas, with sometimes even no boiling water to make tea. By 1944 – rather late in the war – the military authorities became aware that living conditions and discipline needed to improve. However, the absence of even minimal home comforts disillusioned men who were already badly spooked by the negative omens dogging Central Asia. Just two days before Hitler invaded the Soviet Union, the tomb of regional hero Timur in Samarkand was opened. Allegedly, inside the tomb was found the inscription: 'Whomsoever opens my tomb shall unleash an invader more terrible than I.'[78] Many Soviets, including those from Russia and Central Asia, were highly superstitious and took the curse at face value. Apparently an icon of the Virgin Mary in an Orthodox church in Talas, Kyrgyzstan, was moved to Przheval'sk in the east of the country just before the war started. When it arrived in its new home, it allegedly started crying tears of blood, another sign that something terrible was about to happen to the country and its people.[79] No wonder gullible future soldiers listening to rumours or superstitions were afraid for their short-term future.

Refugees and evacuees also experienced the moral dilemma of whether to go to war or not, having already escaped from occupied parts of the Soviet Union or other occupied countries. Regina Chanowicz, for example, a Polish Jew living in Uzbekistan, followed her father to the town hall in Osh, in southern Kyrgyzstan, when he was taken by the NKVD for conscription into the Soviet Red Army. She successfully argued that her father was too old and ill to serve, only to find that he was picked up once again and taken to the station where a train was waiting to take him to military headquarters. Only her quick thinking saved him, when, dressed as a nurse, she commandeered a horse-drawn ambulance to collect her father and took him to hospital as a supposed heart attack victim. Only at this stage did he receive a formal certificate of medical exemption from Red Army service. This type of ingenuity saved lives. Mehal Kesler, another Polish refugee, could not escape conscription and was taken to a training camp in Samarkand, Uzbekistan. His enterprising sister followed him with a false passport, which he successfully employed once she had sprung him from the train dressed as a coal-shoveller.[80]

Journey into the unknown

There was no escape from the inevitable for the majority, however. The crossing of Lake Issyk-Kul' was the first stage in the long journey westwards to the front for men like Rakhmanov, as they set off for basic training and onward deployment. From Frunze, the capital of Kyrgyzstan, most conscripts were directed either to Alma-Ata in Kazakhstan or to Tashkent, the headquarters of the Soviet army in Central Asia.

They knew that active service would not be easy, but already there was a sense of foreboding as the barges inched their way out of the port at Pristan'. New troops were usually transported in the depths of winter after the annual autumn round of conscription. This led to serious delays: for example, Vasilii Kaikin from Tiup was twice turned back from the jetty in January 1942, due to bad weather conditions.[81] Kaikin's third attempt at the crossing would sadly be his last: little did he know then that he was never to return to the mountains he called home.[82]

The cloud often descended from the mountains and visibility could be dangerously low, although the lake fortunately never froze. Enveloped in fog, the barges were in danger of collision, causing accidents to happen, such as when one troop-carrying barge left its moorings in January 1943, crashing into a post. Two tugs, the *Ob'* and the *Kirov*, were implicated in the collision, which also involved the steamer *Komsomol* and caused the loss of ten hours in the overall transport schedule. Luckily, nobody was injured, although the young soldiers were sitting huddled together on the deck throughout the winter's night with no shelter from the icy wind as they chugged westwards.[83]

Since the start of the purges in the 1930s, the Soviet Union had gained comprehensive experience in moving large numbers of people east to the Siberian forced labour camps of the GULag system. From 1939 an increasing volume of troops had been moved in the opposite direction – westwards into Eastern Europe. This number rapidly accelerated as millions were deployed to the front. Five large barges were requisitioned for the movement of troops and heavy goods across Lake Issyk-Kul', an operation which became more efficient as the war progressed.[84] In 1943, for example, the new tranche of 440 conscripts was ready to leave Pristan' on 8 January, due to arrive in Rybach'e the following day. Major Borisov, the military commander in Przheval'sk, telegraphed ahead to confirm the arrangements for their reception. Following a quick check of footwear, clothing and documents, the men were to be dispatched by train to military headquarters in Frunze on the evening of 12 January, on their way to join the 368th Rifle Division in Samarkand. Tracking the men's progress across Kyrgyzstan, Major Borisov suddenly received an amended order from Tashkent, causing the men to be diverted to the 211th Rifle Regiment in Fergana. Despite this initial uncertainty, these Kyrgyz men eventually reached Europe to make their mark on the outcome of the war. After the large numbers of the January mobilization, a further trickle of small groups of around twenty conscripts made their way across the lake. One young man, Nikolai Mukhovikov, called up later than his official cohort, travelled alone in November 1944, ready to start basic training by the New Year.[85]

Basic training

A network of training points was set up across Central Asia, from Tashkent to Alma-Ata. In Kyrgyzstan, most men were sent to Frunze in the north or Osh in the south for their basic training. On arrival, they underwent a disinfection process in a steam bath, before being issued with their military uniform, consisting of green woollen jacket and trousers with a warm coat and boots if available. New soldiers took an oath after a ceremonial march-past on joining the Red Army, often on 23 February, the anniversary of the formation of the Red Army in 1918. Everyone was issued with a small cylindrical Bakelite cartridge in which were kept details of the soldier's identity and contact details of his family in case of his death in action – the Red Army equivalent of the British or American 'dog tag'. This information was handwritten in tiny letters on thin paper, which was rolled up to slot inside the cylinder. Many young men avoided this exercise, however, leaving the paper intentionally blank, fearing superstitiously that by providing this information they were sealing their own death warrant.[86]

In theory, all Soviet men should have received some pre-conscription training either at school, summer camp, on their collective farm or at Komsomol meetings in main towns across Central Asia. This comprised civil defence lessons and basic military skills, such as marksmanship, grenade-throwing, anti-aircraft defence and anti-chemical warfare. In practice, this paramilitary training was compromised as most of the population

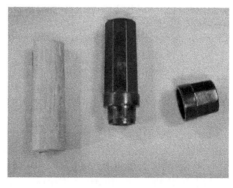

FIGURE 2.1 *Red Army identity cartridge. On display in the Panfilov museum, Almaty.*

in Kazakhstan and Kyrgyzstan lived on rural farms and were unable to attend regularly.[87] Instructors tended to be political officers without much experience of warfare, while also lacking the clout to provide training materials and weapons. As the war progressed, the situation improved as wounded veterans returned from the field to conduct pre-conscription training in the rear. The pressure to turn out new conscripts was such that only a half of Kazakh soldiers had used a rifle before being called up.[88]

The other main disadvantage was the poor literacy and lack of knowledge of the Russian language – both spoken and written – of Central Asian men in general. Many had attended school for only two or three years, and the Cyrillic alphabet (introduced into Central Asia only in 1940) was alien to those who had some degree of literacy but who were more familiar with the traditional Latin or Arabic script. Education was seen as key for the success of a modern army of mixed ethnicity, although top secret documents reveal huge misgivings at the preparedness of men at the onset of war in the Issyk-Kul' province. Schoolchildren in the town of Przheval'sk enjoyed a relatively good education, but 29 per cent of school-leavers in the Tiup district were judged to be barely literate, while over 90 per cent in the Ton district had no knowledge of Russian at all. As a consequence, it was felt necessary to deliver survival courses in Russian (plus extra political lessons) for future conscripts. These measures helped a great deal in Kazakhstan and Kyrgyzstan, although they were deemed less successful in Uzbekistan. Once again, improvements were made as the war progressed and post-conscription training gradually became better organized.[89]

Most of the training time, though, concentrated on the practical and theoretical aspects of warfare. Comprehensive courses had been developed in 1939, which crammed 300 hours of general military training into the first seventy-five days, without a break. Physical fitness was important culturally in the Soviet Union, not only in the army. The garrison in Tashkent prioritized sporting competition by training men to run faster and further under field conditions (e.g. to pick up a wounded comrade), firing on the run or throwing a hand grenade. For the final part of their training, conscripts moved to outlying camps for a further twelve full days and nights of practical warfare in all weathers, after which they were judged ready for combat.[90]

By the autumn of 1941, this course was condensed in an effort to expedite training and get as many men into the field as quickly as possible. Training concentrated on the tactics of war, weapons, construction and chemical warfare, with slightly less time devoted to political theory. The reality of war ensured that a few brief hours of new topics were added to the initial training course, including attacks specifically with rifles or tanks, in forests or at night, and organizing defensive positions.[91]

Despite the poor literacy of most men, instructors complained about the lack of literature for conscripts to study, while training camps also lacked weapons and sufficient junior officers. In a region famed for its horses, the best had already been sent to the front, leaving too few for cavalry training.

Basic military training June 1941 (hours)

FIGURE 2.2 *Basic military training June 1941 (hours). IKSA:146/1/1/75–8.*

Many men were already competent hunters, familiar with mountain sharpshooting, but training camps had to rely on old weapons, if any. Few conscripts dared complain about the lack of grenades or the amount of political content in the training, although their confidence suffered badly when other topics seen as more vital to survival were squeezed out of the course. Morale also plummeted as they experienced a lack of beds, food, toilets and soap, with many men suffering from food poisoning, lice and boils.[92]

As previously conscripted men fell or were wounded in the field, new cohorts were trained somewhat more efficiently to replace them, if often without the luxury of experienced instructors. Initial training was reduced by 50 per cent to 150 hours in 1943, to include military preparation (seventy-five hours in total), a technical speciality (forty-five hours) and Marxist-Leninist ideology (reduced to only thirty hours). Targets for specialities were introduced, including the training of female snipers used to working in the mountains. Men were increasingly assessed for previous experience in order to direct them into the cavalry, tank crew, artillery or the air force, each involving some specialist training. With this in mind, a certain Aleksandr Golovanev and his friend were dispatched to Saratov in Russia for training on the BT-7 tank, while another Kyrgyz man, Mikhail Bibikov, finished his training in Tashkent, where he was inducted in the use of anti-tank artillery.[93]

Radio operators were like gold dust and were trained with special care: after all, a mistake keying a letter or coded symbol in a radio message or order could cost lives. Their course was broken down into bite-sized chunks, with two or three hours on each page of the instruction manual. Firstly they had to learn how to set up a field radio station, then how to operate the microphone. Morse code followed with lessons in signalling, vital for reporting and controlling troop movements in the field. Men gradually built up familiarity with letters, then numbers, finally progressing to text, at which point they were mobilized to the front without further ado, to put their new skills into action.[94]

Officer cadets, who had completed their secondary or university education, were issued with a pistol and a wristwatch on embarking on a more advanced, if equally brief, training course concentrating on tactics in the field. With developing leadership skills, they were occasionally released from training on Sundays in the summer to help on the collective farm.[95]

Basic training completed, conscripts from Central Asia were deployed as riflemen, sappers, machine-gunners, tank personnel, mine-layers, drivers or radio and telegraph operators. These men joined others mobilized from elsewhere in the Soviet Union to build up the Red Army by an additional 29 million over the course of the war to produce a fighting force that was formidably large, if flawed with serious weaknesses once facing the enemy.[96]

Mobilization

Once their initial training was finished, troops from Central Asia were dispersed across the region and beyond as new military units were formed or men were sent to replace others in existing units. For the first few months of the war, Central Asians were largely sent to labour battalions operating in the rear or on border patrol in the mountains, while Red Army veterans and those of Russian or Ukrainian nationality were immediately directed to the front. As the war progressed, this situation changed according to need, with some men even going to support partisans in occupied western areas of the Soviet Union.

Within a few days of the start of the war, almost 200 new divisions had been raised across the Soviet Union, as new armies were formed and sent into battle. One and a half million men from Central Asia were mobilized during the first six months of the war. As military leaders had noted that men from Central Asia spoke little Russian and differed culturally from Slavic troops, full integration into the new divisions proved difficult. With this in mind, the creation of discrete national units became official policy from November 1941. The units raised in Central Asia were mainly rifle divisions, the Soviet term for ground troops or infantry. It is sometimes argued in Kyrgyzstan that men with hunting experience and proved marksmanship were ideal for the rifles, although military commanders probably considered that this was the most appropriate destination for troops whose loyalty and effectiveness remained questionable and whose lives could be squandered if necessary. In any case, deployment to a rifles unit was the default position for men with no obvious speciality. Over time, both Kyrgyz men and women became snipers, while many Central Asian conscripts were deployed as tank crew or joined the artillery after training, as a much smaller number joined the air force or navy.[97] Only a small percentage of elite specialists were recruited from ethnic Central Asians in comparison with their Slavic counterparts. Nonetheless, ten Kyrgyz men were sent to the aviation unit in Novosibirsk, twenty-five for submariner training and a further twenty-five to parachute regiments. These top secret troop movements were meticulously detailed in a pink school exercise book, evidence of the paper shortages across the Soviet Union during wartime.[98]

Reminiscent of the separate Gurkha battalions contributing to the British war effort, sixty-six new national units were created by the middle of November 1941, when it became apparent to Stalin that any initial qualms about the use of Asian forces were an indulgence that could no longer be afforded as the enemy marched inexorably towards Moscow. Although it was recognized that national units were preferable in maintaining comradeship and in the understanding of orders, all Central Asian divisions contained at least 30 per cent Slavic troops in an attempt to keep the men under close, trusted supervision and to dilute any potential disloyalty.[99] After all, many of these men were from families which had opposed conscription and fought against the Russians during the First World War, the *Basmachi* revolt or during the collectivization process of the 1930s. As the war progressed and Asian troops became more embedded in their new postings, many of the original battalions were dissolved or merged with mainstream army units from 1943. This was not only a question of maintaining political ideology, but also a pragmatic solution to the huge number of deaths during the first two years of the war and a need to restructure armies and replace losses after the devastation of the Battles of Moscow and Stalingrad. Similarly, divisions formed largely of Slavic volunteers from Central Asia at the onset of war in 1941 were gradually incorporated into regular units as the war progressed.[100]

During the course of the war, twelve rifle divisions, four cavalry divisions, seven brigades and over fifty various regiments and specialized battalions were raised in Kazakhstan. Retrospectively the most famous Central Asian division was the 316th Rifle Division, raised in southern Kazakhstan and northern Kyrgyzstan, where three national rifle divisions were raised alongside two cavalry brigades and two air regiments. By November 1941 fourteen national brigades had been raised in Uzbekistan, including the 99th to 102nd Cavalry Divisions, while the 116th Air Regiment was based in Stalinabad (Dushanbe), the capital of Tajikistan.[101]

Officers were mainly from the same areas as their men in an attempt to maintain efficient communication and instil better discipline. According to reports, one new rifle battalion benefited from three political officers but only six junior officers were in place out of the intended full complement of thirty. Despite the apparent organization of new conscripts, at the beginning of 1942 military commanders were still looking to identify a further four political officers and the forty-six junior officers needed for the smooth running of a further battalion, an issue which continued to plague all the Central Asian units. In contrast, the deployment charts demonstrate considerable planning, even at this early stage in the war, with a careful distribution of technical skills.[102]

These national units were sometimes, however, accused of physical weakness and even cowardice, and were not allowed into combat until it became absolutely necessary to boost decreasing numbers at the end of 1941. These claims probably became self-perpetuating, as Moscow's ongoing reluctance to deploy Central Asian troops added to the overall perception that they were actually more guilty of cowardice than other ethnic minorities. This, in turn, adversely affected the morale of Central Asian soldiers, who realized that they were seen as inferior in many ways to ethnic Slavs.[103]

By the end of 1941 nurses were being sent to the front line in large numbers, as the army struggled to deal with the increasing number of men who were wounded in action.[104] In addition, all qualified veterinary surgeons and nurses were sent to Tashkent as soon as possible and thence straight to the front to serve as a *vetfel'dsher* (veterinary paramedic) to nurse stricken, but valuable, animals back to full health. Civilian administrators, also, took the same route westwards as the serving troops. A certain Klavdiia Drutska, a soldier's wife, was granted a travel permit to Opalikha, not far from Moscow, by special request from the brigade headquarters where she was to work.[105]

As for Lieutenant Colonel Nikolai Liashchenko, as the war began in earnest he set off for Odessa as second in command of the 737th Rifle Regiment, to be posted soon afterwards to command the 972nd Reserve Rifle Regiment in Dnepropetrovsk (Dnipro), where he was joined by young Jumabek Rakhmanov in his first posting to the 424th Rifle Regiment of the 18th Rifle Division.[106] At the beginning and during the war the state successfully avoided most of the conscription difficulties encountered in 1916. Rakhmanov was just one of nearly 4 million men from Central Asia who answered the call to duty from the Soviet motherland, which had previously seemed so remote. Only time would tell how they would cope in the heat of battle.

Notes

1 John Barber and Mark Harrison, *The Soviet Home Front, 1941–1945* (London and New York: Longman, 1991), 406; Rodric Braithwaite, *Moscow 1941: A City and Its People at War* (New York: Knopf, 2006), 47–8; Hosking, *Russia and the Russians*, 492–3; and A. V. Veka, *Istoriia Rossii* (Moscow: Kharvest, 2003), 882.

2 Barber and Harrison, *The Soviet Home Front*, 16–17.

3 Braithwaite, *Moscow 1941*, 46; and Catherine Merridale, *Ivan's War: Life and Death in the Red Army, 1939–1945* (New York: Picador, 2006), 69–70.

4 Braithwaite, *Moscow 1941*, 50.

5 Barber and Harrison, *The Soviet Home Front*, 17.

6 Membership of the Komsomol was expected for young people aged from 14 to 28. See also Nikolai Liashchenko, *Gody v shineli* (Frunze: Kyrgyzstan, 1974), 37, 41 and 50; Kaptagaev, et al., *Sbornik*, 170; Kerimbaev, *Sovetskii Kirgizstan v Velikoi Otechestvennoi voine*, 33; and IKSA:119/1/8/112.

7 Liashchenko, *Gody v shineli*, 55, 153–200 and 220–30; and Hosking, *Russia and the Russians*, 493.

8 Merridale, *Ivan's War*, 55.

9 IKSA:146/1/1/23.

10 IKSA:119/1/7/10 and 14.

11 Braithwaite, *Moscow 1941*, 47–8; and Merridale, *Ivan's War*, 49–50 and 403 (note 2).

12 IKSA:119/1/7/12, 25, 47, 51 and 65; IKSA:146/1/2/8; and IKSA:146/1/4/16.

13 IKSA:119/1/8/296; and IKSA:146/1/6/2 and 169–7.

14 Braithwaite, *Moscow 1941*, 50; and Hosking, *Russia and the Russians*, 492–3.

15 Braithwaite, *Moscow 1941*, 49; and IKSA:146/2/5/70–8.

16 See Roger Moorhouse, *The Devils' Alliance: Hitler's Pact with Stalin, 1939–41* (London: The Bodley Head, 2014).

17 *Issyk-Kul'skaia Pravda (IKP)*, 11 June 1941, 4; 13 June 1941, 4; and 15 June 1941, 4.

18 *IKP*, 13 June 1941, 1; and 15 June 1941, 1.

19 Barber and Harrison, *The Soviet Home Front*, 59–60; and Braithwaite, *Moscow 1941*, 5.

20 *IKP*, 25 June 1941, 1–2; Barber and Harrison, *The Soviet Home Front*, 60–1; and Paul Stronski, *Tashkent: Forging a Soviet City. 1930–1966* (Pittsburgh: University of Pittsburgh Press, 2011), 74.

21 IKSA:146/1/5/139; Moritz Florin, 'Becoming Soviet through War: The Kyrgyz and the Great Fatherland War', *Kritika: Explorations in Russian and Eurasian History* 17, no. 3 (2016): 495–516, 495; and Stronski, *Tashkent*, 76.

22 IKSA:146/2/5/1.

23 Stronski, *Tashkent*, 75.

24 Kerimbaev, *Sovetskii Kirgizstan v Velikoi Otechestvennoi voine*, 36–7.

25 Stronski, *Tashkent*, 77.

26 *IKP*, 1 August 1941, 1.

27 *IKP*, 3 August 1941, 1.

28 Carmack, *Kazakhstan in World War II*, 20.

29 Stronski, *Tashkent*, 74–5 and 77–9.

30 Kerimbaev, *Sovetskii Kirgizstan v Velikoi Otechestvennoi voine*, 216.

31 Esenaliev, *Zhenishke dank*, 5; Kaptagaev, et al., *Sbornik*, 5; and Kerimbaev, *Sovetskii Kirgizstan v Velikoi Otechestvennoi voine*, 215.

32 Roberto Carmack, 'And They Fought for Their Socialist Motherland: The Creation of the Multi-ethnic Red Army, 1941–1945', *Otan Tarikhi* 64, no. 4 (2013): 35–45, 35; Roberto Carmack, 'History and Hero-Making: Patriotic Narratives and the Sovietization of Kazakh Front-Line Propaganda, 1941–1945', *Central Asian Survey* 33, no. 1 (2014): 95–112, 95; Carmack, *Kazakhstan in World War II*, 18; and information from the Panfilov museum, Almaty.

33 Interview with Kyias Satrovich Moldokasymov, chair of Fond Muras, 10 May 2018. See also Carmack, 'And They Fought for Their Socialist Motherland', 38; and Florin, 'Becoming Soviet through War', 505.

34 Barber and Harrison, *The Soviet Home Front*, 60; and Braithwaite, *Moscow 1941*, 128.

35 IKSA:119/1/17/248–61.

36 IKSA:119/1/17/267 and 296; IKSA:119/1/23/263; and Kerimbaev, *Sovetskii Kirgizstan v Velikoi Otechestvennoi voine*, 207.

37 IKSA:119/1/33/216 and 219.

38 Kaptagaev, et al., *Sbornik*, 8.

39 IKSA:146/1/26/5.

40 IKSA:119/1/23/17.

41 *IKP*, 2 August 1942, 2.

42 Barber and Harrison, *The Soviet Home Front*, 93.

43 IKSA:146/1/38/196.

44 Braithwaite, *Moscow 1941*, 96; and Tranum, *Life at the Edge of the Empire*, 127.

45 Information from historian Prof. Dr Tyntchtykbek Tchoraev (Chorotegin), Bishkek, 12 June 2018. See also Braithwaite, *Moscow 1941*, 96.

46 Carmack, *Kazakhstan in World War II*, 19.

47 IKSA:119/1/8/296; and IKSA:119/1/23/30.

48 IKSA:119/1/17/184 and187.

49 Tranum, *Life at the Edge of the Empire*, 126 and 136; and Kaptagaev, et al., *Sbornik*, 10.

50 *IKP*, 5 July 1944; IKSA:119/1/26/26; and Braithwaite, *Moscow 1941*, 107.

51 IKSA:119/1/17/190; IKSA:119/1/22/304; IKSA:119/1/23/24, 30, 33, 263, 308, 313 and 315; and IKSA:146/2/5/277. See also Barber and Harrison, *The Soviet Home Front*, 76.

52 IKSA:146/2/13/13–35.

53 Tranum, *Life at the Edge of the Empire*, 145.

54 Interview with 'Zoia' (a pseudonym), 22 May 2018; Tranum, *Life at the Edge of the Empire*, 145 and 149.

55 Tranum, *Life at the Edge of the Empire*, 13–14.

56 Ibid., 30; and IKSA:119/1/8/22 and 57.

57 IKSA:119/1/7/11.

58 IKSA:19/1/26/12.

59 IKSA:119/1/23/313–5.

60 IKSA:119/1/8/4–6 and 20–5.

61 IKSA:119/1/22/290; IKSA:146/2/12/718 and 772; and IKSA:146/2/13/11.

62 Carmack, 'And They Fought for Their Socialist Motherland', 39 and 40.

63 IKSA:146/2/5/281; and IKSA146/2/13/5.

64 IKSA:119/1/43/11.

65 IKSA:119/1/79/73; and IKSA:146/2/13/13 and 22. See also Carmack,
    Kazakhstan in World War II, 23.

66 Stronski, *Tashkent*, 1.

67 IKSA:146/1/1/65–7; and Merridale, *Ivan's War*, 59–67.

68 Information from Prof. Tchoraev. See also IKSA:119/1/33/34; Anne
    Applebaum, *Gulag: A History* (London and New York: Penguin, 2003), 102;
    El'mira Nogoibaeva, *Sud'by: Otkryvaia stranitsy istorii Kyrgyzstana* (Bishkek:
    2019), 58–60; and Tranum, *Life at the Edge of the Empire*, 102.

69 IKSA:119/1/17/248–59; IKSA:119/1/33/30; IKSA:146/2/13/104–6; and
    Tranum, *Life at the Edge of the Empire*, 112–13.

70 Information from Prof. Tchoraev; IKSA:119/1/22/277; IKSA:146/1/38/120;
    and Merridale, *Ivan's War*, 55.

71 IKSA:119/1/23/220; IKSA:119/1/31/8; IKSA:146/2/5/10, 141 and 303; and
    Kaptagaev, et al., *Sbornik*, 18–23 and 28.

72 Moritz Florin, *Kirgistan und die sowjetische Moderne, 1941–1991*
    (Göttingen: V&R, 2015), 43–4; and Dadabaev, *Identity and Memory*, 65.

73 IKSA:119/1/50/132; IKSA:146/2/5/22–209; and IKSA:146/2/20/1–2. See also
    Carmack, *Kazakhstan in World War II*, 25; Merridale, *Ivan's War*, 76; and
    Stronski, *Tashkent*, 295, note 23.

74 Braithwaite, *Moscow 1941*, 131; IKSA:119/1/22/244–74; and
    IKSA:119/1/34/2.

75 IKSA:119/1/34/2; and IKSA:119/1/50/8, 14, 50, 56–9, 130–2 and 239.

76 Florin, 'Becoming Soviet through War', 495 and 499–500; and
    IKSA:119/1/22/276 and 369.

77 IKSA:146/2/20/31; and Tranum, *Life at the Edge of the Empire*, 178–9.

78 IKSA:146/2/13/98; Dadabaev, *Identity and Memory*, 63; and Mark Stratton,
    'Uzbekistan: On the Bloody Trail of Tamerlane', *Independent*, 9 July 2006,
    https://www.independent.co.uk/travel/asia/uzbekistan-on-the-bloody-trail-of
    -tamerlane-5547233.html (accessed 17 December 2021).

79 Interview with church verger at Holy Trinity Church, Karakol, 31 May 2018;
    and IKSA:119/1/50/130–1.

80 Regina Kesler, *Grit: A Pediatrician's Odyssey from a Soviet Camp to Harvard*
    (Bloomington: AuthorHouse, 2009), location 888–922; and Michael Kesler,
    Shards of War: Fleeing to and from Uzbekistan (Durham: Strategic Book
    Group, 2010), location 1839.

81 Esenaliev, *Zhenishke dank*, 100.

82 Kaikin died a hero's death in 1945.

83 IKSA:885/1/2/1.

84 Braithwaite, *Moscow 1941*, 114; and Kaptagaev, et al., *Sbornik*, 10.

85 IKSA:119/1/6/98, 111 and 118; and IKSA:119/1/61/3–13.

86 Kerimbaev, *Sovetskii Kirgizstan v Velikoi Otechestvennoi voine*, 208–9; Liashchenko, *Gody v shineli*, 226; and Merridale, *Ivan's War*, 56–8.

87 Carmack, 'And They Fought for Their Socialist Motherland', 36–7; and Carmack, *Kazakhstan in World War II*, 7.

88 Carmack, 'And They Fought for Their Socialist Motherland', 36–40; Merridale, *Ivan's War*, 55; and Stronski, *Tashkent*, 80.

89 Information from Prof. Tchoraev. See also IKSA:119/1/19/113 and 178–80; IKSA:279/1/1/125; Carmack, 'And They Fought for Their Socialist Motherland', 40; and Bhavna Dave, *Kazakhstan: Ethnicity, Language and Power* (London and New York: Routledge, 2007), 22, 45 and 46.

90 IKSA:146/1/1/75–8; and IKSA:146/1/28/3.

91 IKSA:146/2/7/43, 50 and 75–91.

92 Merridale, *Ivan's War*, 59.

93 IKSA:146/1/27/9, 12, 46–7 and 63–7; and Tranum, *Life at the Edge of the Empire*, 31 and 75–6.

94 IKSA:119/1/61/215; and IKSA:146/1/27/9, 12, 46–7 and 63–7.

95 Merridale, *Ivan's War*, 58; and *IKP*, 22 July 1943, 2.

96 IKSA:146/2/7/75; Carmack, 'And They Fought for Their Socialist Motherland', 38; and Kerimbaev, *Sovetskii Kirgizstan v Velikoi Otechestvennoi voine*, 209–10.

97 Braithwaite, *Moscow 1941*, 129; Carmack, 'And They Fought for Their Socialist Motherland', 39; Kaptagaev, et al., *Sbornik*, 7; Keller, *Russia and Central Asia*, 204; and IKSA:119/23/23/30.

98 IKSA:146/1/38/135–41; and Carmack, *Kazakhstan in World War II*, 31.

99 Carmack, 'And They Fought for Their Socialist Motherland', 39; Carmack, *Kazakhstan in World War II*, 27; and Florin, 'Becoming Soviet through War', 505.

100 Braithwaite, *Moscow 1941*, 112.

101 Zh. Abylkhozhin, et al., eds, *Istoriia Kazakhstana*, vol. 4 (Almaty: Atamura, 2010), 467.

102 IKSA:146/2/7/1 and 22.

103 Carmack, *Kazakhstan in World War II*, 19 and 35.

104 Ibid., 20.

105 IKSA:146/1/17/1; and IKSA:146/2/13/1 and 4.

106 Liashchenko, *Gody v shineli*, 230; Kaptagaev, et al., *Sbornik*, 170 and 209; and Rakhmanov family archive.

3

At the fighting front

Viktor Mishin from Kyrgyzstan was already an experienced soldier when war broke out, having taken part in the Finnish war soon after he joined up in 1937. On 22 June 1941 he and his platoon were taking part in military exercises outside the city of Brest in Belarus when out of the blue their camp was bombed. Mishin and a few comrades managed to escape into the forest, where they successfully evaded the advancing Germans for twelve days and nights, eating mushrooms and berries to survive. He eventually rejoined Soviet lines in time to take part in the Battle of Moscow.[1] Mishin was just one of the men from Central Asia plunged into a life-and-death situation for the duration of the war.

The invasion of the Soviet Union at first threatened only its western, Slavic republics – Belarus, Ukraine and western Russia. In an effort to encourage distant Central Asians to join up and play an active role in the war, the state propaganda machine constantly reminded them that the enemy posed an indirect threat to their own families, ancestral lands and descendants. Rather than being made to feel inferior to their Slavic older brothers, they found that they were in fact their equals, urgently needed to come to the assistance of fellow countrymen in the west. In this way, Central Asians were targeted by a non-stop campaign highlighting the state's pervading communist ideology and urging them to join the Red Army in a distant war against the common fascist enemy. Only twenty-five years after the recruitment disaster of 1916, this indeed represented a distinct change of tone on the part of the state.

With historical irony, Slavic residents of Central Asia, whose families had chosen to move eastwards and settle in Central Asia in the nineteenth century, returned westwards towards their ancestral homelands in Ukraine and Russia, supported by their new Asian compatriots from the former tsarist colonies. At the same time, descendants of peasant families, who had migrated from the depths of Siberia to the fertile lands of the warmer south, marched north-eastwards to defend the Soviet Far Eastern Front on the Pacific coast and the Manchurian border. Even some prisoners who, just a few years earlier, had been exiled to Siberian or Kazakh GULag camps, found themselves caught up in a huge wave of population displacement. Like travellers of old traversing the Silk Road, they covered vast distances, this time often by train but also sometimes marching on foot towards their inevitable encounter with the enemy. Not only men but also tanks, munitions, horses, clothing, food and fodder joined the mass movement on an unprecedented scale.

Operation Barbarossa, the sudden German offensive of 1941, could well have led to a speedy defeat for Stalin and his *Stavka* (chiefs of staff). However, despite inroads into Ukraine and the Baltic States, enemy forces were stopped before they reached Moscow and just failed to take the country's second city, Leningrad, which remained besieged by enemy troops until 1944.

The year 1942 saw further enemy advances, but most historians agree that the Battle of Stalingrad was the turning point of the war. Stalingrad (Volgograd), a key industrial city on the River Volga, was the gateway to the Caucasus and the rich oilfields of the Caspian Sea. This decisive battle raged in harsh conditions throughout the autumn and winter of 1942 until the enemy was finally surrounded and defeated at the beginning of February 1943. The Soviet counter-attack had begun, as the Red Army gradually clawed back occupied territory in the west of Russia and Ukraine in 1943, pressing on to relieve Leningrad and the Baltic States the following year. Poland and Hungary also fell to Soviet troops, as the enemy was split on several fronts. As the Allies advanced from the west and south, the Red Army pushed from the east through Czechoslovakia, Austria and East Prussia, staging the final assault on Berlin at the end of April 1945.

Following the capitulation of Berlin in May 1945, many men, particularly those newly conscripted from Central Asia, were then rapidly deployed to the far east, to concentrate on the war with Japan and Manchuria which was not concluded until four months later. Those troops who had been on active service since 1939 were demobilized relatively quickly, but many men were forced to remain in uniform for up to five or six years until they were finally free to return to civilian life.

Many volumes have been written about the war on the Soviet Western Front.[2] The following pages do not aim to offer a detailed military history of the Soviet role in the Second World War. Rather, they highlight the part played by Central Asians in the conflict. Disadvantaged at first by a lack of equipment and racial prejudice, troops from these republics nevertheless experienced a similar war to those from other regions of the Soviet Union, bringing them state acknowledgement for their role. In many notable ways the war years changed these participants, bringing them closer to the rest of the Soviet Union, while giving them skills which were used on their return home to assist in building up the modern independent republics which exist today.

Battle of Moscow

As soon as war was declared, Soviet troops were dispatched post-haste to the front lines to engage the enemy advancing through Belarus and Ukraine. The German offensive was so fast and well planned, however, that the Red Army immediately found itself on the defensive, with insufficient equipment and manpower. The first Kyrgyz units reached the front in August 1941, where Moldokmat Bulanbekov, a sniper with the 336th Rifle Regiment, bemoaned having to share just one rifle between two men.[3] This was typical of the problems facing Central Asians particularly in the first two years of the war, when they suffered a lack of equipment ranging from sturdy boots to binoculars.[4] These naïve young men with little schooling were at first poorly equipped to fight a modern war, barely understood orders shouted or written in Russian and were completely out of their depth living and fighting amongst men from a totally different culture, who often regarded them as outsiders. Morale was understandably low when men faced the bitter cold fuelled only with meals of pork, in principle off the menu for Muslims who preferred their usual *chuchuk* (horsemeat sausages).[5] Despite the official proclamations of the friendship of the peoples of the Soviet Union – the so-called *druzhba narodov* – these Asian troops suffered substantial discrimination from officers and NCOs. Desertion rates were high, and many were suspected of defection to the enemy, an accusation which only confirmed initial prejudices against them.[6]

In an effort to address the disaffection of ethnic minorities plunged into this nightmare situation, official war correspondents were directed to boost morale. Il'ia Erenburg, writing for the Red Army newspaper *Krasnaia Zvezda* (The Red Star), published a major propaganda piece in the autumn of 1941 as the reality of war was starting to bite. Listing a string of ethnic minorities serving in the Soviet armed forces, he emphasized that all the republics were fighting together against the common enemy. The so-called fascist 'Hitlerites', he told readers, wished to squash minority cultures by promoting a divisive hatred. Quoting Stalin's nationalities policy, he reminded them that 'friendship between the peoples of the USSR is a great and serious conquest. For as long as this friendship exists, the peoples of our country will be free and remain unvanquished'.[7]

Mavlian Matniiazov, born in 1914 to an Uzbek family living in Przheval'sk, was one of the first Kyrgyz conscripts to whom his political officer would have read this and similar articles. Illiterate and without any formal schooling, this new private joined the 407th Rifle Regiment as a machine-gunner. By the autumn of 1941 he was part of the 316th Rifle Division fighting in freezing conditions to the west of Moscow in a desperate bid to halt the German advance (known as Operation Typhoon) before it reached the capital.[8]

At least most Soviet troops were used to the low temperatures. Many Germans and Uzbeks suffered, however, and Matniiazov missed his hot tea. Not only supplies and sufficient weapons were missing, however. At the start of the war the severe shortage of junior officers remained: indeed, it is estimated that the country as a whole lacked around 55,000 officers. The hole was filled as quickly as possible by the rapid deployment of young men with little military training and barely in a position to command the older men in their platoons.[9] However, relatively few Central Asians spoke good enough Russian to be made officers; neither were they educated or trusted enough for leadership positions. Consequently, most of the 10,000 officer cadets who left Kazakhstan for the front during the war were ethnic Russians.[10]

Umarzhan Churukov from Przheval'sk was one budding Kyrgyz officer. He was already at military academy training for duty in a tank regiment at the time of the German invasion. Aged only twenty, the young lieutenant took command of a tank brigade at the Battle of Moscow. Unsurprisingly, his war career ended in an early death, and he was laid to rest in a communal grave in 1943.[11]

One distinguished Kazakh officer was somewhat luckier, or perhaps simply more experienced. Senior Lieutenant Baurzhan Momysh-uly, born in 1910 to a family of nomadic herders, was a former teacher who had already served in the army before the war as commander of a squad of a mountain cavalry regiment in Termez, Uzbekistan. Following demobilization in 1934 he worked in a bank, only to be recalled to the army alongside other trusted Central Asians who had already seen service and earned relatively quick promotion. At first he was sent to the Russian far east as commander of an anti-aircraft battery platoon, then subsequently posted to Ukraine as the assistant commander of a regiment. Momysh-uly put in for a transfer to Kazakhstan in January 1941 to work as a senior instructor in the conscription service. Following the German invasion, as a mature and experienced soldier he was put in command of the 1st Rifle Battalion of the 1073rd Rifle Regiment raised in the Kazakh town of Talgar, a unit of the 316th Rifle Division under the command of Major General Ivan Panfilov. Although not an indigenous Central Asian, Panfilov had formerly served as the military commander of the Kyrgyz republic, a deputy of the Frunze province and a senior politician in the city of Frunze. As a soldier, he was highly rated by senior Soviet generals for his tactical skill, intelligent humour and respect for his men.[12]

Panfilov's motorized infantry division was originally formed of 11,750 men in three rifle regiments, two of which were raised in Alma-Ata (Kazakhstan) and one in Frunze (Kyrgyzstan). It was supplemented by an additional two artillery regiments and a small reserve tank company comprising just two of the famous T-34 tanks and a few smaller armoured vehicles.[13] Alongside the Kazakh 310th Akmolinsk, 312th Aktiubinsk and the 314th Petropavlovsk Rifle Divisions, the 316th was part of the 52nd

Army building defensive positions on the Soviet north-west front. However, by the beginning of September 1941, they faced an increasing enemy threat from Germans on the south of Lake Ladoga outside the city of Leningrad, causing the 310th and 314th Rifles to retreat. Shortly after Leningrad came under siege many remaining Soviet units fell back, leaving Leningrad to its fate and marching south to the urgent defence of Moscow.[14]

After quite a slow start to their war, Panfilov's division was deployed to reinforce General Konstantin Rokossovskii's 16th Army to the west of Moscow following the protracted battle around Briansk. The 316th was selected to defend an overextended line of 41 kilometres across the major road running eastwards through the town of Volokolamsk towards Moscow, the so-called Volokolamsk Highway. The 316th went into battle from 14 to 18 October 1941, establishing several defensive areas around the town. Strengthened by three anti-tank and heavy artillery regiments, Panfilov's division took part in a protracted battle in which Senior Lieutenant Momysh-uly's 700 men reportedly distinguished themselves. The Germans counter-attacked on 22 October, encircling the area where Momysh-uly had gathered the wounded and artillery into the centre of a defensive formation. Gaining some advantage to the rear of the German advance on Moscow, the 316th were, however, bombarded by enemy aircraft and artillery, taking heavy losses. With morale plummeting at the obvious superiority of the enemy, they eventually retreated in some disorder on 28 October, flouting a direct order from Stalin and incurring the temporary wrath of Rokossovskii.[15]

Panfilov's division regrouped and prepared for renewed battle. The German advance on Moscow by a total of fifty-one divisions and the 46th Panzer Corps was slowed to an extent on 16 November, helped by the action of an anti-tank platoon of the 1075th Regiment near the village of Dubosekovo. With retreat on this occasion never an option, it was later claimed that dozens of enemy tanks were destroyed in what was described as heroic action on the part of twenty-eight of Panfilov's men, most of whom died in the engagement. The 1073rd Regiment deployed nearby similarly helped to stall and deflect the invaders at high cost.[16] As the German advance lost momentum due to the freezing weather, the responsibility for thousands of Soviet prisoners of war (POWs) and overstretched supply lines, Moscow was narrowly saved from invasion.

The 316th Rifle Division was awarded the Order of the Red Banner and renamed the 8th Guards (Panfilov) Rifle Division. Panfilov himself, however, was mortally wounded on 17 November, to be made a posthumous Hero of the Soviet Union. In a successful propaganda campaign, twenty-eight men of the 1075th Regiment were also made Heroes of the Soviet Union for their action at Dubosekovo, as the state propagandists searched out ethnic minorities to mythologize. While at first it was claimed by the state that all twenty-eight men had died in the defence of Moscow, this was later found to be untrue, but did not alter the developing myth around the action. This

FIGURE 3.1 *A group of soldiers from the 316th 'Panfilov' Rifle Division. Reproduced with permission from the Issyk-Kul' State Archives.*

encounter with the enemy, exaggerated for public consumption, served to underline further the friendship of the various nationalities across the Soviet Union, demonstrating the key role of Central Asian troops in the defence of Moscow, the Russian and Soviet capital.[17]

The 316th Rifles were returned to the rear in December 1941 and reformed as the 8th Guards in 1942 under a series of new commanders. Despite the state's original intention to keep regional minorities together, most of the initial national units were dismantled within a few months of their formation, while the men were usually amalgamated into other pan-Soviet fighting forces. This was not necessarily an attempt to undermine the concept of national divisions, but rather a pragmatic recognition that their manpower had been severely reduced. By the end of the war, the division originally raised in Central Asia contained over 5,000 men of thirty different nationalities.[18]

Stalingrad

The main Kyrgyz units fought their way westwards and northwards from Volokolamsk, but men from Central Asia were also allocated to regiments close to the action on the River Volga as the Germans advanced south-east towards the industrial city of Stalingrad. Only 500 kilometres separated Stalingrad from western Kazakhstan, which came increasingly under threat from German bombers during 1942, bringing the war much closer to home for some. Indeed, Kazakh troops were constantly reminded by radio of their important role: 'In defending the great Russian River Volga, you are defending your own sunny Kazakhstan.'[19] As well as motivating Central Asians to fight for their families, it was also felt important by the *Stavka* to integrate them as much as possible into regular Red Army units. This was effected by instructing commanders to treat all their men equally, but also by a series of propaganda letters from Russians to ethnic minorities on the front line, continuing to highlight the importance of their role in the war. In reiterating the friendship of the peoples, these official letters implicitly emphasized the hierarchy of ethnicities in the Soviet Union, with Russians clearly outranking Central Asians.[20]

By September 1942 the Red Army had reached the centre of Stalingrad. Three hundred and twenty Soviet units took part in the protracted Battle of Stalingrad, including five rifle and cavalry divisions from Kazakhstan, plus specialist mine-laying regiments and a battalion of bridge-builders, many of which formed part of the 64th Army. New divisions – the 10th and 4th Guards Rifles – each including Kyrgyz and Uzbeks, were hurriedly raised in Frunze in an effort to meet the mortal challenge posed by the enemy.[21] The Soviet offensive became more difficult as November saw the onset of deep snow, with troops fighting to the death over every inch of ground and enormous losses on both sides. Facing summary execution from Stalin's 'Not one step back' Order Number 227 of July 1942, retreat was not an option for the Soviet troops. Military police stationed just behind the lines were even ordered to arrest stragglers and shoot anyone retreating without orders, while officers who failed to hold their units together were sent to the infamous penal battalions.[22]

Discipline may have been tight, but morale suffered badly in the atrocious winter conditions. Teenage Kyrgyz machine-gunner Apysh Makeev, conscripted only at the start of 1942, claimed responsibility for the deaths of over a hundred Germans, while watching his comrades fall on a daily basis. He was fortunate enough to survive the conflict, eventually receiving the prized medal 'For the defence of Stalingrad'.[23] Alabakov Karif, who joined the army in 1938, was already an experienced soldier. He had served in the original Panfilov 316th Rifle Division, having played an important role in the Battle of Moscow as a senior sergeant in an anti-aircraft artillery regiment. Karif was posted to Stalingrad as a scout with the aim of pinpointing enemy positions in order to guide the heavy artillery with some accuracy towards their target. As they became more skilled, reconnaissance troops were also credited with estimating the strength and capability of enemy forces, and even gauging their morale.[24]

Casualties

Nearly half a million Soviet soldiers and airmen died during the Battle of Stalingrad, a figure exacerbated by the inexperience of junior commanders.

The full information was suppressed for decades by the Soviet regime, which also significantly under-reported the number of wounded.[25] Kyrgyz Bakas Japarov was sent to Stalingrad before having had the chance to complete his officer training. With ten years of formal schooling, he was obvious officer material, but reached the front line as a sergeant. Such was the shortage of junior officers that he was promoted to Junior Lieutenant after his very first experience of action. In this exposed position, he was soon wounded and hospitalized in the rear for months. His comrade, Fedor Emel'ianov from the Fergana military academy in Uzbekistan, was in a similar position, being wounded within a short time of arriving at Stalingrad, which entailed a six-month stay in hospital before he was fit to return to battle.[26]

Twenty-year-old Tenti Tamashaev from Tiup in eastern Kyrgyzstan equally missed out on most of the action. He had been conscripted in December 1941 and was rapidly promoted to senior sergeant. After cursory basic training he set off for the front, covering the final 400 kilometres from Kazakhstan on foot, walking at night and resting by day to avoid enemy planes. Tamashaev and his Kyrgyz and Kazakh comrades eventually reached Stalingrad, where he received a leg wound necessitating treatment in a military hospital in Saratov for six months before he was sent home.[27]

Kurmankul Azhinaev from the Issyk-Kul' province never even made it to Stalingrad. He journeyed westwards from Central Asia by train, as German planes strafed and bombed his troop convoy night after night. Even armoured carriages carrying tanks were badly damaged before Azhinaev's train was stopped short just 15 kilometres from Stalingrad. His carriage suffered a direct hit, but Azhinaev was able to jump out of the train, despite his clothes being on fire. The flames were fortunately extinguished by another soldier, enabling the two men to run into a nearby wood. Desperate for cover, they were bombed all night long, finding in the light of dawn that they were surrounded by scores of dead bodies and badly injured men. Medical orderlies eventually gathered together the seriously wounded, leaving Azhinaev – who had been hit in the left leg and burnt on the left side of his body – to make his own way to a medical station under canvas. Not surprisingly, it took five months for him to recover once the shrapnel had been removed and he had been treated for the burns in a field hospital, by which time the Red Army had retaken Stalingrad.[28]

Petr Chervonnykh from Kyrgyzstan started his war in Ukraine and arrived in Stalingrad from the west. He was badly wounded in November 1942, losing an eye. After eight months' treatment in an 'evac' hospital in the rear, he faced protracted periods in other specialist face hospitals, finally being discharged from the army in February 1944. Classified unfit for active service, he returned home, along with thousands of other war wounded, or 'invalids' in the Soviet system.[29] The impact of the arrival at home of so many disabled war veterans is examined in Chapter 4.

Friendship of the peoples?

Many ethnic Central Asians continued to fight at the front, while also suffering from discrimination and racism at the hands of Slavic officers and even rank-and-file soldiers in their new multiethnic units. General Nikolai Belov employed in his diary the derogatory term used by some Russians for Kazakh men – *iusupy* (literally, Josephs). He amplified this term of abuse by noting that 'they are members of a cruel people, not knowing which way to turn when under fire, like a flock of sheep', effectively bemoaning the ineffectiveness of Kazakh troops at Stalingrad. He went on to attribute losses in his battalion to the defection of several Kazakh men, *iusupy* and *eldashy* (comrades) to the enemy in June 1943, despite the fact that they would have risked execution if caught.[30] This attitude was common amongst commanding officers, who sometimes treated Central Asians as inferior to their Slavic comrades due to their lack of both education and a good command of the Russian language. They were therefore often consigned to menial roles in their units.[31]

Ethnic minorities were sometimes dismissed by Russian servicemen as *natsmen*, using the Russian abbreviation for minority nationalities. Blaming them for the vagaries of war was not uncommon amongst Red Army officers, particularly in multiethnic units.[32] A certain Amantur Tektonazarov recalled after the war how his commanding officer had despised his fellow Kyrgyz as small and weak, forcing them to carry 42-kilogram shells in a deliberate attempt to humiliate them. It was clearly not only the high command who mistrusted Central Asian troops. Political officers still tried to uphold the official doctrine of the brotherhood of nations by carrying out Communist Party education in an effort to integrate men of different ethnicities, but endemic racial prejudice usually won out and many Central Asians were sent back to the rear in October 1943, once the tide of war had turned in favour of the Soviet Union.[33]

The long months of the Battle of Stalingrad witnessed a low point in the morale of the Soviet Union, amongst both the troops and those in the rear. As the fierce fighting on the Volga reached its climax, the first news finally reached the public through the press in early December 1942, when a short report was complemented by photographs of the devastation.[34] In an effort to encourage the loyalty of Kyrgyz troops, a further wave of official letters was launched. Each letter, originally signed by 700,000 compatriots, was sent to every soldier in both Russian and Kyrgyz versions. A total of 13,000 copies were dispatched to the front in December 1942, targeted at the 103 army units containing Kyrgyz men. The letter was also published in the Kyrgyz newspaper *Kyzyl Kyrgyzstan* (Red Kyrgyzstan) and *Sovetskaia Kirgiziia* (Soviet Kyrgyzstan), being reproduced in local newspapers to drum up support for the serving troops and to encourage others to enlist. The creative Soviet propagandists judged that the greetings and encouragement of their compatriots at the rear would boost morale, especially if addressed to soldiers of discrete nationalities.[35] At the same time as distinguishing certain ethnic minorities, the Soviet military command endeavoured to foster a unity of all peoples of the Soviet Union, while constructing a dual identity for Central Asian troops and cultivating more Soviet loyalty for Kazakhs in particular.[36] An ostensible response from the Kyrgyz troops at the front was published shortly afterwards, containing an oath pledging to do their utmost for the Soviet motherland.

The new year brought those at home further worrying snippets from the front, tempered by the propagandists' positive spin on the exploits of the Panfilov Division, in an obvious attempt to repair the damage done to morale by the high losses and racism evident on the battlefield.[37] Surprisingly, therefore, some soldiers apparently had the time to write back to their comrades on the collective farms at home to wish them well in their enterprises.[38] This uplifting, if artificial, exchange of congratulatory letters preceded the official news a week later of victory at Stalingrad in a front-page article entitled 'At the Last Minute'.[39]

Servicemen and women

Nikolai Liashchenko from Kyrgyzstan became second in command of the 18th Rifle Division in September 1942, fighting to relieve the siege of Leningrad. If Stalingrad was the biggest artillery battle of the war, the city of Leningrad and its citizens certainly suffered the most protracted siege, lasting a total of 872 long days from 8 September 1941 to 27 January 1944.[40]

Jumabek Rakhmanov, who had started his war on the banks of Lake Issyk-Kul', had rapidly gained combat experience, being promoted to section commander. By the time the tide of war was on the turn at the start of 1943, he was serving as colour sergeant to Liashchenko. Rakhmanov had already been wounded once in October 1942 and again in January 1943, when Liashchenko received a congratulatory telegram from newly promoted Marshal Georgii Zhukov following a significant breakthrough against the enemy forces surrounding Russia's second-largest city.[41] By the summer of 1943 Liashchenko was commanding the 90th Rifle Division, still stationed outside Leningrad. Within the space of three weeks in July 1943, Rakhmanov was wounded twice more. Spotting a German sniper positioned in a tree and successfully taking out Soviet soldiers, Rakhmanov managed to shoot down the enemy. In doing so, he received his final wound, spending the rest of his life with a bullet permanently lodged in the back of his neck. Rakhmanov survived his stay in hospital and received, with others involved in the eventual relief of the siege of Leningrad, the medals 'For the defence of Leningrad' and 'For courage'.[42]

Troops from Central Asia followed different trajectories during the final years of the war. Liashchenko's route took him from Leningrad westwards to Belarus, Karelia and the Baltic States as the enemy retreated in the face of resurgent Soviet armies. The famous 8th Guards (Panfilov) Division marched across western Russia and finally into the Baltic States, helping to take Riga and then Tallinn, while the Kyrgyz 385th Rifle Division fought their way across Belarus and into Danzig (Gdansk), reaching Berlin in the final stages of the war.

In early 1944 Central Asian troops also progressed westwards via Poland, Czechoslovakia and Yugoslavia. At the start of the war, Kalyk Shykyev from Chaek in the central mountains of Kyrgyzstan had been posted to the 309th Rifle Regiment in a division largely formed of fellow Central Asians.

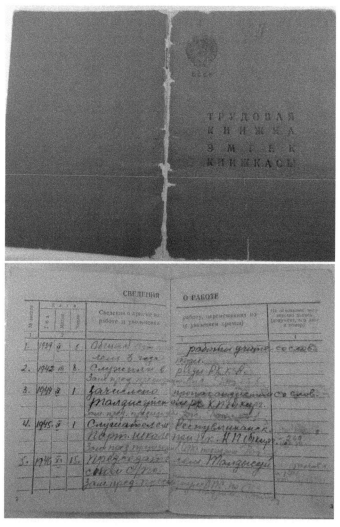

FIGURE 3.2 *Jumabek Rakhmanov's service record. Published with kind permission from the Rakhmanov family.*

Following a short stint in a cavalry regiment he joined the 229th Guards Artillery Regiment, manning field guns. His unit was sent from Pskov, between Leningrad and the Baltic States, south to Ukraine once the Red Army started to claw back occupied territory there. Notwithstanding the loss of an ear to enemy fire in March 1944, he returned to active service to take part in the liberation of Crimea. Another rapid journey north took him back to the Baltic States, with a final quick change in direction to end the war in Romania.[43]

Others were already embedded deep behind enemy lines, serving with local partisans – especially prevalent in occupied Ukraine. Strategic roles were also played by radio operators, parachutists, medical orderlies, interpreters and even war artists and musicians entertaining the troops. Slavs and ethnic minorities from across Central Asia saw service in an increasingly complex logistical operation across Europe and Asia. Men with family roots in China, such as Dungans Bagi Abdullaev and intellectual Abdrakhman Kalimov, joined Officer Cadet Aziz Narynbaev, a Uighur former baker. They fought alongside Cossack, Tatar, Tajiki, Kyrgyz, Uzbek and Kazakh comrades in this multiethnic – but ostensibly atheist – communist environment. Soldiers of all nationalities were often heard in prayer before a major encounter, whether Russian Orthodox, Muslim or Buddhist believers.[44]

Omor Asankozhoev was already a relatively experienced soldier when the Soviet Union was invaded, having seen service in Lithuania since his conscription in 1939. By October 1941 he had been posted to the 224th Artillery Regiment as a radio operator, acting also as a topographer specializing in mapping the landscape to direct Soviet fire. He remained in the north until the relief of the siege of Leningrad, when his unit moved west through Ukraine, Belarus, Poland and East Prussia.[45]

Nikolai Shuba was born in 1925 into a peasant family which had emigrated from Ukraine in the nineteenth century to the village of Ak Suu in eastern Kyrgyzstan. He was working as a builder on a collective farm when he was called up at the beginning of 1943. He had not even completed basic training when he was suddenly deployed to the 13th Parachute Brigade. Shuba also became involved in the Leningrad offensive, often – as a parachutist – first into any action. His trajectory took him from Leningrad through Belarus and on to Austria, Czechoslovakia and Hungary.[46]

It was Obil Nazirov's linguistic knowledge which dictated his wartime role. Rushed through officer training in 1942, the former Tajik primary school teacher was sent to Iran as an interpreter. Speaking not only Tajiki and Persian but also Russian, Tatar and Kyrgyz – languages acquired in the melting pot of cultures in his home country – he even helped to deal with an alleged American spy. With a shortage of junior officers at the front, however, he was posted as a young lieutenant to Kursk followed by service in Ukraine and Romania.[47] Another interpreter was Kyrgyz Azhimatov Ylyrys, who served most of his war in the 2nd Battalion of the 8th Guards (Panfilov) Division, commanded at that time by Momysh-uly. As the war progressed, he used his college German to interrogate POWs. In this capacity, he spent most of his time at regiment headquarters, usually out of range of enemy artillery.[48]

Keeping up the morale of the troops was vital. Kazakh Vasilii Kudinov, from the shores of the Aral Sea, took his accordion with him to the front to entertain others in his platoon during the quiet spells between action. Nicknamed 'Vasilii Terkin' after Aleksandr Tvardovskii's popular fictional wartime hero, he helped to dispel the considerable homesickness amongst the troops. Tvardovskii's protagonist appeared in the mainstream press from 1942 to the end of the war in a long series of poetic episodes recounting the adventures of an ordinary soldier going through the war with his comrades while nearly always maintaining a cheerful outlook. A testament to Tvardovskii's simple narrative skills was that Terkin appealed to people of all nationalities, as his verses were also broadcast on the radio. More formal concerts for the troops were arranged centrally, including well over a thousand musical events for Kazakh soldiers on active service. Kudinov was eventually ordered to form his own official wind band which toured newly liberated towns playing victory marches. This move to the rear probably saved his life, as his old battalion was wiped out in the final years of the war.[49]

Wounded in action

A talent for drawing determined Konstantin Kulakov's war. Originally from Alma-Ata, he was sent to the Siberian Far Eastern province to study military art for three months after being called up in December 1942. This speciality was no guarantee of a quiet war, however, as most of his work was completed on the front line. Assigned to an artillery regiment, Kulakov had travelled through Belarus and the Baltic States before he was badly wounded in East Prussia towards the end of the war. The worst damage was to his back and head, where shrapnel was deeply embedded. Despite the large quantities of opium poppies harvested and opiates manufactured in Kyrgyzstan for use in military hospitals, there remained an insufficient supply of anaesthetics in field hospitals. With only a tumbler of spirits to numb the pain, he was still conscious as the metal pieces were scraped from his skull. Remarkably, he was back at the front after only six weeks, marching through Danzig and Königsberg (Kaliningrad) into East Prussia with the 96th Regiment of the 216th Guards Division.[50] Similarly, Kyrgyz Tentimish Inazarov, wounded in the leg and dragged to safety by his Russian comrade Ivan, was evacuated by boat across the River Elbe to a nearby hospital in the rear, his shoes soaked in blood. Brandy was administered, and he was held down by two field paramedics as the surgeon extracted the bullet. Inazarov's five-month convalescence took place in Brandenburg at the very end of the war.[51]

Even Obil Nazirov, the interpreter, did not escape the horrors of battle, as war wounds were the rule rather than the exception. He sustained a head injury in Ukraine in October 1943. Following a relatively quick recovery he was cleared for active service, only to be severely wounded again in 1944, this time permanently.[52] Every effort was expended to ensure, firstly that men were healthy enough to go to the front, and secondly to treat their wounds as quickly as possible in order to return them into action, often only for them to return home for further medical intervention after another battle. On occasion, however, a light wound could provide a ticket home for a war-weary soldier. While most were wounded by the enemy, some desperate troops resorted to self-mutilation, thereby risking a punishment much greater than the temporary pain of a shot in the arm or leg.[53]

This constant turnaround of troops in field hospitals and at the rear was the only way to sustain the machinery of war, often thanks to the skills of medical staff and the sheer determination of the men. Kazakh peasant Kozhogul Satybaldiev fled his home village as a child in the early 1930s in order to escape the hunger brought about by the policy of collectivization. Seeking to better himself, he attended the Turkestan Military Technical College after leaving school until he was conscripted as a *feld'sher*, a medical orderly, saving hundreds of lives in his role at the front. These men worked close to the battle, commandeering stretcher bearers, often using sledges in wintry conditions, to transport wounded men to the medical aid station just behind the lines. Following emergency treatment, the injured were sent to the nearest field hospital until they were stable enough to journey back to the rear for long-term rehabilitation.[54]

Women in action

Many women also joined the Red Army in a medical capacity as nurses, orderlies or doctors, with several stationed in military hospitals in the rear. Some were based relatively near home on the Russian–Kazakh border, working in mobile field hospitals under canvas. The Issyk-Kul' local newspaper boasted a photograph of volunteer nurse Liza Koziukova clad in furs and posing on skis in the north of Russia, in an attempt to encourage others to join her.[55] Some women doctors were also allowed to serve in the field. Even General Panfilov's daughter, Valentina, served in a medical brigade, being herself badly wounded in action.[56]

In the early days of the war, women were restricted to non-combat roles. Some volunteered, however, and, as the situation became even more desperate in the second year of the war, women with experience as engineers, telephonists and signallers were conscripted, but only if their employer was in agreement when they had been working in munitions factories under the close management of the NKVD.[57] Eventually, women were permitted to serve in most areas except as infantry in the trenches or tank crew, acting as pilots, snipers, mechanics, anti-aircraft and machine gunners.[58]

FIGURE 3.3 *Valentina Panfilova, nurse in the 8th Rifle Division, with a political officer, 1943. Reproduced with permission from the Issyk-Kul' State Archives.*

Evdokiia Pas'ko was typical of the often well-educated women volunteers. Born in the Kyrgyz village of Lipenka in the Jeti-Oguz district to a family which had emigrated eastwards from Ukraine around 1910, she attended school in Przheval'sk and then completed her education at Moscow State University. Her elder brother Stepan was already an officer in the Red Army, but died in May 1943 at Voroshilovgrad (Luhansk). A second brother, Fedor, met his death in Belarus in February 1944, and her two other brothers, Ivan and Vasilii, were also killed in action. Three relatively small all-female bomber regiments and one fighter regiment were established in the autumn of 1941, operating under demanding conditions, often with open cockpits necessitating low-altitude flying over enemy-held territory. Exceptionally, Senior Lieutenant Evdokiia Pas'ko became a navigator in the 46th Guards Night Bomber Aviation Regiment, dubbed the 'Night Witches' by the enemy. She accrued over 800 missions over the course of the war and made her final landing in Berlin.[59]

Kazakhstan alone sent over 5,000 women to the front, with a further 1,395 from Kyrgyzstan. However, these figures indicate that, proportionally, fewer Central Asian women were deployed during the war in comparison with the total of around 800,000 Soviet women who joined the Red Army. This relatively low take-up is no doubt due to the cultural and social issues keeping women close to home in Muslim society, with the majority of women conscripts from Central Asia being of Russian or Ukrainian backgrounds.[60]

FIGURE 3.4 *Lieutenant Evdokiia Pas'ko. Reproduced with permission from the Issyk-Kul' State Archives.*

Heroes of the Soviet Union

The majority of Soviet military personnel were decorated for their war service, with most receiving campaign medals. The Soviet Union rewarded the most courageous feats of heroism with the highest military honour, the gold star of a Hero of the Soviet Union. While 182 Victoria Crosses were awarded to British troops in the Second World War and 7,000 Knight's Crosses to Germans, over 11,600 Soviets were honoured with the highest award. Whether for genuine or sometimes artificially exaggerated acts of heroism, most heroes and their stories were exploited for propaganda purposes, in order to boost morale amongst the troops and motivate civilians in the rear either to join up or to perform similarly remarkable feats in their farms and factories.[61]

As most members of the Red Army were ethnic Russians, the majority of Soviet heroes were of Russian nationality and relatively few Central Asians were awarded the gold star. It is estimated that of the 100,000 Kyrgyz soldiers who were decorated and received a letter of thanks from Stalin, their commander-in-chief, only 74–78 were made Heroes of the Soviet Union.[62] Of these, just fifteen hailed from the remote Issyk-Kul' province. Commensurate with its larger population, 497 citizens of Kazakhstan were made Heroes, the majority (325) being of Russian or Ukrainian nationality. Only ninety-seven ethnic Kazakhs received the highest award, four of them on two separate occasions.[63]

The heroism of troops from ethnic minorities was normally exploited as a means of integrating these regions into the war effort. The recognition of heroes in the press was an important tool in the Soviet propaganda machine which continued to emphasize the brotherhood of the peoples, and considered vital in the process of Sovietization of Central Asia. From mid-1942, the central propaganda bureau realized that it would be useful to recognize the war effort of ethnic minorities, with popular local heroes especially singled out. Following the pre-war Stalinist repressions, Central Asians had been at risk of alienation from the centre, as Russian culture increasingly dominated intellectual and political life. Therefore, the unity as well as friendship of peoples was constantly stressed by Abdy Suerkulov, Kyrgyz Secretary for Agitation and Propaganda, as more ethnic Kyrgyz and Kyrgyz residents of Russian or Ukrainian nationality were added to the expanding list of local heroes. According to the official interpretation, these men were fighting for a common earth, a common motherland and a common cause with other Soviet citizens.[64]

Newspaper editors eagerly carried stories of the epic actions of compatriots. In anticipation of courageous exploits by locals, *Issyk-Kul'skaia Pravda* called on all its readers to become heroic in their actions: '*Budem geroiami*' (Let us become heroes!), as men started to leave for the front line.[65] The most revered Central Asia Hero of the Soviet Union was without doubt Major General Ivan Panfilov, who lost his life in the Battle of Moscow. Panfilov's death was reported in *Issyk-Kul'skaia Pravda* on 28 November 1941, and he was given a hero's burial, while not being officially posthumously decorated until 12 April 1942.[66] The twenty-eight men who were alleged to have fallen at Dubosekovo in the defence of Moscow were also awarded posthumous heroes' gold stars a few months later.[67]

Although they were named in *Pravda* on 27 January 1942, it was not until April that the full list of Panfilov's twenty-eight men was published in *Issyk-Kul'skaia Pravda*.[68] Billed as comrades of Grigorii Konkin, a local man, they included the name of Nikolai Anan'ev from the village of Sazanovki on the northern shore of the lake. Anan'ev merited his own article a few days later, when the paper interviewed his grieving sister, Matrena. The thirty-year-old Anan'ev, who had worked on the Issyk-Kul' collective fishing farm with his five siblings, helping to support them after the death of their parents, was by then being hailed as an immortal Hero of the Soviet Union.[69]

Other heroes were awarded their gold star for exploits in different spheres of battle. Vasilii Kaikin, for example, who had been delayed in his journey across Lake Issyk-Kul' in 1942 (see Chapter 2), was, just like Anan'ev, responsible for a young family following the death of his parents when he was only nine years old. Forced to become a herdsman in the summer and a farm worker in the winter, he received some schooling and became a tractor driver at the Tiup MTS (*mashino-traktornaia stantsiia*), the communal machine and tractor station from which tractors and other heavy machinery could be borrowed by local collective farms. Kaikin was sent for cavalry training as a young officer in Stalinabad in Tajikistan before heading for Stalingrad. Having survived the battle there, he was in command of a machine-gun platoon in Poland in January 1945 when he was surrounded by hundreds of 'Fritzes'. With little ammunition left and fearing being taken prisoner, he apparently used his remaining anti-tank grenade to kill himself and five Germans. A school was named after him in his home town of Tiup.[70]

Young Kyrgyz pilot Ismailbek Taranchiev was only twenty when he deliberately flew his stricken plane into a column of German tanks in Estonia. A similar feat was attributed to experienced Kazakh pilot Nurken Abdirov from Karaganda, who died near Rostov-on-Don in December 1942. Many more Kazakh pilots distinguished themselves in the Baltic States and Belarus in the latter months of the war, notably L. I. Beda and I. F. Pavlov, who were each awarded two gold stars for their heroism in the skies.[71] It is notable, however, that most Red Army pilots from Central Asia were ethnic Slavs, evidence once more of some discrimination – or just lack of opportunity – against ethnic minorities. The claims of Taranchiev and Abdirov to the highest award were no doubt promoted as they were rare examples of Central Asian pilots.

It was not necessary always to receive the gold star posthumously. Andrei Titov of the Kirov fishing collective farm on Lake Issyk-Kul' was called up in January 1942, already in his late thirties. He had his baptism of fire in the 60th Cavalry Regiment at Stalingrad, being wounded during a raid behind

FIGURE 3.5 *Nikolai Anan'ev. Reproduced with permission from the Issyk-Kul' State Archives.*

FIGURE 3.6 *Grigorii Konkin. Reproduced with permission from the Issyk-Kul'*
State Archives.

FIGURE 3.7 *Vasilii Kaikin. Reproduced with permission from the Issyk-Kul' State*
Archives.

enemy lines. Titov earned his hero's medal on the River Dnieper, where he took out three machine-gun posts and two enemy tanks. Titov was one of many soldiers who were able to return home, visiting collective farms in Jeti-Oguz and in Przheval'sk in a recruiting and information campaign.[72]

Nor were all Heroes of the Soviet Union men. Women were singled out for wide press coverage in a probable effort to increase the number of volunteers and to validate the communist ideology of equality. Evdokiia Pas'ko received her gold star for her numerous aerial sorties over enemy territory. Two Kazakh soldiers became arguably more famous, however, if for exploits which may not have merited such a high decoration in a Russian male soldier. Machine-gunner Manshuk Mametova died at the age of twenty in October 1943. Aliia Moldagulova, a sniper in the 54th Rifle Brigade, was one year younger when she died of her wounds near Pskov in January 1944.[73] Both young women were commemorated in film and song and in a monument in Almaty.[74]

Penal and labour battalions

Many men and women died a hero's death. Too many others, though, were deemed to be fit only for cannon fodder. Typical of many, Azat (a pseudonym) was arrested in the Stalinist pre-war purges. A relatively wealthy man, he lived in a mountain village but had no servants. It therefore fell to the master of the house to ride on horseback from Kyrgyzstan to the distant Aral Sea on the Uzbekistan–Kazakhstan border to obtain the salt vital for the health of his animals. On his return Azat was arrested, judged to be a rich man because he could afford such a trip, and sent to a Siberian prison camp, leaving his wife to give birth to their son alone shortly afterwards. When the war started the state declared an amnesty for some prisoners in order to recruit more troops. In common with many who had committed minor crimes he was released from prison and sent to a *shtrafbatal'on* (penal battalion) immediately after the outbreak of war. In this way men were catapulted out of the frying pan into the fire, including some army officers who had been imprisoned before the war. The state was not so desperate as to liberate repeat offenders or political prisoners, however: they still selected their future troops relatively carefully.[75]

Usually organized by the NKVD, these penal units were largely composed of men who had been serving time in prison or had relations who had been caught up in the purges and who were therefore 'enemies of the people', serving time in the camps of the GULag system. Penal battalions were sent to pave the way for regular troops at the front, often clearing minefields and suffering the most dangerous conditions of all. Very few weapons were available for these most inferior of troops. Fighting in appalling conditions in the most vulnerable situations at the front, a high percentage died within weeks, demanding a constant supply of reinforcements and causing a huge turnover of troops. The ideological excuse for such treatment was that it offered an opportunity for former prisoners to atone for their offences. Those who survived only had to serve for a few months before being officially rehabilitated for their efforts for the motherland.[76]

Ex-convicts were joined in due course by soldiers who had acted in a so-called 'cowardly' fashion on the battlefield. Men who retreated or deserted were usually shot – including 13,500 men who were executed on the battlefield at Stalingrad alone – while their officers were treated rather more leniently and sent to punishment battalions for a spell of a few months. Once there, they were reduced to the ranks and lost the right to wear any medal already awarded.[77] Despite this harsh treatment, many men were said by propagandists to have become more patriotic and even earned the praise of their commanders for their hardiness. Remarkably, while men were serving in penal battalions, the state still ensured that their families retained their right to financial and material aid.[78]

Meanwhile, some men suffered the lesser punishment of serving in labour battalions in the rear. The elderly, the physically weak and those Central Asians whom the state most distrusted were made to work as labourers on road and railway construction, building defence fortifications and working in underground mines. Active Muslims were often targeted, as were any who may have been seen as potential trouble-makers. Ninety-five thousand indigenous Central Asian conscripts were allocated to such work in 1941, often retained in the rear for long spells with the excuse that their Russian-language skills were poor.[79]

Once it became evident at the start of 1942 that more frontline soldiers were needed, places in labour battalions were increasingly filled by prisoners and interned ethnic minorities in order to release other Central Asian troops for combat duties, despite any prior misgivings displayed by the state. As the Ministry of Defence claimed first refusal of men, there was the real danger that infrastructure development, especially in Kazakhstan, would be delayed. In some cases, this change resulted in an unseemly fight for human resources, as local authorities were often reluctant to lose men who were probably more useful in industrial, administrative or professional positions at home. In the end, however, the maxim 'everything for the front' prevailed, and few able-bodied men were granted the right to remain in the rear. As the war progressed, more labour battalions were formed from 1943 as a considerable number of Central Asian troops were no longer deployed on active service.[80] A total of 700,000 men from Kazakhstan alone saw service in labour battalions during the course of the war.[81]

Soviet prisoners of war

Stalin's Order Number 270 came into force on 16 August 1941, ordering Red Army troops to fight to the death. Surrender in the face of superior enemy forces would not be an option for commanders in the field, who would face serious penalties for their men's perceived cowardice, which would henceforth be treated as desertion. Despite the threat of execution, many Soviet soldiers turned and fled the enemy during the first year of the war. By the following summer, as a consequence of months of huge losses, Order Number 227 was issued on 28 July 1942. Commanders read the uncompromising words to their men: 'Ne shagu nazad' (Not one step back), with the implication that neither retreat nor surrender to the enemy was ever sanctioned. The NKVD, firmly in charge of army discipline, considered any soldier allowing himself to be taken prisoner the equivalent of a deserter or traitor.[82]

By the time the Soviets were facing the Germans at the decisive Battle of Stalingrad, discipline had been tightened to such an extent that military police deployed behind the front line were positioned to arrest and execute any man retreating from the battle zone or even failing to keep up with his comrades. It is claimed that, although some Kyrgyz officers tried to support their troops in the case of a relatively ordered, if illegal retreat, some Central Asian military leaders, caught firmly between the enemy and their own ideological leaders, chose to take their own lives rather than be sent to the GULag camps for disobeying orders.[83]

Despite these threats from above, many Soviet prisoners of war (POWs) were indeed taken in the early months of the war. The NKVD arrested anybody suspected of having been held prisoner or of disloyalty to the state in any form, even soldiers finding themselves cut off from their platoons behind enemy lines during the fast-moving action. Accused of treason, former POWs were held to have betrayed the motherland and summarily executed, leaving their families at home deprived of a military pension.[84] This cruel fate is portrayed by Aleksandr Solzhenitsyn of his protagonist Ivan Denisovich. While the fictional Ivan was briefly captured by the Germans during the war and subsequently accused of spying for them on his escape, Solzhenitsyn himself, who was an artillery officer in the Red Army, was sentenced for his (private) criticism of Stalin. Arrested months before the end of the war, he was subsequently sent to the Karaganda corrective labour camp in Kazakhstan to join thousands of other political and criminal prisoners detained in the GULag camps. It was this experience which informed his later literature.[85]

Life was no better for those Soviet troops held in German POW camps, where exhaustion, typhoid fever, cold and hunger also prevailed. Fed on starvation rations, they supplemented their thin soup with insects where possible and allegedly some resorted to cannibalism. Living in tents even in the bitter cold, they were used as slave labour, digging trenches despite their physical weakness. Those who were simply too ill to work were killed or sometimes buried alive without any documentation. Those men deemed untragbar (unacceptable), mainly Jews, political commissars or members of the intelligentsia, were often taken to extermination camps. In such appalling conditions, a far higher percentage of Soviet POWs died in captivity than those of any other Allied nation. The mass murder of Soviet troops decreased somewhat as the war progressed and the need for more forced labourers in industrial areas of Germany increased, especially in armaments factories. Supplemented by civilians brought to Germany from Poland and Ukraine, so-called *Ostarbeiter*, even officers were employed as slave labourers, in violation of international law.[86]

Red Army prisoners were treated more harshly than the European Allies in captivity, who were not made to work and even received Red Cross parcels to supplement their prison diet. German POW camps sometimes employed Soviet volunteers as guards with the promise of better rations for this unpalatable duty. Some Uzbeks apparently agreed to these conditions, alleged in a few documented cases to mete out even worse punishments to their former comrades than their German captors.[87]

Soviet prisoners were held in camps across Europe. If the Soviets were treated badly in comparison with other allies, the Central Asians amongst them suffered even more inhumane treatment. One particularly extreme example was the camp located outside the town of Amersfoort in the Netherlands. Many Dutch members of the resistance were incarcerated here with 101 Uzbek POWs in September 1941. Treated as *Untermenschen* (racially inferior sub-humans) and exposed in a cage to local onlookers the Nazis wished to convert to their cause of ethnic extermination, the Uzbeks were eventually starved or murdered and buried in a communal grave. Also buried in Amersfoort are 691 former Soviet POWs marched there from other concentration camps in the mass movement of prisoners towards the end of the war, many of whom died of illness or starvation.[88]

Just before the end of the war it was agreed at the Yalta Conference of February 1945 that all Soviet citizens incarcerated in Europe should be repatriated without delay to the Soviet Union. Former POWs were therefore sent east, often against their will, following triage and interrogation in NKVD filtration camps set up within days of the end of the war. Many chose not to return home, however, realizing that they would spend ten or twenty-five years in a Siberian camp if they did. Several had escaped from POW camps and proved their worth in Eastern Europe by fighting alongside local partisans. Even these men were accused of collaboration or disloyalty to a Soviet state which feared that anyone who had experienced life in the relative freedom of the West may deduce that the standard of living there was considerably higher than in the Soviet Union.[89]

One such unfortunate Red Army conscript was Kudaibergen Kojomberdiev from Kyrgyzstan, who later assumed the pen-name Azamat Altay. Altay was captured and imprisoned in 1941, spending most of the war either in prison or working with teams of partisans while evading captivity. While in a concentration camp near the Belarus border, Altay suffered at first hand the inhumane treatment regularly meted out to Soviets. Starvation rations often amounted to only 700 Calories a day, allegedly because the Germans felt no need to provide the internationally agreed 2,200 Calories, as the Soviet Union had not ratified the 1929 Geneva Convention on the treatment of POWs.[90]

Keen to return to Kyrgyzstan after the war, Altay took the train out of western Europe, noting with relief the posters advertising that 'Prisoners of Nazism, your motherland awaits you'. However, this positive message changed tone abruptly as the train reached eastern Germany, where it was surrounded by Soviet guards. Altay linked this change in mood with the advice he had received from other ex-prisoners about the treatment awaiting them at home. Making his way into the British zone of Germany, he travelled back to Paris, where he was able to live while carefully avoiding any contact with Soviet authorities.[91]

Altay was neither a collaborator nor an enemy of the Soviet Union, but was nonetheless treated as a traitor once he decided not to return to Kyrgyzstan. The assistance offered to prisoners on the run in Europe was varied. Some were rebuffed as the locals feared recriminations, while others received small amounts of food and shelter. Kyrgyz Baltakun Kendirbaev was permitted to sleep in a barn, looking after the farm animals. Aleksandr Golovanev, an ethnic Russian from Frunze, had travelled from the Baltic States through Belarus and onwards to Prague, where he was wounded in the eye. His comrades left him in the home of a Czech woman, where he stayed until taken by the enemy and sent to a series of POW camps. He narrowly escaped death by working as a cook for a German who had befriended him. He was then moved to Hanover, where he was set to work in a factory – dangerous work in view of the Allied bombing raids on the city.[92]

Golovanev was able to return home at the end of the war, but other Central Asians did not survive the repatriation process. Many had learnt some German during their period in captivity, which condemned them to the death penalty simply for knowing too much. Others were forced to return home having been wounded during the war, often while serving with partisan companies. Some, like Altay, remained indefinitely in Western Europe or forged a new life for themselves in America after the war.[93]

Nearly 6 million Red Army soldiers were captured by the Germans during the course of the war, half of whom were taken during the first six months. Over 4 million died of starvation, cold, illness, overwork or by execution.[94] Almost 2 million returned to the motherland after the war, of whom over one and a half million were sentenced to lengthy periods in the GULag camps or labour battalions in equally uninviting areas of Siberia or Kazakhstan. One of these men was Shambetaly Soltonkulov from the remote mountain village of Kyzart in central Kyrgyzstan. Conscripted at the start of the war aged thirty-six, he was soon taken prisoner and spent most of the war in a German camp. It was just a year after his release that Soviet authorities caught up with him, sentencing him to twenty-five years in Siberia. This term was cut short in the spate of amnesties following the death of Stalin in 1953, enabling him to return home before the end of his sentence. Tragically, he was so scarred by both the prison camp in Germany and the Siberian labour camp that Soltonkulov, along with many others, felt unable to take advantage of the compensation offered by Germany in the 1990s to former POWs. Fearing a further stretch in Siberia, he failed to present his documents to the relevant Kyrgyz authorities, thereby missing out on his rightful claim to reparations.[95]

Deserters and traitors

Some soldiers would do anything to avoid being killed in battle or taken prisoner by the enemy. Several absconded even before being officially conscripted, but far more deserted once they had experienced frontline action. They fled their positions, despite the threat of Orders Number 270 and 227,

FIGURE 3.8 *Shambetaly Soltonkulov. Published with kind permission from the Soltonkulov family.*

leaving their families at home liable to arrest. Over the course of the war, nearly a million men were sentenced by military courts for desertion, with 400,000 being fined and sent to penal units.[96]

It was recorded by the military authorities that higher rates of desertion took place amongst soldiers of ethnic minorities, including Central Asians. An official, if probably prejudiced, report showed that around 80 per cent of all cases were by non-Russian troops. This is surprising in view of the fact that, officially, the Soviet authorities proclaimed the 'friendship of the peoples' and worked hard to promote ethnic equality, even recognizing that more mentoring and work on ideology were needed to promote the Soviet consciousness of ethnic minorities. There is no doubt, though, that many Russian officers and men considered themselves to be 'first amongst equals', despising and discriminating against Uzbek and other Central Asian troops. Even Lavrentii Beriia, head of the NKVD, felt that Kazakh cavalry were too undependable and cowardly to defend strategic positions.[97]

There may have been some truth in the accusations of cowardice. Many more Central Asians were executed in the field than any other nationality.[98] This may have been due to their basic discontent, possibly stoked by a German propaganda machine which targeted disaffected ethnic minorities. The distinct military prejudice against Central Asians certainly did not help to keep them onside. Central Asians tended to be quieter and more gentle than Russian troops, keeping themselves to themselves in small ethnic and linguistic cliques. They were distinctly demoralized by the harsh weather conditions at the front, while their poor Russian prevented integration and led to accusations of backwardness – deficiencies for which they were definitely not to blame. Central Asians were certainly useful scapegoats when things went wrong. Just as 'wreckers' and 'saboteurs' were accused of ruining the output of factories, which was usually due to unrealistic demands from above, poor equipment or managerial inefficiency, so groups of ethnic minorities were accused of being infiltrators working for the enemy. This deliberate targeting no doubt exacerbated the misery of Central Asian soldiers at the front, particularly Uzbeks, such that they were driven to desertion. The numbers increased markedly as the war progressed, with the highest desertion figure for Kyrgyz troops recorded in June 1943, probably as the summer months proved most attractive for long journeys on foot. German propagandists capitalized on Soviet racial prejudice and accusations of cowardice to promote even more ethnic tension and discord in the ranks.[99]

Two men from the Issyk-Kul' province, who had been serving since 1939, left their units in the 315th Regiment of the 19th Rifle Division in the Voronezh area in August 1941, after it became increasingly obvious that the war was taking its toll on the Red Army. Like many deserters, they were older men with family responsibilities.[100] Many headed straight for home and family, while others remained outside their communities with few support mechanisms, fearing the military tribunal and certain punishment waiting for them if caught by the ever-watchful NKVD. Survival outside the towns and villages was tough, where food was harder to obtain, although it was easier to avoid re-capture. Some small bands of deserters in Kyrgyzstan even resorted to plundering villages, alienating themselves from both their compatriots and the Soviet authorities. In Kazakhstan, almost 10,000 deserters were discovered in hiding during the war and duly punished for their dereliction of duty.[101]

Some soldiers who deserted the army ended up joining local partisans, especially in Ukraine. In contrast, others were tempted to throw in their lot with the enemy. Uzbeks were particularly singled out as defectors, becoming traitors in the eyes of the Soviet military authorities and often treated worse than animals if taken as POWs. However, despite the German opinion of captive Uzbeks as *Untermenschen*, this view changed as it became evident that the German Wehrmacht needed to recruit supplementary forces if it was to overcome the constantly replenished Red Army. Realizing that many Uzbeks and other Tatar minorities were more than disaffected with life in the Red Army, the Wehrmacht offered them not only supervisory jobs in POW camps but also some administrative positions in exchange for better food and treatment.

The ultimate offer was a post in the Turkestan Legion.[102] Formed in January 1942, this was a series of battalions attached to Wehrmacht divisions comprising largely of Muslim Turkic men from the Soviet Union who agreed to fight for the Germans. The decision to change sides was not necessarily a difficult one, as it was simply a matter of survival for men suffering the cruel treatment meted out to POWs. Some Turkestan battalions were deployed at Stalingrad, although this winter experience resulted in several men defecting back to the Red Army. After 1942, they were mainly sent to western parts of Europe, further from home, while others were used in Yugoslavia. The deployment of their own citizens against the Soviet Union was a political triumph for Germany. However, many of the surviving 16,000 members of the Turkestan Legion were captured by the Allies towards the end of the war, only to suffer the terrible consequences of repatriation to the Soviet Union and the subsequent charge of treason.[103]

Berlin and beyond

Tenti Tamashaev from Kyrgyzstan returned to action following a prolonged recuperation from his leg wound at Stalingrad. He was promoted to captain and deployed to assist with interrogating enemy POWs in Warsaw, as he spoke some German. It was not long before he, like Pas'ko, was one of the first to arrive in Berlin after the final offensive, exchanging tentative greetings with British and American troops.

There is still some controversy over who actually raised the Soviet Red Flag on the Reichstag building in central Berlin on 30 April 1945. It is likely that the iconic victory photograph by Evgenii Khaldei was staged the following day using Russian Sergeant Mikhail Egorov with Georgian Sergeant Meliton Kantariia, in a strategic duo of nationalities which paid tribute to the friendship of peoples, while acknowledging Stalin's Georgian ancestry. However, it is claimed in the Kazakhstan State National museum in Almaty that the flag was raised by Kazakh soldier R. Koshkarbaev, assisted by a certain Comrade Bulatov. The fact is that many men from different units and with different ethnicities took turns to raise their military standards in what provided powerful and inclusive victory propaganda material for several nationalities. Berlin finally fell on 2 May, with an end to war in Europe declared in the Soviet Union following the liberation of Prague on 9 May.[104]

If the Reichstag was the epitome of Soviet success, the systematic rape of innocent German civilians by Soviet troops represents the nadir of the victors' retributive action. It has been alleged that over 2 million women suffered sexual assault at the hands of unrestrained soldiers. The rape of the local population also occurred in other theatres of war. For example, after the Normandy landings in June 1944, French sources claimed that around 3,500 women were violated, mainly at the hands of American troops, some of whom were hanged for their offence. However, in Germany it was claimed that the most vicious offenders had Asian faces, dubbed 'Mongols' by those assaulted. It is possible that all Soviet soldiers looked non-European to their German victims; Goebbels had indeed incited popular hatred of the enemy by referring to Soviet troops collectively as 'Mongols'. There was in reality a very small percentage of Central Asian troops in Germany, but it is likely that any evidently foreign intruder could be taken for Asian. However, this smear against Central Asian troops had the effect of further staining their already poor military reputation. Certainly, evidence suggests that Uzbek and Turkmen soldiers had no qualms about looting, while expressing naïve amazement at the sophisticated items they plundered.[105]

Victory in Europe marked the end of the war for most, but some Central Asians found themselves rapidly deployed to the far east, where the war against Japan was still raging. The Soviet Union finally entered the action in this theatre of war on 9 August 1945, exactly three months after the end of war in Europe. This was the natural outcome after several cross-border incursions by the Japanese had violated the non-aggression treaty signed in 1944 between the Soviet Union and Japan. Fighting took place for a few short weeks in north-east China, North Korea, South Sakhalin and the Kuril Islands, where it made logistical sense to deploy Asian troops who were likely to be based closer than most to this region. Kyrgyz parachutist Nikolai Shuba travelled to Manchuria from Hungary via Moscow, while Kazakh musician Vasilii Kudinov celebrated his birthday in China on 3 September, the day after Japan finally capitulated to the Soviet Union. At this late stage in the war, Soviet losses in the Asian sphere were far fewer than those in the

European conflict. Technical support was better, and by 1945 men and their leaders had gained valuable experience.[106]

Ismail Jusupov from the Osh province of Kyrgyzstan was one of those who found himself fighting the Japanese for the second time. Shortly after his initial conscription in 1938, he had seen action in Mongolia at the Battle of Khalkhin Gol, defending the Siberian–Manchurian border from Japanese expansionism in the summer of 1939. After several years fighting on the Soviet Western Front, Private Jusupov was posted back to the region during the final month of the war, receiving his 'Victory over Japan' medal following his demobilization in November 1945.[107]

Demob happy?

The Second World War accelerated the change of identity forced upon the people of Central Asia as their integration within the USSR was cemented. In a few short decades they had mutated from colonial subjects of expansionist tsarist Russia to supposedly equal citizens of the new Soviet Union. Men who at the start of the war had demonstrated some understandable degree of hesitancy about serving in the Red Army returned home as victors, fully aware – thanks to their ideological exposure – that they had successfully defended their Soviet motherland against the common enemy.

About 8.5 million men were demobilized shortly after the end of the Great Patriotic War.[108] The official demobilization process took place in phases from June 1945 until February 1948, although some men were retained for five years or more after the end of the war.[109] Older men were sent home relatively quickly, as were those who had been conscripted before the start of the war – men who had been in uniform since 1939 or even earlier. However, officers, younger men and those who had only been conscripted in the final two years of the war were retained for longer, often remaining in Germany or Eastern Europe for a further three or four years.[110]

Demobilization took place under a strict protocol, managed minutely by the military authorities. Returnees and their dependants were largely treated well, with families alerted in advance of the date of their arrival. Streets in Frunze were hung with flags, posters and bunting, while station platforms, buffets and waiting rooms were similarly decorated. The first tranche of demobilized men returned to Przheval'sk as early as 23 June 1945.[111] Groups of friends and family from across the Issyk-Kul' province gathered together at the jetty in Pristan' to meet the returning soldiers, greeting them with flowers and applause. Details of any Heroes of the Soviet Union were recorded in full, presumably for potential propaganda purposes. Once the official welcome was over, fleets of droshkas or sledges, according to the season, transported the weary men back home to their new life in peacetime.[112]

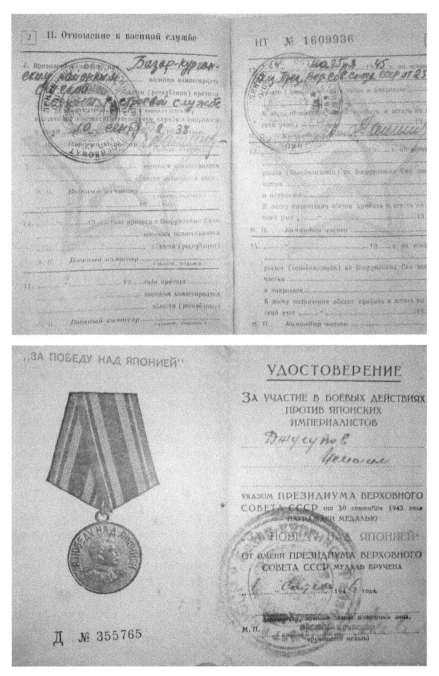

FIGURES 3.9–10 *Private Ismail Jusupov's service record and certificate for the award of his 'Victory over Japan' medal. Published with kind permission from the Jusupov family.*

Others came home for a period of well-deserved leave, bringing with it the temptation to remain at home more permanently. Those who failed to rejoin their units were judged absent without leave. Perhaps understandably, after such a long war and in the middle of winter, Corporal Sadyk Usenov failed to return to his company. He disappeared without trace in December 1946 during a short period of leave in Kyrgyzstan, with the Issyk-Kul' military police on his tracks.[113]

Returning soldiers must have experienced some disillusionment once at home. They almost certainly found their homes not quite as they had left them, especially in the case of the city of Tashkent, which had been forced to accommodate the bulk of the evacuees to Central Asia from areas in the western Soviet Union. Most towns and villages had undergone a marked deterioration in their absence, with few resources and little manpower to effect repairs. In most cases, however, the war had equipped men from Central Asia with the skills to reintegrate successfully into civilian life. Many soldiers spoke and even read Russian considerably better than at the onset of war, and were more familiar with the communist ideology which would often later provide them with a job within the party. For this reason, returnees were altogether in a better position than before the war to find employment, particularly as the population had decreased dramatically.

Of the 34 million serving in the Red Army during the war, nearly 9 million died. In all, the Soviet Union lost around 27 million of its total population, including civilians and those who later died of their wounds or who went missing in action.[114] Various estimates of the numbers of the fallen from Central Asia have been made since the end of the war, but the exact statistics are still hard to pin down. An unknown number of troops were missing in action (*propali bez vesti*). Some men were buried in mass graves in the field, with no official notes made of their place of burial. Others fell in the snow or the mud, left to the elements as their comrades retreated in haste. Identity cartridges were often useless, particularly in the case of air crew whose bodies were often incinerated as their planes crashed. Search teams scouring the battlefields of the Soviet Western Front are still digging up the remains of men from Central Asia, which are then exhumed and reinterred at home.[115] Of those taken prisoner, many died in captivity with records destroyed, while a minority escaped to the West and never returned home. Others died of their wounds some time after the war in the GULag camps or at home. In these cases their deaths were not always attributed to their war service. Deaths occurring in hospitals were similarly seldom added to the total list, particularly once field hospitals had been dismantled and records lost or destroyed. Some injured men were known to the medical staff simply by their first names; other names were sometimes wrongly transcribed, so that their death certificates remained unattributed.[116]

Only 60 per cent of conscripts and volunteers from the Issyk-Kul' province returned home after the war. The total number of troops from

Kyrgyzstan to lose their lives in the war is variously estimated, with figures ranging widely from 27,000 to 240,000.[117] On a greater scale, around half of the 1.2 million men from Kazakhstan serving in the Second World War met their death in action or shortly afterwards, while over 400,000 of the 1.4 million from Uzbekistan who went to war failed to return. Of these, traces of 100,000 have still not been found.[118] Recent sources claim that 300,000 left Turkmenistan for the war, of whom 86,000 gave their lives for the motherland. The figures were similar in Tajikistan, with losses of around 30 per cent.[119]

In the whole of Central Asia, therefore, deaths may be estimated at around one and a half million, perhaps 40 per cent of those who went to war. This figure represents the cream of the younger generation, men aged from eighteen to fifty who had been responsible for most of the economic output of the region. Some of their work had been taken over by women and incoming evacuees and refugees. However, there still remained a dearth of healthy people to keep the region on its feet.

Despite the number of available positions, it was recognized by the authorities that men may need assistance to find jobs upon demobilization. In the Issyk-Kul' province a new commission was created in July 1945 to collate a list of job vacancies in factories and collective farms, and to encourage veterans back into peacetime employment. Thanks to this help, many men were able to use skills acquired in the army to find jobs as engineers, accountants, electricians or tractor drivers.[120] Others used their new literacy skills and ideological education to become teachers, Communist Party leaders, village elders or managers on the farm or in industry.[121]

Officers also needed support, once they started to return home to Central Asia a year later. Some were placed directly into industry, others on training courses with the intention that they would rapidly gain new qualifications to equip them for managerial positions in factories. Some officers chose to remain in the army, however, often training new conscripts or working in the party hierarchy. Others had no choice: Mikhail Bibikov from the Chui province of Kyrgyzstan, for example, stayed in Belarus to train new recruits to drive tanks, only being demobilized in 1951.[122]

Nikolai Liashchenko elected to continue his successful military career, attending military academy and serving in the North Caucasus before returning to Central Asia in 1957. He finally became the military commander of the Central Asia military district in Tashkent before retiring to the Issyk-Kul' province in Kyrgyzstan, where he often visited his former colour sergeant, Jumabek Rakhmanov. Rakhmanov worked for a time as a school teacher upon his return, but was subsequently offered a good position in the Communist Party thanks to his wartime leadership experience.[123]

Work on the collective farm was the default position for most soldiers after demobilization. For far too long jobs had been completed by women, children and elderly men, or even left undone. Much catching up remained to be done when the more able men returned home. Sergeant Vasilii Kudinov, the accordionist, returned home to the collective farm, augmenting his income by playing in his newly formed wind band which performed at local dances.[124] Tractor and combine harvester drivers were always in big demand on the farms. Many men with experience in tanks or armoured vehicles found work with the area's MTS, the communal support base from which a group of farms would borrow bigger agricultural machinery. Dungan Bagi Abdullaev, whose family roots were in China, returned to his collective farm in the Jeti-Oguz district of the Issyk-Kul' province as a qualified driver once demobilized in 1947. Amantur Tektonazarov received his driving training in Jena in East Germany in 1946. Once demobilized in 1950, six years after being conscripted and still aged only twenty-four, he continued this relatively profitable work.[125]

Other men took advantage of offers of further training. Tentimish Inazarov decided to go to agricultural college rather than remain on his home farm. Military artist Konstantin Kulakov had appreciated his brief course of military art before he was sent to the front. After demobilization in 1951, he opted to continue his studies before settling down in Przheval'sk.[126]

Those who showed some advanced literacy and academic merit were encouraged to become school teachers. During the war women and many wounded men had held this occupation, but more teachers were needed once the post-war baby boom increased the size of the younger generation. Obi Nazirov, a Tajik former officer, had worked in Iran as an interpreter for most of the war, but, once demobilized, returned to his pre-war post as a primary school teacher in Tajikistan. Tenti Tamashaev returned home earlier than most to become a Kyrgyz language teacher. He soon became a headmaster, then went on to work for the Communist Party in Przheval'sk and Tiup. The pinnacle of his post-war career was as editor of party promotional material.[127]

Some had been conscripted from universities for officer training, whereas others were foiled in their academic aspirations and had to wait years to complete their education. Petr Berdnik from a peasant family in Kazakhstan was called up virtually straight from school. Following a stint at the Voronezh military academy in Samarkand he had served as platoon commander and head of communications in an artillery regiment. His unit was deployed to Simferopol (Crimea) after the end of the war and he was finally demobilized with the rank of captain in March 1947. Berdnik's obvious next step was to go straight to university in Alma-Ata, where he eventually achieved a doctorate in Russian language in 1956 which led to a new post in a university in Kamchatka. Following decades of mobility across the Soviet Union, he eventually returned to Central Asia to found the Russian-language faculty in Przheval'sk State University.[128]

Dungan intellectual and linguist Abdrakhman Kalimov also moved frequently in pursuit of his career, which was interrupted by the war. Having decided to become a teacher, he attended the literary faculty of the Kyrgyz Pedagogical Institute for a year. He had just embarked on a doctoral course when he was conscripted in 1943. After the war Kalimov was able to take advantage of the social mobility opportunities offered by the Soviet Union to study in Leningrad, finally gaining his doctorate in Dungan grammar in 1951.[129]

Another member of an ethnic minority, Uighur Aziz Narynbaev, was highly influenced by his Chinese grandparents. He was studying history at the Przheval'sk Pedagogical Institute when he volunteered for the army in 1942 at the age of eighteen. After a year's officer training in Frunze, he became an artillery officer in the 50th Army, serving at the Battle of Kursk. Demobilized early due to wounds sustained in 1944, he returned to his studies and joined the history faculty as a lecturer in 1947.[130]

Others took advantage of vocational training during the war to start a new post-war career. Tatar Khamit Bashirov from Ukraine remained in the army after cessation of hostilities, eventually becoming a veterinary technician when he returned to work on a collective farm near Przheval'sk in 1946. Kazakh Kozhogul Satybaldiev served as a medical orderly during the war, having previously trained at a military medical technical college. He eventually achieved his ambition of becoming a doctor in 1961 following several years' more study.[131]

Navigator Evdokiia Pas'ko had volunteered for service from her mathematics course at Moscow State University. After the war, this Hero of the Soviet Union returned to university, achieving a doctorate in mathematics which qualified her to spend the rest of her career teaching at the prestigious Baumann Technical University in Moscow.[132] Other educated women found jobs in education or with the Communist Party, not all returning to their home towns. The wartime experience had changed many Central Asian women's lives for ever, as those involved in the military had led substantially less sheltered lives than previously, becoming more independent and empowered to pursue their own careers.

Not only did the war increase population mobility across the Soviet Union and beyond, enabling soldiers to see other parts of Europe and Asia but it also offered substantial opportunities for people to improve their lot by the development of new jobs and educational prospects. With the experience of increased contact with other Soviet citizens of various nationalities, they had become better integrated within the Soviet system, enabling them to move further afield with their families to take advantage of the opportunities inherent in a burgeoning post-war economy.

Having played an integral part in the war as citizens of the Soviet Union, the troops of Central Asia had been subjected to a barrage of propaganda materials seeking to persuade them to embrace communist ideals, partly to spur them into combat and also in order to justify the enormous sacrifices made during the conflict. Both the war and the propaganda drive accelerated the process of Sovietization of the Central Asian republics, started albeit cautiously in the 1930s. Despite the 'friendship of the peoples' policy with its rhetoric of equality, the impact of the participation of troops from Central

Asia on the military outcome of the war was arguably small and broadly in proportion with the population of the region. It has even been claimed that any success of Central Asian troops in the war was largely due to the leadership of their Slavic officers.[133] It may well be true that the men of Central Asia were just pawns at the mercy of the generals and politicians, but they certainly experienced a steep and all too dangerous learning curve, again accelerating their overall assimilation into the Soviet Union. This process, in turn, significantly altered the pre-war patriarchal relationship between Russia and the republics of Central Asia. Moscow still remained the centre of the union, but the overarching colonial approach to the outlying republics gave way – if not to a true brotherhood of nations – at least to a more co-operative and less antagonistic relationship in the post-war years.

Notes

1   Esenaliev, *Zhenishke dank*, 129.

2   For example: Antony Beevor, *Berlin: The Downfall 1945* (London: Viking, 2017); Antony Beevor, *Stalingrad* (London: Penguin, 1999); Braithwaite, *Moscow 1941*; Alan Clark, *Barbarossa: The Russian German Conflict 1941–1945* (London: Cassell, 1965); and Keith Cumins, *Cataclysm: The War on the Eastern Front, 1941–45* (Helion: Solihull, 2011).

3   Esenaliev, *Zhenishke dank*, 62.

4   Carmack, *Kazakhstan in World War II*, 28; and Merridale, *Ivan's War*, 51.

5   Information from Prof. Tchoraev.

6   Carmack, *Kazakhstan in World War II*, 40–2; and Max Hastings, *All Hell Let Loose: The World at War 1939–1945* (London: Collins, 2012), 386.

7   Il'ia Erenburg, 'Krasnaia armiia sil'na velikoi druzhboi narodov', *Zvezda*, 16 September 1941, 1.

8   Barber and Harrison, *The Soviet Home Front*, 27.

9   Merridale, *Ivan's War*, 71.

10 Carmack, *Kazakhstan in World War II*, 32; and Abylkhozhin, *Istoriia Kazakhstana*, 450.

11 Esenaliev, *Zhenishke dank*, 186.

12 Braithwaite, *Moscow 1941*, 109; Florin, 'Becoming Soviet through War', 503; and Kerimbaev, *Sovetskii Kirgizstan v Velikoi Otechestvennoi voine*, 67 and 216.

13 Information from Director of the Panfilov museum, Almaty.

14 Abylkhozhin, *Istoriia Kazakhstana*, 467–8.

15 Braithwaite, *Moscow 1941*, 209; and Kerimbaev, *Sovetskii Kirgizstan v Velikoi Otechestvennoi voine*, 219 and 222.

16 Braithwaite, *Moscow 1941*, 267; Kerimbaev, *Sovetskii Kirgizstan v Velikoi Otechestvennoi voine*, 220 and 222–4; and Merridale, *Ivan's War*, 124.

17 For a full account of the historical events behind the myth, see Alexander Statiev, '"La Garde meurt mais ne se rend pas!": Once again on the 28 Panfilov Heroes', *Kritika: Explorations in Russian and Eurasian History* 13, no. 4 (2012): 769–98.

18 Abylkhozhin, *Istoriia Kazakhstana*, 469–75 and 490; Carmack, *Kazakhstan in World War II*, 30; Florin, 'Becoming Soviet through War', 503; and Kerimbaev, *Sovetskii Kirgizstan v Velikoi Otechestvennoi voine*, 175, 217, 220 and 226.

19 Karel Berkhoff, *Motherland in Danger: Soviet propaganda during World War II* (Cambridge, MA: Harvard University Press, 2012), 216.

20 Brandon Schechter, 'The People's Instructions: Indigenizing the Great Patriotic War among Non-Russians', *Ab Imperio* 3 (2012): 109–33.

21 Abylkhozhin, *Istoriia Kazakhstana*, 477; and Kerimbaev, *Sovetskii Kirgizstan v Velikoi Otechestvennoi voine*, 216 and 240.

22 Barber and Harrison, *The Soviet Home Front*, 31; and Braithwaite, *Moscow 1941*, 143.

23 Esenaliev, *Zhenishke dank*, 120.

24 Ibid., 29.

25 Merridale, *Ivan's War*, 188.

26 Esenaliev, *Zhenishke dank*, 68 and 80.

27 Ibid., 162.

28 Interview with Tenti Tamashaev, 15 May 2018. See also Esenaliev, *Zhenishke dank*, 23–4.

29 Ibid., 183; and Z. G. Saktaganova, 'Povsednevnye problem evakogospitalei Tsentral'nogo Kazakhstana v gody Velikoi Otechestvennoi voiny', in *Istoriia. Pamiat'. Liudi: Materialy VIII Mezhdunarodnoi nauchno-prakticheskoi konferentsii 16 sentiabria 2016 g.*, eds M. S. Makarova, et al., 187–92 (Almaty, 2017), 187.

30 Hastings, *All Hell Let Loose*, 386.

31 Carmack, *Kazakhstan in World War II*, 32–8.

32 Merridale, *Ivan's War*, 154–5.

33 Esenaliev, *Zhenishke dank*, 166. On dismissive behaviour towards ethnic minorities in the Red Army, see Carmack, *Kazakhstan in World War II*, 32–8; and Merridale, *Ivan's War*, 288.

34 *IKP*, 6 December 1942, 1.

35 *IKP*, 28 January 1943, 2.

36 Carmack, 'History and Hero-Making'.

37 *IKP*, 1 January 1943, 1.

38 *IKP*, 28 January 1943, 2.

39 *IKP*, 7 February 1943, 1.

40 Kaptagaev, et al., *Sbornik*, 170.

41 Ibid., 209.

42 Rakhmanov's personal archive.

43 Information from Kalyk Shykyev, June 2017.

44 Esenaliev, *Zhenishke dank*, 10–13, 52, 102, 114 and 134.

45 Ibid., 44.

46 Ibid., 189.

47 Ibid., 133.

48 Ibid., 22.

49 Ibid., 112.

50 Ibid., 114.

51 Ibid., 95.

52 Ibid., 133.

53 Tranum, *Life at the Edge of the Empire*, 76–8; and Carmack, *Kazakhstan in World War II*, 25.

54 Esenaliev, *Zhenishke dank*, 152; and Albert Axell, *Russia's Heroes 1941–45* (London: Robinson, 2002), 235.

55 *IKP*, 19 April 1942.

56 Information from her daughter (Panfilov's granddaughter), Alua Baikadamova, 2 May 2018.

57 Braithwaite, *Moscow 1941*, 99; Merridale, *Ivan's War*, 165; and IKSA:146/2/12/625.

58 Anna Krylova, *Soviet Women in Combat* (Cambridge: Cambridge University Press, 2011).

59 Information from Dr Narynbek Alymnugov, 11 May 2018. See also *IKP*, 11 October 1945; Svetlana Alexievich, *The Unwomanly Face of War: An Oral History of Women in WWII* (London: Random House, 2018); Axell, *Russia's Heroes*, 59–60; Kaptagaev, et al., *Sbornik*, 156–8; and Bruce Myles, *Night Witches: The Amazing Story of Russia's Women Pilots in WWII* (Chicago: Academy Chicago, 1990).

60 Abylkhozhin, *Istoriia Kazakhstana*, 508–11; Kerimbaev, *Sovetskii Kirgizstan v Velikoi Otechestvennoi voine*, 215; Merridale, *Ivan's War*, 165; and Liza Mundy, 'The Significant, Neglected Role of Russian Women in World War II', *The Washington Post*, 4 August 2017.

61 Abylkhozhin, *Istoriia Kazakhstana*, 499; Carmack, 'History and Hero-Making', 103; and Merridale, *Ivan's War*, 190.

62 Abylkhozhin, *Istoriia Kazakhstana*, 499–500. The ongoing debate depends on the exact criteria used to define 'Kygyz'. Although many men were resident in Kyrgyzstan immediately before the war, they were in fact ethnic Russians, according to historian Dr Alymnugov. Some heroes were born in Kyrgyzstan, but moved out of the region before the war; others only relocated to Central Asia after the war.

63 Director of the Panfilov museum; Abylkhozhin, *Istoriia Kazakhstana*, 500; and Carmack, 'History and Hero-Making', 104.

64 Carmack, 'History and Hero-Making'; and Florin, 'Becoming Soviet through War', 502–5.

65 *IKP*, 19 October 1941, 3.

66 *IKP*, 28 November 1941, 4; and Florin, 'Becoming Soviet through War', 503.

67 M. M. Kozlov, ed., *Velikaia Otechestvennaia voina: 1941–1945. Entsiklopediia* (Moscow: Sovetskaia entsiklopediia, 1985), 606.

68 'Pust' kazhdyi znaet ikh imena', *IKP*, 12 April 1942, 1.

69 B. Vorzukov, 'Odin iz 28', *IKP*, 17 April 1942, 2.

70 Esenaliev, *Zhenishke dank*, 100.

71 Abylkhozhin, *Istoriia Kazakhstana*, 493–4.

72 Esenaliev, *Zhenishke dank*, 163; Kaptagaev, et al., *Sbornik*, 136–7; and Kerimbaev, *Sovetskii Kirgizstan v Velikoi Otechestvennoi voine*, 238–9. For more details of soldiers' visits home, see Chapter 6.

73 Carmack, 'History and Hero-Making', 104–5.

74 Mazhit Begalin's film *Pesn' o Manshuk* appeared in 1969. Roza Rymbaeva famously sang about Aliia in the 1970s.

75 Information from Gulzat Abdykadyrova, 4 June 2018. See also Applebaum, *Gulag*, 402–3; Barber and Harrison, *The Soviet Home Front*, 117; and Alexander Statiev, 'Penal Units in the Red Army', *Europe–Asia Studies* 62, no. 5 (2010): 721–47.

76 Information from Prof. Tchoraev. See also IKSA:119/1/23/263; Barber and Harrison, *The Soviet Home Front*, 117; and Braithwaite, *Moscow 1941*, 142.

77 Statiev, 'Penal Units in the Red Army'; Applebaum, *Gulag*, 404; Barber and Harrison, *The Soviet Home Front*, 31; and Braithwaite, *Moscow 1941*, 142.

78 Applebaum, *Gulag*, 404–5; and Braithwaite, *Moscow 1941*, 142.

79 IKSA:146/1/173; Carmack, *Kazakhstan in World War II*, 77–80; and Keller, *Russia and Central Asia*, 204.

80 Carmack, *Kazakhstan in World War II*, 74, 76–80 and 90; and Barber and Harrison, *The Soviet Home Front*, 62.

81 Director of the Panfilov museum, Almaty.

82 Merridale, *Ivan's War*, 112 and 157.

83 Information from Prof. Tchoraev. See also Barber and Harrison, *The Soviet Home Front*, 31.

84 Barber and Harrison, *The Soviet Home Front*, 28 and 31.

85 Aleksandr Solzhenitsyn, *One Day in the Life of Ivan Denisovich*, trans. R. Parker (London: Victor Gollancz, 2000). See also Joanna Lillis, *Dark Shadows: Inside the Secret World of Kazakhstan* (London: I.B. Tauris, 2019), location 3017.

86 Information from the Document Centre, Nazi Party Rally Grounds, Nuremberg.

87 Beevor, *Berlin*, 85–6.

88 Remco Reiding, *Kind von et Erefeld* (Zwolle, The Netherlands: D33 Publicaties, 2012); and E. Myachinskaya, N. Demers and B. Demers, 'Soviet Field of Honour, Leusden, the Netherlands: Then and Now', *Scandinavian Philology* 18, no. 1 (2020): 198–212.

89 Jeffrey B. Lilley, *Have the Mountains Fallen?* (Bloomington: Indiana University Press, 2018), 62; and Beevor, *Berlin*, 423.

90 Altay's experience is documented in Lilley, *Have the Mountains Fallen?*.

91 Lilley, *Have the Mountains Fallen?*, 60–3.

92 Tranum, *Life at the Edge of the Empire*, 31–5.

93 Interview with Mairamkul Kendirbaeva, 4 June 2018.

94 Barber and Harrison, *The Soviet Home Front*, 41.

95 Information from the family of Shambetaly Soltonkulov, 15 April 2020.

96 Axell, *Russia's Heroes*, 172; Barber and Harrison, *The Soviet Home Front*, 28; Braithwaite, *Moscow 1941*, 150–1; and Carmack, *Kazakhstan in World War II*, 25.

97 Carmack, 'And They Fought for Their Socialist Motherland', 40–2; Carmack, *Kazakhstan in World War II*, 25; and Roger Reese, *Why Stalin's Soldiers Fought: The Red Army's Military Effectiveness in WWII* (Lawrence: University Press of Kansas, 2011), 141–8.

98 Carmack, *Kazakhstan in World War II*, 35.

99 IKSA:119/1/50; Carmack, 'And They Fought for Their Socialist Motherland', 41–2; Carmack, *Kazakhstan in World War II*, 25; and Stronski, *Tashkent*, 131.

100 IKSA:146/2/5/146.

101 Florin, 'Becoming Soviet through War', 495 and 500; and Carmack, *Kazakhstan in World War II*, 25.

102 Turkestan was the pre-Soviet name for Russian Central Asia.

103 Information from Prof. Tchoraev. See also Carmack, *Kazakhstan in World War II*, 112; and Dadabaev, *Identity and Memory*, 70.

104 For a full discussion, see Jeremy Hicks, *The Victory Banner over the Reichstag: Film, Document and Ritual in Russia's Contested Memory of World War II* (Pittsburgh: Pittsburgh University Press, 2012). See also Kerimbaev, *Sovetskii Kirgizstan v Velikoi Otechestvennoi voine*, 271; and Berkhoff, *Motherland in Danger*, 220.

105 Antony Beevor covers the topics of rape and looting extensively, for example Beevor, *Berlin*, 35, 224, 326–7, 410 and 418; and Antony Beevor, 'They Raped Every German Female from Eight to 90', *The Guardian*, 1 May 2002. See also Lilley, *Have the Mountains Fallen?*, 92; and Francis Patard, *100 Jours pour la Liberté* (Cherbourg: Société Cherbourgeoise, 2019), 117.

106 Abylkhozhin, *Istoriia Kazakhstana*, 497–8; Axell, *Russia's Heroes*, 151–2; Barber and Harrison, *The Soviet Home Front*, 38–9; and Esenaliev, *Zhenishke dank*, 189 and 112.

107 Information from the Jusupov family, 17 March 2021.

108 Natalia Danilova, 'Veterans' Policy in Russia: A Puzzle of Creation', *PIPSS (The Journal of Power Institutions in Post-Soviet Societies)* 6, no. 7 (2007): para. 5.

109 Manley, *To the Tashkent Station*.

110 IKSA:146/1/39/18; and Kaptagaev, et al., *Sbornik*, 151.

111 Ibid.

112 IKSA:146/1/39/3; and Kaptagaev, et al., *Sbornik*, 151 and 154–5.

113 IKSA:146/2/45/6–9 and 45.

114 Axell, *Russia's Heroes*, 246; and Barber and Harrison, *The Soviet Home Front*, 41.

115 Svetlana Lapteva, 'Istoriia semei pogibshikh bez vesti i veteranov voiny', *Sud'ba soldata* Conference (Moscow, 2019). See also Chapter 9.

116 Svetlana Lapteva, 'Sostavlenie banka dannykh po gospital'nym spiskam, gospital'nym zakhoroneniiam po Kirgizskoi SSR 1941–1946 gg.', *Sud'ba soldata* Conference (Moscow, 2019); and Nurbubu Mambetakunova, 'Sbor dannykh po voennym gospitaliam i gospital'nym zakhoroneniiam na territorii Chuiskoi oblasti dlia uvekovecheniia pamiati pogibshikh', *Sud'ba soldata* Conference (Moscow, 2019).

117 It is probable that the actual figure is around 200,000. Information from Kyias Moldokasymov, Chair of Fond Muras, 10 May 2018. See also President A. Akaev, 'Introduction', in *Kyrgyzskaia Respublikanskaia Kniga pamiati 1941–1945*, eds K. I. Isenbekov et al. (Bishkek: Kyrgyz entsiklopediiasynyn Bashki redaktsiiasy, 1995); Esenaliev, *Zhenishke dank*, 5; Florin, 'Becoming Soviet through War', 505, note 58; Kaptagaev, et al., *Sbornik*, 5; and Lilley, *Have the Mountains Fallen?*, 12.

118 Abylkhozhin, *Istoriia Kazakhstana*, 499–500; Dadabaev, *Identity and Memory*, 64; Keller, *Russia and Central Asia*, 206; and Yerbolat Uatkhanov, 'Military Parade Commemorates Fatherland Defenders' Day, Victory Day Marked', *The Astana Times*, 10 May 2017.

119 'Den' Pobedy v Turkmenistane', *Calend.ru*, https://www.calend.ru/holidays /0/0/40/9/ (accessed 10 May 2019); and '9 maia: Den' Pobedy v Velikoi Otechestvennoi voine', *Sputnik Tajikistan*, https://tj.sputniknews.ru/trend/ Den_Pobedi_v_stranah_SSSR_6052016/ (accessed 10 May 2019).

120 Kaptagaev, et al., *Sbornik*, 151–2.

121 Ibid.; and Moritz Florin, 'Faîtes tomber les murs! La politique civilisatrice de l'ère Brežnev dans les villages kirghiz', *Cahiers du monde russe* 54, no. 1/2 (2013): 187–211, 202.

122 IKSA:146/1/49/18; Kaptagaev, et al., *Sbornik*, 151 and 156; and Tranum, *Life at the Edge of the Empire*, 78.

123 Information from the Rakhmanov family personal archive.

124 Esenaliev, *Zhenishke dank*, 112.

125 Ibid., 10–13 and 166.

126 Ibid., 95 and 114.

127 Ibid., 133; and personal interview with Tenti Tamashaev, 15 May 2018.

128 Esenaliev, *Zhenishke dank*, 57–8.

129 Ibid., 102.

130 Ibid., 134.

131 Ibid., 52 and 152.

132 Information from Prof. Tchoraev.

133 Abylkhozhin, *Istoriia Kazakhstana*, 449–538; and Carmack, *Kazakhstan in World War II*, 20–1.

PART II

The impact of war on the home front

4

Wartime economy

Everything for the front! Everything for victory!

The whole of the Soviet Union suffered incredible hardship during the war years. In many respects, life was no different in Central Asia than in other parts of the vast country. In some ways, though, Central Asia was more fortunate. This region lay thousands of kilometres away from the occupied territories: it did not have to put up with the humiliation and inherent danger of Nazi occupation. Nor did Central Asia suffer from the partial isolation felt in much of north-eastern Siberia, where communications with the centre were often compromised. In conjunction with the Urals, Central Asia enjoyed support and investment from Moscow for the exploitation of its crops and mineral resources, providing secure employment for all. The moderate climate of much of the region was a benefit, helping to maximize the amount of crops available for those eking out a meagre existence. The region also welcomed thousands of incoming evacuees who brought their skills and talents to what was once considered a backward region, thus bridging any perceived distance from the centre while developing the scientific community and enlivening cultural life to the advantage of the local population.

However, Central Asia was certainly over-exploited by Moscow in many areas. Stripped of its assets by the increasing impact of state requisitions, it left its citizens to fend for themselves in some of the most inhospitable circumstances. Moreover, it was inundated with incomers – not only evacuees but also refugees and deportees, who proved as much a drain on the region as a help, bringing with them disease and infestation as well as the need for food and accommodation.

As the war progressed, the citizens of Central Asia became more and more resigned to the deteriorating conditions on the home front, as they were increasingly Sovietized by the constant propaganda from a centre which needed to keep the region onside. At stake was the very existence of the communist Soviet Union, which under these threatening circumstances risked the development of cultural, linguistic and political fault lines across its peripheral Asian regions.

Life in the rear

While those fighting the war at the front experienced the very real danger of close combat with the enemy, those left at home also underwent huge deprivation. Around 16 million Soviet civilians died during the war, falling victim to enemy bombs, slave labour camps, disease or starvation. The challenges of wartime were felt across the Soviet Union in different ways. Those in the western regions experienced the cruel reality of enemy occupation, imprisonment and forced labour, whereas their counterparts in the centre and easternmost areas of the vast country had to bear the brunt of sustaining a state at war. Central Asia may have been perceived in Moscow as one of the safest places for strategic assets and potential retreat, the so-called *glubokii tyl* (deep rear), but the extreme demands of the war effort there were also acknowledged: not for nothing was this region, alongside the Urals, recognised as the *trudovoi front* – the labour front.

Much has been written since 1945 about the occupation in the west of the Soviet Union. Little has appeared, however, about civilian life during the war in the unoccupied regions,[1] and even less is available about the special challenges facing the ordinary people of Central Asia. Although this region had much in common with the Urals, which also received factories and their personnel evacuated from occupied territory and where ordinary citizens worked without ceasing for the war effort, special conditions pertained in the Central Asian republics.

In the early days of the Soviet Union, resources were pumped into the region to enable the shipment of cotton and coal to other parts of the Soviet Union. Intent on nurturing class equality, the state nevertheless flooded Central Asia with Slavic and Jewish administrative and professional personnel, leaving the local workers to menial jobs on the farms, in the mines or in the new factories. This left a big division between the Soviet governing elite and those whom they perceived as backward Asians. The citizens of Central Asia may have been viewed as inferiors in the Soviet pecking order, but the fruits of their labours and the resources of their lands were essential to the state in wartime.

These indigenous inhabitants had only recently been introduced to the 'civilizing' influence of the Soviet state, which suddenly depended upon them not only for the production of the mineral resources, but also for the food needed to keep the vast Red Army in action. This interdependency of front and rear served to strengthen the region's identity with respect to the war effort, while at the same time undermining the ability of its own inhabitants to survive. The legacy of the sudden surge in exploitation of mines for the production of rare minerals, coal and oil, remains evident even today. Furthermore, the remoteness of much of the region rendered it ideal for the testing of new technology and armaments, which continued in secret locations until the collapse of the Soviet Union.

With most of the able-bodied men fighting in the army, the urban and rural economy was severely disrupted. Women, children and elderly men kept the farms, pastures and factories in action night and day, as their own animals, food and other materials were requisitioned by the state. Thanks to the loss of their menfolk and with little left to eat as the authorities sucked the land dry, a depleted population struggled to stay alive during the harsh war years. The arrival of evacuees, refugees and deportees from west of the Urals brought more mouths to feed, despite a limited increase in able-bodied manpower. Seen by the military authorities as a safe haven, Central Asia was gradually bled of its lifeblood in order to meet the single wartime priority: that the army might survive to fight another day.

The war had a profound impact on the relations of the public with the state. For the first time since the introduction of collectivization and the Stalinist purges of the 1930s, all were in it together, working towards the common goal of victory against a shared enemy. A surge of patriotism did much to mitigate the increased suffering of the ordinary people of Central Asia, as individuals, just like the state, became embroiled in a fight for sheer survival. Appalling living accommodation in many places across the region matched the meagre food rations upon which most were forced to survive. For civilians, it was a case of either adapting to the new conditions by the adoption of survival strategies or succumbing to despair and even starvation.

Despite the common cause, people had different experiences of hardship according to their status in the hierarchy and whether they lived in an urban or rural environment. Across the region bureaucratic demands were imposed inconsistently with consequent impacts on homelessness and employment opportunities. The ethnic Russian population lived mainly in the larger urban centres, while indigenous citizens were largely found in villages, on the farms or the alpine *jailoo*, still following the seasons in the traditional manner.

The central military headquarters (SAVO) of the region were located in Tashkent, the largest and culturally most advanced of Soviet cities in Central Asia.[2] The Uzbek capital was situated at the crossroads of Central Asia – a hub of the ancient Silk Road, which fused its Soviet development with the different cultural identities of its many ethnicities. Occupied before the war by Uzbeks, Tajiks, Russians, Jews, Koreans, Armenians, Tatars and Germans, it acted as a magnet for incoming refugees and evacuees until the city was overflowing. In this melting pot of humanity, ordinary residents gradually came to accept their role as Soviet citizens with little real objection possible.

Despite huge pre-war plans for urban development, the administrative authorities in Tashkent struggled to cope with the increasing population.[3] In contrast, the main problems in Kazakhstan revolved around the determination of the precise location of potential labourers and conscripts, scattered thinly over the vast steppe. Whether living in a small adobe hut on the collective farm or in a communal dormitory adjacent to a factory, workers were driven by the local authorities to physical extremes and privation as every ounce of collective energy was directed towards the war effort. This goal was unfortunately often in conflict with the personal aim of every resident of the region – simply to survive the war years.

The home guard

Most of Central Asia may have been located well away from frontline fighting, but areas of western Kazakhstan were close enough to the city of Stalingrad to experience aerial attack by German bombers during the autumn of 1942. Systematic enemy flights over the Soviet rear on the lower Volga seriously disrupted the Urbach–Astrakhan railway line. The towns of Janybek, Saikhin and Shungai each suffered over twenty raids during which a total of over 300 civilians lost their lives, with many more wounded. Even hospital trains on the branchline from Stalingrad were targeted, seriously limiting the evacuation of troops eastwards and the movement of reinforcements to the west.[4]

However, Central Asia remained unoccupied by the enemy, with most of the region geographically – if not politically – thousands of kilometres from the front, such that the direct impact of the conflict remained limited. With the region still surviving under relatively safe circumstances, it was difficult for the government to transmit the urgency of the threat to the western Soviet Union, while at the same time not spreading alarm and potentially causing an uprising in Central Asia. Little real news about the war reached the ears of those at home as newspapers failed to appear for weeks at a time and the few permitted communal radios reported a highly sanitized version of the truth. Civilians listened with dread to the spreading rumours that the Soviet Union would never win the war, just as Central Asian soldiers were similarly demoralized once they saw action.[5]

In order to engage the public, authorities reported that enemy agents and diversionary groups had managed to enter western Kazakhstan, although the extent of this alleged infiltration was probably extremely limited. It did provide propaganda material for locals, however, impressing a sense of urgency about the need to defend the Soviet motherland. Citizens were made aware that the danger of aerial attacks further into the region was not impossible, in which case Tashkent itself could be in danger of bombing raids. As the population became more conscious of the imminent approach of war, civil defence training was introduced. Originally intended as pre-conscription training for males aged between sixteen and fifty, training was stepped up to prepare a greater proportion of the population up to the age of sixty, with the limited exception of the war wounded or those employed in reserved industries vital for the war effort. Similar in nature to the courses undergone by soldiers, men were trained in basic military skills, the use of guns and grenades, anti-tank warfare and in the defence against aerial or chemical attack. These comprehensive 100-hour courses suffered, however, from the defects identified by newly conscripted men – a shortage of rifles and other vital equipment, plus the marked inadequacy of trainers.[6]

Even civilians not already co-opted into the civil defence units were targeted and trained to an extent via the local press. *Issyk-Kul'skaia Pravda* optimistically published articles such as 'What you should know about civil defence groups' and 'Be prepared for chemical warfare', in the hope that (literate) citizens would read them. By the middle of September 1941 it was evident that most residents of the Issyk-Kul' province had indeed learnt their lessons. A realistic exercise took place in Przheval'sk from 12 to 15 September, requiring the complete black-out of all buildings, even canteens and vehicles. The local Red Crescent manned first-aid posts and the police checked duty rosters. After completion of the exercise it was declared that it had gone well, with residents responding promptly to chemical warfare attack signals.[7] However, children were adversely affected by propaganda about the 'people-eating fascists'. One man later recalled that the village elder would scare them by shouting 'The Germans are coming!' to encourage them back to work.[8]

As the Battle of Stalingrad took its toll, a secret communiqué of 15 September 1942 from military headquarters in Frunze to local anti-aircraft defence units (MPVOs) revealed the desperation of the situation on the Volga and the potential repercussions for Central Asia. Urging a fight against complacency, it ordered that sirens and radio transmitters were checked, while emergency food distribution networks, medical support and evacuation procedures should be put in place immediately. The formation of civil defence groups was also ramped up. People working in industry and educational institutes were mobilized in an effort to protect the civilian population of Kyrgyzstan, its industry, transport systems, collective farms and state institutes from attack. Preparations were taken seriously: fire-fighters were added to those being trained for emergency action, while more support was enlisted from branches of the Red Cross and Red Crescent. The existing 'Organization for the promotion of defence, aviation and chemical industries', *Osoaviakhim*, also provided training for civilians in Kazakhstan.[9]

Women aged eighteen to fifty were urged to take part in the civil defence movement unless they were mothers of children under the age of eight or were more than thirty-five days pregnant. Their duty to family and community was invoked by the authorities, who reminded women that, by enrolling as locally based nurses, they would be helping their compatriots at the front.[10]

Students in further education were also trained to provide emergency relief in war, being taught how to perform parachute landings, transporting food and medical supplies.[11]

With the war sometimes thousands of kilometres away, support for the state took some time to build up in Central Asia, as families struggled with the desperate conditions associated with the war effort. It was only when members of their own families were killed, and the wounded and deserters started to stream eastwards, that the full implications of war were appreciated and civilians began to work almost at one with the state on the home front.[12]

The labour front

State employment policy

The invasion of June 1941 was soon followed by an industrial crisis as the Germans occupied the most productive regions of the Soviet Union. The coal mines of the Donbass area of eastern Ukraine fell into enemy hands, as did many key industrial plants vital for the production of Red Army equipment. Central Asia was one of the main parts of the country, along with the Urals and parts of Siberia, where new supply bases could be established and evacuated factories rebuilt. The region became a large arsenal in the rear, providing armaments for the troops. As the population worked to supply soldiers at the front, the city of Tashkent became the focal point of the civilian war effort, the growing industrial centre of the region. The coal mines and oil refineries of Kazakhstan were expanded, and the extraction of valuable mineral ores increased rapidly across the region.[13]

It was recognized early in the war that, unless new supply chains could be introduced quickly, the enemy would command an early victory. With the very survival of the state at stake, the government took the definitive decision to prioritize the needs of the army over those of civilians. Everything was put in place so that industrial wheels could keep turning, as all financial, human and material resources were directed to the defence industry, building on successive five-year plans which had promoted rapid industrialization in an effort to render the country independent of imports in all essential areas.[14]

Acting promptly to place the economy on an official war footing, the state announced in a directive to all managers of industry the increase in the length of the working day on 26 June, just days after war was declared. In Central Asia, as across the union, up to three extra hours were required, increasing the normal working day to eleven hours. This was a dramatic response to the need to raise productivity by one-third without a commensurate increase in the number of workers. Even children under the age of sixteen were liable to two hours of overtime, although pregnant women were excluded from this directive from their sixth month of pregnancy and for the first six months of breastfeeding. As a fifty-five-hour working week became the norm, the only advantages about the new system were that workers were paid at 1.5 times the normal rate, while previous maternity and pregnancy leave continued to apply.[15] At the same time, though, annual holiday entitlement was almost entirely axed and the state took upon itself the right to redeploy workers to another place of work without their agreement. These severe instructions took some time to be completely absorbed into daily life, even after it became obvious the following week that Stalin meant serious business in his broadcast to the nation on 3 July demanding 'All for the front'.[16]

A mass mobilization of labour ensued, as workers became tied to their posts, unable to move at will to another job in order to fulfil the demands of a command economy operating under martial conditions. Men were deployed to factories, mines and oil fields, several of them in other republics. Seven thousand Kyrgyz men were redeployed to lumber-jacking in the forests, with others marched off to help build new hydro-electric power (HEP) stations. Conditions were harsh, with the added element of racist abuse and discrimination towards Central Asian labourers based in the Urals. Posters appeared across Kyrgyzstan in an effort to attract women workers to sign up for manual jobs in support of 'our fathers, brothers, husbands and sons' at the front. Pensioners and war invalids also helped by filling the posts left vacant by army conscripts.[17]

As the economy nose-dived in the autumn of 1941, the search for additional manpower widened, as able-bodied men, civil servants and older children were redeployed to vital industry or transport services; even children as young as fourteen found themselves in underground coal mines as part of the State Labour Reserve.[18] Shortly after the initial measures, those already working in reserved professions, for example the defence industry or transport and communications, were officially exempted from military service, with many more 'conscripted' to join them.[19] By February 1942, the situation was so serious that more and more industries were placed under martial law, including key railway and river transport employees. Anybody caught leaving their job was treated as a deserter, facing a military tribunal and a prison sentence of five to eight years. Virtually everybody not already fully employed was mobilized for the duration of the war, even those deemed unfit for military service, but with the continuing exception of mothers with young children and students undergoing training or higher education.[20]

With most able-bodied men already serving in the army, a marked shortage of workers in the rear developed as the economy declined over the first year of the war. Perversely, it was often the most experienced and skilled men who were conscripted, as the region was bled of both manpower and resources. Factory managers were even spotted dragging their men away from army recruitment offices as an unseemly tug-of-war for the physically fit ensued. As some men were snatched from the arms of the army, others insisted on enlisting, being either extremely patriotic or preferring the salary and conditions of army life to the long working week on the factory floor. With such a huge demand for labour, young people underwent curtailed training courses in an effort to push them through into jobs for which they were barely equipped. In the meantime, labour battalions were also deployed to work on defence structures and infrastructure projects, where they were declared to be 'working like the troops'.[21]

By 1943, as more and more of the western territory of the Soviet Union was liberated from occupation, many men from Central Asia were sent there to re-establish industries and re-build factories. However, this significant achievement was at the expense of the workers and their families, who suffered badly in the struggle to keep the war effort at home on track.[22]

Industrial development

The Soviet authorities diverted both money and resources into Central Asia in an effort to boost existing industrial plants, to establish new industries vital for the defence of the country and to re-establish industrial plants and factories evacuated from the occupied western regions. In return they expected an increasing supply of armaments and other goods heading west to equip, feed and clothe the military. At the top of the priority list was investment in heavy industry and energy production as the country was put on a war footing.[23]

Building upon the existing cotton monoculture in Uzbekistan, the fishing and food canning industry in Kyrgyzstan, and the mining industry across most parts of Central Asia, new industries were developed in the early months of the war. Some factories were re-directed to the strategic production of defence materials to help the war economy. Mining was re-booted where necessary and new mines opened to meet the demand for coal and rare metals. The search for and extraction of oil similarly became urgent to fuel both tanks and aircraft.[24]

The population of most towns increased substantially. Tashkent, the capital of Uzbekistan, rocketed in size as workers flooded in to fill positions in the newly established factories, with qualified engineers most in demand. It was a particularly popular destination for incomers – much more so than Siberia or the Urals – thanks to its clement climate and once thriving food markets, which proved a great attraction in view of the ubiquitous food shortages. The local authorities eventually started to exercise more social and racial discrimination, imposing a cap on the number of new workers arriving in the city. Despite these measures, the population increased from 600,000 in 1941 to around 1 million in 1944, badly straining the city's infrastructure. Unskilled workers and former criminals were evicted from the city along with ethnic Germans, condemned to a daily struggle away from the mainstream. In an effort to maintain some control over the population explosion, the city was divided into zones for specific types of industry. Despite these measures, more room for industrial purposes was needed in an already bursting urban centre, leading to the closure of some academic institutes and buildings used for leisure purposes, which were then converted into factories or dormitories for workers in the defence industry.[25] Similar, if less dramatic, expansion took place in towns across the region. Smaller townships and villages sprang up around new industrial plants, for example, the town of Khaidarken, which was formed in the Osh province of Kyrgyzstan in February 1942. Overall, the urban population of Kyrgyzstan increased by 8.7 per cent by 1945, with a permanent change in the republic's demographics.[26]

The huge coal mines at Karaganda in Kazakhstan were expanded to supply the metal plants in the Urals, despite the lack of experienced miners, most of whom had been conscripted as sappers into the Red Army. Largely manned by prisoners incarcerated at the enormous Karlag facility, with a significant number of additional women and young people, Karaganda's coal production per person at first declined. The manual work was unenviable: both strenuous and dangerous, with little regard for health and safety. Many workers were not able to continue in such physically demanding circumstances: some stayed away, while others performed poorly under slack management supervision. Living conditions for the workers, often in communal barracks, were appalling. According to employment regulations, the personal living space in a coal mine barracks should be 4.5 square metres, whereas workers often found themselves sleeping in a cramped 1.5 square metres in an unsanitary, unheated dormitory with limited access to clean water but an unlimited supply of bedbugs. Unable to work efficiently in such inhumane conditions, many risked their lives by absconding to the mountains or even across the Chinese border, causing a marked decrease in industrial output. A substantial increase in wages was deemed necessary in August 1942 to retain workers suffering such poor conditions, resulting in an eventual increase in output of 70 per cent. The smaller Suliutkii, Kok-Jangak and Tash-Kumyr mines in Kyrgyzstan were united for efficiency under the overall name of 'Kirgiz-ugol' (Kyrgyz Coal), with production increasing following an advertising promotion to attract more young people using the slogan: '*V tylu – kak na fronte*' ([Working in] the rear is like being at the front).[27]

As discipline increased across the board, people were increasingly imprisoned for minor infringements, leaving work or shirking, largely *pour encourager les autres*. Workers in Tashkent faced particularly hard conditions, causing a high leakage of employees. Some had originally been press-ganged into jobs in the capital and away from their families. Like fish out of water, they were forced to work in an industrial environment where Russian was the working language, and training poor. No doubt assuming that the food and living conditions would be better on the land, many chose to return home, often being pursued for so-called 'desertion'. Those who identified them enjoyed a degree of praise. One hard-working

Comrade Nikolai Kharichev, a model worker at the coalface of a mine in the Issyk-Kul' province, came to the notice of the authorities in March 1942 for identifying 'enemy elements and some criminals', including four deserters subsequently labelled 'traitors of the motherland'.[28]

Twenty-four new mines and eleven new factories were set up in Kazakhstan during the war years. Copper and lead output was increased across the region, which supplied much of the state's needs. The zinc factory at Ust'-Kamenogorsk in Kazakhstan also stepped up its production in response to the new demand. Rare metals were very important for the war effort. It was claimed that the new Vostochno-Kounrad molybdenum mine, opened in June 1942, produced an unbelievably high 60 per cent yield of the metal ore from the mined rock, helping meet the state's production of high-quality steel. Uzbekistan also contributed to the production of molybdenum, while the rapidly constructed Jezdinsk manganese mine in Kazakhstan again served to improve steel production. In both Uzbekistan and Kyrgyzstan the supply of tungsten for the manufacture of steel, bullets, grenades, rockets and shells was dramatically increased. In fact, the majority of new positions in Kyrgyzstan involved working underground in the newly developed mining industry. The production of chemicals was also increased, with new plants established for the manufacture of synthetic rubber in Kazakhstan and for artificial fertilizers in the agricultural area of Chirchik, Uzbekistan. Two hundred and eighty industrial enterprises were established in Uzbekistan alone during the war, with a further thirty-eight new mines, power stations and other large plants in Kyrgyzstan.[29]

As the war made an increasing impact on the people of Central Asia, military air bases such as the Kant air base on the northern plain of Kyrgyzstan were established. Further east, Lake Issyk-Kul' provided a ready-made testing ground for submarines and torpedoes. Top secret and heavily guarded, the Kirov defence factory was built here in 1943 by 500 construction workers. Engineers and technical specialists arrived with their families to find a small settlement developing to house them at Pristan' on the lakeside outside Przheval'sk. Further factories specialized in other types of armaments, for example, mortar bombs and hand grenades.[30]

The Frunze mechanical factory was transformed by special decree at the very start of the war to produce military goods, while more cement for construction purposes was manufactured in Kant and on the north shore of Lake Issyk-Kul'. The oil production facilities at Aktiubinsk (Aktobe) and Emba in Kazakhstan were further developed to exploit this 'liquid gold'. The new Petrovskii construction factory and oil refinery were built in the Caspian Sea port of Gur'ev (Atyrau), with an emphasis on the production of fuels for the military.[31]

There was a correspondingly rapid increase in light industry to meet the needs of the army, building on the cotton and textile industry in Uzbekistan and to a lesser extent in the south of Kazakhstan. Factories which had once produced household clothes were successfully diverted to the manufacture

FIGURE 4.1 *Preparing mortar bombs for the front, 1942. Reproduced with permission from the Issyk-Kul' State Archives.*

of military uniforms, boots and saddles. Kyrgyz factories produced over 6 million uniforms and greatcoats, an additional 2 million sweaters and 628 million pairs of shoes during the war, mainly in the southern provinces of Osh and Jalal-Abad, while leather for belts and straps was produced in Naryn. The production of woollen fabric was almost halved in order to concentrate on the output of silk for the production of parachutes. Sacks for the transport of sugar and flour were also at a premium, as were bandages and dressings for the wounded.[32]

A similar change of gear in the food canning industry took place in Kyrgyzstan, as the pace of agricultural output gradually increased alongside industrial capacity. Although agriculture was deemed slightly less important than industry, food processing plants were vital for the preservation of products destined for the front and hence for the overall success of the war. Their output increased by over 120 per cent during the war, ensuring millions of tons of sugar, sausages, preserved meat and tobacco for the troops. For example, one factory in Frunze produced 23 million tins of preserved meat in 1943 alone, a record output, while the huge factory in Tokmok produced sugar from the locally grown sugar beet. A new fish-canning plant with an annual capacity for 3 million tins opened in Przheval'sk to take advantage of the natural resources of Lake Issyk-Kul'.[33]

The horse meat factory in Cholpon-Ata on Lake Issyk-Kul' continued production, despite the loss of many experienced staff – and horses – to the army.[34] As senior men left their posts, younger and even considerably underage youths took over, while others were rapidly trained to take their places. People under the age of twenty-five made up 38 per cent of the Kyrgyz workforce at the beginning of 1945. Young people from rural collective farms were even forced from their alpine *jailoo* into work underground, comprising a large proportion of Kyrgyz miners. Unused to this type of working environment, they understandably failed to flourish.[35]

Similar issues affected workers in the towns. Tension arose in Tashkent with its huge, mixed population of incomers and indigenous workers. With an influx of army deserters and some criminals, and many residents affected by severe hunger, here was a recipe for instability. Desperate people, stricken by diseases prevalent in conditions of poverty and communal living, vied for food and other resources as Moscow concentrated its efforts on the troops rather than the support needed by vulnerable civilians.[36]

Under these impossible circumstances, it is a testament to the concerted effort of the state, the discipline of local authorities and the tenacity of the human spirit that industrial production in the Soviet Union became more successful than in Germany by mid-1943. By the end of the war, Uzbekistan alone had produced over 2,000 military aeroplanes, 22 million mines, 560,000 shells, 1 million grenades and 330,000 parachutes. Mainly thanks to the effective mobilization of its vast natural resources, this output was also due to the carrot and stick propaganda campaign around industrial output. Much was published in the war years about Stakhanovites in the workplace – single-minded people who broke all production records – as others were urged to emulate their remarkable feats. On the other hand, cautionary reminders were deemed necessary to a relatively small meat factory about the risk of falling standards of production.[37]

Women in the workplace

Despite the marked personal cost to citizens working in the rear, the tight control of centralized planning succeeded in effecting the swift and successful reorganization of industry to meet the requirements of war. Part of this strategy was the use of women in the workplace, replacing their husbands, fathers and brothers conscripted into the army. Alongside their new employment, women had to bear the heavy domestic burden of maintaining sometimes large families without the help of their menfolk. Women took on men's jobs across most industries, even to the extent of going down the mines, driving trains and operating machine tools in factories. In

Kyrgyzstan a staggering 8,000 women were employed in the Kyzyl Kii coal mine alone, for example, while a significant 36 per cent of workers in the gold industry at Kirgizzolotoredmet were females.[38] In this respect, their roles changed dramatically, much more than their counterparts in Britain, for example.[39]

Women also played a vital role in light industry, particularly in textile and food factories. Those looking for work often migrated to the larger centres such as Tashkent, Samarkand and Osh, where there were both more employment opportunities and training courses.[40] While 78 per cent of jobs in the Osh silk industry and 87 per cent in the Frunze meatworks were soon occupied by women, others took up employment in food canning factories. Women were also enlisted to work on building and construction sites, increasing in significance from 15 per cent of the workforce in Kyrgyzstan in 1941 to 52 per cent in 1944, but declining again at the end of the war as the men returned to take their place.[41]

In contrast, in Tashkent a much smaller proportion of women entered factory employment, preferring more traditional occupations such as care roles in the many orphanages springing up in the war. Uzbek women were culturally quite conservative: unskilled and less open to new challenges. Fewer Uzbek women therefore entered heavy industry in comparison to their Russian, Ukrainian and Jewish compatriots. With very low wages coming into the home, they were consequently less able to purchase necessary foodstuffs and household materials such as soap or medicine.[42]

Although some Uzbek women held down jobs in transport and industry, cultural barriers and the long-standing perception of gender-specific roles prevented many from working outside the home, especially if the language demanded in the workplace was Russian. Some were attracted onto the factory floor by the huge propaganda effort, however, sometimes being shamed into action when the hardship of females at the front was highlighted. This forced cohesion between front and rear drove some courageous women to accept more responsibility at home by the formation of sanitation brigades to keep Tashkent clean and their homes somewhat less squalid.[43]

In Kyrgyzstan a similar campaign in September 1941 aimed to attract women into industry, if with a subtle difference. Here, women were told that Hitler was denigrating German women, destroying their right to a family life as their husbands were sent off to war. Furthermore, they were claimed to have been relegated to production machines for pure-blooded Aryan children. In contrast, propagandists extolled the characteristics of dignified Soviet motherhood, as women sacrificed their own sons to the war. And then came the crux: Kyrgyz women were reminded that they worked to very high standards – whether on the farm, in heavy industrial plants or smaller factories, as they took on the jobs of their menfolk. According to a local newspaper three weeks later, one woman 'almost ran' to the wood manufacturing factory to join her friends already working there. This report may be taken with a pinch of salt, as no mention is made of the pressure probably applied to the poor woman to hurry her off to the factory gate.[44]

Life on the farm

Agriculture in the Soviet Union was governed by the practice of collectivization introduced in the early 1930s, often with disastrous consequences. Nomads, who had for generations wandered the vast expanses of Kazakhstan with their herds of camels, sheep and horses, were forced to endure a more settled existence on either a large state or collective farm (*sovkhoz* or *kolkhoz* respectively) with invented names varying from the mundane 'Stalin', 'Kirov' and 'Pioneer', to the more ideologically correct. The latter often began with the word 'red' in either Russian or the indigenous language, such as 'Krasnyi vostok' (Red East in Russian) or 'Kyzyl Oktiabr" (Red October in Kyrgyz), after the 1917 revolution.

The hardship which ensued from the destruction of the traditional land economy with the introduction of this social experiment had barely been overcome before the war brought about a further set of extreme circumstances for farmers. Ilhomjan Karimov, an elderly Uzbek man born in 1924, recalled decades later:

> Almost everybody [in my village] was sent to the war and those who weren't were sent to the mines. There was no one left to farm. We were starving, there was no food. Only a few tractor drivers were left in the village and we farmed everything [by hand]. [. . .] It was a difficult time.[45]

Agriculture under martial law

By the end of 1941, the German army had occupied much of Ukraine and other food-producing regions of the western Soviet Union. With a loss of 38 per cent of the area normally used to grow grain and 84 per cent of the former sugar beet fields, the supply of produce for both troops and civilians dried up quickly, leaving the state to turn to the fields and grazing pastures of Central Asia for survival. To ensure a sustainable flow of food to the front and to hard-pressed regions of the country, the government immediately increased grain requisitions in a manner reminiscent of conditions during the First World War and the 1917 revolution. In addition, it proclaimed that the duty of every Soviet patriot was 'to give more meat, oil and wool' to the country and the army.[46]

However, as soon as the state started to conscript able-bodied men into the Red Army or the defence industry, the manpower upon which the farms traditionally depended dried up almost overnight. Villages were emptied, as the cream of the rural supply of tractor drivers and combine harvester operators left the region. The only consolation was that, after 1941, the annual recruitment drives only took place after the autumn harvest.[47]

Not only the men but also most of the farming vehicles disappeared from the landscape, as they were requisitioned for army haulage purposes. The degree of mechanization of agriculture in Kazakhstan was halved, as farms were forced to resort to horses, oxen and camels to work the fields as in the past. In Tajikistan the situation was somewhat less dire, as many more camels and asses were bred to plug the gap left by the requisition of farm trucks. As agriculture became more labour intensive than ever, there remained fewer people to share the increased burden. One Kyrgyz man recalled the first tractor appearing in his village as late as 1943, which helped to improve the situation somewhat as it was no longer necessary to do all the manual work by hand.[48]

In its drive for more productivity, the state continued to squeeze those upon whom the lives of millions depended. In 1940 farms occupied a massive 88 per cent of the area of Kyrgyzstan. Before the war, farmers had earned very little for themselves, receiving only a proportion of the total farm income, once outgoings such as seeds and tractor hire had been taken into account. When it became evident that the fewer remaining farms were needed to produce even more for the state, individual workers were forced to work an increasing number of (even longer) days before they were given a wage. Those living in the countryside soon saw a marked deterioration in their already small earnings.[49]

Less concentrated work was expected of farmers in more industrialized areas, where a variety of crops ensured work throughout the year. This gave workers longer periods of employment and hence a greater accrued salary than their counterparts working solely on a sheep farm or in the cotton fields. Minors had to meet lower annual targets, with a minimum of fifty days per year expected of them. If a person failed to meet the required number of days, they were sent to court, usually resulting in part of their pay being confiscated. There was little point in banishing offenders from the farm, when every hand was necessary.[50]

As they worked harder and harder, farm workers suffered more and more. The state needed more produce to feed the army, requisitioning grain for the troops and taking farmers' personal cows and horses. Urban residents were issued with ration cards and many possessed their own modest vegetable plots. Especially army families and the war wounded enjoyed this privilege, with over half the population of Frunze – around 84,000 families – working individual patches in 1944. The situation was slightly better in Alma-Ata, with its milder climate and abundant fruit harvests. Even there, though, individuals were forced to dig up any lawn or spare ground to grow potatoes and other vegetables. This was not comparable with the measures taken by families in Britain, for whom 'digging for victory' was a way to supplement official rations, but necessary for sheer survival. The rural population had no ration cards, having to rely on their own personal allotments for fruit and vegetables. However, much land was taken from individuals in an effort to increase overall production. Furthermore, those farmers who had previously grown food to sell at market were forbidden from 1943 to conduct this activity any longer. This disadvantaged both the farmers who produced the food and the urban population who no longer had access to it. Prices rocketed as the traditional food supply dried up, causing many deaths by starvation and driving citizens to extraordinary measures to keep their families alive.[51]

Mixed farming and monocultures

The region of Central Asia is geographically and climatically diverse, with its varied topography of isolated mountainous terrain, deserts, lush oases and river valleys dictating different types of farming. Some food crops were grown around the desert oases of Uzbekistan and the Fergana Valley, where a settled mode of agriculture prevailed involving cotton and textiles. In contrast, the northern republics of Kazakhstan and Kyrgyzstan with an emphasis on pastoral farming still retained aspects of their traditional nomadic culture.

The mass drive to wholesale cotton production in the west had caused substantial changes to the traditional mixed mode of agriculture. The cotton monoculture in much of Uzbekistan and the Osh and Jalal-Abad areas of Kyrgyzstan was a great advantage to a state wishing to become self-reliant in textiles, but undoubtedly disadvantaged fishermen in the Aral Sea whose water supply was diverted to irrigate the cotton crop. Farmers were forced to supply the state with cotton while selling surplus stocks in order to buy their own food, which they had once produced themselves. As Uzbek farmers complained, you can't eat cotton.[52]

Sugar beet was a key crop in the northern valleys of Kyrgyzstan, with the precious sugar sent by train convoy from Frunze to Moscow, presumably to meet the ration entitlements of civilians as well as keeping the troops fed and fuelled. Large poppy plantations located in the Issyk-Kul' province with its optimum climate produced vital opium derivatives for the pain relief of wounded troops. Grain, rice and potatoes fed the ordinary citizens of the region, while grapes, tobacco, honey, water melons, apples from Alma-Ata, pears, peaches, strawberries, tomatoes and medicinal herbs added variety on a smaller scale.

The nomads of Central Asia had always concentrated predominantly on their herds, which were moved seasonally from pasture to pasture across the region. Cattle, horses, sheep, goats, pigs and camels kept families supplied with meat and dairy products, including *kumis* (mare's milk). As animals were requisitioned for the war effort, farmers were forced to 'sell' their stock of cattle, horses, sheep and goats to the state for a risible sum. This loss of many mature animals led to a proportionate increase in young animals left on the farm, not yet ready for reproduction or farm work. The small amount of meat that was still retained in some households from before the war did not last long. After the requisitions in 1943, only 28.7 tonnes of meat – just 1.3 per cent of that year's produce – remained to feed all the inhabitants of Kyrgyzstan.[53]

By the end of the war 69 per cent of Kyrgyz collective farmers no longer possessed sheep or goats, and 46 per cent had no cow to their name. Dairy products became a distant memory, as farmers struggled to feed their children with little recourse to protein. As the cattle were taken for meat, the Przheval'sk dairy product factory was also left in short supply, resulting in a noticeable decrease in output. In a blatant exercise of naming and shaming, Comrade Goncharov, the unfortunate factory manager, was publicly accused of inefficiency as the quality of his products also deteriorated.[54] However, horses were the main target for the army, being used for the cavalry or haulage at the front as well as for meat if luxury permitted. They were also at high risk of death at the front, so replacements were demanded from Central Asia throughout the war, as fewer and fewer remained for use at home. At the end of the war, a staggering 93 per cent of Kyrgyz farmers had either sold or lost their last horse to the army – or eaten it in desperation.[55]

Women to the rescue

In the early days of the war, it was obvious that fewer men than usual would be available to bring in the harvest that summer. Preparations for a difficult season were being made as soon as the Nazis started to roll into the western Soviet Union. In the Issyk-Kul' province of eastern Kyrgyzstan farmers were urged by the local newspaper to bring in the harvest as early as possible and with increased vigour, as 'Stakhanovite labour is necessary for a victory over the enemy'. Furthermore, equating workers in the rear with the troops at the front, patriotism was invoked as farmers were urged to 'attack' the fascist enemy in order to win the 'battle for the harvest'. According to the newspaper, their hard work would surely reflect the 'honour, pride, glory and heroism of all sons and daughters of our socialist Fatherland'.[56] The urgency implied by the article suggested that farmers were working quite slowly at that point and needed a sudden change of gear before all was lost.

Those men not already conscripted were dispatched speedily to the countryside in an urgent effort to bring in the harvest that was needed to sustain the country over the coming winter. With the army's food supply at stake, men were sent to the alpine meadows to help bring down the animals in the annual transhumance. Children, already used to helping with the harvest, spent their two months' summer holidays on the farm.[57] The message at home again equated this work with that of the military:

> Soviet people in the rear feel as if they are at the front. All our strength is directed towards bringing in the rich harvest quickly, efficiently and without loss.[58]

As their menfolk gradually left for the war or the defence industry, the number of male agricultural workers decreased by over 50 per cent in Kyrgyzstan, substantially altering the age profile of those left behind. Most able-bodied men were conscripted, especially those able to handle machinery such as tractor drivers or combine harvester operators. Thousands of able-bodied teachers and some older students were therefore ordered into the fields – that is, until they too were needed to join the army.[59]

As early as the summer of 1941, the Priozernyi grain farm in the Tiup area employed a team ('brigade') composed entirely of sixty women for the fortnight's back-breaking work in the fields to bring in the harvest.[60] Women were increasingly left in the position of having to take on more responsible jobs, from labourers in the fields to team leaders (so-called 'brigadiers'), sometimes even learning to drive tractors. Within two months of the start of the war, over 1,000 women from the Issyk-Kul' province had been trained as MTS operatives, responsible for operating, maintaining and repairing machinery in the local collective machine and tractor centres. A certain Ekaterina Gordienko of the Osoaviakhim collective farm had previously occasionally driven a tractor alongside her husband. As instructions for his mobilization arrived, she determined to master the combine harvester at the Issyk-Kul' MTS station in order to take his place. Combine harvester courses took over three months, but by August 1942, she had brought in her first grain crop, covering 285 hectares.[61]

In the absence of their menfolk, women and girls took over the fishing duties of the Issyk-Kul' collective fish farm in Anan'evo. Even in the depths of winter they worked 8 kilometres offshore to bring in an important catch of scaly osman, a species of carp found at a depth of over 50 metres in high-altitude Asian fresh-water lakes. Women also became members and even chairmen of the Communist Party management bodies for farms. Whereas only seven women led collective farms at the start of the war, by January 1944, 114 women had taken on this responsibility.[62]

Women were also left largely in charge of the household as well as carrying out physically demanding work such as building stone walls. Some lenience was shown towards mothers of small children, permitting them to work nearer the home, for example drying potatoes or sugar beet for the troops. Some left for the towns, where employment was more varied and often better paid, so that sometimes it was necessary to consolidate rural households in order to free up more women for work. This led to a decrease in the average number of households on a collective farm during the war, from 186 at the beginning to 162 at the end in Kyrgyzstan. While the number of farms remained broadly stable, agriculture overall took a huge blow.[63]

As work on the farm reverted to older methods without the aid of mechanized vehicles or draft animals, women and children worked the fields by hand – digging, sowing, cutting hay and bringing in the harvest. The ground was sometimes used in new ways, as crops were farmed differently in an effort to avoid the need for an urgent rush to complete a large task to a deadline. Students still able to attend university were expected to work in the fields during the summer vacation. One Polish refugee became experienced in digging potatoes and picking cotton in the Osh area, trying to ignore the ubiquitous mosquitoes and receiving peaches and apricots instead of wages.[64] By 1944, nearly 70 per cent of farm workers were women, working alongside children and elderly men.

Press propaganda

Despite the military action in the west, the yearly cycle of agriculture continued relentlessly, as the press printed a torrent of seasonal articles to emphasize that life carried on as normal. The transhumance had to take place with children rather than men often acting as summer shepherds on the *jailoo*. The loss of a lamb was always a catastrophe for the farmer, so that the news that shepherds caught a she-bear in the act of taking a young animal made the headlines in August 1943. The safe return of the stock

FIGURE 4.2 *Preparing dried fruits to send to the Red Army, 1941. Reproduced with permission from the Issyk-Kul' State Archives.*

towards mid-September was always a relief for the farms, as they welcomed their well-fed animals safely back into the fold.[65]

The state machine worked almost as hard as the farmers to maintain the flow of food to the front. Propagandists employed four main tactics to encourage higher production rates: by congratulating well-performing farms and farmers, encouraging competitiveness between farms, naming and shaming poor performers, and offering advice on farming methods.

The default setting for the press was to publish good news to maintain the morale of the region's hard-pressed farmers. In the Issyk-Kul' province people read constantly of the 'enthusiasm' of farmers and their patriotic wish to exceed the 'norms' (the production targets dictated by the five-year plan), that is, to exceed often artificially and unrealistically set objectives. Political 'agitators' – often wounded soldiers and occasionally even politically inclined women – were dispatched to hold informative discussions and to read newspaper articles to collective farmers. Every effort was taken to get them to recognize the emergency conditions of wartime and encourage them to increase their productivity by identifying with their family members on active service. Komsomol members also played an active role in disseminating the party's ideological agenda.[66] As well as giving lessons in communist ideology and reading articles to farm workers, Komsomol activists on the Orto-Aryk farm were apparently organized enough to increase the yield by arranging for better storage of produce on the fields before it was taken inside for the winter.[67]

Communist Party slogans and ideological vocabulary were scattered liberally across the press, which was quick to report political work on the farm. Agitators went out to 'harness the initiative of the masses', to 'light huge fires [of Communism] in the fields of collective farms', while 'only the Bolshevik power of labour' would eventually win the war.[68]

Issyk-Kul'skaia Pravda, the official newspaper for the province, constantly ran good news stories. Only two months after the outbreak of war, they were lauding two Komsomol members, Comrades Toktobekov and Kol'baev of the Karajal collective farm, who had exceeded the target for harvesting opium poppy plants by 200 per cent.[69] Shortly afterwards, everybody on the once mediocre Toktoian farm in the Tiup area was singled out for praise. Apparently the farm had improved so much over the previous few months that everybody there knew their own role, working from dawn to dusk so that not a single grain was lost. Other farmers were shown no longer relying on combine harvesters, but taking up their scythes to ensure that as much hay as possible was collected.[70]

Quoting Stalin's demand that farms go the extra mile to help those at the front, team leader Mironenko of the 'Gornyi gigant' (Mountain Giant) farm in southern Kazakhstan was reported as urging on his team, saying:

> We will not complain about anything in our fight against the cruel enemy – our energy, our wealth and our lives are given to the motherland for the common good.[71]

It was indeed the common wealth of collective farms which was important for individual farmers. Some farms implemented such dramatic changes that the farm's collective income increased substantially, to the benefit of all its farmers. Thanks to firm discipline and excellent veterinary support, the Budennii farm reportedly increased its annual income to 1 million roubles. Specializing in sheep rearing, the farmers managed to shear their sheep so efficiently that each animal allegedly gave an astonishing 3.1 kilograms of wool, rather than the average of 1.6 kilograms per head. Their cows were apparently similarly heroic, yielding over one-third more milk than usual.[72]

Military expressions were often introduced into press articles, in an effort to unite those working in the rear with those at the fighting front. For example, as the war dragged on into 1942, farmers were told that 'in the Issyk-Kul' province the "spring-work in the fields" front widens day by day,' as people 'mobilize' their inner resources. A propaganda poster informed workers that 'every tonne of grain equates to one more shell in our arsenal', as ever more produce was requisitioned. The papers went further, as people read that 'each extra tonne of grain in this year's harvest equates to more shells, bombs and mines' to defeat the enemy. Just like the soldiers, farm workers could also receive special awards for outstanding performance. Comrades Shirnonol'skaia and Kirillova of the Frunze collective farm received the award 'For excellence in animal husbandry' (*Otlichnik zhivotnovodstva*) by achieving overall milk yields of 25 per cent above average. While Soviet troops were engaged in hand to hand combat in the rubble of Stalingrad, Kyrgyz farmers could rest assured that they had collectively fulfilled the state plan for the supply of corn to the Red Army for the coming winter.[73]

It was naturally the harvest which attracted the most attention, being vital for both the war effort and to keep the whole population alive, if not always healthy. At the appropriate season, the newspaper urged farms to complete the harvest as quickly and efficiently as possible. The 'Novyi put" (New Path) collective farm made the front page in 1943 for bringing in its grain harvest ahead of all the other farms in the province, under the leadership of communist Comrade I. F. Golovchenko.[74]

The poppy harvest was much publicized, as nobody could deny the vital importance of opiate drugs to soldiers wounded in action. At least here there was no conflict of interest between front and rear as to who received the most food. The poppy seeds were normally sown at the start of May, once the ground was snow free and warm enough for germination. The plants grew for around four months, with the seed pod appearing and slowly ripening in the final stages as the petals fell. It was the unripe seed pod which was harvested at exactly the right time for its milky opium-containing sap to be extracted. Plantation workers would cut the seed pod early in the morning, returning in the evening to collect the hardened gum, which was then refined to produce the pain-relieving drugs. Any discarded seed heads were eagerly collected by children, who took them home to supplement their food.[75]

Already in the autumn of 1941, exceptional efforts were being put into the important poppy harvest. By April 1942 the motivational and organizational skills of three brigade leaders on the Shevchenko farm were highlighted, as they aimed to complete the first tranche of poppy sowing well before the traditional date of 1 May. Similarly, the Kyzyl-Tuu farm in the Jeti-Oguz district finished its second round of weeding on the poppy plantation on 30 May, two days earlier than anticipated in the farm schedule. It was closely followed by the Deishin farm teams, which succeeded in the back-breaking work of weeding an area of 20 hectares in only three days. One farm labourer singled out for her extraordinary devotion to duty was a certain Liubov' Vasil'eva from the Voroshilov farm, who harvested 78 per cent more poppy heads than projected, earning a commensurate extra bounty of 2,860 roubles.[76]

Nothing could compare with the devotion to duty of Comrade Volynkin of the Issyk-Kul' district, however. A teacher during the day, he turned his talented hand to farm work during the hard spring season in the fields. He not only drove a tractor but also repaired tractors and organized tractor teams. And as if that was not enough, he apparently also found time to train snipers.[77]

In addition to state encouragement – with some motivational threats – the press created competition between farms in a further measure to increase productivity. A so-called 'board of honour' on the front page of the local paper displayed the names of farms reaching certain milestones ahead of others. For example, towards the end of August 1942, *Issyk-Kul'skaia*

FIGURE 4.3 *Poppy plantation, Issyk-Kul' province, Kyrgyzstan. Reproduced with permission from the Issyk-Kul' State Archives.*

Pravda published regular progress reports from the farms in the province as they completed the poppy harvest, including the percentages by which each had exceeded their targets. There was even a board of honour outlining the achievements of individual combine harvesters.[78]

Bad results were also made public, in a concerted campaign of naming and shaming poor performance. In 1945 the poppy harvest was reported to be of particularly poor quality. All farms with poppy plantations were urged to prepare well ahead for 1946, when even more opium would be needed. Some shirkers were called out on the Molotov farm in the Tiup area, when all the hay harvested in 1942 had been used by the end of the year, leaving nothing for the animals for the winter. During the first few months of 1943, 370 cattle consequently died, leaving the farm with insufficient meat to meet the state's demands and absolutely nothing left over for their own needs. Shortly afterwards, it was reported that a certain Comrade Malyshev, the leader of the Molotov farm, had allowed low standards of discipline to take root. Furthermore, the grain harvest was brought in much too slowly, as workers put in only four to six hours a day. The newspaper reader is left to wonder why this should be so, when every grain was vital to life. It can only be imagined that either the poor workers were so physically debilitated that normal work had become impossible, or that the labourers prioritized working their own plots above the farm, making sure that their families had sufficient to eat during the winter, rather than sending the results of their efforts straight into the hands of the state. According to the newspaper, had Malyshev not been publicly rebuked, this practice could have continued unnoticed. In some cases, political education was the response to poor yields, linking political awareness to agricultural productivity. However, the ideological lecture delivered on the Krupskaia farm attracted only eight attendees from a community of 300 farmers, illustrating the constant wartime tension between what farmers *should* do and what they actually *could* do under impossible circumstances.[79]

The area around Lake Issyk-Kul' proved ideal for the cultivation of potatoes, being free from common blights and diseases. In spite of the excellent soil, though, some farms in the Anan'evo area did not return as high a yield as expected. This may have been because some potatoes were hidden away for use by individual families, or because there was simply not enough manpower to dig up the potato harvest at the end of the season. With little food available for its families, one farm even resorted to the desperate measure of eating their seed potatoes over the winter – potatoes which had been intended for planting the following spring. In an effort to educate the farmers, the local Communist Party sent in high-ranking 'agro-personnel' to supervise the next spring planting.[80]

Despite the occasional holding to account, though, the press definitely employed more carrot than stick with regard to local collective farms. A widespread campaign throughout the war succeeded in disseminating useful information and advice to those farmers who could read, as articles appeared by veterinary surgeons and directors of research institutions working to ascertain the optimum conditions for improving yields.

Most experienced veterinary surgeons had been conscripted for the front, where they were needed to ensure the health of war horses. In the rear, the work was often left to barely qualified practitioners, such as vet's assistant Mehal Kesler. Based in Tashkent, he would travel by horse, riding through orchards, rice paddies and cotton fields to reach the collective farms on the outskirts of the city, where his work included the supervision of anti-eczema baths for sheep and the castration of lambs.[81]

The Kyrgyz biological institute farmed 2 million hectares for its research, which included best practice in the sphere of animal husbandry. There was a college of horse husbandry in Przheval'sk in Kyrgyzstan, and itinerant staff would also teach farmers about animal husbandry in general and how to build yurts on the summer pastures. The newspapers published regular seasonal issues devoted to farming advice, including, for example, lengthy sections on pigs, sheep and even camels at work on the collective farm. It is likely that most ordinary farmers were virtually illiterate, so this material would have been read to them possibly by a village Komsomol member. In all probability, the target audience would then have returned to traditional tried and tested ways of caring for their stock.[82]

The results of scientific research on crops were also published, being somewhat easier to digest. Instructions on the harvesting and protection of crops from autumn frosts were followed by advice on the optimum conditions for preserving seeds over the winter. Whole four-page issues were devoted to the most common crops: cotton, sugar beet and potatoes, while advanced trout science was outlined for the fishermen and women of Lake Issyk-Kul'.[83]

The institute researching medicinal herb and poppy cultivation was evacuated from Moscow to Chimkent (Shymkent) in southern Kazakhstan at the beginning of the war. Its aim was to identify the most productive varieties of poppy and the best conditions for an optimal yield. High on the recommended list were the Przheval'skii-222, the Przheval'skii-D250 and the Przheval'skii-133 types, each with a slightly different harvesting period.[84]

On a much smaller scale, experiments were conducted in Przheval'sk on four different varieties of water melon to establish which may be suited for cultivation on the sandy soil in the high-lying north-east of Kyrgyzstan. Murashko melons were compared with early Uzbeks, early Americans and the so-called 'Crimean Victors', with the most promising selected for future crops. In similar experiments with tomatoes, a variety from the Krasnodar province in the south-west of the Soviet Union was found to yield the plumpest, sweetest and tastiest fruit under the environmental conditions of the Issyk-Kul' province.[85] This type of research continued in the post-war years, to the advantage of crop cultivation across Central Asia.

In general, agricultural output in Central Asia did not let the army down, in spite of a dramatic loss of manpower and machinery and considerable personal hardship for farming communities. In Kyrgyzstan overall yields increased by an average 20 per cent, despite a smaller area of land coming under cultivation towards the end of the war. More was produced and a much greater proportion was given to the state than in pre-war years. It is claimed by Brezhnev-era sources that the weight of vegetables produced overall increased by an almost unbelievable 107 per cent and even the amount of parachute silk taken by the Red Army increased by 60 per cent. The press, obviously, lauded these triumphs of the war effort on the agricultural front, thanks to – but equally to the detriment of – the impoverished citizens of Central Asia.[86]

With the state prioritizing the army and the defence industry over farmers, Central Asia was affected worse than most areas of the Soviet Union by food shortages as the region became increasingly exploited. As the amount of grain taken by the state increased, resistance from farms and individuals sometimes became physical. In addition, food and animals were occasionally stolen by groups of ruthless army deserters roaming the land, some with no qualms about depriving farming compatriots who had very little themselves. If a collective farm refused or was unable to produce the requisitioned crops or animals, larger armed uprisings sometimes ensued, leading to the dispatch of troops to arrest and discipline the rebels. Some protesters were even supported by local Communist Party leaders who allowed them to escape into the mountains. It is surprising that most collective farm workers put up with these conditions, despite being constantly reminded that their sacrifices kept the army moving, in the interest of a forthcoming victory. As the war developed, though, they became more lethargic and unable to offer any real resistance as the effects of malnutrition took hold.[87]

After the war, it took some years before the men returned to the farms and life gradually became more stable. Once bled of men, animals, crops and resources, Central Asia benefited from post-war investment as Moscow's Virgin Lands campaign of 1954 to 1963, overseen by Nikita Khrushchev and implemented by Leonid Brezhnev, inflicted further dramatic changes on the landscape of Central Asia, boosting the local economy for a time and flooding Kazakhstan with new farmers, if with mixed success.[88]

Altruism in action

On the one hand highly valued by the state, but on the other over-exploited and singled out as inferiors to western Slavs, the citizens of Central Asia suffered exceptionally badly on the home front as collective farms and individual families were progressively and systematically squeezed. Not only was food commandeered for the army but money was also extracted to help fill the government's war chest. Another way in which the rear supported the war effort was by the collection of items for the men at the front, the donation and reception of which served further to consolidate front and rear throughout the hard war years, as the republics of Central Asia played their part in ensuring the economic survival of the Soviet Union.

The state was well aware of the serious need for supplementary funds and material goods to help equip an army lacking in most areas – provisions, uniforms and military hardware. Calling upon those in the rear across all the unoccupied territories of the Soviet Union to fill these gaps, it united all Soviet citizens, while including all the Central Asian republics in a common cause against the fascist enemy. Wartime propaganda managed to portray the vast state as one huge family threatened by the invaders, as the much-vaunted ideology of the 'brotherhood of peoples' enabled a link between the farmers of Central Asia and the mainly Russian factory workers of the Urals, all battling to keep the troops fighting fit.

A so-called Defence Fund (*Fond oborony*) was established at the onset of war in all the Soviet republics, with the aim of collecting and distributing contributions from regions in the rear to the front and later also to the occupied and economically devastated western territories upon their liberation. The state issued *obligatsii* (war bonds) in exchange for monetary donations, while people were encouraged to gift gold and silver items, food and clothing to soldiers and their hard-pressed families.

The idea that the impoverished peasants of Central Asia would give voluntarily to the Defence Fund is highly improbable, until it is remembered that they were fighting not only for their country but also for the lives of their husbands, fathers and sons on active service. The state's call to patriotic citizens convinced many to support the effort, at least in the early days, until the 'voluntary' donations had sometimes to be extracted by force to meet the Communist Party's demand for a certain sum. Euphemistically branded as 'gifts' and usually wrapped up in parcels as 'presents', these extra requisitions overstretched an already struggling population. In its propaganda spin, the state introduced a degree of competition between towns and villages as they were forced to stump up aid – at first more or less willingly, but then with more and more difficulty as the war progressed, causing an increasing degree of unrest in some areas.[89]

In order to render giving psychologically more palatable, a human face was introduced as Asian donors and Russian recipients were artificially linked by the press as Soviet 'brothers'. Not only did propagandists create an invisible emotional bond between front and rear in the battle for victory, but also between areas and cities. Kyrgyzstan, for example, was 'twinned' with the city of Leningrad even before the war, as Leningrad adopted the role of patron to the young republic, helping to develop its industrialization by dispatching machines and tools made in the city's factories. Many of the new Kyrgyz intelligentsia were educated in Leningrad's universities and institutes of technology, so that it is not surprising that the citizens of Kyrgyzstan were asked to reciprocate by supplying extra food to the city once Leningrad found itself under siege.[90] This link was further strengthened as Leningrad children were evacuated eastwards to Central Asia at the same time as goods were transported westwards to the occupied area on special train convoys.[91]

Kazakhstan, for its part, 'sponsored' the civilians of the liberated areas of Kursk, Orlov, the Donbass, Krasnodar and Stavropol' by the provision of tractors and combine harvesters to assist the regeneration of agriculture, while the whole of Central Asia was urged to provide material support for the troops at Stalingrad during the winter of 1942–3. This practical exercise in the friendship of the peoples did much to level out the former inherent primacy of the European regions of the Soviet Union, as the citizens of Central Asia came to the rescue of the western Slavs of Russia, Belarus and Ukraine.[92] Thus Dogdurbai Kachikeev, a Kyrgyz shepherd from Przheval'sk, was able to boast later that, although the Second World War 'did not touch Central Asia directly [. . .] we helped the war effort by making socks and coats and by harvesting wheat and sending it to the front'. He accepted that 'this resulted in a scarcity of clothing and food here in Central Asia', but was nonetheless proud of his countrymen's generosity.[93]

The local Issyk-Kul' press went to great lengths to report this type of patriotism, with frequent exemplar reports of altruistic activity in the province. The establishment of the Defence Fund was advertised in September 1941:

At this desperate time of mortal danger threatening our country, a mighty patriotic movement involving millions of people has been born.

FIGURE 4.4 *Knitting and sewing for the front. Reproduced with permission from the Issyk-Kul' State Archives.*

FIGURE 4.5 *Warm clothes collected for the Red Army, 1942. Reproduced with permission from the Issyk-Kul' State Archives.*

FIGURE 4.6 *Parcels for the front. Reproduced with permission from the Issyk-Kul' State Archives.*

The paper suggested that 'the people' had given two or three days' pay plus warm clothing and items made of precious metals, a prompt intended to inspire others to contribute. As it became apparent that Red Army troops would be unprepared for the coming winter, the women of Przheval'sk town led the way, sending off eight parcels of knitted woollen underwear and socks.[94]

Collections of warm clothes and bedding started in the autumn of 1941, as winter approached on the Western Front. Przheval'sk's residents contributed again, sending over 300 individual parcels, each containing a personal letter, in time for New Year 1942.[95] Individuals and groups pitched in as the momentum gathered, providing shirts and blankets, while some offered to teach others sewing skills. Older women apparently needed no further encouragement. One reporter caught a certain Agrafena sitting on her porch in the Tiup district, leading a group of younger women knitting socks and gloves. Elsewhere, in Pokrovka village, women's 'caring fingers' prepared more parcels containing the usual range of woollen items. Even relatively young girls across Central Asia were made to knit simple garments, while the parcels prepared by older women seemed to contain finer items: pillows, pillowcases and blankets. Some women provided the material themselves, while others received supplies of wool from female members of the NKVD and militia, who had 'collected' it from others. One

FIGURE 4.7 *Gifts from Central Asia for the Panfilov Division, 1941. Reproduced with permission from the Issyk-Kul' State Archives.*

can only imagine the pressure applied on farmers to part with this valuable and saleable commodity.[96]

Individual farms at first added to the gifts, including, for example, lamb's meat, salt, medicinal herbs or apples. Parcels sometimes contained soap and toothpaste for the men's personal hygiene, which were becoming very hard to source during the war, plus 'high-quality cigarettes' for the soldiers' downtime. As the war dragged on, this latter item was replaced by *makhorka*, the coarse Soviet tobacco which the men used to roll their own cigarettes.[97]

As the provision of parcels for the troops became embedded in the war culture of Central Asia, the Communist Party started to organize shipments on a large scale. Przheval'sk town singled out the Stalin factory in Leningrad for support, receiving in return a telegram of thanks for their parcels. A few months later, it was the wounded soldiers of the Battle of Stalingrad who benefited, as students of the Kyrgyz agricultural college sent footwear and warm clothes for the hospitalized men. At the same time, the successful push to liberate occupied Ukraine revealed the need for aid there. Substantial quantities of medical equipment were transported westwards, where they were used to refurbish hospitals and first-aid points. A group of highly qualified nurses, armed with medical literature and laboratory equipment, followed close behind.[98]

It is understandable that this type of action provided a huge amount of propaganda material. A train comprising seventeen goods wagons left Frunze in October 1943, in the charge of Communist Party Secretary Comrade Suerkulov. Taking a cargo of grain, meat and oil from 'the workers of Kyrgyzstan' to Ukraine, it also contained pastries and even gifts of wine for the coalminers in the newly liberated Donbass basin. When the delegation arrived four weeks later in Stalino (Donetsk), they met with local Stakhanovites in the mines and on collective farms.[99]

The first train from Kyrgyzstan to Leningrad was dispatched as early as February 1942 when the city was at its lowest point. The fifty vital freight wagons were loaded with flour, meat, rice and fruit to help the starving, besieged citizens through the harsh winter. A further convoy under the leadership of Comrade Tokobaev, the chair of the Presidium of the Upper Chamber of the Kyrgyz Republic, left Frunze in October 1943, addressed to 'the defenders of Leningrad'. In addition to the thousands of parcels, they contained gifts from the Narimanov collective farm in Osh intended for the factory with which it was twinned. When this delegation eventually arrived in the north, its members visited factories, industrial plants, warships and schools. They even met Kyrgyz soldiers on the front line, who, they reported back, were apparently well clothed, amply fed and armed. The war reporter obviously milked this opportunity for the people at home, with the rather contrived observation that the troops 'gave an artillery salute to nearby Germans' in honour of the delegation's visit. The more peaceful conclusion to this visit was a concert featuring songs by the Kyrgyz bard Toktogul.[100]

Parcels sent regularly to the army, often to the Central Asian 8th Guards (Panfilov) Division, were gratefully acknowledged in letters of thanks from the men or their commanders. The donation of food and clothing also enabled established local Communist Party branches to support the families of soldiers and evacuees, contributing to the war economy alongside more traditional methods.[101]

The helping hands of young people, often Komsomol members, were set to collecting scrap metal, as in Great Britain and the United States, if on a lesser scale due to the relative poverty of the population of Central Asia. Official letters sent to the head teacher of every school in the Issyk-Kul' province reminded them of the hundreds of tonnes of metal demanded by the state from this province alone. Pupils were sent to every household to collect anything that was not for immediate use – items which were then delivered to metal factories to be melted down and reconstituted as ships or tanks. In the Issyk-Kul' province, children and teachers took part in 'Operation *Kolosok* (Wheel)' to collect as many old metal wheels as possible from the farming community. Despite the urgency of the initial request, further official demands chased the original notice until every kilogram of scrap metal had been extracted from local households.[102]

This type of material aid, provided in a timely fashion from all the unoccupied regions of the Soviet Union, substantially improved the lot of those in the west, reinforcing the notion of the Soviet Union as a brotherhood of peoples. It also relieved the government of much of the responsibility for the proper care of the Red Army, soldiers' families and evacuees, releasing its precious funds for armaments, tanks, aircraft and warships. The collection of money for the Defence Fund proceeded in an equally organized fashion. Just as Britain's campaign to build a Spitfire from public donations took off, schools in Kyrgyzstan were encouraged to crowdfund the construction of an aircraft named 'Red Army Teacher'. The Kazakh Republic named its tank columns after its official sponsors, for example, 'Shakhter Karagandy' (Karaganda miner) or 'Kolkhoznik Kazakhstana' (Kazakhstan collective farmer), while a Kyrgyz-sponsored tank was unsurprisingly named 'General Panfilov'.[103]

Not only was a spirit of competitiveness engendered in donations from various areas, but the state also took pains to recognize the contributions to the Defence Fund by nationality, highlighting the overall role played by the Kyrgyz, Kazakh or Uzbek people as members of the Soviet brotherhood of peoples. Importantly, contributions, however small, to the Defence Fund nurtured a feeling of 'all in this together', as individuals in the rear were recognized for doing 'their bit' for the state in its hour of need.[104]

Infrastructure projects

There may have been a marked increase in industrial and agricultural output, but the infrastructure necessary for the state to capitalize on its increased productivity was totally inadequate. In a war where the timely delivery of food, clothing, munitions, tractors, horses and key raw materials was all important, it was vital to be able to rely on the efficient transport of goods westwards to the centre and onwards to the front. Supply lines from the east to the west of the Soviet Union were relatively poor in comparison with those lost to the enemy in Ukraine and Belarus. Deficiencies were particularly noticeable in Central Asia, which was suddenly propelled to become one of the vital regions of the rear. Nor was its urban infrastructure able to cope with the influx of evacuees and refugees flooding eastwards in search of a safe haven. The state's commitment of significant financial resources was complemented by the conscription of the workforce necessary to complete the huge infrastructure projects identified by a country at war, which urgently needed to construct new mines, hydro-electric power stations, railways, roads and canals.

The influx of evacuees and refugees, added to the increase in industrial capacity built up in Central Asia, necessitated the expansion of major towns,

FIGURE 4.8 *Tanks produced in the name of Kyrgyz workers, 1942. Reproduced with permission from the Issyk-Kul' State Archives.*

as workers were redeployed from farms and villages to larger centres. The multiethnic cities of Tashkent, Samarkand, Frunze, Osh and Alma-Ata were particularly important in this respect, being already on Moscow's to-do list for urban development before the war, thanks to their narrow and often insanitary streets. The region's largest city and de facto capital, Tashkent, was approximately divided into two parts. The older, Muslim sector was inhabited by indigenous Uzbeks, Kyrgyz and Kazakhs, with its bazaars and flimsy, thatched homes often constructed of dried mud bricks. In contrast a newer, relatively modern 'European' sector, intended for government officials, managers and other professional staff, offered more spacious thoroughfares with more substantial buildings and community facilities.[105]

Much has been written about the development of Tashkent during the war years.[106] The Central Asian military headquarters were housed here, making it the largest transit hub in the whole of the region. With its warm climate and thriving agricultural environment, it was perceived by many evacuees and refugees as a metaphorical and geographical oasis in the desert, the garden of Central Asia and therefore the optimum destination east of Moscow. Tashkent had also benefited from some pre-war investment in its water supply due to its status as a colonial capital and its strategic importance in the growth and manufacture of cotton.[107]

However, as the city grew to bursting point, it became obvious that its infrastructure was inadequate for the necessary expansion, and many workers were forcibly expelled to the Uzbek interior, including Soviet ethnic Germans and the unemployed. By 1943 many residents were compelled to share their squalid accommodation, such that each one of the city's citizens enjoyed on average 2.6 square metres of living space as the Muslim sector became completely overcrowded – not only with humanity but also with the camel trains and donkeys providing its transport. On the other hand, the more Russianized, colonial sector benefited from further modernization, including trams for public transport, with the promise of public parks and larger factories once the shortage of construction materials could be overcome.[108]

The conversion of Tashkent into a modern, Soviet city was, however, put on the back burner as the war progressed. Plans for fresh water supplies and large hospitals were put aside, as disease spread in the polluted city, where people and animals often lived in the same accommodation. The city's infrastructure was completely overstretched as it became increasingly industrialized; however, it was only in 1944 that the authorities managed to make inroads into creating more streets, reservoirs and power stations. New construction within the city was still very much subjugated to the war effort and had to wait for peacetime until it could be seriously considered again.[109]

The city of Tashkent was divided into its two sectors by the Ankhor canal. In 1942 further canalization took place in order to irrigate land given over to the military to enable it to produce more food for its soldiers. As the population of Tashkent increased, so did the pollution of its waterways, with industrial and animal effluent coursing along its stinking canals at the height of summer, causing the proliferation of disease. Beyond the city boundary, the cotton fields of Tashkent and Osh demanded plentiful irrigation. Even in the modest Issyk-Kul' province, a good water supply was significant for the success of the harvest. A key irrigation channel, the Kundui, ran across the Karakol state collective farm. However, farmers had permitted their herds to cross the canal over the years, leading to the erosion of its banks and the loss of precious water into the surrounding fields. As a knock-on effect, the farms downstream in Cholpon-Ata experienced a serious water shortage, similar if less drastic than that of the fishermen of the Aral Sea who had lost their aqueous lifeblood to the Uzbek cotton fields. Accordingly, the Karakol farm was ordered in no uncertain terms to sort out the problem and repair the canal forthwith.[110]

Undoubtedly the most important waterway for irrigation in Kyrgyzstan was the Grand Chui Canal around Frunze on the republic's northern border with Kazakhstan. Started in 1940, work was accelerated at the start of war, using the manual labour of navvies to complete the project. With the canal in place, it was then possible to build more sugar factories in the Tokmak area with a huge increase in sugar production. The construction by 1943 of the Lebedinov hydro-electric power station on the canal represented a further important boost to the development of wartime industry in northern Kyrgyzstan.[111]

It had become very clear at the onset of hostilities that a much greater supply of electricity was necessary for the increased industrial output needed to sustain the war. The mountainous geography of Central Asia – and Kyrgyzstan in particular – rendered it especially suitable for the construction of hydro-electric power stations. Electricity generated in Central Asia not only powered local factories, but also assisted with the supply consumed in the southern Urals and the Volga. The Karaganda power station contributed to the 70 per cent increase in electricity generated in Kazakhstan, while the Farkhad HEP station in Uzbekistan helped that republic to increase its output by 350 per cent during the war. Seven new power plants were constructed in Uzbekistan, with five in Kyrgyzstan, and six in Alma-Ata in Kazakhstan. Most of the power generated was prioritized for industrial plants rather than civilian residential accommodation.[112]

As with the canalization of rivers and building of new roads, the construction of power stations also involved a huge labour force. Engineers estimated, for example, that a total of 80,000 man-days would be needed for the construction of the new plant on the River Karakolka above Przheval'sk, intended to supply all the electrical power needed by local industry, community services, housing and streets in the provincial capital for years to come. Water flowing down from the mountains was diverted into a canal and then a reservoir, with the turbines located at the bottom of a 400-metre-high waterfall. However, construction was compromised by the lack of available concrete and steel, leaving only home-grown lumber as a construction material. As the demands of industry became critical, Communist Party officials blamed the overseers for a lack of proper planning. Managers who had 'badly underestimated requirements' were chastised as precious time was wasted in the construction of the new plant. As deadline after deadline was missed, students from the evacuated shipbuilding institute were enlisted in the task, along with their lecturers, in order to speed up the final delivery.[113]

In the early years of the war, a Catch-22 situation developed as it became necessary to increase the pace of infrastructure construction. Even if manual labour was employed, robust infrastructure was first needed in order to move the construction materials to the project site in a timely manner. The primitive roads from the forests of Siberia into Central Asia were improved with some urgency, as more and more heavy lorries transported wood to the south. A mountain road between Barskaun and the Bedel' Pass was built to enable the transport of heavy military equipment to defend the border between Kyrgyzstan and China, using a local workforce drawn from nearby collective farms to supplement an army sapper division. However, road repair in general was delayed by the lack of men and materials. During this period there were few cars in use and buses for civilian purposes were also rare. The supply of drivers was the limiting factor, as most were diverted to the army. The total number of buses in Kyrgyzstan decreased from just over ninety in 1941 to a minimal provision of thirty-nine in 1945, with only five remaining in service in Frunze itself.[114] The use of trams and trolleybuses was compromised by the constant attention necessary for the elderly vehicles. In Alma-Ata the repair yard previously used for their maintenance was given over to new factories, so that, by the end of the war, less than half of the original coaches were in working order, rendering travel around the city a more complex and much slower process.[115]

For the most part, however, the railroad was the chosen means of transport, constantly moving troops and freight across the Soviet Union. Soldiers, armaments, clothes and food were rapidly moved from eastern parts of Kyrgyzstan towards Frunze, Tashkent and further west, taking precedence over the movement of construction materials into Central Asia. The main line between Groznyi in Chechnia and Baku in Azerbaijan was in danger of enemy bombing in the summer of 1942, so oil vital for fuelling the front line had to be transported by a more circuitous route: by sea from Baku to Krasnovodsk (Turkmenbashi) in Turkmenistan, and thence to Ashkhabad and Tashkent, whence it was directed onwards to Ural'sk in Kazakhstan and eventually to Stalingrad, where it was urgently needed. The Caspian Sea route became increasingly important as the oil refinery at Gur'ev was considerably expanded. Important main lines were also constructed in Kazakhstan to enable the efficient transport of coal and oil across the republic. It was only in October 1943, however, that work started on the railway line from Kant to Rybach'e on the western end of Lake Issyk-Kul', in order to link this industrial centre with the source of raw materials in the Issyk-Kul' province and the high Tian' Shan' mountains.[116]

With improved infrastructure, more robust telephone links became available for the military. Telegraphic communication remained more important, however, with provision in Kyrgyzstan for around 20 million words per year, at a rate of about thirty-five to forty words per minute. For the ordinary citizen, though, letter and parcel post remained a lifeline between the men at the front and those left at home.[117]

For the first year of the war, four steamers belonging to the Issyk-Kul' Steamer Company plied the lake from Pristan' to Rybach'e carrying food, animals and lumber. With identities as original as those of many collective farms, they were named *Issyk-Kul'*, *Sovetskaia Kirgiziia* (Soviet Kyrgyzstan), *Piatiletka* (Five Year Plan) and *Komsomol*. The steamer *General Panfilov* joined the fleet mainly as a troop transporter, named in tribute to the famous hero. Five barges equally capable of carrying heavy loads also transported construction materials and troops. Working under the jurisdiction of the Soviet River Fleet, they achieved a modest increase in the tonnage of goods transported by 1944, while the number of foot passengers increased dramatically as successive tranches of men were conscripted. The work of these ships and their crews was lauded in a newspaper article as they struggled at the height of winter. Captain Comrade Rabochikh of the steamer *Piatiletka* is described in military fashion as if standing at the helm of a warship, while Captain Denis Advolodkin of the *Sovetskaia Kirgiziia* was commended for joining the Communist Party.[118]

Both *Sovetskaia Kirgiziia* and *General Panfilov* were singled out for praise when they won monetary prizes for their performance at the end of 1944. This was the exception rather than the rule, however, as local archives reflect the degree of official dissatisfaction with many of the crews. The captain of the *General Panfilov* had incurred a fine earlier in 1944, while the manager of the Steamer Company itself, a certain Comrade Goroshevskii, was reprimanded for allowing the chimney of his flat to catch fire in the middle of the night in December 1944. This was no doubt because he had left his fire burning overnight in the harsh winter weather, but the only defence he could muster was to blame the poor quality of chimney bricks and a blockage caused by poor maintenance.[119] Worse problems were caused by collisions on the lake, often in winter, causing potential danger to the precious loads.[120]

It had become eminently clear by the beginning of 1943 that the country's infrastructure was to be one of the deciding factors in an eventual victory, as the supply chain between the food-producing and industrial centres of the rear became better connected with the army fighting at the front. On 15 April 1943 new legislation involving the introduction of military discipline on the railway came into force, as workers were placed under martial law. By May, all shipping transport on lakes, rivers and the open sea was included under the same emergency legislation, including employees of the Issyk-Kul' Shipping Company.[121]

Life was not all plain sailing, however, with several cases of desertion of duty taking place as the new military conditions struck home. Treated as severely as industrial workers leaving their employment, ships' crews could not afford to shirk their duty under the threat of a lengthy term in a prison camp for just one day's absence without leave. Many of these workers were women, performing some of the shipping jobs previously undertaken by men. A certain Ekaterina Ignat'eva, for example, was conscripted to the steamer company at the age of nineteen, just a month before the militarization of her employment came into force. Three months later she left her post on the *Sovetskaia Kirgiziia*, jumping ship while on a few hours' shore leave in Przheval'sk. Just over six months later the reason for her absconding became evident, as she was discovered, still in Przheval'sk, and married to an injured war veteran named Chuiko. By then Ekaterina was six months pregnant. Treated as a deserter when arrested, she was sentenced – despite her pregnancy and the medical needs of her husband – to eight years in a labour camp, a much worse fate than working on the lake in the summer months.[122]

Another woman was sentenced for negligence of duty thanks to a man's laziness. A valuable male member of crew named Plastinin was arrested for desertion by the river police and sent before a military judge, Comrade Plekhanov. As he was only missing from duty for a few days in comparison with Ignat'eva, he was sentenced to the lesser term of eighty-five days in prison. However, his superior officer, Lieutenant Chernikova, was accused of not having supervised him closely enough, nor even having questioned his prison sentence, which meant that he was unavailable for useful work for even longer. For this offence, she herself was sentenced to three days in prison, while, in a growing comedy of errors, the judge himself was severely censured by the local Communist Party for his original judgement in removing an able-bodied man from the workforce.[123]

Despite the inefficiencies in the implementation of ambitious new projects, Central Asia benefited from much improved infrastructure by the end of the war, with new canals, dams and HEP stations boosting the economy and overall modernity of the region. By the 1950s new construction was once again evident in the region. Postponed development projects were realized in the main regional centres, including – in order of state priority – new factories, homes, urban transport networks, parks and swimming pools, as city life gradually improved in the post-war years.[124]

Forced labour in the rear

The conflicting needs for manpower of the army, industry, construction projects and other essential services were very much in evidence in the rear.

Indeed, a tug-of-war situation sometimes developed, as the military vied with industrial and transport managers for the relatively able-bodied. For a state trying to manage a full-scale war with all its challenges, while also attempting to maintain industrial output and supply lines, the question of sufficient cheap labour was very much at the forefront of decision making. One solution lay in the huge numbers of prisoners already serving their terms in the east of the country, alongside the deployment of some dubious conscripts, citizens deemed unfit for military service and enemy POWs.

Existing prisoners languishing in the camps of the GULag were amongst the first to be targeted as the state considered its options for non-military labour. Several of the so-called *zeks* were victims of the political purges of the late 1930s, while many others had been imprisoned for relatively minor infringements. The latter were often redeployed to army penal battalions, as were some former army officers, where they were offered the chance of rehabilitation if they distinguished themselves – always assuming that they survived the dangerous missions they were ordered to undertake. It is likely that some prisoners even volunteered for frontline action, seeking not only eventual rehabilitation but also better food rations in the interim. Other prisoners, often victims of Stalin's purges, were sent to labour camps alongside industrial plants or to infrastructure projects, where they worked in mines, road building and railway construction. Those remaining in prison suffered increasingly from malnutrition and even starvation as they sank to the bottom of the priority list for rations while being expected to work even harder as the prison population gradually dwindled.[125]

From the very start of the war, the Soviet Union took pains to identify existing prisoners of foreign origin and to impose an even harsher regime by removing their privileges, especially those concerning the right to correspondence and access to newspapers. A rapid campaign also victimized and imprisoned various suspect categories of citizen, for example, people who had travelled abroad before the war. Some ethnic minorities were also targeted, despite the fact that their families may have lived peacefully in the country for generations. Ethnic Germans living in the Volga area, for example, suddenly became *persona non grata* as the Soviet Union declared war on Germany. Some had even been in the Red Army before war was declared, but in 1941 all were treated as enemies of the state, basically POWs.[126]

Most Volga Germans with other potentially suspicious ethnic minorities were assigned to industrial plants and infrastructure projects. Germans, Romanians, Hungarians, Finns, Italians and Koreans, to be joined by many other deportees in 1944, were compelled to perform exhausting manual work under extreme conditions. Guarded by the NKVD, they laboured in industry, coal mines, forests or farms, living in bare, unhygienic military-style barracks. Discipline in these prison-like internment conditions was harsh and often brutal, with barracks even infiltrated by NKVD informants to report potential plots. Mortality rates increased as epidemics of typhus and dysentery went largely uncontrolled. Few managed to escape a regime where deprivation and abuse were common and prisoners were fed only according to their daily output. As the working day was extended, the weakest struggled to cope on starvation rations, leaving only the strongest to survive. Only as the turning point of the war arrived with the victory at Stalingrad were food rations finally increased. Despite this slight amelioration, the death toll in the prison camps during the war was enormous: over 2 million men and women succumbed to the harsh conditions.[127]

Groups of ethnic Koreans were made to slave on the construction of the Kyrgyz Chui Canal, while in Uzbekistan the Sazlag camp, established in 1934 as part of the growing GULag system, was notorious for its brutality in forcing men to work. Many prisoners were sent to work in industry, except in more sensitive areas such as munitions manufacture. In Kazakhstan the major destination for ethnic minorities was the Karaganda coal basin which drove the economy. The enormous Karlag prison complex also housed women, often the families of political prisoners arrested during the purges. Within the ALZHIR camp – the Akmola camp for the wives of traitors of the Motherland – women were made, amongst other tasks, to sew uniforms for Red Army soldiers.[128]

A constant influx of enemy POWs were also incarcerated in Central Asia – a major dumping ground for these unfortunates, too – where they were mainly forced to work in mines or infrastructure developments. Their camps were not part of the notorious GULag system but still operated an exceedingly harsh regime, possibly in part to repay the Germans for the brutal treatment meted out to Soviet POWs in Germany and viewed by Stalin as a type of reparation. Over 3 million German and other Axis prisoners were joined by 600,000 Japanese POWs in 1945, all receiving a political re-education while in Soviet custody until their often delayed repatriation after the end of the war.[129]

Little concrete information about these men is available, as their imprisonment was subject to high security and top secret classification, but glimpses remain of their forced contribution to the Central Asian landscape. One centre about which some records are available was Prison Camp No. 29 in Kazakhstan, located in the southern cotton fields. Opened in March 1943 to house some of the 91,000 Germans taken at the Battle of Stalingrad, it received thousands of malnourished, diseased prisoners who arrived after a long, slow journey from western Russia. Plagued also by a typhus epidemic shortly after arrival, about one-fifth of the newcomers died. Those who lived suffered, like the civilian population, from a lack of protein, but the relatively liberal regime in the camp meant that a farm was established there, where fruit and vegetables for the prisoners could be grown. With the additional incentive of a small wage, they worked on the

Pakhta-Aral cotton farm and helped in the construction of a new irrigation canal. Over 10,000 prisoners occupied the camp between 1943 and its closure in 1948.[130]

Other POWs laboured under less fortunate conditions. In Tajikistan, Japanese and German prisoners were made to work on the Farkhad dam, while Japanese prisoners were deployed to construct the large Bekobod metallurgical complex in Uzbekistan. They also laboured on construction projects around Karaganda, infrastructure projects in the hills above Alma-Ata in Kazakhstan and built the road in Kyrgyzstan from Kant to Lake Issyk-Kul', partly crossing a low mountain range. Japanese POWs in captivity in Tashkent were set to work on the new Navoi opera house, which was opened in 1947. Few records remain of this achievement, to the extent that the history of its construction is mainly propagated as an urban myth. Similarly, it is believed that German prisoners were made to build the Frunze opera and ballet theatre and the railway station in the Kyrgyz capital. German POWs are also alleged to have helped in the construction of the railway from Frunze to Rybach'e and the Grand Chui Canal. In the Przheval'sk area, new roads emerged thanks to German POWs, while Japanese prisoners constructed a new hospital and factory in the town and others cleared forests on the shores of Lake Issyk-Kul'. It is even reported that 125 Japanese POWs built the Tamga military sanatorium on the south shore of Lake Issyk-Kul', where, years later in 1961, the astronaut Iurii Gagarin recuperated after his first flight into space.[131] Furthermore, 114 German POWs worked in uranium mines in southern Kyrgyzstan, forced to extract ore for the Soviet nuclear programme.[132]

The total number of POWs held in Central Asia is still unknown and the topic is rarely raised, even by local researchers, although one estimate indicates that 3,000 Japanese were retained in captivity in Kyrgyzstan until 1948.[133] It is also known that German and Austrian POWs were held towards the end of the war in the village of Kajy-Sai in the Issyk-Kul' province. A few, flimsy records remain of some of the fatalities in POW camps, although many men were buried in unmarked, communal graves. Again, only a little is to be found locally about the repatriation of prisoners after the end of hostilities, with sparse information about POWs available in the open Kyrgyz archives.[134]

Living memory helps fill in the gaps, however. It is recalled that German POWs arrived in 1947 to start a new life in a remote part of south-western Kyrgyzstan, still wearing their military uniforms. Despite a Soviet agreement with West Germany in the 1950s to allow prisoners home, many chose to marry local women and remain in Central Asia, although now it is almost impossible to establish when they first arrived. Other German-speaking people still live in the region: possibly Volga Germans who chose not to return home on the reunification of Germany and the collapse of the Soviet Union, or, less likely, men who had served in the German Turkestan Legion or alongside the German occupiers of Ukraine. It is even reported that one former Japanese POW returned to Przheval'sk (now named Karakol) in 2015. Aged over ninety, he undertook a memorial pilgrimage to the site of his slave labour during the period of his wartime captivity.[135]

Victory!

The depleted and exhausted population of Central Asia bent its ears to the radio with unqualified relief to hear Stalin announce the cessation of hostilities – except, that is, for some remote rural communities in southern Tajikistan with no access to radio or electricity, who remained in ignorance of the end of the war for weeks![136]

Between them, the women, children and elderly men of the region had held the home front together, while providing the army with huge amounts of food and material resources. Women had become experienced in managing both family life and collective farms, while many came to terms with the demands of industrial work as in other allied countries in the West. Women had also held significant roles within the Communist Party as they filled the positions left vacant by their menfolk on active service. In this respect, the citizens of Central Asia had much in common with their compatriots in the Urals, despite the initial cultural reticence of many more conservative Muslim women to work outside the protection of the home.

Victory Day was greeted as a day of unmitigated celebration, as the sunshine of 9 May was equated with the symbol of Kyrgyzstan, the Sunshine republic of the Soviet Union. Crowds united by the years spent toiling together with only one aim sang the Soviet national anthem, at one with the other Soviet republics and their victorious leader, Joseph Stalin. In Przheval'sk, war hero Nikolenko and Communist Party leader Vagov made speeches as the public shed tears of relief that their fathers, husbands and sons would soon be home.[137] Within a few short weeks, the railway station in Frunze was prepared for the return of the first of the soldiers, as its platforms and waiting rooms were decorated with flags, posters and placards. On 18 July the first of the Kyrgyz soldiers stepped off the train to the acclaim of the population.[138]

The happy period was short-lived, however, as the demobbed troops cast their eyes around at the changed town. In Tashkent, complaints were made about the state of the city, while in Przheval'sk it was quickly realized that the refurbishment of dilapidated apartments intended for the returnees and their families had not been carried out. Across the Soviet Union, soldiers were left in a vulnerable position as they attempted to settle back into civilian life, re-acquaint themselves with their families and find new jobs. It took time for new homes to be built, food production to be stepped up and diverted back to the region, clothing to be distributed and vegetable plots to be allocated.[139]

As the page turned into an often more privileged new life for many war veterans, others returned home with life-changing wounds, having to rely on the welfare state and their families as never before. The women of Central Asia, who had also made huge sacrifices during the war, faced a return to a more domestic role as primary carers, having in many cases to give up the jobs they had held down during the war years. As in many Western European countries taking part in the conflict, working relations between men and women could not easily, if ever, return to the status quo. In this way women had perforce become integrated into a more Soviet socialist way of life with substantially more independence than previously.

As the country faced the enormous transition from the demands of war to those of peacetime, the whole population of Central Asia took time to settle into its new role as a more equal part of a Soviet Union transformed by the joint experience of war. The region was fortunate that the war had brought none of the devastation wreaked on the western part of the country. Yes, its civilians had laboured and suffered, but some opportunities had also opened up to the citizens of Central Asia. The improvements to infrastructure and agricultural science alongside the scaling up of industrial processes forced through during the war had laid the foundations for the further economic development of Central Asia over the next thirty years.

Notes

1 See notably Barber and Harrison, *The Soviet Home Front*; and Mark Edele, *Stalinism at War: The Soviet Union in World War II* (London: Bloomsbury, 2021).

2 See Manley, *To the Tashkent Station*; and Stronski, *Tashkent*.

3 Stronski, *Tashkent*, 5, 7, 9 and 139.

4 Abylkhozhin, *Istoriia Kazakhstana*, 480.

5 Florin, *Kirgistan und die sowjetische Moderne*, 43.

6 Carmack, 'And They Fought for Their Socialist Motherland', 36; Kaptagaev, et al., *Sbornik*, 20; and Stronski, *Tashkent*, 79–80.

7 *IKP*, 3 August 1941, 4; *IKP*, 22 August 1941, 1; and 'Itogi uchebno-vozdushnoi trevogi v Przheval'ske', *IKP*, 17 September 1941, 2.

8 Ibid., 4; Kaptagaev, et al., *Sbornik*, 123–4; and Tranum, *Life at the Edge of the Empire*, 152.

9 IKSA:476/1/1/1–4; and Carmack, 'And They Fought for Their Socialist Motherland', 36.

10 Kaptagaev, et al., *Sbornik*, 20; and Stronski, *Tashkent*, 80.

11 Kesler, *Grit*, 975.

12 Abylkhozhin, *Istoriia Kazakhstana*, 480; and Stronski, *Tashkent*, 74–9.

13 Stronski, *Tashkent*, 31 and 73.

14 Barber and Harrison, *The Soviet Home Front*, 8 and 43.

15 'O rezhime rabochego vremeni rabochikh i sluzhashchikh v voennoe vremia', *IKP*, 29 July 1941, 2.

16 Barber and Harrison, *The Soviet Home Front*, 61; Hosking, *Russia and the Russians*, 497; and Kerimbaev, *Sovetskii Kirgizstan v Velikoi Otechestvennoi voine*, 92.

17 Carmack, *Kazakhstan in World War II*, 66; and Kerimbaev, *Sovetskii Kirgizstan v Velikoi Otechestvennoi voine*, 94. On racism in the Urals, see Wendy Goldman and Donald Filtzer, *Fortress Dark and Stern: The Soviet Home Front during World War II* (Oxford: Oxford University Press, 2021), 198, 204, 207–11 and 226.

18 Kerimbaev, *Sovetskii Kirgizstan v Velikoi Otechestvennoi voine*, 113.

19 Barber and Harrison, *The Soviet Home Front*, 76.

20 Ibid., 62, 63, 90–1 and 96; and Kerimbaev, *Sovetskii Kirgizstan v Velikoi Otechestvennoi voine*, 96–8.

21 *IKP*, 24 September 1941, 3; Barber and Harrison, *The Soviet Home Front*, 62, 75, 97 and 147; and Carmack, *Kazakhstan in World War II*, 75.

22 Hosking, *Russia and the Russians*, 497 and 499.

23 Barber and Harrison, *The Soviet Home Front*, 140.

24 Kerimbaev, *Sovetskii Kirgizstan v Velikoi Otechestvennoi voine*, 163.

25 Stronski, *Tashkent*, 57, 90, 94–5 and 136.

26 Kerimbaev, *Sovetskii Kirgizstan v Velikoi Otechestvennoi voine*, 100 and 130.

27 Abylkhozhin, *Istoriia Kazakhstana*, 512; Barber and Harrison, *The Soviet Home Front*, 166–7; Carmack, *Kazakhstan in World War II*, 70–1 and 79; M. K. Kozybaev, et al., *Istoriia Kazakhstana (s nachala XX v. po nastoiashchee vremia)* (Almaty: Mektep, 2013), 123; and O. Dzh. Osmonov, *Istoriia Kyrgyzstana: Osnovnye vekhi* (Bishkek: Insanat, 2012), 144.

28 IKSA:174/2/48/16; Barber and Harrison, *The Soviet Home Front*, 164–5; and Stronski, *Tashkent*, 131.

29 Abylkhozhin, *Istoriia Kazakhstana*, 513–14; 'Istoriia', *Ministerstvo inostrannykh del Respubliki Uzbekistan*, https://mfa.uz/ru/uzbekistan/98/ (accessed 15 March 2020); Kerimbaev, *Sovetskii Kirgizstan v Velikoi Otechestvennoi voine*, 100 and 131; and Kozybaev, *Istoriia Kazakhstana*, 123.

30 Kaptagaev, et al., *Sbornik*, 10.

31 Abylkhozhin, *Istoriia Kazakhstana*, 513; Barber and Harrison, *The Soviet Home Front*, 133; Kaptagaev, et al., *Sbornik*, 9; Kerimbaev, *Sovetskii Kirgizstan v Velikoi Otechestvennoi voine*, 120; and Kozybaev, *Istoriia Kazakhstana*, 123.

32 The output of silk fabric was increased from 44,000 metres in 1941 to 142,000 metres in 1945; see Kerimbaev, *Sovetskii Kirgizstan v Velikoi Otechestvennoi voine*, 120 and 133. See also Barber and Harrison, *The Soviet Home Front*, 134–5; and M. K. Imankulov, *Istoriia Kyrgyzstana: XX–XXI vek* (Bishkek: Ministerstvo obrazovanniia i nauki, 2017), 115–16.

33 Kaptagaev, et al., *Sbornik*, 9; and Kerimbaev, *Sovetskii Kirgizstan v Velikoi Otechestvennoi voine*, 96.

34 'Cholpon-Atinskii konezavod', *IKP*, 27 March 1942, 2.

35 Kerimbaev, *Sovetskii Kirgizstan v Velikoi Otechestvennoi voine*, 96.

36 Ibid., 130; and Stronski, *Tashkent*, 120.

37 Abylkhozhin, *Istoriia Kazakhstana*, 513–14; 'Istoriia', *Ministerstvo inostrannykh del Respubliki Uzbekistan*; and IKSA:146/2/5/6.

38 Imankulov, *Istoriia Kyrgyzstana*, 115.

39 Kaptagaev, et al., *Sbornik*, 7; Mira Peck, *What My Parents Told Me about Siberia, Kirgizia and the Holocaust* (Poland: CreateSpace, 2017), 37; and Stronski, *Tashkent*, 82.

40 Stronski, *Tashkent*, 75.

41 Imankulov, *Istoriia Kyrgyzstana*, 115; Kerimbaev, *Sovetskii Kirgizstan v Velikoi Otechestvennoi voine*, 95; and Stronski, *Tashkent*, 81–2.

42 Imankulov, *Istoriia Kyrgyzstana*, 115; Kerimbaev, *Sovetskii Kirgizstan v Velikoi Otechestvennoi voine*, 194–5; and Stronski, *Tashkent*, 81.

43 Stronski, *Tashkent*, 75 and 81–3.

44 'Ko vsem zhenshchinam nashei oblasti', *IKP*, 19 September 1941, 3; and 'Geroicheskie budni', *IKP*, 5 October 1941, 3.

45 Tranum, *Life at the Edge of the Empire*, 127.

46 'Dat' strane i frontu bol'she miasa, masla, shersti – boevaia zadacha sovetskikh patriotov', *IKP*, 27 March 1942, 3; and Osmonov, *Istoriia Kyrgyzstana*, 144.

47 Imankulov, *Istoriia Kyrgyzstana*, 116.

48 Abylkhozhin, *Istoriia Kazakhstana*, 517; Barber and Harrison, *The Soviet Home Front*, 169; Imankulov, *Istoriia Kyrgyzstana*, 116; Flora Roberts, 'A Time for Feasting? Autarky in the Tajik Ferghana Valley at War, 1941–45', *Central Asian Survey* 36, no. 1 (2017): 37–54, 4; and Tranum, *Life at the Edge of the Empire*, 118.

49 Imankulov, *Istoriia Kyrgyzstana*, 118; and Kerimbaev, *Sovetskii Kirgizstan v Velikoi Otechestvennoi voine*, 102.

50 Barber and Harrison, *The Soviet Home Front*, 168–9; and Imankulov, *Istoriia Kyrgyzstana*, 117.

51 Isaak Grinberg, *Evrei v Alma-Ate: kratkii istoricheskii ocherk* (Almaty: Iskander, 2005), 85; and Imankulov, *Istoriia Kyrgyzstana*, 118.

52 Hosking, *Russia and the Russians*, 467.

53 Imankulov, *Istoriia Kyrgyzstana*, 118–19.

54 'Gotovit'sia k sezonu maslodeliia', *IKP*, 7 April 1944, 2.

55 Kerimbaev, *Sovetskii Kirgizstan v Velikoi Otechestvennoi voine*, 153; and Osmonov, *Istoriia Kyrgyzstana*, 146.

56 'Stakhanovskii trud – reshaiushchee uslovie pobedy nad vragom', *IKP*, 29 June 1941, 1.

57 Barber and Harrison, *The Soviet Home Front*, 62; and Kerimbaev, *Sovetskii Kirgizstan v Velikoi Otechestvennoi voine*, 194.

58 'Boevye zadachi sovetskoi shkoly', *IKP*, 31 August 1941, 4.

59 Imankulov, *Istoriia Kyrgyzstana*, 116–17.

60 'Bystro ubiraiut urozhai', *IKP*, 15 August 1941, 2; and Imankulov, *Istoriia Kyrgyzstana*, 116–17.

61 'Osennie raboty provesti v szhatye sroki', *IKP*, 31 August 1941; 'Zhena frontovika', *IKP*, 20 August 1942, 2; Imankulov, *Istoriia Kyrgyzstana*, 115; and Kerimbaev, *Sovetskii Kirgizstan v Velikoi Otechestvennoi voine*, 114.

62 'Glubinnyi lov osmana', *IKP*, 8 March 1943, 2; and Kerimbaev, *Sovetskii Kirgizstan v Velikoi Otechestvennoi voine*, 116–17.

63 Kerimbaev, *Sovetskii Kirgizstan v Velikoi Otechestvennoi voine*, 103; and Tranum, *Life at the Edge of the Empire*, 69.

64 Kaptagaev, et al., *Sbornik*, 147–8; Kesler, *Grit*, 944 and 956; and Kozybaev, *Istoriia Kazakhstana*, 123.

65 'Skot peregoniaiut na jailoo', *IKP*, 8 July 1943, 2; A. S. Belik, 'Na jailoo', *IKP*, 5 August 1943, 2; 'V gorakh Tian'-Shania', *IKP*, 8 August 1943, 2; 'O razmeshchenii skota na zimnikh pastbishchakh', *IKP*, 19 September 1943, 2; and 'Zima i zhivotnovodstvo', *IKP*, 30 September 1943, 1.

66 'Agitatsiia v Issyk-Kul'skom raione', *IKP*, 3 September 1941, 3.

67 'Uroki pervykh dnei seva', *IKP*, 8 April 1942, 1.

68 'Agitator dolzhen uchit' liudei kak zashchishchat' nashu rodinu', *IKP*, 7 September 1941, 3.

69 'Na 200–300 protsentov', *IKP*, 20 August 1941, 3.

70 'Vse dlia pobedy nad fashizmom', *IKP*, 7 September 1941, 1.

71 'Prizyv tovarishcha Stalina k kolkhoznoi derevne', *IKP*, 12 November 1941, 1.

72 'Przheval'skii raion v dni voiny', *IKP*, 12 November 1941, 3.

73 'Uroki pervykh dnei seva', *IKP*, 8 April 1942, 1; 'Bor'ba s poteriami – bor'by za pobedu!', *IKP*, 20 August 1942, 1; 'Materi-rodine!', *IKP*, 7 November 1942, 1; 'Peredovye zhenshchiny Tiupskogo raiona', *IKP*, 9 May 1944, 2; and Osmonov, *Istoriia Kyrgyzstana*, 145.

74 'Frontovoi zakaz kommunistam sela', *IKP*, 19 August 1943, 1.

75 Information from the Director of the Issyk-Kul'l State Archives, 11 March 2021.

76 'Chem my pomagli frontu', *IKP*, 15 October, 1941; 'O trekh devushkakh i rukovoditeliakh odnoi MTS', *IKP*, 22 April 1942, 3; 'Zhenshchiny jety-oguzkogo raiona', *IKP*, 8 March 1943, 1; 'Zakonchili vtoruiu propolku maka', *IKP*, 5 June 1944, 1; and O. Kulachenko, 'Zakonchili vtoruiu propolku maka', *IKP*, 10 June 1944, 2.

77 'Sel'skaia intelligentsiia', *IKP*, 12 December 1943, 1.

78 'Doska pocheta', *IKP*, 13 August 1942 and 16 August 1942, 1; and *IKP*, 7 October, 1943, 1.

79 'Zheleznaia distsiplina – zakon voennogo vremeni', *IKP*, 8 August 1943, 1; 'Plokho rabotaiut v kolkhozakh Kuturgi', *IKP*, 3 October 1943, 1; *IKP*, 12 October 1944, 1; and S. Karimov, 'K sebu lekarstvennogo maka – podgotovit'sia', *IKP*, 11 August 1945, 2.

80 'Pod"em kul'tury kartofelia', *IKP*, 14 April 1944, 2; and Kerimbaev, *Sovetskii Kirgizstan v Velikoi Otechestvennoi voine*, 146.

81 Kesler, *Shards of War*, 1204 and 1240.

82 IKSA:331 and IKSA:297/1/145/184; *IKP*, issues of 27 March 1942 and 5 April 1942; and Kerimbaev, *Sovetskii Kirgizstan v Velikoi Otechestvennoi voine*, 164.

83 *IKP* issues of 19 July 1942 and 28 July 1943; 'Forel' v Issyk-Kule', *IKP*, 17 January 1943, 2; 'Po uborke i zagotovkam kartofelia i ovoshchei', *IKP*, 28 July 1943, 3; and *IKP*, 21 December 1944, 2.

84 Vsesoiuznyi institut lekarstvennykh i aromaticheskikh rastenii. See also Ekaterina Korinenko, 'Istoriia pokrytaia makom', *Izvestiia*, 30 October 2018.

85 'Arbuzy v nashei oblasti', *IKP*, 14 February 1943, 2; 'Pomodory v Issyk-Kul'skoi oblasti', *IKP*, 11 March 1943, 2; and Kerimbaev, *Sovetskii Kirgizstan v Velikoi Otechestvennoi voine*, 108.

86 One centner was equal to 100 kilograms. See also '45 tysiach tsentnerov sakhara', *IKP*, 5 November 1943, 2; Imankulov, *Istoriia Kyrgyzstana*, 116 and 119; and Kerimbaev, *Sovetskii Kirgizstan v Velikoi Otechestvennoi voine*, 146 and 147.

87 Florin, *Kirgistan und die sowjetische Moderne*, 44.

88 Leonid Brezhnev, *The Virgin Lands* (Moscow: Politizdat, 1978).

89 Carmack, *Kazakhstan in World War II*, 73.

90 Kaptagaev, et al., *Sbornik*, 9.

91 See Chapter 7.

92 Abylkhozhin, *Istoriia Kazakhstana*, 519; Carmack, *Kazakhstan in World War II*, 104–6; and Imankulov, *Istoriia Kyrgyzstana*, 120 and 125.

93 Tranum, *Life at the Edge of the Empire*, 146; and Kaptagaev, et al., *Sbornik*, 9.

94 A. Alekseeva, 'Zhenshchiny goroda pomogaiut frontu', *IKP*, 28 September 1941, 4; and A. Alekseeva, 'Zhenshchiny-frontu', *IKP*, 5 October 1941, 3.

95 Kaptagaev, et al., *Sbornik*, 8.

96 'Posylki boitsam Krasnoi Armii', *IKP*, 5 September 1941, 4; 'Podarki boitsam', *IKP*, 10 September 1941, 1; 'Liubov' k rodine bezgranichna', *IKP*, 24 September 1941, 1; and Alekseeva, 'Zhenshchiny-frontu'.

97 'Posylki boitsam Krasnoi Armii'; 'V fond oborony', *IKP*, 14 September 1941, 3; and 'Podarki tyla idut na front', *IKP*, 7 October 1943, 2.

98 'Ot Nevy do Jergalana', *IKP*, 5 July 1942, 2; 'Ranenym boitsam i komendiram', *IKP*, 11 February 1943, 1; and 'Meditsinskaia pomoshch' osvoboditennym raionam', *IKP*, 23 February 1943, 1.

99 'Podarki trudiashchikhsia Kirgizii', *IKP*, 1 November 1943, 2; 'Delegatsiia Kirgizii v Leningrade i Donbasse', *IKP*, 28 November 1943, 2; and Abylkhozhin, *Istoriia Kazakhstana*, 518.

100 'Podarki trudiashchikhsia Kirgizii', *IKP*, 1 November 1943, 2; 'Delegatsiia Kirgizii v Leningrade i Donbasse', *IKP*, 28 November 1943, 2; and 'Deleglatisiia Kirgizii v Moskve', *IKP*, 16 December 1943, 2. See also Kaptagaev, et al., *Sbornik*, 9; and Osmonov, *Istoriia Kyrgyzstana*, 149.

101 Kaptagaev, et al., *Sbornik*, 128 and 132; and Osmonov, *Istoriia Kyrgyzstana*, 148.

102 IKSA:279/1/145/263 and IKSA:119/1/66/17.

103 Information in the Panfilov museum, Almaty. See also V. Meshcheriakov, 'Postroim eskadril'iu "Solnechnyi Kirgizstan"', *IKP*, 4 January 1942, 1; Abylkhozhin, *Istoriia Kazakhstana*, 517–18; Florin, *Kirgistan und die sowjetische Moderne*, 53; and Kaptagaev, et al., *Sbornik*, 8–9 and 130.

104 Florin, 'Becoming Soviet through War', 502.

105 Kesler, *Grit*, 541; and Stronski, *Tashkent*, Chapter 2.

106 See especially Stronski, *Tashkent*; and Manley, *To the Tashkent Station*.

107 Stronski, *Tashkent*, 1–2.

108 Manley, *To the Tashkent Station*, 172–3; and Stronski, *Tashkent*, 42, 48 and 61.

109 Manley, *To the Tashkent Station*, 173; and Stronski, *Tashkent*, 62 and 89.

110 'Vosstanovit' kanal Kundui', *IKP*, 17 March 1944, 1; and Stronski, *Tashkent*, 70 and 130.

111 Osmonov, *Istoriia Kyrgyzstana*, 143–4.

112 Abylkhozhin, *Istoriia Kazakhstana*, 512 and 514; Dadabaev, *Identity and Memory*, 69; 'Istoriia', *Ministerstvo inostrannykh del Respubliki Uzbekistan*; and Kerimbaev, *Sovetskii Kirgizstan v Velikoi Otechestvennoi voine*, 120–1 and 131; and Z. G. Saktaganova, 'Alma-Ata v gody Velikoi Otechestvennoi voiny: evakuatsiia, zhilishchnyi vopros, kommunal'nye i drugie problem', in *Istoriia. Pamiat'. Liudi: Materialy IX Mezhdunarodnoi nauchno-prakticheskoi konferentsii 27 sentiabria 2018 g.*, eds K. Sh. Alimgazinov, et al., 167–72 (Almaty: 2019), 169.

113 'Chto meshaet stroitel'stvu GES', *IKP*, 8 August 1943, 2; 'Vysokogornaia gidroelektrostantsiia na reke Karakolke', *IKP*, 5 March 1944, 2; and 'Korablestroiteli na stroitel'stve GES', *IKP*, 19 April 1944. See also Kaptagaev, et al., *Sbornik*, 138; and Kerimbaev, *Sovetskii Kirgizstan v Velikoi Otechestvennoi voine*, 164.

114 Kaptagaev, et al., *Sbornik*, 10; Kerimbaev, *Sovetskii Kirgizstan v Velikoi Otechestvennoi voine*, 139; and Peck, *What My Parents Told Me*, 37.

115 Saktaganova, 'Alma-Ata v gody Velikoi Otechestvennoi voiny', 170.

116 Abylkhozhin, *Istoriia Kazakhstana*, 512–13; Kerimbaev, *Sovetskii Kirgizstan v Velikoi Otechestvennoi voine*, 137; and Osmonov, *Istoriia Kyrgyzstana*, 144.

117 Kerimbaev, *Sovetskii Kirgizstan v Velikoi Otechestvennoi voine*, 139–40; and Osmonov, *Istoriia Kyrgyzstana*, 144.

118 IKSA:885/1/6/26; 'Na Issyk-Kule', *IKP*, 4 December 1941, 3; Kaptagaev, et al., *Sbornik*, 10; and Kerimbaev, *Sovetskii Kirgizstan v Velikoi Otechestvennoi voine*, 138.

119 IKSA:885/1/6/19, 125 and 140.

120 IKSA:885/1/2/1 and 6–14.

121 Barber and Harrison, *The Soviet Home Front*, 63; and Kerimbaev, *Sovetskii Kirgizstan v Velikoi Otechestvennoi voine*, 136–7.

122 IKSA:885/2/42/20 and 23.

123 IKSA:885/1/4/9.

124 Saktaganova, 'Alma-Ata v gody Velikoi Otechestvennoi voiny', 171–2.

125 Applebaum, *Gulag*, 403 and 405–6; and Barber and Harrison, *The Soviet Home Front*, 117–18.

126 Information from Dr Alymnugov. See also Applebaum, *Gulag*, 374 and 382–3; and Carmack, *Kazakhstan in World War II*, 125–8. See also Chapter 8.

127 Applebaum, *Gulag*, 375–6; Barber and Harrison, *The Soviet Home Front*, 69; and Carmack, *Kazakhstan in World War II*, 129–34.

128 Saya Mailibayeva and Anar Khassenova, 'ALZHIR, a Place of Remembrance', *Voices on Central Asia*, 31 January 2020, https://voicesoncentralasia.org/alzhir-a-place-of-remembrance (accessed 4 March 2020); Applebaum, *Gulag*, 102, 374 and 391; and Carmack, *Kazakhstan in World War II*, 130.

129 Applebaum, *Gulag*, 389 and 391–3; and Beevor, *Berlin*, 86.

130 Aimar Ventsel and Baurzhan Zhangultin, 'Prison Camp No. 29 for Prisoners of War from the Second World War on the Territory of Kazakhstan between 1943–9', *Electronic Journal of Folklore* 63 (2016): 9–28; and Applebaum, *Gulag*, 390.

131 Information from the Director of the Issyk-Kul'l State Archives, 30 November 2019, and Dr Alymnugov. See also Arstanbek Sargalbaev, '600 dnei very', *Esimde*, 7 July 2020, http://esimde.org/archives/2212 (accessed 7 July 2020); Dadabaev, *Identity and Memory*, 69 and 78–9; Robbins, *In search of Kazakhstan*, 219; and Stronski, *Tashkent*, 102.

132 Chynara Israilova-Khar'ekhuzen, *Esimde*, http://esimde.org/archives/3023 (accessed 21 December 2020); and Dadabaev, *Identity and Memory*, 69 and 78.

133 Sargalbaev, '600 dnei very'.

134 Records remain only in the Kyrgyz GKNB (National State Security) archives, see Israilova-Khar'ekhuzen, *Esimde*.

135 IKSA:146/2/50/13; Tranum, *Life at the Edge of the Empire*, 200–1; also information from the Director of the Issyk-Kul'l State Archives, and Dr Alymnugov.

136 Roberts, 'A Time for Feasting?' 4.

137 Kaptagaev, et al., *Sbornik*, 148–50.

138 Ibid., 151.

139 Stronski, *Tashkent*, 145 and 151–2.

5

Society in wartime

The family, health and education

The Churukov family hailed from Jarkent in Kazakhstan, a province which was renamed Panfilov in 1942 in honour of the military hero. In 1920 Imrazi and Azharbu moved south to Kyrgyzstan and settled in Przheval'sk, where Umarzhan, their eldest son, was born the following year. Lieutenant Umarzhan Churukov was already in the army as commander of a tank unit when the war began. Having survived the Battle of Moscow, he met his death during the offensives of early 1943 in the north-west of the Soviet Union. The young officer's mother had just a single, faded photograph of her son by which to remember him.[1]

This chapter examines the impact of war on individual families – in particular the women and children left at home. At the most basic level, each person faced their own struggle in order simply to survive the war years despite the huge disruption to normal family life. Not only the people of Central Asia faced these hardships, of course, but certain specific issues were met here by ordinary families, who had within the course of just one generation been forced to come to terms with significant changes to their traditional lifestyles as they became part of the new Soviet Union and a new relationship between state and society was gradually forged. The massive influx of evacuees, refugees and deportees affected the lives of many citizens, particularly in the larger towns of the region. In contrast, the sparse populations of the predominantly rural areas of Central Asia fought to make a living on the land in the absence of their able-bodied menfolk. Examples of altruism and generosity were matched by acts of greed and desperation in communities supposedly facing a common enemy. The very fabric of this patriarchal society came under severe threat, as women and children either rose to face the new challenges or succumbed to the hardship thrust upon them by the not-so-distant war.

Disruption of the family unit

Umarzhan Churukov was one of six children.[2] The traditional family unit
in most parts of Central Asia was large, reflecting the tendency for many
generations to live together, often with several children under the same
roof and sometimes with different wives in polygamous marriages residing
around the same courtyard or on neighbouring farms. With the nomadic
lifestyle discouraged under Soviet rule, families were forced increasingly
to take up residence on collective farms or in towns, still retaining the
inherently strong ties within their close-knit communities.[3]

The most serious issues of the rapid drive to Sovietization in Central Asia
were caused by the Europeanization of women's place in Muslim society by
the new socialist state with its emphasis on gender and social equality. The
emancipation of women included not only schooling but also the abolition
of the traditional practices of child marriage and polygamy. The final straw
in the increasing level of Soviet social micro-management in the region for
the more religiously conservative western areas of Muslim Uzbekistan and
Tajikistan was the forced renunciation of the veil for women; for tribes in the
north and east this did not provoke quite so much opposition, as nomadic
women had often already dispensed with some constraints of Islamic dress.
In its drive for modernization, the Soviet state also started to impose its
communist, atheist ideology on a Muslim society traditionally based around
the mosque, driving remaining religious activities underground as places of
worship were closed.

By 1941 the Soviet campaign to 'civilize' the Islamic societies of the
region was well under way, but still had a long way to go in the process of
modernization. The indigenous peoples of Central Asia were perceived as
backward by the Europeans, in need of pulling into the twentieth century
with comprehensive education in the communist ideology. At the outbreak
of war, the issues of low literacy rates and poor sanitation were only just
being addressed by the state, as measures were being discussed for better
town planning and an increase in the standard of living across a region
which was being gradually developed in order to maximize its contribution
to the prosperity of the overall Soviet economy. For the first time, the
systematic registration of all births and deaths was introduced, albeit with
sometimes spasmodic implementation in a region where the population was
often very diffuse.[4]

The patriarchal family structure suffered substantially as the younger,
able-bodied men were conscripted. Traditional notions of gender were
increasingly cast aside, as the new Soviet policy of equality took on a fresh
significance, with women forced to take on roles of which their – albeit
often absent – husbands sometimes disapproved. In a fight for survival,
however, women increasingly had to work outside the home, even in ultra-
conservative areas of Uzbekistan, as families desperately needed an income

on which to live. Even in farming communities, it was impossible to be self-sufficient when money was needed to buy precious commodities such as soap and medicine.[5]

Some families lost the majority of their offspring to military service, leaving a much depleted household behind. Within the smaller family units, the eldest son left at home often took on his father's responsibility to support the women and children. As young men were conscripted, this adult role increasingly fell on the shoulders of younger teenagers, typically fourteen-year-old boys, who worked on the farm during daylight hours and helped at home in the evening. Stronger women and boys worked non-stop, as girls took over domestic duties while also joining family members in the fields at key times. One Kyrgyz man testified to women's manual labour, recalling that women 'plastered, hauled stones, and built walls'. Wives and mothers of serving soldiers also formed brigades at work to emulate their menfolk's platoons on the front line.[6]

It was well-nigh impossible for soldiers to dispatch their wages back to their homes. Indeed, one of the main reasons for conscripts to desert was not out of cowardice but to support their struggling families in the rear. Periods of home leave were rare, and communications in general between soldiers and their families were difficult: contact was often completely lost with men who were not able to get messages home. Towards the end of 1944, the Issyk-Kul' province authorities were actively seeking news of the whereabouts of young officers on behalf of their wives and mothers: Jamil' Motanov was registered as searching for Captain Diushenbi Motanov; Mariia Shukhgalter wanted news of Lieutenant Zegfrid Shukhgalter; and Almokan Saryeva had lost contact with Lieutenant Mukash Saryev.[7]

Although soldiers on active service were in theory able to write to relations and to receive post, men in working battalions labouring in mines and factories did not have the right to correspondence.[8] The triangular, folded letters from the field were rare and often took several weeks to reach home. Political officers and their teams at the front assisted with reading and writing messages when the soldiers themselves struggled. Similarly, very few families possessed sufficient skills to read the precious incoming mail, often relying on educated mullahs or children of the new Soviet generation who had benefited from some schooling. The arrival of a letter, which should have been received with joy, was often viewed with suspicion, as its delivery sometimes heralded official notification of the injury or even death – in the case of a 'black letter' – of a close family member.[9]

Lieutenant Churukov's family was notified of his death by a delegation from the Przheval'sk war committee. Although he was an officer, he had been buried – like most fighting fiercely on the front line – in a communal grave with other men from his unit.[10] At least his family had certain news of his death. Twenty-year-old Duishen Shamenov's relations received the official *pokhoronka* (death notification) stating that he had fallen 'without news' (*bez vesti*), apparently lost in action. The last letter they had received

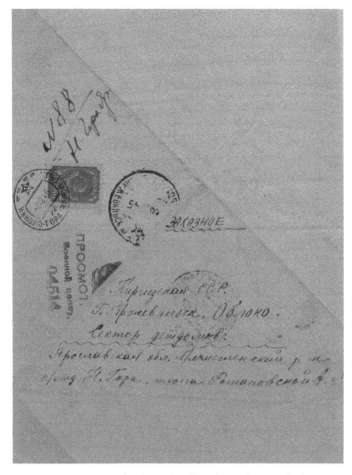

FIGURE 5.1 *Wartime triangular letter heading from the Iaroslavl' area to Przheval'sk, bearing the stamp of the official censor. IKSA:279/1/295/40.*

from him was from the deadly area around Kursk, but his children in Kyrgyzstan never discovered their father's fate.[11] In a region where funeral rites were very important for the family, it was highly distressing when a soldier's body was not brought home for burial. Russian and Muslim tradition dictates an early burial, with familial rituals by the grave at prescribed intervals after the funeral. In the absence of a body over which to mourn, Turkmen women created their own lamentations, sung during the mourning period as the women gathered together after work to lament their fallen menfolk.[12]

The lengthy separation of family members exacted a huge emotional toll on Soviet citizens across the country as the family unit came under increasing stress. Although some families enjoyed brief visits from their menfolk on leave, most remained isolated from news and visits for years.

At the onset of war, a surge in weddings took place as conscripts prepared to leave for the front line. This sudden upturn in marriage did not continue beyond the first couple of summer months, however, followed by a marked decrease in weddings over the course of the war. Interestingly, considering the problems of absence, no immediate significant change in the divorce rate was apparent. However, the state legislated to make divorce more difficult in the final year of the war, in an effort to boost the family and the Soviet population. Consequently, dissatisfaction within a marriage more often manifested itself by other informal arrangements.[13]

Wartime marriages changed in nature as well as number, as the remaining men in Central Asia sought wives. Childhood marriages had been the norm in more conservative areas, but children of the war years were too occupied with playing an enhanced role in the wartime economy for such marriages to continue to be viable. As young men were conscripted, the number of eligible husbands diminished, leaving more unmarried women and widows available for marriage to sometimes much older men. By 1944, the state was so eager to boost marriage that unmarried men over the age of twenty-five were taxed into conformity.[14]

There was also a significant rise in informal cohabitation arrangements, as pragmatic decisions took over under the strain of separation. It was not unknown for wives, suffering from the prolonged absence of their husbands, to engage in extramarital relationships and even embark on polygamous marriages, while their husbands in their turn took solace in the arms of another woman in a distant region. Facing loneliness on the one side or impending death on the other, both men and women sought comfort outside their marriage to alleviate the psychological and emotional toll of war.

Mikhail Bibikov from the Chui province of Kyrgyzstan asked his girlfriend to wait for him as he left for war. He was not the only soldier to return home to find that his girl had married another man in his absence. Following a prolonged recovery from wounds sustained in battle, Tenti Tamashaev from Tiup found that his eventual pleasure at returning home was marred by the fact that his young wife had left him for another man. In contrast, Aleksandr Tereshchenko, wounded at Stalingrad, returned home to Kyrgyzstan for convalescence, where he met and married the widow of a soldier who had recently died in action.[15]

The poor nutrition of many women adversely affected their fertility. This biological disruption, together with the long-term absence of their soldier husbands, had significant repercussions on the birth rate from 1942. It has been noted that, in peace time, more births took place in village communities where families depended on having many children. In contrast, the birth rate was traditionally lower in towns, as fewer children were necessary to work on the land. During the war, however, rural populations were decimated, as people flocked to the towns for better work opportunities and a higher income. For this reason, perhaps, farming families were often keen to foster or adopt children evacuated to the region, arousing some cynicism about the real motive for such apparent altruism.[16]

The situation became so problematic that the state felt it necessary to intervene in an attempt to manipulate the demographics across the Soviet Union. Deploying wartime terminology, they announced that new privileges would be awarded from July 1944 to every *mat' geroina* (heroine mother) of ten or more children, while mothers of more modest families of over four children received the *Orden materinskaia slava* (Order of maternal glory). Both these military-style awards entitled the bearer to extra food and some financial assistance in recognition of their 'patriotic work in the rear', whereas families with only one or two children were made to suffer an extra tax burden.

For example, Aidarova Suidum, living on a collective farm in Kyrgyzstan, had raised ten children, of whom the two eldest sons were in the Red Army. From 1936 until the end of the war she received a total of 32,000 roubles in benefits from the state for her work in raising the upcoming generation, the equivalent of ten years of the average annual wage. Advertising the need for larger families, the newspaper *Issyk-Kul'skaia Pravda* made much of the case of 42-year-old Kul'tsunai Urkumbaeva of the Talapker farm in the Tiup area. In order to qualify for benefits, mothers had to raise their children until at least their first birthday. Urkumbaeva was able to point to her nine children, the eldest of whom was twenty-one. Thanks to state benefits since 1936 amounting to 40,000 roubles, Urkumbaeva exceptionally owned her own home, plus both a cow and a horse. When pressed, she was quick to praise the state and to contrast her own relatively happy situation with that of her mother, who had given birth to eight children. Six of these had died of disease and starvation, leaving only two, herself included, reaching adulthood.[17]

Mothers caring for several small children were still expected to work, but were often allocated less onerous jobs. For example, one woman was allowed to dry potatoes and sugar beet rather than digging them up, in preparation for their shipment to the front.[18] Aid was also granted to single mothers, who had the right to state care for their offspring in children's homes, reflecting the need for women to take on employment despite the wartime phenomenon of births outside wedlock.[19]

With the main breadwinner away from home, soldiers' families enjoyed financial and material assistance, ordered by the state but implemented locally. For most families it was relatively easy to provide the documentation needed to prove that their family member was indeed a serving soldier, which also exempted them from tax payments; others, though, had to resort to friendship and kinship networks to convince the authorities of their eligibility. The number of dependent children was also recorded in an effort to plan the necessary number of nurseries and other support services for the family.[20] Needless to say, families were all too often failed by the local authorities and struggled to provide for their children without timely state support.

The state acknowledged that substantial social welfare support would be needed. A decree of June 1941 published the rates of payment to various categories of dependent families of Red Army, Navy and NKVD NCOs and other ranks. Benefits were awarded on a sliding scale, according to the number of members in the family who were unable to work: for example the disabled, children under the age of sixteen, fathers over sixty and mothers over fifty-five. A family with a mother and two children would receive a state subsidy of only 150 roubles per month, about half the average wage and sufficient to buy only ten loaves of bread or eight litres of milk. More helpfully, families of soldiers killed in battle or even those lost without trace would continue to receive these benefits until a military pension was granted.[21]

By March 1943 almost 186,000 military families were eligible for state support in Kyrgyzstan. Many enjoyed tax relief and widows received military pensions where relevant. Support systems included the establishment of canteens in factories, often manned by the Komsomol. The movement 'Aid for the front' created professional organizations to help the families of servicemen, while also providing help to incoming evacuees where necessary. Local communities collected money and food, clothes, shoes and even animals, while the authorities were expected to offer housing and repair existing homes where necessary.[22]

By 1944, social assistance was being received by 19,043 families of serving soldiers in the Issyk-Kul' province of Kyrgyzstan. 8,039 families were given clothes: mothers typically benefited from underwear, skirts and coats, while 1,422 growing children received new shoes. Benefits paid to families consisted not only of the regular monthly payment but also one-off gifts of flour, potatoes, eggs and even meat. In addition, mothers and teenage children were supported in accessing training to equip them for work.[23]

In theory, the payment of benefits as well as the distribution of social welfare to military families was appreciated by the recipients. However, delays in payment only added to the extreme stress and hardship experienced by several family units. Most of the payments made were not authorized locally, being instructed via military headquarters in Tashkent and further slowed down by the bureaucratic process in the provinces. The cavalier treatment of some families in the early months of the war flew in the face of the positive propaganda, being recorded in secret NKVD documents which demanded urgent local action. A certain Comrade M. I. Maletskaia had not received the benefits due to her family as quickly as she had hoped by September 1941. Her complaint to a higher authority caused the prompt dispatch of terse instructions to the local NKVD in Przheval'sk to action an immediate payment of the monthly sum of 150 roubles. Even worse, in October 1941 sixty-year-old Comrade Rakhmaniuka, a soldier's mother, was actually forced to pay 494 roubles in tax rather than receiving a similar sum in state support in the absence of her son. It appears that these were not isolated cases, as the authorities struggled to cope with the huge administrative task associated with the payment of benefits. Deliveries of sacks of grain and the issue of one-off payments to isolated farming families took its toll on the poorly staffed systems, until such delays were no longer secret. Eventually, the editor of the local Issyk-Kul' newspaper, normally hand in glove with the authorities, took it upon himself to openly criticize the bureaucrats by championing military families left in severe hardship through no fault of their own.[24]

Following a decree of 16 August 1941, however, if a soldier was taken prisoner of war, benefits to his family ceased immediately, as he was accused of cowardice or even treason in the face of the enemy. These families experienced untold material deprivation added to the psychological stress of not knowing whether the soldier was dead or alive and the social stigma attached to imprisonment by the enemy. For most, though, benefits and social welfare for military families and those of men fighting alongside the partisans continued even after the war had ended, subjecting the state to a huge debt of honour.[25]

Once the war was over at last, towns and villages across Central Asia prepared as far as possible the necessary food, medical and 'cultural services' for returning soldiers. In the Issyk-Kul' province, a commission was specially created in July 1945 to examine all family accommodation, repairing flats where possible and even building new houses as returning soldiers and their families were prioritized for accommodation. Household goods were offered to families so that they could better care for their menfolk as they adjusted to civilian life. Clothes were scarce, necessitating a further distribution of warm jumpers in particular.[26] However, many centres were badly organized in the early days, especially when it came to food, resulting in an urgent demand for an improvement in the supply of bread. Wounded veterans were desperately in need of assistance before their pensions could be arranged. Easier to arrange were tickets to the theatre and medical breaks in sanatoria, such as those on the shore of Lake Issyk-Kul', to aid their recovery. Records indicate that large numbers of families of wounded and deceased soldiers indeed received substantial support, even to the extent of help with their children's education, as soldiers' children were prioritized for scarce university places in Central Asia.[27]

For some families, however, the happy day of a husband's or son's return from the war never arrived. One woman waited patiently for news of her son, finally concluding that he may have been killed in action. The letter bringing news of his fate eventually arrived, as she learned that he had just been released from a slave labour camp in France and would soon be home.[28] News was extremely slow to filter back home in many cases. One man, who had been deemed unfit for action, remained at home in Kyrgyzstan during the war, after watching his four brothers leave for the front. Two of them returned home, but two remained missing. He therefore took on responsibility for the children of the missing men, hoping secretly that no news was an indication that they may have wisely decided to stay in the West with new wives and families.[29] Many families were decimated in this way, the awful truth only appreciated in the aftermath of victory. Mutaliap Aubakirov from northern Kazakhstan, for example, lost all seven of his brothers in the war.[30]

Most men were at least granted some leave once the conflict had ceased, and it is noticeable that the birth rate in the Soviet Union increased dramatically after 1946, although it remained lower than in the pre-war period, as so many lives had been lost during the conflict. Jumabek Rakhmanov from the Issyk-Kul' province was already married before he left for the Red Army, but his first child was only born after the war ended. Whereas many returned to their families, others found that their wives had betrayed them in their absence. Some got married immediately after demobilization, having waited years for the event. One man aged thirty came home anxious to find a wife and have children, and soon married a girl of sixteen. Others were chastened to return to their existing wives, having left behind them memories of wartime affairs with European women.[31]

Return of the wounded warriors

Mukhammed Malikov, a recently qualified electrician, was conscripted into the Red Army shortly after the start of the war, joining an artillery regiment in the Astrakhan area of the Russian–Kazakh border. Wounded five times during military engagements, he was awarded three medals and promoted from the ranks to become a Senior Lieutenant in command of a battery. His sixth wound outside Berlin in 1945 was the most severe, leading to a two-month hospitalization and his discharge from the Red Army into the care of his family on the Kyrgyz collective farm where he was born and raised.[32]

It is estimated that over 15 million Soviet troops (44 per cent) serving in the Red Army were wounded during the war. Following triage in field hospitals and treatment in the rear, a large percentage of Central Asians were returned to active service, in a desperate attempt to rebuild the number of troops on the front line. However, at least 2.6 million veterans, like Mukhammed Malikov, remained permanently disabled (so-called invalids), nearly half a million of whom had at least one amputated limb.[33]

The heavy number of casualties flooding into Central Asia risked overwhelming the relatively small numbers of hospitals and medical workers in the first months of the war. During the Battle of Stalingrad patients arrived daily by train, severely overloading nurses who worked without rest to care for mortally wounded men. The wounded usually required surgery either in field hospitals or once safely back in the rear, meaning that hospital stays tended to be long as they were slowly nursed back to health. Some took time to recover their lost memory, while many had lost legs, requiring wheelchairs and the fitting of one of the sought-after wooden prosthetic limbs.[34]

Several new hospitals were established across the region, most of them in 1941. One hundred and fifty-five were set up in Kazakhstan alone, about a half of which had been transferred from occupied regions of the Soviet Union. The first new hospitals to open were in Karaganda and Petropavlovsk, closely connected to the railway line from the front, while eight hospitals were evacuated to Alma-Ata.[35] In Alma-Ata, twelve of the existing fifty-one schools were occupied by newly established hospitals, while sanatoria and other public buildings were also converted.[36] A remarkable twelve new hospitals for the war wounded were built in the Chui province of Kyrgyzstan, exactly half of the total number of such facilities in the republic. The northern location was preferred for easy access from the war zones as the railway from the west arrived in this area. Conditions in the hospitals were poor, though, with an acute shortage of beds, exacerbated by the presence of some POWs who received treatment alongside the Soviet wounded.[37]

Akram Valiev returned to his home city of Osh when he was wounded at Stalingrad. His injuries required an eight-month stay in hospital before he was invalided out of the Red Army.[38] Many men were successfully treated physically, although little attention was paid to the mental illness sometimes caused by their experiences at the front. A proportion of the hospital patients died of their wounds or from associated infections like tuberculosis, necessitating the establishment of cemeteries with communal graves next to each hospital.[39]

Once the urgent phase of their treatment was over, the wounded were usually discharged into the typical Soviet convalescent homes or santoria across the region, sometimes financed with the help of sponsorship from local firms or enterprises. Clothing was provided from a communal collection for the homes for the wounded located on various collective farms in the Issyk-Kul' province. Once recovered from their wounds and convalescent fatigue, soldiers had to appear before a local military commission, where a doctor would assess their condition. If they were still unfit for active service, this would be repeated on a monthly basis until it was confirmed whether they were ever able to return to the front. Those who had made a good recovery were directed according to official instructions on where to send the wounded men after their medical leave, dependent on their military specialisms. Many were sent to Alma-Ata, Tashkent or Petropavlovsk to be deployed to their new units. On the other hand, men whose health was still adversely affected by their wounds were permanently discharged from the army and sent back to civilian life.[40]

The state acknowledged as early as 1940 that pensions would be required for any war wounded, thereby pre-empting any disaffection or even civil unrest which may have manifested itself. Pensions were not actually issued until 1944, when the state had regained some control over the course of the war. This gesture was not as generous as it sounds, however, as the meagre benefits issued were not sufficient for the wounded to live their future life without substantial poverty. These pensions depended on the veteran's professional background and previous salary, his military rank and – most of all – on the degree of disability. Category One wounded were the most seriously affected, unable to work at all due to their severely compromised health. Those in Category Two were still unable to work for the moment, albeit somewhat less seriously wounded, while Category Three veterans were only lightly affected, could undertake some type of unskilled work and were therefore virtually ignored by the pensions authorities.[41]

Although most wounded veterans suffered a future of deprivation and hardship, some good news was reported in *Issyk-Kul'skaia Pravda* on 23 February 1944 – the anniversary of the creation of the Red Army in 1918 and the date traditionally linked with service personnel. According to journalists, some disabled veterans benefited from time in picturesque resorts (*kurorty*) in the mountains or on the banks of the lake – a luxury for the moment not available to those living in Moscow.[42]

The state was anxious to return as many of the wounded as possible to productive employment, in an effort to boost the war economy and to minimize the drain on resources of unemployed dependent veterans. Before identifying suitable vacancies and enlisting the veterans on retraining courses, it was felt necessary to ensure their correct political education – probably in an effort to avoid any unrest on the part of a significant minority of former military personnel. It was originally intended to use some of the more educated wounded for political instruction, but this plan was abandoned when it was found that most of the returnees were not suited for this work, whether for educational or psychological reasons. Measures were then put in place to re-educate the returnees for their 'general cultural welfare', involving systematic political indoctrination. Local authorities were instructed to organize talks and discussions about the international situation and the duty of every Soviet citizen in the rear to support the front, a series of lectures relieved by the occasional concert. Men on the ground were reminded to check amongst the wounded for any known deserters, who should be dealt with accordingly. Most important of all, though, was the advice to remove immediately any service weapons still in the hands of returnees, who, it seems, could no longer be trusted to bear arms. Indeed, it was noted by the authorities in April 1942 that some of the wounded men were already behaving in a distinctly anti-social manner, to the extent that collective farm chairmen were warned to be alert to possible disruption in their communities.[43]

The only way to manage financially for most Category Three wounded was to take a job. The case of one Kyrgyz man who went back to working in the fields despite the loss of a leg is typical of many. Most men found that the only work they could perform was of a lower status than their pre-war positions, with a concomitantly lower salary. However, any formal work entitled the wounded person to become a member of a union, with its associated privileges, so it was better than the life of begging outside bazaars and railway stations to which many urban veterans were reduced.[44]

Training courses took some time to establish in Central Asia. Deaf and, to some extent, blind veterans coped relatively well with new jobs set up by work co-operatives, often in the food industry or alongside institutes for the wounded. However, most found that vocational training was inaccessible, as they were simply too injured to benefit. Substantial numbers were nevertheless trained for jobs such as basket makers, cobblers, car drivers or watch repairers. An article in *Issyk-Kul'skaia Pravda* in June 1944 reported the start of a three-month course for wounded collective farm workers to retrain as accounts clerks. Mukhammed Malikov, the electrician, recovered sufficiently to work in the electrical power station on his collective farm, while also maintaining the electrical network and repairing motors. He was just one of the 22,464 war wounded who had returned to Kyrgyzstan by the summer of 1944, a number dwarfed by the probably underestimated 81,000 disabled veterans in Kazakhstan.[45]

Most of the longer-term war wounded were left to heal – as far as possible – out of public sight at home in the care of wives or mothers. This placed a great strain on families and the farm communities around them, but was usually the least worst option. For those who remained completely dependent on others but without any relatives at all, state institutions or hospices were the only answer, where the wounded lived in primitive dormitories lacking most amenities and even basic entertainment.

The wounded largely remained silent reminders of the tragedy of war, being written out of the official post-war state narrative, unless their exploits could be used in propaganda material to label them as Soviet heroes, or they could be shown to have forged a successful new life for themselves as solid Soviet citizens. Some of the wounded from cities such as Moscow were removed even further from public sight to distant areas of the Soviet Union: some were even relocated to the Karaganda labour colonies in Kazakhstan as a cynical reward for their wartime service.[46] The war wounded represented the sad price of victory, a negative reminder of total warfare, as the extent of the predicament was kept hidden from public discourse. Occasionally mocked by the public, with double amputees likened to *samovars* as they laboured in awkward wheelchairs, the men who had lost their health fighting for their country usually disappeared from society into the darkness of their own homes or special institutions, to be gradually forgotten by the state. These mostly young men were left to manage as well as they could, often turning to alcohol as a crutch, while around them the healthy population started to rebuild their post-war lives without them.[47]

Malnutrition and starvation

The civilian population of the Soviet Union also suffered from substantial medical issues during the war. Little official material is freely available to document the extensive famine and widespread starvation in eastern parts of the Soviet Union, including Central Asia and extending into Mongolia. Some NKVD records dating from early 1945 recognize the scale of the problem, however, which is also widely acknowledged through the memories of those elderly citizens of post-Soviet Central Asia who, as children, experienced extreme hunger and lived with the spectre of starvation.[48]

Klara, born in 1931, well recalls the deprivation of wartime. At the onset of war, her family was living in Tashkent, having moved there from Kyrgyzstan. Tashkent was a magnet for incomers, known across the Soviet Union as 'the city of bread' (*khlebnii gorod*) by a naïve Soviet population. Once Klara's father had been conscripted into the army, the family had little to eat, surviving mainly on millet and grass, as most food was sent to the front. Realizing that they were on the verge of starvation, her father insisted that they return to their village in Kyrgyzstan, where at least there was a cow and people to help them. It was this move that saved their lives.[49]

The older generation maintains that today's younger generation simply cannot understand the importance of bread to those civilians who survived the war in spite of severe food shortages.[50] In a simple narrative, one man from Bazar Korgon in Kyrgyzstan stated: 'During the war we ate anything we could get [. . .] Sometimes, during the difficult times, we didn't even get bread.'[51]

Although not as pervasive or all-encompassing as the famine in Kazakhstan induced by enforced collectivization during the early 1930s, when a man was reportedly willing to sell his wife for a bag of grain, such memories indicate a side of the war on the home front not openly acknowledged by the authorities or reported in the newspapers. How galling it must have been for people to read in newspapers articles praising the number of sacks of flour sent off to the Red Army, while they struggled for every single grain of wheat and, driven by hunger, had to sell precious scraps of clothes or bed linen for a day's food.[52]

Requisitioning and rationing

The food supply in the region was badly depleted for several reasons: not only had the able-bodied men normally working on the farm been conscripted, leading to lower yields in general, but the urban population rocketed with the influx of evacuees and refugees. To make matters worse, stringent taxation and requisitioning of food and animals stripped farmers of their stores across most of the region. Evidence suggests, however, that parts of Tajikistan suffered slightly less deprivation than the other republics, as tribal networks remained strong and many of the outlying mountainous areas remained out of reach of state control.[53]

Elsewhere, though, local officials visited farms and individual households to demand a certain number of goats, sheep and cattle, only to leave with more than this quota. Animals and grain were nominally 'sold' to the state for much less than their market value, leading to the loss of mature livestock and leaving many farms with no dairy animals or seed for the next sowing season. Extra 'donations' were also required to feed frontline troops. Food parcels sometimes contained a ready-made mixture of flour, eggs and butter, to be cooked at the front, with all the ingredients taken from the precious stocks of peasant families.[54]

Although rationing was not deemed necessary in the countryside, from November 1941 it was introduced in urban centres through a system of ration cards and vouchers.[55] The largest rations went to manual workers in defence factories, mines, the oil and energy industries and the railways, who each received 800 grams of bread per day, plus 500 grams of sugar per month. Other industrial employees were entitled to 600 grams of bread per day, with the same amount of sugar, although it was nearly impossible for most of them to find enough food to fulfil their due quota, even after queuing for hours. Many factory, mine and hospital workers were given their meals in a workers' canteen, reducing their dependency upon rationed food. Most people, however, only received 400–500 grams of bread per day, and some as little as 300 grams, as women and children were given less than working men. Families supplemented their often meagre rations with fruit and vegetables grown in their personal gardens or allotments, usually no larger than the official 0.15 hectares (1,500 square metres). Military families had preferential treatment in the allocation of allotments, for example in 1942 soldiers' families in Tashkent received plots of land watered by the new city canal. By 1944, when conditions had improved, more than half the population of Frunze had their own private patch.[56]

The situation was far worse in the countryside, however, as farm workers often did not possess their own plot of land and depended upon help from the collective community. Personal income diminished rapidly as collective farms earned very little once their produce had been requisitioned. For example, in Kyrgyzstan, a family may have earned the equivalent of 1.6 kilograms of grain and 300 grams of potatoes per working day in 1940, only to see its income reduced to 1.3 kilograms of grain and 90 grams of potatoes in 1941, shrinking to a miserly 0.8 kilograms of grain and 30 grams of potatoes in 1942. By 1944, a typical family received only 0.4 kilograms of grain and 27 grams of potatoes per day to feed all its members. Furthermore, from 1943 farmers were forbidden to sell home-grown produce in town bazaars – a bureaucratic nicety, as they simply could not afford to part with any of their own food.[57]

While manual workers just managed on their rations, wartime children recall that growing teenagers suffered badly, receiving a bread ration of around 500 grams per day, just sufficient to avert starvation. Similarly, the 400 grams of black bread allocated to Regina Kesler in Osh was not deemed to be enough for an adult female to survive in the medium term, while the unemployed received no state support whatsoever. Food supplies remained

problematic for some time, with meat and butter being unheard of for the
duration. Milk, usually reserved for infants, remained rationed for years
after the war.[58]

Even if people wished to buy extra food in local bazaars, it was usually
priced beyond their means as supply failed to match demand, particularly
in Tashkent with its growing refugee population. Salt, for example, was an
incredibly valuable commodity for landlocked countries, both for animals
and people. It had to be transported over large distances to most communities,
commanding extremely high prices. With trucks requisitioned by the army,
most food was transported by camel or donkey. People's savings did not
go as far as previously: the rouble was able to buy less and, with rampant
inflation, low salaries failed to cover even essential items. It is no wonder
that some turned to criminal activity to feed their families. An illegal taxi
driver, for instance, was able to buy some milk, cheese and butter, while a
rare few resorted to murder in order to obtain their next meal. The Timofeev
brothers, for example, ably assisted by their extended family, were responsible
for the murder of at least thirteen innocent citizens in northern Kazakhstan
until eventually brought to justice by detective Vladimir Rozentsvaig. In a
region where the ethos was on sharing, this type of breakdown in social
values was an indication of the desperation of the population. The black
market in food and other collective farm assets flourished, as criminals used
stolen ration cards. Farm animals were also targeted by heartless thieves
who deprived their owners of their most precious asset. By 1943 it became
necessary to introduce a ten-year prison term or even the death sentence for
the theft of food. With nothing further to lose from committing more serious
infringements, the crime rate in Central Asia rose rapidly during the war, a
fact which went under-reported by the ever-optimistic press, which probably
exercised considerable self-censorship in this respect.[59]

The fight for survival

Central Asia was not the only region of the Soviet Union to experience
deprivation during the war. Indeed, it enjoyed a more benign climate than
many parts of the country and most residents were able to grow at least
some of their own food. However, food prices were so high and government
requisitions in the region so demanding that the rural population laboured
on the farms for their very survival.

Obstacles included the daily queue for bread in the towns, with some older
children taking on this task to help their mothers, despite the occasional
cruelty of other adults who were not reticent to push children out of their
way as the fight for survival took hold. Children would walk for several
kilometres to collect wood for the fire or to gather mushrooms, in common
with most other Soviet citizens. One man recalled as a child collecting
individual grains left in the fields after the harvest, despite the fact that they

officially belonged to the farm and his family would have suffered a penalty had he been caught. He similarly tried to locate any remaining potatoes left in the frozen ground over the winter. They were not good quality, but apparently made passable pancakes for a hungry family. Most families were reduced to selling possessions to buy food, from jewellery and pieces of cloth to the family home or even their own blood. Although illegal, it was also tempting to trade the monthly kerosene ration for food. In extremis, families found it impossible to eke out their provisions if there were many mouths to feed.[60]

It was only the inventiveness of desperate individuals and communities which kept most of the population alive during the war years as they lived from hand to mouth, with women often taking less for themselves in order to feed their growing children. Many individuals resorted to eating boiled grass from the fields or berries from the forest, as testified by Ilhomjan Karimov, who was a teenager in the war:

> Then the mulberries ripened and we ate them and waited for the wheat to ripen. But we couldn't wait until it was fully ripe. We used to cook half-ripe wheat and eat it. [. . .] We survived somehow.[61]

Wartime diets included an unusual range of 'food': grasshoppers and slugs provided at least some protein, while old, rotten potatoes were either eaten as vegetables or dried and ground for flour. Hot water was helpful to stave off hunger pangs, with *atala* (thin soup) or tea made from ground grain, crushed fried barley or oat flour. In the end, almost any type of leaf or root from wild plants was used, whether safe for human consumption or not, including the *algy* plant, an onion-like vegetable which could, if not properly prepared, actually poison the drinker.[62]

The hardest decision was to consume seeds or seed potatoes, or even to eat the fodder upon which farm animals depended. Refugee Zofia Właźnik, for example, delivered bread in Osh, Kyrgyzstan, by camel, whose hay she resorted to sharing. On another occasion, she sold her horse's harness and stole its wheat to buy food. When the horse died of starvation, having only been offered water to live on, she overcame any remaining scruples and ate its meat.[63]

Despite the ingenuity of the population, many civilians died during the war – mainly young children and the elderly, who often did not survive the first couple of years. Infant mortality, as high as 52 per cent in rural parts of the Issyk-Kul' province in 1941, increased over the first two years of the war as food shortages became more marked. People had to bury their neighbours and even children were enlisted in the burial process if they had the strength to help dig a grave. Rations in labour camps were increased a little in January 1943, as it became apparent that productivity had been adversely affected thanks to the starvation rations introduced in the early months of the war. Other citizens had to wait until mid-1944 for some improvement in their food supply. Overall, people became too lethargic through malnutrition and exhaustion to do much to alleviate the situation, as the years slowly passed until victory was announced. Even then, the drought of 1945 caused acute grain shortages, particularly in the south-east of Kazakhstan, where some Uighur farmers, faced with starvation, summoned what little energy they still possessed to relocate to China. It was not until 1946 that many in Kyrgyzstan began to feel some relief from the effects of protracted malnutrition, despite the brief celebrations to mark the end of the war, when a sheep was cooked and enjoyed in some communities.[64]

Community spirit was credited by many for their survival, despite the antisocial behaviour of some city-dwellers. Soup kitchens provided for some of the population, notably in Kazakhstan, but were not able to relieve the distress of the majority. The hunger experienced by most of the population was widely acknowledged in private, although nothing appeared in Kyrgyz newspapers and contemporaneous official documents remained largely silent.[65]

Community health

In contrast, the Soviet state did acknowledge health problems amongst the population of Central Asia. It was apparent in the city of Tashkent that the overcrowded streets harboured germs which were readily transmitted from person to person in the unsanitary conditions prevalent at the time. Particularly in the Asian part of the city, the health of the indigenous Uzbeks was endangered by the lack of clean drinking water, with canals contaminated by the free disposal of household waste in addition to industrial pollution. The grand Soviet designs for spacious roads, new apartment blocks and cleaner canals were largely put on hold during the war as the city became even more crowded with refugees. To a lesser extent this scenario was repeated across the region, as increasing strain was experienced by a stretched health system lacking both medicines and medical personnel. The few doctors, nurses and paramedics left in the region had to deal not only with wounded soldiers and the effects of malnutrition in the population, but also the highly transmissible diseases introduced by evacuees and returning soldiers.[66]

As many existing doctors and nurses had been conscripted into the army, people left at home had to rely increasingly on very elderly doctors who were not eligible for active service. Women doctors evacuated from Ukraine and other occupied areas were also drafted in to staff military muster stations in Central Asia.[67] In Przheval'sk, for instance, Karl Sukhonos, a senior *fel'dsher* (a paramedic trained to deliver first aid) took charge of the local population, while community nurse Comrade Shmatova delivered pre-conscription lectures to young men.[68]

The few hospitals catering for civilians were desperate for qualified medical personnel. At the onset of war a system was set up to train volunteers as medical assistants. Once the wounded started to flood back home from the Battle of Moscow in November 1941, the cottage hospital in Sazanovka introduced training courses for nurses. Forty graduated in the first intake, with a second tranche early in 1942. The evening classes, covering topics such as practical nursing, X-rays and the running of rural surgeries, were timed to attract industrial or farm workers who were busy during the day, with participants including a teacher and even a middle school pupil. A refugee in Osh similarly followed a short course teaching her to give injections and change dressings, enabling her to obtain a position as an assistant nurse in a city hospital.[69]

The training of doctors was hampered in Kazakhstan and Uzbekistan by the lack of indigenous instructors and medical textbooks in local languages.[70] The only medical college in Kyrgyzstan added to the number of qualified doctors in Central Asia: the first graduates emerged in the summer of 1943, although many were immediately conscripted into the army. The few able to remain in their home republic were highly valued, as they were familiar with the everyday living conditions of the Kyrgyz people. In an effort to produce more doctors, even students who had not completed middle school were accepted for training, being supported by a special foundation course. As many needed to live away from home in Frunze, they benefited from a hostel and a canteen at the medical college.[71]

Once in position, the thinly spread new doctors were expected to 'mobilize all their strength and energy to increase help for the front and improve medical services for the population', as a means of increasing productivity in wartime. This involved caring for the wounded, attending defence industry factories, conducting prophylactic work with children and supporting health services on collective farms.[72]

Fulfilling all these demands was no mean feat, especially as the whole region was struck by regular outbreaks of disease. Although much of the Soviet Union remained free of epidemics during the war, Central Asia and the prison camps of Siberia and Kazakhstan were prone to large-scale infection. Typhus was the main killer, spread by fleas or lice breeding in overcrowded conditions with poor sanitation. Prevalent in Tashkent and Frunze from the beginning of 1942 as refugees arrived after long journeys from the western parts of the Soviet Union, it caused regular epidemics amongst poorer people and in prison camps. People – the majority young children – died in their dozens, with communities often lacking traditional funeral shrouds in which to wrap them.[73]

In addition to typhus, cholera and dysentery plagued the region, with tuberculosis and scrofula also endemic. Malaria was present around the waterways in hot areas of Uzbekistan and Kyrgyzstan, while episodes of measles periodically hit the whole of the Soviet Union. Trachoma, an easily transmissible bacterial eye disease, also thrived in the dirty and unhygienic conditions in Osh and Tashkent. While locals hoped to prevent infection by eating spicy peppers and herbs, one refugee resorted to stealing quinine from a hospital to treat malaria, as medication for most diseases was in short supply. Precious stocks were diverted to the army, while remaining supplies were severely stretched due to the increasing civilian population of Central Asia.[74]

The Soviet authorities also targeted what they perceived as the backward habits of the population, for example, spitting or sitting on the floor to eat. The state's health budget was increased during the first years of the war to educate the people in cleaner cultural habits. Public health education was prioritized as the war progressed through local newspapers, posters and leaflets. An early newspaper article, for instance, urged mothers to protect their infants from microbial stomach organisms by feeding them with breast milk. Animal milk was notoriously prone to infection, so milk centres were established later in the war as well as consultations for parents who needed advice in this area.[75]

Children were very susceptible to infection, especially those living in communal institutions, which were liable to lice infestations and typhus epidemics. Local authority advice early in 1942 to Kyrgyz children's homes and boarding schools emphasized the importance of regular weekly baths for all children and staff using hot water and soap, followed by a mandatory change of bed and personal linen. Children's cleanliness should be inspected daily, according to medical officials, concentrating on their hands, neck and underwear, with a weekly inspection of their outer clothing. Girls' hair should be checked regularly for nits and boys' hair cut once a month to keep it short; more drastic head shaving was advised in cases of infestation. The ever-present danger of typhus was taken very seriously. If a child was found to have a temperature above 37.5C, they should be sent to the institution nurse and isolated. In the case of confirmed typhus, the child's bed linen should be destroyed, baths disinfected and every resident monitored for twenty days.[76]

Parents were similarly cautioned to be meticulous about personal hygiene using a similar range of preventative measures. Additionally, the hems and seams of clothes were to be checked regularly for lice. If discovered, the clothes should be thoroughly washed with soap and the seams pressed with a hot iron. If hair was found to harbour nits or lice, it was to be washed with soap and kerosene to stamp out the infestation. Food hygiene was particularly important in the summer, when diarrhoea and dysentery were common in groups of children, particularly in outdoor summer camps, when food, water and milk could easily be infected by flies around rubbish bins. Leaders were advised to boil water and milk and to wash fruit and vegetables with boiled water. In the case of microbial illness causing loose, sometimes bloody stools, doctors recommended offering the child only boiled water to drink, followed by a little boiled rice after twelve hours or so.[77]

One of the big constraints with observing personal hygiene was the ubiquitous lack of soap across the Soviet Union. Whereas soap was merely rationed in Britain during the war, in the Soviet Union it was almost impossible to source. Central Asia was no exception, often necessitating home-made production using lye from wood ash and animal fat, when and if available.[78]

Public sanitation and disinfection points were therefore established in collective farms across the region. Sanitation control points were also set up at stations and more public baths were introduced for the population in general. In Tashkent sanitation brigades were formed, with women leading the push to educate others in hygiene, while also inspecting the degree of cleanliness of the city's streets. In Przheval'sk, systematic cleaning of the urban area was demanded by the authorities in advance of the spring thaw of 1944. Citizens were instructed to sweep the streets and clear them of grass and leaves after the winter snow in a mass spring-cleaning effort to take place between mid-March and mid-April. Personal rubbish bins and all private courtyards were included in the purge, which was followed in the summer by orders to the public to sweep all streets, pavements and markets on a daily basis. Inside the home, residents were advised to wash up their crockery after meals, launder their underwear regularly and not to keep domestic animals in close proximity to the house. Water cleanliness was to be preserved by avoiding the use of public canals to water private gardens and the order never to dump private waste into the town's waterways.[79]

State resources were ploughed into a mandatory vaccination programme for children starting in 1941. Treatment stations were also established to fight malaria and tuberculosis where it was prevalent. Vitamin C deficiencies were tackled by the use of supplements manufactured in Jalal-Abad from unripe walnuts harvested from the nearby forests of Arslanbob. These were distributed to military hospitals and children's homes across the republic, while individuals sometimes obtained their dose from dried fruit or vegetables.[80] Overall, however, the situation was less severe in warmer parts of Central Asia than in other regions of the Soviet Union, where scurvy became increasingly prevalent as the war progressed.[81]

Most of the population and many medical personnel resorted to the use of medicinal herbs growing on the hills and in the forests, often gathered by schoolchildren. In principle controlled by the medicines office, they were traditionally used by the locals for relief from illness. Plants such as aconite, taken orally or applied to the skin, were employed to treat fevers. Unfortunately, many were toxic and their successful use depended on substantial experience. Safer options included henbane and mint, gathered by children and dried for the treatment of digestive ailments. As the war took its toll, doctors had recourse to more modern drugs, including the newly discovered sulfapyridine for the treatment of diarrhoea and dysentery in children. Medical trials were even conducted by Soviet doctors in Przheval'sk, eliciting encouraging results. Apparently, the new drug decreased the recovery time from an average of nine days to around three days – a positive step in the advancement of conventional medicine in Central Asia.[82]

Wartime children

With the able-bodied men away at the front, children in Central Asia sacrificed much of their childhood to help their families survive. Traditionally, these young people matured early: older children helped their mother with younger siblings in an often large family, while boys and girls tended to marry at a young age. The demands of life in wartime meant that they took on additional responsibilities in the household and on the collective farm. It was virtually impossible to shield children from the effects of war: they, too, suffered from hunger, disease and the trauma of witnessing family funerals.[83]

Children suffered psychologically, alongside the rest of the Soviet Union. 'Why was there so much rage?' asked one Kyrgyz man rhetorically. 'Because we lost so much in the war.' This sense of loss was ever present – of missing fathers and brothers, the food they needed for a healthy development and the material possessions which had to be sold to make ends meet. This anger was projected onto the invisible common enemy – the 'Hitlerites', the 'fascist occupiers', the Nazis. The genuine fear of the enemy was harnessed by parents who threatened naughty children with being taken by the Germans. Encouraged by the propagandists, even children sang songs about the enemy.[84]

Despite the prevalent uncertainty and stress of the war, most reports indicate a supportive atmosphere within close communities. Indeed, some guarded optimism about the outcome and a sense of normality took over in the final year of the war, by which time people were used to the austere conditions and had more or less learned how to manage. The seasonality of life in Central Asia remained regular, even punctuated by a few minor celebrations, for example, Labour Day on 1 May or when the harvest had been taken in. On these days, recalls one Kyrgyz woman, the young people would dress up and walk to the nearest town to enjoy a meal with friends and relations. She enjoyed herself so much on these outings that she was married at the tender age of sixteen in 1944.[85]

However, life at home generally remained primitive and crowded, with few amenities and no electricity. Children were often engaged in foraging for food and had few, if any, material possessions. Many were forced to go barefoot, and clothes were a big issue, as garments were repaired and handed down from one child to another within the family. Schools and other organizations constantly tried to procure aid for struggling families, particularly fur hats and warm trousers for the winter. It was not nearly enough to satisfy all needs, but every little helped as poorer families lived from hand to mouth. Some children had only hay to sleep on, having to wait until the post-war period to enjoy the comfort of a real bed.[86]

What childhood there was did not last long. Children over the age of eleven and students in colleges and universities had to work on the farm after school and during the holidays to meet the new requirement introduced in

February 1942 for a minimum number of days' labour for the common good. Children over the age of fourteen who had left school had to work a six-hour day for a modest salary, with many progressing to underground work in the mine with the adults. Training schemes for teenagers were introduced in July 1942 at so-called F30 establishments – technical colleges which prepared teenagers for work in factories, on the railroad or as mechanics. This helped fill the shortage of civilian tractor drivers and factory workers and the additional income generated was essential for families who had lost their main breadwinner.[87]

Most children, though, were dispatched to work on the fields with the women, forming the majority of farm workers. Indeed, in Kyrgyzstan in 1942, 89 per cent of farm labour was carried out by children. With food shortages and genuine hunger, even small children were sent out to collect leftover grain remaining in the field after the main harvest. A total of 10,502 schoolchildren from the Issyk-Kul' province helped out in the fields during the summer of 1942. Kyrgyz boys were sometimes sent further afield to work as shepherds on the summer *jailoo*, while, in more traditional Uzbekistan, girls would sit and sew blankets and warm clothing for Red Army soldiers. With a regularity dominated by the seasons, schoolchildren would head for the fields as soon as the 'last bell' of the academic year rang out, only returning to the classroom as the 'first bell' announced the start of a new school year at the beginning of September.[88]

Farm work undertaken by children under fourteen went largely unpaid, as it was not officially recognized by the state, although children usually received their meals at work. There was a tacit agreement between the state and the family that the Soviet Union badly needed its children, who were deliberately targeted in newspaper articles and by youth organizations.[89]

Membership of the Komsomol organization was encouraged and indeed expected of older school children and students aged from fourteen to twenty-eight. Younger children aged from nine to fifteen were similarly able to become Young Pioneers. In 1941 in Kyrgyzstan alone there were 3,445 local Komsomol groups, including 108 in the Issyk-Kul' province. This was the generation first targeted for conscription, with 85,000 of the 96,704 members called up during the war. Of these, Duishenkul Shopokov was one of the twenty-eight Panfilov heroes, while Komsomol member Cholponbai Tiuleberdiev was mythologized for shielding his comrades by using his body to cover an enemy machine-gun.[90]

The Komsomol reflected the structure of the Red Army with its system of brigades and sections. It was very much a political body, engaged in the propagation of communist ideology to young people on collective farms and in schools. Fifty-six Komsomol members from Przheval'sk, escorted by middle school teacher Comrade Anisimova and nurse Comrade Krutovetskaia, formed a delegation travelling to Stalingrad shortly after its liberation, answering the call to hundreds of thousands of young people across the Soviet Union to rebuild the city. At home, annual conferences were held for Komsomol leaders, where they presented their ideas and exchanged views.[91]

Komsomol members formed the spearhead of the Kyrgyz republic's initiative to encourage young people to work on the fields during school holidays. For example, Comrade Malinovskaia led two brigades of twenty children from Przheval'sk to the Dyishin farm in Irdyk village to help weed the poppy fields in the summer of 1942. Apparently, the children arrived full of 'enthusiasm and jollity', only to be treated after work to lessons from Komsomol agitators on the textbook approved by Stalin for children's ideological development, *A Short Course in the History of the Communist Party*.[92] Lectures to expand their horizons were obligatory for Komsomol members, covering science, politics and history. Topics included in the summer course of 1945 included 'Is there life on other planets?', 'Was there a start of the world and will there be an end?' and the edifying 'A young person's moral outlook'.[93]

The newspapers portray Komsomol organizations as very eager to help the war effort on both the ideological and practical front. Neither Komsomol members nor newspaper editors held back from naming and shaming underperformers, whether schools or collective farms. For example, when crop yields fell in the Piatiletka collective farm in the Tiup area, a team of twenty-seven Komsomol members was deployed to pull the farm out of its previous inadequacy. In addition to farm work, clearing rivers and forests and helping in sawmills, Komsomol members used their powers of persuasion to acquire the loan of horses for farming plots. They managed to extract scrap metal for the Defence Fund, even succeeding in sourcing guitars, balalaikas and other musical instruments to add to the typical content of parcels destined for soldiers at the front. At harvest time, some Komsomol members were deployed to look after children too young to help in the fields, while others, encouraged by the local press, were called upon to conduct repairs and otherwise use their initiative to save the state from wasting precious resources.[94]

A further group of young people helped out in cases of need – Timur teams, or '*Timurovtsy*', formed mainly of children belonging to the Young Pioneers organization. Timur teams came into their own during the war, the brainchild of children's author Arkadii Golikov (1904–41). Golikov was a former Red Army officer who later became a journalist, writing under the pen-name 'Gaidar'. Perhaps recalling his own intrepid youth and his military service in the far east of the Soviet Union, Gaidar created his most famous protagonist in 1940 – thirteen-year-old Timur Garaev. 'Komissar' of a band of young teenagers in *Timur i ego komanda* (Timur and his Gang), Timur was a member of the Young Pioneers, sporting the uniform red neckerchief with a red star on his chest. Named after the famous fourteenth-century Uzbek military leader, Timur tasks his team to assist families of Red Army soldiers, often involving secret nocturnal activities. Thanks to a widespread intelligence network, war games and paramilitary manoeuvres,

Timur's gang succeeds in helping out worthy cases, while rooting out a nest of local 'hooligans'. A product of the imagination of a former soldier, whose own son was named Timur, the story is set against the pre-war background of a country already mobilizing its troops. Examples of military leadership abound, alongside the constant trope of helping others in need.[95]

Timur was adopted by schoolchildren across the entire Soviet Union during the war, but was especially beloved in Central Asia, thanks to the significance of the protagonist's name. Following the fictional Timur's example, real Timur teams offered practical help tending orchards, repairing flats and sweeping courtyards, generally assisting the war effort in their own way.[96] *Issyk-Kul'skaia Pravda* and the local Communist Party praised their work, for example, when a group of year six children, aged around twelve or thirteen, helped out a woman who was ill by cooking for the household and looking after her four young children, while also digging up vegetables in the garden.[97]

Education

When Central Asia became incorporated into the newly formed Soviet Union in the early 1920s, very few of the population were educated except seminary students taught by mullahs about the Muslim religion. The 1897 census indicates a much higher literacy rate in Russia (28 per cent) than in Central Asia. Indeed, it is estimated that by 1914 literacy levels in Kyrgyzstan were still as low as 0.6 per cent, probably the lowest figure in the region. Rates were marginally higher in Uzbekistan, where the centres of Samarkand, Bukhara and Khiva housed a few Islamic schools, and even remote Tajikistan saw more meaningful education for its inhabitants. These figures largely relate to male literacy, as it was most uncommon for girls to receive any education at all.[98]

The newly formed Soviet Union had to address a situation where the pan-Turkic Jadid movement was starting to promote education across the Islamic region from Crimea to Central Asia. The religious connotations were underlined by the fact that the small literate minority employed the Arabic script, serving to alienate the new Central Asian republics from Moscow. Lenin was nonetheless anxious to grant the republics of Central Asia some degree of autonomy. Conscious that any 'nation' depends for its survival on a coherent culture and a shared history, Lenin formulated his policy of *korenizatsiia*, which is sometimes translated as 'indigenization'. The ideology of *korenizatsiia* embraced the retention of the unique culture of an ethnic minority on its home territory, alongside partial self-governance and some devolved administrative authority. Following the 1917 revolution, Moscow attempted to convince the people that they were no longer simply powerless subjects of the tsar, but equal citizens in the brand new Soviet project. Lenin underlined the fact that the one-time colony of Central Asia had become valued as an integral part of the new Soviet Union. Each republic was therefore encouraged to develop its own internal structures, its own language, literature and artistic culture. These new rights mitigated many of the previous century's colonial impositions by imperial Russia, rendering the new republics in principle relatively independent of Moscow.

Despite the new *korenizatsiia* policy, the pan-Turkic movement sweeping across a region united by a common religion and mostly similar Turkic languages inherently posed a potential threat to Moscow's overall political and linguistic hegemony. The Soviet policy to improve the education – and thus the future prospects – of the people often perceived as backward and uncivilized was therefore not just taken for benevolent reasons. The state wished to forge new Soviet citizens in the Slavic, rather than the Turkic, cultural mould, while removing any hint of religious influence from their lives.

The Bolsheviks embarked on a mass educational programme as soon as 1919, as part of their modernization agenda. A literacy drive was deemed to be important politically as well as socially, if the new Soviet citizens were to be inducted in the state's communist ideology. State funding was provided for new primary schools, while newspapers, theatres and clubs were established. Seen by Moscow as both an ideological and a civilizing mission, the introduction of Western culture to a region based mainly on an oral tradition proceeded gradually, especially in the traditionally intellectual centres of Samarkand, Tashkent, Alma-Ata and Frunze.[99]

The education system was a highlight of Soviet modernization, even encouraging lessons in the local language to the perceived disadvantage of Slavs who had settled in Central Asia. Young people benefiting from a Soviet education were able to continue their higher education in Moscow, eventually becoming the new regional elite. Here was the supply of new leaders for the Central Asian republics, who would go on to work within the Communist Party structure at the local level. Despite their new status, they were in fact Moscow's puppets, acting under political domination while enjoying some modest degree of independence to govern their own people.[100]

As Stalin started to make his leadership felt after the death of Lenin, it was dictated that the Latin alphabet would be introduced in Central Asia from around 1928 to the frustration of Muslim clerics in the region.[101] Thanks mainly to Stalin's tight grip on the ethnic minority republics, their real degree of independence was further diminished in the 1930s. The freedom to celebrate indigenous culture was very much curtailed, as the region's history was re-written in accord with Moscow's revolutionary version. Other aspects of culture were denigrated by Russians, who considered most Central Asians to be primitive and child-like in clinging to an oral culture and nomadic tradition. Far from being equal in the eyes of western Soviets, these new citizens were viewed as inferior and in need of substantial cultural and political guidance from the centre. Books, art and methods of learning were often prescribed, in contrast to Lenin's original policy which had promised free rein to the region to retain its own traditions.

The move to educate the children of Central Asia developed momentum from 1930, when it was aimed to educate all children in schools, although in reality children in urban centres benefited more quickly from the new policies than those in rural areas.[102] Kazakhstan, with its highest proportion of Russian speakers in the region, also had the highest pre-war literacy rate at around 84 per cent, with Tajikistan trailing furthest behind at 63 per cent.[103] This was the situation in 1940, when the state suddenly decided to change the rules again with the introduction of the Cyrillic alphabet for these peripheral languages. By then Stalin was seriously reconsidering the benefits of multinationlism and rewriting the rules for the minority republics, as the benefits of *korenizatsiia* for the autonomous regions were acting against any central drive to unite the Soviet Union as an ideological, linguistic and cultural entity. The barely hidden aim towards cultural hegemony was obvious.

Without changing the languages of the republics, a further alphabet reform was an interim measure to align indigenous and Russian script. The political agenda is obvious, as Central Asians would be more exposed to communist propaganda and a gradual encroachment of the Russian language itself in a creeping Sovietization of the region. The Cyrillic script employed by Russian speakers of the Soviet Union became mandatory in Central Asia on the eve of war, as the urgency to raise adult literacy in the drive to produce cultured and complete Soviet citizens took hold.[104] The result of the two drastic alphabet changes was to confuse further those adults who were able to read. It also reduced temporarily the supply of books in schools, until newer material in the Cyrillic script could be produced.

The state school system

For the youngest children the lack of reading material was not an immediate problem. Since its establishment, the Soviet state had always aimed to provide childcare in order to enable women to work independently outside the home as much as men, although this was easier to implement in the western Soviet cities than in rural Central Asia, where more traditional roles were adopted. The provision of free *detsad* (nursery) care for young children under the age of seven was key to freeing women for the war effort. The stated objectives of pre-school education in January 1941 were:

- to organize nature outings, walks, creative work, games and drawing;
- to keep a close eye on all children;
- to encourage an afternoon nap;
- to keep children healthy and well fed;
- to encourage conversation;
- to promote physical education and activities;
- and to introduce toys for creative play.

In this way, the state set out to provide *vospitanie*, a social and moral upbringing for young children outside the home, as opposed to *obrazovanie*, or formal school education. All education, however, was subject to the political tone of the era, with the main aim of all schools being 'to raise fiery patriots'.[105]

Staffed by personnel with minimal qualifications, these nursery schools were set up alongside factories and on collective farms. This system worked well outside the cities, as the *detsad* network gradually expanded during the war, but insufficient places were available for young children in Tashkent, thanks to its influx of refugees. Whereas only 3,659 children received pre-school care in 101 nursery schools in Kyrgyzstan in 1940, by the end of the war the state looked after nearly 10,000 children in 187 establishments, freeing mothers to bring in a necessary income. Comrade Sharokhina ran the Tiup district nursery school in the Issyk-Kul' province, organizing games, music and movement, singing, dancing and even poetry recitals for the sixty children. Other establishments operated seasonally, when all the adults were needed on the farm. State assistance continued in the holidays, as Pioneer camps and summer sanatoria constructively occupied children of school age.[106]

The phased introduction of schooling for the whole population was almost complete by the start of the war, although there remained many older children who had received little or no formal schooling. The goal of the Soviet third five-year plan, starting in 1938, was for all children to attend school from the age of seven to fourteen. At this stage, after seven years of formal education, teenagers would either leave for work or continue for a further three years at school until they were seventeen and eligible for vocational college or university. To the credit of the Soviet state, even Kyrgyzstan, where only 1 per cent of children completed seven years at school in 1939, managed to achieve remarkable progress during the war such that one-fifth of school-leavers reached their seventh year. In general, by 1941 most villages and collective farms had access to a primary school, teaching pupils from the age of seven to eleven, while towns normally had at least one 'seven-year school', taking pupils from seven to fourteen. The aim was to increase the provision to seven years of education in villages, with full ten-year 'middle' schooling in towns.[107]

Some children lived in isolated villages, farms or herding communities, far from the nearest school. The introduction of boarding schools enabled older children to live there during the working week, avoiding what was often a lengthy walk to school every day. At the start of the war there were twenty-nine such schools in Kyrgyzstan, increasing to as many as eighty-nine by the end of the war, as families strained to cope with managing the education of their offspring. Great lengths were taken to ensure that wartime children had a good diet at school, although the ration recommended for each pupil by the education authorities in the 1942/3 academic year was exceedingly ambitious under the straitened wartime circumstances.[108]

The urgency of the school situation was exacerbated by the requirement of the Red Army for literate, Russian-speaking conscripts. Although the alphabets had been harmonized, Central Asia retained its dual system of schools according to mother tongue. Kyrgyzstan, for example, had both Kyrgyz- and Russian-speaking citizens, along with other minority residents. Russian was made an integral part of the school curriculum across the Soviet Union in 1938. In most schools, though, the language of instruction was Kyrgyz, in line with Soviet *korenizatsiia* policy, with just a few lessons of Russian per week. Many of these offered only the first seven years of education. Children in the north of the country, however, for example in Frunze and Przheval'sk, often attended schools where lessons were conducted in Russian. These were the 'middle school' establishments which were more capable of catering for pupils wishing to remain at school until the age of seventeen before proceeding to a high-status profession for which a knowledge of Russian would be a distinct advantage. However, many students with ten years of formal education under their belt were conscripted into the army, leaving few to proceed to higher education and partly contributing to a dearth of qualified teachers to educate the wartime generation of schoolchildren. Although the number of teachers decreased by 10 per cent in Kazakhstan during the war, there was also a disproportionate decrease in pupils of 30 per cent, partly as more young people were engaged in work of some description, while others may have been too ill or poorly equipped to attend school. Similarly, in Kyrgyzstan the number of pupils fell by 20 per cent, although in Uzbekistan the rolls were boosted by incoming refugees.[109]

Further problems served to reduce the number of schools across Central Asia, as former school buildings were appropriated for other purposes. In Uzbekistan in particular, the urgent need to accommodate evacuated factories meant that schools and some libraries were converted into industrial premises and accommodation for workers. Hospitals were also established in some educational buildings, causing the eviction of teachers and their pupils into less suitable premises, often outside the town. The situation in Kyrgyzstan was not quite so desperate for schools, as fewer evacuees travelled so far east. Acknowledging the transient nature of the change in use of schools, the Kyrgyz authorities determined to reclaim all school buildings for children by the beginning of 1944, once refugees and evacuated factories and institutions started to return home.[110] In fact, the state's commitment to education in Central Asia continued in the post-war period, when several postponed plans to build new schools were finally implemented.[111]

Although the uncertainties of war caused temporary issues for schools, in many ways children and their families were protected by the state, as it continued to introduce more comprehensive teaching and literacy measures for adults. However, the war certainly created serious difficulties in the sphere of education, with insufficient textbooks, exercise books, writing materials, visual aids, laboratory equipment and substantially fewer qualified teachers.[112]

The trouble with teachers

Schools were badly understaffed in the war, as many experienced teaching staff were conscripted into the Red Army for officer training. Furthermore, even those school-leavers not taken into the army hesitated to consider a career in teaching, often wishing to bring in an immediate wage.

In an effort to fill the gaps, teacher training courses were shortened from three to two years in 1942. Despite the shortage of qualified staff, the Kyrgyz State Pedagogical Institute in Przheval'sk remained at first discriminating in its selection of seventeen-year-old students. A second teacher training college opened in Przheval'sk in 1942 to address the need, offering places for 150 students in key curriculum areas: physics and mathematics vital for engineering; history, deemed politically important for ethnic and national identity; and the shortage subjects of Kyrgyz and Russian language and literature. It was anticipated that 60 per cent of the places would be for those of Kyrgyz nationality, reflecting the importance attributed to teaching in the mother tongue.[113]

Despite the urgent need for teachers, too many staff were left without accommodation provided by the state, nor the important fuel oil necessary for them to survive the winter weather in Kyrgyzstan. In warmer Tashkent, the prime accommodation for academics too often went to incomers from Moscow, who led the housing pecking order. A teacher's job was not easy, as they were also expected to contribute to the war effort outside school hours and in the 'holidays'. Lev Spektorov, the headmaster of Tiup middle school, even completed a combine harvester operator course, as his local collective farm had no relevant expertise. Being literate members of society, many teachers also held administrative posts on the farm. Once the harvest was completed, teachers then had to turn their skills to repair work in their school buildings, painting classroom walls and taking in deliveries of coal and precious fuel oil to keep their classes warm during the winter, as the first day of the new academic year approached. Teachers were also expected to donate their salary from a few working days to the Defence Fund, while also working for the common good on *subbotnik* days – Saturdays when the whole community tackled various necessary projects together.[114]

Stalin ordered that the main task of teachers was 'to prepare the soldiers of tomorrow, nurturing in them the patriotic qualities of fearlessness, courage, determination and the ability to withstand any hardship, confident in the defeat of the German occupiers and eventual victory over the enemy'. Teachers were meticulously guided in their lesson plans, in order 'to make maximum use of every second to ensure the best results for participants', as inexperienced teachers were recommended to record full details of their lessons. Acknowledging 'the increasingly important role of the Soviet teacher in wartime' and with the Soviet Union determined to increase the standard of education in Central Asia, school inspections were carried out annually to ensure that the agreed curriculum was being properly delivered.[115]

During the first year of the war, Issyk-Kul' province education authority inspectors recognized the fact that schools were bursting at the seams, while coping with a lack of specialist teachers for older children, high staff turnover and insufficient textbooks, especially those in the Kyrgyz language. Furthermore, it was found that there were not enough teachers of foreign languages, in addition to a shortage of Kyrgyz and Russian specialists. Indeed, it was found that Russian was taught to Kyrgyz children by teachers who themselves possessed only middle school qualifications, while no specialist Kyrgyz language teachers were employed in some schools. Even worse, mathematics was not taught at all well, as many teachers of this subject had been conscripted into engineering corps, while others were absent due to ill health – possibly stress-induced, as the load on them had become intolerable. Similarly, chemistry and physics were taught at a very superficial level by teachers who did not always entirely understand the subject themselves due to their mediocre qualifications. The most serious deficiencies were found in schools where overstretched head teachers failed to spend enough time observing the lessons of their colleagues or even to prepare the schools for the coming academic year. In the Lenin Middle School in Przheval'sk, for example, head teacher Comrade Sokolenko had failed to prepare the school sufficiently, leaving some children disorganized and consequently obviously unhappy. In contrast, Comrade Elena Siausova of the nearby Przheval'sk School had ensured that her premises were welcoming, freshly painted and with posters on the walls.[116]

On the positive side, the Lenin School, where the teaching academic elite were based, provided excellent lessons. Outstanding lesson plans put in place by Comrades Kiselev and Mal'gin (in history and geography respectively) included examples relevant to the war effort. Comrade Lysenko of the physics department employed examples of the laws of physics in self-defence, while in chemistry his colleague Comrade Druzhikhina outlined the principles of chemical warfare and even mentioned the racist theories inherent in fascism. Turning to oral lessons wherever possible because of the shortage of writing materials, children were encouraged to give talks on 'the patriotism of the Soviet people and the atrocities of fascism' in language lessons, while Russian literature classes in the Przheval'sk Middle School concentrated on a dramatic production of Gogol"s *Taras Bul'ba*.[117]

If these teachers were applauded for their outstanding lessons, some were singled out as 'Stakhanovites'. One such paragon was 22-year-old Baialy Aldaiarbekova of Karashar primary school, who had been a Komsomol member since 1932 and a teacher since 1937. During the 1941/2 academic year her class reportedly made remarkable progress. In addition, this community-centred woman worked as a political agitator on her collective farm, being particularly vocal at harvest time, while in her spare time lending a hand in the construction of the Bystrovka-Rybach'e railroad, where it was claimed that she exceeded the expected daily norm by over 500 per cent![118]

Schools in the service of the state

Even during wartime, a child's first day at school was a day for celebration, as mothers dressed their offspring in their best clothes, making sure that they carried the traditional bouquets of flowers for their new teachers. Most seven-year-olds entered the first class of one of the 121 schools in the Issyk-Kul' province, catering for a total of around 25,000 children during the war. Of these, seventy-four were middle schools taking children up to the age of seventeen, whereas forty-seven were 'incomplete' middle schools offering only seven years of education. The most prestigious schools were in the main town of Przheval'sk, which boasted five ten-year middle schools, one seven-year school and one primary school. In common with many schools across the Soviet Union, their names included the ubiquitous Lenin School, Il'ich School (also named after Lenin), Stalin School, Kirov School and Chekhov School.[119] The signs of Russian colonialism were very much in evidence.

Most of the ten-year middle schools were concentrated in urban areas, but some villages were also well provisioned. For example, in the outlying Tiup area, a total of sixty-nine teachers managed the education of 1,146 pupils, including music, art and physical education specialists. However, in rural areas a sizeable 18 per cent of children – mainly boys – left school at the age of eleven to help at home and on the farm. Furthermore, up to 20 per cent of children were made to repeat one or two years of schooling. This was possibly caused by the high rate of absenteeism in schools during the war, discussed herein. For example, the first year in the collective farm school in Kurmenktin comprised twenty-seven children aged from seven to eleven. Here it was probable that the younger children would sit at the front of the class, with the repeaters at the back, a recipe for a breakdown in discipline. It is unsurprising, therefore, that an average of only four pupils per year went on to study beyond the age of eleven. Very few pupils returned to the eighth year at the age of fourteen with a view to completing their middle school education, even if this facility was offered.[120]

The state was determined that children should be taught in their own native tongue where possible, while also ensuring that everyone also mastered the Russian language. Schools tended therefore to be either 'Kyrgyz', 'Kazakh' and so on or 'Russian' depending on the language of instruction. Some establishments even managed to segregate the pupils into two streams to accommodate different mother tongues, especially in the final three years of education. The families living in the Issyk-Kul' province included children of Kyrgyz, Kazakh, Russian, Tatar, Ukrainian, Jewish and German nationalities. Most village schools usually taught through the

medium of Kyrgyz, such as in Tepke, where only 2 per cent of the pupils
were Russian-speaking. Russian schools were largely populated by incomers
from Ukraine or Russia, often refugees or evacuees, as in Nikolaevka or
Mikhailovka, where a substantial minority were Jewish families originally
from Ukraine. Moreover, detailed archival statistics reveal that Kyrgyz
language schools catered for very few older pupils, with only four tenth-
year classes across the province. In stark contrast, nine Russian language
tenth-year classes provided for five times the number of pupils with Russian
as their native tongue, and those who wished to pursue further or higher
education through the medium of Russian – the gateway to professional
advancement in the Soviet Union.[121]

Bizarrely, although the best education was no doubt delivered through the
medium of Russian, there was a shortage of teachers of the Kyrgyz language
in so-called 'Russian' schools. Once again evidence of the determination of
the Soviet leaders to accommodate all nationalities, the Kyrgyz language
was an integral part of the school curriculum in all schools. Kyrgyz was
taught with reading and writing in the first year in Kyrgyz schools, but
was not introduced until the fifth year (at the age of eleven) in Russian
schools. In contrast, and indicative of the real priority attached to the two
languages, Russian, started naturally in the first year of Russian schools,
was introduced in the second or third year of Kyrgyz schools, with lessons
in Russian literature in the final three years of middle school in both
systems.[122]

In other areas of the curriculum, primary children studied mainly
arithmetic and physical education, with geography and nature – later
becoming biology – added at the age of nine and history at ten. Once in
year five, children started to add extra subjects, with geometry, physics,
chemistry and a foreign language in year six, and a one-year course in the
constitution taken in year seven (the final year of compulsory education),
ensuring that early leavers would have at least some grounding in Soviet
citizenship. Additional subjects included painting and drawing, singing and
courses in military preparation, while in Kazakhstan older pupils received
lessons in agriculture, with courses on tractor driving and combine harvester
operation for those above the age of fourteen. After school, extra-curricular
activities sometimes included craft, drama clubs, choirs and literary circles
tackling a range of politically approved books. In all activities, from the
early days of the war, teachers were instructed to increase the degree of
vospitanie in the school day, not forgetting the main instruction to imbue a
sense of 'fiery patriotism' in their charges.[123]

Schools also had to fulfil the overall state plan for education, involving
the measurement of the degree of success of their pupils at the end of each
academic year. In the Issyk-Kul' province the schools with the best results
were predictably the Russian middle schools, where it was often found that
98 per cent of the annual cohort passed their examinations. In contrast, the
performance of children in village schools decreased as the war continued,

with a disturbing rate of failure. Results in the key subjects of Russian, Kyrgyz and arithmetic remained relatively good across the province in 1942, but this figure masks the far better performance of older children and the much worse situation in primary schools. The primary school on the Tashkiia collective farm in the Przheval'sk area, for example, was named in the local newspaper as bringing up the rear in the league table. By the following year the situation had noticeably declined, particularly in village schools, with further implications across the board for children's learning in general as the war progressed.[124]

This comes as no surprise in retrospect, as the children must have become progressively more tired, hungry and malnourished. They were also surrounded by families suffering the loss of key members, no doubt causing instability and concern. The local authorities also struggled to obtain sufficient fuel oil to keep classrooms warm. Education authorities acknowledged some of the main reasons for the poor results, as they had already recognized that schools were suffering from a high turnover of often young and inexperienced staff. Together with the shortage of qualified staff in key subjects, children were at a real disadvantage, which was compounded by the lack of equipment in all schools.[125]

Academic progress was also hampered by absenteeism and poor discipline. Even at the start of the war, Uzbek children tended to avoid school, whereas their counterparts in Kyrgyzstan seemed to attend relatively regularly until the middle of 1942, when the demands of the farm became overbearing. By June 1942, 20 per cent of the pupils in the Issyk-Kul' province were absent from school. As may be expected, the outlying rural areas were worst affected, with only a 10 per cent decrease in attendance in the town of Przheval'sk. As the war progressed, schools were taken to task for pupil absences, with the accusation that teachers did little to build meaningful relations with families, despite the fact that parents' committees were set up in all schools. This may well have been true, as hard-pressed head teachers had quite enough on their plate. However, some schools still served as beacons of excellence. The Chekhov School in Przheval'sk, for example, established a parents' *aktiv*, a group of relatively energetic adults who helped to repair the school where necessary in the holidays. Comrade Sinusova of a village school apparently visited her pupils regularly at home to build up relationships with the family, while her colleague, Comrade Miniakhmetov, held classes for parents on the importance of school routine, punctuality and personal hygiene. These were exceptional cases, however, and the decline in attendance is probably evidence rather of the effects of the deprivation of the war years on children who were becoming badly malnourished, suffered from disease (often measles or typhoid) and who had little in the way of warm clothing or boots to wear to school.[126]

As the war became more and more disruptive for family life and tired teachers struggled to maintain interest and control, so pupils themselves became more disruptive in class. Schools had been praised for the excellent level of discipline in the summer of 1942, thanks, inspectors concluded, to a high degree of *vospitanie* and the nurturing of a 'strong Soviet patriotic attitude to study'. No schools were found to have a discipline problem, although a few instances of bad behaviour had led to minor sanctions. Even some older pupils from the Lenin School in Przheval'sk were excluded both from school and the Komsomol organization for 'hooliganism'. Similarly letting off steam, four teenagers from the Voroshilov School in the Balykchin area were disciplined for drunkenness. By the following year, though, discipline had become a problem across the province, where pupils seemed to have lost the Soviet 'culture of obedience and respect for teachers'. The situation was not helped by the Komsomol, whose naïve and inexperienced members insisted on 'helping' young teachers with their preparation for lessons on political ideology, while at the same time criticizing head teachers and their staff. Komsomol authorities tactfully suggested that their members should stick to more practical help, such as getting in fuel oil and carrying out repairs ready for the winter term.[127]

Teachers indeed faced huge difficulties in maintaining the interest of tired, cold and hungry pupils. Local authority inspectors reinforced the need for teaching materials, notably textbooks and exercise books. Some textbooks existed, but were not yet in the Cyrillic script, which muddied the water for Central Asian pupils trying to learn to read and for parents trying to help them. School libraries stocked few books, most of which, again, were in the old Roman alphabet and did not really support the learning process. Russian-language material seems to have been available, but suppliers were chastised for failing to supply books in the Kyrgyz language. The situation with exercise books was dire, due to chronic paper shortages, as evidenced by the scraps of paper used for official returns in the archives. Threats were made to suppliers as repeated demands were made. The province ordered 570,000 new exercise books in the summer of 1942, with no realistic chance of delivery. Wall maps used in history and geography lessons were similarly absent, and practical science work was badly compromised by the lack of laboratory equipment. Urban schools may have held some stocks of material, but, as always, it was the rural schools which suffered most.[128]

By the start of the autumn term in September 1943, insufficient food for hot breakfasts, clothes and footwear were top of the list of deficiencies, as academic issues – this year including pens, pencils and ink – took second place to pupil welfare. Local industry had been ordered to meet the task of providing children with the necessary equipment, but apparently had scandalously failed to expend sufficient energy on this important task. By October, shipments of exercise books were on the way, as the Communist Party banged heads together and threw money at the problem. For the vast sum of 2,000 roubles, 8,000 exercise books were on order, sufficient only to scratch the surface of the shortage. This unhelpful, but understandable, situation continued until well after the end of the war. All the archival evidence paints a picture of a theoretically sound system intended to improve the education of Central Asian children, yet placed under huge stress due to the acute shortage of staff and materials linked to the strain on the wartime generation of children themselves.[129]

War games

Substantial progress was made, however, in the relatively new curriculum area of military-political training, which was linked with physical education lessons. Staffed initially by physical education specialists who themselves were often conscripted, classes were later taught by former military personnel, including lightly wounded veterans. This subject came into its own in the war years, at first preparing older pupils for conscription, but from the autumn of 1942, military-political training was extended to all pupils of school age. Primary school children spent most of their thirty-three lessons per year on sport, games and 'military gymnastics', while older pupils had lessons on political ideology, first aid, tackling incendiary bombs and even radio communications in year nine, when 165 lessons were devoted annually to the subject.[130]

The focus on military-political training was increased as the war progressed. By early 1943 schools were instructed to deploy only the best staff for this curriculum area, who should deliver lectures on war news from the Western Front; work at home in the rear; the Soviet Union's allies in the war against Germany and its fascist allies; and the atrocities committed by the Nazis in occupied countries. On the ideological front, lectures included 'Twenty-five years of the Red Army' (in 1943), 'Sixty years since the death of Karl Marx' (in 1943) and, to include history nearer to home, 'The heroic tradition of the Kyrgyz people'. Resources were also collected by pupils to imbue the spirit of patriotism fostered in these lessons, for example, stories of Red Army heroes cut from the newspapers.[131]

Once again, though, a lack of equipment was evident, as with soldiers during their initial training. Komsomol members came into their own in this case, making mock rifles, machine-guns and hand grenades. These 'weapons' were put to good use during quasi-military manoeuvres held during the winter holidays early in January 1942, when older pupils from the Lenin School organized a simulated landing operation in conjunction with groups from the Stalin and Przheval'sk schools. These tactical exercises involved 'soldiers' wearing camouflage gear, some bearing machine-guns and hand grenades. Others were the landing troops themselves, while a further group of pupils provided first aid to the 'wounded'. At the same time, groups of pupils from other schools tackled a 15-kilometre ski trail. Physical fitness was an integral part of military-political courses, as pupils were relentlessly prepared for their future life in the Red Army.[132]

Extra-curricular provision

Holiday activities and summer camps for children were an integral part of life in the Soviet Union. While some pupils were taking part in military exercises in January 1942, others were occupied by a daily programme of cultural activities. Outings to the cinema were an important part of this largely indoor programme of *vospitanie*, where the focus was clearly on inculcating a hatred of fascists and a desire to defeat the enemy occupiers. To facilitate the organization of these propaganda film shows, some teenagers were trained as 'young cinema mechanics'. Children also attended lectures about the war, with talks on defence, anti-aircraft measures and chemical warfare high on the agenda. In addition, they had meetings with soldiers, another important part of the Soviet strategy for educating the younger generation about the war. As light relief, there was the opportunity for creative art and to sing songs about heroes by Soviet composers, with some games and dances at the end of the very full days.[133]

During term time, the occasional weekend programme was organized by schools. The middle school in Sazanovka sent all its boys over the age of fifteen on military exercises one Sunday in mid-October 1941, just as the attack on distant Moscow was at its height. At the same time, girls and younger boys were sent off to the hills to pick rose hips, an important ingredient of rose-hip syrup or tea, providing vital vitamin C. To cap off the special day, teachers put on the play *Bez viny vinovatye* (Guilty without Fault) by Aleksandr Ostrovskii, with all ticket proceeds going to the Defence Fund.[134]

Summer camps for children of all ages continued during the war years, freeing up parents for work on the farm. Pupils aged fifteen and sixteen, together with some older students, experienced a fortnight's military training in the summer of 1943. Here they worked on building fortifications under field conditions, practised their response to a chemical attack and studied topography. Written work was also expected of seventeen-year-olds. Some wrote about the Kyrgyz epic poem *Manas*. Others produced 'splendid essays' on the subject 'We are proud of the valiant Red Army', a title which seems to have answered its own premise with little room for debate. These and similar activities were intended to instil discipline in the young people as they approached school-leaving age.[135]

Summer camps for Young Pioneers (*Pionerskie lageri*) focused on the picking of medicinal herbs, an activity which continued on a monthly basis throughout the year. This gave town children from Przheval'sk the chance to spend long days in the countryside, the nearest thing to a holiday which could be provided. Some children had to remain in a more formal setting, however, as collective farms organized summer schools for children. In July 1943 fifty-three such schools were in operation across the Issyk-Kul' province, with some children receiving care and tuition in larger centres. By the summer of 1945 children were more free simply to play as children, as organized holiday clubs offered the ubiquitous cinema programme (*detskie kinoseansy*), excursions, fishing trips and games, although it was still deemed necessary to continue the collection of medicinal herbs and berries for the health of the nation. Throughout the war it was considered a necessary part of summer camps to encourage children into the fresh air and to feed them well with milk, berries and fruit. The authorities were keen for the children to put on weight, with the focus on making up any deficit in nutrition over the winter months, thus leaving them better able to face the health challenges of the coming autumn term.[136]

Adult literacy

The campaign to improve adult literacy in Central Asia continued through the war. The Uzbek Foreign Office states that the literacy rate in Uzbekistan in 1941 was an incredible 95 per cent, while one Soviet source claimed a literacy rate of 70 per cent had been achieved in Kyrgyzstan by the end of the war from what had been almost a standing start. These claims seem to overstate the case, however, when compared with contemporaneous archival evidence.[137] Some children of the pre-war period had still not benefited from any formal education, while one Uzbek tractor driver recalled only three years at school, less than the complete primary education. For adults the situation was compounded by the changes in alphabet from Arabic to Roman to Cyrillic over the course of just a decade. Certainly, the pressures of wartime exacerbated the situation for many barely literate adults, whose reading skills caused them to underperform in the Red Army. Indeed, local authority inspectors concluded that not enough was being done during the war to overcome the disadvantages of adult illiteracy.[138]

Statistics reveal that, for the academic year 1940/1, 25,000 children in the Issyk-Kul' province left school with very weak literacy skills. As may be expected, the smallest numbers of illiterate school-leavers were in Przheval'sk town, with the largest numbers in the rural Jeti-Oguz district. The degree of illiteracy was higher for females than for males, as it was girls who largely took on the responsibility of household work at a very young age. However, it is also true that those girls who did attend school tended to stay longer than boys, who were often withdrawn to help on the farm.[139]

A big adult literacy drive was announced in Kyrgyzstan in March 1941, before the official onset of war with Germany. The campaign was concentrated mainly on farms, in an acknowledgment that it was women who needed intervention in a Muslim society where at least some men had previously been educated in a religious environment. Schools helped adults, who sometimes attended school lessons alongside the children, but who could also visit so-called *likpunkty*, centres intended to 'liquidate' illiteracy. When ordinary teachers were on holiday, Komsomol members stepped in to continue the classes. Despite this, only around 40 per cent of the targeted population sought help, being no doubt fully occupied at work and in the home.[140]

Libraries were set up in 'reading huts' or 'red yurts' across the province, containing literature, newspapers, posters and artwork to stimulate the local community, also housing political and literary clubs.[141] By mid-1944 it is evident that the measures had had some effect and the scale of illiteracy had decreased a little, although it was still the female population who were badly disadvantaged. Even more surprisingly, the decrease in illiteracy was greater in villages than in the town, probably thanks to direct local intervention. Villages even managed to collect some books in 1943 to send to similar 'red huts' in liberated areas of Ukraine, even though there were not many to spare. After the war, a network of libraries and cultural centres sprang up, offering opportunities for self-improvement for all generations, but it would not be until many years after the war that illiteracy was finally conquered in Central Asia.[142]

Signs of social progress

The impact of war on the ordinary families of Central Asia was huge, despite efforts on the part of the state to provide support through welfare benefits for some families. Reduced to near-starvation in many cases, women struggled on in the rear in the absence of their menfolk and in increasingly desperate conditions. As the war became a more distant memory, many people recalled the camaraderie of communities helping each other out; others, however, remember only the fight for survival during the darkest time of their lives.[143] Even once the war was over, living standards remained low for several years, rising only in the 1950s in common with the rest of the Soviet Union. There were signs of progress, though, as information campaigns continued to alert communities to health issues inherent in their traditional behaviour. Measures were introduced across the region to keep infection levels as low as possible in view of the arrival of vast numbers of disease-carrying refugees and evacuees. New medical research also heralded the use of a new generation of drugs to complement the traditional remedies employed in indigenous communities.

Across the region it also became evident that the state was intent both on educating the population as a whole and on nurturing its youngest members, the future citizens of a more modern and integrated Soviet Union. With the successful implementation of the Cyrillic script across Central Asia, the introduction of new schools and better opportunities for further education, the region became increasingly aligned culturally with the dominant Slavic republics in the west. The Soviet project in the southern republics was finally on the road to success.

Notes

1 Esenaliev, *Zhenishke dank*, 186.

2 Ibid.

3 Kesler, *Shards of War*, 1293; and Stronski, *Tashkent*, 5 and 78.

4 Kaptagaev, et al., *Sbornik*, 27; and Stronski, *Tashkent*, 6–7.

5 Stronski, *Tashkent*, 78 and 82.

6 Tranum, *Life at the Edge of the Empire*, 14, 64, 74 and 105; Dadabaev, *Identity and Memory*, 65; and Kerimbaev, *Sovetskii Kirgizstan v Velikoi Otechestvennoi voine*, 124.

7 IKSA:119/1/56/87.

8 Information from Prof. Tchoraev.

9 Florin, *Kirgistan und die sowjetische Moderne*, 52; Lilley, *Have the Mountains Fallen?*, 11; Stronski, *Tashkent*, 138; and Tranum, *Life at the Edge of the Empire*, 212.

10 Esenaliev, *Zhenishke dank*, 186–7.

11 Ibid.

12 Carole Blackwell, *Tradition and Society in Turkmenistan: Gender, Oral Culture and Song* (London and New York: Routledge, 2013), 31 and 158–9; and Catherine Merridale, 'Russia', in *Encyclopedia of Death and Dying*, eds Glennys Howarth and Oliver Leaman, 390–1 (London: Routledge, 2001).

13 Barber and Harrison, *The Soviet Home Front*, 91 and 93.

14 Ibid., 93.

15 Interview with Tenti Tamashaev, 15 May 2018; Esenaliev, *Zhenishke dank*, 162; and Tranum, *Life at the Edge of the Empire*, 75 and 78.

16 See chapter 7. Barber and Harrison, *The Soviet Home Front*, 92–3; Goldman and Filtzer, *Fortress Dark and Stern*, 281; and Stronski, *Tashkent*, 140.

17 Aidarova Suidum, 'Bol'shaia zabota o materiakh', *IKP*, 26 July 1944, 1; and 'Mat' deviati detei', *IKP*, 10 February 1945, 4. Details of wages in the Soviet Union are given in Janet Chapman, 'Real Wages in the Soviet Union, 1928–1952', *The Review of Economics and Statistics* 36, no. 2 (1954): 134–56, 144.

18 Tranum, *Life at the Edge of the Empire*, 69.

19 *IKP*, 8 July 1944; and Barber and Harrison, *The Soviet Home Front*, 93.

20 IKSA:146/1/17/22; Manley, *To the Tashkent Station*, 178; and Stronski, *Tashkent*, 135–6.

21 'O poriadke naznacheniia i vyplaty posobiia sem'iam voennosluzhashchikh riadovogo i mladshego nachal'stvuiushchego sostava v voennee vremia', *IKP*, 29 June 1941, 1. For typical food prices, see Irina Mukhina, *The Germans of the Soviet Union* (London and New York: Routledge, 2007), 74–5.

22 'V pomoshch' sem'iam voennosluzhashchikh', *IKP*, 1 April 1943, 1; Abylkhozhin, *Istoriia Kazakhstana*, 518; Kaptagaev, et al., *Sbornik*, 8; and Kerimbaev, *Sovetskii Kirgizstan v Velikoi Otechestvennoi voine*, 47 and 192.

23 IKSA:119/1/49/89; 'Pomoshch' sem'iam voennosluzhashchikh', *IKP*, 27 May 1943, 2; 'Issyk-Kul' – sem'iam frontovikov', *IKP*, 23 February 1944, 2; and 'Pomoshch' sem'iam frontovikov', *IKP*, 7 February 1945, 2.

24 IKSA:119/1; 'Zabotit'sia o semiakh krasnoarmeitsev', *IKP*, 26 November 1941, 4; Kaptagaev, et al., *Sbornik*, 22–3; and Stronski, *Tashkent*, 134 and 139.

25 Barber and Harrison, *The Soviet Home Front*, 91.

26 Kaptagaev, et al., *Sbornik*, 151–2.

27 IKSA:146/1/39/4; and IKSA:146/2/47/5–7; Kaptagaev, et al., *Sbornik*, 135 and 151; and Manley, *To the Tashkent Station*, 261.

28 Kaptagaev, et al., *Sbornik*, 151 and 153–4.

29 Interview with Gulsara Nurmatova, 11 May 2018.

30 Aisulu Zhumagulova, 'Ikh bylo vosem' brat'ev, v voine vyzhil odin', *Sputnik*, 9 May 2018, https://ru.sputniknews.kz/society/20180509 /5553978/kazakhstan-vojna-den-pobedy-istoriya-frontovika.html (accessed 8 November 2019); and Dadabaev, *Identity and Memory*, 65.

31 Interview with 'Saltanat', 31 May 2018. See also Barber and Harrison, *The Soviet Home Front*, 93; and Stronski, *Tashkent*, 145.

32 *IKP*, 13 September 1945; and Kaptagaev, et al., *Sbornik*, 155–6.

33 Beate Fieseler, 'The Bitter Legacy of the "Great Patriotic War": Red Army Disabled Soldiers under Late Stalinism', in *Late Stalinist Russia: Society between Reconstruction and Reinvention*, ed. Juliane Fuerst, 46–61 (Abingdon and New York: Routledge, 2006), 46–7; Abylkhozhin, *Istoriia Kazakhstana*, 518; Axell, *Russia's Heroes*, 246; Kerimbaev, *Sovetskii Kirgizstan v Velikoi Otechestvennoi voine*, 174–5; and Stronski, *Tashkent*, 91.

34 Sarah Phillips, '"There Are No Invalids in the USSR!": A Missing Soviet Chapter in the New Disability History', *Disabilities Study Quarterly* 29, no. 3 (2009), paragraph 11, quoting Fieseler, 'The Bitter Legacy of the "Great Patriotic War"', 54. See also Dadabaev, *Identity and Memory*, 66; Imankulov, *Istoriia Kyrgyzstana*, 235; and Kesler, *Grit* , 541, 641 and 877.

35 Saktaganova, 'Alma-Ata v gody Velikoi Otechestvennoi voiny', 168; and Saktaganova, 'Povsednevnye problem evakogospitalei', 188.

36 Grinberg, *Evrei v Alma-Ate*, 93.

37 Abylkhozhin, *Istoriia Kazakhstana*, 518; Phillips, '"There Are No Invalids in the USSR!"'; G. D. Salyk, 'Arkhivnye dokumenty Akmolinskogo regiona ob evakuatsii i bezhentsakh', in *Istoriia. Pamiat'. Liudi: Materialy VIII Mezhdunarodnoi nauchno-prakticheskoi konferentsii 16 sentiabria 2016 g.*, eds M. S. Makarova, et al., 216–20 (Almaty: 2017), 219; and Elena Zubkova,

Russia after the War: Hopes, Illusions, and Disappointments, 1945–1957, ed. and trans. Hugh Ragsdale (Armonk and London: M. E. Sharpe, 1998), 24.

38 Esenaliev, *Zhenishke dank*, 94–5.

39 Mambetakunova, 'Sbor dannykh po voennym gospitaliam'.

40 IKSA:146/1/38/226–7; Abylkhozhin, *Istoriia Kazakhstana*, 518; Kaptagaev, et al., *Sbornik*, 12; Kerimbaev, *Sovetskii Kirgizstan v Velikoi Otechestvennoi voine*, 174–5; and Zubkova, *Russia after the War*, 24.

41 IKSA:146/2/5/8; Phillips, '"There Are No Invalids in the USSR!"'; Beate Fieseler, '"La protection sociale totale": Les hospices pour grands mutilés de guerre dans L'Union soviétique des années 1940', *Cahiers du Monde russe* 49 (2009): 419–40, paragraphs 5, 6 and 15; and Zubkova, *Russia after the War*, 24.

42 'Zabota ob invalidakh Otechestvennoi voiny', *IKP*, 23 February 1944, 2; Fieseler, '"La protection sociale totale"', paragraph 30; Phillips, '"There Are No Invalids in the USSR!"'; and Kaptagaev, et al., *Sbornik*, 135.

43 IKSA:146/2/20/13.

44 Interview with the veteran's great-grandaughter, 1 May 2018. See also Phillips, '"There Are No Invalids in the USSR!"'; and Zubkova, *Russia after the War*, 24.

45 'Zabota ob invalidakh Otechestvennoi voiny'; 'Kursy dlia invalidov Otechestvennoi voiny', *IKP*, 22 June 1944, 2; and *IKP*, 13 September 1945. See also Hisayo Katsui, 'The Challenges of Operationalizing a Human Rights Approach to Disability in Central Asia', in *Disability in Eastern Europe and the Former Soviet Union: History, Policy and Everyday Life*, eds Michael Rasell and Elena Iarskaia-Smirnova, 204–25 (Oxford and New York: Routledge, 2014), 205; Phillips, '"There Are No Invalids in the USSR!"'; Abylkhozhin, *Istoriia Kazakhstana*, 518; Kaptagaev, et al., *Sbornik*, 135 and 155–6; Kerimbaev, *Sovetskii Kirgizstan v Velikoi Otechestvennoi voine*, 194; and Zubkova, *Russia after the War*, 24.

46 Fieseler, '"La protection sociale totale"', paragraphs 11, 18–21, 23, 25–7 and 30; Hisayo Katsui, 'The Challenges of Operationalizing a Human Rights Approach to Disability in Central Asia', 205; and Phillips, '"There Are No Invalids in the USSR!"'.

47 A samovar is a large, traditional Russian urn used to make tea. See also Fieseler, '"La protection sociale totale"', paragraphs 2–3 and 31; Hisayo Katsui, 'The Challenges of Operationalizing a Human Rights Approach to Disability in Central Asia', 205; Phillips, '"There Are No Invalids in the USSR!"'; and Zubkova, *Russia after the War*, 24.

48 Applebaum, *Gulag*, 376; and Florin, *Kirgistan und die sowjetische Moderne*, 44, note 132.

49 Oral history recounted by Klara's daughter, 6 June 2018.

50 Interview with Dr Alymnugov.

51 Tranum, *Life at the Edge of the Empire*, 130.

52   For example, 'Khleb nuzhen frontu', *IKP*, 10 December 1943, 2; Guljanat
     Kurmangaliyeva Ercilasun, 'Famine in Kyrgyzstan in the 1930s and 1940s', in
     *Kazakhstan, Kyrgyzstan and Uzbekistan: Life and Politics during the Soviet
     Era*, eds Timur Dadabaev and Hisad Koatsu, 39–51 (New York: Palgrave
     Macmillan, 2017), 39 and 45; Grinberg, *Evrei v Alma-Ate*, 87; and Tranum,
     Life at the Edge of the Empire, 134.

53   Roberts, 'A Time for Feasting?' 3.

54   Ercilasun, 'Famine in Kyrgyzstan in the 1930s and 1940s', 42; and
     Imankulov, *Istoriia Kyrgyzstana*, 119.

55   See particularly Goldman and Filtzer, *Fortress Dark and Stern*, 96.

56   Barber and Harrison, *The Soviet Home Front*, 83–4 and 169; Dadabaev,
     Identity and Memory, 73; Florin, *Kirgistan und die sowjetische Moderne*, 45;
     Imankulov, *Istoriia Kyrgyzstana*, 117–18; Manley, *To the Tashkent Station*,
     170 and 189; Stronski, *Tashkent*, 130; and Tranum, *Life at the Edge of the
     Empire*, 134.

57   Imankulov, *Istoriia Kyrgyzstana*, 118; and Kerimbaev, *Sovetskii Kirgizstan v
     Velikoi Otechestvennoi voine*, 102.

58   Tranum, *Life at the Edge of the Empire*, 101, 134 and 155; Barber and
     Harrison, *The Soviet Home Front*, 81; Dadabaev, *Identity and Memory*, 74;
     and Kesler, *Grit*, 933.

59   'Raskhititelei – v tiur'my', *IKP*, 11 March 1943, 2; Barber and Harrison,
     The Soviet Home Front, 89–90; Dadabaev, *Identity and Memory*, 74;
     Grinberg, *Evrei v Alma-Ate*, 139–41; Kesler, *Grit*, 585 and 596; Manley, *To
     the Tashkent Station*, 166–7; Peck, *What My Parents Told Me*, 38; Stronski,
     Tashkent, 124 and 130; and Tranum, *Life at the Edge of the Empire*, 127–8
     and 156.

60   Tranum, *Life at the Edge of the Empire*, 20, 69, 88, 110 and 146; Dadabaev,
     Identity and Memory, 74–5; Ercilasun, 'Famine in Kyrgyzstan in the 1930s
     and 1940s', 42 and 46; Kesler, *Grit*, 585; Peck, *What My Parents Told Me*,
     36; and Stronski, *Tashkent*, 130, 135 and 168.

61   Peck, *What My Parents Told Me*, 35 and 121; and Tranum, *Life at the Edge
     of the Empire*, 127–8.

62   Tranum, *Life at the Edge of the Empire*, 20, 145–6, 152, 155, 200, 217 and
     223; Dadabaev, *Identity and Memory*, 75; Ercilasun, 'Famine in Kyrgyzstan
     in the 1930s and 1940s', 43–4; and Peck, *What My Parents Told Me*, 36.

63   Peck, *What My Parents Told Me*, 98 and 100.

64   Tranum, *Life at the Edge of the Empire*, 20–1, 110 and 146; Ercilasun,
     'Famine in Kyrgyzstan in the 1930s and 1940s', 43–4; Carmack, *Kazakhstan
     in World War II*, 69, 70 and 72; Applebaum, *Gulag*, 376; Barber and
     Harrison, *The Soviet Home Front*, 89; Florin, 'Becoming Soviet through War',
     495 and 500; Kaptagaev, et al., *Sbornik*, 27; Peck, *What My Parents Told Me*,
     101; and Tranum, *Life at the Edge of the Empire*, 20.

65   Ercilasun, 'Famine in Kyrgyzstan in the 1930s and 1940s', 46–7; and
     Carmack, *Kazakhstan in World War II*, 71.

66 Stronski, *Tashkent*, 5–6, 8, 48, 59, 62, 74 and 98; and Kaptagaev, et al., *Sbornik*, 13.

67 IKSA:119/1/22/304; IKSA:119/1/126/26; IKSA:146/2/5/277; *IKP*, 5 July 1944; and Braithwaite, *Moscow 1941*, 107.

68 'Gotoviatsia k sanitarnoi oborone', *IKP*, 20 August 1941, 4.

69 Ibid.; 'Podgotovka medsester', *IKP*, 4 January 1942, 4; and Kesler, *Grit*, 630, 641 and 651.

70 Keller, *Russia and Central Asia*, 197.

71 'Gotovit' vrachei-kirgizov', *IKP*, 27 June 1943, 2.

72 *IKP*, 25 January 1945; and Kaptagaev, et al., *Sbornik*, 144.

73 Tranum, *Life at the Edge of the Empire*, 110 and 145–6; Applebaum, *Gulag*, 376; Barber and Harrison, *The Soviet Home Front*, 87–8; Carmack, *Kazakhstan in World War II*, 71; Florin, *Kirgistan und die sowjetische Moderne*, 45; Kerimbaev, *Sovetskii Kirgizstan v Velikoi Otechestvennoi voine*, 174–5; Kesler, *Shards of War*, 2029; Manley, *To the Tashkent Station*, 192; and Stronski, *Tashkent*, 63 and 84.

74 Barber and Harrison, *The Soviet Home Front*, 88; Kaptagaev, et al., *Sbornik*, 14; Goldman and Filtzer, *Fortress Dark and Stern*, 70–4; Kesler, *Grit*, 782 and 837; Manley, *To the Tashkent Station*, 165; Peck, *What My Parents Told Me*, 32 and 102; Stronski, *Tashkent*, 63 and 126; and Tranum, *Life at the Edge of the Empire*, 110.

75 *IKP*, 22 April 1942, 4; 'Gosudarstvennaia pomoshch' materi i rebenku', *IKP*, 18 November 1944, 1; Barber and Harrison, *The Soviet Home Front*, 88; Kerimbaev, *Sovetskii Kirgizstan v Velikoi Otechestvennoi voine*, 172; and Stronski, *Tashkent*, 63–4 and 130.

76 IKSA:279/1/145/103–4.

77 'O bor'be s letnimi detskimi ponosami', *IKP*, 12 August 1944, 2; and 'Sypnoi tif i bor'ba s nim', *IKP*, 10 February 1945, 3.

78 'Kogda zhe budet mylo?' *IKP*, 19 August 1943, 2; Manley, *To the Tashkent Station*, 192; and Tranum, *Life at the Edge of the Empire*, 110.

79 'Meditsinskoe obsluzhivanie na poliakh', *IKP*, 15 April 1943, 1; 'O meropriiatiiakh po sanitarnomy blagoustroistvu g. Przheval'ska', *IKP*, 3 March 1944, 2; Barber and Harrison, *The Soviet Home Front*, 88; Kaptagaev, et al., *Sbornik*, 13; and Stronski, *Tashkent*, 75.

80 Barber and Harrison, *The Soviet Home Front*, 88; Kaptagaev, et al., *Sbornik*, 13; and Kerimbaev, *Sovetskii Kirgizstan v Velikoi Otechestvennoi voine*, 162.

81 Goldman and Filtzer, *Fortress Dark and Stern*, 100 and 117–18.

82 'Usilit' sbor lekarstvennykh trav', *IKP*, 23 August 1942, 2; 'Shkol'niki sobiraiut lekarstvennye travy', *IKP*, 1 July 1944, 2; 'Novye sredstva lecheniia', *IKP*, 26 December 1944, 2; and Kaptagaev, et al., *Sbornik*, 11.

83 Stronski, *Tashkent*, 138; and Tranum, *Life at the Edge of the Empire*, 120, 122 and 200.

84 Tranum, *Life at the Edge of the Empire*, 120 and 122.

85   Ibid., 116; and testimony of Asel Imankulova.

86   'Odezhda i obuv' dlia shkol'nikov', *IKP*, 14 October 1943, 2; Tranum, *Life at the Edge of the Empire*, 88, 148 and 201; and Kesler, *Grit*, 498.

87   Tranum, *Life at the Edge of the Empire*, 74, 88 and 163; Kerimbaev, *Sovetskii Kirgizstan v Velikoi Otechestvennoi voine*, 97, 108 and 113; and Barber and Harrison, *The Soviet Home Front*, 97.

88   'Tiupskaia molodezh v dni otechestvennoi voiny', *IKP*, 5 September 1941, 3; 'Gorodskie shkol'niki na poliakh kolkhozov', *IKP*, 5 July 1942, 1; 'Itogi uchebnogo goda i zadachi v letnii period', *IKP*, 5 July 1942, 2; and 'Shkol'niki vyshli na polia', *IKP*, 10 June 1943, 2. See also Kerimbaev, *Sovetskii Kirgizstan v Velikoi Otechestvennoi voine*, 107; Stronski, *Tashkent*, 81; and Tranum, *Life at the Edge of the Empire*, 19 and 122.

89   Tranum, *Life at the Edge of the Empire*, 19.

90   IKSA:279/1/109/12 and 34; 'Komsomol'tsy Issyk-Kulia v dni voiny', *IKP*, 29 October 1943, 1; and Kerimbaev, *Sovetskii Kirgizstan v Velikoi Otechestvennoi voine*, 47.

91   'V fond pomoshchi detiam frontovikov', *IKP*, 5 September 1944, 2; 'Komsomol'tsy Przheval'ska vyekhali v Stalingrad', *IKP*, 16 August 1943, 2; and 'Komsomol'tsy Issyk-Kulia v dni voiny'.

92   Kratkii kurs istorii VKP(B).

93   'Molodye kolkhozniki', *IKP*, 26 November 1941, 2; 'Shkol'niki na vstrechu vesne', *IKP*, 23 February 1943, 4; 'Komsomol'tsy Issyk-Kulia v dni voiny'; 'Komsomol'tsy, molodezh'!', *IKP*, 7 July 1944, 2; 'Shkol'niki na kolkhoznykh poliakh', *IKP*, 16 August 1944, 2; 'Lektorii dlia molodezhi', *IKP*, 15 June 1945, 1; and 'Gorodskie shkol'niki na poliakh kolkhozov'.

94   'Tiupskaia molodezh v dni otechestvennoi voiny', *IKP*, 5 September 1941, 3; 'Shkol'niki – frontu', *IKP*, 1 April 1942, 4; 'Pomoshch' roditelei shkole', *IKP*, 27 May 1943, 2; *IKP*, 16 September 1943, 2; 'Komsomol'tsy odnogo kolkhoza', *IKP*, 3 October 1943, 2; 'V fond pomoshchi detiam frontovikov', *IKP*, 5 September 1944, 2; and Kaptagaev, et al., *Sbornik*, 126 and 132.

95   A. P. Gaidar, *Timur i ego komanda* (Moscow: ROSMEN, 2017), 3, 24, 30 and 103.

96   Kerimbaev, *Sovetskii Kirgizstan v Velikoi Otechestvennoi voine*, 193.

97   'Sovetskie deti–frontu', *IKP*, 12 November 1941, 4.

98   Mark Dickens, *Soviet Language Policy in Central Asia* (Self-publication, 1988), 2–4.

99   İğmen, *Speaking Soviet with an Accent*, 25 and 30; and Keller, *Russia and Central Asia*, 195–7.

100 Florin, *Kirgistan und die sowjetische Moderne*, 39; Hosking, *Russia and the Russians*, 432; İğmen, *Speaking Soviet with an Accent*, 23; Keller, *Russia and Central Asia*, 14; and Lilley, *Have the Mountains Fallen?*, 22, 28 and 34.

101 Information from Prof. Tchoraev. See also Dickens, *Soviet Language Policy in Central Asia*, 10.

102 Florin, *Kirgistan und die sowjetische Moderne*, 35; and Kerimbaev, *Sovetskii Kirgizstan v Velikoi Otechestvennoi voine*, 27.

103 Dickens, *Soviet Language Policy in Central Asia*, 6.

104 Information from Prof. Tchoraev. See also Dickens, *Soviet Language Policy in Central Asia*, 8–12.

105 'Boevye zadachi sovetskoi shkoly', *IKP*, 31 August 1941, 4; and IKSA:279/1/80/overview.

106 'V pomoshch' materiam kolkhoznitsam', *IKP*, 28 July 1944, 2; 'Dva detskikh sada', *IKP*, 21 September 1944, 2; 'Gosudarstvennaia pomoshch' materi i rebenku', *IKP*, 18 November 1944, 1; and 'Otkryt kolkhoznyi detskii sad', *IKP*, 13 June 1945, 1. See also IKSA:279/overview/2–3; Kerimbaev, *Sovetskii Kirgizstan v Velikoi Otechestvennoi voine*, 96 and 193; Kesler, *Grit*, 738; and Stronski, *Tashkent*, 91.

107 Florin, *Kirgistan und die sowjetische Moderne*, 35; and Tranum, *Life at the Edge of the Empire*, 126.

108 IKSA:279/1/145/35; Goldman and Filtzer, *Fortress Dark and Stern*, 269; and Kerimbaev, *Sovetskii Kirgizstan v Velikoi Otechestvennoi voine*, 172.

109 IKSA:279/overview/2–3; Abylkhozhin, *Istoriia Kazakhstana*, 519; Dave, *Kazakhstan*, 63; Dickens, *Soviet Language Policy in Central Asia*, 15; Florin, 'Becoming Soviet through War', 501, note 31; Florin, *Kirgistan und die sowjetische Moderne*, 32–3 and 35.

110 IKSA:885/1/4/17; Kerimbaev, *Sovetskii Kirgizstan v Velikoi Otechestvennoi voine*, 172; and Stronski, *Tashkent*, 90–1.

111 IKSA:274/1/6/13; IKSA:279/1/285/8; and IKSA:282/1/3/6.

112 IKSA:204/1/15/2.

113 'Novyi otriad molodykh pedagogov', *IKP*, 17 September 1944, 1; 'Uchitel'skii institut v Przheval'ske', *IKP*, 23 September 1944, 2; IKSA:146/2/13/18–19; IKSA:279/1/145/15; IKSA:279/1/234/26; Kerimbaev, *Sovetskii Kirgizstan v Velikoi Otechestvennoi voine*, 173; and Kozybaev, *Istoriia Kazakhstana*, 129.

114 'V shkolakh przheval'skogo raiona', *IKP*, 20 August 1941, 4; 'Boevye zadachi sovetskoi shkoly', *IKP*, 31 August 1941, 4; 'Shkol'niki – frontu', *IKP*, 1 April 1942, 4; 'Oblastnoe soveshchanie uchitelei', *IKP*, 16 September 1943, 2; IKSA:279/1/100/18; and IKSA:279/1/145/15 and 30. See also Dadabaev, *Identity and Memory*, 76; and Stronski, *Tashkent*, 92.

115 IKSA:279/1/100/12; and IKSA:279/1/145/1–4.

116 'Oblastnoe soveshchanie uchitelei', *IKP*, 16 September 1943, 2; 'Pervyi den'', *IKP*, 3 September 1944, 2; and IKSA:279/1/100/15–16 and 21.

117 IKSA:279/1/100/16 and 22.

118 IKSA:174/2/48/28.

119 'Pervyi den'', *IKP*, 3 September 1944, 2; IKSA:119/1/49/92; and IKSA:204/1/28/1 and 11.

120 IKSA:119/1/49/92; IKSA:274/1/6/3; IKSA:274/1/6/9; IKSA:282/1/3/1–2; and Dadabaev, *Identity and Memory*, 76.

121 'Boevye zadachi sovetskoi shkoly', *IKP*, 31 August 1941, 4; IKSA:274/1/6/15; IKSA:279/1/109/22; IKSA:279/1/100/13 and 68; and IKSA:282/1/3/3–5, 14 and 20.

122 IKSA:274/1/6/1; and IKSA:279/1/145/7.

123 'Boevye zadachi sovetskoi shkoly', *IKP*, 31 August 1941, 4; IKSA: 274/1/6/1; IKSA:279/1/109/12 and 32; IKSA:279/1/145/7; and Abylkhozhin, *Istoriia Kazakhstana*, 519.

124 'Itogi uchebnogo goda i zadachi v letnii period', *IKP*, 5 July 1942; 'Gotovit'sia k novomu uchebnomu godu', *IKP*, 20 June 1943, 1; IKSA:279/1/100/59; and IKSA:279/1/109/4, 26 and 31.

125 'Gotovit'sia k novomu uchebnomu godu', *IKP*, 20 June 1943, 1; and IKSA:279/1/109/4–5.

126 'Oblastnoe soveshchanie uchitelei', *IKP*, 16 September 1943, 2; IKSA:279/1/100/15–18 and 21; IKSA:279/1/109/2–3 and 16; and Kesler, *Grit*, 804.

127 'Na novuiu, vysshuiu stupen' v rabote shkoly', *IKP*, 23 September 1943, 2; 'O rabote Komsomola v shkole', *IKP*, 16 June 1944, 2; IKSA:279/1/100/17–18; and IKSA:279/1/109/7 and 33.

128 IKSA:279/1/100/20 and 24; IKSA:279/1/109/7, 17 and 35; and Tranum, *Life at the Edge of the Empire*, 37. See also Kerimbaev, *Sovetskii Kirgizstan v Velikoi Otechestvennoi voine*, 172.

129 'Uchebnyi god nachalsia', *IKP*, 2 September 1943, 1; 'Vypolnit' zakaz shkoly', *IKP*, 9 September 1943, 2. 'Tetriadi, per'ia, karandashi', *IKP*, 14 October 1943, 2; and Dadabaev, *Identity and Memory*, 77.

130 IKSA:204/1/15/2; IKSA:279/1/109/9–11; IKSA:279/1/145/22; and Kaptagaev, et al., *Sbornik*, 129.

131 IKSA:279/1/45/43 and 121.

132 'Voennaia ucheba v shkolakh', *IKP*, 4 March 1943, 2; 'Fizkul'turniki gotoviatsia k svoemu prazniku', *IKP*, 9 July 1944, 2; and IKSA:279/1/109/10 and 32.

133 IKSA:132/1/8/2.

134 'Voskresnyi den' v Sazanovskoi shkole', *IKP*, 19 October 1941, 4.

135 'Itogi uchebnogo goda i zadachi v letnii period', *IKP*, 5 July 1942; and 'Letniaia voennaia ucheba shkol'nikov', *IKP*, 27 June 1943, 2.

136 'Pionerskie lageri', *IKP*, 17 June 1943, 2; 'Letnii otdykh detei', *IKP*, 4 July 1943, 2; 'Zabota o detiakh frontovikov', *IKP*, 22 July 1943, 2; 'Zabota o detiakh', *IKP*, 12 August 1944, 2; 'Letnii otdykh shkol'nikov', *IKP*, 13 June 1945, 1; and IKSA:279/1/145/219.

137 'Istoriia', *Ministerstvo inostrannykh del Respubliki Uzbekistan*; and Kerimbaev, *Sovetskii Kirgizstan v Velikoi Otechestvennoi voine*, 27.

138 IKSA:279/1/100/23; and Tranum, *Life at the Edge of the Empire*, 114 and 126.

139 IKSA:279/1/80/35–6; and IKSA:279/1/121/3 and 15.

140 IKSA:279/1/121/11–12; IKSA: 279/1/208/1, 17, 18, 21, 44, 45 and 47; and Tranum, *Life at the Edge of the Empire*, 19.

141 IKSA:279/1/100/25; and IKSA:279/1/145/184.

142 IKSA:274/1/6/13; IKSA:279/1/145/126; IKSA:279/1/208/1, 7, 21, 44 and 47; IKSA:279/1/285/8; IKSA:282/1/3/6; and Florin, *Kirgistan und die sowjetische Moderne*, 35.

143 Tranum, *Life at the Edge of the Empire*, 210–11.

6

Propaganda and the culture war

Over the course of a few days early in November 1938, 137 bodies were dumped into a mass grave near the remote village of Chong Tash in the hills above Frunze. Each dispatched by a bullet to the back of the head, these were once the cream of the Kyrgyz intellectual elite who fell victim to Stalin's Great Terror, the purges which claimed the lives of hundreds of writers and experienced Communist Party leaders across Central Asia.[1]

As the process of centralized Sovietization and modernization progressed, Lenin's policy of *korenizatsiia* was increasingly eroded under Stalin, who displayed a cold lack of regard and even fear of the Soviet ethnic minorities during his drive to homogenize the Soviet republics in the interests of building socialism. Through a build-up of arrests in 1937 and 1938, Stalin effectively purged Central Asian society of high numbers of so-called 'class enemies' or 'counter-revolutionaries' – wealthier farmers, members of the intelligentsia and religious clerics, thereby dismantling Lenin's vision of home rule. Thousands of Central Asia's home-grown politicians were killed or imprisoned as 'nationalists', only to be replaced by Moscow's men in a resumption of colonial practices which threatened to alienate the very people whom Moscow wished to bring into the Soviet fold.

Following the disappearance of many political and cultural leaders at the hands of the NKVD, it became an uphill struggle to win over the hearts and minds of the Central Asian republics. With the start of the war, though, the pendulum moved back in the direction of *korenizatsiia*, as the state rapidly came to appreciate that it needed to get the region onside in the fight against the enemy if complete annihilation of the Soviet Union were to be avoided. The official policy changed from one of repression and execution to the embrace and active encouragement of the region's ethnic minorities. The overriding Communist Party line of the 'friendship of the peoples' emphasized the role played by indigenous Central Asians as equals in the struggle against the common enemy. The party recognized their identity as ethnic Kazakhs or Kyrgyz, for example, but also as fully fledged citizens of the Soviet Union, in common with their Slavic brothers. The stark contrast with race-obsessed Nazi Germany was all too evident.[2]

Several of those writers still remaining in the region were conscripted into the Red Army, many as propagandists or war correspondents, while actors and musicians were gathered into troupes performing plays and concerts for the soldiers.[3] This exodus left relatively few of the former cultural intelligentsia based in Central Asia during the war. However, the gap was more than plugged by the waves of evacuees arriving from the western parts of the Soviet Union, notably Moscow and Leningrad. Their presence was so significant that the region became a veritable hub of cultural creativity during the first years of the war, as writers, poets, musicians, artists and cinematographers rubbed shoulders in the cosmopolitan centres of Tashkent, Alma-Ata and Frunze. Harnessing the power of the thriving artistic colonies, the Soviet authorities ensured that literature and the arts were deployed as potent weapons in the fight against the enemy.[4]

As a result of the Terror, the remaining members of the region's intelligentsia became superficially increasingly patriotic – either in self-defence against potential threats from Moscow, or in genuine acknowledgement of the needs of a state in real danger of defeat. Away from the close oversight of Moscow, it occasionally became possible for both indigenous and incoming writers to question the state in small ways, although most remained overtly loyal to the centre, with the majority producing and endorsing the propaganda promulgated by the state to convince the people to play their part in the war against the invader.[5]

Propaganda

The Soviet Union already possessed a robust *agitprop* (agitation and propaganda) network even before the war, intended to further the legitimacy and aims of the Communist Party. At the onset of hostilities propaganda fast became the weapon of choice for the State Defence Committee in its campaign to gain the loyalty and support of the people of Central Asia. Propaganda material took many forms: pamphlets and newspaper articles, talks and lectures from Communist Party leaders, radio programmes, plays and literature. Bombarded with information from Komsomol groups on the farm or factory floor, citizens were exposed to clear, simple explanations of why the Soviet Union needed their support in the war. Black-and-white caricatures were drawn of the virtuous Red Army fighting against the evil fascist occupiers who threatened the very existence of the *Rodina*, the sacred Soviet Motherland. This anti-German narrative was intended to instil fear of the enemy in the population, while evoking a strong desire to fight, either in the armed forces or on the home front. At the same time, citizens of Central Asia were depicted as integral members of the Soviet Union, fighting shoulder to shoulder with their Russian and Ukrainian counterparts.[6]

The appeal to patriotism was rendered as accessible and relevant as possible to ordinary people. Portraying the public as militant and heroic in the mould of their ancestors, the state resorted at first to examples of Russian history and then increasingly to episodes of Central Asian history which were intended to inspire the population in battle in the same way as past heroes. Linking the history of Central Asia with that of Russia – although conveniently omitting details of tsarist military oppression – the state increasingly tailored its propaganda to the five individual republics from the middle of 1942.

The 1916 rebellion across Central Asia against Russian imperial forces during the First World War was invoked, portrayed for the Second World War as the epitome of the struggle of hard-working peasants against the oppressive invader. Similarly, the participation of Central Asians in the Civil War following the 1917 revolution was presented as a 'movement of national liberation', a previous occasion when Central Asians had successfully supported the Bolsheviks in a military struggle.[7]

In this way, history was re-written for the purpose of engaging the republics of Central Asia with the Soviet centre. As the war progressed, even the course of the conflict was distorted and re-interpreted, as defeats were rarely reported and any news from the front was given a positive spin. War correspondents became adept at milking the grim military bulletins for the smallest acts of courage, which were then exaggerated for popular consumption. These heroic exploits were brought to public attention, including the feats of the Panfilov Division and other (usually dead) Central Asian heroes such as Cholponbai Tuleberdiev. By 1943 even the series of defeats during the first months of the war was being portrayed in a more rosy light, while reports which alluded to the less than courageous attitude of the Panfilov Division were strenuously suppressed.[8]

Workers on collective farms and in factories were expected to attend lectures and evening classes to inculcate in them a sense of patriotism. Communist leaders believed that an acquaintance with the ideology behind the Soviet Union's stance in the war would help the citizens of Central Asia to become more productive participants in the war effort in the rear. An obligatory series of classes was established in Przheval'sk in August 1943 to study the published work containing Stalin's speeches and most significant orders during the war. Apparently, members of the twenty-three newly established study groups in the town showed 'a great interest in Comrade Stalin's book about the Great Patriotic War'. Group leaders were usually briefed beforehand by Professor Comrade Eroshenko in an introductory seminar to ensure that the party line was strictly followed. Evidence shows that, while people's sense of patriotism and loyalty to the Soviet Union increased with the unrelenting exposure to such propaganda measures, they unsurprisingly begrudged the time spent at evening lectures and tended to mistrust local Communist Party leaders, while largely failing to understand the intricacies of communist ideology. This tendency increased as the domestic situation became too difficult to sustain any additional demands, but it is probable that the desired message had already been instilled in most citizens of the region, as evidenced by the much publicized anti-fascist rallies held in many cities in February 1943. In contrast, anti-war disturbances were relatively minor, and any rumour mongers, such as those propagating the notion that Turkey was joining the war alongside Germany, were dealt with robustly by the NKVD.[9]

If the drip of news coming into the region from refugees fleeing the Nazi occupiers in the western Soviet Union may often have been despondent, letters from family members on the front line were sufficient in many cases to imbue in those remaining at home a sense of common purpose which was endorsed by the constant flow of propaganda. The most direct influence was through the medium of soldiers returning, often temporarily, from the front line. Local heroes, such as Andrei Titov, were enlisted to speak to collective farms and factories in the Issyk-Kul' province. Although Titov was an ethnic Russian, it was felt necessary for him to address farmers in the Kyrgyz language, the better to motivate them to increase their productivity to help the war effort. Speaking to groups and giving newspaper interviews under the control of the local and military authorities, these new mouthpieces of the state disseminated the official line about the progress of the war.[10]

Of course, only good news was presented in this fashion. Three other Kyrgyz soldiers returned home in the final year of the war on well-earned

FIGURE 6.1 *Andrei Titov. Reproduced with permission from the Issyk-Kul' State Archives.*

leave, to the acclaim of friends, family and local Communist Party leaders, with their stories captured by the press as excellent propaganda material. Tashmamat Jumabaev returned to the Fabrika collective farm in the Issyk-Kul' province in January 1944. Dair Asanov from Naryn, who had taken out several tanks and armoured vehicles outside Khar'kov (Kharkiv) in January 1943, was afforded a hero's welcome on his visit to Przheval'sk in April 1944. Finally, Sergeant Efrem Kurochkin came back to Przheval'sk only in January 1945, having been decorated for allegedly single-handedly killing ten Germans and capturing fifty. Kurochkin had been in the army since he was called up in 1940, surviving the Battle of Stalingrad and the more recent push into East Prussia before he could be spared for a motivational trip back to Kyrgyzstan.[11]

Those soldiers not able to return home on leave were enlisted to endorse letters of encouragement to their home republics. These propaganda messages, meticulously reproduced in the press, were tailored specifically for each individual republic in Central Asia, referring to their national traditions and culture. For example, Cavalry Captain Razuvaev wrote to the Issyk-Kul' provincial authorities in July 1944 to praise one of his men, a certain Sharshe Toktosunov, a Communist Party member from Jeti-Oguz. Serving in the political section of his unit, he was decorated for his bravery in the liberation of Sevastopol'. Following the party line in encouraging ethnic minorities, Captain Razuvaev cited his case as an example of the

FIGURE 6.2 *Efrem Kurochkin. Reproduced with permission from the Issyk-Kul' State Archives.*

'friendship of the peoples', expressing his gratitude to the Kyrgyz people for having raised such a courageous soldier.[12]

Furthermore, a letter to the Kyrgyz people from a Komsomol member wounded on the Dnieper urged his compatriots to fight for the final push, just as they were fighting to get the herds to eat as much as they could before they descended from the mountain pastures in the autumn. It was also necessary to grow the most effective feed for them over the winter months, he reminded them. Adding that they were engaged in a war for their cultural and political traditions, he encouraged them to read Stalin's works so that their work in the rear could support the heroic exploits of their comrades at the front.[13]

Vasilii Lagutin, once a secondary school teacher and secretary of a Komsomol branch, served in the political section of his battalion. His letter, addressed to his motherland from his unit in the Balkans, was also published in the local newspaper *Issyk-Kul'skaia Pravda*. Detailing his battalion's journey across Eastern Europe – from Stalingrad to Ukraine and back via the Black Sea to Romania and Bulgaria – his message of hope for an early victory was intended to keep up the motivation of his countrymen in the rear during the final months of the war.[14]

People remaining in the rear were also encouraged to send letters to their troops at the front, consolidating the connection between front and rear and the unity of all Soviet peoples in the conflict. Letters from home were exploited as propaganda material for the troops, as they were written in their own language and linked the men to the people in the distant homeland for whom they were fighting. 'The People's Instructions' (*Nakaz naroda*) was a series of letters written on a mass scale at the worst stage of the war in 1942, with the aim of retaining the loyalty of ethnic minority troops. Thus workers of the Issyk-Kul' province wrote at the height of the Battle of Stalingrad 'to our young men in the Red Army', urging them to do their utmost in the fight against the common enemy.[15]

There was almost no escape from state-controlled propaganda. The all-embracing message delivered from the centre to the republics of Central Asia represented an attempt to forge and retain the loyalty of the people. As the war progressed citizens became used to the style and terminology of the Soviet propaganda message, especially when presented in a familiar language and idiom. Furthermore, Russian propaganda vocabulary became gradually incorporated into the other languages of Central Asia. Most people became used to considering themselves Soviet citizens and knew precisely against whom they were fighting. However, those living in outlying areas were less exposed to the prevailing narrative. In addition, some found the language and the new Cyrillic script hard to understand, for instance in the Uighur areas of Kazakhstan. The failure of propaganda to reach every corner of the region was exacerbated by the relatively poor level of education and even motivation of those Communist Party members who conducted the ideological campaign. There remained, however, a genuine thirst for any information about the war, which was assuaged to some extent by radio broadcasts and local newspapers.[16]

Mass media

The mass media were a potent weapon in the state's propaganda arsenal. Controlled by *Sovinformbiuro* (the Soviet Information Bureau), media reports were disseminated through the official state news agency, TASS (*Telegrafnoe agentstvo Sovetskogo Soiuza*). Other items underwent a strict censorship process, so that news reaching private citizens often bore little resemblance to the true facts behind the stories. Although many people became adept at reading between the lines of state propaganda, others seemed to accept news reports at face value, optimistically accepting the party line about the progress of the war.[17]

At the start of the war all private radios held by individuals for their personal use were taken by the authorities – ostensibly requisitioned for military purposes, while also removing the means from ordinary citizens to tune in to unofficial or even foreign transmissions. The easiest access to news was to visit the nearest community listening post, where a loudspeaker broadcast programmes relayed from a fixed official radio. It is estimated

FIGURE 6.3 *Listening to news from the front in Kyrgyzstan, 1941. Reproduced with permission from the Issyk-Kul' State Archives.*

that there were around 150,000 of these in Kazakhstan, which enjoyed a greater provision than Kyrgyzstan, where the state only provided a radio post for around one in ten communities. Gathering together in a public space, people would listen to the news, Stalin's official speeches, patriotic music and authorized literary programmes. Broadcasts were often in Russian and at first relatively short although the output increased in the final two years of the war, once there was better news to report. Despite the brevity of the programmes, people came to rely on the radio for news. Evacuees in particular, desperate for updates from the western part of the Soviet Union, crowded around the main listening post in Tashkent. The radio was the people's main means of communication from Moscow and its importance was recognized from 1945 with its own place in the Soviet calendar – Radio Day, 7 May, two days before Victory in Europe was finally announced to the whole Soviet population.[18]

Radio broadcasts were often preferred to newspapers, as bulletins were scheduled daily and remained as up to date as was possible under the prevailing circumstances. The central Moscow papers – including the main government mouthpieces *Pravda* (Truth), *Izvestiia* (News) and *Komsomol'skaia Pravda* (Komsomol Truth) – inevitably suffered delays in transport across the country, such that the news they carried was stale on arrival in Central Asia. The individual republics also had their own press, for example *Pravda Vostoka* (Truth of the East) in Uzbekistan, *Kazakhstanskaia Pravda* (Kazakhstan Truth) and *Sovettik Kyrgyzstan* (Soviet Kyrgyzstan). In addition, papers such as *Issyk-Kul'skaia Pravda* (Issyk-Kul' Truth) disseminated local information to the public. The latter two titles were published both in Russian and in Kyrgyz, rendering them more accessible to literate members of the indigenous community.

Illiterate citizens curious for news had to rely on the help of others who read the articles to them, just as schoolchildren were sometimes enlisted to read letters arriving from the front.[19] Advice to propagandists fulfilling this task required them to read to their audience daily, 'selecting the most important current events' of the day. It was further advised to prepare carefully for the session, practising beforehand in front of a smaller audience of perhaps twenty or thirty people. Appreciating that readings were not always well performed, party officials advised readers to choose only the most obedient and docile people for their audience, who would listen well. These were usually the most 'literate and politically developed' of the community. The propagandist should be prepared not only to read the day's material but also to offer explanations in case the audience failed to understand everything. For this reason, as delegated mediators of news reaching the rear, they were advised to select only the simplest, clearest items, ideally those about work in the rear, which would further motivate the attendees.[20]

Material published during the war was subject to strict examination by the official censor charged with the protection of state secrets and the political tone of any propaganda messages.[21] Ensuring that citizens were told sufficient to satiate their need for information, but not enough to cause serious disquiet or unrest, censors worked with reporters and newspaper editors to produce clear and straightforward narratives which kept both state and subjects relatively content as losses were downplayed while even the smallest of victories was magnified. The population of Central Asia, in common with their compatriots across the Soviet Union, may have suspected that they were not being told the whole truth, but the news disseminated by the mass media was mostly all that they received and any doubt on their part was best left unvoiced.[22]

Works of literature had to be submitted to the scrutiny of Glavlit,[23] the official censor charged with the protection of state secrets. At the beginning of the war broadcasters and newspaper editors were reminded that they had to check out any printed reports before publication with the MPVO (local air defence), a branch of the NKVD. A string of 'mistakes' had led to misleading articles 'alerting the population to the widespread installation of gas-proof chambers in blocks of flats', a proposal which had apparently already been rejected by the time it appeared in print. This type of article in the local press probably caused widespread panic, whereas the report of 11 July 1941 in *Turkmenskaia Pravda* (Turkmenistan Truth) about the need to decontaminate food by the use of bleach was deemed particularly reckless.[24]

Stringent instructions about the maintenance of state secrets were issued and re-issued to newspaper editors, with threats of five or ten years' imprisonment for those flouting the law or publishing classified material.[25] Censors were provided with reams of practice and exemplar material to make sure that they also followed the official guidelines – bizarrely redacted in places as the examples quoted were sometimes deemed too sensitive.[26] Any printed material revealing details which may be of use to the enemy or disloyal citizens was totally censored. Similarly, strategic information about the transport network was absolutely forbidden. The local paper in Alma-Ata was singled out for criticism for printing an article which revealed some details of the railway timetable. Even worse, in the paper *Ontustyk Kazakhstan* (South Kazakhstan), repairs to the railway line were announced, leading to the censure of the censor, who should have billed them merely as 'prophylactic' maintenance. Another local paper from northeast Kazakhstan detailed the huge number of livestock losing their lives in a wild fire. Such negative news was best delayed by a month, according to senior censors, suggesting the cautious wording 'With the start of the dry weather, several herds lost their lives', while avoiding full details of the enormity of the disaster. Similarly, negative news such as the chronic lack of soap was best left out of the public domain – as if people were not already well aware of the shortages.[27]

In Kyrgyzstan, *Issyk-Kul'skaia Pravda* was a relative newcomer to the printed press, having been founded only in 1939. In the first two years of its existence, the front page was devoted to Soviet news – usually a major speech by Stalin or another notable government official. Local news was situated in the centre two pages, while international war news was relegated to the back page. Once the Soviet Union joined the war, however, war news was moved forwards for the first couple of months of the war. As the news from the west became unbearable, very little was published, with much of the front page devoted to provincial reports in the early months of 1942. Very few editions were published in 1942 – either due to the serious shortage of paper, or because the state wished to prevent readers from discovering the true progress of the war and the military failures of the Red Army. Thus no copies of *Issyk-Kul'skaia Pravda* were available from the beginning of January to the end of March 1942, when the paper suddenly became much more locally oriented. Local papers again disappeared in the province from the end of April to the beginning of July; and once more from the end of August to the beginning of November of the same year. Upon their return they shrank to two pages of non-war news, only reverting to four pages on 7 February 1943, immediately after the victory at Stalingrad. It may be fair to conclude, therefore, that the newsprint dried up only when there was bad news to hide from the general population. In addition, however, instructions to editors of local papers show that they were forced to cut the print runs by 10 per cent from 1 March 1943, evidence that a shortage of materials also had a role to play.[28]

The appearance of newspapers was notoriously unreliable. People wishing to read the local news, available in libraries, reading huts or palaces of culture, often found that they appeared even later than the national dailies, if at all. Initially sold at fifteen kopecks per edition, *Issyk-Kul'skaia Pravda* increased in price to forty kopecks in 1943 as paper became more expensive. However, on occasions when the usual four pages were reduced to two, the price was similarly reduced to twenty kopecks. By 1944 it was rare for an individual to be able to purchase a newspaper, as, according to the editor, 'in spite of the large print run of our local papers, it is impossible to satisfy the high demand of the population'. Acknowledging that 'reading the papers has become a most important necessity for millions of Soviet people', the editor recognized that 'papers have to be employed widely by propagandists and party officials to ensure that they are used to their full potential'. Each edition should therefore be available to as wide an audience as possible in reading huts, collective farms and so on. With this in mind, it was proposed that glass display cabinets containing the local paper should be erected across the province at key sites, to enable ease of access by passers-by.[29]

Not all papers, however, were deemed worthy of such showcasing. *Kyzyl-Kunchigish* (Red Sun of the East), the local publication of the Tonsk area in the Issyk-Kul' province, was spectacularly named and shamed. According to *Issyk-Kul'skaia Pravda* its editor, Comrade Orozakunov, did not fulfil his duty at all well, being content to oversee a product of poor technical quality, with many errata and printing mishaps. Furthermore, the paper had little of the required content: not much on the rural economy appeared in its pages in the first half of 1944, which also lacked comments by collective farm chairmen and animal husbandry specialists. Criticized for its dearth of analytical content, it was required to make a rapid improvement. Such minor papers contained very little material about the war apart from its immediate effect on the local community. With this one exception, articles were usually written in a very positive way, however, and many tended to contain good advice for farmers and citizens in general.[30]

All the papers, regional and national, included copious articles on Stalin's stirring speeches and important anniversaries in the history of the Soviet Union. For example, the whole of the edition of *Issyk-Kul'skaia Pravda* of 14 November 1943 was devoted to a lecture delivered by Stalin, while the New Year's Day issue in 1944 boasted a large photo of Stalin on the front page, together with the words of the national anthem of the Soviet Union. Nor was approved history forgotten. November 1942 brought the celebration of the twenty-fifth anniversary of the Russian Revolution of 1917, when papers suddenly re-appeared in the Issyk-Kul' province after an absence of over two months. Articles about the revolution and its ideological significance occupied the local press for almost two weeks, after which the newspaper resumed publication in its minimalist version of just two pages. Indeed, the anniversary provided the opportunity for Stalin to remind all citizens of the continuity of the struggle against oppression.[31] Similarly, on 14 September 1941 the Kazakh daily *Kazakhstanskaia Pravda* published a special edition covering the 1916 rebellion across the region, presenting it in the newly agreed manner as a fight against tsarist colonialism and oppression.[32]

Despite the reality of war on everyday lives, most of the content of local newspapers concerned work and events on the home front. News about the progress of the war was, not surprisingly, sparse during the first few months, as it was not deemed wise to let the Soviet people appreciate the true extent of the enemy advance. Information about the Battle of Moscow, raging throughout the month of October 1941, was slow to reach the public in the distant Issyk-Kul' province, arriving only on 8 November 1941. Even then, the virtually defeated Red Army was presented as being on a liberating mission, quite the opposite of the tragic truth. Even the death of local hero General Panfilov was not reported until 28 November, a full ten days after the actual event.[33] The first widely disseminated stories about the Battle of Moscow of course related to the men of the Panfilov Division, who were said to have given their lives in the defence of the capital and thus provided a heroic spin to the narrative.[34]

Although at the start of the war such articles usually related to Slavic heroes, as the war progressed the feats of soldiers from Central Asia were increasingly reported in *Issyk-Kul'skaia Pravda*. Articles about the exploits of heroes were written by war correspondents in the field who were attached to the political sections of specific units. State-approved authors, poets and writers were usually given an honorary military rank during the war. These special correspondents were under implicit instructions to 'fight with the pen' by covering positive and heroic events while suppressing, diluting or just delaying the dissemination of bad news.[35] While never achieving the status of famous Soviet journalists such as Konstantin Simonov, Vasilii Grossman or Il'ia Erenburg, Central Asian correspondents included Kazakh officer Dmitrii Snegin in their number.[36] Snegin's poem 'Na zapad!' (Westwards!), mythologizing the Battle of Moscow, was published in *Issyk-Kul'skaia Pravda* on 1 May 1943.

Когда-нибудь кто-то расскажет
О битвах за нашу Москву . . .
[. . .]
Гвардейцы – на запад, на запад!
В далеких нас ждут городах.
Там смерти и тления запах,
А счастье – на наших штыках.

Sometime or other someone will recount tales
Of the battles for our Moscow . . .
[. . .]
Guardsmen – westwards, westwards!
They are waiting for us in distant towns.
There is the smell of death and decay
On our bayonets – and even happiness.

Unlike Snegin, not all correspondents who wrote about Central Asians were themselves from the region. Il'ia Erenburg wrote a trilogy of articles in the autumn of 1942 for the Red Army publication *Krasnaia Zvezda*. At the time of the first anniversary of the Panfilov exploit, when the Battle of Stalingrad was well under way, he described in his pieces the exploits of several soldiers from Uzbekistan, Kazakhstan and Kyrgyzstan. Although the press in general and Stalin in particular made few comments about Asian citizens of the Soviet Union,[37] Erenburg's series of articles was particularly well timed to appeal to soldiers who may have been tempted to desert as their loyalty was severely tested under the harsh conditions of winter under fire in Stalingrad. Probably under instructions from Communist Party propagandists to emphasize the 'friendship of the peoples' by highlighting the contribution to the war of troops of ethnic minorities, Erenburg's formulaic articles each cover a ticklist of topics as he invokes various propagandistic tropes in an effort to appeal to the emotions, honour and sense of history of the Uzbek, Kazakh and Kyrgyz people. These obviously deliberately judged pieces tailored to each nationality were designed to be read by political officers to soldiers at the front, who would then pass on the content to families at home.[38]

Each article lists several reasons to fight for the Soviet Union in the Red Army, preaching about solidarity and defence of the homeland. Soviet soldiers are depicted as defending the honour of loved ones at home, who would no doubt be violated if the enemy managed to advance into Central Asia. This thought apparently inspires young Kazakh soldier Oshim Koskabaev to attack and kill a group of Germans, despite his serious wounds. The enemy is portrayed as uncouth and dangerous – the foreign 'Fritzes' with their square heads, the evil child-slayers who needed to be defeated and driven out of the Motherland.

In contrast, Erenburg reminds his readers that Uzbeks possess the 'heart of a lion', according to the national poet Islam Shair, while Kyrgyz 'roar like a lion'. Recounting numerous episodes of bravery, Erenburg illustrates these claims, citing examples to which other Asians could aspire. In his introduction to the piece on Kazakhs, Erenburg imagines the thoughts of a German soldier: 'We had scary soldiers [fighting] against us – no firing could stop them, they ran straight after us. Afterwards I heard that they were Kazakhs.' Here the implication is that the Germans knew that 'Russia' [sic] was a big country, but not that it contained numerous different nationalities. No doubt some of his readers would have been aware of the treatment of ethnic minorities by the Nazis.

In this way, Erenburg underscores the friendship of the peoples, reminding the readers that they have been friends of the Russians since the time of the revolution. Acknowledging that they are fighting for the Russians and Ukrainians of the western Soviet Union, far away from home, he gives numerous examples of Asians who have helped to liberate Russian villages and people, fighting shoulder to shoulder with Russian compatriots. The long-standing friendship of one Kazakh soldier who had met a Russian sailor at the time of the 1917 revolution was apparently rekindled during the war. The Kazakh, by then chair of a collective farm, had allegedly killed twenty-four German soldiers within three weeks of joining the Red Army. According to Erenburg, 'Kazakhs fight alongside Russians. We are heroes together. [. . .] Together we'll rejoice on the first morning of victory.'

Erenburg employs the trope of the comradeship of individual soldiers to illustrate the friendship of the peoples in general. Taking this to extremes, he selects the Uzbek teacher Akhad Akhmedov, a sniper commander, whose name – by coincidence – has the same initials as his Russian friend, the reconnaissance scout Anatolii Asoskov.

Different spheres of battle are mentioned. Kazakh soldier Diagan Kokvalin was a defender of the Russian city of Leningrad, while another Kazakh, a certain Private Torunsabaev, assimilates both Kazakh and Soviet identities, as he defends 'nearby' Kazakhstan from his position on the banks of the River Don. Leading an attack on the enemy, he shouts 'For the Motherland!' in both Russian (*Za Rodinu!*) and Kazakh (*Otan ushin!*). In a similar vein, his Uzbek counterpart cries '*Vatan uchun!*', while defending the common motherland which stretches from the Carpathian mountains in the west to Uzbekistan's Fergana Valley in the east. The Russian forest may be a complete contrast to the Kyrgyz steppe, but Kyrgyz lads still come to the aid of their Russian comrades, while Moscow recognizes the loyalty of their friends.

Rather than invading a different country, the men of Central Asia were depicted as acting sincerely in the defence of their own homeland and their families. Each article contains references to specific people, places and environmental highlights – from crops to the sunny weather – which both distinguished their republics and were worth fighting for. Similarly the Kazakhs are shown to be defending their homeland's cotton and water melon fields from potential German invasion, while Uzbeks from the Fergana Valley live under a starry sky. Uzbek soldier Tashtamirov invokes the rocky cliffs of the Pamir mountains of his homeland to illustrate the strength of his friendship with the Russians, whose besieged city of Leningrad he is defending. In contrast, the Uzbek Fergana Valley is 'as green as paradise', possessing a 'fairy-tale bounty' of apples and vegetables thanks to its hot sun. Similarly, Uzbeks are told they are fighting for the 'gardens of Tashkent', which the Germans must not be allowed to capture.

Loved ones were most definitely worth fighting for, as Erenburg includes both fathers and mothers giving advice to the young men departing for the front, while also mentioning a string of Uzbek female names, potential lovers, who the men have left behind; thus Khanina, Khalime, Liailia, Giul'nar and Saodat were waiting at home for their men to return. The correspondence of one – probably fictional – soldier in the Panfilov Division, nineteen-year-old Sultan Khojikov, demonstrates the loyalty and warm-heartedness of a Kazakh writing to Esfir, the girlfriend he loves. In contrast, 'the beautiful women of sunny Uzbekistan' write to their men to tell them how proud they are of their menfolk, the 'brave sons of Uzbekistan defending their loved ones on the banks of the Volga'.

National bards and heroes from history are also brought into the narratives, as evidence of the continued courage of today's men of Central Asia. Examples of heroic deeds are littered throughout the articles. Ancient Kazakh bards would sing about heroes of old, who are now compared with the twenty-eight men of the Panfilov Division, who succeeded in thwarting the German advance on Moscow. Kyrgyz soldiers are similarly compared with their traditional hero, Manas. According to Erenburg, whether he really lived or not, this immortal hero embodies a representation of the Kyrgyz people.

Erenburg pays a final tribute to the men of Central Asia as he describes their outstanding national characteristics. The Kazakhs may be used to horse-riding across the steppe, but are also adept at crawling, running, navigating mountains and crossing marshes. Uzbeks are both hard-working and friendly; under normal circumstances these 'peaceful' people would never dream of carrying arms, but at this time of danger are fighting alongside other peoples of the motherland to 'defend our life, breath, traditions, dreams and liberty'. Kyrgyz men are 'burnt by the sun of the Kyrgyz steppe', excellent riflemen – calm and level-headed, courageous and loyal as a local '*jigit*' (lad). They are indeed brave warriors who have saved the lives of many Russian girls. In this way the journalist also reminds the Slavic soldiers serving alongside Central Asians that they should be, if not necessarily respected, certainly tolerated as comrades-in-arms.

Summarizing both the reasons for fighting and the 'friendship of the peoples', Erenburg concludes with the example of a famous Central Asian sniper, who went on to kill dozens of enemy troops during his war career. Although Uzbek by nationality, Mamadali Madaminov was born in Kyrgyzstan and served in the Panfilov Rifle Division.

> Every man and child in flowery Uzbekistan knows that, if the Germans fail in their mission, it is because, far away in the west, Russians and Ukrainians, Kazakhs and Tatars are fighting the evil enemy. And every Russian woman in Moscow will thank Mamadali Madaminov for the eighty-four Germans he killed, who are no longer able to slay their Russian children.[39]

It has been noted that the role of soldiers of different nationalities was downplayed in the national press. However, this series of articles by a respected war correspondent in the main military newspaper suggests that this tacit policy was reversed at a crucial period in the Battle of Stalingrad, when it became necessary to clarify and specify the 'friendship of the peoples' to ensure that all ethnic minority troops identified with the Soviet cause. Confirming this interpretation, Tatar poet Akhmed Erikeev published his poem, 'Druzhba' (Friendship) in 1942. The friends are 'two Soviet riflemen' – Akhmed, a Tatar, and Stepan, a Russian – who fall into the hands of the enemy. Despite the attempts of a German officer to get Akhmed to denounce Stepan, noting that 'he is your and my enemy', Akhmed remembers that 'Lenin was also a Russian' and retorts that his only enemy is their captor. After the Germans have shot 'the two Soviet heroes', their officer realizes that he may have killed Soviet prisoners, 'but he could not kill their honour or their friendship'. The same trope was repeated in the poems 'The Threesome' by the Kyrgyz poet Temirkul Umetaliev, about Azerbaijani, Kyrgyz and Russian comrades-in-arms going into battle together; and in Joomart Bokonbaev's 'Druzhba – vershina schast'ia' (Friendship, the height of happiness). However, despite the relative liberty of writers during the war to express the official state policy of the 'friendship of the peoples' when it was necessary at the time of most danger to the state, the situation was reversed across the board shortly after the war, as the ideology of the one Soviet people took hold.[40]

Literature

Throughout the Soviet period the state kept a careful watch over the literature available in shops and libraries, publishing lists of approved and non-approved books. During the war the authorities distributed details of novels and plays to be removed from circulation, while endorsing those deemed fit for consumption under communist rule. These included the classic poets Lermontov, Pushkin and Tiutchev, and even novels in translation by John Galsworthy and Jack London, which seemed to fit the state's requirements for literature. Poets from Burns and Byron (lauded by Lermontov and Pushkin) to Kipling were given shelf space amongst authors such as William Shakespeare, Jonathan Swift and Walter Scott.[41]

Many works were not approved for inclusion in Soviet libraries and bookshops, however. Books in foreign languages were particularly suspect and amongst those which were carefully inspected at regular intervals by the censor to ensure that their contents were in harmony with the state's demands for literature containing no anti-Soviet or anti-communist matter. Books in German were particularly targeted, especially those published since 1933. While technical literature dating from before 1933 was permitted, any German books appearing under the 'fascist regime' were liable to be destroyed on the spot. These stringent rules meant that the shelves of libraries, reading huts and the few bookshops were relatively thinly stocked, although apparently one village library in the Issyk-Kul' province boasted 3,000 books, of which 300 were on loan at any one time. Probably wishing to portray the local Kyrgyz readers as cultured Soviet citizens, *Issyk-Kul'skaia Pravda* points out that Pushkin and Turgenev were the most widely read authors – in Russian, of course.[42]

Not only fiction proved popular. Works by British physicist Isaac Newton and economist Adam Smith remained on the shelves, while the first Russian–Kyrgyz dictionary was published in 1944, listing 40,000 words. A new textbook, *The History of the Kazakh Soviet Socialist Republic*, appeared in 1943 after a collaborative propaganda exercise between Moscow and Kazakhstan. At first it was highly praised, ticking all the *agitprop* boxes and portraying Kazakh men as brave as warriors of the past, in an effort to persuade them to join the Red Army and increase productivity on the home front. However, 'mistakes' soon emerged, as the book was judged to be anti-Soviet and the whole print run destroyed. The main author, Ermukhan Bekmakhanov, was ruled to be an enemy of the people and sentenced to twenty-five years, as the rest of the authorial team was instructed to re-write the whole volume, which had apparently failed to do justice to Russia's imperial past while over-emphasizing its colonial expansion.[43]

As the state's attempts at inclusivity began to take hold in 1942, Central Asian myths of the past were dusted off and assimilated for Soviet wartime use, promoting national identity within Soviet guidelines. Academic research on the collection and collation of different versions of the *Manas* epic resumed, including a new publication, after it had been banned from 1937 to 1941 at the time of the purges alongside much traditional regional literature. As well as the ancient warrior Manas, classical Kyrgyz and Kazakh bardic poetry revived other heroes of old, who became once again central to the region's literature. Similarly the Tajik intellectual Sadriddin Aini, part of the Soviet establishment in Stalinabad, invoked the eighth-century religious leader Al-Muqanna in a parallel with contemporary military heroes, while also comparing Hitler with Genghis Khan, the infamous invader of old.[44]

The main task of the writers of Central Asia, however, was to toe the party line by invoking contemporary heroism at the front and in the rear, in order to encourage loyalty and Soviet identity amongst the population. Literature was seen by the state as a valuable weapon in the war effort, situated squarely on the defence line. Most of the writers remaining in the region, who had to be authorized members of their republic's writers' union, tacitly agreed to produce the formulaic material demanded by the state. The output of novels, plays and poetry was prolific, although Kyrgyz writers were berated for the lack of material produced for young people during the war. As evacuated Russian intellectuals began to stream into the region from western occupied areas, there was no shortage of people to translate Asian texts into Russian for wider consumption across the Soviet Union.[45]

Many of the approved Soviet authors won prizes and awards for their wartime works, as long as they met the state's aims for writers. Published works which had passed the censor often had a war theme, such as *The Taking of Berlin* by Vsevolod Ivanov, a Central Asian war correspondent for *Izvestiia*, and *Soldat iz Kazakhstana* (The Soldier from Kazakhstan) by Gabit Musrepov. Other Kazakh prose treated coming of age and the advent of communist consciousness, including the autobiographical novel *Shkola zhizni* (The School of Life) by Sabit Mukanov. *Put' Abaia* (Abai's Journey) by Mukhtar Auezov was the first of four volumes fictionalizing the life of the famous Kazakh poet, Abai Kunanbaev, detailing life on the Kazakh steppe at the end of the nineteenth century. Aleksei Tolstoi, the famous Soviet author, was evacuated to Uzbekistan, where he wrote his powerful historical play about Ivan the Terrible. Although banned in Moscow, the work was read privately to fellow-writers in the literary salons of Tashkent. The capital of Uzbekistan may have been thousands of kilometres from Moscow, but censorship still managed to reach the relatively isolated intellectual society which gathered there.[46]

Lengthy Russian prose was difficult for the ordinary people of the region to digest, especially during wartime. Poetry, in contrast, offered more immediate satisfaction than novels or non-fiction, tugging at the heartstrings and stirring emotion in a manner which appealed both to the propagandists and the reader or listener in equal measure. Central Asia boasted a heritage of nationalistic bardic song and poetry, in which oral performers often accompanied themselves on the *dombra*, a traditional type of lute. This tradition was discouraged under Soviet rule, although permitted to re-emerge during the war, when the heroes of old were once again invoked as a testament to the courage of those conscripted into the Red Army. Although themes recalling Russian colonial oppression were largely discouraged, some Kyrgyz poetry exceptionally managed to escape the censor.[47]

The Kyrgyz poet Kubanychbek Malikov wrote about the soldier Kurban Durdy, who was made the first Turkmen Hero of the Soviet Union in November 1941. Delineating his ancestral line in a manner typical of the region, Malikov depicts the protagonist of his poem 'Kurban Durdy' (1942) recalling the empty sands and rushing rivers of his homeland. Malikov's work not only covers the attributes of the hero, but also those of the poet himself, styling himself as a Central Asian *akyn* (bard), while describing the hero in a traditional manner in order to appeal to a popular audience:

> And poets, the people's friends,
> Sing about the heroes
> Praising their souls and wisdom
> Praising their military prowess![48]

Most poetry of the period was written in the native language and occasionally translated into Russian, but some – usually Kazakh – poets wrote in Russian for a wider audience. Dmitrii Snegin, for example, translated the Kazakh poem 'Sary-Arka' (1943) by Kasym Amanzholov, which appeals to the young man's emotions as he leaves his homeland for war. Just as Malikov describes the geographical attributes of Turkmenistan, so Amanzholov extols the 'golden meadows', steppe, mountains and rivers of Kazakhstan, as the poem's newly conscripted soldier swears never to forget the skies of his native land. 'My country! I am your son for ever.' 'Adieu, my native Kazakhstan! But I will return, I shall return.' In a similar vein, Kyrgyz war correspondent Joomart Bokonbaev wrote in his poetic letter to his girlfriend from the front 'Liubimoi s fronta' (To my loved one from the front) of the happy life he has left behind. 'Will I forget how bright life was?' Encouraging compatriots to join up, Bokonbaev's soldier notes that, although he misses his girlfriend, he knows that she is proud of him: 'Hold your head high, my friend, and be proud that your loved one is at war.' Giving a reason for young men to fight – for their homeland or their women – these poems epitomize the propaganda aims of the Soviet Union.[49]

Further reasons for Kyrgyz men to go to war for the Soviet Union were advanced by Aaly Tokombaev in his poem 'The Blessing' (1944). As chair of the Kyrgyz Writers' Union, Tokombaev was conscious throughout the war of the demands and concerns of Soviet propagandists in Central Asia. Acknowledging that new conscripts may be frightened for their future, the poet reminds them: 'Do not be afraid of death! Everybody dies.' Death is advanced as a better fate than potential slavery under the enemy:

> Do not become a slave!
> Die for truth and freedom
> For your people, my son.

And finally, appealing to the Kyrgyz sense of chivalry:

If it is necessary, boldly sacrifice your life
In the name of truth, gallantry and honour.[50]

The moral superiority of the people of the region is expressed in the popular poem 'Leningradtsy, deti moi!' (Citizens of Leningrad, my children) (September 1941) by Kazakh bard Jambul Jabaev. In this work, the reason advanced for Central Asian men to go to war is to help the besieged citizens of Leningrad. Once again the poet proclaims his own status as a senior folkloric bard: he was well into his nineties when the poem was written. Going over some of the recent history of Leningrad, Jabaev recalls the city's politician Sergei Kirov, who had visited Kazakhstan before his unexplained death in 1934. According to the poet, ongoing links rendered the citizens of Leningrad as close to the country as brothers and sisters. For this reason, the people of Kazakhstan are ready to send their soldiers to die for Leningrad, sending quantities of aid: 'Rivers of oil flowed to you, Black coal, red honey.' In this way, Jabaev reverses the Russo-centric rhetoric in which the people of Central Asia are seen as primitive and child-like, needing to be civilized by the centre. Here, it is the people of Leningrad who are addressed as children, needing help from their compatriots in the east, who freely give the produce of their land and the lives of their own children. Powerful propaganda, indeed![51] Wartime children were also the topic of the well-known Uzbek poet G'afur G'ulom, who recorded in verse the case of the Uzbek family which adopted fourteen evacuated children of various nationalities. 'You are not an orphan' was translated into Russian for a wider audience by poet Anna Akhmatova, herself evacuated to Tashkent from Leningrad in the autumn of 1941.[52]

Literature in Uzbekistan during the war was dominated by western writers often gathering unofficially around the Akhmatova household.[53] Suffering a degree of censorship, Akhmatova still managed to publish some of her work, as long as it was overtly patriotic. Her short poem 'Muzhestvo' (Courage), symbolically written on 23 February 1942, the Soviet anniversary of the foundation of the Red Army in 1918, falls into this category. Lauding the bravery of the Soviet Red Army, it was published in *Pravda* two weeks later on 8 March, International Women's Day. There is a poetic twist, however. This short work not only speaks of the courage of the troops defending (specifically) Russia, but also the right to express oneself in Russian, a language implicitly in danger of being extinguished by the advancing enemy.

We shall preserve you, Russian speech,
The great Russian word,
We shall carry you forward, free and pure,
And pass you on to our grandchildren, and save them from captivity.
Forever!

Here, surely, is a swipe at the Soviet censor, who, Akhmatova seems to imply, forbids many types of self-expression, also endangering free speech just as obviously as the invaders from the west. These heartfelt lines must even represent the poet's longing to return to her Leningrad home, where she would be surrounded by only the Russian language, rather than the confusing and loud multilingual babble in the streets and markets of cosmopolitan Tashkent.[54]

Pleasing the censor in a similar vein, Akhmatova's poem 'Pobediteliam' (To the victors) (rather prematurely written in 1943) lists the Russian soldiers – with their diminutive, familiar names – at war to save the country, people's 'grandsons, younger brothers, sons'. 'Pobeda' (Victory) (commenced in 1942 in Tashkent and finished in 1945), however, clearly acknowledges the pain of the anticipated victory, as women lift high their remaining children, 'saved from the thousands of thousands of deaths' to greet the long-awaited return of their sailor husbands.[55] While this poem clearly reflects the poet's love for her maritime Russian home, her other wartime works offer a closer – if less politically correct – insight into Akhmatova's exile in Central Asia.[56]

The performing arts

The literary soirées in wartime Tashkent continued to offer recitals of unofficial new plays to the intelligentsia, while the public were able to attend performances at the theatres and opera houses of Central Asia. Concerts were even offered closer to home on the collective farm or at the local MTS station. Several dramatic and operatic companies were evacuated to the region, being encouraged to continue performing for a new audience.[57] For this reason, Russian theatre dominated advertising posters and newspaper reviews, appealing to a cultured audience during the winter season.

A snapshot of cultural life in Kyrgyzstan indicates a variety of old and new dramatic works – a mixture of classical and modern Soviet plays. For example, the new Kyrgyz theatrical company in Frunze performed translations of Shakespeare's *King Lear* and *Twelfth Night*, while also offering Konstantin Simonov's contemporary play, *Russkie liudi* (Russian People), a staple across the region as soon as it appeared in 1942.[58] Even in distant Przheval'sk the theatre was full, as audiences had little choice but to appreciate one of the rare types of wartime entertainment. Relatively well known classics such as Maksim Gork'ii's *Poslednie* (The Last Ones) and Ostrovskii's *Pridannitsa* (Without a Dowry) were complemented by more recent works written to please the wartime propagandists. Aleksandr Afinogenov's *Mashen'ka* taught the audience the best way to bring up a teenager, showing the increasing child-awareness of old academic Okaemov as he takes in his granddaughter Mashen'ka. Criticized by the newspaper reviewer as a little too emotional and melodramatic, the play addressed 'every person's second profession' as a parent, as the war took its toll on family life. In contrast, the popular play *Chrezvychainyi zakon* (The Exceptional Law) by Lev Sheinin and the Tur brothers satirized the concept of a strained wartime marriage.[59]

Just as in other areas of Central Asia, the local population was able to take advantage of the presence of evacuees, with Ukraine's modest Donetsk Theatre Company also able to entertain the people of the Issyk-Kul' province. On a wider scale, twenty-three theatre companies were evacuated to Kazakhstan. In Uzbekistan, the Moscow Jewish State Theatre found a new lease of life in Tashkent, where its famous director, Solomon Mikhoels, developed a truly international enterprise through his Yiddish plays. Thus the people of Tashkent attended the performance of *Tevya the Milkman* – later reincarnated as *Fiddler on the Roof* for the Western stage – while also enjoying plays which reflected the life of wartime Uzbekistan and its people.[60]

Non-Russian speakers were also catered for, if to a lesser extent. Mikhoels collaborated with the Uzbek writer Khamid Almijan on a production of his play *Mukanna* about the Central Asian hero. The *Manas* theme played an increasingly important role in Kyrgyz wartime dramatic productions, while Aaly Tokombaev's work *The Oath* once again ticked all the boxes required by the Soviet censor, depicting 'the best sons of the Kyrgyz people', courageously fighting at the front shoulder to shoulder with their Russian comrades. Indeed, Tokombaev wrote prolifically for the theatre during the war, relishing his position as Kyrgyzstan's leading living playwright, while helping to redress the balance of local versus Russian works on the Central Asian stage and furthering a pragmatic friendship of the peoples.[61]

Back in Przheval'sk, cultural items were usually relegated to the last page of the local newspaper, *Issyk-Kul'skaia Pravda*. Exceptionally, the director of the Przheval'sk theatre, Comrade Liubanskii, wrote to the paper to complain about the nature of its drama coverage. He was apparently aggrieved that many plays went without a review; furthermore, he was angry that, even if an article did appear, it more often than not concentrated on the inadequacies of the play rather than its positive aspects. Citing the need for balanced reporting for the cultural benefit of the good citizens of the town, he also bemoaned the plethora of spelling and grammatical mistakes in the paper. This dramatic turn of events was presumably only possible once the area's cultural offerings had taken on more significance in the final year of the war, when people had somewhat fewer other worries and more opportunity to take advantage of entertainment.[62]

Perhaps by then the diet of Soviet propagandist plays had become too repetitive, boring or formulaic for the locals to digest. Concerts of the time were easier to access and probably did a lot more to improve the mood of the population during the long hard years of the war, being more difficult to censor or restrict than plays or the written word. It was not necessary to go to an opera house or even to a local palace of culture to enjoy a concert. Filmed concerts were often available at the cinema, while peripatetic concert brigades were formed across the region. Many members of these groups were also trained as paramedics, so that, in a civil emergency or at the front, they could be flexibly redeployed. Sometimes working with troops on active service, they usually travelled from military or conscription centres in the rear to collective farms and even sanatoria to entertain people with light music. These travelling musical and drama companies often included Central Asian musicians, an *akyn* and players expert on the *komuz*, a stringed instrument.[63]

More popular light music was widely available in concert programmes across the region. The Kyrgyzstan 'Toktogul Satylganov' Philharmonia, for example, included in its repertoire the patriotically themed concerts 'Arts in the service of the front', 'Komuz' and 'For our Great Motherland', while in Przheval'sk the programme for January 1942 included a concert by a Caucasian ensemble. Patriotic music had pride of place, with many stirring instrumental and emotional lyrical works being composed during the war. Kyrgyz *akyn* and *komuz* player Atai Ogonbaev wrote both 'Panfilov, the Hero' and 'Longing', while prolific composer Zhumamudin Sheraliev's song 'The White Wave' contrasted with his rousing march 'Victorious People'. In contrast, Abdylas Maldybaev composed Asian music for the popular Soviet war poem 'Zhdi menia' (Wait for Me) by Konstantin Simonov.[64]

During the winter season, those living in the towns had the opportunity to attend the opera, the ballet or a concert. Tchaikovsky's comic opera *Cherevichki*, based on Nikolai Gogol's play, *The Night before Christmas*, was hugely popular, as was Tchaikovsky's classical work *Eugene Onegin*. The new Kyrgyz operas *Patriots* and *Kekiul* were premiered in 1942, with the ballet *Cholpon* in 1944, whereas in Uzbekistan composer Mukhtar Ashrafi premiered his 'Heroic Symphony (No. 1)' in Tashkent in November 1942, the first Uzbek work for a Western-style orchestra. This was followed in 1944 by his similarly military second symphony 'Glory to the Victors'. Meanwhile, in Kazakhstan, the famous musician Sergei Prokofiev composed his ballet *Cinderella* (Opus 87) during the war years.[65]

Cultural life in Central Asia developed increasingly along Soviet and international lines as evacuated orchestras and opera companies contributed to the artistic scene, for example, the Leningrad conservatoire which was moved to Tashkent for the duration. On a smaller scale, part of the Donetsk Russian Musical Theatre (Donmuzteatr) was evacuated in 1942 from its home in Stalino, Ukraine, to the village of Anan'evo in the Issyk-Kul' province of Kyrgyzstan. Given the considerably reduced company and the lack of space, it proved a challenge to put on any performances. In spite of the lack of soloists and musicians, they managed to entertain the people of the Przheval'sk area with Puccini's *Madame Butterfly* and Offenbach's operetta *Lischen et Fritzchen*, renamed for Soviet audiences *Lizetta i Filidor* (Lizetta and Filidor) with a Russian libretto by V. Timofeev. As they settled down into their new surroundings, their repertoire expanded to include more demanding operas such as *Rigoletto*, *Eugene Onegin* and *La Traviata*.[66]

Despite the overwhelmingly European programme of classical opera, the poet Joomart Bokonbaev translated the libretto of *Carmen* into Kyrgyz for the 1944/5 season in Frunze. The importance of raising a new generation of home-grown local musicians for the future was recognized by the opening of a Kyrgyz branch of Moscow's Tchaikovsky conservatoire. In addition, senior Kyrgyz performers actively sought out young singers and dancers for the opera and ballet. There is no doubt that, while drama remained culturally exclusive and largely a Soviet art during the war, mainly performed in Russian, music remained more accessible. With hundreds of thousands of attendees annually at concerts on collective farms and in towns, music had a popular appeal for all the citizens of Central Asia who were seeking some distraction from the war.[67]

Cinema

Cinema was even more widely accessible and popular across the region than concerts or the theatre. It was therefore fully exploited as the most useful cultural outlet for propaganda purposes.[68] Recognizing from the onset of war the key ability of film to appeal to the masses, Soviet propagandists rapidly implemented a concerted campaign to increase the number of cinemas and viewers. Cinema production was already established in Central Asia, but Alma-Ata rose to become the film-producing capital of the Soviet Union in the war years, thanks to the evacuation there of the main studios from the west. Of the nearly seventy films produced in the Soviet Union during the war, most were filmed in the region, although official approval was only granted once they had been previewed by Stalin himself.[69]

As early as August 1941 the power of cinema as a propaganda tool was officially endorsed by the Soviet authorities under Andrei Zhdanov, the state's culture supremo, in a statement of intent:

> Cinema, as an effective propaganda weapon during wartime, should serve the aims of the fatherland war of liberation. In showing documentaries and films about the heroic deeds of the Soviet people, cinema will help to forge victory over the enemy.[70]

Adopting the catchy new slogan: 'Every cinema is a propaganda centre; every cinema technician is an agitator', the Communist Party set about harnessing cinematography into war service, with the aim of inspiring 'millions of patriots and conscripts'. From city centres to the humblest collective farm, the people of Central Asia were to be fed a diet of Soviet heroism and ideology second to none.[71]

One of the most relevant documentary films for Central Asian audiences covered the exploits of the 8th Guards (Panfilov) Rifle Brigade. *8-ia Gvardeiskaia* (The Eighth Guards) (1943), recounts the famous story of the Panfilov Division from its journey to the front to its recognition with the Order of the Red Banner. Most of the half-hour film is a collage of war reportage depicting the operation of troops in the Russian winter. The thrust of the first part of the film is that, thanks to the friendship of people of different ethnicities, men from Kazakhstan and Kyrgyzstan helped in the defence of the Soviet capital, Moscow. The action is interspersed with scenes of the troops singing and playing Kazakh music on a record player in the field, as their minds return to their homeland. The viewer finally learns how the group of dead Panfilov heroes had destroyed a total of fifty enemy tanks, as their young faces appear on the screen at the same time as a funeral ceremony takes place for them. Targeted mainly at Kazakhs on the home front, this educational film also shows coal mining, women hard at work sewing, and shells for the front rolling off the factory production line. Parcels from home are distributed to grateful men with Asiatic faces, containing cigarettes and sausages, wine and oversized apples from Alma-Ata – presumably encouraging further donations. The men's success is intended to motivate those at home to increase production, as selected women address their relations via a radio link from Alma-Ata. The final scenes show the presentation of the Order of the Red Banner to Major General Vasilii Reviakin, Panfilov's successor, with other honoured members of the division also receiving awards, notably Senior Lieutenant Momysh-uly and Panfilov's daughter, Valentina.[72]

Films were usually shown in a dedicated *kinoteatr* (cinema), in palaces of culture or in temporary venues in villages, on collective farms and MTS stations. The target of increasing the number of cinemas was achieved somewhat more slowly than desired by the state, often let down by the creaky old projectors. As the first winter of the war approached, it was realized that physical access to cinemas was not always up to standard in Kyrgyzstan, with instructions issued to ensure a hard path or road was in place right up to the cinema door in case of deep snow or sudden thaw.[73]

The number of film programmes was also dramatically increased. These measures in themselves were not deemed to be sufficient, however. Propagandists instructed that, in order to maximize the efficacy of the offerings, a range of advertising should be employed. Posters were to be displayed on cinema walls, with comprehensive displays of 'anti-fascist' or defence material in the foyer. Advertisements should also be placed on the local radio and in newspapers, institutes, shops and canteens at least five days before a new film was shown. Furthermore, it was advised to hold lectures about the forthcoming programme before the start of every film, with the addition of documentary war footage for extra measure, so that audiences would be familiarized with the progress and ideology of the war.[74] Despite the fact that the cinema in Przheval'sk was berated in the early days for its poor implementation of the new recommendations, attendance improved during the harvest period of 1942. Apparently over 28,000 collective farm viewers in the Issyk-Kul' province visited the cinema at this time, being fed a diet of suitable educational and inspirational material. Numbers gradually increased, such that, in the spring of 1943, a grand total of almost 50,000 villagers attended 432 film programmes on 72 collective farms over an eleven-week period.[75]

In order to meet the manufactured demand for patriotic films, the security of the domestic film industry had to be ensured. Both the Mosfil'm and the Lenfil'm studios were evacuated to Central Asia in October 1941, when enemy forces were threatening the main cities of Moscow and Leningrad. Merging in Alma-Ata to form the new Central Combined Cinema Studio (TsOKS) in November that year, they produced a total of twenty-three films during the war, the vast majority of the output of the Soviet Union. Most of the predominant directors and actors of the era joined the studio, notably Sergei Eizenshtein whose historical film *Ivan Groznyi* (Ivan the Terrible) (1944) with its score by Sergei Prokofiev portrayed the period in the sixteenth century when Russia first united into one great nation.[76]

Many of the films produced in Alma-Ata portrayed, in true propaganda fashion, the heroic war of the Soviet people against fascism, aiming to increase the morale of the population. A typical example is *Zoia* (1944), directed by Leo Arnshtam, about the young partisan Zoia Kosmodem'ianskaia who was 'martyred' for her role with partisans. Similarly, the heroine of *Ona zashchishchaet Rodinu* (She defends the Motherland) (1943), directed by Fridrikh Ermler, is driven to join the partisans after the death of her husband and son, single-handedly halting a tank in its tracks in an act of revenge. The promotion of female protagonists served to enlist the support of women for the war effort by implying that, if women proved themselves to display typically Soviet courage in the face of the enemy, then men should follow suit. Most films depicted the Nazi enemy as cowardly and dastardly. This is not to say that lighter films had no place during the war. Gerbert Rappaport's *Vozdushnyi izbozchik* (Taxi to Heaven) (1943) tells the romantic story of a pilot and an opera singer at the start of the war, while Leonid Trauberg's musical *Aktrisa* (The Actress) (1943) tugs at the heartstrings, as a Soviet actress falls in love with a wounded veteran.[77]

The war correspondent Konstantin Simonov also spent time in Alma-Ata working on the screenplay for his popular play *Russkie liudi* (1942). Appearing in 1943 as *Vo imia Rodiny* (In the name of the Motherland), it proved extremely popular in the war years. Even more important was the film *Zhdi menia* (Wait for me) (1943) based on Simonov's emotional poem of the same name, which lauds the loyalty of a woman waiting for her soldier boyfriend when everything indicates that he has been killed in action. Alma-Ata was also the temporary home of other famous artists, including author Mikhail Zoshchenko, director Sergei Mikhalkov and actress Liubov' Orlova, while the esteemed Soviet director Mikhail Romm worked in Tashkent. Other film studios relocated to Ashkhabad, Stalinabad and Frunze, further establishing Central Asia as the hub of the cinema industry in wartime. The pan-Soviet institute of cinematography was also located in Alma-Ata, where the Kazakh film acting school offered four-year courses for budding actors.[78]

The war provoked an artistic collaboration between Russians and Ukrainians from the west of the Soviet Union with members of the local Central Asian cultural elite. Appealing to a local audience was the film *Batyry stepei* (Knights of the Steppe) (1942), linking the contemporary Red Army with the Central Asian hero Tulegen Tokharov. Similarly *Pesni Abaia* (The Songs of Abai) (1945), directed by Efim Aron and Grigorii Roshal', was the film version of the novels by Kazakh author Mukhtar Auezov. With special significance for Kyrgyz audiences, the studio in Alma-Ata released (in both Russian- and Kyrgyz-language versions) Konstantin Isaev's film *Semetei – syn Manasa* (Semetei, son of Manas) (1945) with an input from Kyrgyz poet Joomart Bokonbaev. Tashkent Studios also produced a range of films, including Iakov Protazanov's popular comedy *Nasreddin in Bukhara* (1943), based on a novel by Leonid Solov'ev. Reinforcing the 'friendship of the peoples' trope, Vasilii Pronin's *Syn Tajikistana* (Son of Tajikistan) (1942) depicts a Tajik soldier mourning his dying Russian comrade.[79]

Possibly the most famous overtly Kazakh film of the war was the quasi-documentary *Tebe, Front* (To you, the Front), commissioned early in 1942 to show the effect of work in the rear on those fighting on the front line. Originally named *Kazakhstan–frontu* (Kazakhstan to the front), it was one of several wartime films directed by Dziga Vertov. In this instance, though, Vertov had to contend with repeated editing by the Communist Party before the film was passed for release. *Tebe, Front* employs Central Asian tropes to bring home the reality of war to the population of Kazakhstan. An old folk-singer, the *akyn* Nurpeis Baiganin, frames the narrative while playing the *dombra*. The tension between the *akyn* singing in Kazakh about the wife of a soldier at the front, and the Russian voice and text with the sound of guns firing, emphasizes the dissonance between the archaic, oral (Kazakh) tradition, and the modern, written (Russian). The contrast between the historic past and the Soviet present, with the promise of the socialist future to come, is underlined by the work of the soldier's wife in the lead mine where he used to work. Her labour brings the work in the rear to the fore, as she becomes a Stakhanovite heroine in her own right, breaking all production records. On the collective farm, too, peasants are shown collecting every grain, working as hard as their compatriots on the front line to a background of martial music, while a fake song in Russian is designed to resemble traditional Kazakh music for the pan-Soviet audience. The propaganda message of the film is clear: that the (female) workers of Central Asia could and should work harder – both collectively and individually – to become more productive, for the sake of their men at the front. In this way, the future (implied) victory would be due to a collaboration of front and rear, of men and women, of traditional Central Asian and modern Soviet methods.[80]

As the output of the film studios changed to a war footing, so the programmes offered in cinemas reflected the demands of the propagandists for 'defence of the motherland', 'anti-fascist' and 'historical military', educational themes. Details of new releases could be found in the journal *Kino*, while local cinema networks compiled programmes tailored to the season. Agricultural films were deemed most suitable for the harvest period, while in the run-up to the twenty-fourth anniversary of the foundation of the Red Army on 23 February 1942 military topics on heroism and defence dominated the bill. For example the Vasil'ev brothers' *Oborona Tsaritsyna* (The Defence of Tsaritsyn) (1942) served as a reminder to the population that Stalingrad had been taken by the Bolsheviks during the civil war. Other films also referred to success in earlier wars: Eizenshtein's powerful film *Aleksandr Nevskii* (1938) about the defeat of foreign invaders in the thirteenth century was shown in 1942, while the Vasil'ev brothers' *Chapaev* (1934) reminded viewers of the eponymous civil war hero. To dilute the menu of war films, the cinemas in the Issyk-Kul' province also screened *Sovetskaia Kirgiziia* (Soviet Kyrgyzstan) (1944), a film released by the Kyrgyz film studio about the natural resources of the republic. For pure escapism, though, Ivan Pyr'ev's musical comedy *Svinarka i pastukh* (The Swineherd and the Shepherd) (1941) topped the bill.[81]

The cinema was always an important part of the community's offering for children in the early January winter holidays, an indoor contrast to the outings and camps keeping them entertained in the summer season. Providing a cinema 'service' for children, the provincial cinema in Przheval'sk established a daily afternoon film programme aiming to 'educate' (*vospityvat'*) children while developing in them a spirit of Soviet patriotism and willingness to work for the common cause. Unashamedly utilized as a propaganda vehicle, the programme was specially selected, often including the film version of *Timur and His Gang*. *Kliatva Timura* (Timur's Oath) (1942) was produced in Stalinabad, the capital of Tajikistan, thanks to the evacuation from Moscow of the Soiuzdetfil'm studio which specialized in children's cinema. Towards the end of the war the menu became markedly lighter in tone, including such classics as Grigorii Aleksandrov's oft-repeated musical *Veselye rebiata* (Jolly Fellows) (1934), starring famous actress Liubov' Orlova. *Zolotoi kliuchik* (The golden key) (1939), the Russian adaptation of *Pinocchio* by writer Aleksei Tolstoi, also proved a hit amongst the youngsters.[82]

Some children had the opportunity to take on a less sedentary role in the cinema, being trained in clubs to become *kinomekhaniki* (cinema technicians). Recognized by propagandists as 'not only a means of getting schoolchildren to start work, but also a way of attracting them into further education in the field of cinema technology in order to take it up as a career', these clubs offered courses largely for year eight pupils, particularly those of Kyrgyz ethnicity, including girls. Most technicians remained adults, however, who increasingly found that they had to travel from farm to farm to complete their schedule of programmes. Mandatory training came with the job, as technicians were often the people also delivering pre-film ideological talks to the captive audience. Professional requirements included a familiarity with the guidelines on anti-aircraft and chemical defence methods. As the job became more demanding, so the pay of technicians increased, causing in turn an increase in the price of a cinema ticket from around 1.5 to 2 roubles by January 1942. Most cinema technicians proved outstanding, maintaining the equipment well, according to reports of June 1942. However, a minority proved less reliable. Checks on fire safety in cinemas across the Issyk-Kul' province showed significant deficiencies even before the war, with a certain Comrade Mikhailov in the village of Pokrovka being singled out for criticism in 1941. Improvements were slow to be effected, however, and just a year after inspection, a fire broke out in one of the other cinemas of the provincial network. The culprit was, apparently, the film *The Defence of Tsaritsyn*, with the fire starting during a change from the third to the fourth reel. It was fortunately contained, but not before destroying both the fourth and fifth reels. The projector and the cinema itself were saved and, after some local repairs, the programme recommenced later that evening with a showing of a somewhat less demanding film, Ivan Pyr'ev's *Liubimaia devushka* (The Beloved Girl) (1940). The consumption of cinematic culture on the home front could provide a welcome distraction from everyday concerns during wartime, but occasionally proved to be a potentially dangerous activity.[83]

Fine art

If the cinema portrayed the war in black-and-white movies, other types of visual art presented static, if colourful and equally dramatic images to the public. None were more evident in palaces of culture and recruitment stations than official posters of brave military heroes, contrasted with satirical portrayals of the cowardly enemy. One of the prime propagandist's tools, war art was sometimes displayed in exhibitions in the larger cities, which took place despite the privations of wartime because of their political utility. Local and evacuee artists were invited to submit their works on the usual themes of war, patriotism, great historical leaders and work in the rear, including more poster art as the war progressed. The exhibition 'Ten years of Kyrgyz artists in the Soviet Union' was held in Frunze in 1942, with a follow-up exhibition in 1943 arranged by famous Kyrgyz artist Semen Chuikov. Reflecting 'the military history of the Kyrgyz people in their fight for independence, the growth of local agriculture and culture during the Soviet period, and the participation of Kyrgyzstan in the fight against the enemies of the Motherland', this exhibition included sculptures of Stalin and a series of paintings of farm life, showing off 'the achievements of animal husbandry on Kyrgyz collective farms'.[84]

Two similar events in School Number 28 in Alma-Ata were organized by the Kazakh artists' union on the first and second anniversaries of the start of the war. The exhibitions were on an impressive scale, including several submissions from Moscow, Leningrad and Khar'kov (Kharkiv), although a minority of local artists also took part. The judging panels, too, included some local artists, who were able to do justice to the variety of media covering paintings, sculpture, graphic design and posters.[85]

It is not surprising that several works were dedicated to 'The Twenty-eight'. Both B. Belopol'skii's painting 'The Approach to Moscow' and M. Lysenko and L. Muravin's sculpture were dedicated to the Panfilov heroes. Aleksandr Rittikh, whose German name and education could have caused him problems during the purges of the 1930s had he not already been living in Kazakhstan, submitted the painting 'The Last Grenade', which was later re-titled 'The Heroic Exploit of the Twenty-eight Panfilovites Blocking Fifty Enemy Tanks on the Approach to Moscow' – just in case of any ambiguity. This painting proved so successful in Central Asia that 10,000 prints were made soon after the 1942 exhibition. On the home front, Professor Abram Cherkasskii, an evacuee from Ukraine, displayed his latest work 'Komsomol lads – future guardsmen', while Mariia Lizogub portrayed workers collecting 'Presents for the guardsmen'.[86]

Aleksandr Rittikh rather hogged the 1943 exhibition with his sixty-eight submissions, including forty-two pencil sketches of animals. M. Lipkin had managed to bring with him some of his smaller pictures as he was evacuated from Leningrad. His 'Leningrad in Wartime' series proved as popular with citizens of Alma-Ata wishing to visualize the war as I. Gurvich's series 'The Leningrad Front'. This type of art won the unanimous approval of the judges, who demanded earthy portrayals of the reality of war. In contrast, landscapes were not generally permitted, as it was felt that citizens had no right to admire the beauty of nature during wartime. Only the Kazakh artist Abdylkhan Kasteev, a former shepherd and largely self-taught, was praised for his great observation skills with his detailed and nuanced portrayals of nature. Other artists were deployed to various areas of the republic to collect material about working life in the rear, producing realistic paintings of factories and oil refineries, fishermen and farms.[87]

With these and other wartime exhibitions held in SAVO, the regional military headquarters in Tashkent, the reputation of Central Asia as the artistic hub of the Soviet Union was confirmed. Many of the best Soviet artists had, however, been sent to the front lines as war artists, where several even lost their lives. Conditions for creative artists remaining at home were also difficult across the region, with a lack of materials and very little studio space available. The Uzbek artist Kh. Abdullaev, for example, lived with six other people in one room in a private flat with no separate studio where he could continue his work. The only support on offer for the artistic community was a few dedicated canteens and a guaranteed pay packet as long as the artists produced the type of product dictated by the state, such as posters and portraits of war heroes and Stakhanovites. Aleksandr Liubimov specialized in heroes, depicting 'I. V. Panfilov at the front' (1942), holding binoculars and astride a horse in the snow. Hard work in the rear was vividly depicted in Ivan Gal'chenko's painting 'Na stroike BChK' (Building the Grand Chui Canal) (1943), showing men still hard at work at night-time, toiling in the light of floodlights, in an effort to complete the canal as quickly as possible.

Throughout the war there was a mass production of motivational posters, propaganda sheets and cartoons in which political satire was directed against the fascist enemy, often depicted as wild animals. The average print run of posters on display in recruitment centres, barracks and hospitals was over 70,000. Samarkand-based M. Avetov was one of the main propaganda artists based in Central Asia, together with V. I. Kozlinskii in Fergana, whose busy team produced a phenomenal 400 different posters in the first three months of the war. As the war progressed, larger works were commissioned with a commensurately bigger pay packet: the rates for calendar drawings or postcards were better, for example, than those for pictures appearing in newspapers or children's books.[88]

The subjects of propaganda paintings changed markedly after the war. An immediate postwar still life 'Frukty Kirgizii' (Fruits of Kyrgyzstan) (1946) by Evgeniia Maleina depicts a complete recovery from the austere years with a water melon, apples, grapes and a basket and sack brimming over with healthy produce. Changed living conditions are evident in Leonid Deimant's 'V novyi dom' (Into the new house) (1949), where women and children are happily moving into a static home, not a temporary yurt, with piles of food on display, symbolizing not only the permanence and bounty of Soviet rule, but also the death of the traditional lifestyle. A precursor to Aleksandr Laktionov's 'Moving into the new flat' (1952), it also includes a child carrying a pile of books, demonstrating to the people of Central Asia the cultural modernity brought to the republics by the Soviet education system.

Religion

Central Asia represents a melting pot of religions – from the shamanism which dominated the region for centuries, celebrating the sun and the moon with the natural world, to later arrivals such as Buddhism, Islam, Judaism and Christianity. Despite the building of many Russian Orthodox churches by the tsarist expeditions conquering the region in the nineteenth century, in the twentieth century the majority of the region's residents professed themselves Muslim, if only by cultural tradition. Viewed from Moscow, Central Asia may have seemed to be one large Muslim entity. Although most were Sunni Muslims, a more conservative form of Islam was practised in Uzbekistan and Tajikistan than in Kazakhstan or Kyrgyzstan, and most intellectuals were traditionally based in the ancient Uzbek cities of Samarkand, Bukhara and Khiva.

The atheist authorities of the newly formed Soviet Union regarded Islam as the antithesis of communism with its ideological emphasis on equality. Considering Muslims as over-patriarchal, primitive and reactionary, they stressed in their policies the equality of the sexes, ensuring that both boys and girls received an education. With the enforced secularization of Central Asia following new laws against religion in 1929, the clergy were repressed as enemies of the people, with many executed, sent to the GULag camps or fleeing abroad. Muslims were forced to conduct prayer clandestinely, leaving mosques unattended. The change of alphabet, alienating the Arabic script used in most Islamic texts, was a further threat to the region's traditional religion. This suppression was not unique to Islam, however, as, in common with mosques, churches and other places of worship across the Soviet Union were repurposed as schools, libraries or storage facilities. Even the Holy Trinity Russian Orthodox church in Przheval'sk was closed to believers and used for children's sport from 1933.[89]

Defiance to the state continued underground, for example, in the isolated regions of conservative Tajikistan and Uzbekistan, where women continued to wear the veil and polygamy was still practised in the 1930s.[90] Fifteen per cent of the Soviet state's population was Muslim, a powerful 30 million people who were concentrated in the southern regions, in republics in which there was a strong nationalistic tendency. From the Crimean Tatars of the Black Sea to the Caucasian republics, it could have been easy for Islamic insurgents to spread into Central Asia. There therefore remained a genuine fear on the part of the authorities of organized Islam in the pre-war Soviet Union.

Stalin's campaign of sometimes violent religious persecution continued until after the start of the war, when it was soon acknowledged that policies of repression would do little to help the conscription of men from Central Asia into the Red Army. As the need to bring the republics of Central Asia onside became increasingly urgent, the state suppression of religion was relaxed somewhat from 1942 and some co-operation between state and those remaining religious leaders evolved.[91]

At the same time, enemy forces were also coming to appreciate the necessity of wooing Soviet Muslims as they pushed into Crimea and the Caucasian republics. A war for the hearts and minds of Muslims in occupied territories ensued, with the Germans trying to entice the local population to collaborate or even to join their armed forces, while the Soviet leaders looked on, for the moment powerless to counteract the enemy's message of conciliation. The Germans waged an initially successful propaganda war vis-à-vis the local populations, courting popularity by reinstating Islamic festivals and re-opening mosques and madrassas which had previously been closed by the Soviet regime. Occupying German and Romanian soldiers often failed to carry out the conciliatory orders of their officers, however, mistaking some Muslims for Jews in Crimea and executing them indiscriminately.[92]

German atrocities against Muslim citizens were seized upon by Soviet propagandists in Central Asia as a warning to Muslims there of what to expect if the enemy succeeded in pushing further east. Seeking to placate both Muslim soldiers in the Red Army and citizens in the rear, the authorities embarked on a propaganda campaign to harness the power of Islam in Central Asia for the war effort, acknowledging that some co-operation with religious leaders was necessary if they were to remain loyal to the state. This change in attitude was implemented during 1942, and by 1943 significant concessions were evident for both Soviet Muslims and Christians in the region.[93]

With Islam rehabilitated as the traditional religion of most of Central Asia, Muslim culture was appropriated by the state for the war effort. State propaganda demonstrated the anti-fascist nature of Islam, uniting religion and the state in a common cause. As faith finally became compatible with communist ideology, Muslims were targeted by the conscription centres with a new reason for joining the Red Army – a strong sense of Soviet patriotism and the opportunity it offered for the expression of religious faith through the martyrdom rooted in Islamic culture.

Citizens were allowed to observe their religion privately, but mosques had no legal rights over their communities and were not permitted to govern themselves. In this way, the Muslims of Central Asia were attracted into the Soviet fold as they adopted their new Soviet identity. As good Soviet citizens, their sense of patriotism was extended beyond their republic to incorporate allegiance to the Soviet Union and Islam as a whole. Building on an expanded belief system which could then incorporate the collective sacrifice needed to defeat the common enemy, a fragile co-operation between state and religious society developed, to the mutual advantage of all concerned. The Muslim values of sharing and giving were also exploited by a state which needed all the financial and material help it could get. Muslim communities in Central Asia collected charitable funds for soldiers' families and their counterparts in the recently liberated areas, including Crimea and the Caucasus.[94]

The co-existence of state and religious society was assisted by Islamic leaders and intellectuals, with the main centres of Islamic learning of Samarkand and Bukhara in Uzbekistan key to the success of the campaign. Thus SADUM (the Spiritual Directorate of Muslims in Central Asia) was established in Tashkent in 1943, representing the new official version of Islam in the Soviet Union, in contrast to other more traditional and conservative Islamic groups which were undermined by the Soviet authorities. Muslims were thereby subject to three types of authority: that of the regime, the military and their religious leaders. With mutually reinforcing propaganda from all directions, religious imagery and culture was employed for the benefit of the state and the army. A key rallying call to arms against 'the enemy wolves of Hitler' was made to the Muslims of Central Asia in October 1943 by Ishan Babakhanov, a senior Muslim cleric and leader of

SADUM in Tashkent, who, like many religious leaders, had served time in the GULag camps during Stalin's purges.[95] With a continuation of the animal metaphor, Muslims learnt from respected Tajik intellectual Sadriddin Aini that Hitler was the 'dog that desecrated the mosque', as Islamic leaders often conveniently forgot that Stalin had ever waged a war on religion or consigned thousands of religious leaders to the GULag. This attitude naturally fed down to the ordinary village mullah, whose wisdom and authority was generally respected. With prayers for the Red Army's 'sacred struggle' against the Germans who were credited, falsely, with seeking to destroy Islamic culture in Central Asia, Muslim clergy bowed to pressure from above, eventually equating Soviet patriotism with their faith. They were forced to spell out the links between Communism and Islam by opening their sermons with the following words: 'Soviet authority is given by Allah. Therefore everyone who turns against Soviet authority turns against Allah, and Muhammad, his Prophet.' In this way, the generally peace-loving Sunni Muslims of Central Asia were called to *jihad*, a holy war against the enemy – and even potential martyrdom – in the interest of defending their country and their faith from the infidel.[96]

This loose marriage of convenience between Soviet and Islamic leaders was damaged, however, once Crimea had been completely liberated from enemy occupation in May 1944. Muslim clerics in the occupied territories were deemed to have been enemy collaborators and were immediately executed. A few days later, all the remaining Crimean Tatars were deported to Central Asia, following the Chechens and other Caucasian ethnic groups as victims of ethnic cleansing and Stalin's search for ethnic minority scapegoats.

As the war drew to its conclusion, the need for Muslim military assistance in the army and co-operation in the rear was no longer essential and the fragile dynamic slowly collapsed. With people of faith across the Soviet Union, Muslims were once again banned from their places of worship during the gradual post-war clampdown on religion. The wartime relaxation of controls on religion and the consequent truce in hostilities between the state and religious leaders had lasted just a few short years, after which intellectuals of Central Asia were forced to drop their overt Muslim allegiance in the renewed conflict between state and religion. Access to the Koran was severely restricted for ordinary citizens, and the Dungan mosque in Przheval'sk was made to shut its doors to the public early in 1946, ostensibly due to local conflicts between Uzbek and Tatar religious leaders. The manufactured antagonism between different religions and nationalities led to an official withdrawal of privileges for all, as the state dropped all pretence of conciliation with citizens of faith, compelling Muslims to re-evaluate the reasons which had led them to support the communist regime during the war.[97] The temporary wartime truce had, however, served to reconcile many Muslims to the Soviet state, opening up a dialogue between Moscow and local leaders, thus defusing the potential threat of a pan-Islamic anti-Soviet movement. Furthermore, more women were included in religious activity than previously, as they increasingly laid claim to a more open role in the new Soviet society.[98]

A cultural revolution

The war prompted a reset of the relationship between the state and society in Central Asia, as the need for the region's support became apparent. Rather than alienating sectors of the population as in the Stalinist pre-war purges, Moscow was obliged to increase conscription and encourage goodwill amongst families struggling to survive in the rear – all with the aim of defeating a common enemy. To this end a concerted propaganda campaign was waged to remind the people of Central Asia of their identity as valued members of the Soviet Union. As the regime necessarily espoused its 'friendship of the peoples' policy, wartime propaganda specifically tailored to Central Asian traditional values and history succeeded in delivering a message of inclusivity, despite the varying connotations of the concept of patriotism for which the people of the region were fighting. A degree of historical revisionism permitted the adulation of Central Asian heroes old and new, with a marked reinterpretation of the events of 1916 and 1917.

As the war progressed, there was less chance of Central Asia remaining isolated from the news, with communications from Moscow increasing in volume and efficacy. The exposure to wartime propaganda was ubiquitous across the Soviet Union, as the state ensured that western Slavic and Asiatic cultures were surprisingly successfully meshed together – if not on an entirely equal footing, at least with somewhat less condescension shown to the indigenous citizens of Central Asia than previously. A gradual normalization of practices and expectations of the people was created, as citizens came to know where they stood within the state and adapted to their new Soviet, communist identity. In this respect Moscow's propaganda war was largely successful.

The arrival of millions from the western parts of the Soviet Union helped to trigger a cultural revolution, as the Russian language increased its stronghold on the region. The assimilation of Soviet values in Central Asia was greatly assisted through cultural propaganda, with the accessibility and entertainment value of cinema and the participation of the mullahs offering the greatest opportunities for indoctrination. As a little religious tolerance was once again sanctioned, Moscow turned a blind eye to some traditional cultural and religious practices which were permitted again, if under communist control and only for the duration of the war.

Having experienced the army and the Slavic culture imported with the evacuees, the population of Central Asia became more cosmopolitan in outlook, encouraged by a higher standard of education and supported by an ongoing campaign of modernization offering more opportunities. By the end of the Second World War the population of Central Asia was better integrated into Soviet society. This had been the first experience of the whole of the Soviet Union working collectively in a common cause – to defend the motherland, regardless of nationality or ethnicity. With some degree of cultural freedom and a moratorium on the Stalinist internal purges in Central Asia came an increased expectation of citizens' responsibility to the state in the fight against the enemy. However, this same state dashed any expectations of continued relaxation once victory had been achieved. Contrary to the hopes of many intellectuals, Moscow clamped down on its peripheral republics shortly after the war, as histories were revised in a Soviet mould and religious beliefs and practice were once more alienated from the state.

By the time the external enemy had been repelled, the little cultural freedom temporarily permitted to Central Asia was curtailed and the 'friendship of the peoples' policy was exposed as the political expedient it really was. This firm re-imposition of control by the centre after a few short years of pragmatic indulgence was reminiscent of the colonial measures of the tsarist era, except that, by the late 1940s, the population of Central Asia had expanded their original parochial identity to include a greater cultural and ideological alignment with their comrades across Stalin's increasingly modern Soviet Union.

Notes

1 Keller, *Russia and Central Asia*, 200–3; and Lilley, *Have the Mountains Fallen?*, 89 and 221–3.

2 Florin, 'Becoming Soviet through War', 496; and Florin, *Kirgistan und die sowjetische Moderne*, 64.

3 Around ninety Kazakh writers and poets were conscripted (Abylkhozhin, *Istoriia Kazakhstana*, 522). See also Kerimbaev, *Sovetskii Kirgizstan v Velikoi Otechestvennoi voine*, 164.

4 Florin, *Kirgistan und die sowjetische Moderne*, 60–6.

5 Carmack, *Kazakhstan in World War II*, 101; Florin, *Kirgistan und die sowjetische Moderne*, 61 and 65; Hosking, *Russia and the Russians*, 433; and Kerimbaev, *Sovetskii Kirgizstan v Velikoi Otechestvennoi voine*, 164.

6 On propaganda in general, see Berkhoff, *Motherland in Danger*; and Jeffrey Brooks, *Thank You, Comrade Stalin! Soviet Public Culture from Revolution to Cold War* (Princeton: Princeton University Press, 2001). See also Barber and Harrison, *The Soviet Home Front*, 68–9; and Florin, *Kirgistan und die sowjetische Moderne*, 47–8.

7 Carmack, *Kazakhstan in World War II*, 52–3, 55–6 and 102; Aminat Chokobaeva, *Frontiers of Violence: State and Conflict in Semirechye, 1850–1938*, PhD thesis (Australian National University, 2016), 8–9; and Florin, 'Becoming Soviet through War', 502.

8 Florin, 'Becoming Soviet through War', 502–3; and Merridale, *Ivan's War*, 189 and 414 note 6.

9 'Obrashchenie antifashistskogo mitinga predstaviltelei trudiashchikhsia Uzbekistana, Turkmenii, Tajikistana, Kazakhstana, Kirgizii k narodam Uzbekskoi, Turkmenskoi, Tajikskoi, Kazakhskoi, Kirgizskoi Sovetskikh Respublik', *IKP*, 7 February 1943, 3; 'Izuchaiut knigu tovarishcha Stalina o velikoi Otechestvennoi voine', *IKP*, 16 August 1943, 2. See also Carmack, *Kazakhstan in World War II*, 107; Florin, 'Becoming Soviet through War', 495–7 and 501; Florin, *Kirgistan und die sowjetische Moderne*, 47 and 49; and Stronski, *Tashkent*, 12.

10 Florin, 'Becoming Soviet through War', 505; and Kaptagaev, et al., *Sbornik*, 136–7.

11 'Geroi Sovetskogo Soiuza Tashmamat Jumabaev', *IKP*, 16 January 1944, 2; 'Geroi Sovetskogo Soiuza Dair Asanov v Przheval'ske', *IKP*, 16 April 1944, 1; 'Geroi Sovetskogo Soiuza tov. Kurochkin E. G. v Przheval'ske', *IKP*, 18 January 1945, 2; 'Vstrechi przheval'tsev s Geroem Sovetskogo Soiuza t. Kurochkinom', *IKP*, 21 January 1945, 2. See also Kerimbaev, *Sovetskii Kirgizstan v Velikoi Otechestvennoi voine*, 237 and 261.

12 *IKP*, 19 July 1944; Kaptagaev, et al., *Sbornik*, 139; and Stronski, *Tashkent*, 83.

13 *IKP*, 10 September 1944; and Kaptagaev, et al., *Sbornik*, 140–1.

14 *IKP*, 23 November 1944; and Kaptagaev, et al., *Sbornik*, 143.

15 IKSA:146/1/38/265–6; Berkhoff, *Motherland in Danger*, 217; and Schechter, 'The People's Instructions'.

16 Carmack, *Kazakhstan in World War II*, 95 and 98; and Florin, 'Becoming Soviet through War', 515.

17 See for example Kesler, *Shards of War*, 1366.

18 Barber and Harrison, *The Soviet Home Front*, 65; Carmack, *Kazakhstan in World War II*, 97; Florin, *Kirgistan und die sowjetische Moderne*, 52; Manley, *To the Tashkent Station*, 199; Peck, *What My Parents Told Me*, 103; and Kristin Roth-Ey, *Moscow Prime Time: How the Soviet Union Built the Media Empire that Lost the Cultural Cold War* (Ithaca and London: Cornell University Press, 2011), 136–7.

19 Florin, 'Becoming Soviet through War', 504–5; Florin, *Kirgistan und die sowjetische Moderne*, 52; and Manley, *To the Tashkent Station*, 199.

20 'Kak organizovat' kollektivnuiu chitku gazety', *IKP*, 26 May 1944, 2.

21 IKSA:212/1/3/101–31 details preparations for the censorship of state secrets in June 1941, even before the start of the war.

22 Merridale, *Ivan's War*, 189.

23 Glavlit: *Glavnoe upravlenie po okhrane gosudarstvennykh tain v pechati pri SM SSSR* (Main Directorate for Literary and Publishing Affairs).

24 MPVO: *Mestnaia protivovozdushnaia oborona*. IKSA:212/1/1/28.

25 IKSA:212/2/1/115–28; and IKSA:212/6/1/1.

26 See, for example, IKSA:212/2/3. For a lengthy document about guarding state secrets issued by Moscow in November 1943, see IKSA:212/2/1/115–28.

27 IKSA:212/2/1/115–28.

28 IKSA:212/2/2/33.

29 'Gazetu v massy', *IKP*, 25 November 1944, 2. See also Abylkhozhin, *Istoriia Kazakhstana*, 520; Carmack, *Kazakhstan in World War II*, 96; and Florin, 'Becoming Soviet through War', 504.

30 'Tonskii raion ne rukovodit svoei gazetoi', *IKP*, 18 June 1944, 2.

31 'Velikaia data', *IKP*, 1 November 1942, 1–2; *IKP*, 7 November 1942, 1; and *IKP*, 11 November 1942, 1.

32 Carmack, *Kazakhstan in World War II*, 52.

33 'Za Moskvu, za Rodinu', *IKP*, 8 November 1941, 1; and 'Velikaia osvoboditel'naia missiia Krasnoi armii', *IKP*, 16 November 1941, 1.

34 For example, *IKP*, 28 November 1941, 4; 'Odin iz 28', *IKP*, 17 April 1942, 4; and *IKP*, 1 January 1943, 1.

35 Vicky Davis, *Myth Making in the Soviet Union and Modern Russia: Remembering World War II in Brezhnev's Hero City* (London: I.B. Tauris, 2017), 56–8.

36 Abylkhozhin, *Istoriia Kazakhstana*, 520; and Kerimbaev, *Sovetskii Kirgizstan v Velikoi Otechestvennoi voine*, 165.

37 Berkhoff, *Motherland in Danger*, 216.

38 Il'ia Erenburg, 'Kazakhi', *Krasnaia Zvezda*, 18 October 1942; 'Uzbeki', *Krasnaia Zvezda*, 20 October 1942; and 'Kirgizy', *Krasnaia Zvezda*, 3 November 1942.

39 Il'ia Erenburg, 'Uzbeki', *Krasnaia Zvezda*, 20 October 1942.

40 S. Narovchatov, ed., *Pobeda: Stikhi voennykh let* (Moscow: Khudozhestvennaia literatura, 1985), 161; Brooks, *Thank You, Comrade Stalin!*, 188; Florin, 'Becoming Soviet through War', 504; and Kerimbaev, *Sovetskii Kirgizstan v Velikoi Otechestvennoi voine*, 165.

41 Prof. P. N. Berkov, 'Kul'turno-istoricheskie sviazi Anglii i SSSR', *IKP*, 26 July 1942, 2; and IKSA:212/1/3/61–85.

42 'V sel'skoi biblioteke', *IKP*, 18 April 1943, 2; IKSA:212/1/3/86–99; and IKSA:212/2/1/25, 27–9.

43 Berkov, 'Kul'turno-istoricheskie sviazi Anglii i SSSR', *IKP*, 26 July 1942, 2; and Kerimbaev, *Sovetskii Kirgizstan v Velikoi Otechestvennoi voine*, 164. The lengthy controversy over the Kazakh history book is discussed in Carmack, *Kazakhstan in World War II*, 52–4; T. T. Turlygul, et al., *Istoriia Kazakhstana: Vazhneishie periody i nauchnye problem* (Almaty: Mektep, 2015), 193; and Harun Yilmaz, 'History Writing as Agitation and Propaganda: The Kazakh History Book of 1943', *Central Asian Survey* 31, no. 4 (2012): 409–23.

44 Abylkhozhin, *Istoriia Kazakhstana*, 522; Florin, 'Becoming Soviet through War', 496 and 502–3; Florin, *Kirgistan und die sowjetische Moderne*, 61 and 65; Kerimbaev, *Sovetskii Kirgizstan v Velikoi Otechestvennoi voine*, 164; and Nazar Shokhin, 'Arts during the War: Central Asia', *Voices on Central Asia*, 10 May 2018, available online: https://voicesoncentralasia.org/arts-during-the-war-central-asia (accessed 18 June 2020).

45 'Oboronnaia konferentsiia pisatelei Kirgizii', *IKP*, 27 March 1942, 4. See also Florin, *Kirgistan und die sowjetische Moderne*, 61 and 65; and Kerimbaev, *Sovetskii Kirgizstan v Velikoi Otechestvennoi voine*, 164.

46 Abylkhozhin, *Istoriia Kazakhstana*, 522; Kerimbaev, *Sovetskii Kirgizstan v Velikoi Otechestvennoi voine*, 165–6; and Manley, *To the Tashkent Station*, 148, 192, 208 and 217.

47 Florin, 'Becoming Soviet through War', 503.

48 Narovchatov, *Pobeda: Stikhi voennykh let*, 301; and Rafis Abazov, *Historical Dictionary of Turkmenistan* (Lanham: Scarecrow Press, 2005), xxxvi.

49 Narovchatov, *Pobeda: Stikhi voennykh let*, 29 and 65.

50 Ibid., 515.

51 Ibid., 138.

52 Ibid., 129.

53 For a detailed description of the literary scene in wartime Tashkent, see Manley, *To the Tashkent Station*.

54 Anna Akhmatova, *Iz semi knig: Stikhotvoreniia, Requiem* (Saint Petersburg: Azbuka-klassiki, 2004), 201; O. Gorbovskoi, *Stikhi i pesni o voine 1941–1945* (Moscow: Klassika v shkole, 2016), 8; and Narovchatov, *Pobeda: Stikhi voennykh let*, 40. See also Manley, *To the Tashkent Station*, 208 and 217.

55 Akhmatova, *Iz semi knig*, 203; and Gorbovskoi, *Stikhi i pesni o voine*, 10 and 12.

56 See Chapter 7.

57 Kerimbaev, *Sovetskii Kirgizstan v Velikoi Otechestvennoi voine*, 169–70.

58 'Russkie liudi', *IKP*, 16 August 1942, 2; and Kerimbaev, *Sovetskii Kirgizstan v Velikoi Otechestvennoi voine*, 168.

59 A. Sergeev, '"Mashen'ka"', *IKP*, 12 April 1942, 4; *IKP*, 15 July 1943, 2; *IKP*, 10 October 1943, 2; and '"Chrezvychainyi zakon" v oblastnom teatre', *IKP*, 11 June 1944, 2.

60 'Dva goda', *IKP*, 15 February 1944, 2. See also Kozybaev, *Istoriia Kazakhstana*, 130; and Manley, *To the Tashkent Station*, 220.

61 Kerimbaev, *Sovetskii Kirgizstan v Velikoi Otechestvennoi voine*, 165; Manley, *To the Tashkent Station*, 220–1 and 229; and Osmonov, *Istoriia Kyrgyzstana*, 165.

62 'Shire osveshchat' deiatel'nost' teatra', *IKP*, 5 May 1944, 2.

63 'Artisty v kolkhoze', *IKP*, 12 April 1942, 4; *IKP*, 5 August 1943, 2; and 'Kontserty na poliakh', *IKP*, 21 July 1944, 2. See also Kerimbaev, *Sovetskii Kirgizstan v Velikoi Otechestvennoi voine*, 166–7; and Turlygul, *Istoriia Kazakhstana*, 208.

64 *IKP*, 4 January 1942, 4; and Kerimbaev, *Sovetskii Kirgizstan v Velikoi Otechestvennoi voine*, 169.

65 *IKP*, 10 October 1943, 2. See also Abylkhozhin, *Istoriia Kazakhstana*, 522–3; Kerimbaev, *Sovetskii Kirgizstan v Velikoi Otechestvennoi voine*, 166; Osmonov, *Istoriia Kyrgyzstana*, 164; and Shokhin, 'Arts during the War'.

66 'Pervyi vypusk kirgizskoi konservatorii', *IKP*, 18 July 1943, 1; 'Dva goda', *IKP*, 15 February 1944, 2; and Manley, *To the Tashkent Station*, 137.

67 'Teatral'naia zhizn'', *IKP*, 18 July 1943, 2; and 'Opera "Karmen" v Kirgizteatre', *IKP*, 11 June 1944, 2.

68 See Peter Kenez, 'Black and White: The War on Film', in *Culture and Entertainment in Wartime Russia*, ed. Richard Stites (Bloomington: Indiana University Press, 1995).

69 Roth-Ey, *Moscow Prime Time*, 29.

70 IKSA:132/1/8/38–9.

71 Ibid.

72 *8-ia Gvardeiskaia*, dir. M. Slutskii (USSR:1943).

73 IKSA:132/1/8/4–5, 20 and 37; and IKSA:132/1/10/184. See also Kenez, 'Black and White', 166.

74 IKSA:132/1/8/37–8; and IKSA:132/1/10/121.

75 'Kino na poliakh', *IKP*, 6 August 1942, 2; IKSA:132/1/8/95; IKSA:132/1/10/54; and IKSA:132/1/11/31–2.

76 *Ivan Groznyi*, dir. Sergei Eizenshtein (Alma-Ata: TsOKS, 1944); Abylkhozhin, *Istoriia Kazakhstana*, 520 and 522–3; Kozybaev, *Istoriia Kazakhstana*, 130–1; and Turlygul, *Istoriia Kazakhstana*, 207–8. See also 'Tsentral'naia ob"edinnaia kinostudiia (1941–1944gg.)', *Kinoentsiklopediia Kazakhstana*, available online: https://csdfmuseum.ru (accessed 15 June 2020).

77 Kenez, 'Black and White', 168; Peter Rollberg, *Historical Dictionary of Russian and Soviet Cinema* (Plymouth: Rowman and Littlefield, 2016), 567 and 750; and 'Tsentral'naia ob"edinnaia kinostudiia'.

78 'Tsentral'naia ob"edinnaia kinostudiia'; Abylkhozhin, *Istoriia Kazakhstana*, 522–3; Florin, *Kirgistan und die sowjetische Moderne*, 41; Kozybaev, *Istoriia Kazakhstana*, 130; Manley, *To the Tashkent Station*, 233; and Turlygul, *Istoriia Kazakhstana*, 208.

79 'Kinofil'm "Semetei syn Manasa"', *IKP*, 20 March 1945, 1; Shokhin, 'Arts during the War'; and 'Tsentral'naia ob"edinnaia kinostudiia'.

80 Zh. A. Sataeva, 'K voprosu izucheniia istorii sovetskogo kino v gody voiny', in *Istoriia. Pamiat'. Liudi: Materialy IX Mezhdunarodnoi nauchno-prakticheskoi konferentsii 27 sentiabria 2018 g.*, eds K. Sh. Alimgazinov, et al., 218–22 (Almaty: 2019), 220–2; and Nariman Skakov, 'Folklore as Device: Dziga Vertov's "To You, the Front!"', in *Central Asia in Russian Language and Culture* (University of Oxford Conference, 2018).

81 'Kino na poliakh', *IKP*, 6 August 1942, 2; 'Fil'm o bogatstve Kirgizii', *IKP*, 8 September 1944, 2; IKSA:132/1/8/38–9; IKSA:132/1/10/133 and 142; and IKSA:132/1/11/13 and 84.

82 'Detskie kinoseansy', *IKP*, 7 January 1945, 2; and IKSA:132/1/8/2.

83 IKSA:132/1/8/2, 3, 24, 37 and 39; ISKA:132/1/9/32; ISKA:132/1/10/1–2, 5 and 181; and ISKA:132/1/11/91.

84 'Vystavka izobrazitel'nogo iskusstva Kirgizii', *IKP*, 18 March 1943, 2; and Kerimbaev, *Sovetskii Kirgizstan v Velikoi Otechestvennoi voine*, 170–1.

85   G. N. Syrlybaeva, 'Krupneishie vystavochnye proekty Soiuza khudozhnikov
     Kazakhskoi SSR v gody Velikoi Otechestvennoi voiny. 1942–1943 gg. Pervaia
     Respublikanskaia khudozhestvennaia vystavka "Velikaia Otechestvennaia
     voina"", in *Istoriia. Pamiat'. Liudi: Materialy VIII Mezhdunarodnoi nauchno-
     prakticheskoi konferentsii 16 sentiabria 2016 g.*, eds M. S. Makarova, et al.,
     126–36 (Almaty: 2017); and G. N. Syrlybaeva, 'Krupneishie vystavochnye
     proekty Soiuza khudozhnikov Kazakhskoi SSR v gody Velikoi Otechestvennoi
     voiny. 1942–1943 gg. Vtoraia Respublikanskaia khudozhestvennaia vystavka
     "Velikaia Otechestvennaia voina"', in *Istoriia. Pamiat'. Liudi: Materialy VIII
     Mezhdunarodnoi nauchno-prakticheskoi konferentsii 16 sentiabria 2016 g.*,
     eds M. S. Makarova, et al., 137–44 (Almaty: 2017).

86   Syrlybaeva, 'Pervaia Respublikanskaia khudozhestvennaia vystavka "Velikaia
     Otechestvennaia voina"'; and Grinberg, *Evrei v Alma-Ate*, 118.

87   Syrlybaeva, 'Vtoraia Respublikanskaia khudozhestvennaia vystavka "Velikaia
     Otechestvennaia voina"', 137–44.

88   Syrlybaeva, 'Pervaia Respublikanskaia khudozhestvennaia vystavka "Velikaia
     Otechestvennaia voina"', 126 and 129; M. S. Tukhtaeva, 'Povsednevnaia
     zhizn' evakuirovannykh khudozhnikov Moskvy i Leningrada v Uzbekistan v
     1941–1943 gg.', in *Istoriia. Pamiat'. Liudi: Materialy VIII Mezhdunarodnoi
     nauchno-prakticheskoi konferentsii 16 sentiabria 2016 g.*, eds M. S.
     Makarova, et al., 112–18 (Almaty: 2017); and M. S. Tukhtaeva, 'Tvorcheskaia
     zhizn' khudozhestvennoi intelligentsii Leningrada i Moskvy v evakuatsii
     v Uzbekistan (1941–1943 gg.)', in *Istoriia. Pamiat'. Liudi: Materialy VIII
     Mezhdunarodnoi nauchno-prakticheskoi konferentsii 16 sentiabria 2016 g.*,
     eds M. S. Makarova, et al., 118–26 (Almaty: 2017).

89   Keller, *Russia and Central Asia*, 202; I. P. Lipovsky, *Central Asia: In Search of
     a New Identity* (North Charleston: CreateSpace, 2012), 87–8; Andrea Schmitz,
     'Islam in Tajikistan: Actors, Discourses, Conflicts', SWP Research Paper, Berlin,
     2015, 7; and Eren Murat Tasar, 'Islamically Informed Soviet Patriotism in
     Postwar Kyrgyzstan', *Cahiers du Monde russe* 52, no. 2/3 (2011): 387–404,
     400.

90   Eden, *God Save the USSR*, 22; and Kesler, *Shards of War*, 1297.

91   Carmack, *Kazakhstan in World War II*, 108–10; Florin, *Kirgistan und die
     sowjetische Moderne*, 66; and David Motadel, 'Islam and Germany's War in
     the Soviet Borderlands, 1941–5', *Journal of Contemporary History* 48, no. 4
     (October 2013): 784–820, 787.

92   Interviews with Sanie Zevadinova, 10 May 2010 and 19 March 2011. See
     also Jeff Eden, 'A Soviet Jihad against Hitler: Ishan Babakhan Calls Central
     Asian Muslims to War', *Journal of the Economic and Social History of the
     Orient* 59 (2016): 237–64, 240–1; Motadel, 'Islam and Germany's War in the
     Soviet Borderlands', 784, 789, 793–4, 796, 803, 805–6, 809 and 815–6; and
     Bryn Glyn Williams, *The Crimean Tatars: From Soviet Genocide to Putin's
     Conquest* (London: Hurst, 2015), chapters 5 and 6.

93   Motadel, 'Islam and Germany's War in the Soviet Borderlands', 784 and 817.

94   IKSA:347/1/2/1 and 4; Carmack, *Kazakhstan in World War II*, 111–13; Eden,
     God Save the USSR, 89–91 and 99; Florin, *Kirgistan und die sowjetische*

Moderne, 67–8; and Tasar, 'Islamically Informed Soviet Patriotism in Postwar Kyrgyzstan', 397–8, 400 and 404.

95 Eden, *God Save the USSR*, 75.

96 Eden, 'A Soviet Jihad against Hitler', 241–9, 252 and 254–6; Motadel, 'Islam and Germany's War in the Soviet Borderlands', 819; and Tasar, 'Islamically Informed Soviet Patriotism in Postwar Kyrgyzstan', 387 and 392.

97 IKSA:347/1/2/72; and Florin, *Kirgistan und die sowjetische Moderne*, 70–4.

98 Eden, *God Save the USSR*, 126–8.

PART III

Comings and goings

The movement of a displaced population

7

Seeking sanctuary in Central Asia

Evacuees, refugees and VIPs

As the German army pushed through Belarus and western Ukraine in the deadly summer of 1941, the Soviet regime oversaw an operation to salvage as much as possible from the military disaster. Amongst the numerous factories and universities to be dismantled and precipitously evacuated was the Nikolaev Shipbuilding Institute. The Black Sea port of Nikolaev (Mykolaiv), lying to the east of Odessa, was once considered to be the cradle of the Russian empire's maritime construction industry. In the unceremonious rush to escape the approaching invading forces in August 1941, the renowned institute headed east to the temporary sanctuary of Stalingrad on the River Volga, thence moving rapidly downstream to the Caspian Sea port of Astrakhan, losing many of its expert engineers to the Red Army in the process. The final stage of this strategic evacuation took the institute with its remaining staff and students across Central Asia to its new home in Przheval'sk on the shore of Kyrgyzstan's Lake Issyk-Kul', where it arrived on 24 December 1941.

As the German guns started their bombardment of the western Soviet Union, planning began for the speedy withdrawal of everything and everybody necessary to maintain the government of the state and the manufacturing capacity of its defence industry. Within a few weeks of the onset of war, a huge feat of logistics enabled the relatively rapid movement of industrial plants, research institutes, evacuees and even farm animals to safe havens beyond the Urals as the enemy increased its stronghold on the western Soviet Union. This frenetic operation complemented the simultaneous mobilization in the opposite direction of enormous numbers of newly conscripted troops, sent off by train in their millions to the front line in the west of the country, chased by convoys of food and munitions. Of course, the state was already geared up for travel on a grand scale, due to the sheer dimensions of the USSR and its relatively recent experience in the 1930s of organizing the transport of hundreds of thousands of convicts east to the camps of the GULag system in Siberia. The flood of civilians heading east in the summer and autumn of 1941 largely followed this same route, either in organized evacuee convoys or as small groups of refugees fleeing Nazi oppression under their own steam.

Many Soviet citizens suffered undue hardship on their journey to reach the alien surroundings of Central Asia: the evacuees transported from besieged Leningrad, the Jewish refugees fleeing the Holocaust in Europe and the deportees forced thousands of kilometres from home by a regime suspicious of potential collaborators amongst ethnic minorities on its borderlands. Several discrete studies have been made of these mass migrations.[1] In this part they are brought together with a wealth of examples in an examination of the impact on individuals and communities of the displacement of war, forced resettlement and its ongoing legacy today.

The evacuation of whole factories, academic institutes, works of art and millions of debilitated civilians who had never travelled more than a few kilometres from home – with the mass evacuation of unaccompanied children – suddenly changed the demographic landscape of Central Asia. As wave after wave of civilian evacuees travelled to the region, their arrival was heralded with the order from the state that they be properly housed and cared for, a big demand from peripheral republics with little to spare by means of food or accommodation. Over the long years of the war, around 3 million incomers brought new skills to the region, enabling some degree of integration. However, the arrival of large groups of desperate deportees and Jewish refugees tended rather to ignite inter-ethnic tensions as they were often excluded from society and the Soviet project in general.

Industry on the move

As the German army overran the western Soviet Union, the main priority for the Soviet government was to safeguard the means of retaliation and food production. An Evacuation Council was established within two days of the German invasion, tasked with the large-scale strategic withdrawal of industrial plants and their experienced workforce. With a massive planning effort under the leadership of Nikolai Shvernik, munitions factories and metal works were dismantled and relocated to the centre and east of the country – to the Volga basin, the Ural Mountains, Siberia and Central Asia beyond.[2] Western Belarus was the first area to fall to the enemy, as Brest, Minsk, Bobruisk and Vitebsk fell like dominoes within a fortnight of the Nazi invasion. With time of the essence, it was simply too late for many factories to consider evacuation. For others, in the haste to reach safety, train convoys were split at key junctions such that parts of some factories arrived in two completely different locations in Central Asia. Archival evidence is limited in view of the chaotic circumstances, but within six months of the outbreak of war, around 2,600 threatened industrial plants and factories had been dismantled and evacuated eastwards, of which just over 300 eventually arrived in Central Asia. In addition, quantities of agricultural machinery and even domestic animals were transported to the rear before they could fall into the hands of the enemy. In all, over 150 factories were relocated to Kazakhstan within a few months, with about 100 arriving in Uzbekistan from 1941 to 1943 and 66 reaching Kyrgyzstan in 1941 and 1942.[3] Of these incoming factories, fifty were up and running in Uzbekistan within the first six months of the war, mainly in the cities of Tashkent and Samarkand, where plants producing materials vital for the war effort were established. In this way Uzbekistan became the new home for an electrical plant from Moscow and a chemical complex evacuated from Stalingrad.[4]

With the defence industry the absolute priority, thirty-eight large industrial plants were evacuated to Kyrgyzstan, manufacturing armaments, torpedoes and mines. Production capacity was increased markedly, for example, of the rare metal molybdenum, whose ore was mined in Kazakhstan and refined in a plant evacuated from Kiev (Kyiv) to Karaganda.[5]

Once relocated in the rear, many evacuated factories were instructed to change their production lines as the Soviet economy was placed on a war footing. Further factories were amalgamated with existing establishments to save space while markedly increasing their capacity. For instance, sewing machinery Factory Number 460 from the Moscow area was evacuated to Kokshetau in northern Kazakhstan, where it was merged with an existing factory, taking over some garage space in the town and renamed Factory Number 621. The new plant then concentrated on turning out mines and grenades as well as sewing machines for the manufacture of Red Army uniforms. Thanks to the simultaneous evacuation of 1,371 workers and their families, including several young children, it was able to function until ordered to stop production in May 1945.[6]

Space was an issue with most incoming factories, as many were forced into unsuitable premises. In a typical attempt to find room in city centres, the metal alloy factory evacuated from the Vladimir area of Russia was split over three smaller sites in different parts of the town of Kalkash in Kazakhstan. No family members were evacuated with the 622 workers accompanying the factory, probably because the workforce was expected to live in tightly packed dormitory accommodation adjacent to the plant.[7]

If the defence industry was the state's main priority, the production of sufficient food for the whole population of the Soviet Union, especially the fighting forces, came a close second. Agricultural machinery plants were evacuated eastwards, such as the factory from Berdiansk in Ukraine, which was erected in the grounds of an existing plant in Frunze in October 1941.[8] On a smaller scale, food canning factories from the west, such as the Mariupol and Kerch' fish factories, arrived in Kazakhstan from Ukraine.[9]

It was also necessary to move the wholesale production and processing of sugar beet to Central Asia. This crop had grown highly successfully in Ukraine, but by 1942 brigades of Uzbek workers were charged with maintaining the traditionally high yields in totally new areas around Tashkent, Samarkand and in the Fergana Valley. A certain Ivan Federenko, based in Khar'kov, was in charge of the evacuation of all sugar beet processing plants from eastern Ukraine to Central Asia. Although he managed to find some of the few seats on a train heading east for his wife, Elizaveta, and their extended family, he was forced to undertake the long journey on foot and horseback once his official driver had fled. As Federenko arrived in Tashkent in April 1942, work on the reconstruction of the Khar'kov sugar beet plant in the city centre was already in full swing. Men laboured for twelve hours a day in the open air during the hot summer, so that the plant was ready in time to process the autumn harvest. In a similar fashion, chief engineer Andrei Kozhushko supervised the transfer of the largest sugar beet plant in Ukraine from Kupiansk to Kokand in the Fergana Valley, thereby safeguarding sugar production in the Soviet Union during the war. This was a painfully slow process, especially crossing the River Volga during enemy bombardment. Once established in Uzbekistan, however, workmen took a further nine months to reconstruct the plant just in time for the autumn crop. By the time eastern Ukraine was liberated towards the end of 1943, there were four sugar beet plants functioning in Uzbekistan.[10]

The sugar produced in Uzbekistan was used mainly for food conservation, but also provided the main resource for a confectionary factory evacuated from Astrakhan on the Caspian Sea to Karaganda in Kazakhstan. During the war it remarkably continued the production of sherbet, fudge and halva, while its popular caramels were sold – to those who could afford them – under topical brand names such as 'Stakhanov' and 'Panfilov'.[11]

Parts of the sugar refineries were sent back to Ukraine immediately after its liberation, to be followed a few years later by all the Uzbek plants, as Soviet policy favoured a cotton monoculture in Uzbekistan from the early 1950s. Sugar refineries remained a mainstay of agricultural production in northern Kyrgyzstan, however, while Kazakhstan went on to be radically re-developed for food production in Khrushchev's so-called 'Virgin Lands' campaign implemented by Leonid Brezhnev.[12]

Light industry on a much smaller scale was less important strategically, but still represented a vital part of the Soviet economy. As Uzbekistan was the centre of the Soviet cotton fields, a Leningrad factory producing textile machinery was relocated here, followed by textile factories themselves.[13] A silk factory was moved from Pavlovskii Posad near Moscow to combine with one in the city of Osh to produce parachutes vital for the air force. A leather factory from Odessa was relocated to Kyrgyzstan, together with a pharmaceutical plant from Khar'kov and a shoe factory from Rostov-on-Don. Another shoe factory headed from Ukraine to Karaganda, where its range of offerings increased dramatically to fulfil the needs of the army and the local population.[14]

Evacuated factories usually brought with them sufficient specialist personnel to ensure their smooth running once established in Central Asia, but then depended upon the enlistment of a local workforce to supplement their numbers. In this way the cities of the region were at the same time rapidly industrialized and some of their inhabitants trained in the technological and engineering skills needed to support the modern Soviet economy. As the infrastructure around most major cities of the region developed, it was more able to supply the new plants with energy and transport links to the rest of the country. Tajikistan, however, remained on the periphery of Sovietization during the war, with its more remote areas hard to access and develop, and therefore less attractive as new locations for evacuated enterprises. This step change in the modernization of most of Central Asia provided a positive post-war legacy: although most of the evacuated factories returned home in 1943 or 1944, some remained in the region, along with a few of the evacuated theatres and film studios. In this way, their mainly Slavic managers became integrated into the local population, advancing its professional capital, while their workers benefited from further Sovietization and future career opportunities across the Soviet Union.[15]

Institutes of higher education

The preservation of intellectual life in the Soviet Union was also a priority for the state. Many students and lecturers at technical, engineering and medical universities were conscripted into the Red Army in the first days of the war, but the government quickly reversed this decision, realising that it was necessary to maintain the means of developing future generations of experts and cadres. Research into fuels and new materials for the defence industry was vital and, similarly, the experimental development of new food crops and methods of augmenting agricultural yields became increasingly important.[16]

Emphasis was placed on the co-operation between research and developmental scientists and the military through the creation of the Soviet Commission for Academic Sciences tasked with developing defence weaponry in Kazakhstan, Siberia and the Urals. Of the twenty-three institutes of higher education evacuated to Kazakhstan, the brightest minds in the country were gathered together in Alma-Ata, where the Soviet State Academy of Sciences was relocated. Several other research institutes joined it there – often complete with their libraries and museums. Key military research into hydro-electric power and materials science took place at the Institute of Physics and Mechanics, the Moscow Aviation Institute and the Moscow Institute for Gold and Precious Metals. The number of academics overall in Kazakhstan increased by a dramatic 470 per cent during the war years.[17]

Twenty-two research institutes with most of their staff and students were evacuated to Uzbekistan, along with sixteen universities and two libraries, mostly concentrated in the city of Tashkent – the so-called 'Soviet Athens'.[18] Thanks to this rapid expansion of educational provision, an astonishing total of 20,000 students graduated in Uzbekistan during the war years. In addition, twelve institutes of higher education were evacuated to Kyrgyzstan, mainly to Frunze, Osh and Przheval'sk. The latter, although far from Moscow, became a new centre for higher education in Central Asia. The Ukrainian Khar'kov Institute for Agricultural Engineering was re-established in Frunze and the Rostov State University in Osh. Kyrgyzstan also accepted educational establishments from Leningrad, including its prestigious veterinary institute.[19]

Once again, Lake Issyk-Kul' came into its own by hosting the research station for high-altitude physical geography on its southern shore, established under the auspices of the newly created Kyrgyz branch of the Academy of Science. Each republic helped to support a philosophy of intellectual investigation and research in the region, albeit mainly through Slavic academic staff evacuated with their institutions from the western Soviet Union. These facilities played an important role in the geological search for rare metals, coal and oil. Similarly, the biology faculty of the Soviet Academy of Science was evacuated to Frunze, while a chemical institute specializing in explosives was also relocated to Kyrgyzstan.[20]

The large numbers of incoming educational institutions contributed greatly to the development of the intellectual life of the region, while simultaneously placing a huge strain on its resources. Suitable buildings were again at a premium, as was the accommodation necessary for academic staff and students alike. The prestige of the newly evacuated western establishments usually accorded them priority in the domestic battle for premises, although some novel arrangements permitted the sharing of accommodation between the rival claims of existing and incoming institutions. The situation was worst in Tashkent, where the Tashkent Institute of Agricultural and Mechanized Irrigation was ousted from its habitual premises by the Moscow Academy for Metallic Machinery. With little sign of advanced planning, local students were evicted to collective farms outside the city, where they struggled to continue their studies. Dormitory housing for trainee teachers at the Tashkent Pedagogical Institute was similarly commandeered for the elite members of the Union of Soviet Writers and academics of the Frunze Military Academy from Moscow. With this step, future Uzbek teachers were relegated to lower ranks in the educational pecking order. The evacuated Academy of Arts in Samarkand was even forced to hold lectures in corridors and on staircases! The authorities in Przheval'sk seem to have been more accommodating to the incoming Nikolaev Shipbuilding Institute, whose students were offered classes from 3 to 11pm in premises shared with the pedagogical institute, which took the morning shift. Evening classes became the norm during the war years, as buildings were exploited to their maximum, being additionally used on Sundays for training courses for tractor drivers and combine harvester operators.[21]

Despite some degree of in-fighting over premises, the evacuated establishments worked quickly to set up shop in their new Central Asian locations, although inevitably the fresh intake of students was somewhat slower to start the new academic year in the autumn of 1942. Fewer academic staff were available to deliver courses, as many had been conscripted and some had already lost their lives in the Red Army. The Nikolaev Shipbuilding Institute, under the directorship of Comrade Chubov, determined to continue its mission in its new home of Przheval'sk, as it prepared future shipping construction engineers, fuel scientists and materials technology specialists for the defence industry. Thanks to the drive of its eight professors and twenty doctoral staff, its 183 students were able to re-start their courses within five weeks of their arrival. Nineteen-year-old Valentina Klimova and her comrade, 21-year-old Anna Farberova, were two of the small minority of women students. Despite all the difficulties engendered by the war, a commendable 84 per cent of them graduated two years later, with a further cohort of 156 graduate engineers by the end of the war. This steady output of highly qualified engineers was enabled by the equipment of specialist laboratories and workshops in the premises made available in Przheval'sk, which included a large canteen adjacent to the student hostel.[22]

The Mikhail Frunze Pedagogical Institute under the directorship of Comrade Sultan Arbaev was also hurriedly evacuated in an internal move from Frunze to Przheval'sk in the autumn of 1941, with a complement of only 670 of its original 1,087 students (having lost the remainder to the army). One hundred and nine of these went on to graduate in the summer of 1942, starting their vital professional careers that autumn. Przheval'sk also became the new home of the Kirov Agricultural College, originally also based in Frunze. In contrast to many institutions which needed to accelerate learning and increase output by decreasing the length of courses, its courses in veterinary medicine, animal husbandry and land management were expanded from two to three years to reflect the academic demands of these specialist qualifications.[23]

The new institutes sometimes catered also for local students, who had previously found it difficult to access higher education, due to the limited academic provision in Central Asia. With the need to replace men killed in action, the state aimed to boost student recruitment by at least 20 per cent in the academic year 1942/3, entailing the refurbishment and expansion of existing premises. Many students enrolling on courses turned out to be those judged unfit for active military service, but still able to consider a future career in teaching, veterinary medicine or engineering.[24]

Although the Soviet Union had embarked on a policy of educational improvement across Central Asia before the war, there is no doubt that the quality and quantity of tertiary education increased in the region during the war, largely thanks to the arrival of evacuated institutes and the state's urgent need to develop specialists in the defence industry. On a micro level, too, the students and even their lecturers helped local communities lacking their menfolk by collecting and preparing medicinal herbs, working on railroad construction, assisting with local defence projects, repairing agricultural machinery and even practising in animal clinics on collective farms. This aid to the region was withdrawn, however, the moment the evacuated educational institutes were repatriated to the western Soviet Union as it was liberated from enemy occupation.[25]

During the war years the number of students in tertiary education increased out of all proportion across the region, for example by an additional 4,600 per year in Kazakhstan alone. However, only a small minority of these were indigenous students, with only 13 per cent of ethnic Kyrgyz students in Kyrgyzstan out of a total of 1,659 during the war years. The Leningrad Veterinary Institute, perhaps unsurprisingly, continued to offer tuition in the Russian language only. In contrast, a further pedagogical institute opened in Przheval'sk in 1944 to meet the need for even more teachers, offering tuition in both Kyrgyz and Russian to accommodate students from across the union. Full literacy was not achieved in Kyrgyzstan until some years after the war, however, when a new generation of children was able to benefit from the substantial educational advances made during the war.[26]

Evacuees

As the German armies pushed through Belarus and approached Moscow and Leningrad, the government finally realized that urgent action was needed to protect the civilian population of the two largest Soviet cities and other urban centres in danger of imminent occupation, for example, Kiev and Odessa in Ukraine. Although Stalin had been opposed to early evacuation, a small degree of preparation had been made in the days preceding the German invasion, and some experience of sudden population displacement had been gained during the First World War and the Stalinist purges. As the movement of civilians away from the danger zones was – to an extent – planned, the term 'evacuees' was coined for those assisted somewhat by the state in their flight; refugees, who took it upon themselves to flee in an unofficial fashion, were labelled 'self-evacuees' and largely left to fend for themselves.[27]

The state Evacuation Council was established shortly after the onset of war to deal with the relocation of civilians according to agreed priorities. Families of Red Army and NKVD officers were first in the evacuation pecking order, alongside Communist Party officials who could re-establish national and local government in the provinces if necessary. Artists and the intellectual elite, able to disseminate the regime's key political ideas, were similarly prioritized, with ordinary workers and their families bringing up the rear.[28] Hospitals, also, were evacuated en bloc, to care for the war wounded in their new destinations in the rear.[29]

During organized waves of evacuation in the summer months of 1941 and 1942, over 16 million Soviet citizens were displaced eastwards, arriving eventually in the safer areas of Central Asia, Siberia and the Urals. Central Asia had to be prepared rapidly for the huge scale of the evacuations hitting the region just a few short weeks after the German invasion. The first wave of evacuees arrived in the summer of 1941 from the north-west of the Soviet Union – Belarus and the Baltic States. Evacuees from Ukraine, Leningrad and Moscow arrived during the autumn, followed by a further wave from the centre and south of Russia – from cities such as Voronezh, Stalingrad, Krasnodar, Rostov and Astrakhan – in the summer of 1942, as the enemy approached the River Volga. The USSR was vast, and it was possible for evacuees to travel thousands of kilometres, while still remaining in their 'home' country – ready to work on the home front in factories and the fields in the forthcoming fight against the enemy. One million civilians were dispatched to Kazakhstan, over half a million to Uzbekistan and 140,000 to Kyrgyzstan. The majority of the evacuees were women, and their numbers included almost a quarter of a million children.[30]

As enemy forces closed in on the city of Leningrad during the summer of 1941, plans were put in place for the evacuation of the civilian elite and those of its population who could best serve the state's war effort in the rear. The government was anxious to retain control of the evacuations, limiting travel to those with official permits and wishing to prevent the expected chaos of 'self-evacuation'. Young people with a potential future in the armed forces were deemed to be more important than the elderly. Evacuation was facilitated for those living in cities with good railway connections to the interior. In contrast, elderly villagers with no access to a train station were often left behind to fend for themselves, along with those in the westernmost reaches of the Soviet Union which had been overrun within the first days of the Nazi invasion. Directed by the security forces of the NKVD, potential evacuees were given little notice of their departure as they quickly packed a few possessions for the long journey east. Many, however, viewed the instructions to depart with suspicion, recalling no doubt the hurried departure of family taken to the GULag camps during the Stalinist Terror only a few years previously. Others felt ashamed to leave their city in its hour of need, especially when it meant abandoning frail relatives.[31]

By the end of August 1941 one and a half million civilians had left Moscow on organized train convoys. The situation in Leningrad was more precarious, as people weighed up the difficulties of travelling against the almost certain risks of remaining in the besieged city. In a large-scale humanitarian operation, children were amongst the first to leave Leningrad that summer, although often without either parent. Women were only permitted on the official transport if they were accompanying children or if they were wives of Red Army personnel. Other evacuees followed a little later, with those departing in the winter taking the frozen 'ice road' over Lake Ladoga.[32]

The Moscow and Leningrad elite were evacuated relatively smoothly, often by air. For most evacuees, though, the journey to an unknown destination was long and arduous in overcrowded trains which were sometimes targeted by enemy bombers. The provision of food at unanticipated halts was at best spasmodic in these difficult conditions. Some were able to claim familial links to citizens in a particular town or area, and were allowed to choose their destination. Tashkent, with its sunny climate and reputation as the 'city of bread', was top of the wish list for many who had enough knowledge of the eastern Soviet Union to form an opinion.[33] Many ordinary citizens similarly hoped for evacuation to another Soviet city, where job opportunities would be greater, although they often found themselves stranded on collective farms in the middle of nowhere. For most evacuees, however, only fate determined where they eventually arrived. The railway route took Ukrainians east across the Caspian Sea into Central Asia, while evacuees from Leningrad took a more northerly route via Siberia into Kazakhstan and Kyrgyzstan, often arriving in Alma-Ata or Frunze. Uzbekistan was only added to the destination list when the scale of the evacuation exercise became overwhelming. Anna Akhmatova, the poet, joined her literary friends there in the autumn of 1941, having travelled by air to Tashkent via Novosibirsk. Other privileged citizens were evacuated to Alma-Ata, for example the wife and daughter of General Konstantin Rokossovskii – one of the main architects of eventual Soviet victory – who arrived from Kiev, and the family of the future leader of the Soviet Union, Leonid Brezhnev.[34]

As the journey east progressed, the evacuees became increasingly aware of their vulnerability, having left their homes and often friends and family at the mercy of the fast-approaching invading armies. Most had no idea of where they were heading or how they would survive, experiencing, despite the promise of state support, the insecurity of the homeless, the cold of approaching winter and pangs of hunger as they travelled. The trains were overcrowded, with little water available for drinking or personal hygiene. No wonder many of the evacuees arrived in Central Asia newly infected with fleas and bedbugs, malaria, cholera, typhus or dysentery.[35]

Their arrival was anticipated by local authorities who set up an *evakopunkt* (evacuation reception centre) at every main station. Despite the bureaucratic wish to process every arrival, official services were often overwhelmed by the influx of evacuees pouring into the region. In due course, though, relative order emerged from the initial chaos. Largely staffed by female Komsomol members, teachers and medical personnel, the task of the *evakopunkt* was firstly to register every evacuee and check their documentation. Surprisingly, despite the trauma of the evacuation process, only 2–3 per cent of the arrivals were without any form of identity documentation. Reception committees then noted the full name, year of birth, place of birth, gender, position in the family, nationality (usually Russian, Ukrainian, Belarusian or Jewish), place of residence prior to evacuation, the Soviet republic from which evacuated, position (if any) in the Communist Party, education and job. Special care was taken with unaccompanied children. The registration process was intended to record the number and date of arrivals, anticipating future enquiries or social needs. It also established the demographics of the evacuees, for instance, the number of unaccompanied children and how many adults were fit for work. Once officially registered, evacuees were made to undergo medical screening and increasingly disinfection and even isolation in quarantine as the evacuations progressed, although many reception facilities lacked the basics of soap and towels. Incomers were offered food vouchers and hot food in winter with clothing where necessary, after which accommodation was arranged in theory – if slowly – and eventually employment found in factories or farms. In the meantime, propaganda activists stationed at the *evakopunkt* handed out written information to the new arrivals.[36]

The dynamics of the population movement are illustrated by records maintained at the large Karaganda *evakopunkt*, which was set up as early as 7 July 1941, although the first evacuees – from Moscow, Kiev and Mogilev – did not arrive until 2 August. By the middle of August the reception centre was flooded with evacuees from Khar'kov, Poltava, Krivii Rog (Kryvyi Rih), Odessa, Bobruisk, Dneprodzerzhinsk (Kamianske), Sevastopol, Vitebsk, Smolensk and Saratov. Of these evacuees, 28 per cent were men, 43 per cent women and 29 per cent children. Overall, however, it is estimated that 75 per cent of adult evacuees to Kazakhstan during the war were women.[37]

Many of the evacuees reaching the Issyk-Kul' province had survived the journey of 5,000 kilometres from Leningrad, often stopping en route to change trains in Kiubyshev (Samara) and Orenburg in Russia, Shymkent or Aktiubinsk (Aktobe) in Kazakhstan, and Frunze. Whole tranches of arrivals are documented on sheet after sheet of official records, each briefly capturing the background of desperate evacuees from the major cities of the European Soviet Union: Kiev, Novgorod, Novorossiisk, Tula, Chernigov, L'vov (L'viv), Kerch', Stalingrad, Riga, Vilnius, Odessa, Moscow, Smolensk, Orlov, Stalino, Evpatoriia, Minsk, Zhitomir, Bobruisk, Taganrog, Belgorod, Kaliningrad, Voronezh, Simferopol, Krasnodar, Tuapse, Khanko, Groznyi, Sevastopol, Kursk, Astrakhan, Odessa and Khar'kov. In this way, dentists, engineers, hairdressers, housewives, musicians, librarians, metal workers, accountants, teachers and factory workers successfully escaped the advancing German forces. Although frail elderly family members had often been left behind, the oldest evacuee to arrive in Przheval'sk seems to have been a 66-year-old from Odessa.

As the weeks progressed from the autumn of 1941 into 1942, the steady trickle of evacuees became a deluge, as trains carried more and more Jews from the west and increasingly former residents of Stalingrad, followed by arrivals from the northern Caucasus and lower Volga areas. In all, over

10,000 people reached the Issyk-Kul' province between 1941 and 1943, to be spread out over the area in towns, villages and collective farms. Many from the same departure point eventually found themselves living in the same Kyrgyz village, such as the large group from Leningrad who were all sent to the Jeti-Oguz area.[38]

Arrivals were gradually processed as their credentials were established by the NKVD. Most evacuees could not prove where they were going to work and live, and had to fight the authorities in order to remain in a large town, sometimes staying there illegally. The author Kornei Chukovskii intervened on behalf of Anna Akhmatova when she arrived in Tashkent, while others found refuge with relations. The privilege of living in the city was reserved for the elite and key workers in order to stem the flow of incomers, particularly those with no professional qualifications. Many with no fixed employment or existing connections to Central Asia were evicted from the city as undesirables, following one of the regular raids on markets and stations in Tashkent or Alma-Ata, being sent to work on collective farms in outlying provinces.[39]

The sudden arrival of thousands of evacuees, often in poor physical condition, fuelled the suspicions of the local population as well as the reception committees at the stations. Despite their evacuation having been organized and executed by the state, not only were they a drain on local resources, needing food and accommodation, but they also presented a real health hazard as carriers of disease. Soviet propaganda had made citizens so aware of the possibility of enemy agents in their midst that they felt threatened by these foreign-looking incomers, sometimes without official papers. Some felt justified in questioning their motives for travelling to Central Asia, dubbing them deserters, cowards or criminals rather than upstanding and traumatized fellow Soviet citizens deserving of sympathy. Indeed, some Russian families already resident in Central Asia decided to return to Russia, fearing the Uzbek people whom they perceived as dangerous and anti-Russian, at exactly the same time as millions were travelling east to avoid the enemy armies.[40]

The state, however, dictated that evacuees should be treated properly, despite the chaotic circumstances of their arrival. Instructions from Moscow to 'look after them' required that they should be supplied with the bare necessities, which in fact proved rather optimistic in reality, when local resources simply could not stretch to state demands. Local authorities acknowledged that the arriving evacuees usually had no means of financial support, with many receiving a small lump sum on arrival in Central Asia with which to embark on their new life, if little else. Military families evacuated from the westernmost borders of the Soviet Union received the most immediate assistance. Planning on a local scale is evident in instructions to provide new arrivals with bread vouchers, sugar, soap and shoes, plus a ration of kerosene with which to heat the often cold and bare rooms they were allocated – not ideal, it was accepted, for the many ill children who were carried off the trains. To supplement the official provision, the organisation 'Aid for the Front' established committees offering help for evacuee families with tangible support for some lucky newcomers.[41]

There is some evidence of an initially smooth evacuation process to Uzbekistan, where local collective farmers were prepared to welcome and take in the homeless, in an overt demonstration of loyalty to the Soviet Union. However, as numbers increased, many locals became unwilling to help and tried to charge the incomers a prohibitively high rent. The situation in larger towns deteriorated rapidly, with severe overcrowding in Tashkent leading to friction between the local population and incomers. With even more evacuees arriving in the spring of 1942, factories found it increasingly difficult to accommodate their workers, relying at first on hostels and later on temporary tents, makeshift outhouses, stables or even primitive shelters constructed of cardboard. In fact, space was at such a premium that some workers at the sugar beet plant in Tashkent slept on the stage of the main theatre when they first arrived in the city.[42]

As Tashkent's population quickly doubled with many unregistered refugees, the newcomers found that they were in competition for housing and food with local residents. Some incomers even preferred to live on the streets of Tashkent rather than move out of the capital – at least a rent-free option. In Kazakhstan, the city of Alma-Ata managed reasonably well when its first few hundred evacuees arrived, but by the spring of 1942 an accommodation crisis had developed as thousands converged on the capital; by the end of the war the population had almost doubled. One situation was recorded where an extended family of twelve relations of one soldier on active service had to share a room of 9 square metres. Not all could sit down at the same time and sleeping simultaneously was not an option. The average living space per person in Central Asian towns during the war years was a mere 3.5 square metres. To help the situation, four of the city's five pre-war hotels were redesigned as modest flats for workers' families. With a torrent of newcomers and cramped living quarters, disease was rife from the winter of 1941 to 1942, as serious outbreaks of typhus broke out in Tashkent and Frunze. Despite the push to maintain hygiene on the streets of Tashkent, many evacuees succumbed to disease and the strain of the journey as the mortality rate soared.[43]

Although the situation was not uniform across the region, the cities bore the brunt of both the accommodation and food shortages. Factories and educational institutes usually had the resources to feed their staff in canteens, but most evacuees struggled to survive from one day to the next. Prices rocketed, leading to accusations of locals capitalizing on the distress of evacuees, even though the situation was equally dire for most residents. Even evacuees billeted on farms found that locals were loath to share their precious commodities, as they resorted to selling or bartering their every possession in order to avoid starvation. Those with friends or family already in Central Asia could depend to some extent on a support network to navigate the bureaucracy and supply limitations. A few even attempted to bribe their way through the system, to the overt disapproval of the local population. For most, however, it was a case of 'out of the frying pan into the fire' as they tried to make ends meet and come to terms with life in exile.[44]

Ethnic tensions added to the stress of both evacuees and local residents, as populations from across the Soviet Union came together in the melting pot of Central Asia. Fear of the unknown foreigners was evident on both sides of the divide, exacerbated by serious linguistic barriers to communication, except in the case of children who picked up a new language relatively quickly. When it came to finding employment or social support, some evacuees were perceived as work-shy, undeserving members of society. Zacharii Miller, for example, expected more from the Soviet system after his years of fighting in the International Brigade in the Spanish Civil War and his time in a German concentration camp. Classed as a political émigré, he was evacuated to Kazakhstan where he was placed on the *Krasnyi vostok* (Red East) collective farm near Alma-Ata. Thanks to the suspicions of the resident farmers, though, he was viewed as at best a foreigner and at worst a German spy. With no warm coat, Comrade Miller was made to stand guard all night over the valuable farm equipment in the freezing winter weather, for which he was 'paid' half a litre of milk a day. No wonder that many evacuees found it hard to settle in Central Asia, clinging on to the hope that their exile would be relatively short-lived. Tashkent in particular, with Frunze and Alma-Ata, was home to evacuees and refugees from across the western Soviet Union and eastern Europe, which proved somewhat of a culture shock to the local population. The Central Asian intelligentsia were amazed at the thriving new social and literary scene around the artistic and musical evacuees: the jazz they brought was something completely alien to many.[45]

Most evacuees arriving in the Issyk-Kul' province of Kyrgyzstan were rapidly directed to the most suitable vacancies in what appears to have been a relatively smooth administrative operation. The majority of incomers were from towns or other urban areas in the western Soviet Union, often office workers, academics or tradesmen. However, large numbers were sent to work on collective farms with their families, even those with no evident experience of physical labour. This was sometimes a temporary fix, as there was little for them to do during the winter months. Factory work was usually the solution, as production was stepped up to meet the demands of a country at war. Food-producing plants always needed extra hands, as did munitions and armaments plants. Over 300 incomers were dispatched to the Grigor'evka area, where they were allocated to the oil factory. Others arriving from eastern Ukraine and the Russian Krasnodar province were taken on by a local fish factory, while some were selected to undergo training for other necessary jobs, including childcare. Several particularly welcome engineers and their families were moved to the villages of Mikhailovka and

Pristan', but it is unclear where the sole male Ukrainian ballet dancer was finally lodged and employed.[46]

Despite the copious lists and attention to detail on the ground, the sheer speed, scale and chaos of the evacuations led to many families and friends being separated, especially when the postal service caused delays in delivery or even the loss of letters. The Central Information Bureau registered data on all evacuees and was also prepared to respond to queries about the whereabouts of individuals. Many serving soldiers completely lost track of where their families had been sent. Writing on postcards from field post offices, they sent desperate enquiries to various potential destinations, including to the main reception centres in Central Asia.[47]

The Issyk-Kul' authorities dealt with their fair share of such entreaties from the autumn of 1941 to the spring of 1943, as the Soviet population endeavoured to rebuild familial links in the face of the crisis. A certain S. Bogdanovich wrote in search of his wife, Mariia, and two children who were evacuated from Lithuania on 23 June 1941. Fellow-soldier Nikolai Makarov also craved news of his family: his wife Liubov', son, daughter and mother, evacuated from Minsk. Iakov Kleiman had been wounded in action and wrote his letter of enquiry while recovering in Cheliabinsk. His family – wife, two children and his father – had left the Ukrainian town of Zhitomir as the enemy advanced. In view of the state of war, replies, usually in the negative, were issued relatively quickly: Iakov Kleiman was not the only man to learn that his family had 'not arrived here'. Other enquiries came from closer to home, from other Soviet citizens evacuated to different parts of Central Asia. As the war entered its second year, pro forma cards were issued to enable a more streamlined service. However, the Kyrgyz NKVD was unable to help a certain A. Zlotnik, based in Stalinabad, Tajikistan, who was hoping to be reunited with his family from Bobruisk in Belarus. Similarly, Mosei Vainberg, originally from Luninets in Belarus, pursued his search for his parents and sister from his new home in Tashkent, and an elderly member of the Glinguk family, also in Uzbekistan, appeared desperate to find her relations from Minsk.[48]

Most replies to these letters were brief and to the point, leaving the searcher to pursue other lines of enquiry. Occasionally, though, some glimmer of hope shone through the darkness. A response to one enquiry revealed that the person in question had been conscripted into the Red Army almost as soon as he stepped off the train in Przheval'sk. Many evacuees went to great lengths to avoid mandatory conscription, which would have meant leaving their dependants alone in Central Asia. For their part, the military authorities worked equally hard to gather together as many men as possible to shore up the army ranks, including a group of twelve evacuees newly arrived in Przheval'sk, most of whom had travelled from Riga and who then, doubtless, would soon be travelling back to the front line in the opposite direction.[49]

Jewish refugees

The bitter smoke of exile
is in my eyes . . .
I am a Jew.[50]

In his timely response to Hitler's invasion of the Soviet Union and the exodus of many Jewish citizens from Eastern Europe, the Uzbek poet G'afur G'ulom bemoaned in 1941 the fate of the Jewish people over thousands of years of repeated episodes of exile. In his poem 'I am a Jew', he demonstrates unity with the Jewish people from the flight out of Egypt to the present day, in an expression of 'me too' empathy with the millions forced to flee eastwards to an alien land, or with those fighting in the Red Army.

Finishing several stanzas with the statement 'I am a Jew' and 'I am a person', in a 'Je suis Charlie' type of solidarity with the Jewish people, G'ulom recalls the friendship of the peoples of the Soviet Union. Furthermore, he emphasizes the equality of all ethnicities and advocates the elimination of racial or class differences on earth. As 'a representative of the human race', G'ulom expresses a clear disapproval of the Nazi ideology of racial supremacy, while also hinting at a degree of anti-Semitism in the Soviet Union.[51]

The particular problem of Jews living in the western regions of the Soviet Union was not highlighted by Moscow during, or indeed for years after the war. The Soviet censors actively suppressed the dissemination of information about the atrocities taking place in Belarus, Ukraine and western Russia as the enemy advanced, in spite of the official Soviet policy to portray the Germans in the worst possible light. Although evidence of Nazi mass executions of Jews had been discovered by the Red Army in Ukraine in 1941, Soviet media mentioned only generalized accounts of German aggression towards civilians. Even the reports of Jewish war correspondents such as Il'ia Erenburg and Vasilii Grossman were censored to the extent that the general Soviet public knew little of the plight of the Jews, although the reaction of cinematographers was occasionally more immediate. The execution of Jews at Kiev's Bab'ii Iar' in 1941, for example, was not fully exposed until much later in the war, when the Soviet Union was forced to confront the issue of Holocaust events in occupied areas. Even in the post-war years, Stalin continued to downplay the Holocaust on Soviet territory, with massacres of Jewish citizens rarely highlighted, being included only in the more ambiguous official narrative of fascist atrocities towards civilians.[52]

Only those in close contact with Jewish families were able to read between the official lines to gauge the depth of the unfolding tragedy. As is evident from G'ulom's poem, the dire straits of Soviet Jews soon became apparent to Central Asians as thousands of Jewish refugees started to arrive in Uzbekistan and Kazakhstan. The adversities they had faced while living under occupation, in addition to some ongoing anti-Semitism in Central Asia, rendered them even more vulnerable than many others arriving in the region.

It is estimated that just under 5 million Jews were living in the Soviet Union in 1939. Of these, about 1.4 million lived in the east, unaffected by the German occupation. Just under 1 million Jews from Germany, Austria and Eastern European countries sought refuge in the Soviet Union from 1938 to 1940. Estimates vary as to how many Jews fled to safety in the eastern regions of the Soviet Union – probably around 2 million – but it is widely accepted that about 25–30 per cent of all evacuees and refugees were Jewish. Most experts agree, however, that about one and a half million Jews arrived in Central Asia in the first two years of the war.[53]

Travelling east

The hairdresser from Odessa, the teacher from Minsk, the accountant from Novorossiisk – all made their way east in their rush to escape the Germans. Those who had not already been evacuated with their workplace became by default refugees, so-called self-evacuees as they did not wait for official permission to flee. Independent of the official evacuation system, they were dependent upon their own resources and at the mercy of the weather, available transport and German bombers. Most of those on the move were in family groups, the majority aged between ten and forty.[54] Many elderly individuals were not up to making the arduous journey; others were more worried about the reality of leaving their home than of the arrival of the Germans. Most, however, realised what the Nazi occupation could mean for them as rumours of mass executions in Minsk, Odessa and Simferopol preceded the enemy's push into Russia itself. Displaying a distinct lack of trust in the Soviet authorities or the Red Army to come to their assistance, they chose voluntarily to leave their homes in search of refuge. It was easier for those relatively wealthy professionals possessing the means to travel. Some even had family connections elsewhere in the Soviet Union or friends who had previously undertaken the journey east and who had written letters of invitation urging a rapid retreat.

A contemporaneous survey indicated that the Jewish population of Eastern Europe largely embraced cosmopolitanism. As the persecution of Jews increased in Nazi Germany towards the end of the 1930s, those with sufficient means and connections were able to join friends and family abroad, forging a new life in the United States or Palestine. Others decided to flee east into the Soviet Union, which at that time was perceived to be a safe destination. Under this assumption, just under a million Jews arrived in Russia from Germany, Austria, the Baltic States, Poland, Czechoslovakia, Romania and Bessarabia, joining Soviet Jews from Ukraine, Crimea and Belarus in the final exodus.[55] In common with most evacuees, they headed to the Urals, western Siberia and Central Asia. Many arrived in Kazakhstan from August 1941 to January 1942, but, as the flood increased, Tashkent (and Uzbekistan in general) became a more popular destination with its reputation for fresh food and a clement climate. Bukhara and Samarkand in Uzbekistan, and Osh in Kyrgyzstan, had long-standing communities of Bukharian Jews, which, although different in many ways from the European Ashkenazy Jews, nonetheless held largely similar beliefs and followed some of the same traditions. Quite a sizeable minority, however, were content simply to go as far as possible out of the reach of the advancing German forces, alighting from their train at any random station in a region which looked, at first sight, totally uniform.[56]

Carrying everything they could manage between them – occasionally even furniture and pianos – families took to trains, lorries and cars as they made their escape. When nothing else was available, some were forced to travel on horseback or even on foot, preferring minor tracks and trails as the Germans continued to strafe major roads and railway lines. Although some commentators credit the Soviet authorities with making every effort to expedite their evacuation, this claim has been strongly refuted by others. Ironically, a government clamping down on 'illegal' travel failed to address the chaos endangering the nation's transport network, as millions of Jews joined official evacuees in their haste to find relative safety in the rear. There was inevitably a huge inadequacy of passenger trains, causing most to resort

FIGURE 7.1 *Refugees travelling to Central Asia. Reproduced with permission from the Issyk-Kul' State Archives.*

to slower goods wagons or cattle trucks and make several changes. Food on the journey was hard to come by, leaving many refugees begging for assistance. Only the lucky ones managed to procure provisions and occasionally even a precious travel permit, if sometimes issued retrospectively.[57]

Employment

Vladimir Sorokin was one of the last to leave Briansk in western Russia, clutching only a briefcase of his most important files. He had been the senior judge in his area, charged with the evacuation of civilians and the destruction of all secret state documents as the bombs started to fall on the town. Sorokin was eventually able to meet up with his large family, who had preceded him on the journey east. They managed to rent a small room in Uzbekistan, but were permanently hungry and forced to send the children to work in the cotton fields at harvest time in order to survive. By 1942 they had suffered enough and decided to move to north-east Kazakhstan, where they started afresh in the town of Leninogorsk (Ridder) in the mountains close to the Russian border. At least there the children were able to attend school. Sorokin was deemed too weak to serve in the army, but managed to find a position in an evacuated hospital and then in a POW camp for German soldiers. By the end of 1942 he had got his feet back on the legal ladder, becoming the assistant to the town's procurator. By 1944 he was in charge of the whole Leninogorsk legal system as chief public prosecutor.[58]

Sorokin was typical of many Jewish refugees in that he had formerly been living in a town rather than the countryside. Most had held positions in commerce, manufacturing industry, medicine, banking, academia or other office jobs, but were eminently mobile and prepared to change direction if necessary. Jewish medical professionals, teachers and academics were quick to find employment, if of a lower status than previously. Many Jewish refugees were totally unequipped, however, for the hard physical work expected of them as they were largely deployed to collective farms or the Karaganda coal fields, with women often allocated to one of the several textile factories in the region.

Self-evacuees by definition fell outside the state-coordinated evacuation system, so that many were left to fend for themselves. With no official state system to support the imperilled Jewish population of the western Soviet Union, those without private funding were all too often left destitute with no official benefits. With a typical salary of little more than 150 roubles per month, sufficient only for a few days' food, the threat of starvation was always present. Even those working on collective farms received an income commensurate with their productivity. As many had no experience in farming, they, too, faced real deprivation. Tenacity paid off in some towns, however. One young Jewish couple worked hard to save enough money to buy their own cotton loom and successfully started their own weaving business at home. In this way Mehal Kesler produced 20 metres of cloth a day which was traded on the black market – always with a wary eye open for the ever-present NKVD.[59]

Kesler was always careful about leaving his home, as he was well aware of cases when the NKVD press-ganged young men into military service.[60] There was always the real possibility of conscription into the Red Army, which took all Jewish refugees fit for active service, before allocating the rest to work in the rear. Even Jewish refugees from other countries were deemed to have become Soviet citizens by virtue of their residence on Soviet territory, and thus became liable for conscription. One and a half million Jewish men and women served in the armed forces in the war, many of whom were volunteers, wishing to defeat the enemy forces which had committed such atrocities amongst their communities. If captured, Soviet Jews were treated even more harshly by the enemy than other POWs. Refugees in Central Asia were more likely to be deployed to a labour battalion, suffering often appalling conditions as they slaved on construction projects in the rear. Those men arriving in the Issyk-Kul' province from the Baltic States, for instance, were sent to mustering points in Russia where they were formed into regiments comprised wholly of their compatriots, thus minimizing any linguistic or cultural issues. Wherever they served, Jews in the army suffered less than ideal conditions, with common instances of jokes and asides which rarely drew the censure of officers, despite official regulations concerning anti-Semitism.[61]

Anti-Semitism

Anti-Semitism was also experienced by civilian refugees in Central Asia, such as the son of Vladimir Sorokin – by then assistant procurator in the Kazakh town of Leninogorsk. On 29 November 1942, fifteen-year-old Grigorii Sorokin penned an open letter to Stalin, published in the newspaper *Kazakhstanskaia Pravda*.

> Dear Iosif [Joseph] Vissarionovich!
>
> It is my duty as a Pioneer to inform you of certain outrageous acts here in Leninogorsk. A Jew is a fully fledged citizen. But it is not possible to walk along the streets, which are covered with graffiti: 'There goes a Jew [*zhid*]' or 'Beat up the Jews and save Russia'! You can't go to the cinema and, if you dare to, you may be attacked. [. . .] I request you, dear leader, to take steps to ensure that this does not continue. I wish you health and strength for the rest of your life, because this is necessary for the peoples of the Soviet Union. Long live the Great Friendship of the Soviet Peoples.[62]

Cases of anti-Semitism in Central Asia have been downplayed by some commentators working on the memoirs of the Jewish cultural elite –

evacuees largely protected by the state. For refugees at close quarters with local residents, however, there is no doubt that anti-Semitism – not a hugely reported problem in the prewar years – increased during the war, permeating the Red Army and affecting many regions in the rear of the country. This inter-ethnic tension badly undermined the harmony advocated by the government's much-vaunted 'friendship of the peoples' policy, as Sorokin Junior reminded Stalin in no uncertain terms.[63]

Manifestations of anti-Semitism such as those described by Sorokin were many. Some employers overtly refused to give jobs to Jews desperately seeking a new position, possibly in the knowledge that many struggled with hard physical labour. Name-calling in the street and anti-Semitic jokes were common. At the market, Jewish refugees were pushed out of bread queues and sometimes refused sales of medicine or other goods. Spitting and stoning were commonplace in Osh, Kyrgyzstan. Worse acts of violence also occurred. Jews were openly attacked on the streets of Tashkent and Leninogorsk, rapes were alleged on Uzbek collective farms, and three murders in Uzbekistan were attributed to anti-Semitism. A concerted pogrom reminiscent of tsarist Russia even took place in Alma-Ata in August 1942.[64]

There is little evidence of prior tension with the resident Jewish community in Central Asia. Jewish families had been present in the region for centuries, usually living along the Silk Road and working in trade or money exchange. During the nineteenth century settlers from imperial Russia started to arrive from the west, amongst them some of the first Ashkenazi Jews, often skilled artisans. Most of the Jewish communities already resident in Central Asia at the outbreak of war had assimilated the indigenous culture and sometimes spoke several local languages, even though they usually lived in their own separate quarters of the main cities.[65]

The reasons behind the considerable growth in tension between local citizens and incoming Jewish refugees, with a marked increase in hostile behaviour during the war period, are various. As Jews formed the largest proportion of new residents in the region, amounting to over sixty per cent of evacuees and refugees in Uzbekistan in 1941, they rapidly became victims of discontent and rumour-mongering as social conditions deteriorated and local residents felt threatened by the flood of newcomers perceived to be taking their accommodation and food. Visibly different from the indigenous population and Slavic residents and evacuees, they formed an easy target for a restless population in search of a scapegoat.[66]

It was not clear to the people of Central Asia why so many Jewish refugees had fled their homes so rapidly. Soviet propaganda made no attempt to explain why this was the case and state policy intentionally avoided the inclusion in the press of explicit details of the mass execution of Jews in the occupied western regions. Central Asians therefore questioned the mass exodus, deeming Jewish refugees cowardly, in stark contrast to the local men who were serving in the Red Army, if usually against their will. As this resentment grew, Jews were accused of intentionally avoiding military service, while paying others to take their place on the front line. Deemed 'Tashkent partisans' by some, they were derided for their lack of physical ability in the field and for preferring employment in safe, relatively warm offices. Popular prejudice was fed by Jewish stereotypes, mixed with accusations of their former Western, capitalist lifestyles, contrary to the tenets of communism. Not only were Jewish refugees hated, they were also suspected of enemy activity in some extreme cases, as Jewish doctors were accused of sending wounded soldiers back to the front too quickly. These wounded troops also brought with them to the rear aspects of the anti-Semitic attitude prevalent in the ranks. It was evident, too, in German propaganda widespread in occupied territory, to the extent that some even considered it beneficial to kill Jewish children as advocated by the Nazis.[67]

In this way, inter-racial hostility and active anti-Semitism were deemed justifiable by the perpetrators, as Jewish refugees became a scapegoat for a wealth of real and imaginary problems. Not only did anti-Semitic violence occur but on many occasions the local police turned a blind eye to the unrest. There were cases when arrests were made, for example after the Alma-Ata pogrom. However, on balance it was the Jewish community who were let down and even accused of their own rumour-mongering to incite panic about the alleged pogroms. This, it was implied, was in order to achieve their anti-communist Zionist goals. Some Jewish refugees were arrested for counter-revolutionary activity and spreading lies about the bourgeois way of life in a complete clash of traditions, leading the local population to believe that they may indeed be alien spies. The violence in Central Asia continued even in 1946, when the majority of Jewish refugees had returned home. The response of the authorities was tepid indeed, calling overtly anti-Semitic attacks 'acts of hooliganism', which often went unpunished. However, in contrast to many episodes, the situation in Leninogorsk was resolved as several dozen anti-Semites were arrested and tried. Furthermore, a public response to young Grigorii Sorokin's letter to Stalin cleared the Jews of any guilt, reinforcing the official line that anybody inciting hatred against the Jews was helping the fascist enemy achieve its goals.[68]

This was indeed the position of the state, which continued to remain silent about mounting evidence of state-sponsored anti-Semitism while simultaneously declaring the 'friendship of the peoples'. The regime no doubt harboured concerns about Jewish nationalism and the influence of Jewish figures in Soviet cultural life. Prominent Jews in the Moscow press lost their jobs, while actors and other members of the film industry in Central Asia lost potential roles and were targeted purely for their ethnicity – a trend of persecution which continued well into the 1950s with the so-called Doctors' Plot of 1953. Stalin accused Jewish doctors of conspiring to murder elite

Communist Party members, leading to the execution of some, while several others were sentenced to lengthy hard labour terms in Kazakhstan as 'enemies of the people'. By the end of the war state anti-Semitism was so prevalent across the Soviet Union that the popular joke about Jews having served 'on the Tashkent front' circulated widely. Soviet leaders continued to do nothing to disseminate information about the Holocaust in Eastern Europe and on Soviet territory for decades, fearing perhaps that international sympathy for the Jewish population at the hands of the Nazis may diminish Soviet claims to national victimhood by virtue of the massive number of Soviet lives lost in the war.[69]

In spite of some anti-Semitism, most Jewish refugees survived the war thanks to their Central Asian hosts.[70] A letter written by teenager Iakov Ryskin vividly expresses his thanks to the people of Akmolinsk (Astana), where his family found refuge, while also educating local citizens about the atrocities from which they had escaped:

Dear Kazakh friends!

Our family is still alive thanks to your help and support. My mother's brother lost his life at the front; fascists shot my mother's sister and her children, with her dead brother and his children in the town of Novozybkov in Briansk province; they burnt down our house in Unecha, where my brother, sister and I were born and raised. I am writing this as I will always remember that we survived the war because the Kazakh people sheltered and cared for us. Our children and grandchildren will always recall with gratitude what you did for the Jewish people.[71]

Thousands of similar cases across Central Asia are testament to the tenacity of the Jewish refugees and to the real lifeline they received in the region. In return, Central Asia benefited from the talents many Jewish workers brought with them which contributed to the cultural and economic development of the region – their academic and medical skills, their craftsmanship and cinematic prowess which enriched the whole of the Soviet Union. After the war, those who remained tended to move to the larger cities of Central Asia, where synagogues were established as Jewish communities developed in the war years.[72]

Evacuated intellectuals

Many of the intellectual and cultural elite enjoyed a relatively easy transit from Moscow or Leningrad to Central Asia, with some even travelling by plane or private car to their preferred destination of Alma-Ata or Tashkent.

As cinematographers and actors gathered in their relocated studios to produce new films, often for state propaganda purposes, an unofficial literary world assembled in Tashkent around authors Kornei and Lidiia Chukovskii, novelist Alexei Tolstoi and Evgeniia Pasternak (wife of poet Boris Pasternak). Nadezhda Mandel'shtam, widow of poet Osip Mandel'shtam, travelled by train to Kazakhstan, where she was forced to spend the winter of 1941 to 1942 working on a collective farm in the south. She was finally permitted to move to Tashkent, carrying with her the precious collection of her husband's manuscripts. Working as a teacher of English, she lived at first in the home of poet Anna Akhmatova. Akhmatova was already at the centre of this group of evacuees from her arrival in November 1941 until her departure for her home in Leningrad a few months after the end of the siege in May 1944.[73]

Some evacuees hated Tashkent with its searing heat and incomprehensible language. It was impossible for them to understand the tea house culture of the city, until they realized that hot tea was far better than water when it came to combatting disease. Alexei Tolstoi dubbed the city the 'Istanbul of the poor', just as Akhmatova similarly described it as 'the pauper's Constantinople' or 'Baghdad'. Of course, Tashkent may have seemed exotic, but it was not exactly foreign, being part of the same state as Leningrad or Moscow, despite its huge distance from the major western cities. It must have been difficult for Russian exiles to cope with the bustle and confusion of different languages, however: only a few of them were able to learn the Uzbek language to help them cope with everyday life. Russian was also the lingua franca of Alma-Ata and Frunze, where most of the residents were Europeans. Many Russian evacuees became exasperated with the day-to-day struggle of life in Uzbekistan, although some were inspired by the onslaught on their senses of this Asian city – the noise of the market, the smell of spices and herbs and the sight of exotic animals and veiled Muslim women. It must have been equally hard for Tashkent residents to empathize with these pale and alien-looking evacuees.[74]

Some writers tended to romanticize Tashkent, with its strange sounds, sights and smells. Despite the problems of conveying the dislocation of the exile getting used to life in a new place, they were surrounded by a tight circle of fellow-evacuees who could appreciate their works, even if written under the radar of the Soviet authorities.[75] For Akhmatova, it was the eastern moon in the dark night sky which reinforced her sense of unity with, and wonder at her Asiatic surroundings in the poems 'A v knigakh ia posledniuiu stranitsu' (But in books I always loved the final page) (1943) and 'Luna v zenite' (The moon at zenith) (1942–4). The former describes the Central Asian moon emitting green rays from a position low in the sky at midnight, said to evoke a soft crying sound when falling on the snow-white walls of her Tashkent home – a stark contrast to her beloved 'house on the Fontanka' in Leningrad. The sound recalled by the poet in the latter poem, when the moon is at its height, is rather that of water in the 'wooden shade' of her 'solid' house in Tashkent, which she vows never to forget.[76]

A secure home was very important to Akhmatova amidst all the insecurities of the Stalin era; she was therefore one of the artistic elite who accepted and made the most of their time in Central Asia. Playing to the senses again, 'cold water' in the searing heat was appreciated by the poet from coastal Leningrad,[77] as were the vividly coloured flowers emerging as 'Tashkent blazed into bloom'.[78] The sight of the city suddenly bursting into scented blossom impressed Akhmatova hugely; gazing at her exotic surroundings, she resolves never to forget the dark-skinned young mothers holding small lambs in their arms – a totally unknown sight in distant Leningrad.[79]

However, Akhmatova was seriously ill with typhus early in her stay in Tashkent, which coloured her attitude to the city.[80] For Akhmatova, the sometimes overwhelming nostalgia for her home city features strongly in her poetry of the war years. Her masterpiece, 'Poem without a hero', started in Leningrad, with the epilogue completed in Tashkent in 1942,[81] contains the following telling lines:

All of us who have nowhere of our own
Peer through others' windows from outside.
Some are in New York, some in Tashkent,
And the bitter air of banishment
To the exile is like a poisoned wine.[82]

Children on the move

In her poem recalling the dreadful effects of the bombardment of Leningrad on children, Anna Akhmatova expresses her compassion for 'the orphans of Peter, my children!' calling the city by its familiar name from its pre-Soviet days.[83] One of these was little Alik Iakovlev, last on the list alphabetically of the 130 evacuees in one of the groups to arrive in the Issyk-Kul' province. Found alone on the street, the seven-year-old orphan had lost his father in action and his mother in the siege of Leningrad. Alik and his group finally arrived in Kyrgyzstan in the autumn of 1942, to be placed in a new children's home in the small village of Kurmenty in the Issyk-Kul' province. Lacking imagination, the local authorities named the establishment after the hometown of its inhabitants: the Leningrad Children's Home.[84]

During the summer and autumn of 1941, thousands of children like Alik were evacuated from Leningrad and other towns in the western Soviet Union, many of them eventually recognized as orphans. Over 200,000 children finally arrived in Uzbekistan, with a further 156,000 travelling to the city of Alma-Ata. In addition, much as London schools were evacuated en masse to safer parts of the United Kingdom, entire boarding schools and children's homes with their full complement of children and adult staff were evacuated to Central Asia. Moscow's School Number 38 for children of Spanish Civil War republicans who had fled to the Soviet Union, for example, was evacuated to Tashkent with all its equipment. Similarly, over 5,000 students from music colleges in Russia's Krasnodar province arrived in Uzbekistan, where they were deployed to institutes in Tashkent, Samarkand and Kokand.[85]

The statistics are a reminder of the large-scale trauma and dislocation inflicted on many Soviet children during the ten years from 1936 to 1946. Not only did existing children's homes shelter newly orphaned children, but also many whose parents had suffered from the pre-war Stalinist purges. By the end of 1942 almost 45,000 children under sixteen from over forty children's homes in Odessa, Leningrad, Moscow, Kursk, Voroshilograd (Luhansk) and Smolensk had arrived in Kyrgyzstan. Uzbekistan took in almost eighty homes during the same period, while a further 149 children's homes and sixteen state boarding schools from Moscow ended up in Kazakhstan. The Khar'kov school for deaf mutes also brought its seventy-eight children with special needs to their new home in Kazakhstan. State policy was usually to keep together evacuated children with a common background, but a lack of premises often mitigated against this, as pragmatic decisions held sway and children were split up.[86]

It is estimated that around 40 per cent of evacuees registered with the Tashkent authorities in December 1941 were children; in general two-thirds of evacuated children were boys, with a substantial minority of girls arriving in Uzbekistan, probably reflecting their extreme vulnerability. The majority of children were in fact teenagers, while only 2.5 per cent were under the age of eight. Far too many children were forced to travel alone, some scooped up from the streets, like Alik, and sometimes even taken directly from Pioneer summer camps – often against the will of their parents – by a state anxious to safeguard its future. Both parents and children were traumatized – the parents because they feared losing contact with their unaccompanied children, and the children who were completely exhausted physically and mentally by the journey east. The parents' concerns were unfortunately all too often justified, as many never saw their children again, despite their and the state's best efforts. The psychological strain on both sides was immense.[87]

Reception centres for children were set up across Central Asia, registering around 200 per day in Tashkent at the height of the evacuations, most of whom arrived dirty and in poor physical shape. Ten-year-old Ksenie arrived alone in Frunze, having travelled to Kyrgyzstan from Crimea, only to be moved onwards to a more permanent home in Naryn. Most children spent the war based on one of the many collective farms of the region, but it seems that offspring of more privileged party officials or key workers tended to be placed in Tashkent in more favourable children's homes. Many, however, found themselves completely homeless and had to resort to living on the streets of major towns and cities, often succumbing to disease in the squalor. The town of Przheval'sk found it necessary to open a reception facility for homeless children, which directed these parentless waifs and strays to a local children's home. Even children evacuated with their families struggled in their new surroundings, often having to work in mines or factories once they reached the age of fourteen. This usually carried the advantage of a meal ticket in the adjoining canteen, which was useful in a family which had lost its main breadwinner. Younger children sometimes had little more to eat than thin soup and bread, compounding the emaciated and diseased state in which many of them arrived in Central Asia.[88] The situation was so dire for some parents that they made the difficult decision to place their children in an institution. This additional demand on children's homes placed an extra strain on facilities which already catered for orphans and the unaccompanied children of parents in the Red Army.

Prior to 1941 there were only three children's homes in the whole of Uzbekistan, so that the first unaccompanied children to arrive in Tashkent were scattered across the republic as efforts were made to place them appropriately after their mandatory period of quarantine. By the end of 1942 there were 154 children's homes in total in Uzbekistan. The strain on resources was immense across the region, with children often sleeping two to a bed. Tashkent's Children's Home Number 22 was opened in 1942 in response to the massive influx of evacuees to the city. Run by director Antonina Khlebushkina, this one home alone received around 500 children during the course of the war, mainly from the besieged city of Leningrad.[89]

A large proportion of younger evacuees were too weak to withstand the journey to Central Asia, causing a high infant mortality rate. Most of the evacuees in the children's homes of the Issyk-Kul' district were therefore over the age of four. Children living in towns tended to attend ordinary schools, but many children's homes in the countryside had their own dedicated school attached, with a structure similar to that of the state boarding schools – mainly seven-year schools with hardly any senior classes. Although many children's homes across the region had to cater for a mixture of mother tongues, Alik Iakovlev's home concentrated on Russian, being one of two orphanages in the Issyk-Kul' province dedicated to children from Leningrad, as the authorities did their best to educate children from the same background together. For example, one school for evacuees in the village of Mikhailovka catered solely for Russian-speaking children, with 72 per cent of its 430 pupils from Ukraine and 22 per cent from Russia. Last-minute arrivals were squeezed into existing schools: for example, thirty-six Jewish children were suddenly added to the roll of the Karl Marx Russian-language middle school in Tiup in September 1943.[90]

Although the state wished to safeguard its younger generation, children's homes suffered from a variety of problems compounded by a huge lack of resources. According to an inspection report of 1944, the village of Chon-Sary-Oi hosted 192 children from Leningrad and Kronshtadt, mainly the offspring of serving Red Army soldiers, in a former sanatorium on the lakeside – once a summer attraction for Kyrgyz citizens. The main issue identified by the inspectors was that the children's home was situated some distance away from the village centre, such that it was removed in sight and mind from the attention of the authorities. It was no easy matter for the staff to get to the bank or to buy food, for instance, and local officials tended to forget the pressing needs of the children under their care. Fortunately the home had three horses for transport needs and the local collective farm provided dairy products in the absence of a cow, even if there was often insufficient bread and the home's allotment was not very productive. The Leningrad Children's Home in Kurmenty was similarly based in a building previously used by workers on leave from the nearby cement factory in the summer. Consequently, it was totally unsuitable for the children during the hard winters, with a universal lack of heating oil exacerbating the situation. In contrast to the home in Chon-Sary-Oi, it possessed just two ancient horses, fit only for light work, meaning that the director had to walk everywhere on his affairs. On the plus side, this home owned six dairy cows, each yielding a creditable average of 20 litres of milk a day. In theory, though, each children's home was supposed to have at least six working horses, ten cows, ten sheep and forty chickens – an inventory judged sufficient for the needs of 100 children. The main issue in the Leningrad Children's Home was that any food other than dairy products had to be provided by the state, as the home had no other animals and no allotment in which to grow its own vegetables. Nevertheless, the inspectors found that the mainly pre-school children enjoyed a good upbringing and even had use of the grand piano, which enabled some jollity through singing and dancing sessions.[91]

Most unaccompanied and orphaned evacuees seemed if not to thrive, at least to survive in the state children's homes, with an adequate education in the circumstances, plus walks and even baths outside in the summer months as in the state boarding schools. However, the state struggled to provide fully for the needs of growing children with a typical lack of provisions, clothing and equipment.[92] Official instructions demanded that the children be fed four times a day, with malnourished or ill youngsters supposed to have supplementary snacks. However, some of the staff were not entirely honest, and the theft of a home's assets was not unusual. The managers usually did their best, though, with the director of the Dzerzhinskii Children's Home in Sary-Oi buying at her personal expense thirty-one pairs of boots for children in her care possessing no winter footwear. This same director, it should be added, was reprimanded by inspectors for failing to provide sufficient political input into the children's daily routine.[93]

In general, children's homes across Central Asia needed considerable support from the local community. In Tashkent members of the Soviet intellectual elite regularly visited homes to read to the children, while a commission set up to help evacuated children was substantially assisted by prestigious volunteers with time on their hands. In rural Kyrgyzstan, practical help was desperately needed from the local population who could ill afford to give it. Collective farms and Komsomol members in the Tiup area supported the Leningrad Children's Home in Kurmenty by the donation of money, food and wool. After the autumn harvest in 1944, for example, 3.7 tonnes of potatoes, 420 kilograms of meat, over 3 tonnes of grain, over 25 kilograms of honey and 261 kilograms of wool were donated, along with vegetables, apples, dried fruit and fish. Most needed by the children's homes, however, were sugar, tea and flour, with salt for the preservation of home-grown vegetables. Children's clothes and bedding were in demand, and children's home staff also needed their own specialist clothing and equipment. As well as the perennial shortage of soap and paper, they required aprons, overalls and a new pair of galoshes every year. Their jobs were highly valued by a Soviet society demanding a thorough, politically correct upbringing for its children, with a mandatory three-month training course for new entrants to the profession.[94]

Copious lists of all evacuees' details were made as far as possible. However, young Zoia Markova arriving from Stalingrad, but originally from Rostov-on-Don, did not know her own age. It is probable that she spent some time in Stalingrad before it became necessary to evacuate her once more as enemy forces approached the city. Similarly, Evgeniia Sinel'nikova, estimated to have been born in 1938, did not even know her own full name, thus making the task of ever reuniting her with her parents more problematic. It was all too often unknown whether a child did indeed have any living relatives, as families were split up during the evacuation process. Errors were compounded also, as the state Central Information Bureau was itself evacuated to the rear in the war, rendering the response to enquiries about missing children relatively slow.[95]

With complex routes to Central Asia, unknown or distorted names and uncertain dates of birth, it was miraculous that many children's homes were in fact able to correspond with parents remaining in the western Soviet Union – on the front line, in Leningrad or other danger zones. One children's home in the Issyk-Kul' province regularly corresponded with nineteen sets of parents, including a certain Lieutenant Verkhovskii, the father of one unaccompanied child, who wrote to express his gratitude for the care of his offspring. Another letter in response to enquiries from Comrade Aleksandr Negodaev about the whereabouts of his son confirms that young Vladimir was indeed alive and well and living in the children's home in Teplokliuchenka near Przheval'sk. A similar letter was received by the parents of Roman Gershgorin, who was being cared for in the children's home in Chon-Sary-Oi. What a relief for their anxious parents![96]

Many children were not so fortunate, with at least half of those arriving in Uzbekistan having no contact at all from parents or other relations. In January 1942 the state recognized the problems faced by such children and proposed plans for their welfare. Fostering or adoption were advised where possible, with groups of women charged with the task of finding suitable homes. Only a lucky minority of orphans were officially adopted by local families during the war, however. Over 5,000 children were adopted in Uzbekistan by the end of 1942, the majority remaining in towns with only

870 going to more remote villages. One thousand adopted children lived in Tashkent alone – sometimes taken in by the Communist Party elite – with about 300 in the whole of Kyrgyzstan. In a very few cases this turned out to be temporary fostering, as they were eventually reunited with their parents after the end of the war.[97]

The poet G'afur G'ulom added to the huge propaganda interest in the Uzbek Shamakhmudov family which was credited with adopting an astonishing fifteen evacuated children of various nationalities. His poem 'You are not an orphan' was translated into Russian by Anna Akhmatova in the interests of promoting friendship of the peoples and persuading other families to do the same. Whether the Uzbek blacksmith and his wife adopted fewer or more than fifteen children is uncertain, as the figure was almost certainly exaggerated. Media interest in the family served to further the cause of adoption during the war, while also helping to underscore the increasing warmth between nationalities and the acceptance of Soviet citizenship and responsibility by ethnic Uzbeks.[98]

Iminakhun Akhmedov and his wife Mairamkhan in Osh were similarly credited with adopting fourteen children, while Khamid Samadov, a wounded veteran from Kattakurgan near Samarkand, apparently took thirteen, and collective farmer Fatima Kasymova housed ten orphaned children. State financial assistance towards the children's upbringing started in January 1942, paying the family fifty roubles per month per child. Some locals claimed that the families took in children simply for the money, but others contended that the children were housed out of Muslim cultural generosity. This was not a totally altruistic gesture on the part of the families, however, as adopted children were often set to work on the collective farm or on the family allotment, helping out in place of other family members who may have been conscripted.[99]

The return home

Children

Shortly after the end of the war in Europe, many of the children from Leningrad were on their way home. The first to leave Kyrgyzstan were those 145 children with known relations at home and young people aged over fourteen who were bound for training establishments in their home city. Each child was provided with two changes of underwear and sufficient food for the long journey. Preliminary planning for the return of other residents of children's homes in the Issyk-Kul' province was evident as early as 1944, when tentative enquiries were made of a certain Comrade Funnikov holding the relevant provincial purse strings which account should be debited for the necessary funds to return children to their parents in Kursk, Ufa or Khar'kov.[100]

For many of the children, however, a return home was out of the question. A large proportion of the unaccompanied children arriving in Central Asia in 1941 or 1942 were already orphans; the parents of others had died during the course of the war. Although several parents had already established where their children were staying, other families had completely lost contact with their offspring, so the children's homes had no alternative but to retain them. Younger children were often badly registered, as nobody knew their name, address or date of birth. Furthermore, most adopted children were given new names once they joined their new families, so that it was almost impossible to reunite them with their relations, if any, once hostilities ceased. Unlike in Western Europe, there was at first little outside assistance such as the Red Cross to track down displaced children. It was only when fathers were eventually discharged from the army and returned home that the quest for their children began in earnest – all too often with a tragic outcome.[101]

As soon as the end of the war was in sight, relations started the attempt to locate their evacuated children. Handwritten queries about their whereabouts flooded into the region, each bearing the usual thirty-kopeck stamp. These desperate searches were documented in the Issyk-Kul' province on scraps of blue and pink school exercise book covers, thin tissue paper, old newspapers or coarse, grey paper with ragged edges. In many cases it was the grandparents who wrote the heart-rending triangular letters if the child's parents had died, the shaky script a testament to the age and suffering of the correspondent.[102]

Comrade Chernov, Inspector of Children's Homes for the Issyk-Kul' province, had his work cut out. A certain Ivan Tovstonog was quick off the mark in the search for his son, Mikhail, who was nine years old when the war ended, having been evacuated from Leningrad in 1942 with his children's home. In July 1945 Ivan had received a letter from his son and from the director of the children's home in Kuranty, but had heard nothing since and was very concerned that something may have happened to the boy. Writing again once he was demobilized in December 1945, Ivan was so keen to see his son that he offered to arrange his return to Leningrad the moment he received word that it was possible. A certain Anna Metulova wrote at the end of May 1946, looking for her two children: Nina (born in 1936) and Vladimir (1941), who, it seemed, had arrived in a children's home in Kyrgyzstan towards the end of 1944, but with whom contact had also since been lost.[103]

The whereabouts of young Tamara Verkhovskaia were indeed known, however. Her father, Lieutenant Verkhovskii, had established that she was in the Kuranty children's home, but he was not able to come to Kyrgyzstan from his current home in Tiumen' in order to collect her. His request was for his daughter to be moved a little further west, ideally to the Siberian town of Omsk, or, failing that, at least to Frunze. Both of these cities were on the railway line and would have made the girl's repatriation to Russia easier. Good news was also received by her sister about Liudmila Smirnova, who was similarly in the Kurmenty children's home. Iurii Solov'ev (born in 1932), was also located relatively easily, although young Elena Udintsova and Gennadiia Starikova's relations, like many other anxious family members, were disappointed by the response from the Issyk-Kul' authorities: 'She is not in our province.' The father of Nikolai Sukharev (born in 1935) tried in vain to find him, later enlisting the help of the Kyrgyz authorities, who suggested that his name may have been changed along the way.

This may have happened to the son of soldier's widow Ekaterina Ol'shanskaia's, Valerii (born in 1940), who had initially been placed in a children's home not far from Voronezh and probably evacuated in 1941, when he was too young to know his own name. Somewhere during the evacuation process it was thought that Valerii Ol'shanskii may have been re-named according to his anonymous status and become one of the many children bearing the name Vania Besfamil'nov (Little Ivan Without a Surname) – a miniature John Doe. Just in case he was found, Ekaterina provided a pathetic description of her missing son as she remembered him: he was blond, with big grey eyes and a small dark mole on his neck.[104]

It is worth going into some detail about the sad case of another Ekaterina and her missing daughter, Anna. In the spring of 1941 Ekaterina Sausha was posted from her work in Leningrad to the town of Vyborg on the Finnish border, leaving her daughter Anna in the care of her mother-in-law. As soon as war broke out, Ekaterina was evacuated directly from Vyborg to the Komi-Permiak area of the Urals, where she was immediately conscripted into the Red Army. During the harsh winter of 1941–2 Anna's grandmother died – probably, like many others, of starvation or extreme cold. The seven-year-old child was placed in the Dzerzhinskii Children's Home, which was then evacuated to Krasnodar in the south of the country in the spring of 1942. As the enemy approached Krasnodar that summer, the children's home with all its residents was re-evacuated to Kyrgyzstan, to be re-established in the village of Sary-Oi in the Issyk-Kul' province.[105]

As no contact had been made with Anna's parents, the following year she was placed for adoption with the family of a certain Sorombai Jel'denov, a worker on the Jany-Aiyl collective farm in the Jeti-Oguz district. By 1944 her real mother, Ekaterina, was taken ill and returned to Leningrad, where she eventually discovered what had happened to her mother-in-law and daughter. Having lost her first husband, she re-married in July 1945, shortly after the end of the war in Europe. Her new husband was Nikolai Eidemiller, who had volunteered for the army at the start of the war, being demobilized following two serious wounds in 1944. It was at this point that Ekaterina enlisted Nikolai's help in tracking down her lost daughter, Anna Sausha.[106]

By August, Ekaterina and Nikolai had discovered through the Leningrad authorities that Anna had been in the Dzerzhinskii Children's Home in Kyrgyzstan, but that she had been placed for adoption. Nikolai wrote to the home's director in September 1945 and then to the head of the Jeti-

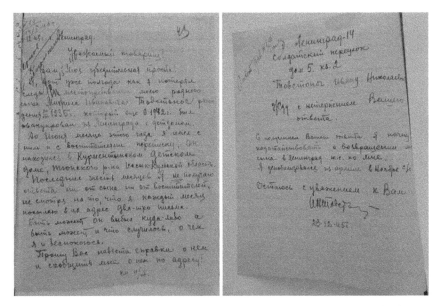

FIGURE 7.2A AND FIGURE 7.2B *A query from Leningrad about Mikhail Tovstonog. IKSA:279/1/295/43.*

Oguz district the following January to ask where she had been placed, but received no reply. By May 1946 he took the drastic decision to write directly to Nikolai Shvernik, Chairman of the Presidium of the Supreme Soviet of the Soviet Union. It had long been a Russian tradition to take one's troubles directly to the country's leader, with letters received from ordinary citizens by the tsar and later by Stalin. It is interesting that Eidemiller decided to write to Shvernik: although he had actually been the head of state for only two months before he received the letter from Leningrad, he in fact held less power than the de facto leader of the Soviet Union, Joseph Stalin. It proved to be a good move, though, as a fortnight later Shvernik's office had instructed the Issyk-Kul' authorities to respond with full details of Anna's case to Comrade Eidemiller.[107]

It was this response of August 1946 which brought the bombshell to Ekaterina and her husband. Apparently, when approached by the investigating authorities, Anna had expressed the strong desire to remain with her new, adoptive parents in Kyrgyzstan – after all, she had not seen her own mother for well over five years and could probably remember little of her pre-war life in Leningrad. The Jel'denov family could not agree more: they had formed firm bonds with Anna over the previous three years and considered her to be their own daughter. Diplomatically, the provincial authorities invited Comrade Eidemiller to come to Kyrgyzstan to discuss the matter in situ. There was no reply from Ekaterina and her husband on this final occasion, although a letter from Przheval'sk to the Leningrad authorities the following month served to tie up any loose official ends on behalf of this one individual. In this tragic case, it was the interests of the child – by then a teenager – which overrode the understandable wishes for a reunion on the part of her mother.[108]

Several other children proved hard to locate because they had been moved more than once. The Leningrad authorities were helpful in discovering where its original homes had been re-established, following initial moves south and then further east. Comrade Grechushkin, the director of children's homes in Krasnodar, also played a part in locating missing children, with information about where some homes in transit had been sent in the tumultuous year of 1942.[109]

Relations persisted in their complex quest for missing children for years after the end of the war. By the end of 1946 a pro forma card was in place, to simplify the sometimes lengthy letters of enquiry. The Moscow-based Red Cross/Red Crescent organization of the Soviet Union became involved by 1947, setting up a centralized system for enquiries and searches for missing people of all ages. As the years passed, it became increasingly likely that the young person was no longer in the care of a children's home, as teenagers were expected to work and usually accommodated in workplace hostels. This was probably the reason why Sof'ia Vasil'eva from Pskov could not locate her niece, Ania, who was born in 1933 and evacuated from Oranienbaum in 1942. By the time her letter reached the children's home in 1947, she already anticipated that the girl would never be found.[110]

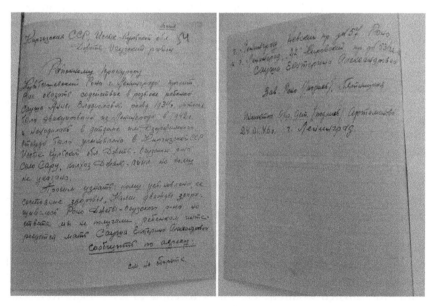

FIGURE 7.3A AND FIGURE 7.3B *One of Nikolai Eidemiller's many letters in search of Anna Sausha. IKSA:279/1/295/54.*

Sadly, many evacuated children remained in homes after the end of the war, including the 1,065 children in the seven homes of the Issyk-Kul' province.[111] Although some parents, such as the mother and step-father of Anna Sausha, probably accepted that they would never see their children again, many continued the search process, despite the enormous psychological burden of prolonged separation. Dedicated radio programmes and newspaper announcements were sometimes invoked, with limited success. The odds were highly stacked against the searchers, however, as records – including those of children who died in care – were often incomplete or kept in distant locations. To this day there are elderly adults still alive in Central Asia – as indeed across most of the former Soviet space – who are still not aware of their own true name and parentage.[112]

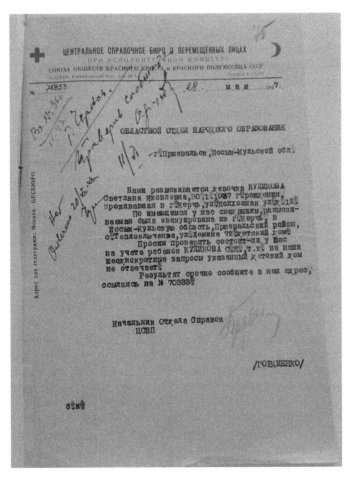

FIGURE 7.4 *A Red Cross/Red Crescent enquiry, dated 28 May 1947.*
IKSA:279/1/295/75.

Adults

Much of the occupied territory was liberated during 1943 and the siege of Leningrad was eventually lifted at the end of January 1944. Most evacuees were then desperate to return home as soon as possible, keen to pick up the pieces of their previous lives. Many displayed what was known as a so-called 'suitcase' attitude, from the Russian idiom equating 'sitting on one's suitcase' with impatience to start the journey.[113] However, the state was anxious for a measured repatriation, as much of the housing and infrastructure in the western provinces had been completely annihilated. Leningrad was a shell of its former self after the lengthy siege, and less than 5 per cent of the buildings in some towns in the Krasnodar province remained standing, thanks to bombing and shelling by both sides. Authorities were extremely cautious about the possibility of homeless, destitute evacuees travelling west before there was a chance to establish better facilities for their reception. Leningrad was particularly well guarded, with few former residents permitted to return, especially orphans who needed more substantial care than the city could offer in its post-war devastation. Furthermore, it was to the state's advantage for some factories and educational institutes to remain in Central Asia as a boost to the local economy.[114]

Most of the evacuated institutes returned home as soon as it was possible, however – indeed often with unseemly haste to escape the relative privations experienced in Central Asia. The prestigious Moscow establishments in Tashkent and Alma-Ata were encouraged to leave promptly, with the Leningrad Law Institution even more eager to vacate its temporary base in Kazakhstan, where space was at a premium for staff and students alike.[115]

The Nikolaev Shipbuilding Institute was one of the first institutes of higher education to leave Kyrgyzstan, shortly after Nikolaev was liberated at the end of March 1944. It headed back to its Black Sea base in August 1944, just in time for the start of the new academic year in the autumn, having seen the graduation of a final 280 students in Przheval'sk that June. The Leningrad Veterinary Institute left somewhat later, returning only in time for the start of the 1945/6 academic year. Promising calls for student registration from Kyrgyz boys and girls were made in April 1945, offering hostel accommodation in Leningrad and even academic scholarships. The entry criteria were high, however, and the timing probably excluded any demobilized soldiers who may have wished to take advantage of a higher education, although applicants were considered up to the age of thirty-five. Students had to have completed at least ten years of secondary schooling, with a good knowledge of physics and chemistry backed up with a positive reference and health certificate. They also had to be fluent in Russian and be prepared to relocate to Leningrad – a great opportunity for a small minority of Kyrgyz students, no doubt, but an insurmountable hurdle for most, who were needed to help re-establish the local economy at home. The Soviet Union had, by taking rapid, if extreme, measures, managed to preserve and extend much of its intellectual capital, but the legacy of the evacuated institutes was a mixed blessing to the local population in Central Asia.[116]

Factories and industrial plants were another matter, with many being forced to remain in Central Asia on a temporary or permanent basis, rather than returning immediately to the west, leaving many of their original workers feeling trapped in Central Asia. The largely planned, phased return – much more measured than the original exodus eastwards at the start of the war – also applied to civilians, who needed to obtain a permit in order to embark on the journey home. The intellectual and party elite, of course, had no trouble leaving Central Asia, as did families of serving soldiers. For others, the difficulties of obtaining travel documents and tickets were almost insurmountable, involving a wait of weeks, with numerous lengthy queues and bureaucracy. Many evacuees and 'self-evacuees' chose to ignore official directives and travelled west regardless, heading home to live an unofficial life on the streets of Leningrad or other cities. The journey itself was hazardous, if not quite as dangerous as the original evacuation. Travellers spent nights sleeping in the open air on the concrete floor of stations, while waiting for trains which arrived intermittently. Most had to change several times, with many evacuees from Central Asia passing through the main railway junction at Arys' in Kazakhstan. There were rarely enough seats for everybody except the elite travellers, with some evacuees resorting to sitting on the train roof – a vulnerable position on a route with so many low bridges. Sanitation and the provision of food and drinking water for train passengers were, as usual, totally inadequate.[117]

In addition to the problems facing most evacuees, Jewish refugees faced further issues on their return home. As many smaller communities had been wiped out, they tended to head for larger towns and cities where there could be employment opportunities. Evidence suggests that increasing state-sponsored anti-Semitism fuelled animosity and local resistance to returning refugees. Competition for housing was rife, with reports of stolen furniture and flats. Perhaps also some past collaborators with the occupying Germans feared that Jews may take revenge for their betrayal. Some returnees also found that they were excluded from their old jobs – a measure which was officially against the law. At any rate, the authorities seemed loath to intervene in what were seen as minor domestic squabbles. Even worse, though, was the manifestation of physical violence to Jews and post-war pogroms, especially in Kiev, which had experienced one of the worst of the Holocaust atrocities at Babii Iar'.[118]

Evacuees without leave to return were forced to remain in Central Asia against their will. Of the 150,000 arriving in Kyrgyzstan in 1941 and 1942, 35,000 evacuees still remained at the end of 1945. Some, though, like Nadezhda Mandel'shtam, wished to remain in Uzbekistan, just as the Soviet artists Abram Cherkasskii (evacuated with his family from Kiev), R. Velikanova and P. Zal'tsman (both from Leningrad) chose to stay in their new home in Kazakhstan. Vladimir Sorokin, too, decided to remain in

Leninogorsk in his new position as town prosecutor, eventually obtaining a degree in law at the university in Alma-Ata. Several academics also stayed in the region. Various reasons informed their decisions: perhaps they had lost all their family at home, or married in Central Asia and put down roots; they may have discovered that the new climate suited them better, or had found more secure employment.[119]

Despite their undoubted suffering in exile and their work in the rear, the evacuees were definitely not a state priority on their return home. The general mood was rather of appreciation for the war veterans who had ensured the recent victory. It was therefore the demobilized Red Army soldiers who were first on the list for housing and post-war employment. Even worse, in contrast to the returning heroes, evacuees were often denigrated by their compatriots, who perceived them as having taken the soft option, away from the fighting front, even dubbed 'deserters' in some cases. There were certainly no medals handed out to evacuees.[120] This type of disapproval had, in fact, been held by Akhmatova herself when in 1922, twenty years before her arrival in Tashkent, she had adamantly refused to leave her beloved Leningrad and scorned those intellectuals who sought a safer life abroad in the aftermath of the revolution and civil war. Proudly, she had proclaimed: 'I am not one of those who cast aside the land/For the enemy to tear to pieces.' Many of the intellectual elite evacuated to Tashkent may have concurred with Akhmatova's 1922 judgement that 'foreign bread smells rotten', although the poet found much to stimulate her senses during her time in Central Asia, feeling quite at home in her 'white house' and even declaring: 'Who dares to tell me that here/I am in a foreign land?'[121]

Ironically, Akhmatova had enjoyed her time in Central Asia more than many, thanking the city and its people in both the Russian and Uzbek languages for their hospitality during her enforced stay: 'Teper' ia vsekh blagodariu' (Now I thank everybody) and, in Uzbek, 'Rakhmat, Toshkent' (Thank you, Tashkent).[122] Despite this, her nostalgia for Leningrad was sometimes overwhelming. She was therefore ecstatic when the time came to leave Uzbekistan for home, once again – as a member of the privileged Soviet elite – by plane. As she described her landing in Moscow, Akhmatova observed the paradoxical sensation of the evacuee greeting her homeland again, while also apparently seeing it as for the first time after her lengthy sojourn in Tashkent – 'as if at once all new and yet well-known'.[123]

This may have been an exceptional reaction, as many evacuees returned to their home towns to find them flattened and barely functioning, bereft of their once thriving atmosphere. During the same period that most evacuees were retracing their route in a westerly direction, Red Army soldiers were also heading back east to Central Asia. Their reaction was probably similar in one important respect – a feeling of relief that the war was finally over and a chance to start afresh, despite the undoubted loss of friends and family over the last few years.

Friendship of the peoples

The evacuations from the west to the east represented a massive relocation from one side of the Soviet Union to the other. They were largely a civilian experience, in contrast to the case of most ordinary soldiers fighting in the Red Army, who had moved from Central Asia to the Western Front. During successive waves of evacuation, citizens from the European part of the Soviet Union were able to see another region of their vast country, experiencing the life and culture of Central Asia.

The suddenness of the dislocation posed a considerable challenge to the authorities in Central Asia, as did the demographic changes and ethnodynamics of war. As millions of able-bodied men left the region for the army, they were replaced by an influx of less physically fit evacuees, who had suffered severe privations on the journey. Predominantly women, children and the elderly, their demographic composition largely replicated that of the population already remaining in Central Asia. Predictably, the number of deaths increased as the birth rate decreased, placing an enormous strain on the region overall. In some compensation, though, the evacuations saved the lives of thousands of children who would otherwise have been lost to the overall Soviet population. Examining the figures for Kazakhstan, for example, of the 6.2 million inhabitants in 1939, 1.2 million were conscripted into the army, to be replaced by over 0.5 million incomers in 1941 and 1942.[124] Most of the arrivals were temporary residents, only staying in the region for two or three years, being replaced from 1943 onwards by thousands of returning, often wounded veterans and a new population of deportees exiled from the west. This mass movement of Soviet citizens changed not only the ethnic composition of Central Asia but also its social, economic and cultural life.

The evacuations to Central Asia took place in the same way as those to other parts of the eastern Soviet Union. Towns in the Urals and villages in Siberia all experienced a similar influx of evacuees, most of whom were accepted as a much-needed help to the local economy, although some families and unaccompanied children in fact became a burden on the local population. The situation in Central Asia was different, however, in that the cultural differences between the local population and incomers were particularly marked. The region's geography and climate rendered it relatively hospitable for the country's defence industry and it received the large majority of the Soviet artistic elite – its cinematographers, writers and poets – as well as its fair share of scientific intelligentsia. Tashkent and Alma-Ata were viewed by many as the most desirable places of exile for any evacuee or refugee, and suffered as a consequence from massive overcrowding and disease. In spite of this, the significance of the evacuations for the success of the war effort is hard to overestimate: they enabled the country's defence and food industries to keep functioning and even expand in productivity, while the Soviet cultural elite were able to survive and, in some cases, even flourish.

The Soviet 'friendship of the peoples' policy ensured that the citizens of Central Asia felt sufficiently Soviet to play an active part in the war as members of the Red Army. The same ideology also called upon Central Asians to offer a basic welcome to fellow-Soviets from the occupied regions in their time of need, even if few had anything much to share. As increasingly onerous demands were made upon them, Central Asians acknowledged that they were all fighting a common enemy and assisted the evacuees to an extent, particularly those who had few friends and family support networks. Highlighted in the propaganda press, however, was the plight of orphaned children, as unaccompanied minors were rarely left in need by their hosts.[125] The enduring remembrance of the evacuations in Central Asia is still the hospitality and support its people showed through the adoption and care of thousands of orphans in the name of friendship, a war myth still prevalent in Uzbekistan in monument, film and literature.

Most evacuees took the necessary steps to integrate sufficiently into the local community in order simply to survive. They were usually given employment and worked, lived and shopped alongside the local population. However, there were very real tensions and cultural divisions in the region, as the competition for limited resources grew and, with it, suspicion of and antagonism towards some incomers, notably Jewish refugees. This inter-ethnic suspicion took the edge off what was politically intended to be a genuine, if pragmatic, brotherhood of different nationalities under the Soviet umbrella, thereby testing the theoretical friendship of the peoples to its limit.

If the 'friendship of the peoples' was not all it was cracked up to be, communist ideology and propaganda at least served to unite locals and incomers sufficiently to ensure the success of the war effort in Central Asia and, in turn, an eventual victory. The union was largely consolidated when it mattered, with a certain degree of integration of citizens from different regions and some cultural assimilation on both sides. Most evacuees left promptly after the war, though, retaining no long-term stakes in Central Asia. Echoing the long caravans travelling along the Silk Roads across Central Asia, the movement of people had enabled genuine cultural and economic exchange. During their stay evacuees had helped to support the local economy and left the region transformed in many ways. Not only the infrastructure had been developed, but Central Asia as a whole had become more ethnically diverse and increasingly an integral part of the Soviet project. Education at all levels, healthcare and industry had been improved, with some social development thanks to a process of Sovietization which had taken place rather more rapidly than may have been possible in peacetime.

Notes

1   See especially Manley, *To the Tashkent Station;* and Williams, *The Crimean Tatars.*

2 Goldman and Filtzer, *Fortress Dark and Stern*, chapter 2.

3 A. M. Podlipskii, 'Evakuatsiia predpriatii Belorussii 1941 g.', in *Istoriia. Pamiat'. Liudi: Materialy VIII Mezhdunarodnoi nauchno-prakticheskoi konferentsii 16 sentiabria 2016 g.*, eds M. S. Makarova, et al., 72–9 (Almaty: 2017), 72 and 75.

4 Sh. D. Batyrbaeva, 'Evakuirovannoe i deportirovannoe naselenie v Kirgizskoi SSR v gody Velikoi Otechestvennoi voiny', in *Istoriia. Pamiat'. Liudi: Materialy IX Mezhdunarodnoi nauchno-prakticheskoi konferentsii 27 sentiabria 2018 g.*, eds K. Sh. Alimgazinov, et al., 25–9 (Almaty: 2019), 26; Carmack, *Kazakhstan in World War II*, 80; Dadabaev, *Identity and Memory*, 67; 'Istoriia', *Ministerstvo inostrannykh del Respubliki Uzbekistan*; Kerimbaev, *Sovetskii Kirgizstan v Velikoi Otechestvennoi voine*, 52; Osmonov, *Istoriia Kyrgyzstana*, 143; and Stronski, *Tashkent*, 57.

5 O. E. Berkun, 'Evakuatsiia promyshlennykh predpriatii v Karagandinskuiu oblast'', in *Istoriia. Pamiat'. Liudi: Materialy VIII Mezhdunarodnoi nauchno-prakticheskoi konferentsii 16 sentiabria 2016 g.*, eds M. S. Makarova, et al., 184–7 (Almaty: 2017), 186.

6 Zh. A. Ermekbai, 'Zavod No. 621 v Kokshetau v gody Velikoi Otechestvennoi voiny', in *Istoriia. Pamiat'. Liudi: Materialy IX Mezhdunarodnoi nauchno-prakticheskoi konferentsii 27 sentiabria 2018 g.*, eds K. Sh. Alimgazinov, et al., 188–94 (Almaty: 2019).

7 A. U. Aupenova, 'Zavod No. 517: Istoriia stanovleniia i razvitiia evakuirovannogo promyshlennogo ob''ekta na kazakhstanskoi zemle', in *Istoriia. Pamiat'. Liudi: Materialy VIII Mezhdunarodnoi nauchno-prakticheskoi konferentsii 16 sentiabria 2016 g.*, eds M. S. Makarova, et al., 229–34 (Almaty: 2017), 229–32; Z. L. Fedorenko, 'Evakuatsiia v Tashkent khar'kovchan s Sakharosveklotrestom', in *Istoriia. Pamiat'. Liudi: Materialy IX Mezhdunarodnoi nauchno-prakticheskoi konferentsii 27 sentiabria 2018 g.*, eds K. Sh. Alimgazinov, et al., 199–205 (Almaty: 2019), 202; and Saktaganova, 'Alma-Ata v gody Velikoi Otechestvennoi voiny', 169.

8 Imankulov, *Istoriia Kyrgyzstana*, 113 and 143; and Kerimbaev, *Sovetskii Kirgizstan v Velikoi Otechestvennoi voine*, 52–3.

9 Berkun, 'Evakuatsiia promyshlennykh predpriatii', 187.

10 Fedorenko, 'Evakuatsiia v Tashkent khar'kovchan s Sakharosveklotrestom'; and E. A. Kozhushko, 'Evakuatsiia Kupianskogo sakharnogo zavoda v g. Kokand', in *Istoriia. Pamiat'. Liudi: Materialy IX Mezhdunarodnoi nauchno-prakticheskoi konferentsii 27 sentiabria 2018 g.*, eds K. Sh. Alimgazinov, et al., 205–8 (Almaty: 2019).

11 Berkun, 'Evakuatsiia promyshlennykh predpriatii', 187.

12 Fedorenko, 'Evakuatsiia v Tashkent khar'kovchan s Sakharosveklotrestom'; and Kozhushko, 'Evakuatsiia Kupianskogo sakharnogo zavoda'.

13 Batyrbaeva, 'Evakuirovannoe i deportirovannoe naselenie', 26; Carmack, *Kazakhstan in World War II*, 80; Dadabaev, *Identity and Memory*, 67; 'Istoriia', *Ministerstvo inostrannykh del Respubliki Uzbekistan*; Kerimbaev, *Sovetskii Kirgizstan v Velikoi Otechestvennoi voine*, 52; Osmonov, *Istoriia Kyrgyzstana*, 143; and Stronski, *Tashkent*, 57.

14 Berkun, 'Evakuatsiia promyshlennykh predpriatii', 186; Imankulov, *Istoriia Kyrgyzstana*, 113 and 143; and Kerimbaev, *Sovetskii Kirgizstan v Velikoi Otechestvennoi voine*, 52 and 53.

15 Florin, 'Becoming Soviet through War', 508–9; Keller, *Russia and Central Asia*, 206; and Kerimbaev, *Sovetskii Kirgizstan v Velikoi Otechestvennoi voine*, 53, 91 and 93.

16 IKSA:146/2/13/20; and Kerimbaev, *Sovetskii Kirgizstan v Velikoi Otechestvennoi voine*, 159.

17 Abylkhozhin, *Istoriia Kazakhstana*, 520–4; Kozybaev, *Istoriia Kazakhstana*, 129; and Turlygul, *Istoriia Kazakhstana*, 207.

18 Manley, *To the Tashkent Station*, 143–4.

19 Dadabaev, *Identity and Memory*, 75; 'Istoriia', *Ministerstvo inostrannykh del Respubliki Uzbekistan*; and Kerimbaev, *Sovetskii Kirgizstan v Velikoi Otechestvennoi voine*, 173–4.

20 Kaptagaev, et al., *Sbornik*, 146; and Osmonov, *Istoriia Kyrgyzstana*, 163–4.

21 Chinara Seidimatova, 'Priissykkul'e v gody Velikoi Otechestvennoi voiny (Evakuatsiia, bezhentsy, pereselenie)', in *Evraziia XXv.: evakuatsiia, pereselentsy, bezhentsy*, eds M. S. Makarova, 275–84 (Almaty: 2017), 282; Stronski, *Tashkent*, 91–3; and Tukhtaeva, 'Tvorcheskaia zhizn' khudozhestvennoi intelligentsii', 119.

22 'Vysshaia korablestroitel'naia shkola', *IKP*, 11 July 1943, 2; 'Novye kadry korablestroitelia', *IKP*, 24 October 1943, 2; IKSA:174/3/36/74 and 79–81; and Kaptagaev, et al., *Sbornik*, 8, 12 and 133–4.

23 'Vuzy na poroge uchebnogo goda', *IKP*, 29 August 1943, 2; 'Chemu obuchaet veterinarnyi institut', *IKP*, 16 July 1944, 2; 'Leningradskii veterinarnyi institut', *IKP*, 23 August 1944, 2; and IKSA/130/overview/1. See also Kaptagaev, et al., *Sbornik*, 9 and 146–7; and Kerimbaev, *Sovetskii Kirgizstan v Velikoi Otechestvennoi voine*, 173.

24 'Vuzy na poroge uchebnogo goda', *IKP*, 29 August 1943, 2; 'K nachalu zaniatii v vuzakh', *IKP*, 10 October 1943, 2. IKSA:146/2/13/20; and Kerimbaev, *Sovetskii Kirgizstan v Velikoi Otechestvennoi voine*, 173.

25 Abylkhozhin, *Istoriia Kazakhstana*, 520; Dadabaev, *Identity and Memory*, 75; Florin, *Kirgistan und die sowjetische Moderne*, 35; and Kaptagaev, et al., *Sbornik*, 9, 11 and 133.

26 IKSA:216/Introduction; Abylkhozhin, *Istoriia Kazakhstana*, 519; and Kerimbaev, *Sovetskii Kirgizstan v Velikoi Otechestvennoi voine*, 97 and 174.

27 Braithwaite, *Moscow 1941*, 114; Rebecca Manley, 'The Perils of Displacement: The Soviet Evacuee between Refugee and Deportee', *Contemporary European History* 16, no. 4 (2007): 495–509, 496; and Manley, *To the Tashkent Station*, 18, 20, 24, 26 and 39.

28 Barber and Harrison, *The Soviet Home Front*, 47; Manley, 'The Perils of Displacement', 501; and Manley, *To the Tashkent Station*, 22, 28 and 30.

29 Twelve evacuated hospitals were re-established in Uzbekistan and four in Kyrgyzstan. See V. G. Iofe and V. A. Petrovskaia, 'Iz istoriia evakuatsii v

Uzbekistan', in *Istoriia. Pamiat'. Liudi: Materialy VIII Mezhdunarodnoi nauchno-prakticheskoi konferentsii 16 sentiabria 2016 g.*, eds M. S. Makarova, et al., 249–61 (Almaty: 2017), 250.

30   Abylkhozhin, *Istoriia Kazakhstana*, 526; Dadabaev, *Identity and Memory*, 73; Florin, 'Becoming Soviet through War', 508; 'Istoriia', *Ministerstvo inostrannykh del Respubliki Uzbekistan*; Manley, *To the Tashkent Station*, 163; and Osmonov, *Istoriia Kyrgyzstana*, 143.

31   Kiril Feferman, 'A Soviet Humanitarian Action?: Centre, Periphery and the Evacuation of Refugees to the North Caucasus, 1941–1942', *Europe–Asia Studies* 61, no. 5 (2009): 813–31, 815; Lisa Kirschenbaum, *The Legacy of the Siege of Leningrad* (Cambridge: Cambridge University Press, 2006), 48; Manley, 'The Perils of Displacement', 498; and Manley, *To the Tashkent Station*, 22, 32, 38, 40, 54, 87, 89, 97, 103 and 115–16.

32   Feferman, 'A Soviet Humanitarian Action?', 815, footnote 4; Grinberg, *Evrei v Alma-Ate*, 86, note 4; Kirschenbaum, *The Legacy of the Siege of Leningrad*, 47–8; and Manley, *To the Tashkent Station*, 32, 36, 55–6 and 58.

33   Tashkent gained its reputation as the 'city of bread' after the publication of Aleksandr Neverov's book of the same name, which was translated into Hebrew and Yiddish in the 1930s.

34   Braithwaite, *Moscow 1941*, 80; Brezhnev, *The Virgin Lands*, 9; Kirschenbaum, *The Legacy of the Siege of Leningrad*, 48; Manley, 'The Perils of Displacement', 501; and Manley, *To the Tashkent Station*, 56, 122, 126, 128, 132, 134, 137, 140, 141, 142, 144, 158 and 202.

35   Manley, 'The Perils of Displacement', 497; Manley, *To the Tashkent Station*, 129; Stronski, *Tashkent*, 126–8; and Tranum, *Life at the Edge of the Empire*, 165.

36   A. U. Aupenova and Zh. E. Isina, 'Masshtabnost' nekotorykh problem evakuatsii grazhdanskogo naseleniia v Kazakhstan v pervye gody Velikoi Otechestvennoi voiny', in *Istoriia. Pamiat'. Liudi: Materialy IX Mezhdunarodnoi nauchno-prakticheskoi konferentsii 27 sentiabria 2018 g.*, eds K. Sh. Alimgazinov, et al., 143–51 (Almaty: 2019), 145; E. B. Chernaiia, 'Iz istorii Karagandinskogo evakuatsionnogo punkta', in *Istoriia. Pamiat'. Liudi: Materialy IX Mezhdunarodnoi nauchno-prakticheskoi konferentsii 27 sentiabria 2018 g.*, eds K. Sh. Alimgazinov, et al., 158–62 (Almaty: 2019); D. M. Inoiatova, 'Pomoshch' Uzbekistana evakuirovannym detiam v gody voiny', in *Istoriia. Pamiat'. Liudi: Materialy VIII Mezhdunarodnoi nauchno-prakticheskoi konferentsii 16 sentiabria 2016 g.*, eds M. S. Makarova, et al., 269–74 (Almaty: 2017), 271; and Z. B. Rakhmonkulova and Sh. Sh. Choriev, 'Upravlenie po evakuatsii naseleniia pri Sovete po evakuatsii', in *Istoriia. Pamiat'. Liudi: Materialy VIII Mezhdunarodnoi nauchno-prakticheskoi konferentsii 16 sentiabria 2016 g.*, eds M. S. Makarova, et al., 63–72 (Almaty: 2017), 64.

37   Aupenova and Isina, 'Masshtabnost' nekotorykh problem evakuatsii grazhdanskogo naseleniia'; Chernaiia, 'Iz istorii Karagandinskogo evakuatsionnogo punkta'; and Saktaganova, 'Alma-Ata v gody Velikoi Otechestvennoi voiny', 168.

38   IKSA:119/1/10; IKSA:174/3/36/1–10, 11–34, 36–8, 43, 45, 50–1, 55–9, 61, 63, 71–2, 114, 116, 225, 238–42, 255–9, 273–83, 308–11; and IKSA:174/3/63/5–7.

39   Manley, 'The Perils of Displacement', 502–3; Manley, *To the Tashkent Station*, 150–3, 155 and 158; Stronski, *Tashkent*, 127; and Tranum, *Life at the Edge of the Empire*, 165.

40   Manley, 'The Perils of Displacement', 499–500; Manley, *To the Tashkent Station*, 152–3; and Stronski, *Tashkent*, 121.

41   IKSA:119/1/10/108–9 and 113–14; and IKSA:146/2/17/1. See also Roberto Carmack, '"A Fortress of the Soviet Home Front": Mobilization and Ethnicity in Kazakhstan during World War II', PhD dissertation (University of Wisconsin-Madison, 2015), 27; Carmack, *Kazakhstan in World War II*, 11; Kaptagaev, et al., *Sbornik*, 8; Manley, 'The Perils of Displacement', 508; and Manley, *To the Tashkent Station*, 156 and 228.

42   Aupenova, 'Zavod No. 517', 229–32; Fedorenko, 'Evakuatsiia v Tashkent khar'kovchan s Sakharosveklotrestom', 202; V. G. Iofe and A. O. Il'ina (Stil'ke), 'Spasenie ot Kholokosta: Evrei iz Pol'shi i Vostochnoevropeiskikh Respublik SSR v Tashkente v dokumentakh mestnykh arkhivov', in *Istoriia. Pamiat'. Liudi: Materialy VIII Mezhdunarodnoi nauchno-prakticheskoi konferentsii 16 sentiabria 2016 g.*, eds M. S. Makarova, et al., 331–40 (Almaty: 2017), 333; K. D. Saipova, 'Vklad uzbekistantsev v pobedu nad fashizmom i tolerantnoe otnoshenie k evakuirovannym', in *Istoriia. Pamiat'. Liudi: Materialy IX Mezhdunarodnoi nauchno-prakticheskoi konferentsii 27 sentiabria 2018 g.*, eds K. Sh. Alimgazinov, et al., 62–8 (Almaty: 2019), 64; and Saktaganova, 'Alma-Ata v gody Velikoi Otechestvennoi voiny', 168–9.

43   Dadabaev, *Identity and Memory*, 68 and 73; Florin, 'Becoming Soviet through War', 509 and 511; Florin, *Kirgistan und die sowjetische Moderne*, 45; Grinberg, *Evrei v Alma-Ate*, 83 and 91; Manley, *To the Tashkent Station*, 31, 177, 193–4; Saktaganova, 'Alma-Ata v gody Velikoi Otechestvennoi voiny', 169; and Stronski, *Tashkent*, 11–12, 50, 57, 124, 129, 130 and 140.

44   Manley, 'The Perils of Displacement', 508; Manley, *To the Tashkent Station*, 30, 157 and 168; and Stronski, *Tashkent*, 84, 124, 129, 130 and 135.

45   Florin, *Kirgistan und die sowjetische Moderne*, 41–2; K. D. Kabdulova, 'Evakuatsiia politemigrantov v Kazakhstan v gody Velikoi Otechestvennoi voiny', in *Istoriia. Pamiat'. Liudi: Materialy IX Mezhdunarodnoi nauchno-prakticheskoi konferentsii 27 sentiabria 2018 g.*, eds K. Sh. Alimgazinov, et al., 133–9 (Almaty: 2019), 138; Manley, 'The Perils of Displacement', 504–5; Manley, *To the Tashkent Station*, 153 and 227; and Stronski, *Tashkent*, 12, 135, 136 and 142.

46   IKSA:174/3/36/50, 244, 247–50, 314, 316 and 321–6; and Kaptagaev, et al., *Sbornik*, 6.

47   Manley, *To the Tashkent Station*, 156 and 180–2.

48   IKSA:174/3/36/141–2, 145–7, 152, 161, 181–3 and 205–6.

49   IKSA:119/1/33/30; and Manley, *To the Tashkent Station*, 153.

50 G'ulom was known in Russian as Gafur Guliam. Gafur Guliam, 'Ia – evrei!' (1941), trans. S. Somova, in *Izbrannye proizvedeniia v 5 tomakh*, vol. 1, 58–64 (Tashkent, 1971).

51 Ibid.

52 For a discussion of Moscow's lack of public recognition of the plight of Soviet Jews, see Davis, *Myth Making in the Soviet Union and Modern Russia*, 198–202.

53 Iofe and Il'ina, 'Spasenie ot Kholokosta', 331–2; N. V. Khlistunova, 'Evakuatsiia evreev vo vremia VOv v Kazakhstan, dr. strany Tsentral'noi Azii i Zapadnuiu Sibir", in *Istoriia. Pamiat'. Liudi: Materialy VIII Mezhdunarodnoi nauchno-prakticheskoi konferentsii 16 sentiabria 2016 g.*, eds M. S. Makarova, et al., 57–63 (Almaty: 2017), 58; and Arieh Tartakower, 'The Jewish Refugees: A Sociological Survey', *Jewish Social Studies* 4, no. 4 (1942): 311–48, 315.

54 Tartakower, 'The Jewish Refugees', 322.

55 Ibid. Note that Bessarabia was partitioned just before the onset of war between the USSR and Nazi Germany.

56 Iofe and Il'ina, 'Spasenie ot Kholokosta', 333; Khlistunova, 'Evakuatsiia evreev vo vremia VOv', 59; and M. Was, 'Perceiving the Others: Some Remarks on the Testimonies of Polish Jews in Soviet Central Asia', in *Istoriia. Pamiat'. Liudi: Materialy VIII Mezhdunarodnoi nauchno-prakticheskoi konferentsii 16 sentiabria 2016 g.*, eds M. S. Makarova, et al., 37–46 (Almaty: 2017), 37–9.

57 Feferman, 'A Soviet Humanitarian Action?', 816; Iofe and Il'ina, 'Spasenie ot Kholokosta', 331–2; Khlistunova, 'Evakuatsiia evreev vo vremia VOv', 57–8; Manley, 'The Perils of Displacement', 499; Manley, *To the Tashkent Station*, 46 and 191; S. Shwarts, *Evrei v Sovetskom Soiuze s nachala Vtoroi mirovoi voiny (1939–1965)* (New York: American Jewish Working Committee, 1966), 45–6; and A. I. Solzhenitsyn, *Dvesti let vmeste* (Moscow: Russkii put', 2002), 342–4.

58 N. V. Kiutova, 'Iz istorii evakuatsii evreev v gorod Leninogorsk Vostochno-Kazakhstanskoi oblasti ili evreiskaia saga Sorokinykh', in *Istoriia. Pamiat'. Liudi: Materialy VIII Mezhdunarodnoi nauchno-prakticheskoi konferentsii 16 sentiabria 2016 g.*, eds M. S. Makarova, et al., 193–9 (Almaty: 2017), 194–5.

59 Grinberg, *Evrei v Alma-Ate*, 104; Iofe and Il'ina, 'Spasenie ot Kholokosta', 333; Kesler, *Shards of War*, 2013–30; Manley, *To the Tashkent Station*, 191; F. N. Miimanbaeva, 'Materialy Natsional'nogo arkhiva Respubliki Kazakhstan o evreiakh, evakuirovannykh v Kazakhstan v gody Velikoi Otechestvennoi voiny', in *Istoriia. Pamiat'. Liudi: Materialy IX Mezhdunarodnoi nauchno-prakticheskoi konferentsii 27 sentiabria 2018 g.*, eds K. Sh. Alimgazinov, et al., 58–62 (Almaty: 2019), 60; K. D. Saipova, 'Istoriia pol'skikh evreev v gody Vtoroi mirovoi voiny', in *Istoriia. Pamiat'. Liudi: Materialy VIII Mezhdunarodnoi nauchno-prakticheskoi konferentsii 16 sentiabria 2016 g.*, eds M. S. Makarova, et al., 415–17 (Almaty: 2017), 416; and Tartakower, 'The Jewish Refugees', 333.

60   Kesler, *Grit*, 735.

61   IKSA:146/2/13/110. See also Iofe and Il'ina, 'Spasenie ot Kholokosta', 332; Kesler, *Grit*, 877; and Merridale, *Ivan's War*, 288–91.

62   Kiutova, 'Iz istorii evakuatsii evreev v gorod Leninogorsk', 196.

63   Manley, *To the Tashkent Station*, 231–2; and Was, 'Perceiving the Others', 44.

64   Florin, *Kirgistan und die sowjetische Moderne*, 46; Grinberg, *Evrei v Alma-Ate*, 109; Kesler, *Grit*, 760; Khlistunova, 'Evakuatsiia evreev vo vremia VOv', 61; Manley, *To the Tashkent Station*, 231; and Stronski, *Tashkent*, 121 and 123.

65   E. V. Chilikova, 'Migratsiia evreev v Kazakhstan v predvoennoe desiatiletie i v period Veliko Otechestvennoi voiny: Region donory i retsipienty, kolichestvennyi sostav', in *Istoriia. Pamiat'. Liudi: Materialy IX Mezhdunarodnoi nauchno-prakticheskoi konferentsii 27 sentiabria 2018 g.*, eds K. Sh. Alimgazinov, et al., 47–54 (Almaty: 2019), 47–9; V. A. Mukhmejanova, 'Ob istorii i kul'turom nasledii evreev v Srednei Azii', in *Istoriia. Pamiat'. Liudi: Materialy VIII Mezhdunarodnoi nauchno-prakticheskoi konferentsii 16 sentiabria 2016 g.*, eds M. S. Makarova, et al., 350–3 (Almaty: 2017), 350; Saipova, 'Istoriia pol'skikh evreev'; Sokol, *The Revolt of 1916 in Russian Central Asia*, 5; Irena Vladimirsky, 'The Jews of Kyrgyzstan', *Museum of the Jewish People at Beit Hatfutsot*, available online: https://www.bh.org.il/jews-kyrgyzstan (accessed 20 September 2020); and S. Ch. Zhumalieva, 'Stanovlenie i deiatel'nost' obshchestva evreiskoi kul'tury Kyrgyzstana', in *Istoriia. Pamiat'. Liudi: Materialy IX Mezhdunarodnoi nauchno-prakticheskoi konferentsii 27 sentiabria 2018 g.*, eds K. Sh. Alimgazinov, et al., 360–8 (Almaty: 2019), 360–1.

66   Kesler, *Grit*, 816; and Manley, *To the Tashkent Station*, 229.

67   Florin, *Kirgistan und die sowjetische Moderne*, 46; Grinberg, *Evrei v Alma-Ate*, 109; Kiutova, 'Iz istorii evakuatsii evreev v gorod Leninogorsk', 196; Manley, *To the Tashkent Station*, 112, 114 and 230–2; Merridale, *Ivan's War*, 289 and 296; Stronski, *Tashkent*, 123; and Vladimirsky, 'The Jews of Kyrgyzstan'.

68   Beevor, *Berlin*, 424; Grinberg, *Evrei v Alma-Ate*, 109–10; Kiutova, 'Iz istorii evakuatsii evreev v gorod Leninogorsk', 195–6; Manley, *To the Tashkent Station*, 230; and Vladimirsky, 'The Jews of Kyrgyzstan'.

69   Manley, *To the Tashkent Station*, 115, 233 and 266; Merridale, *Ivan's War*, 297; and Turlygul, *Istoriia Kazakhstana*, 193.

70   Iofe and Il'ina, 'Spasenie ot Kholokosta', 337.

71   Miimanbaeva, 'Materialy Natsional'nogo arkhiva Respubliki Kazakhstan o evreiakh', 62.

72   Khlistunova, 'Evakuatsiia evreev vo vremia VOv', 61.

73   Manley, *To the Tashkent Station*, 55 and 225; and Stronski, *Tashkent*, 124, 125, 148, 165 and 192.

74   Anna Akhmatova, *My Half-Century: Selected Prose*, ed. and trans. Ronald Meyer (Evanston: Northwestern University Press, 1998), 128; Anna Akhmatova, 'Tashkentskie stranitsy', in *Izbrannoe: Stikhotvoreniia, poemy*

(Moscow: AST, 2006), 427; Manley, *To the Tashkent Station*, 148–9, 163, 221 and 236–40; and Stronski, *Tashkent*, 124.

75 Michael Wachtel, *The Cambridge Introduction to Russian Poetry* (Cambridge: Cambridge University Press, 2004),147.

76 'A v knigakh ia posledniuiu stranitsu' (1943), Akhmatova, *Iz semi knig*, 192–3; 'Luna v zenite' (1942–4), in Akhmatova, *Izbrannoe*, 370–2.

77 'Kogda lezhit luna lomtem chardzhuiskoi dyni' (1944), in Akhmatova, *Izbrannoe*, 376.

78 'Eshche odno liricheskoe otstuplenie' (1943), in Akhmatova, *Izbrannoe*, 373.

79 'Tashkent zatsvetaet' (1944), in Akhmatova, *Izbrannoe*, 378; and Manley, *To the Tashkent Station*, 236. The same image of young, dark-skinned mothers is captured in Anna Akhmatova, 'Teper' ia vsekh blagodariu' (1945), in Anna Akhmatova, *Polnoe sobranie poezii i prozy v odnom tome* (Russia: Al'fa-kniga, 2019), 367.

80 'Smert'' (1944), in Akhmatova, *Izbrannoe*, 375.

81 Akhmatova, *Izbrannoe*, 571.

82 From Anna Akhmatova, 'Poema bez geroia' (1942), ed. Maria Bloshteyn, *Russia is Burning: Poems of the Great Patriotic War* (Ripon: Smokestack Books, 2020), 235.

83 Anna Akhmatova, 'Pamiati Vali' (1942), in Gorbovskoi, *Stikhi i pesni o voine*, 9.

84 S. Dolgov, 'Zabyty tiazhelye dni', *IKP*, 17 January 1943; IKSA:279/1/251/14–17; and Kaptagaev, et al., *Sbornik*, 133.

85 Information from Director of the Panfilov museum. See also V. G. Iofe and G. S. Vedernikova, 'Iz istorii evakuatsii v Uzbekistan', in *Istoriia. Pamiat'. Liudi: Materialy IX Mezhdunarodnoi nauchno-prakticheskoi konferentsii 27 sentiabria 2018 g.*, eds K. Sh. Alimgazinov, et al., 265–7 (Almaty: 2019), 266; 'Istoriia', *Ministerstvo inostrannykh del Respubliki Uzbekistan*; Keller, *Russia and Central Asia*, 204; and G. S. Vedernikova, 'Evakuatsiia: Tiazhelye, no blagorodnye stranitsy istorii', in *Istoriia. Pamiat'. Liudi: Materialy VIII Mezhdunarodnoi nauchno-prakticheskoi konferentsii 16 sentiabria 2016 g.*, eds M. S. Makarova, et al., 79–82 (Almaty: 2017), 81.

86 Abylkhozhin, *Istoriia Kazakhstana*, 526; Batyrbaeva, 'Evakuirovannoe i deportirovannoe naselenie', 26; A. M. Berkimbaeva and D. M. Legkii, 'Oblono ne okhvatilo vsekh evakuirovannykh detei ucheboi: Shkol'noe obuchenie detei iz evakuirovannykh i deportirovannykh semei v gody Velikoi Otechestvennoi voiny', in *Istoriia. Pamiat'. Liudi: Materialy IX Mezhdunarodnoi nauchno-prakticheskoi konferentsii 27 sentiabria 2018 g.*, eds K. Sh. Alimgazinov, et al., 88–93 (Almaty: 2019), 89; Inoiatova, 'Pomoshch' Uzbekistana evakuirovannym detiam', 271; and Zh. Zh. Tursynova, 'Ikh sud'by izmenila voina', in *Istoriia. Pamiat'. Liudi: Materialy VIII Mezhdunarodnoi nauchno-prakticheskoi konferentsii 16 sentiabria 2016 g.*, eds M. S. Makarova, et al., 180–4 (Almaty: 2017), 181–2.

87 Barber and Harrison, *The Soviet Home Front*, 91; Inoiatova, 'Pomoshch' Uzbekistana evakuirovannym detiam', 271; Manley, 'The Perils of

Displacement', 497; and Manley, *To the Tashkent Station*, 20, 185 (footnote 247) and 198.

88   IKSA:279/1/251/52; Berkimbaeva and Legkii, 'Oblono ne okhvatilo vsekh evakuirovannykh detei ucheboi', 89; Kseniia Kerez Zarlykova, *Povest' Zhana Angemeler* (Bishkek: 2007); Manley, *To the Tashkent Station*, 185 and 189–90; and Stronski, *Tashkent*, 50, 90 and 138. Further information from Prof. Tchoraev.

89   Florin, 'Becoming Soviet through War', 509 (footnote 72); Florin, *Kirgistan und die sowjetische Moderne*, 46; Inoiatova, 'Pomoshch' Uzbekistana evakuirovannym detiam', 270–2; Manley, *To the Tashkent Station*, 192; and Tursynova, 'Ikh sud'by izmenila voina', 182. Further information from Tatiana Dubovik, 'Sud'ba soldata' conference, Moscow, 30 November 2019.

90   IKSA:282/1/3/14 and 15.

91   IKSA:174/3/36/261–4; IKSA:279/1/250/11 and 21; and IKSA:279/1/251/62–3. See also Seidimatova, 'Priissykkul'e v gody Velikoi Otechestvennoi voiny', 282; and Tranum, *Life at the Edge of the Empire*, 163.

92   Manley, *To the Tashkent Station*, 188 and 190; and Seidimatova, 'Priissykkul'e v gody Velikoi Otechestvennoi voiny', 282.

93   IKSA:279/1/103/25.

94   IKSA:279/1/105/12; IKSA: 279/1/250/21; and IKSA:279/1/251/21–2.

95   IKSA:174/3/36/261–4; IKSA:279/1/251/62; and Manley, *To the Tashkent Station*, 121, 183–4 and 187. Further information from Chinara Seidimatova, 30 November 2019.

96   IKSA:279/1/251/4, 6, 12 and 17.

97   Inoiatova, 'Pomoshch' Uzbekistana evakuirovannym detiam', 269; Kerimbaev, *Sovetskii Kirgizstan v Velikoi Otechestvennoi voine*, 194; Manley, *To the Tashkent Station*, 224–6; Seidimatova, 'Priissykkul'e v gody Velikoi Otechestvennoi voiny', 282; and Tursynova, 'Ikh sud'by izmenila voina', 182–3.

98   Zukhra Kasimova, 'Adoption and Integration of Displaced Soviet Children during the Great Patriotic War in the Uzbek SSR', *Peripheral Histories*, 2018, https://www.peripheralhistories.co.uk/post/adoption-integration-of-displaced-soviet-children-during-the-great-patriotic-war-in-the-uzbek-ssr; and Keller, *Russia and Central Asia*, 206.

99   Anna Akhmatova, 'Ty – ne sirota', translated from G'afur G'ulom, 'Sen etim emassan'. Gafur Guliam, 'Ty ne sirota', in *Pobeda: Stikhi voennykh let*, ed. S. Narovchatov (Moscow: Khudozhestvennaia literatura, 1985), 129–31; Inoiatova, 'Pomoshch' Uzbekistana evakuirovannym detiam', 272; Keller, *Russia and Central Asia*, 206; Manley, *To the Tashkent Station*, 224–5; and Stronski, *Tashkent*, 140.

100 V. Mikhailov, 'Vozvrashchenie v rodnoi gorod', *IKP*, 5 July 1945; IKSA:279/1/251/7–8; and Kaptagaev, et al., *Sbornik*, 150.

101 Information from Prof. Tchoraev. See also Manley, *To the Tashkent Station*, 265–6.2018.

102 'Perepiska s roditeliami 1945–47 gody', IKSA:279/1/295.

103 IKSA:279/1/295/50.

104 IKSA:279/1/295/7, 58, 59, 69–70 and 76.

105 IKSA:279/1/295/53–7.

106 Ibid.

107 IKSA:279/1/295/53–7 and 68.

108 IKSA:279/1/295/53, 71 and 115–16. See also Seidimatova, 'Priissykkul'e v gody Velikoi Otechestvennoi voiny', 282.

109 IKSA:279/1/295/30, 46, 47 and 51.

110 IKSA:279/1/295/74, 75, 91, 92 and 94.

111 Kerimbaev, *Sovetskii Kirgizstan v Velikoi Otechestvennoi voine*, 193.

112 Maksimova, *Deti voennoi pory*, 1988, 235–308 (cited in Barber and Harrison, *The Soviet Home Front*, 91). Further information from Dr Narynbek Alymnugov, 11 May 2018.

113 M. N. Potemkina, 'Dolgaia doroga domoi sem'i Min'kinnykh', in *Istoriia. Pamiat'. Liudi: Materialy VIII Mezhdunarodnoi nauchno-prakticheskoi konferentsii 16 sentiabria 2016 g.*, eds M. S. Makarova, et al., 284–90 (Almaty: 2017), 284.

114 Davis, *Myth Making in the Soviet Union and Modern Russia*, 177; Manley, *To the Tashkent Station*, 246; and Elizabeth White, 'After the War was Over: The civilian return to Leningrad', *Europe–Asia Studies* 59, no. 7 (2007): 1145–61, 1159.

115 White, 'After the War was Over', 1147.

116 'Kogo gotovit Nikolaevskii korablestroitel'nyi institut', *IKP*, 8 August 1944, 2; Kaptagaev, et al., *Sbornik*, 136, 139 and 146–7; Manley, *To the Tashkent Station*, 238; and Seidimatova, 'Priissykkul'e v gody Velikoi Otechestvennoi voiny', 281.

117 Potemkina, 'Dolgaia doroga domoi', 286–8.

118 Beevor, *Berlin*, 424–5; Y. Gilboa, *The Black Years of Soviet Jewry: 1939–1953*, trans. Yosef Shachter and Dov Ben-Abba (USA: Brandeis University, 1971), 34–6; Khlistunova, 'Evakuatsiia evreev vo vremia VOv', 61; Manley, *To the Tashkent Station*, 262–3; and Merridale, *Ivan's War*, 297.

119 Batyrbaeva, 'Evakuirovannoe i deportirovannoe naselenie', 26–7; Florin, 'Becoming Soviet through War', 509; Grinberg, *Evrei v Alma-Ate*, 118; Kiutova, 'Iz istorii evakuatsii evreev v gorod Leninogorsk', 197; Manley, *To the Tashkent Station*, 238, 251–5 and 259; Syrlybaeva, 'Pervaia Respublikanskaia khudozhestvennaia vystavka "Velikaia Otechestvennaia voina"', 129–30; Syrlybaeva, 'Vtoraia Respublikanskaia khudozhestvennaia vystavka "Velikaia Otechestvennaia voina"', 138; and White, 'After the War was Over', 1145 and 1159.

120 Manley, *To the Tashkent Station*, 258, 260–1, 264, 266 and 268.

121 Anna Akhmatova, 'Ne s temi ia' (1922), in *Iz semi knig*, 145; and 'Luna v zenite', stanza 5.

122 Akhmatova, 'Teper' ia vsekh blagodariu'.

123 'S samoleta' (1944), in Akhmatova, *Izbrannoe*, 379.

124 Ermekbai, 'Zavod No. 621', 188.

125 Florin, 'Becoming Soviet through War', 508; and Manley, *To the Tashkent Station*, 227.

8

Forced deportations
to Central Asia

As evacuees and refugees climbed more or less willingly aboard the trains hastening them eastwards, about 2 million other Soviet citizens were uprooted from their homes under extreme duress. If the evacuations represented the moral highpoint of what the state could do to help its citizens stay safe during the war, the deportations were the absolute nadir of intra-state cruelty. In multiple waves of deportation Soviet civilians of various nationalities were expelled from their homes and unceremoniously dumped in Central Asia, the state's destination of choice for its undesirables. These harsh mass relocations were based on ethnicity alone, ostensibly either to remove certain minorities from the temptation of collaboration with the enemy before any potential occupation or to punish them en masse in the later years of the war for presumed betrayal. In this way, ethnic Germans and Greeks, followed by Islamic Soviet citizens such as Chechens, Ingush and Crimean Tatars, arrived in Central Asia. In addition, just like the millions of prisoners sent to the slave labour camps in Siberia and Kazakhstan before them, Polish soldiers and civilians taken during the campaigns of 1939 and 1940 were re-located to Siberia and Central Asia where they could cause no further trouble to the aims of the expanding Soviet state.

Pre-war deportations

The successive waves of wartime deportations were built on the administrative and logistical experience accumulated during the 1930s, when systemic class warfare resulted in the expulsion of vast numbers of *kulaks* (wealthier peasants), members of the intelligentsia, religious leaders and senior military officers to the Siberian labour camps. Throughout the pre-war period, the state built up an atmosphere of suspicion in which spies and saboteurs supposedly lurked around every corner with the alleged express intention of stealing state secrets and damaging industrial output. Although so-called saboteurs were usually scapegoats for the all-too-frequent missing of state targets in successive five-year plans, it was the state's claims of foreign collaboration and espionage on an industrial scale which led to the deportation of whole ethnic minorities living in the Soviet Union.

Since the early 1920s Lenin had endeavoured to integrate into the newly formed Union of Soviet Socialist Republics those regions which were home to ethnic minorities, while permitting a degree of self-governance through his *korenizatsiia* policy. As the Stalinist state increasingly turned its attention – and growing paranoia – to potential internal enemies during the 1930s, the promotion of the rights of ethnic minorities was tacitly abandoned. During the Great Terror of 1937 and 1938 many local leaders and members of the intelligentsia were executed or imprisoned, to be replaced by the Kremlin's puppets. Against this background of suspicion and increasing Russian dominance, the mass deportations of ethnic minorities began. On this occasion, however, it was not just individual politicians who were the targets but innocent families and whole communities.

The first to come under attack were the Soviet citizens of Korean ethnicity living in the Vladivostok region in the far east of the country. As the state sought to safeguard its borders from enemy infiltration in the second half of the 1930s, these so-called 'unreliable elements' became politically undesirable by virtue of their ethnicity. Strategically located on the Soviet eastern seaboard and rendering the country potentially vulnerable to invasion by Japan, this sparsely populated region represented a back door into the Soviet Union. In the autumn of 1937 around 170,000 ethnic Koreans were deported from their homes near the Korean border to the Soviet interior where they could do no harm to state interests. Indeed, the mass resettlement of a whole nationality was probably seen by Soviet leaders as a positive move rather than merely a means to calm Stalin's paranoia. It was hoped that those sent to Central Asia would make a significant contribution to the local economy, thanks to the healthy work ethic of the Koreans. Furthermore, their presence would serve to dilute the concentration of a population which may have gone on to make its own territorial demands on the Soviet Union had it been allowed to grow unhindered in the far east.[1]

Sofiya Kim was only eight years old in 1937, living with her family in the city of Iman (Dal'nerechensk) on the Russo-Chinese border north of Vladivostok, when they were deported to Ush Tobe near Alma-Ata, an area which had become accustomed to receiving deportees over the years. As the frontier region was systematically cleansed by the NKVD, families were packed onto trains, with the deported Koreans often undergoing journeys of up to a month to their final destinations in Kazakhstan and Uzbekistan. Although probably not intended, many died en route or shortly after arrival, thus permanently removing any potential threat to the state. Meagre compensation for their loss comprised a small plot of land for each family and the materials with which to build a new home.[2] Despite the hardship endured, most families gradually adapted to their new lives by continuing their traditional jobs as rice farmers or fishermen. More Koreans were deported as the war progressed, for example from the northern port of Murmansk, while any already serving in the Red Army were redeployed to labour battalions in the rear, where there was no danger of subversive contact with the enemy. One notable exception to this crackdown was a certain Kim Il-Sung, whose proven record of anti-Japanese guerrilla warfare in Manchuria led to the granting of shelter in Siberia during the war years. He was made an officer of the Red Army 88th Brigade, commanding the 1st Battalion in the final action against Japan in the summer of 1945. With Stalin's backing, Kim returned to Pyongyang later that year to become the new leader of the communist Democratic People's Republic of Korea, the future North Korea, where he was to build his own ruling dynasty.[3]

The deportation of Soviet citizens of Korean nationality was the first internal state action against a whole ethnic group – people who were by and large (given half a chance) both peaceful and hard-working. Over the course of the next decades, the state tried to integrate them more deeply into the Soviet Union and thus remove any remote possibility of treason. Many lost their own culture and language, although Sofiya Kim remained until recently a member of the Korean association in her adopted home of Bishkek.[4]

As the control of border zones tightened, a few hundred Kurds living in southern regions of the Soviet Union close to the borders with Turkey, Afghanistan and Iran were relocated forcibly to Kyrgyzstan and Kazakhstan, while security along the southern borders of Tajikistan, Uzbekistan and Turkmenistan was increased. Similarly, alleged 'alien elements' on other fringes of the Soviet Union, such as Finns from Karelia, Poles from Belarus or Ukraine, some Soviet citizens originally from the Baltic States and Soviet Greeks from the Black Sea coastal areas were deported in the pre-war years simply by virtue of their questionable nationality.[5] These planned, if relatively minor, measures showed a blatant disregard for the official Soviet policy of *korenizatsiia*, while building on the earlier repression of members of the indigenous intelligentsia and political leaders. In this way the stage was set for more drastic waves of deportation affecting not only Soviet citizens but also the overt wartime adversaries of the Soviet Union.

The plight of the Poles

As the tense summer of 1939 in Europe drew to a close, the Soviet Union and Nazi Germany signed a non-aggression pact on 23 August 1939. A few days afterwards, on 1 September, Hitler's forces marched into western Poland, dramatically augmenting the stream of Polish refugees already heading eastwards to seek supposed sanctuary in the Soviet Union. The plight of the Poles was sealed, however, when Stalin ordered his 12th Army west into the

eastern marches of Poland, the Kresy, which the secret pact had allocated
to Soviet power. Trapped in a tight pincer movement, the Polish army stood
little chance of survival, with many officers and men taken prisoner and
transported to the Siberian camps.[6] In the spring of 1940 the Red Army
executed 20,000 Polish officers in Katyn Forest, eliminating at a stroke the
cream of the Polish army.

For the privilege of being overrun, all Poles living in the eastern area
occupied by Soviet forces were deemed to have become Soviet citizens
almost overnight, as it was incorporated into Belarus and Ukraine. Life for
the remaining civilians became increasingly Sovietized as the Red Army
made its presence felt. Places of worship were shut down and property
was confiscated, as landowners and their families were either executed or
deported.[7] Citizens of the Baltic States and Bessarabia (or Moldavia) were
swept up alongside Poles from Ukraine and Belarus in the well-planned
operation to purge the region of the potential threat of these 'enemies of the
state'.[8]

Estimates of the number of deportees from eastern Poland range from
a few hundred thousand to almost 2 million civilians. The true number is
probably around one and a half million Poles who were plucked from their
beds and given just minutes to pack for the journey east. Irena Protassewicz
and eleven-year-old Michał Giedroyć were just two of those packed into
wooden cattle or freight wagons, carrying clothing, bedding, kitchen utensils
and a few portable valuables. Their own food supplies supplemented the
meagre rations provided by the accompanying guards as they travelled for
up to four weeks deep into the Soviet Union to remote areas of the Urals,
Siberia or Kazakhstan.[9]

Those deported Poles who remained alive as they left the train convoy
were transported onwards by truck or sled to their final destination. Zofia
Właźnik was typical of many totally disoriented deportees whose month-
long train journey was followed by one week by truck and a further two days
by horse and cart over snow and taiga.[10] By the end of 1942, 150,000 had
arrived in Kazakhstan, with some 13,000 in Kyrgyzstan. They were mainly
women and children, new citizens of the Soviet Union, whose menfolk were
either languishing in prison camps or had been executed.[11]

All deportees were issued with Soviet passports on arrival, proof that
they had indeed become Soviet citizens of Polish or Jewish nationality.[12]
With able-bodied men often sent to forced labour camps, most women were
allocated to industry, forestry or collective farms.[13] The Karaganda camp in
Kazakhstan benefited from the influx of additional slave labour in the coal
mines, while some children were sent to carry out demanding physical work
in the cotton fields of Uzbekistan. Further north, logging camps were the
norm, even for minors.[14] The Giedroyć family resigned themselves to life
on the remote *Krasnoe Znamia* (Red Banner) collective farm, while others
were placed in the aptly named *Novyi byt* (New Way of Life) farm near
Akmolinsk, both in northern Kazakhstan.[15]

As many of the deportees were from professional backgrounds, including doctors, businessmen and teachers, they found the hard physical labour particularly demanding. In addition, many had no clothing or footwear suitable for the harsh conditions. The freezing winters in northern Kazakhstan brought temperatures as low as –50C, while the summers saw invasions of midges, fleas and mosquitoes. Fuel was hard to come by: the traditional Central Asian dung and straw briquettes were the norm. Very few managed to obtain sufficient food to sustain the expected physical labour. The small amounts of food taken on the journey east did not last long and were supplemented where possible by the barter of personal possessions. However, the local populations were also suffering from starvation rations, even those working on farms. Nobody, it seems, received their full quota, and no wages were offered to deportees. Occasional food parcels arrived from Poland, but bread and thin soup were all that many families could muster as they gradually became too weak to work. Some resorted to begging or stealing food in the struggle to survive, taking the risk in the knowledge that a prison sentence awaited those who were caught. Cases of suicide were not uncommon and illness was rife, leading to more deaths especially during the severe winter months.[16]

Interaction with the local population was often cursory, although incidences of some assistance to deportees have been recorded. Perhaps those Polish children who attended school led the most ordinary existence in the community, as they picked up the local language and integrated quite quickly. Despite this relative normality, the opportunity to receive some sort of education was also at the expense of a degree of Soviet indoctrination.[17] Furthermore, many families found it impossible to support their offspring, who increasingly found themselves in children's homes.[18]

NKVD surveillance ensured that little news from the outside world penetrated these isolated areas, except for the occasional village radio broadcast. Some letters eventually arrived for the deportees, but communications from home were no longer received after the German invasion of the Soviet Union. For this reason the majority of the Polish deportees in Siberia and Central Asia were for several months unaware of the agreement reached in London on 30 July 1941 between Stalin's ambassador to Britain, Ivan Maiskii, and General Władysław Sikorski, the leader of the Polish government in exile. With Operation Barbarossa well under way, the non-aggression treaty between Nazi Germany and the Soviet Union had become null and void, thus changing the status of the Polish deportees and prisoners. As the Soviet Union resumed diplomatic links with the Polish government, they reverted from Soviet citizens to 'refugees, former Polish citizens' with an amnesty proclaimed on 12 August 1941 granting all deportees and POWs their freedom and the permanent right to remain in the Soviet Union.[19]

Naturally the Soviet local authorities, especially the NKVD, were slow to inform Poles in their areas of their new status, wishing to benefit from free labour for as long as possible. Nor was any assistance provided once prisoners had been released from their camps and deportees freed from their farms or factories. By this time, about half of the Polish citizens in the Soviet Union had already died and the Polish government needed to establish the scale of the human tragedy.[20] Polish diplomatic representation was therefore established across the region, tasked with registering Polish citizens and providing practical and financial assistance. A network of information offices in larger towns and at key railway junctions issued passports, as the twenty newly established Polish consulates in the Soviet Union embarked on the enormous task of searching for lost relations.[21] Stuck in the middle of nowhere, many had to barter their remaining possessions in order to beg a ride to the nearest station and buy a train ticket to the closest town where they could register. Irena Protassewicz took months to reach the Jambul (Taraz) field station of the Polish embassy in Kazakhstan, while the Giedroyć family received warm clothes, a food parcel and some money provided by a welfare programme distributing humanitarian aid from the United States and Britain.[22]

Once their situation had stabilized to an extent, many Poles who could not face the thought of another winter in Siberian exile embarked on the long journey south to a warmer climate. Zofia Właźnik received some food and even shoes on her journey as she managed to reach Kyrgyzstan in 1942, following other Poles believing that the climate there would be much warmer. A substantial number of Polish men also headed south to Central Asia because of rumours they had heard about the formation of a Polish army there.[23]

Reaching Anders's army

As part of the Sikorski-Maiskii amnesty pact, it was agreed that a Polish army would be raised in the Soviet Union from Polish citizens living on Soviet soil. Pledging their loyalty to Poland, they would be prepared to fight on the Soviet Western Front under Soviet strategic command. The Polish government further named General Władysław Anders as its leader, under the commander-in-chief of the Polish armed forces, General Sikorski.[24]

Anders, a politically reliable, talented military leader and legendary veteran of the First World War, was no doubt selected for the task due to his extensive prior knowledge of Russia and Russian from his service in the tsar's army. At the beginning of August 1941 Anders was a prisoner of war, incarcerated in the Liubianka (the NKVD's Moscow headquarters), when he was suddenly released under the amnesty. Soon afterwards Anders set up his military headquarters in Uzbekistan, where he deemed the climate more suited to the recuperation of the thousands of men who would be joining him, while being closer to a potential exit route from the Soviet Union.[25]

From his base just outside Tashkent, Anders set up seven infantry divisions across Uzbekistan, Kyrgyzstan and southern Kazakhstan. All the Polish units were subject to NKVD surveillance and under the control of the central Soviet military authorities at SAVO in Tashkent. While rations and military equipment were provided by the Soviets, the army turned to the British for its uniform.[26]

Many men only heard about Anders's army when they registered for their new Polish passports. Men of eighteen and over wishing to volunteer were directed to the nearest conscription centres and mustering stations where regiments were being raised. Confusion reigned, though, as rumours spread about where and how to travel. Some were as quick to volunteer as Zofia Wlaźnik's brother, but others had already been press-ganged into the Red Army before obtaining any information about Anders's army. In the end, sheer ingenuity and dogged perseverance prevailed as thousands of people made their way south by train, truck, boat, raft and even on foot.[27]

Men were keen to enlist to do their bit for their country, once they had heard about the devastation wreaked by the occupying forces. Fear was also a great driver – fear of the Germans, fear of remaining trapped as slaves in Siberia, fear of starvation and disease. In addition more informed deportees saw a glimmer of hope in Central Asia with the so-called 'Persian Corridor' to the south-west providing the light at the end of the escape tunnel. Very few realised, though, that there was a deadline for the journey, as Anders started to negotiate the onward movement of his army.[28]

The long trek south took several weeks for most would-be recruits, who did not know exactly where they were going or what awaited them. Spurred on by the strong motivation to reach the Polish army with its provisions, families traversed the region in an exhausting odyssey. Trading clothes for food, Irena Protassewicz obtained her train ticket illegally for the journey in the depths of winter 1941–2. Hungry and frozen, she arrived in Tashkent only to discover that she had to travel further to Jambul in southern Kazakhstan. Dependent upon sympathetic locals for sanctuary and food, she managed to scrape together a few pieces of coal for warmth. In contrast, the Fedzin family walked most of the way, relying on plant roots and even snakes for food. Like many others, they found no accommodation in Uzbekistan and were diverted into Kyrgyzstan, where they were offered temporary shelter.[29]

The Giedroyć family had a more straightforward, if still taxing, train journey, having received documents entitling them to travel to Guzar on the Uzbek–Afghan border. Despite the usual inquisitive interventions of the NKVD, they travelled for almost a fortnight with the help of forged permits from northern Kazakhstan to Tashkent. The exhausted travellers ran out of food as they crossed the Kyzyl-Kum desert, but eventually arrived in Guzar in the middle of July 1942.[30] These are examples of the fortunate former deportees – those who stayed alive and retained sufficient strength to reach Anders's army.

Enlistment

The rate of recruitment accelerated as Poles gradually managed to reach the relative shelter of the newly established army bases, although officers were thin on the ground – presumably a result of the Katyn massacre. Watslaw Flisinski eventually reached Jalal-Abad in Kyrgyzstan, the headquarters of the new 5th Vilnius Infantry Division, on 22 February 1942. He found the new soldiers in outlying villages, quartered in tents set up under trees for some protection from the fierce sun. First-aid posts had been set up in schools and some private homes to deal with the rampant typhoid fever epidemic. Relations between the soldiers and the locals were friendly, although a minimal NKVD presence still kept a watchful eye on troop movements and a small group of Roman Catholic priests, extraordinarily permitted to conduct services in a makeshift church.[31]

Every effort was made by Polish deportees to join the army. Although the official minimum age was eighteen, some young men claimed to have 'lost' their documents and to be older than they really were.[32] Anders expressed an official preference for those who had seen previous military service, but most physically fit young men were allowed to join up as he aimed to reach the maximum quota of 120,000 soldiers imposed by the Soviet Union. The recruitment strategy was tarnished, however, by widespread claims of anti-Semitism. Allegedly many Polish citizens of Jewish nationality were rejected by the army, especially once the enlistment process got under way, when Jewish recruits were mainly limited to skilled medical professionals and engineers. Doubtless, the Red Army at SAVO had a role to play in the recruitment policy, while ingrained pre-war prejudices amongst Polish officers were probably partly to blame.[33]

Anders had a further challenge to meet in the fitness of his recruits. Most of them had travelled huge distances across the continent, only to collapse in a state of total exhaustion once they reached the army bases. Depleted by malnutrition and months of hard physical labour, they were in a sorry state on arrival. In addition, the majority were debilitated by some form of disease – from the ubiquitous lice and fleas to more serious cases of malaria, typhus, typhoid fever, tuberculosis and dysentery. The facilities often exacerbated the hygiene problems, with water usually drawn from irrigation canals. The testimony of Stanislaw Sobolewski indicates that danger was apparent at every meal.[34] Irena Protassewicz reinforced the squalid conditions suffered during her medical work, after she was accepted into the Polish Women's Auxiliary Service as a nurse in southern Kazakhstan, and then as a patient herself in Uzbekistan, convalescing with the 7th Division near Samarkand.[35] With treatment limited to aspirin, Poles continued to die, leaving relatively few healthy soldiers to dig their graves.[36]

Under these circumstances, training was slow. Anders and occasionally even General Zhukov visited the disparate divisions to observe the new soldiers as they came to terms with Soviet weapons. Discipline was challenged as alcohol abuse was evident amongst the new recruits and some even deserted. A certain Tadeusz Mydliazh of the 5th Division was executed by firing squad after a Polish court martial in February 1942, leading Anders to affirm that 'offensive behaviour, spying and desertion will face the death penalty'.[37]

Anders perceived an increasingly urgent need to leave the Soviet Union in case the state suddenly changed its mind. The army's departure had to wait, however, balanced finely against the need first of all for the recuperation, medical treatment and initial military training of the troops. After lengthy negotiations, it was decided that the Polish army should be deployed to reinforce the British 8th Army in the Middle East rather than be sent prematurely to fight under Soviet command on the Soviet Western Front. Another burden on his shoulders was the enormous number of civilians congregating around the military camps. Anders managed to eke out the food rations supplied by the Soviets to ensure that most family members of recruits had just enough to eat. His hand was forced, however, when food supplies were cut drastically and a quick decision had to be made in the interests of saving the maximum number of Poles. Exploiting the fact that the Soviets were eventually willing to allow the families of troops to leave alongside the army, Anders managed to negotiate the removal of thousands of – if not all – civilians from the realm of Soviet influence and into Iran.[38]

On the move

This magnificent, if bedraggled, escape to freedom was effected between March and September 1942, just in the nick of time, as it turned out. By the spring of 1943 the bodies of thousands of Polish army officers were discovered in the forest at Katyn, near the Soviet city of Smolensk. The eventual attribution of their mass murder in 1940 to the Red Army totally soured diplomatic relations between the Polish government and the Soviet Union for the rest of the war.[39]

Anders was finally credited with the evacuation of over 70,000 soldiers and 44,000 civilians (including over 12,000 children) out of Soviet Central Asia.[40] The Polish army nurse Irena Protassewicz and the Giedroyć family were transported by train across the baking desert of Uzbekistan to the Turkmen port of Krasnovodsk on the Caspian Sea. From there it was a short thirty-six-hour transfer by ship to reach the Iranian port of Pahlevi (Bandar-e Anzali), although the crowded conditions on the old oil tankers and cargo ships proved the final straw for the weakest amongst them. Once out of the Soviet Union, there was time to recover a little. Stanisław Sobolewski was given one pound on arrival, which he used to buy twelve hard-boiled eggs. Others craved the fresh fruit available in Iran rather than the tinned food, mutton and rice offered by the British army, under whose aegis the Polish army was then sheltered.[41] With their basic necessities catered for, the Anders army was ready for further training and their onward transfer through Iraq, Syria and Palestine to Egypt. Many of the Jewish troops with Anders decided to leave the army once in Palestine, although the real reason for their departure has not yet been established. Claims of cowardice on the part of Jews persist, but it is probable that they simply wished to join the Jewish community in Jerusalem and the surrounding areas, having found the anti-Semitism of the Polish army unbearable. As part of the British 8th Army, the Polish Second Corps was subsequently landed in Italy, fighting at Monte Cassino in the push to liberate Nazi-occupied Europe before being finally demobilized in 1946.

After demobilization most decided to stay in the West – in Britain, the United States or Canada. Only 310 soldiers and their families applied to be repatriated to Poland under the new regime, conscious of the fact that it was by then under Soviet communist control. Irena Protassewicz, Stanisław Sobolewski and the Giedroyć family selected the option of life in post-war Britain. General Anders himself lived the rest of his life in London until his death in 1970.[42]

Many of the children who had left Central Asia with Anders were orphaned, finding refuge in other countries as they were scattered across the world from East Africa to Mexico and New Zealand. Vera Lifschitz was one of the so-called Polish 'Tehran Children' eventually cared for in an orphanage set up by the local Jewish community in Iran. From there, they travelled to Karachi in India before finally travelling to Palestine via the Suez Canal. India was also the destination selected by Hanka Ordonowna, a Polish singer and circus performer who found herself in a camp in Uzbekistan following her arrest by the NKVD. Liberated after the amnesty, she offered support to Polish orphans. Antoni Matveichuk, born in 1936, was one of the 400 children she managed to help out of Uzbekistan via Tajikistan, Iran, Beirut and Bombay to Karachi, where the orphanage was housed by an Indian maharajah. These much-travelled children mainly returned to communist Poland after the war, but Antoni and his mother managed to reach Liverpool on a British troop ship after Indian independence, from where they were sent to an evacuee camp near Oxford. Antoni attended reunions in his native Poland of the 'Association of Children of India, 1942–1948' for decades after his departure from Central Asia.[43]

Those left behind

Antoni Matveichuk may have escaped from Central Asia, but his older brother was not so fortunate. As soon as the amnesty was declared, but before knowledge about the Anders army had become widespread, the eighteen-year-old was conscripted into the Red Army. Once the Anders army had left Soviet soil and diplomatic relations between Poland and the Soviet Union had broken down, all Polish citizens remaining in the Soviet Union once again became Soviet citizens by default. As such, they were – once again – liable for conscription into the Red Army. This was the fate of most Polish men remaining in the Soviet Union, including some of those who had been rejected by Anders's army. Some were sent to labour battalions to toil – once again – in the coal mines of Karaganda, or work on the railroads, as was the destiny of one of the Fedzin family. Others, like Antoni Matveichuk's father, a former soldier and freed POW, were conscripted in 1943 into a newly formed division of the Red Army especially for former Polish citizens – the First Tadeusz Kościuszko Polish Infantry Division, the so-called Berling's Army.[44]

Colonel Zygmunt Berling had formerly served in Jalal-Abad as a senior officer in Anders's 5th Division. Mistrusted due to his overt communist leanings, he was passed over for promotion by Anders in 1942 and promptly deserted to join the Red Army. As an experienced officer, he was selected to lead the new Kościuszko Division in April 1943. Whereas joining the Anders army had been voluntary, there was little choice for Poles about service in the new division. Indeed, many Poles preferred not to join up, as, due to a continuing shortage of Polish officers, 70 per cent of the divisional officers were Russian. In addition, the men were expected to swear allegiance to the Soviet state rather than to their homeland, a situation which was replicated in the smaller Czechoslovak Battalion. A further member of the Fedzin family was conscripted into the Kościuszko Division and immediately sent off to the Soviet Western Front. However, the unit was disowned by the Polish government in exile, which accused Berling of treason.[45]

As part of the Red Army, political oversight was embedded into the new Polish division. This was largely provided by the Polish war correspondent and Soviet sympathizer Wanda Wasilewska, a communist activist in the Soviet Union, who had spent much of the war prior to 1943 based in Petropavlovsk in Kazakhstan. A great proponent of the Kościuszko Division, Wasilewska was also involved in the formation of the League of Polish Patriots in the Soviet Union. Under her leadership, substantial social and cultural support was afforded to many of the hundreds of thousands of Poles remaining in and around Central Asia. With the ostensible aim of fighting fascism, the league published cultural material while also sponsoring children's homes and schools for former Polish deportees. In Kazakhstan alone ten homes for a total of 976 children were opened under the auspices of the league. Further south in Kyrgyzstan, where there were fewer Poles, three homes were established in Tokmak, Sary-Bulak and Jalal-Abad, with a further seventeen nurseries for pre-school children. Some provision for special classes in Polish was made in the ordinary schools, but by 1944 a dedicated school for Polish children was opened in Frunze.[46]

The usual problems reared their heads, though: the buildings provided were largely unsuitable for winter conditions and insufficient Polish teachers were available, despite the provision of some Polish textbooks. The Polish teachers managed to set up a Scouts organization in one school, if without the permission of the local educational authorities. The curriculum also included some religious elements and the history and geography of their distant homeland. However, by the end of the 1944/5 academic year fifty Polish teachers from Kazakhstan had attended a two-month professional development course in Moscow, integrating them further into the Soviet educational system with its substantial political content.[47]

Around 150,000 Poles remained in Central Asia when the League of Polish Patriots was formed, quite a significant number, despite the fact that many had left via the Persian Corridor and an even greater number had perished during their time in enforced exile. By the end of the war, well over 2,000 Poles were still resident in Alma-Ata alone, including the poet Aleksander Wat. In Wat's nostalgic poem, 'Willow Trees in Alma-Ata' (1942), he compares the nature of Kazakhstan and his homeland, vowing from his exile never to forget Poland.[48]

The remaining Polish deportees were free to find a job, although the salaries on offer were often insufficient for survival, at around 180 roubles per month. Polish women often found work in light industry, for example, in shoe or textile factories. The enterprising refugee Zofia Właźnik found a job at the Savod sugar beet factory in Kant, not far from Frunze, where she received a bread ration alongside her salary. This was seasonal work, so in the summer she turned her hand to delivering bread by camel. It was not until the spring of 1944 that she and her husband managed to become self-sufficient by growing their own crop of corn in this constant fight for survival. By the end of the war, she was working as a bus conductor, while her husband had become a driver at the sugar factory.[49]

As the war ended, the Poles in the Soviet Union had a choice to make about their future. Around half of all the former Polish deportees elected to return home to communist Poland, clamouring to renounce their current Soviet citizenship and obtain the new Polish passport available only to those who had held Polish citizenship prior to 17 September 1939. Over 100,000 Poles were involved in this administrative change of status in Kazakhstan alone, while in the Kyrgyz Jalal-Abad province almost 2,000 Poles were transported in a trainload of 66 coaches to the town of Medyka on the Ukrainian–Polish border, arriving in their homeland late in the evening of 3 May 1946.[50]

The mass movement west included remaining members of the Fedzin family, who left Jambul in Kazakhstan at the end of April to embark on a two-month journey of 5,000 kilometres. Zofia Właźnik's journey home was delayed, as news of the arrangement was slow to percolate across the region. With her husband and newborn baby, she eventually reached Szczecin, where the International Refugee Organization offered assistance. The International Red Cross also attempted to put family members in touch with each other again, wherever possible.[51]

Unlike those who were quickly repatriated, many Poles in the post-war Soviet Union were either too ill or were living in such remote areas that they were not able to take advantage of the repatriation arrangements. Some managed to return home following further negotiations at the end of 1956, but others found themselves stuck in the Soviet Union until its collapse in 1991. These included some Polish troops who had served in the Kościuszko Division or indeed in other Red Army units, who decided to return to the Soviet Union when they were demobilized in search of their families stranded in Central Asia. In seeking to rejoin their wives and children, these men would forgo the right to repatriation and automatically remain Soviet citizens of Polish nationality.[52]

The impact of the presence of the Poles on Central Asia was limited to their mainly temporary contribution to fulfilling the very real labour demands in the war years. Most of the intelligentsia fled the region as soon as humanly possible. However, traces of the wartime deportees live on in small Polish communities in Kazakhstan, with an estimated 40,000 there in 1989, almost a half in the Karaganda area. The graves of the thousands of Polish citizens who died before they were able to cross the Caspian Sea are scattered across Uzbekistan. Many were buried in communal pits: probably the men performing the burials had little strength and were perhaps anxious about the spread of disease from the bodies. Most date from the first half of 1942, as the exhausted families congregated around the Anders army bases. Just south of Samarkand stands the headstone of a woman bearing the moving inscription: 'Died on April 3, 1942. This foreign land was hard for you in life; may it become light after death.'[53]

The preventative deportations of 1941

Just as the Poles were deemed to be enemies of the state once the Second World War had started in 1939, so the ethnic Germans living within the Soviet Union became the focus of attention as soon as Operation Barbarossa had got under way in June 1941.

Families of ethnic Germans had lived peacefully in the Soviet Union for centuries. Invited to imperial Russia by Catherine the Great with their specialist military, engineering, academic, medical and scientific skills, most chose to settle in the big cities, on the Black Sea coast or along the River Volga. Many of the original immigrant families retained their Catholic or Lutheran religion, while subsequent waves of internal migration encouraged German Mennonites to practise their religion further away from Moscow in Central Asia. By the summer of 1941 there were around 1.5 million Soviet citizens of German nationality in the Soviet Union, including over 90,000 in Kazakhstan.[54] Most of these were concentrated in the German Autonomous Soviet Socialist Republic in the Volga basin. Officially established in 1924, it enabled ethnic Germans to live together with their own local governance, language, religion and culture, according to the *korenizatsiia* policy. With their own schools and German-language books, the population retained high standards of literacy, while remaining relatively isolated from the rest of the population.[55]

Immediately the German army invaded the western Soviet Union, however, the position of the ethnic German Soviet citizens became untenable. Just as families whose ethnicity matched that of the other Axis powers – notably Italians, Bulgarians, Romanians and Hungarians – the Germans were swept up within days and dispatched to the interior where there was no possibility of any spying or collaboration with the enemy. As the occupying army advanced, further batches of Soviet Germans were removed from their family homes and homeland to Siberia or Central Asia. In a similar manner, Germans, Austrians and Italians living in Great Britain, or Japanese Americans from the western seaboard of the United States, suffered internment for the duration of the war. In the case of the Soviet Union, however, these internal deportees received far harsher treatment which endured indefinitely, in some cases until the fall of the Soviet Union in 1991.

At first sight, the stated reason for the deportations was straightforward: the mass collaboration of a whole ethnic group. It did not matter that many of the Soviet Germans were in fact Jewish with no reason to help the enemy, or that very little evidence was actually found of Soviet Germans assisting the invaders: the potential was simply there for them to aid and abet the Nazis in the western regions of the Soviet Union. Even Soviet citizens with German-sounding names were caught up in the pre-emptive cleansing of the frontline areas. Of course, Stalin was constantly on the lookout for a scapegoat, in this case for the state's failure to prepare sufficiently for the sudden invasion. In addition, the mass internal deportations provided hundreds of thousands of labourers for the rear where they were desperately needed. Those Soviet citizens who were deemed most loyal to the state had been immediately conscripted into the Red Army, leaving large gaps in the workforce in the rear – a working population which was already hugely depleted following the devastating effects of collectivization in the early 1930s. Nowhere was this felt more badly than in the Central Asian region, where the collective farms and mines of Kazakhstan, Uzbekistan and, to a lesser extent, Kyrgyzstan, desperately sought additional labour – from the coalfields of Karaganda to the Uzbek cotton fields and the fishing grounds of Lake Issyk-Kul'. By using Central Asia as a dumping ground for deportees, the state was able to utilize the formidable work ethic of its German citizens in the rear, just as with the Koreans before them. The deportation of the ethnic Germans was further evidence of Stalin's aim to abandon the original plurality of the Soviet Union in favour of hyper-centralization. In this way, their previously concentrated cultural influence was considerably diluted amongst the Muslims of their new home, while the potentially trouble-making population of Central Asians themselves was watered down by the presence of a further large ethnic group. With no support mechanism except the state, the Germans had more than enough on their plate to prevent any potential future proactive involvement in the war.[56]

With the onset of war came this further excuse for the state to drop its policy of *korenizatsiia* as the German Autonomous Soviet Socialist Republic in the Volga basin was dissolved in September 1941 and integrated into surrounding provinces.[57] Ethnic Germans who had been serving in the Red Army were removed from frontline service and relegated to labour battalions in the rear as their loyalty to the state was called into question. In a similar manner, no further ethnic Finns, Romanians, Hungarians or Italians were sent into action.[58] The sensitive question of the perceived loyalty of the various ethnic groups meant that only those trusted by the state were posted into action in the early days of the war. Even new Central Asian conscripts were assigned to the rear at first, until the enormous losses at the front led to their redeployment to active service from the beginning of 1942. In the grand Soviet scheme of (once equal) nationalities, the ethnic Germans ranked substantially below Central Asians in terms of their supposed loyalty to the state. For the duration of the war they were deemed fit only to serve as slave labour in the interior.[59]

Of the original one and a half million ethnic German citizens of the Soviet Union, around 80 per cent were deported to the east, leaving only those over the age of sixty and the disabled behind. Estimates vary, but it is probable that well over 400,000 Soviet Germans ended up in Kazakhstan alone, as both men and women were sent to join others slaving in construction battalions, logging or in the mines of Karaganda. Mennonites already living in Central Asia were similarly targeted, if mainly remaining close to their homes.[60]

Men were often separated from their families on the journey east, leaving their women to fend for themselves in their strange new home. Several thousand Germans died in the cattle trucks transporting them east, but even more succumbed to starvation, disease and physical exhaustion at their destination. It is estimated that the death rate was about 9 per cent per annum. Those deportees working on collective farms or in the cotton fields of Central Asia were often allocated the most infertile ground in areas designated for the euphemistically termed *spetspereselentsy* (special settlers). On arrival, most deportees had to build their own makeshift homes with the building materials provided by the receiving local authorities in lieu of the property and possessions they had left behind. Those not able to do this immediately had to make do with primitive, windowless dugouts. As the war went on, a small number of Germans managed to make their way to the larger towns where they found more amenable office employment. The rest, however, were doomed to the harsh conditions, poor food rations and heavy manual work demanded of them. By 1943 it had become clear that so many were physically debilitated that the state intervened to alleviate their conditions to a limited extent, probably in the interests of productivity as much as of humanitarianism. Despite this, the Soviet Germans were often marginalized – targets of abuse from locals subject to the state-sponsored propaganda depicting them as enemies of the Soviet Union and representatives of the national enemy in their midst.[61]

At the end of the war, the deported ethnic Germans were forced to remain in their new homes for decades, still facing general hostility and stuck in their largely manual jobs. After the difficult post-war years, most were eventually allocated adequate housing as the regime of special settlements was relaxed following the death of Stalin in 1953. Finally cleared of treason in 1956, they were able to build a new life in Central Asia, with some degree of integration into their new communities by virtue of their employment and occasional mixed marriages. The children of the war years attended Russian or local schools in Central Asia, losing much of the ability to read and write in German. Their literacy remained lower, however, than that of previous generations, whose families had prided themselves on the retention of their native culture. The concentration of Germanic cultural influence had been lost, never to be regained, with the dissolving of the German Autonomous Republic and the tacit termination of the *korenizatsiia* policy.[62]

After the disintegration of the Soviet Union, the deportees were in theory able to return to the west of Russia or even to Germany itself. However, Germany was a foreign land and not particularly welcoming, while their original homelands had long been lost to others.[63] A substantial number of German families therefore remain in Central Asia, some in the area around the town of Kant in Kyrgyzstan, once a centre for the Mennonites, with others in a community in the Kyrgyz town of Talas.[64] Most still live in Kazakhstan, though, where a large minority population of former Soviet Germans makes its presence felt culturally, if not politically.[65]

The problem of the Pontic Greeks

Zoia Paraskevopulo from Batumi in Georgia was 104 years old when she arrived in Kazakhstan with her family, while Konstantin Tekinidi from Maikop in southern Russia was only eight.[66] They were representative of the demographic range deported from the Black Sea coastal areas of the Soviet Union at the whim of Stalin in a campaign of cleansing lasting from 1937 to 1949. The so-called Pontic Greeks had been living in the Black Sea region for centuries following the gradual migration of traders from Greece. In progressive stages they had travelled along the Turkish coast to Georgia, north to Taman', then around the Sea of Azov to the Crimean peninsula and the sea port of Odessa. While some had been assimilated into Soviet life, many families retained their Greek heritage and language with pride, especially those living in the area set aside in 1930 as the Greek Autonomous District in the Krasnodar Province of south-west Russia.

The problem of the Pontic Greeks is exceptional, showing some similarities with other waves of deportation, while demonstrating its own unique issues. This complex, multifaceted case exemplifies both the inconsistency of Stalin's wartime deportation policy and the limits of the politically expedient 'friendship of the peoples' policy.

As Stalin's suspicion of minorities on the fringes of the Soviet Union grew during the pre-war years, the relatively small population of Pontic Greeks was specially targeted. The Greek Autonomous District was annihilated in 1939 in much the same way as the autonomous republic set aside for the Volga Germans. Following widespread convictions for alleged anti-Soviet and counter-revolutionary activity during the Stalinist Terror of 1937–8, matters unfolded at first in a similar manner to the Germans during the preventative deportations at the start of the war. However it is initially more pertinent to compare the case of the Pontic Greeks with that of the Koreans of the far eastern coast, whose pre-war resettlement to the interior was intended to cleanse the border regions from potential collaborators and spies in the pay of enemy states.

Unlike Germany, Greece was supported in the war by the Allies – particularly the British – as it was invaded by the Italians and Germans. Indeed, Stalin had cause to be grateful to those resistance fighters in Greece who defended their country against the Italian invasion of 1940 so robustly that the German army had to be deployed in strength to ensure the success of the occupation. This distraction, in turn, left fewer German troops available to press home the invasion of the western Soviet Union in 1941. Indeed, although Greek diplomats had been expelled from Moscow early in June 1941, while Stalin was still in principle backing Hitler, an agreement was signed by Greek and Soviet leaders in January 1942 confirming their mutual support of the Allies.

This dichotomy raises the thorny question of the status of the Soviet Greeks of the Black Sea region. Apparently some Greeks were more equal than others under the laws of the Soviet Union. With a dire need for overtly patriotic members of the armed forces, Stalin was content to retain in the Red Army those ethnic Greeks who had been conscripted in 1939. Four of those fighting for their Soviet motherland were the Kokkinaki brothers of Novorossiisk, all of whom had enlisted as pilots before the war. With long track records of military service and Komsomol membership, they were embraced as air force officers and awarded medals for their wartime action in battle.[67]

The view of Soviet military leaders with regard to Greek soldiers changed during the war, however, as most were distrusted in a similar fashion to the conscripts enlisted from Central Asia. Very few were deployed on active service, except for a brief window in the autumn of 1943, once there was little threat of any defection to the retreating enemy. For the rest of the war, though, conscripts were more likely to be sent to work in labour battalions – often in mines or on railroads. Those Greeks removed from active service at the end of 1943 mostly found themselves in Gur'ev, Kazakhstan, building the new oil refinery so necessary to provide fuel for the army which would eventually win the war. Working conditions were tough, with poor food rations and unsafe water leading to dysentery. Even those who could prove that they had fought alongside Soviet partisans were not exempt from deportation.[68] One ethnic Greek resistance fighter, a certain I. Mikhailidi, was arrested by the NKVD in November 1942, tortured and sentenced to ten years in the labour camps.[69]

Suspicion was more likely to fall on ethnic Greeks resident in the Soviet Union whose status was not so secure. These politically 'unreliable elements' were equally likely to hold Greek or Soviet citizenship. Indeed, the citizenship of residents was often unilaterally changed by the authorities with no consultation. In principle, it was those of Greek citizenship who were most at risk, although many others were also targeted in the largely indiscriminate campaign. Similarly, Russian women married to Greek men were seldom spared deportation, once the lorries started to arrive on their doorsteps.

Why, then, were thousands of ethnic Greeks deported from the Black Sea region in 1942, just as Stalin was condoning the release from captivity and subsequent emigration of Polish citizens taken during the first two years of the Second World War? The theoretical support of the British was not able to help the Greeks, who continued to be deemed as politically unreliable as in the 1930s. While the Germans were continuing their advance in the direction of the Volga and the Caucasus, it is likely that Stalin still needed a scapegoat – an ethnic minority which could be accused of espionage long after the Soviet Germans had been removed from the scene. In a continuation of a prolonged and determined campaign waged since the 1920s, many Greeks were dispatched to Kazakhstan and the Krasnoiarsk area of Siberia during the ethnic cleansing of 1942. Like other minorities arriving in Central Asia, they served to supplement the slave labour forces required to boost the war effort.

As Nazi troops entered the Krasnodar and Rostov provinces, traditionally known as the Kuban' region of south-west Russia, preparations were made by the NKVD for the phased deportation of ethnic Greeks, ostensibly to prevent them from serving as enemy agents. Under orders from Lavrentii Beriia to remove 'those serving foreign powers', train convoys of cattle-trucks left specific hubs throughout 1942, full of residents of Greek nationality on their way into exile.[70] At the same time as the Dzerzhinskii Children's Home residents from Leningrad were being evacuated from their temporary shelter in Krasnodar to Kyrgyzstan, others less fortunate were also sent on their journey east. As military leaders were trying desperately to slow the enemy advance, the NKVD was balancing the needs of evacuating the majority of the population – with as many factories and valuable materials as possible – with the simultaneous mass deportation of the ethnic Greeks who comprised the bulk of the alleged 'anti-Soviet, alien and untrustworthy elements' resident in the region.

Konstantin Tekinidi was one of the first to leave, along with his mother and two elder sisters. His father had already been executed as an 'English spy' in 1938, in common with many other men, with the consequence that most of the deportees were once again women, children and elderly men. Testimonies indicate that many families were already prepared for the inevitable, although some optimists hoped they were to be evacuated. Others even celebrated, convinced that they would be expelled to Greece, only to become disillusioned once their train had crossed the Volga. The night-time knocks on the door seem to have been followed by a slightly more humane intervention on the part of the NKVD than usual, with time given to collect items together and some reports of useful advice, for example to take a sewing machine if possible. Konstantin's mother was advised to take a large jar of vegetable oil, while other deportees included clothes, bedding, documents, icons and gold in their luggage. In summer, people took onions, garlic and honey with them, with dried beans, sugar and salted meat which would keep for longer. Many planned ahead: Sofia Lovasova, for example, sold her one cow as the rumours about imminent deportation grew. Some took goods which they could later sell or barter in case of need, including wool and tea. Mark Terzidi from Gelendzhik thoughtfully packed two pairs of warm boots and a fur hat for his journey to Kazakhstan. Other less portable possessions were often left with neighbours pending their owners' eventual return.[71]

Mark Terzidi joined deportees from Kabardinka on the platform at Novorossiisk to await his train, while small groups from Krasnaia Poliana and other inland villages further south were gathered together in Sochi. All convoys were liable to aerial attack by German bombers during the first part of their often circuitous journeys, despite their camouflage cover.[72] Convoys departing from Sochi generally travelled south, away from the military action, by steamer to Georgia, and thence by train to Baku on the Caspian Sea. Having crossed the sea – in the opposite direction to that taken months later by the Poles leaving the Soviet Union – they arrived at the port of Krasnovodsk in Turkmenistan. Those travelling in the summer months were struck by the searing heat in which several children died of thirst, despite the water vouchers issued to the deportees. Some of the Greeks were forced to barter rice and even gold jewellery for extra supplies, while dried beans fetched an amazing 250 roubles per kilogram. Dust storms also affected the vulnerable, killing Kharlampi Kotsailidi's two young sons. The Kolpakidi family lost three children on the journey, while the Aslanidi family put the spade they had taken with them for farming purposes to better use in digging graves alongside the track for impromptu burials. Others preferred to keep the bodies of family members with them until they could be buried closer to their new homes in exile.[73]

Some incidents on the journey similarly led to the loss of family members. One centenarian managed to alight from her train at a halt to relieve herself, only to be run over as the train started to move again. Children were often responsible for fetching water at these stops, always running the risk of being left behind. This was the fate of young Mikhail Kirlakidi from Novorossiisk, whose father, Poros, was forced to jump off the train to look for him. Within seconds, the convoy had left, bearing his wife and three other children. Poros and Mikhail were picked up by a later train, but ended up in Balkashino, Kazakhstan, while the rest of the family were taken to Isakovka, a village several hundred kilometres to the west. Other families were split according to their official citizenship, while sometimes men were sent to labour camps and the women and children to collective farms.[74]

The journey to Central Asia often took over two months, partly due to the lack of direct train lines across Kazakhstan. From Alma-Ata it was necessary to travel north to Talsy, Kurgan and Barnaul and onwards to Novosibirsk. From the capital of Siberia their journey took them west to Petropavlovsk, and finally back south via Osakarovka to Karaganda province, where most deportees were forced to work around the infamous Karaganda camp.[75] Young Konstantin Tekinidi was taken by cart from the train to his family's final destination – the village of Kazagorodok to the west of Karaganda, where they were allocated 'special settler' homes built of traditional mud bricks.[76] Deportees from Tuapse were usually sent to Emba, a common destination alongside Gur'ev for those put to work in the oil industry. Those from Apsheronsk often ended up in Pavlodarsk Province, while the Greeks from Novorossiisk were sent to Kokchetau in North Kazakhstan and the Krasnodar Greeks were destined for Akmolinsk or Kustanai province. Other Greek farmers were sent to the tobacco plantations around Alma-Ata, such as the Panfilov collective farm. This was always a preferred destination, as the weather was somewhat more clement than in central and northern Kazakhstan. In any case, those deportees sent to Kazakhstan in 1942 had a better chance of survival than the minority destined for the banks of the River Enisei in northern Siberia.[77]

The initial waves of wartime deportation of the ethnic Greeks were, in retrospect, merely practice for the larger scale operation which took place in 1944. Once the Crimean peninsula had been liberated from enemy occupation, it was the events there which sealed the fate of the Black Sea Greeks. Not only the Greeks were targeted with these punitive deportations, however. They were just one of several ethnic minorities punished by Stalin for alleged collaboration with the occupying forces. In this case it was impossible to argue that the deportations were ordered as preventative measures. This wave was, rather, a full-scale ethnic cleansing of the minorities, responsible for the relocation of around 225,000 members of targeted ethnic groups to Central Asia.

Ironically, General Georgii Kariofilli was one of the commanding officers of the 18th Army closely involved with ousting the occupying forces from Crimea in the spring of 1944. Although of Greek ancestry, he was a long-term member of the Communist Party and trusted Red Army commander who led the artillery forces in the liberation of Crimea. In addition, several members of the NKVD charged with gathering together the latest tranche of deportees were of Greek ethnicity. About 15,000 new Greek deportees were detained in June 1944, mostly destined for Uzbekistan and Kazakhstan's Gur'ev province where they joined the 8,000 ethnic Greeks deported in 1942 from Krasnodar province, Rostov district and Azerbaijan. Some humanitarian measures were taken to reunite the newcomers with existing relations in exile, although this was probably a futile gesture, in view of the mass movement of people in all directions by the end of 1944.[78] This was not the end of the problems for the Pontic Greeks, however. In 1949 a further large wave of over 50,000 deportees was sent to Kazakhstan, possibly linked to the changing Greco–Soviet relations of the period in the light of the ensuing Greek civil war. The start of the Cold War and the official post-war alignment of Greece with the West served to anger Stalin further and colour his attitude to the ethnic Greeks in the Soviet Union, many of whom were not able to return home until the late 1980s.[79]

The punitive deportation of the Crimean Tatars

Fevzie Jemileva was born in the village of Japerberby near Kerch' on the Crimean peninsula. Married traditionally young, she gave birth to her first daughter at the age of seventeen. Her husband, Jevdet Khojaev, was conscripted into the Red Army at the age of eighteen in 1939, fighting throughout the war years far away from home. On 18 May 1944, a date ingrained in the family's consciousness, 22-year-old Fevzie and her small daughter were deported and sent by cattle train to Uzbekistan. During the month-long journey, the young girl dropped her shoe outside the wagon, but Fevzie was prevented by the NKVD guards from picking it up. For the remainder of the journey she was forced to carry her daughter, who eventually died before reaching their destination of Stantsiia Juma, near Samarkand. Fortunately for Fevzie, her sisters had also been deported and were billeted in a special settlement camp nearby, providing some moral and material support until Fevzie found a job as a teacher.[80]

Fevzie's experience was representative of that of the 200,000 Crimean Tatars who were deported for alleged wholesale collaboration with the occupying forces. Some were sent to Siberia or Kazakhstan, but most arrived in Uzbekistan destitute, having to forge a sparse living in a hostile environment. Fevzie was one who survived to tell the tale. Many others did not, as the so-called *Sürgün* (exile) led to the death by starvation and disease of a large proportion of the Crimean Tatars.[81]

FIGURE 8.1 *Fevzie Jemileva. With thanks to Fevzie's granddaughter.*

Collaboration, actual and alleged

The Muslim khanate on the Crimean peninsula was annexed by Catherine the Great of Russia in 1783, leaving the indigenous Crimean Tatars to face a process of Russian colonization similar to that in Central Asia. Like the Jews, who also populated Crimea, the Tatars were so badly ostracized that emigration became a popular option, although this was stemmed somewhat by Lenin's establishment in 1921 of the Crimean Autonomous Soviet Socialist Republic on their historic homeland. However, with the repressions of the late 1930s Crimean Tatar leaders, nationalists and intellectuals were persecuted in common with those in Central Asia. An ethnic mix of people lived in Crimea, such that on the eve of the Second World War, only 218,000 Crimean Tatars remained on the peninsula, many of whom had no reason to support their Soviet masters. The suspicion was mutual. Stalin deemed those on the edge of the Soviet Union to be particularly dangerous, especially the Muslim Crimean Tatars who could potentially defect to join their kin living in Turkey.[82]

In spite of this official mistrust, about 20,000 Crimean Tatars were conscripted into the Red Army in 1941.[83] One of these was eighteen-year-old Muedin Settarov from Mamat on the Crimean peninsula. Settarov was sent to Irkutsk to train as a military engineer, becoming an officer early in 1942. Lieutenant Settarov reached the front line at Voronezh in March 1942, where his unit – lacking effective weapons – was surrounded and taken prisoner. They managed to escape and head south to Crimea on foot, where Settarov, typical of many, was again taken into captivity by the German army in his home village. Escaping once more, he joined up with the local resistance.[84] The partisan movement was mainly composed of Slavic men, with Crimean Tatars forming only about one-fifth of the strength. They were relatively ineffective at hindering enemy activity, however, even resorting to plundering villages and incurring the wrath not only of the Wehrmacht

FIGURE 8.2 *Muedin Settarov (bottom right) and Red Army comrades in Irkutsk. Published with kind permission from the Settarov family.*

but of some of the Crimean Tatar population.[85] In contrast, many Crimean Tatar POWs were treated so badly by the occupiers that they accepted the offer of relative freedom by joining the Tatar Legion, one of the foreign Wehrmacht units.[86]

Following years of persecution, many of the Crimean Tatars remaining at home actually welcomed the Nazi invasion of Crimea in October 1941, especially when the Wehrmacht went on to permit some degree of religious freedom.[87] While many small shops and businesses had perforce to accommodate German clients, other Crimean Tatars played a more active collaborative role, being dubbed by the Wehrmacht *Hilfswillige*, so-called *Hiwis*. Many Red Army deserters were persuaded by the occupying Einsatzgruppe D to join *Schutzmannschaftsbataillonen* (police protection battalions) which entered into local struggles against the partisans.[88] As the war progressed, some collaborators became disenchanted with the increasingly repressive occupation forces and defected to the partisans, thereby triggering further German reprisals.[89]

The degree of collaboration with the occupying army in Crimea is debatable, although it was on nothing like the scale alleged by Stalin when ordering the deportations of 1944. Of the estimated 20,000 Crimean Tatars who joined the German forces, about 3,700 collaborators were actively engaged in fighting the partisans, involving around 0.5 per cent of the Crimean population. Furthermore, just under 900 Crimean Tatars who had deserted the Red Army defected to the German Wehrmacht, a relatively modest number in view of the estimated 1 million Red Army deserters overall and the much more significant proportion of collaboration in other occupied regions of the western Soviet Union.[90]

The actual collaboration of a small minority of Crimean Tatars was seized upon by Stalin as an excuse for the deportation of the whole population, as it was used as a scapegoat for the initial fall of Crimea and the subsequent humiliation of factional fighting amongst local partisans and protection forces. In fact most of the real Crimean collaborators of all ethnicities had been evacuated in 1944 by the departing Wehrmacht, leaving behind a population of just under 200,000 Crimean Tatars – mainly the elderly, wounded veterans, women and children – to be accused by Beriia of desertion, anti-Soviet activity, mass collaboration and therefore of treason.[91]

It seems probable that Stalin was aware of the mendacity of the charges levelled against the Crimean Tatars after the liberation of Crimea in April 1944. The accusations of wholesale collaboration were never made against Slavs living in other occupied regions: Belarus, Ukraine and western Russia. The collaboration of a minority served rather as an excuse for what amounted to the ethnic cleansing of the Crimean Tatars and other minorities living on the Crimean peninsula, including around 14,300 remaining ethnic Greeks residing in the coastal towns of Sevastopol, Yalta and Kerch'.[92]

Although religion was ostensibly of no importance to the communist state, the Crimean Greeks were Christians, in contrast with most other nationalities targeted in 1944, which were largely Muslim. The so-called 'punished peoples' deported in late 1943 and 1944 from border areas of the Soviet Union, even those only briefly occupied such as Chechnia and Ingushetiia, were therefore not expelled on the grounds of religion alone.[93] Moreover, even though there had been discussions before the war about the formation of a Jewish Autonomous Republic in Crimea, this is unlikely to have been on Stalin's agenda in 1944. It is far more likely that Stalin intended to reserve the most fertile land and the attractive coastal areas for future settlement by Slavic residents – mainly Russians and Ukrainians – whose loyalty to the state was never seriously in question.

In addition, there is no doubt that the peninsula continued to occupy a strategic position in the Black Sea, which the Soviet Union could not risk falling into the hands of foreign powers. The naval base of Sevastopol, in particular, was the largest warm-water port of the country, whose future security could be threatened by an allegiance of Crimean Tatar nationalists with their old allies, Turkey. In fact, Stalin's geopolitical vision for post-war expansion of the Soviet Union could well have included Soviet encroachment on to Greek or Turkish territory, as the Turco-Soviet Treaty of Neutrality signed in 1925 was rescinded in 1944.[94] It is likely, therefore, that the mass deportations towards the end of the war took place as retribution – not for any alleged collaboration, but for any hint of nationalism or disloyalty in the past and as a pre-emptive move to guarantee the strategic security of the peninsula and potentially fulfil the geopolitical ambition of the Soviet leader in the post-war years.

The Black Day

Asanakun Serkebaev from a collective farm in Ak Suu near Przheval'sk was the eldest son in a family of seven children. Called up at the age of eighteen in September 1942 with thirty-seven others from his village, he walked to Pristan' where his group was loaded onto barges for the journey across Lake Issyk-Kul'. From Kyrgyzstan, the train took them across Kazakhstan and the River Volga to the Russian town of Penza. With seven years of schooling behind him, Asanakun was destined for special things, being trained as a rifleman in the NKVD. Throughout 1944 he was involved in the deportation of thousands of fellow-Muslims from the northern Caucasus, largely Chechens from the Groznyi area.[95]

Rifleman Serkebaev was one of several thousand NKVD troops involved in the progressive deportation of ethnic minorities from the southern borderlands, arresting and imprisoning fellow Soviet citizens in the cattle trucks taking them into exile under the most gruelling conditions. The cleansing operation in Chechnia and Ingushetiia took place in February 1944, transferring a total of about 460,000 'enemies of the people' to settlements in Siberia, Kazakhstan and Kyrgyzstan. The operation started ironically on 23 February, Red Army Day, when 100,000 NKVD troops acted under the leadership of Lavrentii Beriia. Accused, like the Crimean Tatars, of mass collaboration, despite only a small area of their mountainous region having been occupied for just a brief period, they followed the 68,000 Karachais from Georgia along the railroads to Central Asia. Once Crimea had been liberated in April 1944, the well-oiled tracks remained busy, until it was finally the turn of the Crimean Tatars.[96]

By the time Beriia signed the orders for the Crimean deportations, the process was already almost mundane – certainly a swift and efficient operation. Thirty-two thousand experienced NKVD officers and men once deployed to the mountainous northern Caucasus region travelled westwards to converge on Crimea in May 1944, with orders to deport over 220,000 ethnic minority residents: mostly Crimean Tatars, but also including smaller numbers of Greeks, Bulgarians, Armenians, Karaims and Germans.[97]

What the Crimean Tatars later named *kara gün* – the black day – started in the early hours of 18 May 1944.[98] Once again, families were taken by surprise, limited to what they could gather together within fifteen or twenty minutes. In practice, few could manage to take the 500 kilograms to which they were apparently entitled, leaving behind homes, animals and other possessions for ever. Goods vehicles transported the deportees to train stations where, as usual, they were packed into cattle trucks, filling sixty-seven whole train convoys over the three-day period of the cleansing operation.[99] Sanie Zevadinova, a twenty-year-old from the village of Mangud, who had been made to work in a Nazi internment camp during the occupation, set off on the longest journey of her young life to spend the next twenty-six years in exile in Uzbekistan.[100]

The Crimean Tatars were scooped up in the operation without exception. A total of 191,000 found themselves locked inside cattle trucks for the journey, mainly easy targets and innocent of any collaboration.[101] The NKVD showed no mercy or discrimination, even deporting former Red Army soldiers who had been fighting alongside the partisans. While his Slavic comrades were left in peace, even Lieutenant Muedin Settarov found himself in a cattle truck heading for Uzbekistan, alongside wounded veterans and the families of soldiers whose husbands had either died in action or were still serving in the Red Army, including Fevzie Jemileva and her young daughter.[102] War correspondent Il'ia Erenburg had earlier praised the heroism of Soviet Tatars at the Battle of Stalingrad, a critical time when the state found it necessary to underline the friendship of the various ethnicities. By May 1944, however, even bearers of the hero's Gold Star were included in the convoys heading east.[103] By this blatant injustice in labelling all the deportees traitors, ethnicity in 1944 counted above all else for a state going to extreme lengths to cleanse its borderlands.

FIGURE 8.3 *Sanie Zevadinova (centre) doing first-aid training, 1940. Published with kind permission from the Zevadinov family.*

For the Crimean Tatars each wagon was like a 'labour camp barracks on wheels', as the cramped passengers struggled to survive the long journey. Although each convoy had its own kitchen wagon with an official requirement for every 'collaborator' to receive 500 grams of bread a day, with 70 grams of meat and 60 grams of buckwheat, these idealistic criteria were never met. Similarly, the services of an isolation wagon with medical specialists on board were rarely offered, as deportees gradually succumbed to dysentery and typhus. Once again, bodies were left by the track, with an estimated 7,000 or 8,000 deaths even before the Crimean Tatars reached their final destination.[104] Despite this, some were afforded a minimum of dignity, as guards were apparently under orders never to threaten children or pregnant women, nor to take any of their belongings. They may have been branded traitors, but the state wanted these prisoners to reach their destination alive and capable of working to help the war effort.[105]

In contrast, reports indicate that the Chechens were treated more harshly than the largely peaceful Crimean Tatars and Greeks, with correspondingly larger losses en route.[106] Charged with mass sabotage rather than collaboration, the population of the Chechen-Ingush Autonomous Soviet Socialist Republic was subject to much harsher conditions, as the NKVD even resorted to murdering any of the weak and elderly who were unable to climb aboard the trucks in the severe winter weather. This discrimination between ethnic groups continued once they reached their destinations in Central Asia.[107]

Sürgün: Life in exile

Towards the end of the long journey, the train convoy carrying Muedin Settarov, Sanie Zevadinova and Fevzie Jemileva crossed Uzbekistan firstly to Tashkent, then traversed the desert to Samarkand, where they were deposited not far from the railhead in Juma.[108] Over 80 per cent of the Crimean Tatars were resettled in Uzbekistan, as by this point in the war it was easier logistically to keep ethnic groups together rather than dispersing them too thinly across the region. They were often dropped in large groups in various provinces – mostly in Tashkent, Samarkand, Andijan, and Fergana in the east of the republic. A minority went directly to the Urals, while smaller numbers were sent onwards to Kazakhstan, the Osh province of Kyrgyzstan, or even Tajikistan as fresh demands for labour emerged.[109]

Kazakhstan again took the lion's share of the next wave of internal deportees, including a significant half a million displaced Chechens and Ingush, with other groups from the North Caucasus and over 100,000 Meskhetian Turks from Georgia, also targets of Stalin's aggressive policy towards Turkey.[110] A total of almost 140,000 of the last tranche of deportees were sent to Kyrgyzstan, including a further 90,000 Chechens and Ingush resettled in the Frunze, Osh, Jalal-Abad and Talas provinces.[111] The distant

Issyk-Kul' province became home to 716 Ingush and Balkar families deported from the Caucasus in 1944.[112]

These additional deportees relocated to Central Asia presented an enormous challenge to the local population, despite the extra free labour they brought to the region. Crimean Tatars, who had never travelled far from their home villages, found themselves treated like slaves. Most were made to labour in construction or the defence industry, often working twelve-hour days. These were the lucky majority: others were forced to slave in the cotton fields of Uzbekistan or Tajikistan, working without shelter under all conditions.[113] In common with some of the 'elite' deportees with a background in engineering or medicine, Muedin Settarov was relatively fortunate in being sent to work as a geologist in a tungsten mine in Uzbekistan.[114]

Of the 2,636 deportees who arrived in Kyrgyzstan's Issyk-Kul' province in 1944, only 912 were capable of doing any manual work. As the two barges loaded with individual 'souls' approached the jetties in Cholpon-Ata, Grigor'evka, Tiup or Przheval'sk, transport was waiting to transfer the newcomers to the collective farms where they were to live. A handful were allocated to the cement factory in Kurmanty or Horse Factory Number 54, while some were deployed to forestry work.[115]

Muedin Settarov and his future wife, Sanie Zevadinova, found themselves living in the communal barracks in Juma, their first home in Uzbekistan. Most of the deportees were housed together in secure settlements, often adjacent to their workplace. Others in larger centres were sometimes housed with local families, while those sent to collective farms had to make do temporarily with heated tents and stables, or the primitive mud huts and dugouts they were forced to construct themselves in order to survive.[116] In reality it was extremely challenging for the local authorities to accommodate everybody, when faced with such a huge influx of destitute people.

The onus was usually on collective farms to provide rooms for new 'settlers', but all too often there was a mismatch between what the state instructed should be provided and what was actually achievable on the ground. Resources were seriously lacking after three years of war, and some of the central funding was probably misappropriated locally.[117] Problems in the Issyk-Kul' province were acute, with only just over a quarter of incoming families accommodated at all.[118] Whereas, officially, the deportees should have received building materials to help them construct their new abode, this was all too often missing. Further instructions were necessary from the Kyrgyz authorities to provide wood and glass to the incoming families and to buy or renovate more houses or flats.[119] According to the authorities, 95 per cent of the 1944 influx to the province received land for an allotment or orchard – land which, however, needed time and effort before it yielded any food.[120] This last big tranche of deportees accordingly suffered more than those deported earlier in the war, who by 1944 had managed to find accommodation and scrape together some sort of subsistence in the region.[121]

Nothing about the issues facing the deportees appeared in the local press, however, although existing residents no doubt resisted the demand to prepare accommodation for or share homes with allegedly treasonous incomers, while officials experienced a constant struggle to fulfil the state's obligations to the exiles.[122] The biggest immediate problem on arrival was food. Those working in the towns usually had some meals provided by the factories to which they were allocated. It was a different matter on farms, however, where the quantity of food given to a family depended on the amount of work completed. Arriving part way through a poor summer season, many families on the land received next to nothing, with no produce as yet from their own plots.[123]

It was the north Caucasians who probably suffered the worst in exile. Less qualified and less used to working in factories or farms, they had usually spent their lives working with animals in their mountainous territory. Often deployed to labour in one of the many mines of Kazakhstan or the oil industry at Gur'ev and the River Emba, they at least qualified for free meals.[124] However, with the bitter conditions in the winter of 1944, many deportees did not live to see the end of the war, as those in Kazakhstan were reduced to eating grass in an effort to survive until the spring.[125] The situation came to a head in December 1944, when Beriia not only had to remind local authorities in Kazakhstan and Kyrgyzstan of their obligations to the deportees but also ordered them to provide some food aid. Although the intention was well meant, not all the meagre rations reached the desperate Caucasians, being diverted by some authorities to needy locals.[126] Evidence from the Issyk-Kul' province demonstrates that some families at least received flour, salt and a little sugar, although it was not until the following year that the state even attempted to replace the animals they had been forced to leave behind with the occasional sheep or goat. The provision of seed loans for the spring planting was also delayed until 1945 in many cases.[127]

It is not surprising, therefore, that the deportee population was badly hit by starvation. The mortality rate across the region in the first few years in exile was correspondingly high, albeit with a marked discrepancy between urban and rural dwellers depending on access to food and much-needed medical care.[128] NKVD records conservatively indicate that about one quarter of the deported Crimean Tatars succumbed to starvation or disease in the first eighteen months of exile. This figure is disputed by the deportees themselves, who estimate that up to 46 per cent may have died prematurely in Central Asia during this period.[129] Similarly, in Kyrgyzstan records indicate that by April 1946 25 per cent of the 1944 deportees had perished.[130] Furthermore, records show that over 100,000 Caucasians died in Kazakhstan alone, a terrible toll and a trend which continued for a few years after the end of the war until conditions improved somewhat as the deportees gradually established themselves in their new homes.[131]

All deportees had suffered a shocking dislocation, existing in exile with their anger, grief and nostalgia. Particular resentment was felt amongst service families, whose husbands and fathers were still fighting on behalf of the Soviet Union. As some small degree of compensation, the state confirmed that military families, even in exile, would continue to be eligible for financial support and pensions, where applicable – upon concrete documentary proof of their status, of course.[132]

During the remaining months of the war, the Soviet emphasis was on the utility of the deportees in their places of work rather than any pretence of their further Sovietization. In this respect, the indigenous inhabitants of Central Asia were able to portray themselves as more Soviet than the incomers, although the medium-term, post-war state aim was to ensure the continued process of Sovietization of the deportees by integrating them into their new societies. For the moment, though, the deportees were usually segregated from the local population in an overt attempt to keep the nationalities apart and prevent the spread of any discontent to the local population. All the deportees experienced a climate of suspicion and surveillance in their new homes, especially those placed in special guarded settlements with orders to present themselves for registration at regular intervals.[133]

Any possibility of integration with the local community was coloured at first by the state propaganda which preceded the deportees to their destinations. Billed as traitors, enemies of the people, collaborators and spies, they were met on arrival by prejudice and sheer hatred by the local population. It is no wonder that the Uzbeks, in particular, were deliberately unhelpful. The situation was not much better in Kyrgyzstan, where ordinary people had little to share with the newcomers, although the experience in Kazakhstan was somewhat less polarized.[134] Some Kyrgyz residents recall the state propaganda which had vindicated the deportations on the grounds that the special settlers were 'traitors' and 'enemies of the people', who either definitely had or may have helped the enemy had they remained at home.[135] The distinct lack of official support and the ostracism of locals led to a complete sense of alienation on the part of many, contributing, no doubt, to the high mortality rate in the first months.

Once again, it was the Caucasians who bore the brunt of the hostility, with organized pogroms directed against them in some areas. Reports of stoning of Crimean Tatars indicate a degree of hostility comparable with that shown towards some Jewish refugees. Even Crimean Tatar children came in for abuse, following rumours that they had devilish horns growing on their heads, with some Central Asians even believing stories of more extreme characteristics. Having been subjected to NKVD propaganda, local residents with little education largely refused at first to help this tranche of incomers, who were treated with much more hostility than earlier waves of deportees.[136]

Most of the Crimean Tatar population, however, already considered themselves to be Soviet citizens by virtue of their education and wartime treatment by the enemy while living under occupation. The treatment by the Soviet regime left innocent, peaceful folk so devastated by their plight that they understandably became alienated from the state which had treated them so cruelly. The newcomers were so shocked by the conditions of exile that any slight hint of independent nationalism they once held was often increased, particularly amongst the north Caucasians who were often restive and unwilling to integrate. Initially disoriented in and depressed by their new living conditions, most Crimean Tatars gradually became resigned to their situation, although they could never have envisaged in 1944 just how long their exile would last.[137]

In general it took years for the simmering mutual hostility engendered by the state to abate, as some degree of tolerance and integration between host and incoming nationalities gradually developed. This has often been attributed to the common Muslim background of indigenous Central Asians, Crimean Tatars and north Caucasians, and no doubt the increased post-war contact between communities only helped matters. Only over a period of decades did a narrative of wholesale welcome and sharing on the part of the local residents emerge – a communal memory nurtured in a similar fashion to that of the hospitality shown to orphans in Uzbekistan. For example, a current school textbook on the history of Kazakhstan reminds schoolchildren that 'local residents received them [deportees] with a deep sense of respect and understanding, in spite of the fact that they themselves were undergoing desperate hunger', demonstrating a complete disconnect between the wartime experience of the deportees and how Kazakhs today wish to recall it. Some Chechens still living in Kazakhstan, however, recall the kindness of the Kazakh families who had shared food and clothing with them in the early days of the *Aardakh* (Exodus). Similarly, one elderly Kyrgyz speaks of a 'friendly and supportive atmosphere' in respect of Tatars and north Caucasians, while another recalls that the Chechens 'received houses here and [. . .] had a good life. Nobody tried to do anything to them. Everyone had the same amount of food. Land was given to all'.[138]

Official documents indicate that the local authorities were encouraged to ensure that deported children received a good Soviet education once housed in their new settlements. This was hard at first, as most children were weak after the journey, malnourished and often diseased – certainly in no fit state to attend school. Once they did set foot inside a school, more problems emerged for the traumatized children, as the younger ones were expected to learn through the medium of Russian, to which many had never previously been exposed. Even though there were similarities between the Turkic languages, for example, Crimean Kipchak and Uzbek, the state insisted on the use of the Slavonic Russian language which was the lingua franca of the Soviet Union. Once the children were in their middle schools, however, the option of the local language became available for some. Any tuition in their mother tongue was strictly forbidden, however, as was the publication of newspapers. This policy, while ensuring some medium-term integration, did little to bridge the gap between nationalities in the early days, with the majority of children not attending school for the first year or so in exile. It was not until the post-war period that Fevzie and Sanie were officially permitted to become teachers in exile – albeit specializing in Russian-language education.[139] By these overt steps at Sovietization, the state intended to assimilate and integrate the deportees into their new communities partly through their children. Furthermore, by the emphasis on the Russian language, the hierarchy of culture was reinforced. By the end of the war, Slavonic culture in general was explicitly presented as more valuable than Central Asian, with the traditions of the deportees regarded as the least important in the nationality spectrum. Unsurprisingly, therefore, much lower levels of literacy were subsequently observed in the children of the deported Crimean Tatars, who had previously enjoyed relatively high levels of education in common with the ethnic Germans.

After the war

During the last year of the war the state was able to facilitate the reunion of some deported families. Where the men had been sent to labour camps or remained in the Red Army, they were usually permitted to rejoin their families if they could be located. This move then condemned them to the same allegedly voluntary deportee status as the original special settlers in their family, despite any successful military track record.[140]

Jevdet Khojaev was one Crimean Tatar who was retained in the Red Army throughout the war, despite being wounded in action. Having undergone treatment in the east of the Soviet Union, he was sent back into active service to fight against the Japanese at the very end of the war. Demobilized only in February 1946 and wearing medals for his war service, he set off in search of his wife, Fevzie, whom he had not seen for years. The two were eventually reunited in Uzbekistan, where they established a life together, Jevdet using the skills he had gained in the army to build a house with an orchard for the growing family after a move to the newly constructed township of Ingichka. There, he added a further two houses to his small estate, which brought in some extra rental income. Their children were brought up in Uzbekistan, speaking Tatar at home, Uzbek at the bazaar and Russian at school.

It was the return of decorated soldiers such as Jevdet at the same time as the local servicemen which brought home to many Central Asians the terrible injustice shown by the state to some of the deportees. Families of all ethnicities were after all facing the same post-war poverty and struggles to rebuild their lives.[141] At the same time as a degree of reconciliation with their neighbours was taking place, the Crimean Tatars, if not necessarily the north Caucasians, realized that the time had come to accept that their exile in Central Asia was permanent. In their homeland, Tatar towns and villages were renamed in Russian, as an annihilistic state set its sights on Crimean Tatar cultural heritage, with the destruction of libraries, mosques and cemeteries. Finally, the Crimean Autonomous Soviet Socialist Republic was relegated in

FIGURE 8.4 *Jevdet Khojaev. Published with kind permission from the Khojaev family.*

significance to a province of Russia, while the Chechen-Ingush Autonomous Republic similarly became Groznyi province, just as had happened with the territory once self-governed by the Soviet German population. In this way, the 'punished peoples' were penalized once more by a state which apparently wished to erase them and their culture from the map.[142]

The death of Stalin marked the start of some relaxation, and the special settler regime was finally dismantled by Khrushchev in 1957, when the deportees were officially pardoned. At this stage the Chechens were allowed back to their Caucasian homes, although many chose to remain in Central Asia where they had established themselves. Even after the collapse of the Soviet Union, return was often not an option for people whose homeland was by then torn apart by war. Even today, a whole village of Chechens remains in Kazakhstan, by now well integrated into Kazakh society, if distanced from extended family in the North Caucasus.[143]

Conversely, many Crimean Tatars spent up to five decades in exile before they were able to leave Central Asia. Crimea remained out of bounds to the deportees, even the younger generations, probably because the state feared the rise of a new wave of nationalism. In most cases, property there had been re-allocated to Slavic incomers, and a return to the peninsula represented simply a dream for many.[144]

It was not until 1967 that the Brezhnev administration rescinded all accusations of collaboration and exonerated the Crimean Tatars of treason.[145] Jevdet Khojaev was one of the first to travel west. Possibly because of his impeccable war record, he received permission for the move in 1968, managing to get as close as possible to his homeland by relocating to Taman' in south-west Russia. His wife and two young daughters joined him shortly afterwards, only to meet with some prejudice from the Russian-speaking community there. Having spent over twenty years establishing themselves in Uzbekistan, in spite of initial suspicion on the part of the local population, they felt equally out of place in Russia. Their time in Central Asia had branded them, if not as collaborators, then unmistakably alien, thanks to their 'foreign' accents. It was rather begrudgingly that the headteacher of one daughter's new school accepted that the child's education and knowledge of the Russian language was excellent. In spite of the official recognition that no wholescale collaboration had taken place by the Crimean Tatar population, history lessons in the late 1960s still maintained that they had committed treason en masse. Recovery from the deportees' individual and collective trauma therefore took the family several more years.[146]

As for Muedin and Sanie, they were at first denied the right to move closer to their homeland. Only when some of his comrades in the Crimean partisan brigade testified on his behalf, backed up by the evidence of a family he helped escape deportation to Germany as slave labourers, was Muedin allowed back into Russia. The family also settled in Taman' in 1970, within sight of the Kerch' peninsula which had once been their home. Two years later they moved further south to the Black Sea port of Novorossiisk, where more suitable work was available for the experienced engineer. At last, after enduring the shelling and occupation of Crimea, deportation and ostracism, they were able to live in safety.[147]

It was only in the final few years of the Soviet Union that any Crimean Tatars were officially rehabilitated and permitted to return to the Crimean peninsula, where some were eventually able to settle again, despite the loss of their previous political autonomy.[148] For around a half of the exiles, however, the only option was to remain in Central Asia where they had built new lives, having lost everything in their homeland.[149]

On a much smaller scale, the fate of the Buddhist Kalmyk ethnic minority deported to Siberia from their homelands around the Caspian Sea in December 1943 also impacted on the indigenous Kalmyks living in and around Przheval'sk during the war. Those who had served in the Red Army during the war were offered, upon demobilization, the option officially to change their nationality to Kyrgyz. About 2,000 agreed, but the 49 who refused were immediately deported to the Urals to join those Kalmyks deported from Russia in 1943.[150]

By the end of the war, around one in ten of the Kyrgyz population was a deportee.[151] Around 50,000 Chechens still live in Central Asia, including some communities in villages north and west of Bishkek, while several north Caucasian families of Chechen, Ingush, Balkar and Darghin descent still remain in the Issyk-Kul' province.[152]

The final straw

The Stalin regime's campaign of wholescale ethnic cleansing at various stages in the war was no doubt genocidal in character – an overt attempt to exterminate many, if not all, of the ethnic minorities concerned, especially the Muslim Crimean Tatars and Chechens.[153] The tragedy of the mass deportations represented the worst possible treatment by the state of its supposedly equal citizens. Refugees and official evacuees enjoyed far more rights and privileges – if this word can be used under such desperate conditions – in their temporary homes in Central Asia. The deportees, however, were stripped of all their possessions and heritage, being denied a salary for their labour and – in the case of the Crimean Tatars – even the right to return home at the end of the war.

Despised and demoralized, the special settlers endured unspeakable hardship, particularly the 870,000 arriving in Central Asia in 1944, for whom preparations were minimal and who took longer to integrate into their new communities than earlier tranches of deportees.[154] Accused of treason or espionage, the deportees were scapegoated and punished. By ridding itself of potentially troublesome peoples in its border regions, the state immediately amassed a wealth of free labour useful in maintaining the war effort in a region decimated of its own men. At the same time, the original concentrated populations of ethnic minorities on the fringes of the Soviet Union were decimated, freeing up land and homes to be occupied by Slavic Soviet citizens re-colonizing the frontier regions. In his long game, Stalin also had an eye to future geopolitical gambits, which would in principle be rendered more straightforward thanks to the removal of potential militants on the edge of his empire.

Despite also sitting on the southern flank of the country, the peoples of Central Asia were by the end of the war more or less trusted by the state to co-operate with its aims – both military and geopolitical – in marked contrast to the Crimean Tatars or the Chechens. This relative degree of state trust was possible because Central Asia never came under enemy occupation, or even the threat of invasion, thus escaping any accusations of collaboration – real or imaginary. However, the deportations put a final, almost unbearable, strain on Central Asia and its people, such that the lukewarm hospitality shown to the earlier evacuees was not offered to subsequent deportees, who were more often treated as social pariahs. The 'friendship of the peoples' policy promoted by the state in the early stages of the war was largely discarded when it concerned relations with so-called 'enemies of the people'.

Ignored by the local communities and the press, the presence of deportees on the periphery of society became a taboo subject until well after the war, as the names of the former autonomous republics were deleted from all records. Even today, there remains a degree of Russian state amnesia with respect to the deportations, which are a largely unstudied topic in Central Asia, while communal remembrance of the *Sürgün* is discouraged in Crimea.[155] From the state's point of view, the unnecessary loss of life thanks to the deportations eventually became subsumed within the overall death toll of the war. Unlike the war veterans or even the evacuees, however, there was little possibility for the deportees to construct their own narrative of patriotic heroism to assuage their losses. Furthermore, it was during the war that particularly the Chechens and Crimean Tatars developed a hatred of the Soviet system, from which the seeds of further nationalistic movements would develop.[156] The mutual distrust of Chechens and Russians led eventually to two destructive Chechen wars after the collapse of the Soviet Union, while the Crimean Tatars were once again persecuted following Russia's invasion of Crimea in 2014. The geopolitical aims of President Vladimir Putin's wars seem to continue those of Stalin before him.

With the arrival of so many evacuees and deportees during the Second World War, the population of Central Asia became ethnically more mixed. This was particularly noticeable in Kazakhstan, that wide empty space on the map of the Soviet Union deemed by the state to be most in need of extra hands and most able to accommodate them. Thanks to the wartime influx of prisoners, refugees and deportees, ethnic Kazakhs became a minority in their own republic. The richness of that multiethnic society is celebrated now on the annual 'Unification of the nationalities day' (1 May) in Kazakhstan, probably the most ethnically diverse of all the Central Asian republics.

The Second World War accentuated a trend of population displacement in Central Asia, which started with the traders of the Silk Road. Mobility has once again become the norm, as many ethnic Russians left Central Asia upon the disintegration of the Soviet Union in 1991. Following them westwards, thousands of indigenous Central Asians became voluntary economic migrants, travelling to Moscow in search of work. Taking the most menial of jobs, many suffered once again the racial discrimination experienced during the war. The Covid-19 pandemic only served to trigger the return of those migrants no longer able to work in Russian cities experiencing less demand for cheap employment. It has been followed, however, by a noticeable exodus of Russian citizens into Kazakhstan, Kyrgyzstan and Uzbekistan, driven by the wish to escape the ramifications of the Russian invasion of Ukraine in 2022, as the republics of Central Asia continue to offer sanctuary to those fleeing war.

Notes

1 German Kim, 'The Deportation of 1937 as a Logical Continuation of Tsarist and Soviet Nationality Policy in the Russian Far East', *Korean and Korean American Studies Bulletin* 12 (2001): 19–44, 19, 30 and 33; Pavel Polian, *Against their Will: The History and Geography of Forced Migration in the*

USSR (Budapest: Central European University Press, 2004), 93, 98 and 101; and Tranum, *Life at the Edge of the Empire*, 112.

2 Tranum, *Life at the Edge of the Empire*, 112–13.

3 Kim, 'The Deportation of 1937', 34; Lipovsky, *Central Asia*, 43; Polian, *Against their Will*, 100–1; Ed Pulford, *Mirrorlands: Russia, China, and Journeys in between* (London: Hurst, 2019), 142–3; Stronski, *Tashkent*, 49; and Tranum, *Life at the Edge of the Empire*, 112–3.

4 Lipovsky, *Central Asia*, 43; and Tranum, *Life at the Edge of the Empire*, 115.

5 Polian, *Against their Will*, 97, 102, and 115–22.

6 See Roger Moorhouse, *First to Fight: The Polish War 1939* (London: Bodley Head, 2019); Moorhouse, *The Devils' Alliance*; and Applebaum, *Gulag*, 389.

7 Norman Davies, *Trail of Hope: The Anders Army: An Odyssey across Three Continents* (Oxford: Osprey, 2015), 17–31.

8 Applebaum, *Gulag*, 383–4; Kenneth Fedzin, *In search of Staszewski* (Market Harborough: Troubador, 2014), location 1216; Moorhouse, *First to Fight*, 160–74; Moorhouse, *The Devils' Alliance*, 60; and Catherine Poujol, 'Poles in Kazakhstan: Between Integration and the Imagined Motherland', *Space, Populations, Societies* 4, no. 1 (2007).

9 Applebaum, *Gulag*, 384; Michał Giedroyć, *Crater's Edge: A Family's Epic Journey through Wartime Russia* (London: Bene Factum, 2010), 31–45; Moorhouse, *The Devils' Alliance*, 60–3 and 251; and Irena Protassewicz, *A Polish Woman's Experience in World War II: Conflict, Deportation and Exile*, eds. Hubert Zawadzki and Meg Knot, trans. Hubert Zawadzki (London: Bloomsbury, 2019), location 3387–442.

10 Peck, *What My Parents Told Me*, 91. Further harrowing examples are included in Davies, *Trail of Hope*, 33–4.

11 Kozybaev, *Istoriia Kazakhstana*, 127.

12 Davies, *Trail of Hope*, 87; and Giedroyć, *Crater's Edge*, 64.

13 Norman Davies includes a map of the camps where the Polish deportees were held. In Central Asia, most worked in and around Karaganda, Tashkent, Frunze and Alma-Ata. See Davies, *Trail of Hope*, 52–3.

14 Applebaum, *Gulag*, 384; Davies, *Trail of Hope*, 68; Fedzin, *In search of Staszewski*, 1548; and Peck, *What My Parents Told Me*, 92.

15 Chilikova, 'Migratsiia evreev v Kazakhstan', 52.

16 Davies, *Trail of Hope*, 40, 44, 71 and 72; Fedzin, *In search of Staszewski*, 2109 and 2114; Giedroyć, *Crater's Edge*, 55, 62, 71–3; Grinberg, *Evrei v Alma-Ate*, 107; Protassewicz, *A Polish Woman's Experience in World War II*, 3504 and 3511; and N. V. Stepanenko, 'Ot deportatsii do reevakuatsii byvshikh pol'skikh grazhdan 1940–1946 gg.', in *Istoriia. Pamiat'. Liudi: Materialy IX Mezhdunarodnoi nauchno-prakticheskoi konferentsii 27 sentiabria 2018 g.*, eds K. Sh. Alimgazinov, et al., 75–9 (Almaty: 2019), 76.

17 Davies, *Trail of Hope*, 33–4 and 71. See Giedroyć, *Crater's Edge*, 65–70, for a full account of his schooldays in Kazakhstan.

18 Grinberg, *Evrei v Alma-Ate*, 108; and Stepanenko, 'Ot deportatsii do reevakuatsii', 76.

19 The news did not reach the Issyk-Kul' province until a week later, see *IKP*, 6 August 1941, 1. See also Davies, *Trail of Hope*, 54; Giedroyć, *Crater's Edge*, 71 and 73; Grinberg, *Evrei v Alma-Ate*, 108; and G. M. Kenebaeva and D. M. Legkii, 'K voprosu ob izmenenii statusa pol'skikh grazhdan v gody Vtoroi mirovoi voiny', in *Istoriia. Pamiat'. Liudi: Materialy IX Mezhdunarodnoi nauchno-prakticheskoi konferentsii 27 sentiabria 2018 g.*, eds K. Sh. Alimgazinov, et al., 80–4 (Almaty: 2019), 80.

20 Giedroyć, *Crater's Edge*, 125.

21 Grinberg, *Evrei v Alma-Ate*, 108; Kenebaeva and Legkii, 'K voprosu ob izmenenii statusa pol'skikh grazhdan', 82; and Stepanenko, 'Ot deportatsii do reevakuatsii', 76.

22 Fedzin, *In search of Staszewski*, 2168; Giedroyć, *Crater's Edge*, 75 and 78; Kenebaeva and Legkii, 'K voprosu ob izmenenii statusa pol'skikh grazhdan', 82; and Protassewicz, *A Polish Woman's Experience in World War II*, 3736.

23 Peck, *What My Parents Told Me*, 96–7.

24 Davies, *Trail of Hope*, 54–5 and 57; Fedzin, *In search of Staszewski*, 2148; and Israel Gutman, 'Jews in General Anders' Army in the Soviet Union', in *Yad Vashem Studies Volume 12*, 231–96 (Jerusalem: 1977).

25 Giedroyć, *Crater's Edge*, 75; and Moorhouse, *First to Fight*, 86–7 and 153–4.

26 Davies, *Trail of Hope*, 58, 87, 95 and 98; and Poujol, 'Poles in Kazakhstan', paragraph 18.

27 Davies, *Trail of Hope*, 108; Fedzin, *In Search of Staszewski*, 2175; Kenebaeva and Legkii, 'K voprosu ob izmenenii statusa pol'skikh grazhdan', 82; Peck, *What My Parents Told Me*, 96; and Protassewicz, *A Polish Woman's Experience in World War II*, 3573.

28 Was, 'Perceiving the Others', 37–8.

29 Fedzin, *In Search of Staszewski*, 2196, 2201 and 2242; and Protassewicz, *A Polish Woman's Experience in World War II*, 3586–723.

30 Giedroyć, *Crater's Edge*, 79, 97 and 102–5.

31 Fedzin, *In Search of Staszewski*, 2256; and K. S. Ibragimow 'Okrinnaia Diviziia Pekhoty v Ferganskoi doline v 1942 god', *Esimde*, 29 May 2019, available online: http://esimde.org/archives/1367 (accessed 24 June 2020).

32 Information from Dr Narynbek Alymnugov, 11 May 2018.

33 For the debate on anti-Semitism in the Anders army, see Davies, *Trail of Hope*, 86–9, 141 and 176; and Gutman, 'Jews in General Anders' Army'. For a further instance of rejection of Polish Jews in Leninabad, see O. Medvedeva-Natu, 'Vospitannik Ianusha Korchaka v tadzhikskom Kurkate', in *Istoriia. Pamiat'. Liudi: Materialy IX Mezhdunarodnoi nauchno-prakticheskoi konferentsii 27 sentiabria 2018 g.*, eds K. Sh. Alimgazinov, et al., 106–24 (Almaty: 2019), 113.

34 Davies, *Trail of Hope*, 59, 126–7, 147–8; Ibragimow 'Okrinnaia Diviziia Pekhoty'; and the testimony of Stanislaw Sobolewski, *Imperial War Museum*

Collection, available online: https://www.iwm.org.uk/collections/item/object /80012766, reel 3 (accessed 9 November 2020).

35 Fedzin, *In search of Staszewski*, 2215; Giedroyć, *Crater's Edge*, 106–7; and Protassewicz, *A Polish Woman's Experience in World War II*, 3748–978.

36 Davies, *Trail of Hope*, 59, 126–7 and 147–8; Stanislaw Sobolewski, *Imperial War Museum Collection*; and 'Uzbekistan: The Forgotten Polish Divisions of Central Asia', *Eurasianet*, 2 June 2016, available online: http://www .eurasianet.org/node/79056 (accessed 17 January 2017).

37 Ibragimow 'Okrinnaia Diviziia Pekhoty'.

38 Davies, *Trail of Hope*, 90–1, 95, 125, 129, 132, 149, 156, 157, 159, 170 and 175; Fedzin, *In Search of Staszewski*, 2201, 2208, 2215, 2277 and 2283; Giedroyć, *Crater's Edge*, 98–9 and 106; and Protassewicz, *A Polish Woman's Experience in World War II*, 4326.

39 Applebaum, *Gulag*, 390; Davies, *Trail of Hope*, 183; Fedzin, *In Search of Staszewski*, 2290, 2297 and 2303; Giedroyć, *Crater's Edge*, 125; and N. V. Stepanenko, 'Sotsial'naia deiatel'nost' Soiuza Pol'skikh Patriotov (1943–1946 gg.)', in *Istoriia. Pamiat'. Liudi: Materialy IX Mezhdunarodnoi nauchno- prakticheskoi konferentsii 27 sentiabria 2018 g.*, eds K. Sh. Alimgazinov, et al., 85–8 (Almaty: 2019), 85.

40 For a detailed breakdown, see Davies, *Trail of Hope*, 177.

41 Davies, *Trail of Hope*, 162–78; Giedroyć, *Crater's Edge*, 98 and 107–9; Ibragimow 'Okrinnaia Diviziia Pekhoty'; Protassewicz, *A Polish Woman's Experience in World War II*, 4003, 4010 and 4017–40; and Sobolewski, *Imperial War Museum Collection*.

42 Davies, *Trail of Hope*, chapter 19; and Fedzin, *In Search of Staszewski*, 2921, 2942, 2955 and 2962; Fedzin, *In Search of Staszewski*, 2657–825; Giedroyć, *Crater's Edge*, 175 and 186; and Protassewicz, *A Polish Woman's Experience in World War II*, 4017–40 and 4094–267.

43 Fedzin, *In Search of Staszewski*, location 2680–4; V. P. Reshetov, '"Chuvstvuiu sebia poliakom!"', in *Istoriia. Pamiat'. Liudi: Materialy IX Mezhdunarodnoi nauchno-prakticheskoi konferentsii 27 sentiabria 2018 g.*, eds K. Sh. Alimgazinov, et al., 481–6 (Almaty: 2019), 483–5; 'The Doll "Lala" ("Ilana") that Vera Lifschitz Received in the Transit Camp in Karachi, India', *Yad Vashem Museum Collection*, available online: https://www.yadvashem .org/yv/en/exhibitions/bearing.../doll-lala.asp (accessed 28 October 2020); and 'The "Teheran Children" and the Jewish Soldiers in Anders' Army', *Yad Vashem Museum Collection*, available online: https://www.yadvashem.org/yv/ en/exhibitions/bearing-witness/tehran.asp (accessed 28 October 2020).

44 Applebaum, *Gulag*, 408; Fedzin, *In Search of Staszewski*, 2343 and 2350; Reshetov, '"Chuvstvuiu sebia poliakom!"'; and Stepanenko, 'Ot deportatsii do reevakuatsii', 77–8. See also the plight of M. Kesler in Kesler, *Grit*, 877; and another conscript in Medvedeva-Natu, 'Vospitannik Ianusha Korchaka v tadzhikskom Kurkate', 117.

45 Davies, *Trail of Hope*, 58, 134 and 183; Fedzin, *In Search of Staszewski*, 2343, 2350 and 2388; Ibragimow 'Okrinnaia Diviziia Pekhoty'; and Merridale, *Ivan's War*, 286.

46 Kerimbaev, *Sovetskii Kirgizstan v Velikoi Otechestvennoi voine*, 172;
    Stepanenko, 'Ot deportatsii do reevakuatsii', 77; and Stepanenko,
    'Sotsial'naia deiatel'nost' Soiuza Pol'skikh Patriotov', 85–7.

47 Berkimbaeva and Legkii, 'Oblono ne okhvatilo vsekh evakuirovannykh detei
    ucheboi', 91–2.

48 Davies, *Trail of Hope*, 183–4; Giedroyć, *Crater's Edge*, 125; and Kenebaeva
    and Legkii, 'K voprosu ob izmenenii statusa pol'skikh grazhdan', 83.

49 Grinberg, *Evrei v Alma-Ate*, 108; Iofe and Il'ina, 'Spasenie ot Kholokosta',
    333; Peck, *What My Parents Told Me*, 97–102; Poujol, 'Poles in Kazakhstan',
    paragraph 19; and Saipova, 'Istoriia pol'skikh evreev', 416.

50 Fedzin, *In Search of Staszewski*, 2363; Ibragimow 'Okrinnaia Diviziia
    Pekhoty'; Poujol, 'Poles in Kazakhstan', paragraph 19; Protassewicz, *A
    Polish Woman's Experience in World War II*, 4017–40, 4593 and 4608; and
    Stepanenko, 'Ot deportatsii do reevakuatsii', 78.

51 Fedzin, *In Search of Staszewski*, 2377 and 2403; Stepanenko, 'Ot deportatsii
    do reevakuatsii', 78; and Stepanenko, 'Sotsial'naia deiatel'nost' Soiuza
    Pol'skikh Patriotov', 88.

52 Poujol, 'Poles in Kazakhstan', paragraphs 18 and 20; and Stepanenko, 'Ot
    deportatsii do reevakuatsii', 79.

53 Applebaum, *Gulag*, 408; Poujol, 'Poles in Kazakhstan', paragraph 5; and
    'Uzbekistan: The Forgotten Polish Divisions of Central Asia'.

54 Andrew J. Brown, 'The Germans of Germany and the Germans of
    Kazakhstan: A Eurasian Volk in the Twilight of Diaspora', *Europe-Asia
    Studies* 57, no. 4 (2005): 625–34, 626–7; and Mukhina, *The Germans of the
    Soviet Union*, 16 and 18.

55 Mukhina, *The Germans of the Soviet Union*, 19, 30 and 31.

56 Carmack, *Kazakhstan in World War II*, 119; Mukhina, *The Germans of the
    Soviet Union*, 32–4; and Polian, *Against their Will*, 124–5.

57 Brown, 'The Germans of Germany and the Germans of Kazakhstan', 627;
    Hosking, *Russia and the Russians*, 504; and Polian, *Against their Will*,
    128 and 131.

58 IKSA:146/2/13/104–6; Mukhina, *The Germans of the Soviet Union*, 48; and
    Polian, *Against their Will*, 137.

59 Carmack, *Kazakhstan in World War II*, 130–1; and Polian, *Against their Will*,
    137 and 139.

60 Applebaum, *Gulag*, 387; Brown, 'The Germans of Germany and the Germans
    of Kazakhstan', 627; Carmack, *Kazakhstan in World War II*, 117, 125 and
    129; Davies, *Trail of Hope*, 83; Kozybaev, *Istoriia Kazakhstana*, 127; and
    Polian, *Against their Will*, 124 and 126–7.

61 Braithwaite, *Moscow 1941*, 249; Carmack, *Kazakhstan in World War II*,
    120–30 and 134; Mukhina, *The Germans of the Soviet Union*, 57, 64–5 and
    67; and Polian, *Against their Will*, 132.

62 Brown, 'The Germans of Germany and the Germans of Kazakhstan', 627;
    Carmack, *Kazakhstan in World War II*, 124; Isabelle Kreindler, 'The Soviet

Deported Nationalities: A Summary and Update', *Soviet Studies* 38 (1986): 387–405, 397; Mukhina, *The Germans of the Soviet Union*, 57, 87, 93, 95, 96, 134, 139 and 140; and White, 'After the War was Over', 1158.

63 Mukhina, *The Germans of the Soviet Union*, 163–8.

64 Information from Gulsara Nurmatova, 11 May 2018. Over 350,000 Germans were still living in Kyrgyzstan in 1991.

65 Brown, 'The Germans of Germany and the Germans of Kazakhstan', 62–6.

66 I. Dzhukha, *Spetseshelony idut na vostok: Istoriia repressii protiv grekov v SSSR. Deportatsii 1940-kh gg.* (St Petersburg: Aleteiia, 2008), 60; and Isabelle Ohayon, 'Ego-récits de l'Intégration: Deux itinéraires de déportés au Kazakhstan soviétique', *Slovo* (2017): 239–52, 240.

67 *Krylataia sem'ia* (Krasnodar: Diapazon, 2005).

68 I. A. Papush, 'Greki priazov'ia v gody Velikoi Otechestvennoi voiny 1941– 1945 gg.', *Azovskie greki* (2000), available online: https://www.azovgreeks .com/library.cfm?articleId=107 (accessed 8 January 2021), 2 and 19.

69 Dzhukha, *Spetseshelony idut na vostok*, 17.

70 Ibid., 4–7.

71 Ibid., 11–12 and 68–9; and Ohayon, 'Ego-récits de l'Intégration', 240 and 242.

72 Dzhukha, *Spetseshelony idut na vostok*, 5, 10 and 17.

73 Ibid., 71–2.

74 Ibid., 61, 63 and 66.

75 Ibid., 17, 62 and 71–2.

76 Ohayon, 'Ego-récits de l'Intégration', 242–6.

77 Dzhukha, *Spetseshelony idut na vostok*, 18 and 79.

78 Ibid., 23, 74, 79 and 93.

79 Ibid., 73.

80 Fevzie's story was recounted to me by her daughter, Saide (25 April 2018).

81 Rory Finnin, 'The Crimean Tatar Sürgün: Past and Present', *University of Cambridge*, 20 May 2014, available online: http://www.cam.ac.uk/research/ discussion/the-crimean-tatar-surgun-past-and-present (accessed 8 December 2021).

82 An excellent history of the Crimean Tatars is provided in Williams, *The Crimean Tatars*. See also Juliette Denis, 'De la Condamnation à l'Expulsion: La construction de l'image de masse durant la Grande Guerre patriotique', in *Les Déportations en Héritage: Les peuples réprimés du Caucase et de Crimée hier et aujourd'hui*, eds A. Campana, G. Dufaud and S. Tournon, 29–51 (Rennes: University Press of Rennes, 2010), location 548; Peter Potichnyj, 'The Struggle of the Crimean Tatars', *Canadian Slavonic Papers* 17, no. 2/3 (1975): 302–19, 302–5; and Greta L. Uehling, *Beyond Memory: The Crimean Tatars' Deportation and Return* (New York: Palgrave McMillan, 2004), 30–40.

83 Williams, *The Crimean Tatars*, 91.

84 Sanie and Muedin Settarov shared their remarkable, if not unusual, story with me in a gradual process over several years between 2001 and 2019. After their death, other family members took up the narrative on their behalf.

85 Denis, 'De la Condamnation à l'Expulsion', 696–711; Potichnyj, 'The Struggle of the Crimean Tatars', 307; Williams, *The Crimean Tatars*, 94; and Brian G. Williams, 'The Hidden Ethnic Cleansing of Muslims in the Soviet Union: The Exile and Repatriation of the Crimean Tatars', *Journal of Contemporary History* 37, no. 3 (2002): 323–47, 329.

86 9,225 Crimean Tatars joined the Crimean Legion; see J. Otto Pohl, 'The False Charges of Treason against the Crimean Tatars', *International Committee for Crimea* (2010), available online: http://www.iccrimea.org/scholarly/ pohl20100518.pdf (accessed 10 December 2021). See also Denis, 'De la Condamnation à l'Expulsion', 711–18; Merridale, *Ivan's War*, 260; and Williams, *The Crimean Tatars*, 92–3.

87 Uehling, *Beyond Memory*, 37; and Williams, *The Crimean Tatars*, 93. See also Denis, 'De la Condamnation à l'Expulsion', 648–64; Motadel, 'Islam and Germany's War in the Soviet Borderlands'; and Potichnyj, 'The Struggle of the Crimean Tatars', 306.

88 Beevor, *Stalingrad*, 184; Denis, 'De la Condamnation à l'Expulsion', 711–18; and Williams, *The Crimean Tatars*, 93.

89 Denis, 'De la Condamnation à l'Expulsion', 673 and 711; and Williams, 'The Hidden Ethnic Cleansing of Muslims', 329.

90 Denis, 'De la Condamnation à l'Expulsion', 602 and 689; Eden, 'A Soviet Jihad against Hitler', 237; and Potichnyj, 'The Struggle of the Crimean Tatars', 306. See also Alan Fisher, *The Crimean Tatars* (Stanford: Stanford University Press, 1978), 153–64.

91 Applebaum, *Gulag*, 387; Denis, 'De la Condamnation à l'Expulsion', 302 and 811; Uehling, *Beyond Memory*, 38; Williams, *The Crimean Tatars*, 95–6; and Williams, 'The Hidden Ethnic Cleansing of Muslims', 329.

92 Dzhukha, *Spetseshelony idut na vostok*, 20.

93 Berkhoff, *Motherland in Danger*, 217.

94 J. Otto Pohl, 'The Deportation and Fate of the Crimean Tatars', *International Committee for Crimea* (2000), available online: http://www.iccrimea.org/ scholarly/jopohl.html (accessed 17 January 2021); Uehling, *Beyond Memory*, 3, 21 and 41; Williams, *The Crimean Tatars*, 97–8; and Williams, 'The Hidden Ethnic Cleansing of Muslims', 331.

95 Esenaliev, *Zhenishke dank*, 153.

96 Carmack, *Kazakhstan in World War II*, 136–7; and Robbins, *In search of Kazakhstan*, 161.

97 Applebaum, *Gulag*, 388; Denis, 'De la Condamnation à l'Expulsion', 820–6 and 86; Polian, *Against their Will*, 152; and Uehling, *Beyond Memory*, 10.

98 Williams, 'The Hidden Ethnic Cleansing of Muslims', 332.

99 Applebaum, *Gulag*, 388; Dzhukha, *Spetseshelony idut na vostok*, 27; Pohl, 'The Deportation and Fate of the Crimean Tatars'; and Uehling, *Beyond Memory*, 38.

100 Motadel, 'Islam and Germany's War in the Soviet Borderlands', 819–20; and Williams, *The Crimean Tatars*, chapter 6.

101 Dzhukha, *Spetseshelony idut na vostok*, 27; Pohl, 'The Deportation and Fate of the Crimean Tatars'; and Uehling, *Beyond Memory*, 38.

102 Information from interviews with Muedin Settarov and his family. See also Merridale, *Ivan's War*, 261; and Polian, *Against their Will*, 125.

103 Il'ia Erenburg, 'Tatary', *Krasnaia Zvezda*, 27 October 1942; and Merridale, *Ivan's War*, 261.

104 Dzhukha, *Spetseshelony idut na vostok*, 27 and 59; Merridale, *Ivan's War*, 261; Pohl, 'The Deportation and Fate of the Crimean Tatars'; and Williams, 'The Hidden Ethnic Cleansing of Muslims', 334.

105 Dzhukha, *Spetseshelony idut na vostok*, 57; and Uehling, *Beyond Memory*, 80 and 83.

106 Applebaum, *Gulag*, 388.

107 Denis, 'De la Condamnation à l'Expulsion', 811 and 852.

108 Interviews with the Settarov and Jemilev families.

109 Iofe and Vedernikova, 'Iz istorii evakuatsii v Uzbekistan'; Pohl, 'The False Charges of Treason against the Crimean Tatars', 4; Williams, *The Crimean Tatars*, 102; and Williams, 'The Hidden Ethnic Cleansing of Muslims', 334.

110 Kozybaev, *Istoriia Kazakhstana*, 127; and Kreindler, 'The Soviet Deported Nationalities', 392.

111 Batyrbaeva, 'Evakuirovannoe i deportirovannoe naselenie', 28.

112 Ibid.; Kaptagaev et al., *Sbornik*, 118; and Seidimatova, 'Priissykkul'e v gody Velikoi Otechestvennoi voiny', 282.

113 Pohl, 'The Deportation and Fate of the Crimean Tatars'; Uehling, *Beyond Memory*, 100; and Williams, 'The Hidden Ethnic Cleansing of Muslims', 335.

114 Interviews with Muedin and the Settarov family. See also Marc Elie, 'La Vie en Déportation (1943–1953)', in *Les Déportations en Héritage: Les peuples réprimés du Caucase et de Crimée hier et aujourd'hui*, eds A. Campana, G. Dufaud and S. Tournon, 53–75 (Rennes: University Press of Rennes, 2010), location 1187–94.

115 Kaptagaev, et al., *Sbornik*, 96–7, 105, 108 and 118.

116 Florin, 'Becoming Soviet through War', 510; Tranum, *Life at the Edge of the Empire*, 69; Uehling, *Beyond Memory*, 96–7; Williams, *The Crimean Tatars*, 87; and Williams, 'The Hidden Ethnic Cleansing of Muslims', 335.

117 Carmack, '"A Fortress of the Soviet Home Front"', 28; and Uehling, *Beyond Memory*, 97.

118 Seidimatova, 'Priissykkul'e v gody Velikoi Otechestvennoi voiny', 282.

119 Ibid., 118–19.

120 Kaptagaev, et al., *Sbornik*, 108 and 118.

121 Mukhina, *The Germans of the Soviet Union*, 59.

122 Elie, 'La Vie en Déportation', 1061.

123 Ibid., 1049 and 1163; Florin, 'Becoming Soviet through War', 510; and Uehling, *Beyond Memory*, 96.

124 Abylkhozhin, *Istoriia Kazakhstana*, 527 and 530; Carmack, *Kazakhstan in World War II*, 143–5; and Elie, 'La Vie en Déportation', 1020.

125 Carmack, *Kazakhstan in World War II*, 138.

126 Elie, 'La Vie en Déportation', 1104.

127 Ibid., 1068–85 and 1113; Kaptagaev, et al., *Sbornik*, 118; and Mukhina, *The Germans of the Soviet Union*, 62.

128 Carmack, *Kazakhstan in World War II*, 138; Elie, 'La Vie en Déportation', 1049, 1102, 1150 and 1163; Uehling, *Beyond Memory*, 38 and 81; and Williams, 'The Hidden Ethnic Cleansing of Muslims', 335.

129 Potichnyj, 'The Struggle of the Crimean Tatars', 308–9; and Uehling, *Beyond Memory*, 38 and 81.

130 Batyrbaeva, 'Evakuirovannoe i deportirovannoe naselenie', 28.

131 Carmack, *Kazakhstan in World War II*, 139; and Elie, 'La Vie en Déportation', 1141.

132 Carmack, '"A Fortress of the Soviet Home Front"', 34–5; Kaptagaev, et al., *Sbornik*, 113; Uehling, *Beyond Memory*, 39; and Williams, 'The Hidden Ethnic Cleansing of Muslims', 335 and 338.

133 Carmack, *Kazakhstan in World War II*, 139; and Williams, 'The Hidden Ethnic Cleansing of Muslims', 338.

134 Carmack, *Kazakhstan in World War II*, 144 and 119; and Elie, 'La Vie en Déportation', 1434.

135 Tranum, *Life at the Edge of the Empire*, 134, 202, 211 and 224.

136 Elie, 'La Vie en Déportation', 1061 and 1418; Uehling, *Beyond Memory*, 29, 83 and 95; and Williams, *The Crimean Tatars*, 102. For an extended discussion on the reception of the deportees in Kyrgyzstan, see Florin, 'Becoming Soviet through War', 510–15. See also Carmack, *Kazakhstan in World War II*, 155; and Stronski, *Tashkent*, 132.

137 Elie, 'La Vie en Déportation', 1401; and Williams, 'The Hidden Ethnic Cleansing of Muslims', 338.

138 Kim, 'The Deportation of 1937', 35; Kozybaev, *Istoriia Kazakhstana*, 128; Lillis, *Dark Shadows*, 3131 and 3200; and Tranum, *Life at the Edge of the Empire*, 101 and 202.

139 Interview with Sanie Zevadinova. See also Applebaum, *Gulag*, 389; Carmack, *Kazakhstan in World War II*, 142; Elie, 'La Vie en Déportation', 1386–1394; Hosking, *Russia and the Russians*, 504–6; Kaptagaev, et al., *Sbornik*, 118–19; and Pohl, 'The Deportation and Fate of the Crimean Tatars'.

140 Elie, 'La Vie en Déportation', 1226; Williams, *The Crimean Tatars*, 102–10; and Williams, 'The Hidden Ethnic Cleansing of Muslims', 337.

141 Williams, 'The Hidden Ethnic Cleansing of Muslims', 337.

142 Polian, *Against their Will*, 150; Turlygul, *Istoriia Kazakhstana*, 216; Williams, *The Crimean Tatars*, 58; and Williams, 'The Hidden Ethnic Cleansing of Muslims', 342–3.

143 Lillis, *Dark Shadows*, 3239.

144 Applebaum, *Gulag*, 389; Rebecca Gould, 'Leaving the House of Memory: Post-Soviet Traces of Deportation Memory', *Mosaic: An Interdisciplinary Critical Journal* 45, no. 2 (2012): 149–64, 154; Uehling, *Beyond Memory*, 38; and Williams, 'The Hidden Ethnic Cleansing of Muslims', 340.

145 Uehling, *Beyond Memory*, 29 and 41.

146 Published with kind permission from the Khojaev family.

147 Information from the Settarov family.

148 For a lengthy coverage of the return of the Crimean Tatars, see Williams, *The Crimean Tatars*, chapter 7. See also Applebaum, *Gulag*, 389; Pohl, 'The Deportation and Fate of the Crimean Tatars'; and Polian, *Against their Will*, 212–15.

149 Williams, 'The Hidden Ethnic Cleansing of Muslims', 345.

150 'Den' v istorii: 28 dekabriia 1943 goda nachalas' deportatatsiia kalmykov', 28 December 2017, *Esimde*, available online: http://esimde.org/archives/729 (accessed 7 January 2021).

151 Florin, 'Becoming Soviet through War', 510.

152 Information from Gulsara Nurmatova (11 May 2018) and the Directors of the Issyk-Kul' archives in Karakol and Tiup (18 May 2018).

153 See Williams, *The Crimean Tatars*.

154 Elie, 'La Vie en Déportation', 1057; and Kozybaev, *Istoriia Kazakhstana*, 127. Smaller overall figures are quoted in Lillis, *Dark Shadows*, 3131; Robbins, *In search of Kazakhstan*, 161; and Williams, 'The Hidden Ethnic Cleansing of Muslims', 341.

155 Information from Dr Narynbek Alymnugov, 11 May 2018. See also Applebaum, *Gulag*, 386; Carmack, *Kazakhstan in World War II*, 158; Finnin, 'The Crimean Tatar Sürgün'; Florin, 'Becoming Soviet through War', 508; and Florin, *Kirgistan und die sowjetische Moderne*, 54.

156 Carmack, *Kazakhstan in World War II*, 151; Elie, 'La Vie en Déportation', 1434; and Williams, *The Crimean Tatars*, chapter 7.

PART IV

The legacy of the Second World War in Central Asia

9

The cultural and social legacy of the war

It took time once the war was over for life to start to return to some semblance of normality – a new, post-war Soviet reality in which the presence of the state was more noticeable than in the pre-war years. There was little time for mourning the dead, as work continued apace in the factories and fields of Central Asia. Indeed, the Soviet regime under Stalin had no wish for displays of remembrance, probably fearing close questioning into the enormous waste of military and civilian lives squandered by the state. Looking determinedly ahead to the continuing task of building socialism in the Soviet Union, there was no political room for the luxury of reflecting on the past, even for peoples who traditionally set great store on the commemoration of their ancestors.

It was only after Stalin's death in 1953 that the relative thaw of the Khrushchev period saw some steps towards communal remembrance and the easing of restrictions on the publication of war memoirs by military officers like Nikolai Liashchenko. However, it was not until the twentieth anniversary of the end of the war in 1965 that the official attitude to memory started to undergo more substantial change following the accession in 1964 of Leonid Brezhnev as General Secretary of the Communist Party. During the Brezhnev era the regime created a countrywide war cult – a memorial environment through which remembrance of the war was encouraged – involving substantial media coverage of war memory, the prolific building of monuments, the increased scale of memorial rituals, the publication of war memoirs and the military–patriotic education of young people. Victory Day on 9 May became an annual public holiday in a political climate which actively promoted commemoration of the past.[1] Within this memorial atmosphere a corpus of literature and film built up around the exploits of the famous Panfilov Division. A reminder to the people of Central Asia that they were valued by the state for playing a key role in the defence of Moscow, despite the extraordinary human cost of the war, the evolving myth of Panfilov's twenty-eight men was presented as exemplifying the epitome of the 'friendship of the peoples'.

The Panfilov myth in the post-war years

Thanks to the Soviet state's propaganda machine, the biggest morale-boosting story of the war for the residents of Central Asia was the exploit of the 316th Division under the leadership of Major General Ivan Panfilov. Instrumental in consolidating the place of Central Asia within the Soviet Union, the myth of the twenty-eight men from the 1075th Rifle Regiment – credited with destroying dozens of enemy tanks during the Battle of Moscow – continued to be exploited in the post-war years. This narrative of heroic sacrifice of men from Central Asia was exploited by the state in its effort to control memory of the war and instil a sense of Soviet pride in the people on its southern flank. Remembrance of the action has been complicated over time by the perpetuation of the deliberate misinformation propagated by contemporaneous journalists, which was ratified by the state and led to the dissemination of the popular narrative across the Soviet Union. Further works of literature which apparently aimed to divulge the 'truth' of the division's exploits during the autumn of 1941 were also compromised when the verbal contract between the war correspondent author and the only indigenous eye-witness he could find broke down over allegations of distortion of the truth. The muddied waters of remembrance of the men of Panfilov's 316th Division have led over the years to a multiplicity of different versions of 'history', raising in Central Asia the important question about who owns the rights to historical memory: the state, the war correspondent or the Red Army officer in the field.

The construction of the Panfilov myth

The first reports to reach the wider Soviet Union about the defence of Moscow by Panfilov's Division were through the newspaper articles of Vasilii Koroteev and Aleksandr Krivitskii, journalists for the military newspaper *Krasnaia Zvezda*.[2] By the end of November 1941, war correspondents were on the hunt for heart-warming stories of valiant behaviour amongst Red Army soldiers, which could be used to mitigate news of the devastating losses as the German army advanced to the very outskirts of Moscow. Using his vivid imagination and some cursory research, Koroteev managed to cobble together the framework of a suitably heroic exploit, which was further embellished by Krivitskii under the guidance of his editor-in-chief Major General David Ortenberg. With the ratification of the state, Krivitskii broke the news in detail on 28 November 1941 in his article 'Zaveshchanie 28 pavshikh geroev' (Testimony of the twenty-eight fallen heroes). In this way, the state's propaganda machine set about the task of turning actual defeat into a propaganda victory in the spirit of the Allied retreat from the beaches of northern France at Dunkirk in 1940.

It was, of course, virtually impossible to confirm that the alleged action had actually happened, as the protagonists had apparently all died on 16 November. Nor was it possible in winter actions, such as the battle for the Volokolamsk Highway, to name or even count the dead. No written reports were available, and confusion existed as to their actual regiment, the number of enemy tanks destroyed and the number of German soldiers killed. The first obviously wildly exaggerated numbers were soon toned down in the interests of credibility as the story built up its own momentum. It was more difficult, though, to identify the names of some men to whom the action could be attributed. Not only spelling mistakes were made, as it became clear that some of the men supposed to have died a hero's death on the day were already dead. Others had survived November's action: some had been taken prisoner, while the platoon's allegedly heroic leader, Sergeant Ivan Dobrobabin, was later identified by the NKVD as a collaborator with the occupying forces in Ukraine. Particularly problematic was the leadership role of the political officer selected for heroism, who suffered a dramatic change of name that winter. In the end, much credit for the action was attributed to the leadership of a certain Vasilii Klochkov, the political officer of the 1075th Regiment, whose questionable name sometimes includes his possible nickname 'Diev'. Nonetheless, Krivitskii followed up his first report with a second article in *Krasnaia Zvezda* on 22 January 1942 in which he named all twenty-eight men who had allegedly died at Dubosekovo. It was these initial articles which laid the foundation for subsequent narratives about the courageous twenty-eight men of one platoon of the 4th Company of the 2nd Battalion of the 1075th Regiment of the 316th Division. They also paved the way for the award of Hero of the Soviet Union status to the largely invented martyrs in July 1942.

Over the months and years after the events of 16 November 1941, a potent myth was constructed with the tacit agreement of the state. The story of the heroic deeds was disseminated across the Soviet Union as part of a propaganda exercise lionizing the courage of Red Army troops – especially those from ethnic minorities. The bare facts remained close to Krivitskii's original template – the self-sacrifice of a whole platoon of twenty-eight (ideologically correct) riflemen from Panfilov's 316th Division, who nonetheless managed to annihilate most of a German tank regiment heading straight for the gates of Moscow. A war myth may be defined as 'a shared and simplified narrative of the past with utility in the present thanks to its enduring emotional and moral appeal'.[3] The myth of Panfilov's twenty-eight riflemen qualified on all counts. With no apparent survivors to tell the tale and reliable eye-witness testimony impossible to find, the alleged exploits of the heroes of the 1075th Rifle Regiment were preserved for posterity through the words of others still living.

The first major literary input in the construction of the myth was thanks to the poetry of the relatively mature and respected Soviet poet Nikolai Tikhonov. In March 1942 his poem 'Slovo o 28 gvardeitsev' (A word about the 28 guardsmen) was published in *Krasnaia Zvezda*. This work is more than just one word, however, but rather a ballad of the engagement, drawn out with much repetition replicating the lengthy hours passing by with increasing tension. The repeated words 'The trench. Twenty-eight guards' indicate time passing slowly at first, and then more urgently as the ranks of enemy tanks come into range: 'Twenty tanks', mentioned three times, to be followed by a further 'thirty tanks'.[4]

The twenty-eight riflemen are introduced sitting together in their trench, shoulder to shoulder. They are men of the motherland, including those from Kyrgyzstan, and Talgar and Alma-Ata in Kazakhstan. In a conversation with his Russian comrade, Ivan Natarov, Kazakh soldier Daniil Kuzhebergenov reminds him that 'Moskvy stoiat za nami steny' (The walls of Moscow stand behind us). This was an expression paraphrasing words attributed to Klochkov about the critical nature of the battle, which had become famous in Kravitskii's first newspaper article: 'Velika Rossiia, a otstupat' nekuda – pozadi Moskva!' (Russia is vast, but there is nowhere to retreat to; Moscow is behind [us]!). In Tikhonov's poem, Daniil recalls his sunny homeland, where his girlfriend is waiting for him. Ivan declares that he, also, is just a young worker fighting for his motherland. Ivan justifies the battle as fulfilling the will of Stalin, the 'father of the peoples', sitting in the Kremlin with the wisdom and clear vision of a wise eagle. Ivan appears to realize that they will all die, but is reassured that Stalin will ensure that they will be remembered. His other consolation is that they may die, but at least they will take the enemy with them. As they wait to engage the tanks, every man remembers his family, the sky over his homeland and the girl waiting for him there.

In contrast, however, Tikhonov emphasizes the autumn cold and the snow of their current exposed situation, as twenty German tanks approach in a column of identical machines like a herd of goats or a flock of geese. The animal imagery mocks the German tank drivers, who are looking forward to taking Moscow just as easily as they had entered Paris earlier in the war. It is up to the Soviet men to stop them, thanks to their communist ideology and Bolshevik background. Political officer, Ukrainian Vasilii Klochkov-Diev, plays a key role in the narrative, providing the impetus for the young men by his words of leadership and his friendship, driving them on to victory with his inspiring rhetoric.

As the battle starts in earnest, the troops in the trench throw grenades and Molotov cocktails in heroic combat, standing, according to the modest Tikhonov, in stark contrast to his feeble poetry. The noise and sight of the battle is vividly described, with groaning, explosions, smoke, dust, flame and fire. The battle takes its toll on both sides, as the pure white snow around the trench becomes soaked in Soviet blood, while stricken tanks stand immobile in the snowy field. As the final thirty German tanks roll into view, 'full of evil', the remaining riflemen launch their last grenades. Evening approaches as Daniil throws his own final explosive, taking out one more tank before his life is extinguished with the last light of day. One after another the twenty-eight men die together in their frozen trench.

The engagement could be portrayed as significant a battle as Waterloo or Borodino, both contributing to the defeat of Napoleon. According to Tikhonov, however, these nineteenth-century conflicts had no such courageous men as the twenty-eight riflemen of the Panfilov Division. They had achieved their aim in stopping the German advance and were able to sleep at last in death. Ivan Natarov, however, could apparently still hear, as he lay dying, the voice of his commanding officer, Panfilov, speaking to 'his' rifleman. Ivan sheds tears of joy as he sees in his mind Kazakhstan with its steppe, mountain ranges and villages just as Daniil had described. Finally, in death, he hears the eternal song about Kazakhstan and its most honourable twenty-eight warriors who had done their duty – a song which the poet declared would live on across the Soviet Union.

Panfilov himself features only briefly in the poem. Compared by Tikhonov with both Wellington and revolutionary and civil war hero Chapaev, he is portrayed as a kind leader, with smiling eyes, who is proud of his men. The emphasis throughout, though, is on the political officer, Klochkov-Diev, whose last words were to reassure the others that 'somewhere they will remember us'.

The literature of Aleksandr Bek and Baurzhan Momysh-uly

As soon as details of the engagement became widespread, the memorial baton was taken up by a respected war correspondent of long standing, Aleksandr Bek. Quick to recognize a good story and responding to state demands for the promotion of works about ethnic minorities, Bek seized upon the opportunity to write a fictionalized documentary of the Central Asian 316th Division through the eyes of one Kazakh officer who had survived to tell the tale. Tracing the trajectory of a specific battalion, Bek based his work on a series of interviews with Senior Lieutenant Baurzhan Momysh-uly, commander of the 700 men of the 1st Battalion of the 1073rd Talgar Rifle Regiment in Panfilov's division. Within weeks of the Battle of Moscow, Bek came to an informal agreement with Momysh-uly to fictionalize his unique perspective on the protracted events from 13 October to 20 November 1941. It was *Panfilovtsy na pervom rubezhe* (Panfilov's men on the forward fringe), published from May to June 1943 in *Znamia*, and *Volokolamskoe Shosse* (The Volokolamsk Highway), published in 1944, which cemented the heroism and put flesh on the bones of the 316th in the mind of the ordinary Soviet citizen. This collaboration between Bek and

Momysh-uly made them both famous, while sparking a controversy over the artistic licence of an author who takes control of his subject's personal narrative, while sometimes distorting his source's idea of the 'truth'.

Bek describes himself as a 'conscientious and diligent scribe', merely setting down on paper what Momysh-uly, the soldier and actual participant in the Battle of Moscow, shares with or dictates to him.[5] This modesty belies Bek's ability to write a good story in Russian, implicitly a skill not shared by Momysh-uly, whose talent lies rather in training the men of his battalion and then leading them into action. In the first work, *Panfilov's Men on the Forward Fringe*, the 'scribe' narrates in the first person, describing his notes as a conversation between himself and Momysh-uly. Not always chronological, it describes the training process of Momysh-uly's battalion and its preparation for action, as he knocks his rough men into shape. The second work, *The Volokolamsk Highway*, in contrast, depicts Momysh-uly dictating his story to the 'scribe' in the first person, who faithfully renders his words. In this way the reader learns of the first October engagements of the Battle of Moscow, detailed day by day and hour by hour as Momysh-uly leads his battalion away from the advancing German army to reach Panfilov's divisional headquarters in the town of Volokolamsk.

Building on his initial success, Bek published two sequels to *The Volokolamsk Highway* in 1960. *Neskol'ko dnei* (A Few Days) covers the period immediately following the arrival of Momysh-uly's battalion in the hub of Volokolamsk, while *Rezerv generala Panfilova* (General Panfilov's Reserve) details the key five days of fiercest fighting from 15 to 20 November, when the German army started to advance again and the battalion was ordered to forestall enemy troop movement along the main road to Moscow. In this volume Momysh-uly's men are depicted as battle-hardened troops, of whom he is finally proud. The last book of the quartet retains Momysh-uly as narrator, while returning to the overall author–narrator in the final paragraphs to remind the reader that this was, indeed, the writing of Aleksandr Bek throughout.

The main premise of both men is that the truth should always be told by a serving soldier and, in this case, by the author transcribing his dictation and putting it into words for the reader. As the unwritten contract is negotiated, Momysh-uly explains that he 'can't stand people writing about the war from hearsay', as he asserts that nobody is able to write legitimately about war unless they have experienced it first hand.[6] Momysh-uly finally agrees to the conditions of trust under which he agrees to share not only his memories but also the thoughts going through his head in the heat of battle. According to Bek's hero in *General Panfilov's Reserve*, Momysh-uly even threatens to chop off the author's right hand if he writes any lies.[7]

The potential for cruelty in dealing with others is just one aspect of Momysh-uly's character which Bek brings to the fore in his works: the execution for self-mutilation and cowardice of Sergeant Barambaev is an early example of his philosophy of training the troops by being cruel to be kind.[8] In this way Momysh-uly concerns himself over the evacuation of the wounded where possible but is then quite prepared to shoot them rather than leave his men to fall into the hands of the enemy.[9] In his preparation for the work, Aleksandr Bek had actively searched for an officer from Central Asia who had directly experienced the Battle of Moscow – no doubt to earn credit for emphasizing the state's 'friendship of the peoples' narrative, while avoiding any lingering doubts about the veracity of his accounts. To underscore his protagonist's ethnic background, he describes repeatedly and in detail Momysh-uly's 'Mongolian' appearance: his 'unusually large black eyes' and prominent cheek-bones. This 'proud Kazakh' from a warrior tribe reminds the scribe of a noble savage, such as the 'Indian' described by James Fenimore Cooper in children's books.[10]

Momysh-uly demonstrates the excellent horsemanship of a true nomad, identifying as much with his horse as with his men: 'I, a free Kazakh, an untamed horse of the steppe, who could not suffer a bridle, had become a soldier.'[11] He employs traditional Kazakh sayings with his men, while enjoying parcels from home containing iconic apples from Alma-Ata and recalling the beauty of his homeland and the legend of its creation.[12] Above all, Bek's uncompromising hero represents the *aksakal*, the village elder, in one more cliché about Central Asians from Bek's armoury.

To Russian readers, Momysh-uly comes across as exotic, a man with no surname; however, as the book develops he becomes more comfortable in his role as leader, trying to create his own image as a truly Soviet officer. Momysh-uly insists on speaking Russian most of the time, despite the fact that one-third of his men are Kazakh, thanks to his time in the Red Army, in officers' training college and in higher education in Leningrad. Although portrayed as a man deeply rooted in Kazakh oral tradition ('a born story teller')[13] and culture, he is at the same time a new Soviet man – a gifted singer, conversant with the works of Pushkin, who is kissed on the lips in Russian style in thanks and reconciliation by Major General Zviagin as he succeeds in retrieving the honour of his battalion.[14] This complex character, not yet a member of the Communist Party,[15] is Bek's prototype of a supposedly backward ethnic minority which has been recently modernized thanks to the opportunities offered by Soviet intervention.

Despite being born into a primitive shepherd's family, Momysh-uly has become a professional Soviet soldier. He betrays the loneliness of an officer in action, enjoying particularly the company of other officer comrades from the division on occasion. He is self-contained, honest and loyal, and keen to be seen to be doing his duty to the Red Army. A stickler for discipline, he insists throughout on his men obeying orders, strictly upholding the official 'not one step back' rule in the final days – until, that is, he himself orders a strategic withdrawal from Matrenino in *General Panfilov's Reserve*.

At the same time, Momysh-uly strives to motivate his men, especially those prone to panic or even desertion under fire. Transmitting Panfilov's philosophy that a commander should try to save rather than squander the lives of his men, he reminds them why they are fighting the war.[16] He underlines the basic necessity to kill the enemy in order to survive themselves. This seems to be contrary to Moscow's expectations of Red Army soldiers, which is to sacrifice themselves if necessary for the 'motherland'. Giving up their lives for Moscow may have proved difficult to expect of troops from Central Asia, however. Momysh-uly still tells his men that they are fighting for the 'motherland', which he defines differently from the official version. According to him, it is not some abstract place, or the Soviet Union as a whole, or even their native republic, but the men themselves and their own families.[17] He succeeds in training his troops so well that, when they engage closely with the enemy, they exceed all expectations with fewer deaths than anticipated thanks to their commander's careful strategy. Any deaths are not, however, in vain, as they manage to hold up the German advance until the arrival of reinforcements and the winter weather, which eventually drives the enemy into retreat.[18]

Momysh-uly, according to Bek, makes good use of his reliable political officers who boost morale and are ready to take command if necessary. This positive portrayal of political officers indicated a nod to the official censor. The tone of the whole series of Bek's works follows the officially recommended parameters of socialist realism in Soviet literature of the period. According to this formulaic system, a generally young and spontaneous hero is mentored by an older and wiser character as he strives to overcome almost impossible odds, learns through his mistakes and matures into a stronger, more ideologically committed leader.[19] In this respect, the self-critical and proud junior officer comes of age in Bek's documentaries, increasing in confidence through lessons learned in action and from Panfilov. The men also gain in combat experience, despite some initial wobbles, becoming less afraid of the enemy as their confidence in their leader increases. By the end of the series, Momysh-uly is promoted to command a regiment.[20] By 1945 he had in fact become a colonel, despite suffering from battle wounds which served to shorten his military career. Unlike the Twenty-eight, though, he was not made a Hero of the Soviet Union in his lifetime.

A key aspect of Bek's works is his attention to Momysh-uly's mental processes as he develops his awareness of battle strategy and military tactics. Learning from Panfilov the importance of allocating time to thinking through his battle plan, he also tries to put himself in the mind of the German commander. From the success of volley fire from an audacious defensive 'lozenge' of troops to Panfilov's favourite spiral defensive manoeuvre likened to a coiled spring, Momysh-uly realizes that he is waging a psychological war with the enemy, whose result depends not merely on superiority of manpower or arms.[21] Much of the works are educational from this point of view, as Momysh-uly apparently teaches both his scribe and the reader about modern warfare.

The reader learns the importance of an orderly retreat and the need for the preservation of communications links at the height of battle. Good morale and the self-confidence of the troops are key to both Panfilov's and Momysh-uly's leadership. This is contrasted with the poor discipline of the Germans who are overconfident, sleeping without watch after pillaging a village. Their luxury food items are compared with the sparse Red Army rations, as the defending troops are prepared to eat horse meat when desperate, while the Germans steal food from Russian peasants.[22] Too dependent upon their overstretched supply chains, they further compromise their Blitzkrieg strategy by their lack of winter uniform.

Many socialist realist portrayals of life in the Soviet Union include female companions on the hero's journey to full maturity. Bek's final volume was no exception. Having been ousted from the battalion by Momysh-uly on their first encounter, determined civilian Variia becomes, over the course of just a few days, a combat nurse able to march in the ranks with the men. In her progression she earns the respect of Momysh-uly as both their characters evolve for the better. It is doubtful whether this encounter was based on reality, betraying rather a literary device on the part of Bek, who uses Variia's character to top and tail *General Panfilov's Reserve*. Nineteen-year-old Variia displays an emotion somewhat less than military during her final meeting with Momysh-uly, despite his call to his men to protect her in a paternal manner.[23]

As expected, the father figure to Momysh-uly is none other than Major General Ivan Panfilov, the divisional commander. While not the actual hero of the works, Panfilov is a constant presence looking over Momysh-uly's shoulder and watching his back in the vein of a socialist realist mentor, grooming his protégé for military advancement. A round-shouldered veteran with heavy eyebrows and 'small, almond-shaped eyes', Panfilov is depicted as a Tatar. Despite his wisdom and worries, he enjoys simple pleasures, relishing his superior Kazbek cigarettes, a cup of tea and even a dish of *plov* (rice and meat) eaten Central Asian style with the hands. This agile, if greying, soldier – an artistic hybrid of ethnicities – has full lips, a small Russian nose and Mongolian cheek-bones, and is apparently at home across the Soviet Union.[24]

Panfilov is preoccupied with the passing of time, constantly consulting and rubbing the glass of his watch as he plays for time in keeping the Germans at bay. 'Time', smiles Panfilov in the end, 'We gained time!'[25] As Momysh-uly demonstrates that he has indeed graduated from Panfilov's personal field military academy, it is time for the general to die. Momysh-uly has learnt to treat his men like his horse – gently urging them on and rewarding them, with less harshness than he initially showed. Panfilov, Momysh-uly's personal *aksakal*, dies on 18 November 1941, the day before his division was honoured as a guards unit, to be lauded by the state as an innovator and master of modern defence tactics. Bek even massages the storyline to confect a meeting of the two protagonists the previous day, neatly drawing together the surviving characters and the various threads which run through the four volumes.[26]

Bek's literary creativity vis-à-vis women and imagined conversations is perhaps to be expected of the experienced author who sought – and received – the praise of his peers, while his works of documentary fiction were at the mercy of the official censor. However, his artistic licence and interest in ideology serve perhaps to detract from Momysh-uly's real rather ambiguous character by over-emphasizing the officer's Kazakh background: his subject certainly wishes that Bek would not exaggerate his Asian characteristics.[27] The tone of the 'scribe' is often quite patronizing – that of a Russian superior to an ethnic Kazakh. The scribe's own 'hero' is introduced at the start of *General Panfilov's Reserve*, before the reader finishes the Battle of Moscow alongside him. 'My terrible Baurzhan!' the scribe says laughing at the end, proceeding to reinforce the fact that his character is the fruit of the author's own imagination as his final volume takes leave of 'my Kazakh'.[28]

In this way, Bek, the author, takes over Momysh-uly's very identity, forcing him to speak and act at his will. Momysh-uly, in contrast, entered the agreement as if Bek were in fact just a scribe. Momysh-uly, the military commander, demanded control over his own story, as an active participant, rather than as a junior partner and tool for Bek's literary agenda. Bek's overt slights and literary artifices may have pleased his target audience across the Soviet Union, but they laid the groundwork for future post-war disagreements between the two one-time collaborators.[29]

Baurzhan Momysh-uly, as a respected war veteran, decided to set the record straight and write his own account of his military career, free from any artistic influence. Thanks to his new degree of fame accorded by Bek's oeuvre, Momysh-uly's several memoirs, with the subtitle 'An officer's notes', appeared in the 1950s.[30] It was probably their publication which pushed Bek to complete the last two volumes of his quartet: *A Few Days* and *General Panfilov's Reserve*, several years after his original *Volokolamsk Highway*. These ripostes to Momysh-uly were a product of the Thaw in Soviet literature, a short period in the Khrushchev era when it was possible to publish literature which did not so stringently conform with official Soviet guidelines. Translated into several languages, the eminently readable and personal narratives reached a wide audience.

Unsurprisingly, in this memorial ping-pong of personal memoir versus fictionalized documentary, Momysh-uly responded to Bek's *General Panfilov's Reserve* with a further memoir about General Panfilov.[31] The latter is not only a tribute to the late commander of the 316th Division but also a first-person account by Momysh-uly of his own dealings with the general. Intended for the general public, as a shortened version of his more academic military textbooks, it details – like Bek's version – his initial head-hunting by Panfilov, when Momysh-uly was working as a senior instructor in the Kazakh War Commission at the start of the war, as the 316th was being formed: 'This is how I met Ivan Vasil'evich Panfilov for the first time', writes Momysh-uly, as he defines their relationship in the first person.[32] Momysh-uly takes credit for several conversations with Rokossovkii, commander of the 16th Army but does not support Bek's account of a meeting with Panfilov on the day before his death. A nurse is indeed mentioned at the end of Momysh-uly's work, almost supporting Bek's narrative. The nurse in question is not, however, Variia, but a rather similar-sounding Valia, Panfilov's eighteen-year-old daughter, who was also serving in the 316th Division. Valia (Valentina) Panfilova went on to produce her own memoir of Panfilov: *My Father*.[33]

With his works, Momysh-uly at last had the opportunity to define his own military identity. He wrote in Russian – not so much a denunciation of his ethnicity as to emphasize his Sovietness while appealing to a wider audience than just his fellow Kazakhs. As an amateur writer, however, his readership was not as wide as Bek's more convincing fiction, appealing mainly to military academics and becoming prescribed reading for officers in countries as diverse as Cuba and Israel, particularly his influential work about the psychology of modern warfare which continued to develop Panfilov's maxims.[34]

According to Bek, Momysh-uly states that his story needs to be recorded for future generations, to ensure that 'Those who fall like warriors will not be forgotten by their country'.[35] This may have been a memory war between two men, the author and the officer, but it also played a part in the construction of memory of the Battle of Moscow. Despite the dearth of information about other contemporary events, Bek's work in particular zooms in on one battalion in one small corner of the protracted conflict. While not of the literary stature of Il'ia Erenburg or Konstantin Simonov, Bek nonetheless succeeded in bringing to the attention of the whole Soviet Union the undemonstrative heroism of Central Asian troops, recording how men from Kazakhstan and Kyrgyzstan courageously helped to defend the Soviet capital. It is noteworthy, though, that Bek does not mention the famous twenty-eight riflemen, although Momysh-uly notes, 'Subsequently we learned that the German tanks had been encountered there by another artillery regiment.'[36] Bek was therefore not guilty of jumping on the bandwagon of writers extolling the manufactured heroes, but does allude to several cases when men of the 1073rd Battalion took out small groups of enemy tanks around the same time. In this respect, his works are indeed more truthful than many, while still not living up to Momysh-uly's high expectations of unvarnished (non-socialist) realism in literature.

War films

Leonid Brezhnev's war cult of the 1960s and 1970s also brought a deluge of war films. The Panfilov Division did not escape attention, as plans were made for a film based on the works of Aleksandr Bek, to be directed by Kazakh Mazhit Begalin. More than simply artistic disagreements emerged, however, as Bek realized that Begalin was populating Momysh-uly's battalion with rather more Central Asian actors than he would have liked. As Bek withdrew his support for the project, Begalin, himself a war veteran, turned to Momysh-uly, the original source for Bek's *Volokolamsk Highway* series. Inspired by the professional soldier rather than the writer, Begalin created a rather bland black-and-white film, which nonetheless proved popular across the Soviet Union.[37]

Begalin's *Za nami Moskva* (Moscow is behind us), 1967, takes its name from Momysh-uly's memoir *Za nami Moskva: zapiski ofitsera* (Moscow is behind us: An officer's notes) of 1958. Covering much of the same ground as Bek's four works, it introduces the older veteran Momysh-uly at a ceremony of remembrance at the Eternal Flame in the Aleksandrovskii Gardens adjacent to the Kremlin wall in Moscow. Momysh-uly, walking with the aid of a stick thanks to his leg wound, also attends an exhibition of war memorabilia, which prompts his memories of the Battle of Moscow. Demonstrating his early frustration with his inexperienced and lax troops, the film covers their development into a fighting force to be reckoned with as they take on the enemy on several occasions. Momysh-uly runs constantly from trench to trench during the action, interspersed with a few key meetings with Panfilov and even Rokossovskii. Thanks to Panfilov, he learns the difference between being cruel to his men and demanding of them, as Panfilov urges him to nurture them. While there is no sign of nurse Variia or the execution of Sergeant Barambaev in the film, the viewer is treated to a highly creative episode as the exhausted men march into Volokolamsk singing. The *dombra* signals Central Asian troops, while the Red Army and the German army both enjoy their own musical themes. Successful engagements with enemy tanks are shown, but never a last stand which could have been attributable to the mythical twenty-eight.[38]

With his film, Begalin ably demonstrated the 'friendship of the peoples', showing his pan-Soviet viewers how the state capital, Moscow, was defended thanks to the courage of Central Asians. Militarily, all was not equal, though. The army hierarchy is obvious, with Russians Rokossovskii and Panfilov commanding a Kazakh junior officer – albeit played by Kyrgyz actor Asanbek Umuraliev – in charge of troops from southern Kazakhstan, leaving the Kyrgyz rank-and-file troops in the division out of the picture entirely. In a brief conversation with a young Russian couple the veteran Momysh-uly achieves some seniority and respect, however, as his memory of the war is patently more vivid than the photographs in the exhibition. In this way, memory of the war is successfully transmitted to the younger generation. The war veteran appears to be haunted by his memories, however, as the ghostly faces of the dead men appear in front of him as the film closes.

Begalin was also responsible for a further film about the first famous female Kazakh war hero, Manshuk Mametova. His *Pesn' o Manshuk* (The ballad of Manshuk) appeared in 1970, also produced in Alma-Ata. Depicting the events of Manshuk's final day as she and her comrades take on superior enemy forces, it reinforces Begalin's efforts to promote understanding of the role of Central Asian troops during the war.[39] Manshuk's heroic compatriot, sniper Aliia Moldagulova, was also famously commemorated in poetry and a well-known song performed in both Kazakh and Russian by Roza Rymbaeva in a creative union of two of Kazakhstan's favourite daughters.[40]

Monumental memorialization

A major statue to Major General Ivan Panfilov was erected months after his death in Frunze, where he had been Kyrgyz military commander. This monument in Panfilov Park was the first of several to appear across Kazakhstan and Kyrgyzstan, where Panfilov's division had been raised, notably the statue erected to Panfilov in Alma-Ata in 1968, as the Brezhnev-era war cult started to gain momentum.

Soviet propagandists continued their field day in the post-war period as a street in the Kazakh capital and a town in a nearby area of Kazakhstan were also named after the iconic commander. Furthermore, a modest museum adjacent to Panfilov Park is dedicated to the Panfilov Division and currently run by Panfilov's granddaughter.

Busts of the famous twenty-eight are to be found across southern Kazakhstan and northern Kyrgyzstan, with many examples in today's Almaty and Karakol. Amongst an avenue of memorials in Almaty's Park of the Twenty-eight Panfilov Guardsmen stands one to their supposed leader, Vasilii

FIGURE 9.1 *Panfilov statue in Panfilov Park, Bishkek (1942).*

FIGURE 9.2 *Detail of Panfilov men in action, Panfilov statue, Bishkek.*

FIGURE 9.3 *Panfilov memorial, Panfilov Park, Almaty (1968).*

Klochkov, the political officer. His words of encouragement, as 'recorded' by journalist Krivitskii, are engraved beneath one of the largest monuments in Central Asia: 'Velika Rossiia. A otstupat' nekuda. Pozadi Moskva!' (Russia is vast, but there is nowhere to retreat to; Moscow is behind [us]!). The monument shows Panfilov's fearless twenty-eight men hurling themselves into action in the park in the centre of Almaty named after them. Almost like comic book superheroes, the men burst out of a map of the Soviet Union, denoting both a variety of birthplaces and the super-state they fought to defend. Erected in 1975 on the thirtieth anniversary of the end of the war, it towers over visitors while guarding the eternal flame nearby.

Schools and even small towns were named after the twenty-eight new heroes. The village of Sazanovki in the Issyk-Kul' province of Kyrgyzstan, for example, was renamed Anan'evo in 1942 after its famous hero. Similarly, the village of Konkin lies on the southern shore of the lake, named after another Panfilov hero, Grigorii Konkin. In this way, remembrance of the war was given a positive local spin by the Soviet state anxious to keep its peripheral republics from recalling the dreadful human cost of the Second World War.

In contrast to these local monuments in Central Asia, a Russian memorial to Panfilov's men was erected on the thirtieth anniversary of the end of the war on the alleged spot of their mythical exploit outside Dubosekovo. Depicting groups of men of various ethnicities watching for the enemy's approach, it is less dynamic in style than the dramatic monument in Alma-Ata, covering a vast expanse of open ground relatively accessible to monumental tourists visiting the site on a day-trip from Moscow. In shaping

FIGURE 9.4 *Monument to Panfilov's twenty-eight men, Almaty (1975).*

FIGURE 9.5 *Bust of Grigorii Konkin, Karakol.*

FIGURE 9.6 *Bust of Nikolai Anan'ev, Bishkek.*

FIGURE 9.7 *Monument to the Panfilov heroes, Dubosekovo (1975). Copyright Ivo Mijnssen (2013).*

the visual form of remembrance, the state retained the overall narrative of the war myth, while encouraging the citizens of Central Asia to maintain pride in their own Soviet heroes in an alignment of vested interests.

Post-Soviet international relations

After the collapse of the Soviet Union in 1991, the independent Central Asian states joined many other post-Soviet republics in the newly formed Commonwealth of Independent States (CIS). Once tightly united within the USSR, they inexorably diverged in their own political directions and governance in their new incarnations, remaining loosely connected largely thanks to economic pragmatism. It is evident that all the modern Central Asian states are far less politically isolated now than in the pre-war years, with the exception of Turkmenistan, which still maintains its political distance from the rest of the world.

Leaders of the modern Central Asian republics have increasingly rejected Slavic influence and promoted nationalism through the celebration of their own traditional culture. In a similar manner, the five new nation-states have reclaimed their Islamic religion in a reversal of the Soviet state's suppression of religion. The influence of Turkey, Iran and Saudi Arabia has notably replaced that of Russia in this respect, as new mosques and universities spring up across the region. Islamic sentiment is particularly marked in the south and west, particularly in Uzbekistan and Tajikistan on the border with Afghanistan, while some Russian Orthodox churches remain in Kazakhstan and northern Kyrgyzstan – vestigial reminders of the colonial era serving the remaining minority of ethnic Russians.

All of the new republics retained some use of the Russian language after independence to aid inter-ethnic communication, although Russian remains an official language only in modern Kyrgyzstan and Tajikistan, which have also retained the Cyrillic script for local languages. Cultivating their new identity, Kazakhstan, Uzbekistan and Turkmenistan have rejected the Cyrillic alphabet and have implemented or are in the process of implementing the Roman script for their own languages, thereby disassociating themselves from their Soviet legacy. This move also reflects the increasing dominance of English as the second foreign language for young people, with university courses in German, Turkish, Japanese and Korean catering for new waves of tourism and business opportunities.

Different spheres of influence now dominate Central Asia, as the United Nations, the European Union and the United States plough resources into non-governmental organizations. Where once the Soviet Union prioritized the construction of new roads and railway tracks, dams and hydro-electric power stations, China is now engaged on huge infrastructure projects through its Belt and Road Initiative projects across Kazakhstan and Kyrgyzstan. Many wartime measures to exploit the natural resources of the region are still evident, however, especially the mines and factories which remained after the war to boost the region's Soviet economy. Russian military bases established during the war still exist in Kazakhstan, Kyrgyzstan and Tajikistan. Most house air force units, for example, the Russian bases at Kant in Kyrgyzstan and outside Dushanbe in Tajikistan. Especially prestigious is the space-launching facility at Baikonur in Kazakhstan, dominated by Russia and used by several other countries sending astronauts to the International Space Station. The future of international space collaboration has been called into question, however, since the Russian invasion of Ukraine in 2022.

The submarine research facility developed during the war outside Przheval'sk has moved along the shore of Lake Issyk-Kul' to continue its work testing anti-submarine weapons in waters that never freeze. These strategically placed Russian military establishments demonstrate the interdependence of Kazakhstan, Kyrgyzstan and Tajikistan with modern Russia in matters of defence and security. Uzbekistan and Turkmenistan prefer in principle not to maintain military relations with Russia through the Collective Security Treaty Organization (CSTO), NATO's equivalent in the post-Soviet space, despite Moscow's obvious wish to retain its influence across all of its near neighbours. Uzbekistan has, however, recently approved the construction of a nuclear power station by Russia, a sign perhaps of some economic self-interest in the country. At the same time, migrant workers from Central Asia depend on employment in Russian cities to bolster the domestic economy in Uzbekistan, Tajikistan and Kyrgyzstan, a sign of the continuing uneven relationship between Russia and its southern neighbours.

Although the Kazakh economy has become largely free of dependence on Russia, thanks to its rich coal and oil fields, its main oil pipeline to the West is vulnerable to Russian influence as it reaches the Black Sea at the Russian port of Novorossiisk. It is notable also that Russian troops stepped in to assist the Kazakh government in January 2022, under the CSTO agreement. Relations between Russia and the Central Asian states of Kazakhstan, Uzbekistan and Kyrgyzstan are on a less secure footing since Russia's invasion of Ukraine, however, when these republics welcomed without question an exodus of Russian men fleeing from forced state conscription. In early 2023, Russia's influence seems to be on the wane in Central Asia.

Remembrance and the Soviet legacy

With independence it became possible for the new republics to forge their own identity and re-examine their relationship with Russia with respect to the interpretation of history and remembrance of the Second World War. Crucially, the new nation states had to decide whether to retain the many Soviet war myths around Central Asian participation in the war or to construct their own, revised history of the twentieth century.

Since the accession of President Putin in 2000, Russia has re-introduced state-led collective remembrance, creating a second war cult which has returned remembrance of the war to the heart of domestic politics, as victory in the Second World War remains virtually the only unifying factor across the vast country. Some Central Asian states have followed suit, if to a lesser extent – notably Kazakhstan, whose population retains a significant proportion of ethnic Russians. Others, however, have markedly diverged from Russian memorial policy, preferring to remember the war in their own way, or even to downgrade its memorial importance in favour of other key events in their national history. Just as few Russian history books mention the role of Central Asia in the war, so the Second World War is consigned to very few paragraphs in most Central Asian school textbooks, as if the war in Europe is better forgotten – an aspect of the Soviet past too far away in time and space to merit much historical significance. Remembrance of the Second World War is not a matter of national identity in the modern Central Asian republics, as it is in the Russian Federation. Of all the current post-Soviet republics, it is Russia – with Belarus – which has the largest political investment in the 1945 victory.

Modern monumentalization

Today's memorial climate is evolving fast, as the modern Central Asian republics continue to diverge from the state-sponsored remembrance in Russia. In contrast to the marked tendency to remove Soviet war memorials in Eastern Europe, most monuments in Central Asia still stand. They sometimes remain centres for commemoration ceremonies, if often allowed to fall into disrepair as demands on the region's economies have put pressure on local councils. The ubiquitous eternal flames installed in the Soviet era have also been extinguished in many cases, remaining permanently alight only in major centres. The dilapidated complex in the Kyrgyz village of Konkin, for example, named after one of Panfilov's twenty-eight men, retains the cold ghost of a 'flame' in the centre of a Soviet-style red star, replicating the Red Army symbol on the helmets of the immortalized soldiers keeping watch.

In contrast, the eternal flame beneath the gigantic statue of Panfilov's twenty-eight men in central Almaty is kept constantly alight, a site for wedding photographs and of pilgrimage for the city's residents around Victory Day. The more modern war memorial in central Bishkek, established in 1985 for the fortieth anniversary of the end of the war, highlights rather the national characteristics at the heart of the Kyrgyz nation. Shaped as a stylistic yurt, it incorporates the *tyndyk*, which takes central place on the national flag. This symbol represents the chimney hole at the apex of a traditional yurt – a circular opening which also binds together the wooden poles holding the structure together. The *tyndyk* therefore has both a practical and metaphorical significance, allowing the smoke from the family fire to leave the home, while also binding together the many tribes of Kyrgyzstan represented by the supportive wooden poles. In the Bishkek monument, the

FIGURE 9.8 *War memorial and unlit eternal flame in the village of Konkin, Kyrgyzstan.*

FIGURE 9.9 *Constantly alight: the eternal flame in Almaty's Panfilov Park.*

tyndyk sits majestically above the constantly guarded eternal flame in the central position where the domestic hearth would be sited.

This monument was the site of some perceived disrespect on a chilly November day in 2016, when Bishkek workmen filmed themselves frying potatoes and eggs on the eternal flame.[41] This blatant breach of memorial etiquette incurred some tut-tutting on social media – much less of a response than would have occurred for a similar incident in Moscow, where recent

FIGURE 9.10 *Central war memorial, Bishkek (1985).*

laws enforce the government's line on mandatory respect for veterans and the state's received version of war history and memory.

More obvious differences are evident in Uzbekistan, where former president Islam Karimov's government led a prolonged campaign against Soviet war memorials after independence. Mourning the death of so many Uzbeks pressed into service for the Soviet Union, Uzbekistan prefers to commemorate the dead rather than focus on the celebration of military victory as in Russia. The unopposed destruction of some Soviet war memorials in Ashgabat, the capital of Turkmenistan, has made way for new development, including a new 'People's Remembrance' memorial complex. Similarly, several monuments which had stood in Uzbekistan since the 1970s have been demolished over the years, occasionally being replaced by more generic memorials simply advocating remembrance.[42] In recognition of the sacrifice made by Uzbekistan, rather than of the Soviet Union as a whole, a monument of a grieving mother represents the loss of Uzbek lives. A renewed rapprochement with Russia's President Putin by Uzbekistan's President Shavkat Mirziyoyev with respect to remembrance of the war was signalled, however, with the opening in 2020 of a brand new memorial complex in Tashkent named Victory Park. Consisting of a large Soviet-style monument sitting above a hill resembling a burial mound, it serves both as a focus for commemoration of the dead and an educational museum about Uzbekistan's role in the war.

One narrative of remembrance remains in common with the Soviet times, as Uzbeks take pride in recalling the hospitality shown to evacuees during the war, notably to the fifteen children said to have been adopted by blacksmith Shaakhmed Shamakhmudov and his wife, Bakhri Akramova. Their devotion is commemorated in a distinctive monument originally erected in the centre of Tashkent on Ploshchad' Druzhby (Friendship Square) in 1982 and retained following independence, albeit after relocation.[43] This historical myth remains probably the only way that Uzbekistan can maintain pride in its collective war effort, although the generosity of ethnic minorities has long been written out of Russia's own national war narrative.

Many films produced over the years in Tashkent – a city still famous for its cinema culture – reinforce the official memory of hospitality, tolerance, multiethnicity and simple humanity of the people of Uzbekistan during the war years. In 1982 director Damir Salimov created the stereotypical *Leningradtsy, deti moi . . .* (People of Leningrad, my children . . .), the title recalling the poems of Akhmatova and Jabaev about the evacuees from Leningrad.[44] Continuing the theme, several documentaries have appeared in the years since independence. One of the most recent benefited from an extensive prior advertising campaign. *Bol'shoe serdtse Tashkenta* (Tashkent's Big Heart), 2016, records a series of interviews with evacuees and their descendants, interspersed with wartime footage of evacuation trains amidst the bombing of Leningrad and Kiev. Particularly concentrating on Jewish refugees and children, it employs – if without attribution – John

Williams's haunting music composed for the film *Schindler's List*,[45] inviting a direct cinematic comparison with the rescue of Jews from the Nazi regime under different circumstances. The Soviet operation was on a much larger scale than that effected by Oskar Schindler, however, leading *Tashkent's Big Heart* to examine the history of the evacuations as one of the greatest Soviet wartime achievements. The implication throughout is that Uzbeks alone in the Soviet Union had hearts big enough to welcome strangers into their homes: indeed, the comparison of the warm welcome by Uzbeks of children from the western regions of the country is seen as a *podvig* (exploit) on a par with their compatriots suffering bombardment and exile. The film is in Russian, rendering it accessible to a wide audience. Present-day Uzbek citizens surely have their pride boosted by the film, which portrays Tashkent as a 'saviour city', propagating the national myth of the wartime welcome with no serious interrogation of the privations of children in exile, nor of any racism towards Jewish refugees.[46]

In a similar fashion, in 2012 the city of Bishkek (formerly Frunze) erected a new memorial complex dedicated to the evacuees arriving there from besieged Leningrad. In common with Uzbekistan, this memorial also recalls the indisputable hospitality of Kyrgyzstan during the war years. In the main, however, Kyrgyzstan has chosen more recently to monumentalize the pre-Soviet historical struggle of 1916 at various sites across the country, preferring to focus remembrance on those who resisted colonial Russia rather than on their shared wartime experience, in a re-prioritization of communal memory. Also coming to the fore are the Kyrgyz victims of Stalin's pre-war purges, who are increasingly commemorated, in common with similar monumentalization in Russia itself.[47]

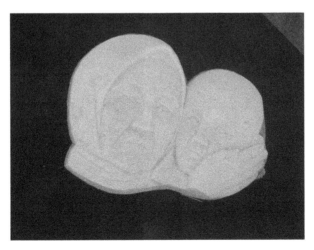

FIGURE 9.11 *Victory Park, Bishkek, 'To the courage of the citizens of Leningrad and the generosity of the Kyrgyz people' (2012).*

This trend is evident in Uzbekistan, too, with the erection of a new memorial complex in 2014 in Tashkent to those victims of Soviet Stalinist repression and the institution of the annual Day of Memory of Victims of Repression on 31 August. In this way the new republics are charting an independent course, celebrating their freedom from colonial oppression.[48] In Kazakhstan, also, the state has opted to customize monumental memory of the war in common with Uzbekistan and Kyrgyzstan in an effort to forge its new identity. The legendary female heroes, Manshuk and Aliia, were finally commemorated in Almaty in 1997, in a period when the newly independent republic of Kazakhstan was actively seeking its own identity outside the Soviet Union.

Although famous in his own right as a Red Army officer and author, Senior Lieutenant Baurzhan Momysh-uly was not made a Hero of the Soviet Union during the war, nor even in his own lifetime, possibly because he was known to the authorities as a Kazakh nationalist. His name does not even appear in the official encyclopaedia about the war published in 1985, notwithstanding the inclusion of items about Aleksandr Bek's works.[49] Once the political climate started to change with the prospect of independence for Kazakhstan, however, he became a prime candidate for a posthumous honour, which was awarded in 1990, eight years after his death. A statue appeared first in Astana in 2008, with a further statue erected in Almaty's Panfilov Park in 2010 on the centenary of his birth. In this way, the legend

FIGURE 9.12 *Memorial to Manshuk Mametova and Aliia Moldagulova, Almaty (1997).*

FIGURE 9.13 *Momysh-uly memorial, Panfilov Park, Almaty (2010).*

of the Panfilov heroes was finally expanded to embrace the man who spent his latter years determined to tell what he always controversially defended as the unvarnished truth about the role of Panfilov's regiments in the Battle of Moscow.

The myth of Panfilov's twenty-eight men today

It is in some respects strange that the story of the twenty-eight Panfilov Division heroes is still current today. A comprehensive post-war investigation held in 1948 proved that the report had been invented by journalists to include an almost random list of supposed participants in the action, who were subsequently made posthumous Heroes of the Soviet Union.[50] The state was so embarrassed at the commission's findings, however, that its conclusions were suppressed for decades, particularly as the myth remained useful in reminding the citizens of Kazakhstan and Kyrgyzstan of the alleged role played by their own war heroes in the defence of Moscow. In the post-war years the myth was set in the stone of multiple monuments and even embedded in the pages of the authoritative encyclopaedia of Soviet war history.[51] As all the protagonists were deemed to have died during the action, nobody was able to cast doubt on the Soviet state's preferred version of events. When a few of the supposed participants did surface after the war, they were rapidly silenced by the state in its usual heavy-handed manner.

The general public only started to become aware of some debate about the veracity of the myth in the increasing governmental transparency of the *glasnost'* period of the late 1980s. By the 1990s sufficient facts were circulating in the newly independent republics for historical revisionists to question the myth entirely. Senior Russian archivist Sergei Mironenko, a whistleblower who exposed the falsity of the myth in 2015, lost his job for his pains.[52] Despite widespread debunking, the myth of Panfilov's twenty-eight men still remains popular in Central Asia, endorsed by President Putin and once again prevalent in the mass media, having captured the public imagination. For the Russian state, the exploit represents a typical David and Goliath story – the success of a handful of men against the overpowering might of the enemy. It also cements the relationship between Russia and Central Asia for the younger generation. National pride ensures that the majority of citizens of Central Asia also cling on to the myth of the self-sacrifice of ordinary servicemen. In the absence of hero-cities in Central Asia, the popular story of contrived heroism continues to provide a positive focus for remembrance of the war dead.

The memorial situation in Russia is still dominated by President Putin's war cult. Remembrance of the Second World War is so crucial to Putin's political success that Russia legally brooks no contradiction of the black-and-white assertion of victory against the enemy. Historians have even been accused of peddling 'false history' for daring to question some less than flattering aspects of Soviet history, for example, the treatment by the state of returning Soviet POWs, or the rape and pillage by Red Army troops in Germany during the final weeks of the war. With the threat of potential criminal charges, some Russian historians now apply a degree of self-censorship in their publications.

The debate about the Panfilov myth resurfaced in 2016 with the production in Russia of a new film: *Dvatsat' vosem' panfilovtsev* (Panfilov's Twenty-eight).[53] The film prompted a new conversation between viewers of all generations in Russia and Central Asia, as historical purists argued with proponents of a black-and-white artistic version of the exploit as originally reported by war correspondents. It is relevant that the film was made in St Petersburg rather than Kazakhstan: the war cult of the Putin era demands straightforward examples of idealized patriotism and national (i.e. Soviet) heroes as role-models for the youth of today.[54] The appropriation of Kazakh heroes by Russian film-makers did not seem to cause any embarrassment for former president Nursaltan Nazarbaev,[55] however, although Kazakhstan recently screened its own television series around Aleksandr Bek's works promoting Momysh-uly's role in the 316th Division's action around Volokolamsk.[56]

In both Kazakhstan and Kyrgyzstan, a deliberate distortion of memory continues as the Panfilov myth is presented in school textbooks to the younger generation as uncontested fact. For over sixty years the exploit of Panfilov's twenty-eight men has been embedded in school curricula, tugging at the emotions of budding patriots with an unnuanced moral appeal. Despite the fact that old, Soviet-era school history textbooks are very gradually being replaced by newer editions, year nine pupils in Kazakh schools read, for example, that 'the immortal exploit of a group of anti-tank troops from the 1075th Rifle Regiment, who stopped the enemy in November 1941 at Dubosekovo station, is known to all the world'. Two years later, older students are taught through modern history textbooks more about Momysh-uly's path to hero status, alongside details of Manshuk and other famous national heroes.[57]

History of the Second World War in Kyrgyzstan is similarly taught through the perspective of heroic deeds. Here, year nine pupils are taught about the heroic leadership of political officer Vasilii Klochkov at Dubosekovo station, as his men showed 'fearless courage in the fight against the enemy'. A detailed description of the action reveals how the men of Panfilov's division deployed anti-tank weapons, grenades and Molotov cocktails to destroy large numbers of enemy tanks and troops. As in the equivalent Kazakh text, Klochkov's alleged motivating words are cited: 'Russia is vast, but there is nowhere to retreat to; Moscow is behind [us]!' Year eleven students in Kyrgyzstan go on to read more details of individual heroes, a Soviet-style approach to the teaching of history which is also evident in some aspects of university research.[58]

In an effort to draw attention to their own national heroes, these highly patriotic – if partly unreliable – Kyrgyz texts are closely based on Soviet-era works and dominated by the biographies of heroes, including Nikolai Anan'ev and Grigorii Konkin from the Issyk-Kul' province. A further Panfilov hero, Duishenkul Shopokov, had a town and a school named after him and a postage stamp published. It is evident from the erection of a new bust of Shopokov in Volokolamsk as recently as 2015 that the attitude to Panfilov's men in both Central Asia and Russia remains in general almost as unquestioningly positive as in the days of the Soviet Union, supported by leaders and the majority of the population basking in the prestige accorded by the ghosts of Panfilov's heroes.[59]

The teaching of history in universities

Despite many continuities in the teaching of history during the Soviet era and in the independent republics of Central Asia, Kyrgyzstan, at least, is endeavouring to rid itself of some of the old Soviet myths while promoting its own pre-Soviet past. The Kyrgyz presidential *Muras* (Legacy) commission was established in Bishkek in 2012 to reconstruct the history syllabus in schools and universities in order to reflect the state's revised priorities. This marked what the president hoped would be a renaissance in the transmission of the republic's cultural and historical heritage to the younger generation.[60] Similarly, former president Nazarbaev of Kazakhstan instigated an educational programme to promote the 'modernization of collective knowledge' in order that Kazakh students should become more familiar with their own national history.[61] These measures are an attempt to reverse the trend amongst young people perceived by most history teachers to absorb historical 'facts' from Western and Russian films, and to inculcate in them a sense of patriotic pride.

Across the region, the interpretation of Central Asia's role in the Second World War is open to revision in the context of world, rather than Soviet history. In this respect, the treatment of the history of the war contrasts with that currently legally enforced in Russia, where the law restricts any research or the dissemination of so-called 'subversive' historical narratives which may be at odds with the state's official version.

In Central Asia, though, the lack of nuance in teaching about the war at higher levels is gradually being addressed, as research lacunae are filled, despite the lack of state financial support and archival resources on home soil, as most Soviet military records remain in Moscow. Academics are starting to investigate more controversial topics, such as the treatment of POWs (on both sides), the involvement of the Turkestan Legion, collaboration in the occupied regions and the huge topic of the deportations which remained taboo throughout most of the Soviet period. Despite this new resolve and annual conferences devoted to the subject, however, academics are failing to change popular opinion about the war, which still relies largely on information disseminated from Soviet and Russian sources.

Victory Day

Victory Day in Russia largely follows the Soviet model of military parades in cities across the country. In Central Asia, however, Victory Day commemorations represent a barometer of political relations with Russia and President Putin himself. Over recent years, each individual republic has varied the circumstances of the events of 9 May depending on their desire to distance themselves from Soviet colonial history and prevailing Russian politics.

Some degree of divergence has been evident in Kazakhstan over recent years, where the parade is now held on 7 May, the anniversary of the creation of the independent republic's armed forces. Known as 'Defender of the Fatherland Day', it is entirely analogous to the anniversary in the former Soviet Union and today's Russia marked on 23 February. Commemoration of the war is still important on 9 May, if on a less military scale. The divergence of the two dates also affords an opportunity for the leaders of Russia and Kazakhstan to attend each other's ceremonies if wished. An insight into the measure of the political importance of the military parades in the two countries is afforded by the decisions in 2020, the seventy-fifth anniversary of the end of the war, to cancel the event in Kazakhstan, whereas in Russia it was merely postponed.

In Kyrgyzstan no commemorative events around Victory Day were held during the Covid-19 pandemic. Traditionally, though, Russian air force troops from the base in nearby Kant join the parade in Bishkek, while a further Russian uniformed presence from the military base on Lake Issyk-Kul' is usual in Karakol. Victory Day is not so clear-cut in Uzbekistan, though. In 1999 it was rebranded by President Karimaov – in a deliberate divergence from Russia – as the 'Day of Remembrance and Honour', instilling memory of the war dead with respect for those Uzbek war veterans still living.[62] As in all the Central Asian states, war veterans still receive gifts from the state on this occasion, although their number is now dwindling. The Day of Remembrance and Honour echoes the memorial square in Tashkent renamed accordingly in 1999.

In a similar fashion, President Saparmurat Niyazov of Turkmenistan renamed Victory Day in 2000 as the 'Day of Remembrance of the National Heroes of Turkmenistan in the 1941–5 war'. Appropriating memory of Turkmenistan's own fallen soldiers, few similarities with the Russian version were evident until 2020, when the first-ever military parade was held in Ashgabat, despite the Covid-19 pandemic (whose existence the country vehemently denied). Once again, tribute was paid in this way to Russia, as the impoverished state wooed its post-Soviet counterpart in a bid for economic and political support. Tajikistan followed suit in the same year, despite previous snubs to Russian influence on its national remembrance. In 2021, autocratic president Emomali Rahmon was the only foreign leader to attend Victory Day commemorations in Moscow.[63]

FIGURE 9.14 *Victory Day banner in Almaty, 2018, bearing Soviet symbolism.*

Despite some rapprochement between the post-Soviet nation states of the region and Russia, largely due to the pragmatic economic urgency to renew relations with the wealthier nation after the pandemic, memorial matters took a sudden change in direction in 2022, following Russia's controversial military invasion of Ukraine. In a noticeable sign of disapproval, parades were halted across the region except for minor events in Tajikistan. In this way the general lack of support for Moscow's war was made evident through the deployment of memory politics, as President Putin's latest war became openly ostracized in much of Central Asia. Allegiances continue to evolve, however. In May 2023 it was noticeable that the presidents of the five Central Asian republics were the only foreign leaders to attend Victory Day in Moscow, alongside the presidents of Armenia and Belarus.

The meaning of memory for the young

As the proportion of school time spent on learning about the Second World War has been reduced in most Central Asian states,[64] many pupils are becoming less interested in the topic as it becomes more and more distant in historical time. The main exception is the increase in participation of teenagers around Victory Day.

In 2005 a new tradition took root across Russia, when the orange-and-black-striped St George's ribbon was introduced as a symbol of war memory around Victory Day commemorations. Based upon the much older award made to military personnel in the reign of Catherine the Great, it is also a reminder of Stalin's Order of Glory, the medal awarded to rank-and-file soldiers during the war. Over the years of Putin's presidency, the St George's ribbon has become a symbol not only of remembrance and respect for war veterans but also of inter-generational social and political cohesion around Victory Day across much of the former Soviet Union and in Russian expatriate communities worldwide.[65] More recently, however, it has evolved into a nationalist symbol in the war against Ukraine, sometimes twisted into the 'Z' shape linked with Russian military forces.

The commemorative ribbon at first became relatively popular in some parts of Central Asia, especially in Kazakhstan with its higher density of ethnic Russians. Some customization of memory has become apparent, however, with the rise in nationalism and the concomitant desire to throw off aspects of Soviet history and domination. In Kazakhstan, for instance, a new ribbon appeared in 2015 – on the seventieth anniversary of the end of the war – in national blue and yellow colours, incorporating the motif from the country's flag.[66] Both ribbons were available for sale or distributed freely, although the new ribbon is far more acceptable to Muslim citizens, who find it difficult to accept the colonial-style imposition of a symbol involving the Russian Orthodox patron saint of Russia. According to some Kazakhs, their new ribbon commemorates specifically the war dead from Kazakhstan, as the republic strives to distance itself from a joint Kazakh–Russian military past.

New ribbons have been introduced in Kyrgyzstan, too, in the national colours of red and yellow. Here commemorative ribbons are less apparent than in Kazakhstan and often worn with a traditional Kyrgyz felt hat, the *kalpak*. A similar situation prevails in Uzbekistan, where a vocal minority opposes symbols connected to Stalin, seen as the arch-oppressor of the Uzbek people.[67] Uzbekistan also has taken the decision to avoid use of the Soviet term 'Great Patriotic War', preferring to locate the war globally as the 'Second World War'. As the states of Central Asia re-examine their relationship with their Soviet past, the external symbols of remembrance are being customized and re-defined for the younger post-colonial generation.

The Immortal Regiment

The death of most Second World War veterans has necessitated the introduction of new modes of remembrance across the republics of the former Soviet Union. Ordinary people have increasingly started to research their own family history – stimulated by school lessons and a burgeoning number of memorial websites. Russia's President Putin has appropriated

FIGURE 9.15 *Compromise in evidence in a combination of colours: Schoolchildren in Almaty on 7 May, wearing Russian St George's ribbons on their school blazers in Kazakh national colours, 2018.*

one new aspect of Victory Day from the ordinary people who instigated it in 2012. The *Bessmertnyi polk* (Immortal Regiment) procession takes place in major towns and cities across the post-Soviet sphere, as people march to a central war memorial holding portraits of their family members who took part in the war.[68] This subsidiary ritual soon became popular in Central Asia, providing virtually the only focus for family remembrance. Promoted in schools and universities, it attracted a high proportion of young people, often wearing replica Red Army uniforms. The main exception to this movement was in Tajikistan, where, after a trial run in 2016, it was declared the following year that it was contrary to Islamic culture to portray images of the deceased.[69] Just a few hundred dedicated citizens appeared on the streets of Dushanbe in 2018 and 2019, only for the procession to be reduced to an online presence in 2020 and 2021 as the Covid-19 pandemic swept across the region. Uzbek authorities are also concerned about the march – and indeed any public gatherings which may have a political agenda. Numbers in Tashkent – mainly young people again – therefore remain small.[70] Kazakhstan and Kyrgyzstan, though, always more closely aligned with Russia, have fewer religious scruples when it comes to such a popular and unifying inter-generational ritual. By 2022, however, attitudes to the Immortal Regiment procession, as indeed to Victory Day itself, had changed in Kazakhstan in line with its opposition to Russia's war in Ukraine. The Immortal Regiment was relegated to an online event, with no more rivers of citizens processing in the main cities.

Before the pandemic took hold in Central Asia, the Immortal Regiment attracted tens of thousands of participants in Bishkek, where the tradition was launched in 2013.[71] Taking their lead from the Kyrgyz president, school teachers accompanied their classes, groups of young friends processed together, while family groups took turns to hold aloft photographs of their ancestors. Fourteen-year-old Zhyklyz had always questioned her mother for watching the ubiquitous menu of war films broadcast on television in the lead-up to Victory Day, but was intensely moved by her first experience of participating in the march in Bishkek with a photograph of her grandfather.[72] Adults, too, had their own family stories to impart: the woman whose father had died outside Moscow in 1942, or the family whose grandfather had served in the Soviet Pacific Fleet based in Vladivostok. One woman carried pictures of both her father and uncle, with only the latter returning home after the war.

In Kazakhstan and Kyrgyzstan society deems it important, as in Russia, to propagate memory of the Second World War across generations. This has been noticeable during the days surrounding Victory Day, when schools introduced 'patriotic education', going to great lengths to involve children in activities teaching them about the war and the role of their own ancestors in it. Now this type of activity is severely reduced in Kazakhstan, in line with the state's lack of support for Russia's war with Ukraine. In previous years in the days leading up to Victory Day, school museums

FIGURES 9.16–9.19 *The Immortal Regiment, Bishkek, 2018.*

would spruce up their collections, with additional posters designed by participating classes. Many schools had their own 'wall of memory', where images of great-grandparents looked down upon their descendants. This memorial activity was supplemented by the plethora of digital memory sites which housed the stories of Soviet citizens as provided by their proud families. Those who were awarded medals were commemorated on official, centralized lists of honour. Older students donned military uniform to take turns standing on guard duty at key memorial sites in Almaty, for example in front of the monument to Manshuk and Aliia. Most children had the opportunity to enter war-themed competitions or to produce their own piece of creative writing, while some were invited to view war films. In contrast, some teachers now prefer to promote the theme of a 'peaceful world' to counteract the former emphasis on death and violence in evidence in early May. In the Bobuk School in Almaty, for example, the pacifist song 'Blowing in the Wind' provides a counterpoint to the military music played in previous years.[73]

On Victory Day itself, many schools used to assemble their youngsters for further commemorative events. Those few local veterans still alive are still invited to attend school concerts, while others receive charitable gifts. School-leavers from the Bobuk School in Almaty lay a wreath at the eternal flame, reciting poetry in Russian. In complete contrast, students from the Lenin School in Karakol attend a ceremony in Victory Park to hear a local mullah read prayers for the dead from the Koran in Arabic.

According to their teachers and parents, children vary in their response to these national ceremonies. Even before it was officially discouraged, one boy in Almaty refused to wear his St George's ribbon because he disliked the colonial connotations of the Soviet hammer and sickle adorning it,[74] while a girl in Bishkek was moved to tears when reciting a poem about the war dead in her school's museum.[75] Most children, however, now seem ambivalent, if not enthusiastic, about Victory Day, despite calls to accord it the respect demanded by the older, Soviet generations.

Still searching

It may seem obvious that, with fewer remaining war veterans and a decreasing appetite amongst the political leadership of some Central Asian states for remembering the Second World War with its links to colonial repression, commemorative events will diminish in future years – in marked contrast to the apparent situation in Russia. The individual soldier, a relatively unimportant person in the war, has not been altogether forgotten, however. One area of concern remains common to all former Soviet states: groups of interested people still continue to take part in search operations to recover bodies of the war dead from communal graves in the battlefields of the Soviet Western Front and give them a decent burial at home. Once a fallen Red Army soldier's body is exhumed, attempts are made to identify it before re-interment closer to home. A so-called *pasport zakhoroneniia* (burial passport), including the victim's name, nationality, date and place of birth, is then issued to any remaining family members.

Thanks to the perseverance of many search organizations and individual squads operating across the former battlefields in Russia and Belarus, some cold cases are solved, even today. Svetlana Lapteva, a prominent Bishkek journalist, is the coordinator of the official Kyrgyz search movement, *Nasha Pobeda* or *Bizdin Zhenish* (Our Victory). She has made it her mission to uncover and publish as much information as possible about former Kyrgyz Red Army soldiers still missing in action, seeing it as the civic duty of citizens to honour their ancestors, even if it means that today's generation have to bear the cost of the repatriation of their compatriots over eighty years after their death.[76]

One group of military pilots, for example, was trained in Frunze, as their training school was transferred to the rear from Odessa in 1941. Even today, the fate of around 1,500 pilots of three air force regiments, dispatched to the Leningrad front line to assist in the defence of the besieged city, is unknown, despite the fact that five of their number were honoured as Heroes of the Soviet Union.[77]

In contrast, the bodies of Uzbek POWs have been exhumed from a communal grave alongside their prison camp in Amersfoort in the Netherlands, where they were executed with some Dutch and almost 1,000 Russian POWs. Journalist Remco Reiding devoted years trying to identify the men before notifying their living relatives and arranging for them to be re-interred in appropriately marked graves.[78] Of the 1.4 million Uzbek soldiers who died in the war, over 100,000 are still missing, although the Uzbek state does not seem to prioritize search work, remaining passively content with the efforts of others.

A whole industry of search work still exists, thanks to volunteers across Central Asia and their colleagues in the west of the former Soviet Union. Although Kazakh teams enjoy no state financial support for their work, some state support is available in Kyrgyzstan to help metal detectorists, archivists and activists erecting memorial plaques and monuments. Communal graves next to former military hospitals are also being excavated, with the bodies exhumed linked to the names of patients from any existing records. Unfortunately, however, records often included only the surname of the soldier, often poorly transcribed. Some men were referred to only by their given names, as they were too weak to iterate their full names. For this reason, it is almost impossible to trace living relatives.

Where possible, the names of any exhumed soldiers are carefully included in the burgeoning number of *knigi pamiati* or *knigi rekviem* (books of memory) in most urban centres across Central Asia. The first book in Uzbekistan appeared in 1995, to be followed by the publication of three dozen further volumes, as more and more names of participants in the war come to light.[79] The Kyrgyz Issyk-Kul' province's book of memory comprises three volumes, with an introduction by the former president Askar Akaev acknowledging the over 100,000 men who died from this province alone.[80] The search movement in Uzbekistan, *Tashpoisk*, publishes its own version, plus an online book of memory with similar, regularly updated information. This type of material is a valuable resource for the descendants of Red Army soldiers researching the fate of their ancestors. Investigations are still hindered by different ways of writing surnames according to the various pronunciations and alphabets used at the time.

An explosion of electronic databases and memorial websites has occurred over the last fifteen years, again sponsored by the state in Kyrgyzstan. Schools often encourage their pupils to investigate the role played by their ancestors online, although the information freely available on the internet is not always correct. Requests for information on social media have also proliferated recently, with some small degree of success. This type of social activity is an indication that living relatives are still reluctant to forget their ancestors who fought and were 'lost without news' in combat. Building on the oral tradition in Central Asia, whereby it is usual for most people to be able to recite the names of their family's predecessors for several generations, remembrance rituals such as the Immortal Regiment bring a sense of personal connection for the young to what is fast becoming a distant period in history.

Reclaiming history

The cultural legacy of the war with respect to the heroism of Panfilov's division may have suffered from the propagandists' exaggeration of a fabricated episode, complicated by the lack of credible eye-witness accounts. In contrast, however, there is no doubt that those who lived through the war on the home front were in a much better position to produce literary works informed by their own experiences. Over the final three decades of the Soviet Union, the fiction of Kyrgyz author Chingiz Aitmatov – a twelve-year-old child when war broke out – played a key role in shaping remembrance of the war as it affected ordinary people in Central Asia.

The conflict in Aitmatov's work between tradition and modernity replicates that between the colonized republic and its Soviet overlords. Yet Aitmatov's narratives smooth over any potential dichotomy between the two. Here is an author from an ethnic minority who manages to minimize any tension between Central Asia and Moscow, just as he managed to bridge the cultural divide himself by the publication of his books in both Russian and Kyrgyz.

In his works, Aitmatov tackles once politically controversial topics such as wartime collaboration, theft on the home front, cowardice, betrayal, desertion from the Red Army and extramarital love. In his unique way, Aitmatov deals with the universal problems of truth and conscience as he explores issues of social conflict, community, loyalty and maturity against a background of a world at war, exposing as he does the many flaws embedded in human nature.[81]

In their own right, however, Aitmatov's works served to shape remembrance across the Soviet Union and beyond around the experience of war on the home front, sometimes succeeding in blatantly contesting the official version of recent history. Although Aitmatov did not always toe the party line in his depiction of the war, it usually suited the Soviet government to be seen to be permitting and even applauding works by a Kyrgyz author during a period when the friendship of the peoples concept was at risk of becoming a mere platitude.

For his part, Aitmatov recognizes in his works that the relationship between history and memory is never straightforward. In *I dol'she veka dlitsia den'* (And a day lasts more than a century), 1980, Aitmatov deploys the image of the mythical *mankurt*, artificially deprived of all memory and enslaved physically and ideologically.[82] In this case, the *mankurt* is a captured Kazakh youth, whose memory is removed in order to render him more biddable to his oppressors. Here is an overt criticism of the perceived Russification and concomitant eradication of social collective memory of the new Soviet generations of Central Asians, along with the loss of their cultural heritage and ethnic identity. In this way the colonial overlords are criticized by Aitmatov for the resulting cultural amnesia and even the loss of their native languages threatening the peoples of Central Asia. The dilemma posed is that the subjects of such an extreme colonial strategy would suffer from such a degree of imposed social amnesia that they would not necessarily appreciate that their past had been systematically erased.

Aitmatov understood that, in seeking to integrate Central Asia into the Soviet Union, its leaders restricted opportunities for traditional, oral cultural discourse. The political subjugation of the region and its assimilation into the Soviet Union in the twentieth century changed the social landscape permanently, as Moscow implemented a modernizing educational policy, threatening the cultural and linguistic heritage of the Central Asian republics as the Russian language and Slavic culture came to enjoy a privileged position. At the same time the predominant Muslim religion was suppressed as part of a campaign of social and cultural changes, held by the state to have been for the good of the people on the periphery as they were gradually assimilated into a largely Russian-dominated sphere.

After the repressions of 1938, Moscow held a much tighter grip on the cultural and political elite in all the Central Asian republics. Sovietization had progressed to the extent that centralized propaganda was effective in convincing sufficient of the population of Central Asia that there was no alternative to joining the common fight against the fascist invaders in 1941. This resulted in less meaningful opposition to conscription than may have been anticipated by the authorities after the experience of the regional uprisings and resistance of 1916 during the First World War. Central Asia went on to play a crucial, if unsought, role in the Second World War, providing conscripts for the trenches, sanctuary for refugees, food for the troops and valuable resources for industry. Through its deployment of the 'friendship of the peoples' narrative, the state continued to justify its exploitative demands on the region, milking it dry of men, materials, animals and crops. In some small degree of recompense, the region enjoyed the recognition afforded to its military heroes and the thanks of refugees as it was pulled more and more forcefully into the Soviet fold.

By the end of the war, the people of Central Asia had broadly embraced the state's propaganda of the common cause in the fight for victory. Families had learned perforce how to work both within and outside the official system in order to survive. The cost of eventual victory was huge – as was the case across the whole of the Soviet Union. In Central Asia, however, not only were lives and health sacrificed, but huge tracts of the region suffered from large-scale population displacement. The intermingling of waves of citizens from various parts of the vast country reshaped society, accelerating the integration of the people of Central Asia into the Soviet project and playing a key role in the formation of today's multiethnic states.

The history of the Soviet Union is now being examined in the West in all its complexity, just as the people of Central Asia are struggling with its legacy. With independence, a new narrative is coming to the fore, whereby the peoples recall their historical fight against the oppressor and are starting to revive their own languages, culture and pre-colonial history. In this environment, it is hardly surprising that there is an ambivalent attitude towards remembrance of the Second World War. On the one hand, families of veterans need, and indeed wish, to recall with gratitude their courage in battle. The war is very much part of Russian national identity and is also remembered with pride by the minority of ethnic Russians still living in the region. On the other hand, the forced drafting of those members of the population who were most necessary to the agricultural survival of the region led to huge sacrifices for those left behind as it was bled dry by the Soviet regime. The common enemy which united most of the Allied countries was a distant foe rather than a close reality to the people of Central Asia. This was simply not their war. There are more important aspects of modern history which many now prefer to remember with a greater patriotic pride than the Second World War, despite its enormous impact on their lives at the time. The reclaiming and reconstruction of history by the newly independent states now appears to privilege other events at the expense of the Second World War, as they choose to reconstruct their pre-tsarist and twentieth-century history with an emphasis on the struggle *against* rather than *alongside* the Soviet Union, more often now depicted as the colonial oppressor.

These are countries still attempting to disentangle themselves from what may be viewed as Soviet colonialism in some areas of joint history. As the people of Central Asia seek to forge their own paths in the twenty-first century and reclaim their own pre-Soviet culture, they are pursuing a post-colonial campaign in defence of their own pre-colonial history, traditions and culture.[83] However, the right to independence and self-determination was won at the expense of the relative economic and political stability offered by the former Soviet Union. As the 'new' republics mature, a more complex relationship with Moscow is emerging, as choices are made over which aspects of their Soviet past to remember. Despite some popularity amongst the young of both President Putin and Russian-influenced rituals in some cities, thanks to the ubiquity of Russian television in Kazakhstan and Kyrgyzstan, for many Central Asians remembrance of the war is fading into the (political) past – alongside the once-ubiquitous eternal flames. The official history of the Second World War still mainly coincides with that of modern Russia, as Central Asia largely accepts the colonists' spin on history, if with a Central Asian slant. It is now relegated to a few pages in the history books, though, where it serves to place Central Asia in a newly defined global context, while maintaining indelible links with a dubious period in the past.

Historical memory today is becoming quite crowded, as other significant events of the twentieth century seem to be taking priority – events which, moreover, depict Russia and Stalin's Soviet Union in a negative light. In Kyrgyzstan, for example, the Urkun tragedy of 1916 is increasingly to the fore in monumental memory and research. Similarly, the victims of the Stalinist repression are recalled at the Ata Beiit (Fathers' grave) memorial complex outside Bishkek, commemorating the execution in 1938 of high-ranking Communist Party officials, including Törökul, the father of Chingiz Aitmatov. Looking further back, the heritage park at Ruk Ordo celebrates traditional Kyrgyz culture. As electronic resources proliferate, the new 'Esimde' website declares its mission 'to promote a social shift in understanding the history and memory of the Kyrgyz Republic during the twentieth and twenty-first centuries'.[84] As Central Asia grapples with its post-Soviet legacy, the struggle for the appropriation and revision of historical memory continues.

A rich, new tapestry of social memory is in the process of construction. It is only occasionally contested, although evidence suggests that it is sometimes hard to reconcile troublesome aspects of the Soviet past with the post-Soviet present, particularly for those states still choosing to remain more closely within the Russian sphere of political and economic influence. As for those special sons of Central Asia, there is no apparent desire to exorcize the ghosts of the Panfilov heroes still lingering in the shadow of major war memorials. They remain a constant reminder of the region's continuing pride in their mythical exploit and the price paid by ordinary local men for their adopted motherland.

Notes

1 Davis, *Myth Making in the Soviet Union and Modern Russia*, 19.

2 The most comprehensive and reliable account of the coverage of journalists and the history of the construction of the myth of the Twenty-eight is to be found in Statiev, '"La Garde meurt mais ne se rend pas!"'. Rodric Braithwaite also mentions the myth in Braithwaite, *Moscow 1941*, 267–8.

3 Davis, *Myth Making in the Soviet Union and Modern Russia*, 17.

4 'Slovo o 28 gvardeitsev', *Krasnaia Zvezda*, 22 March 1942.

5 A. Beck, *On the Forward Fringe: A Novel of General Panfilov's Division* (London: Hutchinson, 1945), 5.

6 Ibid., 5–6.

7 A. Bek, *La Réserve du Général Panfilov* (Paris: Gallimard, 1963), 229.

8 Beck, *On the Forward Fringe*, 24.

9   Ibid., 187; and Bek, *La Réserve du Général Panfilov*, 203.

10   James Fenimore Cooper's work *The Last of the Mohicans* (1826) includes the eponymous indigenous American character Chingachgook; see Beck, *On the Forward Fringe*, 8

11   Beck, *On the Forward Fringe*, 54.

12   Bek, *La Réserve du Général Panfilov*, 17 and 201.

13   Beck, *On the Forward Fringe*, 9.

14   Momysh-uly sings Pushkin's 'Zimnii vecher' in Bek, *La Réserve du Général Panfilov*, 7 and 227.

15   Bek, *La Réserve du Général Panfilov*, 81.

16   Beck, *On the Forward Fringe*, 29–32.

17   Ibid., 32.

18   Bek, *La Réserve du Général Panfilov*, 207 and 223.

19   Katerina Clark, *The Soviet Novel: History as Ritual* (Bloomington and Indianapolis: Indiana University Press, 2000), 183 and 253.

20   Bek, *La Réserve du Général Panfilov*, 228.

21   Beck, *On the Forward Fringe*, 82, 129 and 220–4.

22   Ibid., 185.

23   Bek, *La Réserve du Général Panfilov*, 10.

24   See especially Beck, *On the Forward Fringe*, 35–44.

25   Ibid., 236.

26   Bek, *La Réserve du Général Panfilov*, 218 and 221.

27   Beck, *On the Forward Fringe*, 79.

28   Bek, *La Réserve du Général Panfilov*, 7 and 229.

29   For more insight into the controversy, see Brandon Schechter, *The Language of the Sword: Alexander Bek, the Writers' Union and Baurdzhan Momysh-uly in Battle for the Memory of Volokolamskoe Shosse* (Berkeley: UC Berkeley, 2009).

30   B. Momysh-uly, *Istoriia odnoi nochi: Zapiski ofitsera* (Kalinin: Knizhnoe izdatel'stvo, 1954); and B. Momysh-uly, *Za nami Moskva: Zapiski ofitsera* (1958).

31   B. Momysh-uly, *General Panfilov* (Alma-Ata: Kazakhskoe gosudarstvennoe izdatel'stvo, 1963).

32   Ibid., 5–6.

33   Valentina Panfilova, *Moi otets: Stranitsy vospominanii* (Frunze: Zhazushy, 1971). Panfilova's memoir was also translated into other Central Asian languages, for example Valentina Panfilova, *Menim Atam* (Frunze: 'Kyrgyzstan' Basmasy, 1973). Further memoirs by members of Panfilov's division include Konstantin Drozdov, *Talgarskii polk* (1972).

34   See also Schechter, *The Language of the Sword*, 30.

35   Beck, *On the Forward Fringe*, 8, 21 and 80.

36   Ibid., 217.

37 Aleksei Azarov, 'Soviet-era Film on Battle for Moscow Premiers Again,
    40 Years Later', *Radio Liberty*, 7 November 2011, available online: https://
    www.rferl.org/a/soviet_war_film_with_kazakh_hero_premieres_again
    /24384034.html (accessed 3 July 2021).

38 *Za nami Moskva*, dir. Mazhit Begalin (USSR: Kazakhfil'm, 1967).

39 *Pesn' o Manshuk*, dir. Mazhit Begalin (USSR: Kazakhfil'm, 1970).

40 'Allia', lyrics by B. Tezhibaev, music by S. Baiterekov.

41 'Kyrgyz Authorities Looking for Men Seen Roasting Potatoes on Eternal
    Flame', *Radio Liberty*, 6 December 2016, available online: https://www.rferl
    .org/a/kyrgyzstan-roasting-potatoes-eternal-flame-men-sought/28159240.html
    (accessed 9 July 2021).

42 See, for example, 'Uzbeks Demolish World War II Memorial Ahead of
    Anniversary', *Radio Liberty*, 20 March 2015, available online: https://
    www.rferl.org/a/uzbeks-demolish-ww2-memorial/26911293.html (accessed
    4 August 2021).

43 B. Babaev, 'Podvig uzbekskogo naroda po spaseniiu polutora milliona
    bezhentsev, kotorye obreli vtoroi dom v Uzbekistane v gody Velikoi
    Otechestvennoi voiny', in *Istoriia. Pamiat'. Liudi: Materialy IX
    Mezhdunarodnoi nauchno-prakticheskoi konferentsii 27 sentiabria 2018 g.*,
    eds K. Sh. Alimgazinov, et al., 268–71 (Almaty: 2019), 271.

44 *Leningradtsy, deti moi . . .*, dir. Damir Salimov (USSR: 1982).

45 *Schindler's List*, dir. Steven Spielberg (USA: 1993).

46 *Bol'shoe serdtse Tashkenta*, dir. Khaji-Murat Valiev (Uzbekistan: Favvora Film,
    2016). See also Babaev, 'Podvig uzbekskogo naroda'; and A. Slonim, '"Bol'shoe
    serdtse Tashkenta" vpechatliaet i raduet', in *Istoriia. Pamiat'. Liudi: Materialy
    IX Mezhdunarodnoi nauchno-prakticheskoi konferentsii 27 sentiabria 2018 g.*,
    eds K. Sh. Alimgazinov, et al., 271–6 (Almaty: 2019).

47 For example, the modern monument at Ata Beiit, Kyrgyzstan.

48 'The Enduring Commemoration of Ancestors', *Ministry of Foreign Affairs of
    the Republic of Uzbekistan*, 2 September 2019, available online: https://mfa.uz
    /en/press/news/2017/11/12974/ (accessed 2 November 2017).

49 Kozlov, *Velikaia Otechestvennaia voina*.

50 The conclusions of the enquiry are recorded in the Russian Federation
    State Archives, GARF, in *fond* (collection) R-8131, available online: https://
    statearchive.ru/607 (accessed 25 January 2022). See also Braithwaite, *Moscow
    1941*, 268; and Statiev, '"La Garde meurt mais ne se rend pas!"', 770.

51 Kozlov, *Velikaia Otechestvennaia voina*, 526 and 606.

52 Goldman and Filtzer, *Fortress Dark and Stern*, 447, footnote 46.

53 *Dvatsat' vosem' panfilovtsev*, dir. Andrei Shal'opa (St Petersburg: Libyan
    Palette Studios, 2016).

54 For further details about the film in the context of myth making in Russia, see
    Davis, *Myth Making in the Soviet Union and Modern Russia*, 259–60.

55 Harry Bone, 'Putin Backs WW2 Myth in New Russian Film', *BBC News*,
    11 October 2016, available online: https://www.bbc.co.uk/news/world-europe
    -37595972 (accessed 7 August 2021).

56 *Volokolamskoe Shosse* (Kazakhstan: 2013).

57 Kozybaev, *Istoriia Kazakhstana*, 117; and Turlygul, et al., *Istoriia Kazakhstana*, 201–9.

58 Imankulov, *Istoriia Kyrgyzstana*, 108 and Osmonov, *Istoriia Kyrgyzstana*, 132–4.

59 Imankulov, *Istoriia Kyrgyzstana*, 109; and 'Information about the Feat of the Hero of the Soviet Union Duishenkul Shopokov', *Embassy of the Kyrgyz Republic*, available online: https://mfa.gov.kg/en/dm/-Embassy-of-the-Kyrgyz -Republic-in-the-USA-and-Canada/Menu---Foreign-/News/News-and-Events /v-ramkah-serii-publikaciy-posvyashchennoy-75-letiyu-pobedy-v-velikoy -otechestvennoy-voyne-predstavlyaem-materialy-o-podvige-geroya-sovetskogo -soyuza-duyshenkula-shopokova (accessed 6 August 2021).

60 Interviews with Kyias Moldokasymov and Prof. Tchoraev.

61 G. V. Kan, 'Evakuatsiia i istoricheskaia nauka', in *Istoriia. Pamiat'. Liudi: Materialy IX Mezhdunarodnoi nauchno-prakticheskoi konferentsii 27 sentiabria 2018 g.*, eds K. Sh. Alimgazinov, et al., 54–8 (Almaty: 2019), 54.

62 *Den' pamiati i pochestei*.

63 Mukhammadsharif Mamatkulov and Olzhas Auyezov, 'In Nod to Russia, New Uzbek Leader Revives V-day Celebrations', *Reuters*, 9 May 2017, available online: https://www.reuters.com/article/us-wwii-anniversary-uzbekistan -idUSKBN18524O (accessed 10 May 2018); and Catherine Putz, 'How Is Central Asia Celebrating Victory Day?', *The Diplomat*, 9 May 2015, available online: https://thediplomat.com/2015/05/how-is-central-asia-celebrating -victory-day/ (accessed 10 May 2018).

64 With the exception of Tajikistan.

65 Davis, *Myth Making in the Soviet Union and Modern Russia*, 234–7.

66 Paolo Sorbello, 'Victory Day in Central Asia', *The Diplomat*, 11 May 2015, available online: https://thediplomat.com/2015/05/victory-day-in-central-asia/ (accessed 16 August 2021).

67 'Uzbekistan Resists Russia-style Victory Day Memorial March', *Eurasianet*, 8 May 2018, available online: https://eurasianet.org/s/uzbekistan-resists-russia -style-victory-day-memorial-march (accessed 10 May 18).

68 See Davis, *Myth Making in the Soviet Union and Modern Russia*, 228 and 263.

69 'Tajikistan Cancels "Immortal Regiment" March on Victory Day', *Radio Liberty*, 5 May 2017, available online: https://www.rferl.org/a/tajikistan -cancels-immortal-regiment-march-victory-day/28469791.html (accessed 16 August 2021).

70 'Uzbekistan Resists Russia-style Victory Day Memorial March'.

71 'Techet reka "Bessmertnogo polka"', *Vechernii Bishkek*, 11 May 2018, 4–5.

72 Information from Zhyklys and her mother, 10 May 2018.

73 Bobek School, Almaty, 5 May 2018.

74 Student from the Bobek School, 5 May 2018.

75 School Number 62, Bishkek, 5 June 2018.

76 Discussions with Svetlana Lapteva in November and December 2019; and Nurzhamal Ganyeva, 'Svetlana Lapteva: Nevozmozhno ostanki vsekh zakhoronennykh voinov-kyrgyzstantsev dostavit' na rodinu', *24.kg*, 3 February 2016, available online: https://24.kg/obschestvo/27133_svetlana _lapteva_nevozmojno_ostanki_vsekh_zahoronennyih_voinov-kyirgyizstantsev _dostavit_na_rodinu/ (accessed 17 April 2018).

77 Svetlana Lapteva, 'Aktivisty sobiraiut istoriiu po krupitsam', *Sputnik*, available online: https://ru.sputnik.kg/society/20170207/1031645132/pomnim-1500 -kyrgyzskih-letchikov-propali-75-let-nazad-a-ih-vse-ravno.html (accessed 17 April 2018).

78 Reiding, *Kind von et Erefeld*.

79 This book is simply named *Khotira* (Memory); see Iofe and Petrovskaia, 'Iz istoriia evakuatsii v Uzbekistan', 249.

80 K. I. Usenbekov, et al., eds, *Kyrgyzskaia Respublika: Respublikanskaia Kniga pamiati 1941–1945: Issyk-Kul'skaia oblast'* (Bishkek: Kyrgyz entsiklopediiasynyn Bashki redaktsiiasy, 1995).

81 Ch. Aitmatov, *Dzhamila* (Bishkek: Fast print, 2017); Ch. Aitmatov, 'Materinskoe pole', in *Kogda padaiut gory*, 219–330 (St Petersburg: Azbuka, 2017); Ch. Aitmatov, 'Rannie zhuravli', in *Kogda padaiut gory*, 331–446 (St Petersburg: Azbuka, 2017); Ch. Aitmatov, 'Litsom k litsu', in *Chingiz Aitmatov: Polnoe sobranie sochinenii v vos'mi tomakh*, vol. 2 (Bishkek: Uluu Toolor, 2014), 129–225; and Ch. Aitmatov, 'Voskhozhdenie na Fudziiamu', in *Chingiz Aitmatov: Polnoe sobranie sochinenii v vos'mi tomakh*, vol. 2 (Bishkek: Uluu Toolor, 2014), 340–424.

82 Chingiz Aitmatov, *The Day Lasts more than a Hundred Years*, trans. F. J. French (Bloomington: Indiana University Press, 1983).

83 On post-colonialism in Central Asia, see Alexander Etkind, *Internal Colonization: Russia's Imperial Experience* (Cambridge: Polity, 2011). See also Laura Adams, 'Can we Apply Postcolonial Theory to Central Eurasia?', *Central Eurasian Studies Review* 1 (2008): 2–7; Sharad Chari and Catherine Verdery, 'Thinking Between the Posts', *Comparative Studies in Society and History* 51, no. 1 (2009): 1–29; Moritz Florin, 'Beyond Colonialism? Agency, Power and the Making of Soviet Central Asia', *Kritika: Explorations in Russian and Eurasian History* 4 (2017): 827–38; David Moore, 'Is the Post- in Postcolonial the Post- in Post-Soviet?', *PMLA* 116, no. 1 (2001): 111–28; William Pietz, 'The Post Colonialism of Cold War Discourse', *Social Text* 19/20 (1988): 55–75; and Gyan Prakash, 'Who is Afraid of Postcoloniality?', *Social Text* 49 (1996): 187–203.

84 http://esimde.org.

SELECT BIBLIOGRAPHY

Films

8-ia Gvardeiskaia. Dir. Mikhail Slutskii. Alma-Ata: Alma-Ata Film Studios, 1943.
Aktrisa. Dir. Leonid Trauberg. Alma-Ata: TsOKS, 1943.
Aleksandr Nevskii. Dir. Sergei Eizenshtein. Moscow: Mosfil'm, 1938.
Batyry stepei. Dir. Grigorii Roshal'. USSR, 1942.
Bol'shoe serdtse Tashkenta. Dir. Khaji-Murat Valiev. Uzbekistan: Favvora Film, 2016.
Chapaev. Dirs Georgii and Sergei Vasil'ev. Moscow: Mosfil'm, 1934.
Dvatsat' vosem' panfilovtsev. Dir. Andrei Shal'opa. St Petersburg: Libyan Palette Studios, 2016.
Ivan Groznyi. Dir. Sergei Eizenshtein. Alma-Ata: TsOKS, 1944.
Kliatva Timura. Dirs Aleksandra Khokhlova and Lev Kuleshov. Stalinabad, 1942.
Leningradtsy, deti moi... Dir. Damir Salimov. USSR, 1982.
Liubimaia devushka. Dir. Ivan Pyr'ev. Moscow: Mosfil'm, 1940.
Nasreddin v Bukhare. Dir. Iakov Protazanov. Tashkent: Tashkentskaia kinostudiia, 1943.
Oborona Tsaritsyna. Dirs Georgii and Sergei Vasil'ev. Alma-Ata: Lenfil'm/TsOKS, 1942.
Ona zashchishchaet Rodinu. Dir. Fridrikh Ermler. Alma-Ata: TsOKS, 1943.
Pesn' o Manshuk. Dir. Mazhit Begalin. Alma-Ata: Kazakhfil'm, 1969.
Pesni Abaia. Dirs Efim Aron and Grigorii Roshal'. USSR, 1945.
Schindler's List. Dir. Steven Spielberg. USA, 1993.
Semetei – syn Manasa. Dir. Konstantin Isaev. Alma-Ata, 1945.
Sovetskaia Kirgiziia. Kyrgyz SSR, 1944.
Svinarka i pastukh. Dir. Ivan Pyr'ev. Moscow: Mosfil'm, 1941.
Syn Tajikistana. Dir. Vasilii Pronin. Stalinabad: Stalinabadskaia studiia khudozhestvennykh fil'mov/Soiuzdetfil'm, 1942.
Tebe Front. Dir. Dziga Vertov. Alma-Ata: TsOKS, 1942.
Veselye rebiata. Dir. Grigorii Aleksandrov. Moscow: Moskovskii kinokombinat, 1934.
Vo imia Rodiny. Dirs Vsevolod Pudovkin and Dmitrii Vasil'ev. Alma-Ata: TsOKS, 1943.
Vozdushnyi izbozchik. Dir. Gerbert Rappaport. Alma-Ata: TsOKS, 1943.
Za nami Moskva. Dir. Mazhit Begalin. Alma-Ata: Kazakhfil'm, 1967.
Zhdi menia. Dirs Aleksandr Stolper and Boris Ivanov. Alma-Ata: TsOKS, 1943.
Zoia. Dir. Leo Arnshtam. USSR: Soiuzdetfil'm, 1944.
Zolotoi kliuchik. Dir. Aleksandr Ptushko. Moscow: Mosfil'm, 1939.

Primary written sources

Abylkhozhin, Zh., et al., eds. *Istoriia Kazakhstana*, vol. 4. Almaty: Atamura, 2010.

Aitmatov, Chingiz. *Dzhamila*. Bishkek: Fast print, 2017.

Aitmatov, Chingiz. 'Litsom k litsu'. In *Chingiz Aitmatov: Polnoe sobranie sochinenii v vos'mi tomakh, tom 2*, 129–225. Bishkek: Uluu Toolor, 2014.

Aitmatov, Chingiz. 'Materinskoe pole'. In *Kogda padaiut gory*, 219–330. St Petersburg: Azbuka, 2017.

Aitmatov, Chingiz. 'Rannie zhuravli'. In *Kogda padaiut gory*, 331–446. St Petersburg: Azbuka, 2017.

Aitmatov, Chingiz. *The Day Lasts more than a Hundred Years*. Translated by F. J. French. Bloomington: Indiana University Press, 1983.

Aitmatov, Chingiz. 'Voskhozhdenie na Fudziiamu'. In *Chingiz Aitmatov: Polnoe sobranie sochinenii v vos'mi tomakh, tom 2*, 340–424. Bishkek: Uluu Toolor, 2014.

Akhmatova, Anna. *Iz semi knig: Stikhotvoreniia, Requiem*. Saint Petersburg: Azbuka-klassiki, 2004.

Akhmatova, Anna. *Izbrannoe: Stikhotvoreniia, Poemy*. Moscow: AST, 2006.

Akhmatova, Anna. *My Half-Century: Selected Prose*. Edited and translated by Ronald Meyer. Evanston: Northwestern University Press, 1998.

Akhmatova, Anna. *Polnoe sobranie poezii i prozy v odnom tome*. Russia: Al'fa-kniga, 2019.

Anders, Wladyslaw. *An Army in Exile: The Story of the Second Polish Corps*. London: MacMillan, 1949.

Beck, A. *On the Forward Fringe: A Novel of General Panfilov's Division*. London: Hutchinson, 1945.

Bek, A. *La Réserve du Général Panfilov*. Paris: Gallimard, 1963.

Brezhnev, L. *The Virgin Lands*. Moscow: Politizdat, 1978.

Esenaliev, B. Z., ed. *Zhenishke dank / Slava Pobede*. Bishkek: Kutaalam, 2015.

Gaidar, A. P. *Timur i ego komanda*. 1940. Reprinted Moscow: Rosmen, 2016.

Giedroyć, Michał. *Crater's Edge: A Family's Epic Journey through Wartime Russia*. London: Bene Factum, 2010.

Gorbovskoi, O. *Stikhi i pesni o voine 1941–1945*. Moscow: Klassika v shkole, 2016.

Guliam, Gafur. *Izbrannye proizvedeniia v 5 tomakh*. Tashkent, 1971.

Imankulov, M. K. *Istoriia Kyrgyzstana: XX–XXI vek*. Bishkek: Ministerstvo obrazovanniia i nauki, 2017.

Kaptagaev, E. S., Ch. M. Seidimatova, et al., eds. *Sbornik: Issyk-kul'tsy v gody Velikoi Otechestvennoi voiny (1941–1945gg.)*. Karakol: Issyk-Kul'skii oblastnoi gosudarstvennyi arkhiv, 2015.

Kerez Zarlykova, Kseniia. *Povest' Zhana Angemeler*. Bishkek, 2007.

Kerimbaev, S. K., ed. *Sovetskii Kirgizstan v Velikoi Otechestvennoi voine 1941–1945 gg*. Frunze: ILIM, 1980.

Kesler, M. G. *Shards of War: Fleeing to and from Uzbekistan*. Durham: Strategic Book Group, 2010. Ebook.

Kesler, R. *Grit: A Pediatrician's Odyssey from a Soviet Camp to Harvard*. Bloomington: AuthorHouse, 2009. Ebook.

Kozlov, M. M., ed. *Velikaia Otechestvennaia voina: 1941–1945. Entsiklopediia*. Moscow: Sovetskaia entsiklopediia, 1985.

Kozybaev, M. K., K. N. Nurpeis and K. M. Zhukeshev. *Istoriia Kazakhstana (s nachala XX v. po nastoiashchee vremia)*. Almaty: Mektep, 2013.

Liashchenko, N. G. *Gody v shineli*. Kyrgyzstan: Frunze, 1974.

Momysh-uly, B. *General Panfilov*. Alma-Ata: Kazakhskoe gosudarstvennoe izdatel'stvo, 1963.

Momysh-uly, B. *Istoriia odnoi nochi: Zapiski ofitsera*. Kalinin: Knizhnoe izdatel'stvo, 1954.

Momysh-uly, B. *Za nami Moskva: Zapiski ofitsera*. 1958.

Narovchatov, S., ed. *Pobeda: Stikhi voennykh let*. Moscow: Khudozhestvennaia literatura, 1985.

Osmonov, O. Dzh. *Istoriia Kyrgyzstana: Osnovnye vekhi*. Bishkek: Insanat, 2012.

Panfilova, Valentina. *Menim Atam*. Frunze: 'Kyrgyzstan' Basmasy, 1973.

Panfilova, Valentina. *Moi otets: Stranitsy vospominanii*. Frunze: Zhazushy, 1971.

Protassewicz, Irena. *A Polish Woman's Experience in World War II*. Edited by Hubert Zawadzki and Meg Knot, translated by Hubert Zawadzki. London: Bloomsbury, 2019. Ebook.

Solzhenitsyn, A. *One Day in the Life of Ivan Denisovich*. 1962. Translated by R. Parker. Reprinted London: Victor Gollancz, 2000.

Turlygul, T. T., S. Zh. Zholdasbaev, et al. *Istoriia Kazakhstana: Vazhneishie periody i nauchnye problemy*. Almaty: Mektep, 2015.

Tvardovskii, Aleksandr, 'Vasilii Terkin'. In *A. Tvardovskii: stikhotvoreniia i poemy*, 63–256. Moscow: Detskaia literatura, 2003.

Usenbekov, K. U., V. N. Ananenkov, et al. *Kyrgyzskaia Respublika: Respublikanskaia Kniga pamiati 1941–1945: Issyk-Kul'skaia oblast'*. Bishkek: Kyrgyz entsiklopediiasynyn Bashki redaktsiiasy, 1995.

Secondary written sources

Abazov, Rafis. *Historical Dictionary of Turkmenistan*. Lanham: Scarecrow Press, 2005.

Adams, Laura. 'Can we Apply Postcolonial Theory to Central Eurasia?'. *Central Eurasian Studies Review* 1 (2008): 2–7.

Akaev, A. 'Introduction'. In *Kyrgyzskaia Respublikanskaia Kniga pamiati 1941–1945*, edited by K. U. Usenbekov, V. N. Ananenkov, et al. Bishkek: Kyrgyz entsiklopediiasynyn Bashki redaktsiiasy, 1995.

Alexievich, Svetlana. *The Unwomanly Face of War: An Oral History of Women in WWII*. London: Random House, 2018.

Applebaum, Anne. *Gulag: A History*. London and New York: Penguin, 2003.

Aupenova, A. U. 'Zavod No. 517: Istoriia stanovleniia i razvitiia evakuirovannogo promyshlennogo ob"ekta na kazakhstanskoi zemle'. In *Istoriia. Pamiat'. Liudi: Materialy VIII Mezhdunarodnoi nauchno-prakticheskoi konferentsii 16 sentiabria 2016 g.*, edited by M. S. Makarova, A. I. Baron, et al., 229–34. Almaty, 2017.

Aupenova, A. U. and Zh. E. Isina. 'Masshtabnost' nekotorykh problem evakuatsii grazhdanskogo naseleniia v Kazakhstan v pervye gody Velikoi Otechestvennoi voiny'. In *Istoriia. Pamiat'. Liudi: Materialy IX Mezhdunarodnoi nauchno-prakticheskoi konferentsii 27 sentiabria 2018 g.*, edited by K. Sh. Alimgazinov, A. I. Baron, et al., 143–51. Almaty, 2019.

Axell, Albert. *Russia's Heroes 1941–45*. London: Robinson, 2002.

Azarov, Aleksei. 'Soviet-era Film on Battle for Moscow Premiers Again, 40 Years Later'. *Radio Liberty*, 7 November 2011. Available online: https://www.rferl .org/a/soviet_war_film_with_kazakh_hero_premieres_again/24384034.html (accessed 3 July 2021).

Babaev, B. 'Podvig uzbekskogo naroda po spaseniiu polutora milliona bezhentsev, kotorye obreli vtoroi dom v Uzbekistane v gody Velikoi Otechestvennoi voiny'. In *Istoriia. Pamiat'. Liudi: Materialy IX Mezhdunarodnoi nauchno-prakticheskoi konferentsii 27 sentiabria 2018 g.*, edited by K. Sh. Alimgazinov, et al., 268–71. Almaty, 2019.

Barber, John and Mark Harrison. *The Soviet Home Front, 1941–1945*. London and New York: Longman, 1991.

Batyrbaeva, Sh. D. 'Evakuirovannoe i deportirovannoe naselenie v Kirgizskoi SSR v gody Velikoi Otechestvennoi voiny'. In *Istoriia. Pamiat'. Liudi: Materialy IX Mezhdunarodnoi nauchno-prakticheskoi konferentsii 27 sentiabria 2018 g.*, edited by K. Sh. Alimgazinov, et al., 25–9. Almaty, 2019.

Beevor, Antony. *Berlin: The Downfall 1945*. London: Viking, 2017.

Beevor, Antony. *Stalingrad*. London: Penguin, 1999.

Beevor, Antony. 'They Raped Every German Female from Eight to 90'. *The Guardian*, 1 May 2002.

Berkhoff, K. C. *Motherland in Danger: Soviet Propaganda during World War II*. Cambridge, MA: Harvard University Press, 2012.

Berkimbaeva, A. M. and D. M. Legkii. 'Oblono ne okhvatilo vsekh evakuirovannykh detei ucheboi: Shkol'noe obuchenie detei iz evakuirovannykh i deportirovannykh semei v gody Velikoi Otechestvennoi voiny'. In *Istoriia. Pamiat'. Liudi: Materialy IX Mezhdunarodnoi nauchno-prakticheskoi konferentsii 27 sentiabria 2018 g.*, edited by K. Sh. Alimgazinov, et al., 88–93. Almaty, 2019.

Berkun, O. E. 'Evakuatsiia promyshlennykh predpriatii v Karagandinskuiu oblast''. In *Istoriia. Pamiat'. Liudi: Materialy VIII Mezhdunarodnoi nauchno-prakticheskoi konferentsii 16 sentiabria 2016 g.*, edited by M. S. Makarova, et al., 184–7. Almaty, 2017.

Blackwell, Carole. *Tradition and Society in Turkmenistan: Gender, Oral Culture and Song*. London and New York: Routledge, 2013.

Bloshteyn, Maria, ed. *Russia is Burning: Poems of the Great Patriotic War*. Ripon: Smokestack Books, 2020.

Bone, Harry. 'Putin Backs WW2 Myth in New Russian Film'. *BBC News*, 11 October 2016. Available online: https://www.bbc.co.uk/news/world-europe -37595972 (accessed 7 August 2021).

Braithwaite, R. *Moscow 1941: A City and Its People at War*. New York: Knopf, 2006.

Brooks, Jeffrey. *Thank You, Comrade Stalin! Soviet Public Culture from Revolution to Cold War*. Princeton: Princeton University Press, 2001.

Brown, Andrew J. 'The Germans of Germany and the Germans of Kazakhstan: A Eurasian Volk in the Twilight of Diaspora'. *Europe–Asia Studies* 57, no. 4 (2005): 625–34.

Carmack, Roberto. '"A Fortress of the Soviet Home Front": Mobilization and Ethnicity in Kazakhstan during World War II'. PhD diss. University of Wisconsin-Madison, 2015.

Carmack, Roberto. 'And They Fought for their Socialist Motherland: The Creation of the Multi-ethnic Red Army, 1941–1945'. *Otan Tarikhi* 64, no. 4 (2013): 35–45.

Carmack, Roberto. 'History and Hero-Making: Patriotic Narratives and the Sovietization of Kazakh Front-Line Propaganda, 1941–1945'. *Central Asian Survey* 33, no. 1 (2014): 95–112.

Carmack, Roberto. *Kazakhstan in World War II: Mobilization and Ethnicity in the Soviet Empire*. Lawrence: University Press of Kansas, 2019.

Chapman, Janet G. 'Real Wages in the Soviet Union, 1928–1952'. *The Review of Economics and Statistics* 36, no. 2 (1954): 134–56.

Chari, Sharad and Catherine Verdery. 'Thinking Between the Posts'. *Comparative Studies in Society and History* 51, no. 1 (2009): 1–29.

Chernaiia, E. B. 'Iz istorii Karagandinskogo evakuatsionnogo punkta'. In *Istoriia. Pamiat'. Liudi: Materialy IX Mezhdunarodnoi nauchno-prakticheskoi konferentsii 27 sentiabria 2018 g.*, edited by K. Sh. Alimgazinov, et al., 158–62. Almaty, 2019.

Chilikova, E. V. 'Migratsiia evreev v Kazakhstan v predvoennoe desiatiletie i v period Veliko Otechestvennoi voiny: Region donory i retsipienty, kolichestvennyi sostav. In *Istoriia. Pamiat'. Liudi: Materialy IX Mezhdunarodnoi nauchno-prakticheskoi konferentsii 27 sentiabria 2018 g.*, edited by K. Sh. Alimgazinov, et al., 47–54. Almaty, 2019.

Chokobaeva, Aminat. 'Frontiers of Violence: State and Conflict in Semirechye, 1850–1938'. PhD thesis. The Australian National University, 2016.

Chokobaeva, Aminat. 'When the Nomads Went to War: The Uprising of 1916 in Semirech'e'. In *The 1916 Central Asian Revolt: Rethinking the History of a Collapsing Empire in the Age of War and Revolution*, edited by A. Chokobaeva, C. Drieu and A. Morrison, 145–69. Manchester: Manchester University Press, 2019.

Clark, Alan. *Barbarossa: The Russian German Conflict 1941–1945*. London: Cassell, 1965.

Clark, Katerina. *The Soviet Novel: History as Ritual*. Bloomington and Indianapolis: Indiana University Press, 2000.

Cumins, Keith. *Cataclysm: The War on the Eastern Front, 1941–45*. Helion: Solihull, 2011.

Dadabaev, T. *Identity and Memory in Post-Soviet Central Asia: Uzbekistan's Soviet Past*. London and New York: Routledge, 2016.

Danilova, Natalia. 'Veterans' Policy in Russia: A Puzzle of Creation'. *PIPSS (The Journal of Power Institutions in Post-Soviet Societies)* 6, no. 7 (2007). Available online: https://journals.openedition.org/pipss/873.

Dave, Bhavna. *Kazakhstan: Ethnicity, Language and Power*. London and New York: Routledge, 2007.

Davies, Norman. *Trail of Hope: The Anders Army: An Odyssey across Three Continents*. Oxford: Osprey, 2015.

Davis, Vicky. *Myth Making in the Soviet Union and Modern Russia: Remembering World War II in Brezhnev's Hero City*. London: I.B. Tauris, 2017.

'Den' v istorii: 28 dekabriia 1943 goda nachalas' deportatatsiia kalmykov',
    28 December 2017. *Esimde*. Available online: http://esimde.org/archives/729
    (accessed 7 January 2021).
Denis, Juliette. 'De la Condamnation à l'Expulsion: La construction de l'image de
    masse durant la Grande Guerre patriotique'. In *Les Déportations en héritage:
    Les peuples réprimés du Caucase et de Crimée hier et aujourd'hui*, edited by
    A. Campana, G. Dufaud and S. Tournon, 29–51. Rennes: University Press of
    Rennes, 2010. Ebook.
Dickens, Mark. *Soviet Language Policy in Central Asia*. Self-publication, 1988.
Dzhukha, Ivan. *Spetseshelony idut na vostok: Istoriia repressii protiv grekov v
    SSSR. Deportatsii 1940-kh gg*. St Petersburg: Aleteiia, 2008.
Edele, Mark. *Stalinism at War: The Soviet Union in World War II*. London:
    Bloomsbury, 2021.
Eden, Jeff. 'A Soviet Jihad against Hitler: Ishan Babakhan Calls Central Asian
    Muslims to War'. *Journal of the Economic and Social History of the Orient* 59
    (2016): 237–64.
Eden, Jeff. *God Save the USSR: Soviet Muslims and the Second World War*.
    Oxford: Oxford University Press, 2021.
Edgar, Adrienne Lynn. *Tribal Nation: The Making of Soviet Turkmenistan*.
    Princeton: Princeton University Press, 2006.
Elie, Marc. 'La Vie en Déportation (1943–1953)'. In *Les Déportations en Héritage:
    Les peuples réprimés du Caucase et de Crimée hier et aujourd'hui*, edited by
    A. Campana, G. Dufaud and S. Tournon, 53–75. Rennes: University Press of
    Rennes, 2010. Ebook.
Ercilasun, Guljanat Kurmangaliyeva. 'Famine in Kyrgyzstan in the 1930s and
    1940s'. In *Kazakhstan, Kyrgyzstan and Uzbekistan: Life and Politics during the
    Soviet Era*, edited by Timur Dadabaev and Hisad Koatsu, 39–51. New York:
    Palgrave Macmillan, 2017.
Ermekbai, Zh. A. 'Zavod No. 621 v Kokshetau v gody Velikoi Otechestvennoi
    voiny'. In *Istoriia. Pamiat'. Liudi: Materialy IX Mezhdunarodnoi nauchno-
    prakticheskoi konferentsii 27 sentiabria 2018 g.*, edited by K. Sh. Alimgazinov,
    et al., 188–94. Almaty, 2019.
Etkind, Alexander. *Internal Colonization: Russia's Imperial Experience*.
    Cambridge: Polity, 2011.
Fedorenko, Z. L. 'Evakuatsiia v Tashkent khar'kovchan s Sakharosveklotrestom'. In
    *Istoriia. Pamiat'. Liudi: Materialy IX Mezhdunarodnoi nauchno-prakticheskoi
    konferentsii 27 sentiabria 2018 g.*, edited by K. Sh. Alimgazinov, et al., 199–205.
    Almaty, 2019.
Fedzin, Kenneth. *In Search of Staszewski*. Market Harborough: Troubador, 2014.
    Ebook.
Feferman, Kiril. 'A Soviet Humanitarian Action?: Centre, Periphery and the
    Evacuation of Refugees to the North Caucasus, 1941–1942'. *Europe–Asia
    Studies* 61, no. 5 (2009): 813–31.
Fieseler, Beate. '"La protection sociale totale": Les hospices pour grands mutilés de
    guerre dans L'Union soviétique des années 1940'. *Cahiers du Monde russe* 49
    (2009): 419–40.
Fieseler, Beate. 'The Bitter Legacy of the "Great Patriotic War": Red Army Disabled
    Soldiers under Late Stalinism'. In *Late Stalinist Russia: Society between*

Reconstruction and Reinvention, edited by Juliane Fuerst, 46–61. Abingdon: Routledge, 2006.

Finnin, Rory. 'The Crimean Tatar Sürgün: Past and Present'. University of Cambridge, 20 May 2014. Available online: http://www.cam.ac.uk/research/discussion/the -crimean-tatar-surgun-past-and-present (accessed 8 December 2021).

Fisher, Alan W. *The Crimean Tatars*. Stanford: Stanford University Press, 1978.

Florin, Moritz. 'Becoming Soviet through War: The Kyrgyz and the Great Fatherland War'. *Kritika: Explorations in Russian and Eurasian History* 17, no. 3 (2016): 495–516.

Florin, Moritz. 'Beyond Colonialism? Agency, Power and the Making of Soviet Central Asia'. *Kritika: Explorations in Russian and Eurasian History* 4 (2017): 827–38.

Florin, Moritz. 'Faîtes tomber les murs! La politique civilisatrice de l'ère Brežnev dans les villages kirghiz'. *Cahiers du monde russe* 54, no. 1/2 (2013): 187–211.

Florin, Moritz. *Kirgistan und die sowjetische Moderne, 1941–1991*. Göttingen: V&R, 2015.

Ganyeva, Nurzhamal. 'Svetlana Lapteva: Nevozmozhno ostanki vsekh zakhoronennykh voinov-kyrgyzstantsev dostavit' na rodinu'. *24.kg*, 3 February 2016. Available online: https://24.kg/obschestvo/27133_svetlana_lapteva _nevozmojno_ostanki_vsekh_zahoronennyih_voinov-kyirgyizstantsev_dostavit _na_rodinu/ (accessed 17 April 2018).

Gilboa, Y. A. *The Black Years of Soviet Jewry: 1939–1953*. Translated by Yosef Shachter and Dov Ben-Abba. USA: Brandeis University, 1971.

Goldman, Wendy Z. and Donald Filtzer. *Fortress Dark and Stern: The Soviet Home Front during World War II*. Oxford: Oxford University Press, 2021.

Gould, Rebecca. 'Leaving the House of Memory: Post-Soviet Traces of Deportation Memory'. *Mosaic: An Interdisciplinary Critical Journal* 45, no. 2 (2012): 149–64.

Grinberg, Isaak. *Evrei v Alma-Ate: kratkii istoricheskii ocherk*. Almaty: Iskander, 2005.

Gutman, Israel. 'Jews in General Anders' Army in the Soviet Union'. In *Yad Vashem Studies volume 12*, 231–96. Jerusalem, 1977.

Hastings, Max. *All Hell Let Loose: The World at War 1939–1945*. London: Collins, 2012.

Hicks, Jeremy. *The Victory Banner over the Reichstag: Film, Document and Ritual in Russia's Contested Memory of World War II*. Pittsburgh: Pittsburgh University Press, 2012. Ebook.

Hosking, G. *Russia and the Russians: A History from Rus to the Russian Federation*. London: Allen Lane, Penguin, 2001.

Ibragimow, K. S. 'Okrinnaia Diviziia Pekhoty v Ferganskoi doline v 1942 god'. *Esimde*, 29 May 2019. Available online: http://esimde.org/archives/1367 (accessed 24 June 2020).

İğmen, Ali. *Speaking Soviet with an Accent: Culture and Power in Kyrgyzstan*. Pittsburgh: University of Pittsburgh, 2012.

'Information about the Feat of the Hero of the Soviet Union Duishenkul Shopokov'. *Embassy of the Kyrgyz Republic*. Available online: https://mfa.gov .kg/en/dm/-Embassy-of-the-Kyrgyz-Republic-in-the-USA-and-Canada/Menu-- -Foreign-/News/News-and-Events/v-ramkah-serii-publikaciy-posvyashchennoy -75-letiyu-pobedy-v-velikoy-otechestvennoy-voyne-predstavlyaem-materialy-o -podvige-geroya-sovetskogo-soyuza-duyshenkula-shopokova (accessed 6 August 2021).

Inoiatova, D. M. 'Pomoshch' Uzbekistana evakuirovannym detiam v gody voiny'. In *Istoriia. Pamiat'. Liudi: Materialy VIII Mezhdunarodnoi nauchno-prakticheskoi konferentsii 16 sentiabria 2016 g.*, edited by M. S. Makarova, et al., 269–74. Almaty, 2017.

Iofe, V. G. and A. O. Il'ina (Stil'ke). 'Spasenie ot Kholokosta: Evrei iz Pol'shi i Vostochnoevropeiskikh Respublik SSR v Tashkente v dokumentakh mestnykh arkhivov'. In *Istoriia. Pamiat'. Liudi: Materialy VIII Mezhdunarodnoi nauchno-prakticheskoi konferentsii 16 sentiabria 2016 g.*, edited by M. S. Makarova, et al., 331–40. Almaty, 2017.

Iofe, V. G. and V. A. Petrovskaia. 'Iz istoriia evakuatsii v Uzbekistan'. In *Istoriia. Pamiat'. Liudi: Materialy VIII Mezhdunarodnoi nauchno-prakticheskoi konferentsii 16 sentiabria 2016 g.*, edited by M. S. Makarova, et al., 249–61. Almaty, 2017.

Iofe, V. G. and G. S. Vedernikova. 'Iz istorii evakuatsii v Uzbekistan'. In *Istoriia. Pamiat'. Liudi: Materialy IX Mezhdunarodnoi nauchno-prakticheskoi konferentsii 27 sentiabria 2018 g.*, edited by K. Sh. Alimgazinov, et al., 265–7. Almaty, 2019.

Israilova-Khar'ekhuzen, Chynara. *Esimde*. Available online: http://esimde.org/archives/3023 (accessed 21 December 2020).

Kabdulova, K. D. 'Evakuatsiia politemigrantov v Kazakhstan v gody Velikoi Otechestvennoi voiny'. In *Istoriia. Pamiat'. Liudi: Materialy IX Mezhdunarodnoi nauchno-prakticheskoi konferentsii 27 sentiabria 2018 g.*, edited by K. Sh. Alimgazinov, et al., 133–9. Almaty, 2019.

Kan, G. V. 'Evakuatsiia i istoricheskaia nauka'. In *Istoriia. Pamiat'. Liudi: Materialy IX Mezhdunarodnoi nauchno-prakticheskoi konferentsii 27 sentiabria 2018 g.*, edited by K. Sh. Alimgazinov, et al., 54–8. Almaty, 2019.

Kasimova, Zukhra. 'Adoption and Integration of Displaced Soviet Children during the Great Patriotic War in the Uzbek SSR'. *Peripheral Histories* (2018). Available online https://www.peripheralhistories.co.uk/post/adoption-integration-of-displaced-soviet-children-during-the-great-patriotic-war-in-the-uzbek-ssr (accessed 8 September 2023).

Katsui, Hisayo. 'The Challenges of Operationalizing a Human Rights Approach to Disability in Central Asia'. In *Disability in Eastern Europe and the Former Soviet Union: History, policy and everyday life*, edited by Michael Rasell and Elena Iarskaia-Smirnova, 204–25. Oxford and New York: Routledge, 2014.

Keller, Shoshana. *Russia and Central Asia: Coexistence, Conquest, Convergence.* Toronto and London: University of Toronto Press, 2020.

Kenebaeva, G. M. and D. M. Legkii. 'K voprosu ob izmenenii statusa pol'skikh grazhdan v gody Vtoroi mirovoi voiny'. In *Istoriia. Pamiat'. Liudi: Materialy IX Mezhdunarodnoi nauchno-prakticheskoi konferentsii 27 sentiabria 2018 g.*, edited by K. Sh. Alimgazinov, et al., 80–4. Almaty, 2019.

Kenez, Peter. 'Black and White: The War on Film'. In *Culture and Entertainment in Wartime Russia*, edited by Richard Stites, 157–75. Bloomington: Indiana University Press, 1995.

Khlistunova, N. V. 'Evakuatsiia evreev vo vremia VOv v Kazakhstan, dr. strany Tsentral'noi Azii i Zapadnuiu Sibir". In *Istoriia. Pamiat'. Liudi: Materialy VIII Mezhdunarodnoi nauchno-prakticheskoi konferentsii 16 sentiabria 2016 g.*, edited by M. S. Makarova, et al., 57–63. Almaty, 2017.

Kim, German N. 'The Deportation of 1937 as a Logical Continuation of Tsarist and Soviet Nationality Policy in the Russian Far East'. *Korean and Korean American Studies Bulletin* 12 (2001): 19–44.

Kirschenbaum, Lisa. *The Legacy of the Siege of Leningrad*. Cambridge: Cambridge University Press, 2006.

Kiutova, N. V. 'Iz istorii evakuatsii evreev v gorod Leninogorsk Vostochno-Kazakhstanskoi oblasti ili evreiskaia saga Sorokinykh'. In *Istoriia. Pamiat'. Liudi: Materialy VIII Mezhdunarodnoi nauchno-prakticheskoi konferentsii 16 sentiabria 2016 g.*, edited by M. S. Makarova, et al., 193–9. Almaty, 2017.

Korinenko, Ekaterina. 'Istoriia pokrytaia makom'. *Izvestiia*, 30 October 2018.

Kozhushko, E. A. 'Evakuatsiia Kupianskogo sakharnogo zavoda v g. Kokand'. In *Istoriia. Pamiat'. Liudi: Materialy IX Mezhdunarodnoi nauchno-prakticheskoi konferentsii 27 sentiabria 2018 g.*, edited by K. Sh. Alimgazinov, et al., 205–8. Almaty, 2019.

Kreindler, Isabelle. 'The Soviet Deported Nationalities: A Summary and Update'. *Soviet Studies* 38 (1986): 387–405.

Krylataia sem'ia. Krasnodar: Diapazon, 2005.

Krylova, Anna. *Soviet Women in Combat*. Cambridge: Cambridge University Press, 2011.

'Kyrgyz Authorities Looking for Men seen Roasting Potatoes on Eternal Flame'. *Radio Liberty*, 6 December 2016. Available online: https://www.rferl.org/a/kyrgyzstan-roasting-potatoes-eternal-flame-men-sought/28159240.html (accessed 9 July 2021).

Lapteva, Svetlana. 'Aktivisty sobiraiut istoriiu po krupitsam'. *Sputnik*. Available online: https://ru.sputnik.kg/society/20170207/1031645132/pomnim-1500-kyrgzskih-letchikov-propali-75-let-nazad-a-ih-vse-ravno.html (accessed 17 April 2018).

Lapteva, Svetlana. 'Istoriia semei pogibshikh bez vesti i veteranov voiny'. *Sud'ba soldata* Conference. Moscow, 2019.

Lapteva, Svetlana. 'Sostavlenie banka dannykh po gospital'nym spiskam, gospital'nym zakhoroneniiam po Kirgizskoi SSR 1941–1946 gg.'. *Sud'ba soldata* Conference. Moscow, 2019.

Lilley, Jeffrey B. *Have the Mountains Fallen?*. Bloomington: Indiana University Press, 2018.

Lillis, Joanna. *Dark Shadows: Inside the Secret World of Kazakhstan*. London: I.B. Tauris, 2019. Ebook.

Lipovsky, I. P. *Central Asia: In Search of a New Identity*. North Charleston: CreateSpace, 2012.

Mailibayeva, Saya and Anar Khassenova. 'ALZHIR, a Place of Remembrance'. *Voices on Central Asia*, 31 January 2020. Available online: https://voicesoncentralasia.org/alzhir-a-place-of-remembrance (accessed 4 March 2020).

Mamatkulov, Mukhammadsharif and Olzhas Auyezov. 'In Nod to Russia, New Uzbek Leader Revives V-day Celebrations'. *Reuters*, 9 May 2017. Available online: https://www.reuters.com/article/us-wwii-anniversary-uzbekistan-idUSKBN18524O (accessed 10 May 2018).

Mambetakunova, Nurbubu. 'Sbor dannykh po voennym gospitaliam i gospital'nym zakhoroneniiam na territorii Chuiskoi oblasti dlia uvekovecheniia pamiati pogibshikh'. *Sud'ba soldata* Conference. Moscow, 2019.

Manley, Rebecca. 'The Perils of Displacement: The Soviet Evacuee between Refugee and Deportee'. *Contemporary European History* 16, no. 4 (2007): 495–509.

Manley, Rebecca. *To the Tashkent Station: Evacuation and survival in the Soviet Union at war*. Ithaca and London: Cornell University Press, 2009.

Medvedeva-Natu, O. 'Vospitannik Ianusha Korchaka v tadzhikskom Kurkate'. In *Istoriia. Pamiat'. Liudi: Materialy IX Mezhdunarodnoi nauchno-prakticheskoi konferentsii 27 sentiabria 2018 g.*, edited by K. Sh. Alimgazinov, et al., 106–24. Almaty, 2019.

Merridale, Catherine. *Ivan's War: Life and Death in the Red Army, 1939–1945*. New York: Picador, 2006.

Merridale, Catherine. 'Russia'. In *Encyclopedia of Death and Dying*, edited by Glennys Howarth and Oliver Leaman, 390–1. London: Routledge, 2001.

Miimanbaeva, F. N. 'Materialy Natsional'nogo arkhiva Respubliki Kazakhstan o evreiakh, evakuirovannykh v Kazakhstan v gody Velikoi Otechestvennoi voiny'. In *Istoriia. Pamiat'. Liudi: Materialy IX Mezhdunarodnoi nauchno-prakticheskoi konferentsii 27 sentiabria 2018 g.*, edited by K. Sh. Alimgazinov, et al., 58–62. Almaty, 2019.

Moore, David. 'Is the Post- in Postcolonial the Post- in Post-Soviet?'. *PMLA* 116, no. 1 (2001): 111–28.

Moorhouse, Roger. *First to Fight: The Polish War 1939*. London: Bodley Head, 2019.

Moorhouse, Roger. *The Devils' Alliance: Hitler's Pact with Stalin, 1939–41*. London: Bodley Head, 2014.

Motadel, David. 'Islam and Germany's War in the Soviet Borderlands, 1941–5'. *Journal of Contemporary History* 48, no. 4 (2013): 784–820.

Mukhina, Irina. *The Germans of the Soviet Union*. London and New York: Routledge, 2007.

Mukhmejanova, V. A. 'Ob istorii i kul'turom nasledii evreev v Srednei Azii'. In *Istoriia. Pamiat'. Liudi: Materialy VIII Mezhdunarodnoi nauchno-prakticheskoi konferentsii 16 sentiabria 2016 g.*, edited by M. S. Makarova, et al., 350–3. Almaty, 2017.

Mundy, Liza. 'The Significant, Neglected Role of Russian Women in World War II'. *The Washington Post*, 4 August 2017.

Myachinskaya, E., N. Demers and B. Demers. 'Soviet Field of Honour, Leusden, the Netherlands: Then and Now'. *Scandinavian Philology* 18, no. 1 (2020): 198–212.

Myles, Bruce. *Night Witches: The Amazing Story of Russia's Women Pilots in WWII*. Chicago: Academy Chicago, 1990.

Nekrich, Aleksandr M. *The Punished Peoples: The Deportation and Fate of Soviet Minorities at the End of the Second World War*. New York: W. W. Norton, 1981.

Nogoibaeva, El'mira, *Sud'by: Otkryvaia stranitsy istorii Kyrgyzstana*. Bishkek, 2019.

Ohayon, Isabelle. 'Ego-récits de l'Intégration: Deux itinéraires de déportés au Kazakhstan soviétique'. *Slovo*, 22 March 2017.

O'Keefe, Brigid. *The Multiethnic Soviet Union and Its Demise*. London: Bloomsbury, 2022.

Papush, I. A. 'Greki priazov'ia v gody Velikoi Otechestvennoi voiny 1941–1945 gg.'. *Azovskie greki* (2000). Available online: https://www.azovgreeks.com/library.cfm?articleId=107 (accessed 8 January 2021).

Patard, Francis. *100 Jours pour la Liberté*. Cherbourg: Société Cherbourgeoise, 2019.

Peck, M. *What My Parents Told Me about Siberia, Kirgizia and the Holocaust*. Poland: CreateSpace, 2017.

Phillips, Sarah D. '"There Are No Invalids in the USSR!": A Missing Soviet Chapter in the New Disability History'. *Disabilities Study Quarterly* 29, no. 3 (2009). Available online: https://dsq-sds.org/article/view/936/1111.

Pietz, William. 'The Post Colonialism of Cold War Discourse'. *Social Text* 19/20 (1988): 55–75.

Podlipskii, A. M. 'Evakuatsiia predpriatii Belorussii 1941 g.'. In *Istoriia. Pamiat'. Liudi: Materialy VIII Mezhdunarodnoi nauchno-prakticheskoi konferentsii 16 sentiabria 2016 g.*, edited by M. S. Makarova, et al., 72–9. Almaty, 2017.

Pohl, J. Otto. 'The Deportation and Fate of the Crimean Tatars'. *International Committee for Crimea* (2000). Available online: http://www.iccrimea.org/scholarly/jopohl.html (accessed 17 January 2021).

Pohl, J. Otto. 'The False Charges of Treason against the Crimean Tatars'. *International Committee for Crimea* (2010). Available online: http://www.iccrimea.org/scholarly/pohl20100518.pdf (accessed 10 December 2021).

Polian, Pavel. *Against their Will: The History and Geography of Forced Migration in the USSR*. Budapest: Central European University Press, 2004.

Potemkina, M. N. 'Dolgaia doroga domoi sem'i Min'kinnykh'. In *Istoriia. Pamiat'. Liudi: Materialy VIII Mezhdunarodnoi nauchno-prakticheskoi konferentsii 16 sentiabria 2016 g.*, edited by M. S. Makarova, et al., 284–90. Almaty, 2017.

Potichnyj, Peter J. 'The Struggle of the Crimean Tatars'. *Canadian Slavonic Papers* 17, no. 2/3 (1975): 302–19.

Poujol, Catherine. 'Poles in Kazakhstan: Between Integration and the Imagined Motherland'. *Space, Populations, Societies* 4, no. 1 (2007): 91–100.

Prakash, Gyan. 'Who Is Afraid of Postcoloniality?'. *Social Text* 49 (1996): 187–203.

Pulford, Ed. *Mirrorlands: Russia, China, and Journeys in Between*. London: Hurst, 2019.

Putz, Catherine. 'How Is Central Asia celebrating Victory Day?'. *The Diplomat*, 9 May 2015. Available online: https://thediplomat.com/2015/05/how-is-central-asia-celebrating-victory-day/ (accessed 10 May 2018).

Rakhmonkulova, Z. B. and Sh. Sh. Choriev. 'Upravlenie po evakuatsii naseleniia pri Sovete po evakuatsii'. In *Istoriia. Pamiat'. Liudi: Materialy VIII Mezhdunarodnoi nauchno-prakticheskoi konferentsii 16 sentiabria 2016 g.*, edited by M. S. Makarova, et al., 63–72. Almaty, 2017.

Reese, Roger R. *Why Stalin's Soldiers Fought: The Red Army's Military Effectiveness in WWII*. Lawrence: University Press of Kansas, 2011.

Reiding, Remco. *Kind von et Erefeld*. Zwolle, The Netherlands: D33 Publicaties, 2012.

Reshetov, V. P. '"Chuvstvuiu sebia poliakom!"'. In *Istoriia. Pamiat'. Liudi: Materialy IX Mezhdunarodnoi nauchno-prakticheskoi konferentsii 27 sentiabria 2018 g.*, edited by K. Sh. Alimgazinov, et al., 481–6. Almaty, 2019.

Robbins, Christopher. *In Search of Kazakhstan: The Land That Disappeared*. Croydon: Profile, 2008.

Roberts, Flora. 'A Time for Feasting? Autarky in the Tajik Ferghana Valley at War, 1941–45'. *Central Asian Survey* 36, no. 1 (2017): 37–54.

Rollberg, Peter. *Historical Dictionary of Russian and Soviet Cinema*. Plymouth: Rowman and Littlefield, 2016.

Roth-Ey, Kristin. *Moscow Prime Time: How the Soviet Union Built the Media Empire That Lost the Cultural Cold War*. Ithaca and London: Cornell University Press, 2011.

Saipova, K. D. 'Istoriia pol'skikh evreev v gody Vtoroi mirovoi voiny'. In *Istoriia. Pamiat'. Liudi: Materialy VIII Mezhdunarodnoi nauchno-prakticheskoi konferentsii 16 sentiabria 2016 g.*, edited by M. S. Makarova, et al., 415–7. Almaty, 2017.

Saipova, K. D. 'Vklad uzbekistantsev v pobedu nad fashizmom i tolerantnoe otnoshenie k evakuirovannym'. In *Istoriia. Pamiat'. Liudi: Materialy IX Mezhdunarodnoi nauchno-prakticheskoi konferentsii 27 sentiabria 2018 g.*, edited by K. Sh. Alimgazinov, et al., 62–8. Almaty, 2019.

Saktaganova, Z. G. 'Alma-Ata v gody Velikoi Otechestvennoi voiny: evakuatsiia, zhilishchnyi vopros, kommunal'nye i drugie problem'. In *Istoriia. Pamiat'. Liudi: Materialy IX Mezhdunarodnoi nauchno-prakticheskoi konferentsii 27 sentiabria 2018 g.*, edited by K. Sh. Alimgazinov, et al., 167–172. Almaty, 2019.

Saktaganova, Z. G. 'Povsednevnye problem evakogospitalei Tsentral'nogo Kazakhstana v gody Velikoi Otechestvennoi voiny'. In *Istoriia. Pamiat'. Liudi: Materialy VIII Mezhdunarodnoi nauchno-prakticheskoi konferentsii 16 sentiabria 2016 g.*, edited by M. S. Makarova, et al., 187–92. Almaty, 2017.

Salyk, G. D. 'Arkhivnye dokumenty Akmolinskogo regiona ob evakuatsii i bezhentsakh'. In *Istoriia. Pamiat'. Liudi: Materialy VIII Mezhdunarodnoi nauchno-prakticheskoi konferentsii 16 sentiabria 2016 g.*, edited by M. S. Makarova, et al., 216–20. Almaty, 2017.

Sargalbaev, Arstanbek. '600 dnei very'. *Esimde*, 7 July 2020. Available online: http://esimde.org/archives/2212 (accessed 7 July 2020).

Sataeva, Zh. A. 'K voprosu izucheniia istorii sovetskogo kino v gody voiny'. In *Istoriia. Pamiat'. Liudi: Materialy IX Mezhdunarodnoi nauchno-prakticheskoi konferentsii 27 sentiabria 2018 g.*, edited by K. Sh. Alimgazinov, et al., 218–22. Almaty, 2019.

Schechter, Brandon. *The Language of the Sword: Alexander Bek, the Writers' Union and Baurdzhan Momysh-uly in Battle for the Memory of Volokolamskoe Shosse*. Berkeley: UC Berkeley, 2009.

Schechter, Brandon. 'The People's Instructions: Indigenizing the Great Patriotic War among Non-Russians'. *Ab Imperio* 3 (2012): 109–33.

Schmitz, Andrea. 'Islam in Tajikistan: Actors, Discourses, Conflicts'. SWP Research Paper. Berlin, 2015.

Seidimatova, Chinara. 'Priissykkul'e v gody Velikoi Otechestvennoi voiny (Evakuatsiia, bezhentsy, pereselenie)'. In *Istoriia. Pamiat'. Liudi: Materialy VIII Mezhdunarodnoi nauchno-prakticheskoi konferentsii 16 sentiabria 2016 g.*, edited by M. S. Makarova, et al., 275–84. Almaty, 2017.

Shokhin, Nazar. 'Arts during the War: Central Asia'. *Voices on Central Asia*, 10 May 2018. Available online: https://voicesoncentralasia.org/arts-during-the-war-central-asia (accessed 18 June 2020).

Shwarts, S. *Evrei v Sovetskom Soiuze s nachala Vtoroi mirovoi voiny (1939–1965)*. New York: American Jewish Working Committee, 1966.

Skakov, Nariman. 'Folklore as Device: Dziga Vertov's "To You, the Front!"'. *Central Asia in Russian Language and Culture*. University of Oxford conference, 10 March 2018.

Slonim, A. '"Bol'shoe serdtse Tashkenta" vpechatliaet i raduet'. In *Istoriia. Pamiat'. Liudi: Materialy IX Mezhdunarodnoi nauchno-prakticheskoi konferentsii 27 sentiabria 2018 g.*, edited by K. Sh. Alimgazinov, et al., 271–6. Almaty, 2019.

Sokol, E. D. *The Revolt of 1916 in Russian Central Asia*. (1954). Baltimore: Johns Hopkins University Press, 2016.

Solzhenitsyn, A. I. *Dvesti let vmeste*. Moscow: Russkii put', 2002.

Sorbello, Paolo. 'Victory Day in Central Asia'. *The Diplomat*, 11 May 2015. Available online: https://thediplomat.com/2015/05/victory-day-in-central-asia/ (accessed 16 August 2021).

Statiev, Alexander. '"La Garde meurt mais ne se rend pas!": Once again on the 28 Panfilov heroes'. *Kritika: Explorations in Russian and Eurasian History* 13, no. 4 (2012): 769–98.

Statiev, Alexander. 'Penal Units in the Red Army'. *Europe–Asia Studies* 62, no. 5 (2010): 721–47.

Stepanenko, N. V. 'Ot deportatsii do reevakuatsii byvshikh pol'skikh grazhdan 1940–1946 gg.' In *Istoriia. Pamiat'. Liudi: Materialy IX Mezhdunarodnoi nauchno-prakticheskoi konferentsii 27 sentiabria 2018 g.*, edited by K. Sh. Alimgazinov, et al., 75–9. Almaty, 2019.

Stepanenko, N. V. 'Sotsial'naia deiatel'nost' Soiuza Pol'skikh Patriotov (1943–1946 gg.)'. In *Istoriia. Pamiat'. Liudi: Materialy IX Mezhdunarodnoi nauchno-prakticheskoi konferentsii 27 sentiabria 2018 g.*, edited by K. Sh. Alimgazinov, et al., 85–8. Almaty, 2019.

Stratton, Mark. 'Uzbekistan: On the bloody trail of Tamerlane'. *Independent*, 9 July 2006. Available online: https://www.independent.co.uk/travel/asia/uzbekistan-on-the-bloody-trail-of-tamerlane-5547233.html (accessed 17 December 2021).

Stronski, Paul. *Tashkent: Forging a Soviet City. 1930–1966*. Pittsburgh: University of Pittsburgh Press, 2011.

Syrlybaeva, G. N. 'Krupneishie vystavochnye proekty Soiuza khudozhnikov Kazakhskoi SSR v gody Velikoi Otechestvennoi voiny. 1942–1943 gg. Pervaia Respublikanskaia khudozhestvennaia vystavka "Velikaia Otechestvennaia voina"'. In *Istoriia. Pamiat'. Liudi: Materialy VIII Mezhdunarodnoi nauchno-prakticheskoi konferentsii 16 sentiabria 2016 g.*, edited by M. S. Makarova, et al., 126–36. Almaty, 2017.

Syrlybaeva, G. N. 'Krupneishie vystavochnye proekty Soiuza khudozhnikov Kazakhskoi SSR v gody Velikoi Otechestvennoi voiny. 1942–1943 gg. Vtoraia Respublikanskaia khudozhestvennaia vystavka "Velikaia Otechestvennaia voina"'. In *Istoriia. Pamiat'. Liudi: Materialy VIII Mezhdunarodnoi nauchno-prakticheskoi konferentsii 16 sentiabria 2016 g.*, edited by M. S. Makarova, et al., 137–44. Almaty, 2017.

'Tajikistan Cancels "Immortal Regiment" March On Victory Day'. *Radio Liberty*, 5 May 2017. Available online: https://www.rferl.org/a/tajikistan-cancels-immortal-regiment-march-victory-day/28469791.html (accessed 16 August 2021).

Tartakower, Arieh. 'The Jewish Refugees: A Sociological Survey'. *Jewish Social Studies* 4, no. 4 (1942): 311–48.

Tasar, Eren Murat. 'Islamically Informed Soviet Patriotism in Postwar Kyrgyzstan'. *Cahiers du Monde russe* 52, no. 2/3 (2011): 387–404.

'Techet reka "Bessmertnogo polka"'. *Vechernii Bishkek*, 11 May 2018, 4–5.

'The Doll "Lala" ("Ilana") That Vera Lifschitz Received in the Transit Camp in Karachi, India'. *Yad Vashem Museum Collection*. Available online: https://www.yadvashem.org/yv/en/exhibitions/bearing.../doll-lala.asp (accessed 28 October 2020).

'The Enduring Commemoration of Ancestors'. Ministry of Foreign Affairs of the Republic of Uzbekistan, 2 September 2019. Available online: https://mfa.uz/en/press/news/2017/11/12974/ (accessed 2 November 2017).

'The "Teheran Children" and the Jewish Soldiers in Anders' Army'. *Yad Vashem Museum Collection*. Available online: https://www.yadvashem.org/yv/en/exhibitions/bearing-witness/tehran.asp (accessed 28 October 2020).

Tranum, S., ed. *Life at the Edge of the Empire: Oral histories of Soviet Kyrgyzstan*. Poland: CreateSpace, 2012.

'Tsentral'naia ob"edinnaia kinostudiia (1941–1944gg.)'. *Kinoentsiklopediia Kazakhstana*. Available online: https://csdfmuseum.ru (accessed 15 June 2020).

Tukhtaeva, M. S. 'Povsednevnaia zhizn' evakuirovannykh khudozhnikov Moskvy i Leningrada v Uzbekistan v 1941–1943 gg.'. In *Istoriia. Pamiat'. Liudi: Materialy VIII Mezhdunarodnoi nauchno-prakticheskoi konferentsii 16 sentiabria 2016 g.*, edited by M. S. Makarova, et al., 112–18. Almaty, 2017.

Tukhtaeva, M. S. 'Tvorcheskaia zhizn' khudozhestvennoi intelligentsii Leningrada i Moskvy v evakuatsii v Uzbekistan (1941–1943 gg.)'. In *Istoriia. Pamiat'. Liudi: Materialy VIII Mezhdunarodnoi nauchno-prakticheskoi konferentsii 16 sentiabria 2016 g.*, edited by M. S. Makarova, et al., 118–26. Almaty, 2017.

Tursynova, Zh. Zh. 'Ikh sud'by izmenila voina'. In *Istoriia. Pamiat'. Liudi: Materialy VIII Mezhdunarodnoi nauchno-prakticheskoi konferentsii 16 sentiabria 2016 g.*, edited by M. S. Makarova, et al., 180–4. Almaty, 2017.

Uatkhanov, Yerbolat. 'Military Parade Commemorates Fatherland Defenders' Day, Victory Day Marked'. *The Astana Times*, 10 May 2017.

Uehling, Greta L. *Beyond Memory: The Crimean Tatars' Deportation and Return*. New York: Palgrave McMillan, 2004.

'Uzbekistan: The Forgotten Polish Divisions of Central Asia'. *Eurasianet*, 2 June 2016. Available online: http://www.eurasianet.org/node/79056 (accessed 17 January 2017).

'Uzbekistan Resists Russia-style Victory Day Memorial March'. *Eurasianet*, 8 May 2018. Available online: https://eurasianet.org/s/uzbekistan-resists-russia-style-victory-day-memorial-march (accessed 10 May 18).

'Uzbeks Demolish World War II Memorial Ahead of Anniversary'. *Radio Liberty*, 20 March 2015. Available online: https://www.rferl.org/a/uzbeks-demolish-ww2-memorial/26911293.html (accessed 4 August 2021).

Vedernikova, G. S. 'Evakuatsiia: Tiazhelye, no blagorodnye stranitsy istorii'. In *Istoriia. Pamiat'. Liudi: Materialy VIII Mezhdunarodnoi nauchno-prakticheskoi konferentsii 16 sentiabria 2016 g.*, edited by M. S. Makarova, et al., 79–82. Almaty, 2017.

Veka, A. V. *Istoriia Rossii*. Moscow: Kharvest, 2003.

Ventsel, Aimar and Baurzhan Zhangultin. 'Prison Camp No. 29 for Prisoners of War from the Second World War on the Territory of Kazakhstan between 1943–9'. *Electronic Journal of Folklore* 63 (2016): 9–28.

Vladimirsky, Irena. 'The Jews of Kyrgyzstan'. *Museum of the Jewish People at Beit Hatfutsot*. Available online: https://www.bh.org.il/jews-kyrgyzstan (accessed 20 September 2020).

Wachtel, Michael. *The Cambridge Introduction to Russian Poetry*. Cambridge: Cambridge University Press, 2004.

Was, M. 'Perceiving the Others: Some Remarks on the Testimonies of Polish Jews in Soviet Central Asia'. In *Istoriia. Pamiat'. Liudi: Materialy VIII Mezhdunarodnoi nauchno-prakticheskoi konferentsii 16 sentiabria 2016 g.*, edited by M. S. Makarova, et al., 37–46. Almaty, 2017.

White, Elizabeth. 'After the War was Over: The civilian return to Leningrad'. *Europe–Asia Studies 59*, no. 7 (2007): 1145–61.

Williams, Brian G. *The Crimean Tatars: From Soviet genocide to Putin's Conquest*. London: Hurst, 2015.

Williams, Brian G. 'The Hidden Ethnic Cleansing of Muslims in the Soviet Union: The Exile and Repatriation of the Crimean Tatars'. *Journal of Contemporary History 37*, no. 3 (2002): 323–47.

Yilmaz, Harun. 'History Writing as Agitation and Propaganda: The Kazakh History Book of 1943'. *Central Asian Survey 31*, no. 4 (2012): 409–23.

Zhumagulova, Aisulu. 'Ikh bylo vosem' brat'ev, v voine vyzhil odin'. *Sputnik*, 9 May 2018. Available online: https://ru.sputniknews.kz/society/20180509 /5553978/kazakhstan-vojna-den-pobedy-istoriya-frontovika.html (accessed 8 November 2019).

Zhumalieva, S. Ch. 'Stanovlenie i deiatel'nost' obshchestva evreiskoi kul'tury Kyrgyzstana'. In *Istoriia. Pamiat'. Liudi: Materialy IX Mezhdunarodnoi nauchno-prakticheskoi konferentsii 27 sentiabria 2018 g.*, edited by K. Sh. Alimgazinov, et al., 360–8. Almaty, 2019.

Zubkova, Elena. *Russia after the War: Hopes, Illusions, and Disappointments, 1945–1957*. Edited and translated by Hugh Ragsdale. Armonk and London: M. E. Sharpe, 1998.

INDEX